Blood & Ink

William Probert. This original drawing from life, made before his 1825
execution for stealing a mare, was given to the Reverend Mr. Cotton, the
Ordinary, Newgate prison. *Borowitz True Crime Collection, Kent State
University Libraries.* See B.29.

Blood & Ink

An International Guide to Fact-Based Crime Literature

Albert Borowitz

Note by Jacques Barzun

Foreword by Jonathan Goodman

The Kent State University Press

Kent and London

© 2002 by The Kent State University Press, Kent, Ohio 44242

Library of Congress Catalog Card Number 2001000570

ISBN 0-87338-693-0

Manufactured in the United States of America

07 06 05 04 03 02   5 4 3 2 1

Library of Congress Cataloging-in-Publication Data

Borowitz, Albert, 1930–

Blood and ink : an international guide to fact-based crime literature / Albert Borowitz ;

note by Jacques Barzun ; foreword by Jonathan Goodman.

p.   cm.

Includes bibliographical references and index.

ISBN 0-87338-693-0 (hardcover : alk. paper) ∞

1. Crime—Case studies—Bibliography.

2. Criminal investigation—Case studies—Bibliography.

3. Crime writing—Bibliography. I. Title.

Z5703 .B67

[HV6251]

016.364–dc21

2001000570

British Library Cataloging-in-Publication data are available.

Facts! Facts! Dear sir, facts are as we receive them; and then, in the mind, they are no longer facts, but *life*, which appears in one light or in another. Facts become the past when the mind yields them up . . . and life abandons them. Therefore I do not believe in facts.

—Novelist Lodovico Nota, in Pirandello's *To Dress the Naked*, Act III

Where am I? alone! Where's Abel? where

Cain? Can it be that I am he? My brother,

Awake! —why liest thou so on the green earth?

'Tis not the hour of slumber; why so pale?

What has thou!—thou wert full of life this morn!

Abel! I pray thee, mock me not! I smote

Too fiercely, but not fatally. Ah, why

Wouldst thou oppose me? This is mockery,

And only done to daunt me;—'twas a blow—

And but a blow.

—Cain, in Lord Byron's *Cain: A Mystery*, Act III

With love and thanks, to my wife, Helen,

who has put up with this long project and has contributed entries

regarding what is no longer a "singular anomaly,"

the female crime novelist

Contents

Acknowledgments

The dedicated staff of the Kent State University Libraries deserves much of the credit for the emergence and completion of this book. I am greatly in debt to Dr. Jeanne Somers, associate dean of Libraries and Media Services and curator of the Libraries' Department of Special Collections; she has helped me in more ways than I can enumerate, capping all her acts of encouragement and assistance by indexing *Blood and Ink*. My wife, Helen, and I also are eternally grateful to Dean Keller, retired associate dean of Libraries and Media Sciences of KSU, who played a pivotal role in the establishment of the Borowitz True Crime Collection at the University.

I also wish to thank Joanna Hildebrand Craig, editor-in-chief of The Kent State University Press, for her support of *Blood and Ink* and for her generosity in copyediting the manuscript in the midst of her other daunting responsibilities at the Press.

I am touched by the kindness of Professor Jacques Barzun and Jonathan Goodman, who have contributed the elegant Note and Foreword that grace the book and made valuable proposals regarding the selection of works included in the bibliographical entries. Mr. Goodman, together with another friend and colleague, Wilfred Gregg, participated with me in the conceptual thinking and interchange that shaped *Blood and Ink*.

My researches on this project were greatly advanced by antiquarian booksellers on the Internet. In addition, I have received significant documentation regarding the "thieving magpie" and the related "magpie mass" from Willem de Graeve, Public Relations, Centre Belge de la Bande Dessinée; and Jacques Grosbois, Conseiller Municipal Délégué, Membre de la Société Historique; and Martine Bourron, Le Premier Adjoint, Déléguée à la Culture et aux Festivals, of Palaiseau, France.

As my dedication reveals, a secret weapon in accomplishing this undertaking was the help and literary insight of my wife, the distinguished art historian Helen Osterman Borowitz. Helen wrote many of the entries relating to works of women authors and reviewed countless others. Of equal importance was the understanding she showed for my obsession with *Blood and Ink*, and the wrongdoers it memorializes, over a period of more than five years.

NOTE

The Place and Point of "True Crime"

JACQUES BARZUN

The name of the literature superbly inventoried in this book gives a clue to the kind of readers who enjoy it. True crime is the match of crime *fiction*, the detective story, commonly called mystery. It has been said that a seasoned reader of crime fiction graduates to true crime. But such a graduate does not leave the campus and its reading list; he or she only adds a new source of pleasure to the one they have been cultivating.

It should not be supposed that those who read about either sort of crime do so because of a taste for mayhem and gore. To think so is to miss the point. In good crime fiction, the victim is disposed of quickly with a minimum of physical detail. In true crime the detail may indeed form part of the recital, because the body has been found in shocking condition—in a trunk or buried in a cellar. But the evidence is soon left behind in the quest for motive and circumstance. In both genres, the deep interest lies not in whodunit but in how this is ascertained by a close examination of time and means and other probabilities.

I say "the interest," meaning the suspense that must grace any sort of writing from riddles to theology. The *pleasure* is something else again. In both the crime offerings, true and fictional, the pleasure is literary.

This may surprise the addicts themselves, who often think their taste well beneath that of people who read high-brow novels. The truth is that great novels are often inartistic compared with the great works that retell great crimes. The qualities, besides lucid prose, that distinguish true crime are narrative skill, the right order of topics (equivalent to plot), the writer's grasp of character and knowledge of life, wit, and judicial detachment coupled with sympathy.

To bring these talents to bear on the details of an actual crime calls for great powers, greater perhaps than are needed when the writer invents his facts; for the crimes worth writing about are those that present a murky tangle in which essential points may remain forever doubtful. Thus the famous Wallace case of the 1930s in Liverpool bewildered all true-crime fanciers for years, until the genius of Jonathan Goodman solved it by a combination of wide research and brilliant analysis. Before then, an aficionado such as the theater critic James Agate would call up a friend and say, "Come over and we'll talk about the Wallace case."

The exposition of notable crimes, with or without solutions, has a long history; it begins with the earliest pleadings at the bar. Cicero in 66 B.C. gave a splendid example in his defense of Aulus Cluentius; and before him the Athenians heard Socrates pull apart the

xiii

charges of his accusers. In eighteenth-century London there was the Newgate Calendar and street-vendors' broadsides—cheap and crude tales of recent crimes; in the nineteenth it was that fine critic De Quincey, who after a notorious murder wrote a long analysis for the literary public: "On Murder Considered as One of the Fine Arts." But it mainly sang the praises of the killers.

The modern genre, more law-abiding, usually begins with excerpts from the transcript of the trial, where each side gives a version of what happened. How these slanted stories are dealt with by the later critic shows the degree of his art and judgment. Henry James took delight in the accounts by William Roughead of cases that others have written up with dissenting conclusions. In our time, Edward Radin showed that Lizzie Borden was very probably innocent of her parents' murder, which contradicts the accepted view put forth by Edmund Pearson, Mrs. Lowndes, and Victoria Lincoln.

There is no end to the speculative opportunities that an interest in true crime bestows on the devotee. Did Crippen kill his wife by accident, mistaking the right dosage of the sedative hyoscine? Was Steinie Morrison innocent after all, like Oscar Slater, who owed his release from prison to the tireless efforts of Conan Doyle? And then, as Mr. Goodman remarks on a later page, there is the perennial question: Who was Jack the Ripper?

A wag suggested Matthew Arnold, the advocate of "sweetness and light." Unfortunately, Arnold had been dead six months when the killings began. Looking up this little fact shows the attention to detail that is characteristic of the . . . the . . . . What *shall* we call the connoisseur of true crime, that capacious scholarlike mind, attentive to scientific truth and wedded to legal logic? May I venture to suggest a name? As usual, the ancient Greeks had a word for "the actual murderer"; it was *authentes*. Why not adopt *philauthentist* as our proud designation, on a par with *philatelist* and indeed with *philosopher*?

FOREWORD

Some Prescriptions and Proscriptions
for "True Crime"

JONATHAN GOODMAN

The question "What makes a *classic* murder?" is posed almost as often as that other one—
"What makes a *perfect* murder?"

The answer to the latter question is short but comprehensive: a murder is only surely
perfect if it is not recognized as murder. Some, perhaps many, murders go quite unnoticed:
they are tucked away within what the late, great Professor Sir Leon Radzinowicz called "the
dark figure of crime." They—with oh so many other unnoticed or unreported or reported
but uninvestigated crimes—make crime statistics look far less worrying than the reality.

Perhaps the clearest indication that there is less to *murder* statistics than meets the eye is
the fact that, according to breakdowns of the figures (I speak of British ones, but no doubt
American equivalents are as unreliable), murder by poisoning is a dying, near-dead, art.
Nonsense, of course, given that countless bathroom cabinets and medicine chests contain
leftover prescription drugs and the like, which are toxic to some people or, overdosed, to all,
and which are more complex, more difficult to detect after ingestion than the undoubted
and undoubtable poisons used by murderers in the past.

With an insufficiency of forensic experts, meaning that those in practice are overloaded
with work, many deaths that are considered only a mite suspicious either aren't forensically
examined or are examined inadequately. There is a maxim of the forensic sciences (though
not confined to them) to the effect that if you are not searching for *some*thing, you don't
stand much chance of finding *any*thing. And so—distressingly additional to the too many
guilty parties acquitted by peculiar juries, whose peculiarities increase as the selection standards of responsibleness, language comprehension, and impartiality are eroded for unsound
but politically correct reasons, or who take advantage of quaint constraints on the police to
evade the become-even-quainter notion of Justice—too many people are getting away with
murder. (In a metaphorical sense, so are too many people who write about crime; I'll come
to some of them in a minute.)

First, however, I must tackle the former question. There is no cut-and-dried answer to
that one. Considering the lots of foreign-language entries in Albert Borowitz's book, I may
as well depart from my usual English-only style, albeit briefly, just to say *à chacun son goût*.
So far as the classic murder question is concerned, one man's meat axe is another man's

poison. I can only tell you what, in my opinion, *may* be *some* of the ingredients of a classic murder and what is perhaps the single factor that definitely makes a murder *un*classic.

I go along to quite an extent—not all the way—with Alfred Hitchcock's comment that the factual murders that most appealed to him were "like blood on a daisy": a shocking contrast between a killing and its compass. Yes, that quite often puts a murder into, or somewhere near, the classic category: the Borden case, for instance (of the "murder behind lace curtains" kind), or the Theodore Durrant case (murder in a place of worship).

And, instantly arguing with myself (for Durrant murdered twice), I feel that, aesthetically speaking, murder should be as special an event to the murderer as it is to his victim. Serial killers are not my cup of tea. They bore me, not merely through the repetitiousness and the sameness of their crimes, but because they themselves are so deadly boring. A sweeping statement, I know, but I am not going to water down my conviction that it is their boredom with their own dreary existences that turns them into serial killers, seeking cheap thrills at a terminal cost to others, enjoying some feeling of power that they are incapable of experiencing in any normal way, but still staying stuck in a one-killing-after-another rut. (Is it simplistic to wonder along the following lines: since bored people are usually uncreative, and therefore bored psychopaths turning to crime are inclined to commit copy-cat offenses, might there have been fewer serial killers if the gutter media had spread fewer slobber stories about serial killings?)

When I have to read—or, rather, skip through—some account of serial killings, I tend to recall the ticky-tacky tailor's sales talk, pleading with the customer not to be critical of a roll of shoddy material: "Never mind the quality. Feel the width."

The so-called offender-profilers—who get themselves, puffed up like pouter pigeons, onto all the news program when one of their lists of traits proves to be somewhere near the mark, but who are suspiciously tight-lipped when asked about the ratio between their partial successes and their near-complete failures—would surely be well advised to write "boring" at the top of all their lists, ahead of the presently ever-present descriptive item of "loner."

I don't know whether the term "serial killer" was originally applied only to repetitious murderers who kill for, among other pleasures, a sexual one, but that is how it seems to be applied nowadays. I certainly draw a clear distinction between those perverts and the persons ("multicides" used to be the catch-all term for them) who murder more than once for quite reasonable reasons. Once again, I spot classic exceptions to the one-murder-per-murderer criterion: Dr. William Palmer of Rugeley, Staffordshire, whose umpteen poisonings were occasioned by financial scrapes; and that man of several brides, and even more aliases (the cheekiest of which was "Love"), who is so wonderfully summed up in the first stanza of Ogden Nash's altogether perfect "They Don't Read De Quincey in Philly or Cinci":

Consider, friends, George Joseph Smith,
A Briton not to trifle with;
When wives aroused his greed or wrath,
He led them firmly to the bath.
Instead of guzzling in the pub,
He drowned his troubles in the tub.

It may help to make a case a classic if there is a riddle of some kind: whodunit or, questioning whether it was a *criminal* case, whatwasit. (There are also whydidhedoit riddles, but as these are no help at all toward classic status, and as the suggested solutions to motivational mysteries are armchair-psychiatric as opposed to sensible, are no more than jargon-infested guesswork, they can be ignored.)

Whatwasits—cases (perhaps "perfect murders") in which there is uncertainty as to whether death was caused by accident, suicide, or murder—are, I think, my favorites. At least a couple of them are classics: the burning of Evelyn Foster on the Northumberland moors on Twelfth Night 1931; and, in the same year (1931 was a red-letter year for classic cases), the passing of Starr Faithfull, whose body was found on the sands of Long Beach, Long Island, giving rise to legal and journalistic ferretings among her antecedents (and giving John O'Hara the idea for his novel *Butterfield 8*).

Speaking of cases in which someone has been found guilty of murder, there are not many *real* whodunits, ones with the verdict being open to question. In recent years, though, they have become vastly outnumbered by *retrospective* whodunits, concocted by persons, usually conspiracy theorists, determined to make readers believe (which is not at all the same as *proving*) that someone found guilty of murder was perfectly innocent, the framed victim of a miscarriage of justice. Most of these "truth-seekers" are quite content to tell whopping great lies in what they consider to be a good cause (the clearing of a name, I mean; not, perish the thought, the improved chance of selling film rights).

Probably the largest portion of the mob of revisionists comprises the Kennedy assassination confidence-tricksters, who were called to account (though none of them seems to have been listening) by Louis Nizer, the brilliant lawyer who, in retirement, wrote the excellent *My Life in Court* and subsequent books that were less good. Having coined the term "analytical syndrome," he explained its meaning:

It is possible to take the record of any trial and by minute dissection and post-facto reasoning demonstrate that witnesses for either side made egregious errors or lied. Then, by ascribing critical weight to the exposed facts, the conclusion is reached that the verdict was fraudulently obtained. This was the process by which the Warren Commission Report [on the assassination of President Kennedy] was challenged in a spate of books. To cite just one illustration, a constable deputy sheriff described the rifle which had been found on the sixth floor of the Book Depository Building, Dallas, as a Mauser, instead of a Mannlicher-Carcano, which it was. Out of this innocent error, due to ignorance or excitement, sprouted the theory that the real assassin's rifle had been spirited away and Lee Harvey Oswald's rifle planted on the scene to involve him. Multiply this incident by many others, such as someone's testimony that shots were heard coming from the mall, and the "hiding" of the death x-rays of the President (since revealed), and you have a gigantic conspiracy by foreign agents, or government officials, or New Orleans homosexuals, or lord knows what, to fix the blame on an innocent man, Oswald. Of course, all this was nonsense, and subsequent events have confirmed the accuracy of the Report.

The analytical syndrome can be used to discredit any verdict, from the commonest automobile negligence case to the most involved anti-trust or proxy contest.

Much the same chestnut-tree-sprouting-from-an-acorn methods are used by most writers on the Whitechapel murders of 1888, who have turned an interesting story into a sort of parlor game: "Hunt the Ripper"—undoubtedly a Trivial Pursuit.

Some years ago, intending to poke fun at the already excessive number of named Ripper candidates, I included an entry for Peter J. Harpick, complete with a spoof potted biography, in an unserious reference book. I was confident that everyone who saw it would cotton on to the fact that the name was an anagram of Jack the Ripper, especially as I as much as said that it was in the biography, which I was equally confident would be recognized as a spoof, for it was crammed with twaddle. Shortly after the book's publication, I started to get letters, usually written in green ink, from Ripperologists, asking for further information about Peter J. Harpick. Even now, I still get the occasional letter of that sort from people who have come across the entry belatedly. Which goes to show that as I, not intending to deceive, have done so, any intending deceiver can, if he likes, name the Queen of Romania as Jill the Ripper, in the sure knowledge that too many people will be taken in.

The writers that I have referred to in the past few paragraphs, and others like them, are to *true* true-crime writing what acne is to skin. And they don't appear (well, hardly at all) in this book; and so, of course, I am as pleased with what *isn't* in the following pages as with what is.

I had better admit (*boast* is what I really mean) that Albert Borowitz and I are friends; if I don't, some conspiracy theorist will surely assume that the favorable comments I am about to make about his book are insincere, obvious indications of a furtive Old Pals Act. But if I didn't know him so well, I should not be able to *state*, rather than voice the opinion, that no one but he could have composed this book. His qualifications, all in all, are unique.

Whereas with a good many bibliographies at the back of books, one is suspicious that an author, aiming to impress with the ostensible depth of his desk research, has included titles that he has never seen, let alone glanced at, I *know* that Albert Borowitz has read (and nine times out of ten, *re*read) every single work that he has chosen to include. The fact that he, being multilingual, has been able to read every single one of the works, also the many that he has decided to leave out, greatly reduces the number of people who could have even considered taking on the task. And that number is reduced still more—to a solitary one: Albert Borowitz—by the necessity of conversance with the practicalities of crime writing. He is, by far, the best of American crime historians.

As if the talents I have mentioned weren't enough to make him the uniquely qualified composer of this book, he has a fund of knowledge about several arts, particularly the performing ones, and for longer than I have known him has delighted in finding connections between art and crime, artists and criminals.

We—meaning many people as well as true-crime devotees—should be grateful that Albert Borowitz, the only person more than capable of composing this book, was prepared to accept the immense challenge of doing so.

Blood & Ink

Introduction

This guide and its annotated bibliography document the interrelations between crime history and literature. When juxtaposing fact and fiction in this area of study, it may be misleading to pose the familiar question of whether art imitates nature or nature imitates art. Both the criminal act and the creative impulse have their origin in the human psyche, and it may be pure accident whether a germinative concept is first translated into conduct or formulated as narrative.

To illustrate this point, two examples of surprising interplay between crime fact and fiction may be cited from the field of biblical literature. In the first case, a seventeeth-century French poisoning scandal required the "re-editing" of the Old Testament. Marc-Antoine Charpentier, in composing his 1688 opera *David and Jonathan* for the theater of the Jesuits in Paris, utilized a libretto of Père Bretonneau, who felt compelled to doctor the scene of King Saul's visit to the Witch of Endor. The contemporary "Affair of the Poisons," in which wholesale arsenic poisonings had been linked to witchcraft, made stage presentations of conjuration (even of scriptural origin) a risky enterprise. Therefore, in Bretonneau's version, King Saul does not ask the Witch to call forth the spirit of Samuel. Instead, the so-called Prophetess (*pythonisse*) acts voluntarily in summoning a "shade" whose name is never pronounced in the text of the opera. Thus the Bible, despite its accepted divine inspiration, was not immune, at least in public theatrical presentation, to the influence of current crime reports.

If the Charpentier opera shows in its most compelling form the reinterpretation of literature in the light of subsequent criminal conduct, the Book of Tobit in the Apocrypha provides an instance in which religious literature anticipated by two millennia a bizarre category of crimes that we would be likely to regard as an innovation of our own bloody era. Jack the Ripper owes his unending fascination largely to his perpetration of a series of grisly murders in conformity with established patterns regarding the means of killing and choice of victims; he slashed the throats of prostitutes in London's East End and disemboweled them when he had the time. In the Book of Tobit, a serial killer claims seven lives in Ecbatane, a city of Media, pursuant to an even more rigorous design. Ultimately revealed to be a demon named Asmodeus, the murderer falls in love with Sara and strangles her successive bridegrooms in her bedchamber on the wedding night. More effective than the Metropolitan Police of Victorian London, the archangel Raphael expels Asmodeus by instructing the eighth bridegroom, Tobias, to place the heart and liver of a miraculous fish on a fire in

1

Sara's room. Overcome by the offensive fumes, Asmodeus "fled into the utmost parts of Egypt and the angel bound him."

In the remarkable mass family slaying by Pierre Rivière, studied by Michel Foucault and his disciples (see Bibliography Item F.23), it is not even possible to determine whether the idea of the crime first originated as a literary design or as a plan of action. In Foucault's words, the young semi-literate farmer initially intended to "surround" the murder with his memoirs. He planned to begin by writing the narrative that would announce at the outset the crime that was to follow; then he would detail his parents' quarrelsome marriage and his reasons for his plan to defend his father's interests by eliminating his mother. At this point, the murder was to have been committed, and then Rivière's self-incriminating memoirs were to be completed and mailed to the authorities. Foucault refers to Rivière as a "double *auteur*," simultaneous inventor of the crime and the related narrative.

The above examples should caution against making easy assumptions about the direction of currents flowing between crime history and literature. Still, in defining the subject of this guide as "fact-based crime literature," I intend to include two principal groups of works that, despite frequent overlaps and questionable classifications (for example, the "nonfiction novels" of which I will have more to say later), are generally recognizable as distinct genres: (1) nonfictional accounts of crimes and criminal trials, including essays, monographs, journalism, editions of court transcripts, prison histories, and criminal and police biographies and memoirs, as well as autobiographies of victims' relatives, such as novelist Martin Amis's *Experience* (New York: Talk Miramax, 2000), reflecting the disappearance of the author's cousin, Lucy Partington, and her murder by a notorious serial killer, Frederick West; and (2) works of imaginative literature, such as novels, stories, or stage works, based on, or inspired by, actual crimes or criminals. In making a selection of works for inclusion in the bibliography, I have generally emphasized the literary and/or historical achievement of the author or editor rather than the fame of the individual crimes described; this stress on the work rather than on the criminal case is reflected by the organization of the bibliography, which is, with the exception of anonymous, collective, or serial works, arranged alphabetically by author. Yet, because the great writers of fact-based crime have chosen their subjects with a discriminating eye, the bibliography necessarily provides, through comment on significant literature, a survey of many of the most intriguing criminal cases of the last four centuries.

What crimes are included? Here again I have followed the lead of the writers included in the bibliography. Murder has certainly been favored by true-crime authors, as it has been by popular thriller writers, but I have not neglected other categories of wrongdoing that have had a conspicuous place in crime history and related literature since their inception: fraud, piracy, imposture, historical mysteries, treason, conspiracy, and a wide variety of crimes against property, such as theft, burglary and arson. The emphasis is on the study of specific cases in any of these categories rather than on general theories of criminality, although some criminological studies are included when they take as their point of departure the analysis of a single crime or trial record (for example, Foucault's study of Pierre Rivière, mentioned above). Occasionally, the bibliography strays into areas of aberrant or scandalous behavior that are not subject to criminal sanction. In general, I have excluded Wild

West literature, which is the subject of critical bibliographies by Ramon Adams; and I have deemphasized books on organized crime, because of my preference for studies of conduct driven by complex or elusive motives. My entries tend to become sparser with respect to publications after 1980; I believe the value of a crime work can only be judged fairly when it has aged a bit on my shelves.

One narrowing of scope is due to an embarrassment of riches. Only a few annotations have been made regarding works on Jack the Ripper, whose crimes (now seemingly modest in scope when compared to the mass and serial killings of our day) have spawned a literary industry perhaps rivaled only by the exploitation of President Kennedy's assassination. Ripperologists will perhaps forgive my neglect, since, at this writing, Richard Whittington-Egan's definitive Ripper history and bibliography is scheduled to be published soon by Patterson Smith.

The works on which I have commented are, with very rare exceptions, to be found in the Borowitz True Crime Collection, which my wife, Helen, and I have established in the Special Collections Department of the Kent State University Libraries, Kent, Ohio. In some instances, I comment on special features of the Borowitz Collection's holdings, such as important provenance or tipped-in letters or ephemera. Although the Borowitz True Crime Collection has sufficient size and breadth to be representative of the field of fact-based crime literature, it necessarily reflects my personal tastes and cannot be regarded as complete; nor could such a claim be made for any other harvest in so vast a literary field. In one respect, however, this bibliography may be wider ranging than other publications addressed to English-speaking audiences. I have collected, and include in this bibliography, not only works in English but those in many other languages, including the Romance languages, Latin, German, Swedish, and Russian; where, however, an English translation exists, I have generally preferred it to the foreign original, unless there are significant differences between the two editions. The international character of this book is not a personal whim. Although the Anglo-American tradition is one of the chief glories of fact-based crime writing, it is rivaled in scope and achievement by works of French authors and compilers, who can fairly be regarded as having invented the notion of publishing collections of trial narratives (to which they gave the generic title, *causes célèbres*). Other important fact-based crime literature has been produced in German-speaking countries and throughout the world, except where and when totalitarian governments decree for their own doctrinal purposes that crime does not exist.

To summarize the development of fact-based crime literature in various languages, the balance of this introduction will address separately the Anglo-American tradition, French works, and literature in other languages.

THE ANGLO-AMERICAN TRADITION

The strong British interest in true crime has been noted with amazement, even by the French, whose own attraction to this subject must strike an outside observer as equally powerful. I have never been totally satisfied by the common explanation that dismisses reading and writing about violence as a relatively harmless channel through which the well-behaved British vent their suppressed hostility. Without rejecting this thesis out of hand, I have suggested, in *The Woman Who Murdered Black Satin,* that the fascination of the Scots and English with their crimes also has a significant relationship to their genius for narrative expression: "The devotion of the British to their crimes must remain as great a mystery as many of the cases they treasure. It is possible, though, that this national trait . . . is related to other more significant aspects of British culture. The appeal of murder cases draws to some extent on violent instincts, but certainly it also responds to the love of drama and exciting and suspenseful narrative. Fascination with murder cases may proceed from the same facet of the British genius that created the Elizabethan drama and gave birth to the eighteenth-century novel of adventure" (81).

Another principal source of the passion for true crime, in Britain as elsewhere, is the abundance of psychological revelations that can be mined from criminal trial reports. The value of crime narratives in elucidating human motives is eloquently appraised by Friedrich Schiller in his introduction to a German edition of criminal cases published in 1792:

We catch sight here of people in the most complicated situations, which keep us in total suspense and whose denouements provide pleasant employment for the reader's ability to predict the outcome. The secret play of passion unfolds before our eyes, and many a ray of truth is cast over the hidden paths of intrigue. The springs of conduct, which in everyday life are concealed from the eye of the observer, stand out more clearly in motives where life, freedom and property are at stake, and therefore the criminal judge is in a position to have deeper insights into the human heart.[1]

Critic Jacques Barzun, in his preface to Jonathan Goodman's *The Stabbing of George Harry Storrs,* makes a similar assessment of the allure of "true crime":

The appeal of this last-named species of composition is manifold. It presents ordinary human beings under stress: not just the principals, but a hitherto unconnected score of persons suddenly caught in the searchlight of a police investigation. They are buffeted and bruised by newspaper reports and repeated grilling in and out of court; their earlier doings, their secrets, their abilities and pretensions, are made into a public show. It is a grim novel in action, a novel in the mode of Dickens and Dostoevsky, who in fact drew upon just such live materials for their most renowned effects.

Another advantage of the study of criminal cases by historian or novelist is the wealth of detail court testimony gives us about the way people lived in other places and other times. In the preface to *Innocence and Arsenic,* I observed that "nothing tells us more about the way

---

1. Introduction to *Merkwürdige Rechtsfälle als ein Beitrag zur Geschichte der Menschheit. Nach dem Französischen Werk des Pitaval* [Notable Cases as a Contribution to the Human History. After the French Work of Pitaval], 4 vols. (Jena, 1792–95). Translated by the author.

people live than the strange ways in which they are sometimes done to death." An example drawn from the dining room will illustrate the point. If asked what they had for dinner last Thursday, most people would have trouble recalling. No student of crime, however, will forget the predilection of Charles Bravo for burgundy or the gradually deteriorating mutton and broth that were served up to Lizzie Borden's family in the sultry week that preceded the double axe-murders—a menu that was in itself an adequate motive for the crimes. To stay with this culinary theme, who among crime aficionados will fail to cherish the memory of the maid who served dinner to the murderers Thurtell and Hunt after their murder of Mr. Weare near Elstree in 1823? It had been a busy evening for the murderers, what with the disposal of their victim's body and the rest of their chores, but there had still been a social hour before dinner, and Hunt, who was no mean tenor, obliged his hostess Mrs. Probert with a song. At the trial, the maid, who must have been a spiritual ancestress of Chico Marx, was asked whether the dinner was postponed. She replied, "No, it was pork chops."

In England, nonfictional crime literature had its origins in the sixteenth and seventeenth centuries with the appearance of crime and underworld chapbooks and single-sheet "broadsides," in prose or doggerel verse, devoted to primitive accounts of murders, trials, executions, and confessions. From the beginning there was a large measure of fiction in what passed for crime reportage. Many of the broadsides (as I have learned on many occasions to my scholarly embarrassment) are completely bogus and indeed were known to the street vendors as "cocks" (perhaps an abbreviation of cock and bull). One of the most spectacular successes in the marketing of crime fiction in the trappings of fact dates from the early seventeenth century. In 1621 an Exeter merchant named John Reynolds published one of the earliest bestsellers in crime reporting, giving his collection of narratives the portentous title *The Triumphs of God's Revenge Against the Crying and Execrable Sin of Wilful and Premeditated Murder*. Although the author stoutly insisted that his work was a faithful English adaptation of criminal records that had come to his attention while he was traveling on business in Europe, the entire book appears to be a fabrication. There is no indication that the cases of crime and punishment in *The Triumphs of God's Revenge* were anything but Reynolds's own invention. (One story inspired Middleton and Rowley's murder drama *The Changeling*, so that fiction masquerading as fact became melodrama believed by its authors to be grounded in fact.) Moreover, the author's proclaimed horror of the crimes he describes and the religious lesson he draws from providential discovery and punishment of the guilty apply a thin veneer to what is sensationalism pure and simple. However fraudulent and sanctimonious it may have been, Reynold's work certainly found a wide readership. By 1670 it had gone into a fifth edition (the first to be profusely illustrated with woodcuts), and new editions were still appearing a century later. The curious work had not exhausted its appeal by the end of the eighteenth century when the English novel began to reflect social and political didacticism. William Godwin acknowledged Reynolds's "tremendous compilation" as a source of inspiration for his own 1794 novel of murder and repentance, *Caleb Williams*.

In the eighteenth century, successive compilations of reports of authentic criminal cases gave rise to such famous collections as the Newgate Calendar and the State Trials. Gradually, writers in the mainstream of English literature began to take an interest in their nation's eminent malefactors. Capitalizing on the public craving for narratives of criminal exploits, Daniel Defoe, in addition to his *General History of the Pyrates* (1724), wrote short biographies of the housebreaker and escape artist Jack Sheppard and the archgangster of early eighteenth-century London, Jonathan Wild; it was Defoe's remarkable publicity stunt to arrange for criminals to deliver to him in their cells or at the scaffold manuscripts that he had previously furnished to them and that he was to publish immediately as their "authentic" lives.

A hundred years later, England's modern literary tradition of true crime had its birth in the essays of Thomas De Quincey. De Quincey left two distinct legacies to his successors in the genre: black humor and the highly dramatic reconstruction of murder scenes. The first strand in his crime writing is represented by the celebrated two-part essay "On Murder, Considered as One of the Fine Arts" (1827, 1839), an exercise in irony (perhaps influenced by Jonathan Swift's manner in "A Modest Proposal"), in which an imaginary connoisseur of crime lays down mock-aesthetic standards for the evaluation of the "fine murder": "People begin to see that something more goes to the composition of a fine murder than two blockheads to kill and be killed—a knife—a purse—and a dark lane. Design, gentlemen, grouping, light and shade, poetry, sentiment, are now deemed indispensable to attempts of this nature." In 1984 I was delighted to learn that this essay had, at least to a small degree, made its mark on American popular culture. That year I received from a friend a book bag with an imprint of a bloody hand and the following quotation from De Quincey: "If once a man indulges himself in murder, very soon he comes to think little of robbing; and from robbing he comes next to drinking and Sabbath-breaking, and from that to incivility and procrastination. Once begun upon this downward path, you never know where to stop. Many a man has dated his ruin from some murder or other that perhaps he thought little of at the time."

Some readers of De Quincey in his own time and after have been troubled about the linking of humor with crime. In espousing the view that humor, if well targeted and kept within reasonable bounds, may have a place in true-crime writing, I regard myself as a follower and defender of De Quincey. Certainly, violence and personal loss are not in themselves appropriate subjects for relentless facetiousness. However, there is no reason to spare from satire the callousness of criminals, their lack of foresight, or the ludicrous explanations they give for outrageous conduct. Even in the humor of popular crime doggerel, where good taste is not king, the target is often inhumanity rather than the murder itself. To cite the most famous American example, where the joke is at the expense of the murderer's failure to feel an expected remorse:

> Lizzie Borden took an axe
> And gave her mother forty whacks
> When she saw what she had done
> She gave her father forty-one.

In quite a different vein from his essay "On Murder" is De Quincey's postscript of 1854, "Three Memorable Murders," in which he includes a terrifying account of the massacres thought to have been committed by John Williams, the so-called Ratcliffe Highway murderer. It is impossible to forget the scene of Williams stalking the servant Mary in the house of the slaughtered Marr family. This passage, which imaginatively re-creates the horror cumulating within Mary's mind, demonstrates that De Quincey wrote a "nonfiction novel" well over a century before Truman Capote coined the term. To quote De Quincey:

> Still as death she was; and during that dreadful stillness, when she hushed her breath that she might listen, occurred an incident of killing fear . . . . She, Mary, the poor trembling girl, checking and overruling herself by a final effort, that she might leave full opening for her dear young mistress's answer to her own last frantic appeal, heard at last and most distinctly a sound within the house. Yes, now beyond a doubt there is coming an answer to her summons. What was it?
>
> On the stairs, not the stairs that led downwards to the kitchen, but the stairs that led upwards to the single story of bed-chambers above, was heard a creaking sound. Next was heard most distinctly a footfall: one, two, three, four, five stairs were slowly and distinctly descended. Then the dreadful footsteps were heard advancing along the little narrow passage to the door. The steps—oh heavens! *whose* steps?—have paused at the door. The very breathing can be heard of that dreadful being who has silenced all breathing except his own in the house. There is but a door between him and Mary. What is he doing on the other side of the door? A cautious step, a stealthy step it was that came down the stairs, then paced along the little narrow passage—narrow as a coffin—till at last the step pauses at the door. How hard the fellow breathes! He, the solitary murderer, is on the one side of the door; Mary is on the other side.
>
> Now, suppose that he should suddenly open the door, and that incautiously in the dark Mary should rush in, and find herself in the arms of the murderer. . . . But now Mary is upon her guard. The unknown murderer and she have both their lips upon the door, listening, breathing hard; but luckily they are on different sides of the door; and upon the least indication of unlocking or unlatching, she would have recoiled into the asylum of general darkness.
>
> What was the murderer's meaning in coming along the passage to the front door? The meaning was this: separately, as an individual, Mary was worth nothing at all to him. But, considered as a member of a household, she had this value . . . that she, if caught and murdered, perfected and rounded the desolation of the house.[2]

Many distinguished English and Scottish writers followed the path De Quincey had blazed in "Three Memorable Murders." His disciples included the versatile scholar and essayist Andrew Lang; H. B. Irving, the son of famed Shakespearean actor Sir Henry Irving and himself an actor-manager; the barrister J. B. Atlay; Sir John Hall; and the novelist F. Tennyson Jesse, author of the valuable *Murder and Its Motives.* However, the unquestioned master of this true-crime literary school in the first half of the twentieth century is the nonpracticing Edinburgh solicitor William Roughead, whose biography by Richard Whittington-Egan appeared

---

2. Thomas De Quincey, *On Murder Considered as One of the Fine Arts* (London: Philip Allan, 1925), 106–8.

in 1991. To De Quincey's humor and flair for drama, Roughead added impeccable crime scholarship, legal acumen, a deep knowledge of Scottish and English literature, and a keen eye for colorful topographical detail. His work has mesmerized generations of crime aficionados, including his good friend Henry James, who, after reading one of Roughead's witch stories, implored him "to go back to the dear old human and sociable murders and adulteries and forgeries in which we are so agreeably at home."

Roughead's inimitable charm is well exemplified by his comments on the triviality of motives for many famous murders:

> Thomas Griffiths Wainewright, the prince of poisoners, excused the murder of his young sister-in-law on the ground "that she had such thick ankles." But this purely aesthetic motive was doubtless alloyed by the fact that he had insured her life for £18,000. A case where the motive was startlingly inadequate is that of John Watson Laurie, the Arran murderer, with which some of my readers may be acquainted. All he got was a silver watch (which he threw away on the spot), a half-return ticket to London (which he didn't use), and a poor pound or two—if that. Yet he stoned his friend to death, like St. Stephen, upon a mountain, and spent many hours in raising an elaborate cairn to his memory— the body, incidentally, forming the foundation.[3]

Roughead, like Lang, Irving, Atlay, Hall, and Jesse, wrote introductions and served as editor for volumes in the brilliant series of *Notable British Trials* published by William Hodge of Edinburgh beginning in 1905. Among Roughead's ten contributions, one of the strongest is his introduction to the *Trial of Captain Porteous*. John Porteous, captain of the Edinburgh City Guard, was convicted in 1736 of unlawfully commanding guardsmen to fire on a crowd assembled at a public hanging. Porteous's defense that he had acted on prior instructions of superiors was unavailing. (Roughead's extensive account of the case will serve as an effective antidote for moviegoers seduced by the pictorial beauty of the Australian film *Breaker Morant* to accept the dangerous credo that a military commander is entitled to rely on illegal orders as an excuse for murder.)

The second half of the twentieth century has given rise to new generations of true-crime writers, of whom Edgar Lustgarten and Jonathan Goodman are two of the most important. Lustgarten, a barrister, is at his best in recreating famous trials, speculating about disputed verdicts, and analyzing successful defense strategies. The prolific Goodman brings to his oeuvre a broader array of talents, including a gift for detection (witness his famous solution of the murder of Julia Wallace) and a keen sense of times and scenes past.

Although nonfictional crime literature came to full flower in Britain only in the nineteenth century, dramatic works inspired by actual cases had been produced as early as Elizabethan times. Decades ago a theatrical joke used to run around London: "Everyone here has seen *The Mousetrap*, except the Queen, and she thinks she's seen it." There is no need, however, to guess about the taste of the Elizabethan court for crime plays of the sixteenth

---

3. William Roughead, "Enjoyment of Murder," in *Neck or Nothing* (London: Cassell, 1939), 10–11.

century. It is recorded that in the season of 1578 there was played at court before Queen Elizabeth I a thriller with a title worthy of Agatha Christie, *Murderous Michael*. The novelty of *Murderous Michael* was that it did not deal in the rivalries of noblemen or the assassinations of kings but with a domestic murder of no political or social significance that was based on the facts of an actual criminal case of 1550, the slaying of Thomas Arden by his wife, Alice, and her lover. The text of *Murderous Michael* has been lost, but in 1590 a new play on the same subject, *Arden of Faversham*, was first performed. This drama is one of the earliest surviving examples of a work of imaginative English literature based on a true-crime source. Adhering faithfully to the record of the Arden trial, the play chronicles the blundering efforts of a wife and her lover to dispose of her inconvenient spouse; their victim's luck runs out only in scene 14, a truly remarkable endurance record by Elizabethan standards. It was a sign of things to come that *Arden* chronicled a family murder that had no public importance whatsoever. The appearance of the play foretold the singular British passion for lurid crime narrative that became more pronounced over the succeeding centuries. A generation after *Arden,* John Webster wrote his two classic murder plays, *The White Devil* (1612) and *The Duchess of Malfi* (1623). *The White Devil* was the dramatization of actual events that had occurred nearly thirty years before and featured as its protagonist a famous Venetian courtesan Vittoria Accoramboni; *The Duchess of Malfi* was in large part a reworking of Vittoria's fate.

George Lillo, an eighteenth-century playwright who revised the text of *Arden of Faversham*, wrote a crime drama of his own in prose that eclipsed *Arden* in public favor. Lillo's *The London Merchant*, which opened at the Theatre-Royal in Drury Lane in 1731, retold the murder case of George Barnwell, which was the subject of street ballads as early as the late sixteenth century. Apprentice Barnwell was led by the exactions of a "lady of pleasure," Sarah Millwood, to embezzle his master's funds and then to murder his wealthy uncle. Intended as a sermon for apprentices, it also featured an attractive femme fatale, ultimately played by Sarah Siddons; *The London Merchant* racked up 179 performances between 1731 and 1776, oddly becoming the traditional offering for the Christmas and Easter holidays. Theophilus Cibber, who managed the Drury Lane and created the role of George Barnwell, referred to the play as "almost a new species of tragedy, wrote on a very uncommon subject."

Although overshadowed by purely fictional melodramas and thrillers, English dramas based on true-crime characters and material have attracted enthusiastic audiences in subsequent periods. *The Gamblers*, a play based on the Thurtell-Hunt murder of 1823, opened at London's Surrey Theatre before the case was brought to trial and featured the horse and gig allegedly used in the crime; further performances were blocked by court order. H. Chance Newton[4] recalls the production of Sydney Grundy's play, *A Fool's Paradise*, in which the role of poisoning victim James Maybrick was acted by H. B. Irving, later to become one of England's leading crime essayists. In a classic display of failed prognostication, Newton had advised Grundy to change the drama's original name, *The Mouse Trap*, to one "more understandable by the general public." Twentieth-century British masters of fact-based crime

---

4. *Crime and the Drama* (London: Stanley Paul, 1927), 29.

drama include Emlyn Williams (*Night Must Fall, Someone Waiting*, etc.), Terence Rattigan (*The Winslow Boy, Cause Celebre*), James Bridie (*The Anatomist*), and Rodney Ackland (*A Dead Secret*).

Eighteenth-century English writers also introduced criminals into opera and fiction. In 1728 John Gay scandalized Handelian oratorio fans with his underworld satire *The Beggar's Opera*, starring the highwayman Captain MacHeath and his dangerous company. Gay may have named MacHeath's mistress after a London pickpocket subsequently hanged in 1740 for assiduous devotion to her craft. Born Jane Webb, this light-fingered practitioner won her famous nickname "Jenny Diver" because of great dexterity in raiding her victims' pockets. Jenny's underworld colleague Jonathan Wild was immortalized by Henry Fielding's 1743 novel in which the "thief-taker"'s elaborate system of organized crime was compared to the reputed unscrupulousness of Prime Minister Sir Robert Walpole.

It is to the nineteenth century that we owe one of the supreme masterpieces of imaginative literature inspired by true crime, Robert Browning's *The Ring and the Book* (1868–69). Browning based his long narrative poem on a parchment-covered book he found by chance in a flea market in the Piazza San Lorenzo in Florence; the volume was a collection of documents relating to an obscure triple murder committed by Count Guido Franceschini and his henchmen in Rome in 1698. In his work, Browning displays a virtuosic skill in rendering the ambiguity of courtroom testimony. With the poet as his eloquent spokesman, even the villain Guido finds much to say in the defense of a heinous crime. Another more notorious murder case of a century earlier, the murder of Count Francesco Cenci by his daughter Beatrice and her brothers, inspired Shelley to write another of the great nineteenth-century works of crime literature, the poetic drama *The Cenci* (1819), in which Beatrice is converted into a symbolic rebel against institutional repression. Historical criminal cases and personages also figure prominently in many nineteenth-century novels, including the so-called Newgate fiction of William Harrison Ainsworth and Bulwer Lytton, and, of course, the works of Scott, Stevenson, and Wilkie Collins.

Many of the leading British fact-based crime novelists of the twentieth century are women. One is Gabrielle Margaret Vere Campbell Long (1886–1952), whose early historical fiction under the pen-name Marjorie Bowen was much admired by Henry James. Long also wrote a large number of popular novels freely based on criminal cases under the pre–women's liberation name of "Joseph Shearing." A major rival of an earlier generation is Marie Belloc Lowndes (1868–1947), whose most famous novel, *The Lodger* (1913), was the source of the classic silent movie by Alfred Hitchcock and several remakes in the sound era. The Belloc Lowndes novel illustrates brilliantly how a narrative based on criminal history can serve as a touchstone for appraising social responses to deviant conduct and disaster. The "Lodger" himself is obviously a fictional reincarnation of Jack the Ripper; but in Belloc Lowndes's polite post-Victorian version he becomes a fundamentalist teetotaler who murders tippling women and pins notes to their dresses signed with a flourish "The Avenger." The principal focus of the novel, however, is not on the mad prohibitionist but on the reactions of Mr. and Mrs. Bunting, the poverty-stricken householders who give him lodging. As the Lodger's conduct grows stranger and as his unaccountable absences from the house correspond again and again with the times of the Avenger's killings, both of the Buntings are gradually convinced in their hearts that they are harboring the dreaded murderer. However, because of their common realization that the Lodger's rent is all that keeps the wolf from their door, they keep their suspicions from each other until very late in the game. From Belloc Lowndes's devastating portrait of the willingness of onlookers to temporize with evil for selfish considerations, it is not a very long literary step to Friedrich Dürrenmatt's devastating play *The Visit*.

Many modern detective story writers have drawn freely on themes and personalities of crime history without closely following the facts of criminal cases. Having written a book about the trial of the Mannings that inspired *Bleak House* (1852–53), I must give the place of honor to Charles Dickens. No other English novelist has left a richer or more complex body of work on crime and punishment. A firm believer in the existence of the principle of Evil, Dickens imprinted his hatred of the criminal soul on such unrelieved villains as Rigaud in *Little Dorrit* (1855–57) and Mlle. Hortense in *Bleak House*. However, at the same time that he abhorred violence, Dickens felt a strange empathy for criminals, whose impulses seemed to raise an echo from some of the darker recesses of his own personality. His favorite reading on his lecture tours was the murder of Nancy by Bill Sikes, and he persisted in its performance in the face of the advice of his tour manager, Dolby, that the strain of the scene was tearing him to pieces. Dickens displayed a similar ambivalence in his attitude toward hangings. An absolute opponent of capital punishment, at least in his early days, Dickens was nevertheless drawn by what he called the "attraction of repulsion" to attend several executions. In this respect he proved to have a stronger stomach than his less ideological contemporary Thackeray. After attending the hanging of Courvoisier and finding he could not bear to look, Thackeray turned down an invitation to another public execution in the course of travel abroad. He explained his refusal with the comment, "J'y ai été [I've been there already], as the Frenchman said of hunting."

Many of Dickens's characters are based on historical criminals. The hangman Ned Dennis appears *in propria persona* in *Barnaby Rudge* (1841). The portrait of the rascally Fagin may have been modeled after an authentic receiver of stolen goods, Ikey Solomons. In *Martin Chuzzlewit* (1843–44), the ambush of Montague Tigg by Jonas Chuzzlewit was strongly influenced by the Thurtell-Hunt murder case of 1823, and, as noted in my book on the Mannings, *The Woman Who Murdered Black Satin*, Mlle. Hortense is the very image of Maria Manning.

Dickens also wrote a number of insightful newspaper and magazine articles dealing with crime and punishment. These pieces include letters to the *Daily News* and the *Times* against the death penalty and public hanging; his three articles for *Household Words* on the detectives of Scotland Yard; and his perceptive essay on the courtroom demeanor of murderers.

Dickens's voice is instantly recognizable whether he writes of crime and violence in fiction or nonfiction. Compare, for example, his treatment in these two literary modes, of the theme of the "mob," a dominant image in the mind of Dickens, who had strong fears of the loss of social controls. A passage from his early novel *Barnaby Rudge* describes the storming of Newgate Prison by the Gordon Rioters:

Now, now, the door was down. Now they came rushing through the gaol, calling to each other in the vaulted passages; clashing the iron gates dividing yard from yard; beating at the doors of cells and wards; wrenching off bolts and locks and bars; tearing down the door-posts to get men out; endeavouring to drag them by main force through gaps and windows where a child could scarcely pass; whooping and yelling without a moment's rest; and running through the heat and flames as if they were encased in metal. By their legs, their arms, the hair upon their heads, they dragged the prisoners out.

And now another mob, the mob at Horsemonger Lane on November 13, 1849, that had come to see the hanging of Frederick and Maria Manning (described in *The Woman Who Murdered Black Satin*). Dickens, who viewed the scene with friends from a rented rooftop, recorded the scene below:

> I believe that a sight so inconceivably awful as the wickedness and levity of the immense crowd collected at that execution this morning could be imagined by no man, and could be presented in no heathen land under the sun. The horrors of the gibbet and of the crime which brought the wretched murderers to it faded in my mind before the atrocious bearing, looks and language of the assembled spectators. When I came upon the scene at midnight, the *shrillness* of the cries and howls that were raised from time to time, denoting that they came from a concourse of boys and girls already assembled in the best places, made my blood run cold.
>
> ... When the two miserable creatures who attracted all this ghastly sight about them were turned quivering into the air, there were no more emotion, no more pity, no more thought that two immortal souls had gone to judgment, no more restraint in any of the previous obscenities, than if the name of Christ had never been heard in this world, and there were no belief among men but that they perished like the beasts.[5]

Another juxtaposition of Dickens's crime journalism and fiction will demonstrate how he turned a real figure into what we all fondly call a "Dickens character." Dickens was an ardent admirer of the London police and especially of the detectives of Scotland Yard. One of the detectives with whom he was particularly friendly was Inspector Charles Field, whose methodical performance of duty and encyclopedic knowledge of the underworld Dickens described in an account of an evening that he spent accompanying Field on his nocturnal rounds:

> Inspector Field is, to-night, the guardian genius of the British Museum. He is bringing his shrewd eye to bear on every corner of its solitary galleries, before he reports "all right." Suspicious of the Elgin marbles, and not to be done by cat-faced Egyptian giants with their hands upon their knees, Inspector Field, sagacious, vigilant, lamp in hand, throwing monstrous shadows on the walls and ceilings, passes through the spacious rooms. If a mummy trembled in an atom of its dusty covering, Inspector Field would say, "Come out of that, Tom Green. I know you."[6]

5. Letter to the London *Times,* Nov. 14, 1849.

6. "On Duty with Inspector Field," *Reprinted Pieces,* in *The Works of Charles Dickens,* vol. 8 (London: Chapman & Hall, 1881), 357–58.

In the pages of *Bleak House*, Field is deftly transformed into an equally formidable guardian of public order:

> Otherwise mildly studious in his observation of human nature, on the whole a benignant philosopher not disposed to be severe upon the follies of mankind, Mr. Bucket pervades a vast number of houses, and strolls about an infinity of streets: to outward appearances rather languishing for want of an object. He is in the friendliest condition towards his species, and will drink with most of them. . . . Time and place cannot bind Mr. Bucket. Like man in the abstract, he is here to-day and gone to-morrow—but, very unlike man indeed, he is here again the next day.[7]

In this passage, by a Dickensian miracle, Inspector Charles Field of Scotland Yard has been changed into Inspector Bucket, the first police detective in English fiction.

Other nations of the British Commonwealth have made important contributions to fact-based crime literature. Among the finest of Canada's true-crime writers are essayist W. Stewart Wallace (*Murders and Mysteries: A Canadian Series* [Toronto: Macmillan, 1931]); Marjorie Freeman Campbell, who is equally adept in short studies (*A Century of Crime: The Development of Crime Detection Methods in Canada* [Toronto: McClelland and Stewart, 1970]) and in the book-length crime narrative (*Torso: The Evelyn Dick Case* [Toronto: Macmillan of Canada, 1974]). Toronto lawyer Martin Friedland has produced admirable monographs on English and American murder cases. In Quebec, true-crime reports and studies have appeared since the nineteenth century; an excellent collection is Montreal trial judge Dollard Dansereau's *Causes célèbres du Québec* (Ottawa: Leméac, 1974).

A recent masterwork in Canadian fact-based fiction is Margaret Atwood's *Alias Grace* (1996), in which the novelist brings psychological acuity and understanding of Victorian-era household relationships to bear on the enigmatic murder case of servant Grace Marks, convicted in 1843 of helping her fellow servant James McDermott murder their master, Thomas Kinnear, and his housekeeper and mistress, Nancy Montgomery, in the Canadian town of Richmond Hill. Among Canadian murder cases, the nocturnal attack in 1880 on the Donnelly farms in Ontario has been by far the most productive of historical studies, fiction, plays, and folklore. In the raid, which was the culmination of a feud among Irish immigrants, forty disguised men murdered James Donnelly Sr., his wife, two sons, and a niece. At a second trial, the defendants were acquitted. In Australia an equally rich literary heritage stems from the exploits of its cherished armor-clad bushranger Ned Kelly, who also figures in a series of paintings and drawings by Sidney Nolan.

American colonial murder came over on the *Mayflower:* John Billington, who was one of the signatories of the Mayflower Compact, shot a later Plymouth arrival, John Newcomin, in 1630 after the two men quarreled. Governor William Bradford penned the first page of American crime history when he tersely related Billington's case in *The History of Plymouth Colony* (1630–50):

---

7. *Bleak House*, chap. 53.

This year Billington the elder, one of those who came over first, was arraigned, and both by grand and petty jury found guilty of willful murder by plain and notorious evidence, and was accordingly executed.

This, the first execution among them, was a great sadness to them. They took all possible pains in the trial, and consulted Mr. Winthrop, and the other leading men at the Bay of Massachusetts recently arrived, who concurred with them that he ought to die, and the land be purged of blood. He and some of his relatives had often been punished for misconduct before, being one of the profanest families among them. They came from London, and I know not by what influence they were shuffled into the first body of settlers. The charge against him was that he waylaid a young man, one John Newcomin, about a former quarrel, and shot him with a gun, whereof he died.[8]

From this obscure beginning American true crime narratives followed much the same course marked out in England. A retired FBI agent, Thomas McDade, in his indispensable work *The Annals of Murder: A Bibliography of Books and Pamphlets on American Murders from Colonial Times to 1900* (Norman: Univ. of Oklahoma Press, 1961), lists 1,126 trial reports, chapbooks, criminal biographies, broadsides, confessions, ballads, and sermons devoted exclusively to murder cases in the first three American centuries.[9] One of the first gallows sermons to be published was delivered by Increase Mather to currier James Morgan, who was convicted in Boston in 1685 of murdering butcher Joseph Johnson with an iron spit when Johnson intervened to defend Morgan's wife from his drunken abuse. Cotton Mather followed in his father's literary path, publishing a series of cautionary sermons including *Pillars of Salt* (1699), inspired by the conviction of Bostonian Sarah Threeneedles for the murder of her illegitimate infant. Mather used this occasion for the ambitious purpose of creating New England's first criminal calendar; he appended to the Threeneedles sermon "An History of some Criminals Executed in this Land, for Capital Crimes," together with "some of their Dying Speeches; Collected and Published, For the Warning of such as Live in Destructive Courses of Ungodliness."

The criminal chapbook or pamphlet was an important strand in the development of American popular literature. Examples of some of the most picturesque items in this genre are cited by Edmund Pearson in the first section of his two-part article "'From Sudden Death,'" included in his *Queer Books* (Garden City: Doubleday, Doran, 1928). Pearson notes that one of the most prolific true-crime pamphleteers of the early nineteenth century was none other than the mythifier of George Washington's cherry tree, Parson Mason Locke

8. Billington and his mother, fictitiously named Joan and added to the roster of the Plymouth settlers, figure prominently in Stephen Vincent Benét's posthumously published first volume of a projected narrative poem of American pioneers entitled *Western Star* (1943). Toward the end of Book One, a colonist meets Joan Billington at the foot of her son's gallows and joins her in mourning the murderer as "a man who came with the first and should have thriven."

9. In seventeenth-century New England, of course, true-crime writing by more "serious" writers, such as divines and government functionaries, were more likely to address their witchcraft obsession than murder or other common-law offenses. See, for example, *Narratives of the Witchcraft Cases 1648–1706*, ed. George Lincoln Burr (New York: Scribner's, 1914).

Weems. One of Weems's works, titled *God's Revenge Against Murder* (1808), purports to de-scribe Ned Findley's murder of his wife Mary in South Carolina, a crime that McDade be-lieves "could be another of the Parson's whimseys."

An early nineteenth-century case that spawned ten pamphlet entries in McDade's bibli-ography is the trial and hanging of Jereboam O. Beauchamp (the "Kentucky Tragedy"). Colo-nel Solomon P. Sharp had seduced and abandoned Ann Cooke, to whom Beauchamp sub-sequently paid court. Cooke agreed to marry him only if he avenged her honor; after Sharp refused a duel, Beauchamp donned a mask and stabbed him to death. The Beauchamp case is one of the earliest American murders to have inspired a rich store of imaginative litera-ture: Edgar Allan Poe's fragmentary drama "Politian," William Gilmore Simms's *Charlem-ont* (1856) and *Beauchampe* (1842), and Robert Penn Warren's *World Enough and Time* (1950). Another early true-crime curiosity arose from the 1801 stabbing murder of Elizabeth Fales by her frustrated suitor Jason Fairbanks in a birch grove in Dedham, Massachusetts; a sym-pathetic "life and character" of the executed killer has been attributed to Sarah Wentworth Morton, described by historian Daniel A. Cohen as "a beautiful Boston socialite and fre-quent contributor to local literary magazines whose poetical effusions had at one time earned her considerable renown as 'the American Sappho.'"[10] Another literary fruit of the Dedham murder was *Life of Jason Fairbanks: A Novel Founded on Fact*, which Professor Cohen regards as "evidently one of the earliest novels based on an actual murder case." (Unfortunately no copy survives.) The early nineteenth century also marked the appearance of an extensive ghost-written criminal "autobiography" (1807) of the appealing New England crook Henry Tufts, reprieved from hanging for the theft of six silver spoons.

American writers of the nineteenth century, like their British forerunners, began to com-pile books of trials, but they generally favored English or French cases. John Dunphy's *Re-markable Trials of All Countries* (1867) includes only two American murders. As the century progressed, however, worthier studies of American cases were produced by authors famil-iar with the local or regional settings in which the crimes occurred. A pioneer in this genre was the New Hampshire poet Celia Thaxter (1835–1894), whose essay on Louis Wagner's murder of Anethe and Karen Christensen on Smutty Nose Island in the Isles of Shoals ap-peared in the *Atlantic Monthly* in 1875, only two years after the atrocity. Not only Thaxter's title but her imaginative re-creation of emotions declares an allegiance to De Quincey: "He returns to Anethe standing shuddering there. It is no matter that she is beautiful, young, and helpless to resist, that she has been kind to him, that she never did a human creature harm, that she stretches her gentle hands out to him in agonized entreaty, crying piteously, 'Oh, Louis, Louis, Louis!' He raises the ax and brings it down on her bright head in one tremendous blow, and she sinks without a sound and lies in a heap, with her warm blood reddening the snow."

New Orleans novelist George Washington Cable took pains to lend authenticity to the cases retold in a fictional manner in his *Strange True Stories of Louisiana* (1889). Among the

---

10. Daniel A. Cohen, *Pillars of Salt, Monuments of Grace: New England Crime Literature and the Origins of American Popular Culture, 1674–1860* (New York: Oxford Univ. Press, 1993), 188.

illustrations to his book he included some of the manuscripts and court papers on which he relied. The most famous malefactor restored to life in Cable's colorful prose is Delphine La-laurie, who tortured and mistreated slaves in the "haunted house" of Royal Street, New Orleans. Ohio regionalism combines with the horror of the death penalty in "Gibbetted," Lafcadio Hearn's account of the 1876 Dayton execution of nineteen-year-old James Murphy, who murdered Colonel William Dawson, a plow works superintendent, "apparently for no other reason than that he refused a drunken party permission to intrude upon the quiet enjoyments of a private wedding party." After "a hundred days of mental torture," Murphy faced "a hideous death" on the scaffold built in a prison corridor; after the first rope broke, a double noose took the young Murphy's life away. See *The Selected Writings of Lafcadio Hearn*, ed. Henry Goodman, intro. Malcolm Cowley (New York: Carol Publishing Co., 1991), 203–15. In 1874 Hearn also luridly reported the murder and cremation of Herman Schilling in a Cincinnati tannery; crime sketches were drawn by artist Frank Duveneck.

Cleveland-born short-story writer and magazine editor Alfred Henry Lewis (ca. 1858–1914) similarly applied fictive talent to the re-creation of criminal cases in his late work, *Nation-Famous New York Murders* (1914). Dedicated to William W. McLaughlin, retired chief inspector of the New York City Police, this collection of previously published articles includes highlights of the metropolis's criminal annals: the murder of prostitute Helen Jewett; the Draft Riots; the killing of journalist Albert Richardson in the offices of the *New York Tribune*; and the Astor Place Riot. Lewis's fiction-magazine style is exemplified by his summary of Helen Jewett's views on love and marriage: "The unlovely Scroggs was rich, and owned a bank. He went wild with love for Helen, and would have married her. She refused. What said her philosophy? For her no wedding bells should ring, no bridal veils be woven."

The American true-crime essay came into maturity with the publication in 1924 of *Studies in Murder* by Edmund Lester Pearson (1880–1937). Formerly editor of publications at the New York Public Library and a columnist and author on subjects relating to books, libraries, and book collecting, Pearson exclusively devoted the last twelve years of his life to pursuing his interest in murder cases. Strongly influenced by the work of Scottish crime essayist William Roughead, with whom he developed a friendship mainly by correspondence, Pearson brought to his crime studies a wit, stylishness, and brevity of exposition that are still unsurpassed. By his continued literary attention to Lizzie Borden, he contributed to establishing the preeminence of her case in American history and folklore. Pearson must also be credited with introducing American readers to famous French murder cases.

A near-contemporary of Pearson, Herbert Asbury (1891–1963) also blended humor and antiquarian interests in his volumes of short studies drawn from the underworld histories of American cities, including New York, San Francisco, New Orleans, and Chicago. So deeply engaged was Asbury's mind with crimes of the nineteenth century that he viewed the gangster phenomenon as having disappeared from New York City; in his introduction to *The Gangs of New York* (1928), he maintained that, happily, the gangster "has now passed from the metropolitan scene, and for nearly half a score of years has existed mainly in the lively imaginations of industrious journalists, among whom the tradition of the gangster has more lives than the proverbial cat."

Since World War II, highly accomplished book-length studies of individual criminal cases have been published with increasing frequency by America's trade and scholarly presses. Truman Capote's *In Cold Blood* (1966) is an emotionally committed relation of the murder of the Clutter family by Richard Hickock and Perry Smith and of the hangings of the criminals. The work follows the pattern of such nineteenth-century crime essayists as Thomas De Quincey and Celia Thaxter in its fictive reconstruction of the victims' feelings and in a strong evocation of settings. Because of the work of such forerunners, and of more recent imaginative journalism that Capote himself cited in interviews (such as Lillian Ross's *Picture*), there is reason to dispute his claim to have invented a new literary genre, the "nonfiction novel." Still, it would be difficult to point to a book-length crime reportage before Capote's in which the author, to borrow his words, "employed all the techniques of fictional art."

Norman Mailer's mammoth rendering of Gary Gilmore's murders and his welcomed death before a Utah firing squad, *The Executioner's Song* (1977), won a Pulitzer Prize, a recognition that had been denied *In Cold Blood*. Mailer's publisher had apparently intended to signal Capote's work as a precedent by describing *The Executioner's Song* on its dust jacket as "a true life novel." Yet Mailer, unlike Capote, took great pains to conceal his novelist's art, and his distinctive literary voice does not appear in the Gilmore narrative. Instead, the story is told in a flat, unobtrusive style. Novelist Joan Didion praised its "meticulously limited vocabulary and its voice as flat as the horizon . . . the authentic Western voice."

In addition to the works of Capote and Mailer that bestride the conventional lines between fact and imaginative literature, recent decades have been favored by outstanding examples of crime-history monographs presented in more traditional scholarly modes. Many of the works of this class have been published by university presses and tend therefore to deal with criminal cases that illuminate significant episodes or issues in American history. Among the best are Dan T. Carter's *Scottsboro: A Tragedy of the American South* (Baton Rouge: Louisiana State Univ. Press, 1979), a study of the race-angled rape prosecution and ultimate vindication of the "Scottsboro boys"; and Charles E. Rosenberg's *The Trial of the Assassin Guiteau: Psychiatry and Law in the Gilded Age* (Chicago: Univ. of Chicago Press, 1968), an analysis of the conflict between law and psychiatry in the prosecution of President James Garfield's assassin, Charles Guiteau. With the reawakened examination of Thomas Jefferson's relationship to America's racial nightmares, an abiding interest is attached to Boynton Merrill Jr.'s *Jefferson's Nephews: A Frontier Tragedy* (Princeton: Princeton Univ. Press, 1976), studying a case in which two nephews of Jefferson, Lilburne and Isham Lewis, were charged with the murder of a slave. The crime had previously inspired Robert Penn Warren's "tale in verse and voices," *Brother to Dragons* (New York: Random House, 1953).

Worthy of a place among these esteemed crime historians is journalist J. Anthony Lukas, whose *Big Trouble* (New York: Simon and Schuster, 1997) was published shortly after the author's tragic suicide. Lukas's book, bearing the grandiloquent subtitle "A Murder in a Small Western Town Sets Off a Struggle for the Soul of America," focuses on the trial of Western miners' union leader William (Big Bill) Haywood's trial for the 1907 Idaho bombing murder of banker Frank R. Steunenberg, who as governor has obtained the assistance of federal troops in suppressing labor violence in the Coeur d'Alene mining district. Lukas's principal purpose was to "examine that moment in our national experience when we came closest to [class] warfare." In pursuit of that goal, he paints on a historical canvas incomparably vaster than that of *Ragtime*, introducing a cast of characters including Haywood's successful defender Clarence Darrow, President Theodore Roosevelt, railroad magnate E. H. Harriman, actress Ethel Barrymore, and pitching legend Walter Johnson.

Crime histories of this caliber will likely fight a losing battle against "quickie" hackwork for space on the shelves and display counters of American superstores; but they will continue to instruct and entertain many generations. It is a pity, therefore, that the achievements of crime scholars went unmentioned in Alex Ross's dismissive survey (*New Yorker*, August 19, 1996) of true crime's "current traits and tics, virtues and sins, absurdities and accidental truths."

We are indebted to Edgar Allan Poe for the introduction of true-crime elements into significant American fiction. Poe's French sleuth Auguste Dupin is plainly modeled on the detective chief of Paris, Eugène-François Vidocq, despite Dupin's faint praise for his real-life predecessor: "Vidocq . . . was a good guesser, and a persevering man. But, without educated thought, he erred continually by the very intensity of his investigations. He impaired his vision by holding the object too close. He might see, perhaps, one or two points with unusual clearness, but in so doing he, necessarily, lost sight of the matter as a whole. Thus, there is such a thing as being too profound." In Poe's story "The Mystery of Marie Roget," the title character bears, in Gallicized form, the name of Wall Street tobacconist saleswoman Mary Cecilia Rogers, whose dead body was found floating in the Hudson in 1842. Setting his tale in Paris, Poe closely followed the main facts of the unsolved Rogers case and proposed his own solution. Rejecting the theory that the crime had been perpetrated by a gang of ruffians, Poe surmised, through the reasoning of his detective Dupin, that Rogers had run off with a sailor with whom she had eloped before. After the story's first periodical appearance, Dupin's conclusions were slightly altered by his creator to conform to newer investigative findings suggesting that Rogers might have been the victim of a botched abortion.

One of the permanent values of the Poe tale was in Dupin's attack on irresponsible crime journalism. In Dupin's view, "it is the object of our newspapers rather to create a sensation—to make a point—than to further the cause of truth. . . . In ratiocination, not less than in literature, it is the *epigram* which is the most immediately and the most universally appreciated. In both, it is of the lowest order of merit." (What Poe meant by an "epigram" we now term a "sound byte.") In Poe's wake, many of America's most honored novelists have utilized true-crime sources. Images of historical murderesses are reflected by the two principal female characters, Hilda and Miriam, in Nathaniel Hawthorne's *The Marble Faun* (1860). The pure Hilda feels empathy with Guido Reni's supposed portrait of the parricide Beatrice Cenci, with whose fate Miriam, a painter of scenes of violence by women, also identifies her own impulse to murder her male oppressor. Hawthorne also suggests that Miriam was innocently involved in a scandalous criminal case of the recent past; literary scholarship has shown that the historical figure whom Hawthorne had in mind was Henriette Deluzy, a governess unjustly accused of complicity in the Praslin murder in Paris.

Family and maritime history fuses in Herman Melville's *White-Jacket*. The title character, a seaman on the *Neversink*, refers explicitly to the controversy surrounding the summary hanging of three sailors aboard the USS *Somers* in 1842. The men had been sentenced to death for mutiny, despite the absence of overt acts of rebellion, by an informal officers' court presided over by Melville's cousin, Lieutenant Guert Gansevoort, who had reported the supposed mutinous conspiracy to Captain Alexander Mackenzie. White-Jacket comments, "The well-known case of a United States brig furnishes a memorable example, which at any moment may be repeated. Three men, in a time of peace, were then hung at the yardarm, merely because, in the captain's judgment, it became necessary to hang them. To this day the question of their complete guilt is socially discussed."[11] Professor Michael Paul Rogan has shown how Melville returned to the theme of the *Somers* mutiny in *Billy Budd*, written in the last years preceding his death in 1891.[12] In this novella, according to Rogan's analysis, Melville absolved both the condemned Billy and his executioner, Captain Vere, of bad motives. Instead, he argues, the death sentence reflected a rigid, formalistic devotion to the state that was divorced from human feeling and, paradoxically, left uncontaminated the love that Vere and Billy felt for each other.

Frank Norris's Zolaesque novel *McTeague* (1899) based its title character on an unemployed ironworker, Patrick Collins, who murdered his wife, Sarah, in San Francisco in 1893. At the time of the novel's composition, both Norris and the reporter covering the Collins case reflected the influence of Italian criminologist Cesare Lombroso, who believed in the inheritance of antisocial tendencies from parents who themselves either were criminals or had suffered a degeneration of the nervous system due to alcoholism. McTeague's wife, Trina, also appears to be a victim of her genes, owing her miserliness to tightfisted ancestors.

At least from 1914 on, Theodore Dreiser looked into a number of murder cases as possible subjects for a novel, believing that these crimes were often impelled by a drive to rise in a society dominated by materialism. Among the murders he considered were three poisoning trials: the case of Roland Molineux; the 1891 murder of Helen Potts by her lover, a young medical student named Carlyle Harris, who found their socially ill-assorted match an obstacle to his professional aspirations; and Reverend Clarence Richeson's 1911 killing of a young parishioner, Avis Linnell, whose pregnancy threatened his plans to marry a wealthy woman. After writing six chapters based on the Richeson-Linnell case, Dreiser abandoned the project in favor of the Gillette-Brown case of 1906. In that year Chester Gillette, a supervisor in his uncle's skirt factory, drowned his pregnant sweetheart, a fellow factory employee named Grace Brown, in Big Moose Lake in the Adirondacks. In preparation of the sprawling realist novel that, in support of its author's attack on materialistic standards of the good life, was to be titled *An American Tragedy*, Dreiser visited the murder scene and Sing Sing prison. To provide authenticity to the courtroom scenes in the powerful second volume of his work, Dreiser, according to his biographer W. A. Swanberg, "clung to fact when he could, lifting some 30 pages verbatim from old New York newspaper accounts of the court proceedings and the letters between the ill-fated lovers."

11. *White-Jacket*, chap. 72.

12. "The *Somers* Mutiny and *Billy Budd*: Melville in the Penal Colony," *Subversive Genealogy: The Politics and Art of Herman Melville* (New York: Knopf, 1983), 288–316.

Richard Wright's *Native Son* (1940), depicting the murders and execution of a black youth, Bigger Thomas, shows the influence of Dreiser, whom Wright ardently admired. Originally undertaking the work as a study of life in the black slums of Chicago's South Side, Wright incorporated into his draft elements of Robert Nixon's contemporary burglary-murder trial, which the Chicago press covered with a display of undisguised racism. Bigger Thomas, though, is a personality far more complex than the Robert Nixon who emerges from the court record; although Bigger is prone to a violence that is a product of his own fear as an outcast, his first crime, the suffocation of his white "liberal" employer's daughter, is actuated on the unmarked border between accident and malice.

Although of literary merit considerably below the peaks of fact-based crime fiction, many estimable American bestsellers have continued the tradition of borrowing narrative material from famous murder cases. Three leading examples are Meyer Levin's *Compulsion* (1956), a version of the Leopold-Loeb case somewhat marred by psychobabble; Bernard Malamud's *The Fixer* (1966), based on Mendel Beiliss's blood-libel trial in nineteenth-century Ukraine (in which the defendant was charged with having murdered a Christian boy in order to use his blood to make Passover matzos); and E. L. Doctorow's *Ragtime* (1975), in which "Younger Brother" falls in love with Evelyn Nesbit Thaw, the wife of architect Stanford White's demented killer.

In 1798 William Dunlap, America's first professional playwright, staged *André*, a drama about British spy Major John André. However, American drama based on true-crime sources attained its full powers only in the twentieth century. Prior generations of theater audiences in the United States greatly preferred unabashedly fictional melodrama to entertainments drawn from crime history, but occasionally real criminals, victims, or policemen took brief turns on the stage. The kidnapping of Charley Ross, for example, influenced the last two acts of Augustin Daly's popular 1875 play *Pique*. David Belasco dramatized a current bank scandal in his *Men and Women* (1890), his final collaboration with Henry C. De Mille; earlier Belasco had introduced Napoleon III's police chief, Monsieur Claude, to New Yorkers in his adaptation of a French thriller, *The Stranglers of Paris* (1883). The opening of William R. Wilson's *The Inspector* (1890) was delayed for several nights apparently because the police believed that the play caricatured New City's police inspector Thomas Byrnes.

Other true-crime figures to appear on New York stages in the nineteenth century include Britain's Eugene Aram (in 1885), Deacon Brodie (in 1888), and Jack Sheppard (as early as 1871). As the twentieth century was born, current American murder cases were featured in dramatic productions. Victor C. Calvert's *The Great Poison Mystery* (1902) absolved Roland Molineux of the famous Bromo-Seltzer poisoning at New York's Knickerbocker Athletic Club, but the play never reached New York, possibly because the author plainly attributed the crime to Harry Cornish. According to theater chronicler Gerald Bordman, Molineux, a few years later, became "the first American convicted of murder[13] to have a play of his own given a major New York mounting"; in this comment, Bordman made reference to Molineux's play *The Man Inside* (1913), which David Belasco produced unsuccessfully after subjecting the chaotic manuscript to

---

13. The conviction was later reversed, and Molineux was acquitted upon retrial.

substantial revisions. Another American murder case, the killing of Mr. Burdick by his wife's lover at her behest, was reflected accurately in Lawrence Russell's *The Buffalo Mystery* (1903).

From the 1920s on, increasing use has been made of true crime and scandal in the fundamental plot structures of American drama. December 1926 marked the New York City premiere of the comedy *Chicago*, later filmed as *Roxie Hart* with Ginger Rogers and adapted as a musical comedy under its original name with music by John Kander and lyrics by Fred Ebb. The author of the 1926 stage work, Maurine Watkins, based the characters of Roxie Hart and Velma on her own *Chicago Tribune* coverage of the trials and acquittals of Belva Gaertner and Beulah Annan for the murders of their lovers. Two years later, Sophie Treadwell's *Machinal*, employing techniques similar to those previously used by Elmer Rice in *The Adding Machine*, played free variations on the Ruth Snyder–Judd Gray murder case in powerful expressionist scenes showing the doomed killers in the grip of mechanistic fate. In the following decade, Lillian Hellman, in *The Children's Hour* (first produced in 1934), reversed Edgar Allan Poe's feat of turning a New Yorker into the Frenchwoman "Marie Roget"; she seamlessly Americanized and updated an Edinburgh scandal of 1810 in which a girl student accused her schoolmistresses of lesbianism.

In the latter part of the twentieth century, crime dramas that are fact-based but not necessarily bound to chronological storytelling have flourished on and, more often, far off Broadway. The playwrights, addressing audiences much smaller than the readership that hankers after ephemeral crime journalism, achieve greater freedom in developing themes imbedded deeply in real-life tragedies. It is often small-scale works that have left the strongest impressions. Neal Bell's *Two Small Bodies* (1977), later filmed, is a dark two-character fantasy on the troubling Alice Crimmins murder case, in which an increasingly pathological relationship develops between the Crimmins-like suspect and the detective investigating the disappearance of her two children. *Gross Indecency* dexterously interlaces testimony from the trials of Oscar Wilde with comments of his contemporaries and an amusing interview with a modern literary scholar to shed new light on Wilde's deceptions and self-deceptions about the gap between art and conduct. Thulani Davis's play *Everybody's Ruby*, produced at New York City's Public Theatre in 1999, revisits Ruby McCollum's 1952 murder of her white lover, Dr. Clifford LeRoy Adams. Davis juxtaposes two powerful images of rejected African women: McCollum, denied justice by a racist Florida community, and Zora Neale Hurston (a reporter at McCollum's trial), compelled by lack of a receptive public to abandon her literary career.

FRENCH WORKS

Like cuisine, each country's fact-based crime literature tends to have its own flavor and characteristic modes of preparation. The French, innovators in true-crime literature as in so many of the arts, were among the first to find value in collecting narratives of criminal trials and other legal proceedings in series to which they gave the name "causes célèbres." Gayot de Pitaval, an eighteenth-century lawyer whose work was influential in launching this literary genre, explained in a preface to his causes célèbres why he believed trial accounts to be instructive:

The strange and surprising facts in the agreeable stories that are works of the imagination cause us a poisoned pleasure, so to speak, because of the falsity of the events. This feigned beauty is not a true beauty; it astonishes us at first, but the illusion dissipates, and the natural repugnance that we feel for the false revolts us, at the bottom of our heart, against the most beautiful of fictions.

But when the true combines with the wonderful, and when nature offers them to us in a fabric of facts, where it seems to have borrowed from a happy genius for embellishment, then our mind and our heart enjoy a pleasure that is pure and exquisite.

Following Gayot de Pitaval's lead, other authors produced series of causes célèbres without interruption until the eve of World War II. During the nineteenth century, the work of Armand Fouquier was particularly popular, appearing in a Spanish translation and providing the principal source for American Edmund Pearson's essays on French crime. The more modern compilers of French causes célèbres, such as Albert Bataille (who published between 1880 and 1898) and Geo London (who covered trials between 1927 and 1938) based their trial summaries on their own courtroom notes. Unfortunately, only a small portion of French causes célèbres are available in English: two volumes of selections from Albert Bataille's trial reports and Alexandre Dumas *père*'s engaging but highly fictionalized set of *Celebrated Crimes*.

The trial summaries of Gayot de Pitaval and his followers had their antecedents in popular fact-based crime literature that began to appear in France as early as the sixteenth and seventeenth centuries.[14] A principal source of such publications was the Blue Library (Bibliothèque bleue), consisting of chapbooks published between the late sixteenth century and the end of the nineteenth century. First developed in the printing shops of Troyes en Champagne, these booklets, which owed their generic name to their characteristic blue-gray paper covers, constituted for the majority of the population during the three centuries of their production "the most common means of access to written culture."[15] Sold at cheap prices in tens of millions of copies and offering 1,200 titles on subjects as diverse as beggars and the weather, the Blue Library included narratives and ballads celebrating the crimes and executions of such famous murderers as Madame Lescombat and the poisoner Desrues. Among the bestsellers were chapbooks devoted to the smuggler Mandrin and Parisian gangster Cartouche, who were often portrayed as "social bandits" championing the oppressed.

Although French literary interest in true crime had roots in reportage of criminal trials, factual crime writing did not remain a private preserve of lawyers or crime journalists. The French are inclined to examine their crimes as an integral part of a historical or social milieu, and historians of a particular era are as likely to concern themselves with crimes and mysteries of their period of specialization as with its wars or paintings. For example, Georges

---

14. An early true-crime volume in the Borowitz Collection is François de Calvi's *Histoire générale des larrons* [General History of Thieves] (Rouen: Jacques Caillové, 1636).

15. *Histoires curieuses et véritables de Cartouche et de Mandrin*, texts presented by H. J. Lüsebrink (Paris: Arthaud-Montalba, 1984), 3.

Mongrédien, best known for his cultural studies of seventeenth-century France, has also written valuable monographs on the trial of Louis XIV's finance minister, Nicolas Fouquet, for maladministration of public funds and on the Man in the Iron Mask.

Prominent among historical mysteries that are perennially fascinating to French scholars and their readership are identity disputes and impostures. Among the most persistent conundra are the identity of the Man in the Iron Mask and the respective claims of a series of "false Dauphins" to be Louis XVII, escaped (so they asserted) from the Temple Prison during the French Revolution.[16] A modern film and stage musical have given wider fame to the seventeenth-century impostor who claimed to be Martin Guerre, a case that opens the first volume of Gayot de Pitaval's causes célèbres. Another entrant into the charmed literary circle of French impostors is the "woman without a name," who asserted after the Revolution that she was the Marquise Marie de Douhault, regarded as long dead and buried but in fact (she asserted) long imprisoned in revolutionary *oubliettes*. Her avowed ordeal inspired Wilkie Collins's *The Woman in White*.

An admirable tradition of French writers through the ages has been to take up their pens in favor of compatriots whom they have deemed unjustly accused or condemned. Sometimes these literary interventions have entailed considerable personal risks. The most famous example, of course, is Emile Zola's celebrated advocacy of the cause of Alfred Dreyfus, which led to the novelist's conviction of criminal defamation. Zola's action followed a seventeenth-century precedent; Paul Pellisson, secretary to Fouquet, composed eloquent memorials to Louis XIV in defense of the fallen minister, only to receive five years in the Bastille for his pains. An equal show of courage was made by Voltaire in his successful rehabilitation of the reputation of Jean Calas, erroneously condemned and executed for the murder of his son as the result of anti-Protestant prejudice. Novelist Benjamin Constant's campaign in behalf of farmers' advocate Wilfred Regnault, wrongly convicted of murder in 1817, proved to be more timely; Regnault's death sentence was commuted to imprisonment. Other literary intercessions appear to have been quixotic. Balzac's defense of his former journalistic colleague Sébastien Peytel could not shake the strong murder case against him. Before World War II a group of surrealist writers and artists collaborated on a pamphlet in support of Violette Nozières (or Nozière), who faced trial for poisoning her parents; although the surrealists could not suggest a credible defense to the criminal charges, they sought to portray her as a symbol of youth abused by age. As the Peytel and Nozières cases demonstrate, French writers have not necessarily been on the right side of every issue of criminal law, but each of these instances of literary intervention has given rise to significant fact-based crime writings.

Other important categories of French crime nonfiction are police and detective memoirs, the most notable of which are those of Vidocq (who will be discussed further), Goron, and Napoleon III's police chief Monsieur Claude. Another law-and-order bestseller was the ghost-written memoirs of the Sansons, France's hereditary executioners. Beginning in the nineteenth century, descriptions of France's prisons and prison camps abound; many are the works of reformers, culminating in journalist Albert Londres's *Au bagne* [In the Prison

16. A recent DNA test has confirmed that the Dauphin died in prison.

Camp] (1923), which is credited with contributing to the abolition of France's overseas prison colonies. Prison escape literature, exemplified in our time by Henri Charrière's *Papillon*
(1969), has also been highly favored by French readers. Among criminal autobiographies,
the memoirs written by the "poet-murderer" Pierre-François Lacenaire before his execution
in 1836 show a vein of genuine literary talent unhappily absent from his verse. However, the
memoirs of Clarisse Manson (1818), ghost-written by Balzac's mentor Henri de Latouche
for the duplicitous star witness in the Fualdès murder trials, are primarily a hoax that offended Madame Manson but won a large public in many countries.

As in England, the French nonfictional literature of crime burgeoned as the twentieth
century was ushered in. Alexandre Lacassagne, professor of forensic medicine at the University of Lyon, in addition to his scientific texts such as *Précis de médecine légale* (Paris:
Masson, 1909), wrote a study of Joseph Vacher, large-scale serial killer of animal herders;
Lacassagne had confirmed Vacher's sanity to the trial court. In his book, titled *Vacher the
Ripper and Sadistic Crimes* (Lyon: Storck, 1899), Lacassagne compared Vacher to other sadistic killers, including Gilles de Rais and Jack the Ripper. In the first half of the twentieth
century, another great forensic scientist made his mark in Lyon: criminalist Dr. Edmond
Locard, who became known as the "Sherlock Holmes of France." The author of important
treatises on scientific crime detection, Locard also wrote and edited many popular studies
of criminal cases. Another physician, Dr. [Augustin] Cabanès wrote greatly admired series
of antiquarian works on wide-ranging subjects, including many that investigated the medical aspects of historical mysteries.

Focusing on personal tragedies that were overshadowed by cataclysmic public events,
Théodore Gosselin, adopting the pseudonym of G. Lenotre, created a large body of work
that focused primarily on the era of the French Revolution. To his studies of private disaster
he applied the term "little history" (*petite histoire*). Although his themes were often modest,
Lenotre was unsparing in archival documentation. Paul Reboux and Charles Muller, parodying Lenotre's account of the flight of the royal couple to Varennes, supply a footnote furnishing the names of the six horses that drew the carriage. The warmhearted Lenotre formed
a distinguished literary circle, including crime historians Ernest d'Hauterive (son-in-law of
Alexandre Dumas *fils*) and J. Lucas-Dubreton.

Until about 1925, when one of its leading spirits, Pierre Figerou, died, one of the principal animators of French crime history research was a group of aficionados who called themselves the Dinner Club of the Eleven (Dîner des Onze). The members, "attentive to accuracy
and method, decided to gather periodically to chat, over their cups, about their bibliophilic
finds, to recall curious cases and to call new ones to each other's attention, and to exchange
information and recollections."[17] The eleven clubmen were the former president of the Paris
bar, Henri-Robert; the preeminent forensic scientist of the period, dandyish Dr. Charles
Paul, who sported white gaiters; Judge Maurice Gilbert, who presided over the Landru
murder trial; Robert Godefroy, associate justice of France's Supreme Court; crime annalists
Gaston Delayen and Georges Claretie; crime historian Pierre Figerou; appellate lawyer and

17. Pierre de Pressac, Preface to Pierre Figerou, *La belle Madame Lescombat, son amant et son mari* (Paris: Perrin, 1927).

journalist Henri Vonoven; Maurice Reclus, member of France's highest administrative court (Conseil d'État); historian Pierre de Pressac; and Paul Dollfus, journalist on the staff of *Gil Blas*. Many of the club members authored distinguished monographs on crimes of the past, including volumes in the series published by Perrin under the general title *Judicial Puzzles and Dramas of the Past* (Énigmes et drames judiciaires d'autrefois). The Dinner Club of the Eleven appears to set the pattern for the Parisian "Crimes Club" that furnishes the title of William Le Queux's 1927 collection of short stories. The still-vigorous English counterpart of the Eleven is Our Society, of which Sir Arthur Conan Doyle was an early member.

In terms of the quality and volume of his work, Pierre Bouchardon (1870–1950) has a strong claim to first place among France's crime historians. A magistrate by profession, Bouchardon gained initial prominence as an investigator for the Council of War inquiry into the espionage of Mata Hari and after World War II was called on to consider evidence regarding the charges against Marshal Pétain. Despite his busy judicial career, Bouchardon wrote over thirty books (including monographs and collections of essays) devoted to French crimes, generally preferring to deal with "common-law" cases, in which criminal conduct is actuated by personal motives rather than political antagonisms. An idolator of Balzac, from whose work he often culled quotations to serve as epigraphs, Bouchardon is the most literary of the France's leading crime historians. Given to pungent aphorisms, he compares his favorite poisoner Marie Lafarge to Emma Bovary by remarking, "A woman pardons her husband for the loss of her fortune; she does not pardon him for the violation of her modesty or the ruin of her illusions."

A rich harvest of fact-based crime fiction began in the early nineteenth century. An anonymous 1813 novel based on the persecution and murder of the Marquise de Gange (or Ganges) by her husband and her brothers has been attributed to the Marquis de Sade, who uncharacteristically sympathizes with his virtuous heroine. It is, however, Stendhal's *The Red and Black* (1830) that must be regarded as the fountainhead of French romantic fiction based on fact-crime sources. The calculating heart of Stendhal's antihero Julien Sorel, a fictionalized portrait of Antoine Berthet (who attempted to murder Mme. Michoud de la Tour during a church service at Brangues in 1827), is intended to persuade us that, in nineteenth-century France, it was not murder but seduction that was undertaken "in cold blood." Alexandre Dumas *père* drew many of his characters and plots from real life, often preserving the names of historical figures who rubbed shoulders with others who were pure inventions. Among the most successful of his novels based on crime history are *The Man in the Iron Mask, The Queen's Necklace*, and *Le chevalier de Maison-Rouge*, based on the rash adventurer who tried to free Marie Antoinette from prison in the "carnation plot."

A seminal figure in the development of fact-based crime fiction, by virtue both of his own writings and his international influence on other authors, is Eugène-François Vidocq (1775–1857). A brawler in his early life, Vidocq was repeatedly imprisoned for minor offenses and after the last of many daring escapes was pursued relentlessly by the police. Tiring of life on the run, Vidocq made his peace with the law, becoming successively a police spy, head of the Paris Sûreté, and organizer of a private detective agency. In 1828 his memoirs (heavily adulterated by unscrupulous editors) were published and immediately translated into English; they became an international exemplar for police memoirs, in which reality and sensation kept uneasy company. Between 1836 and 1846 Vidocq published three works of mingled fact and fiction based on his knowledge of crime: *The Thieves* (1836), *The True Mysteries of Paris* (1844), and *The "Chauffeurs" of the North* (1845–46), the last title referring not to taxi drivers but to a gang of ruffians who held householders' feet to the fire in order to force them to reveal the hiding places of their valuables. Vidocq's melodramatic career, charismatic personality, and familiarity with the ways of the underworld influenced the work of romantic novelists, including Balzac and Hugo. Balzac admitted that he based on Vidocq the criminal genius and subsequently police chief Vautrin, who haunts the pages of *La comédie humaine*, making his first appearance in *Le père Goriot*. When Hippolyte Castille objected that Vautrin was superhuman, Balzac responded: "I can assure you that the model exists, that he is a person of appalling greatness and that he has found his place in the world of our time."[18] Vidocq was a friend of Victor Hugo and rendered him valuable services as a private detective at two important junctures in the author's complicated love life. Jean Valjean shared many experiences with Vidocq, including his famed rescue of an injured carter as well as the unflagging pursuit by the police long after Valjean had acquitted his debt to society. Vidocq also exercised a decisive influence on the development of the detective story; his features can be recognized in the detectives of Poe and Gaboriau and in Sherlock Holmes.

Among later works of French fiction based on crime history are Alphonse Daudet's charming spoof of the French Academy, *The Immortal* (1888), which draws on the outrageous literary forgeries of Vrain-Lucas, and André Gide's *The Counterfeiters* (1925), which ends with the death of young Boris in a compelled schoolroom suicide drawn from a 1909 tragedy to which the Littleton, Colorado, massacre of 1999 has been compared.

French stage works based on actual crimes were written as early as 1599, when twenty-five-year-old jurist Pierre Matthieu wrote *La Guisiade*, a five-act tragedy lamenting King Henry III's ordered assassination of his political rival, Henri, Duc de Guise, the leader of the hard-line Catholic faction. Matthieu turned reality into drama with blinding speed, rushing his work into print only six months after Guise was murdered by Henri's cutthroats in the Blois Chateau.

Nonpolitical crimes found their way onto the French stage by the seventeenth century. It is assumed, for example, that Molière, in creating Harpagon, the title character in *The Miser*, must have had in mind the lives and sudden deaths of seventeenth-century Paris's renowned miser, Lieutenant-Criminel (police chief) Jean Tardieu and his wife, Marie, who were murdered by a pair of housebreakers in 1665. The beloved Parisian gang leader Cartouche took a bow in a 1721 prose comedy by M. le Grand, *Cartouche, ou les Voleurs* [Cartouche, or The Thieves]. In August 1793 the staging of *The Friend of the People: or The Death of Marat* by Gaussier Saint-Armand inaugurated the long succession of plays in France and elsewhere depicting the murder of Marat by Charlotte Corday.

One of the most famous French fact-based melodramas of the nineteenth century was *Le Courrier de Lyon* (The Lyons Mail) of 1850 by Moreau, Siraudin, and Delacour; English stag-

18. Quoted in Philip John Stead, *Vidocq: A Biography* (London: Staples Press, 1953), 147.

ings of adaptations successively featured Henry Irving and his son H. B. Irving in the dual role of Joseph Lesurques and the Lyons mail murderer Dubosc, for whose crime Lesurques (who closely resembled Dubosc) may have been unjustly guillotined. The French stage has also favored plays featuring swindlers and wheeler-dealers. In 1893 echoes of John Law's "Mississippi Bubble" were heard in Léon Hennique's *L'Argent d'autrui* [Other People's Money], where the plot focuses on an anti-Jewish swindle launched by the speculator Lafontas, a great admirer of Law. The tradition of French true-crime drama is continued by Jean Genet's *The Maids* (1947), inspired by the murderous housemaids of Le Mans, Christine and Léa Papin.

French murder cases have been adapted for many memorable films. Pierre-François Lacenaire, the sociopathic "poet-murderer" of France's Romantic Age, makes a menacing appearance in the classic film *Les enfants du paradis* [Children of Paradise] (1945), written by Jacques Prévert and directed by Marcel Carné. *L'Auberge Rouge* [The Red Inn] (1951), Fernandel's hilarious send-up of France's bloodthirstiest innkeepers, had the distinction of upsetting Boston's censors. Claude Chabrol's *Bluebeard* (1962), with a script on which he collaborated with Françoise Sagan, brought before the cameras serial killer Henri-Désiré Landru, who had previously inspired Charlie Chaplin's *Monsieur Verdoux*. Other notable French films have been based on the murder cases of Pauline Dubuisson (*The Truth* [1960], starring Brigitte Bardot); Violette Nozières (Chabrol's *Violette* [1978]); and France's incomparably bloodier rival of Jack the Ripper, Joseph Vacher (Bertrand Tavernier's *The Judge and the Assassin* [1975]).

WRITINGS IN OTHER LANGUAGES

Ancient Greece and Rome

Criminal trials of Greek and Roman antiquity are documented by a small but instructive body of legal orations. Four Athenian murder trials featuring legal arguments by Lysias and Antiphon are included in Kathleen Freeman's *The Murder of Herodes, and Other Trials from the Athenian Law Courts* (London: Macdonald, 1946). Athenian procedure did not permit lawyers to appear in court, and it became customary for experts in rhetoric and legal principles to draft courtroom speeches for the private parties who appeared as prosecutor or defendant. The gem of Freeman's collection is Antiphon's brilliant argument in defense of Helos, a young man from Mytilene on the island of Lesbos who was charged with the murder of Herodes, a fellow passenger on a ship bound for the Thracian coast. The facts are murky, for Herodes had disappeared mysteriously at night in a port where the two travelers had been forced to change ships due to a storm. A tantalizing mystery clings to all these ancient cases, since the orations were published without any indication of the jury verdict.

Cicero, dreaded by generations of Latin students for his thundering tirades against political conspiracy and administrative corruption, was also one of the great criminal advocates of his day. Of particular interest is his defense of Aulus Cluentius Habitus against the charge of having bribed a jury to convict his stepfather, Appianicus, of attempting to poison him.[19] In this case we have reason to believe that Cicero's defense was successful, since Quintilian, a considerable lawyer and rhetorician in his own right, quotes Cicero as boasting that he had poured darkness in the eyes of the jury that tried Cluentius. The most intriguing case in Quintilian's career as criminal advocate was his defense of Naevius Arpinianus. The published oration does not survive, but Quintilian remarks in one of his other writings that "the sole question in the case of Naevius of Arpinum was whether he threw his wife out of the window or she threw herself."[20]

Germany

The development of indigenous fact-based crime literature in most of modern Europe was strongly favored at the outset by interest in French criminal cases and trial reports. A German translation of Gayot de Pitaval's *Causes célèbres* was published between 1792 and 1795, with a preface by Schiller (quoted above) that extolled the merit of studying criminal cases. Selections from nineteenth-century sets of French causes célèbres appeared in a Spanish-language version in 1835. In Italy, a translated report of France's internationally renowned Fualdès murder trial appeared in 1818.[21] Swedish novelist C. J. L. Almqvist reported from France on the 1840 poisoning trial of Madame Marie Lafarge, and in Czarist Russia, young opera-composer-to-be Modest Musorgsky kept body and soul together by translating French and German criminal cases.

Of all the countries of continental Europe other than France, Germany has created the most voluminous literature of its own causes célèbres. Many German-language translations of Gayot de Pitaval's French causes célèbres were published, including editions by Friedrich Schiller (1792–95) and Hermann Hesse (1922). Between 1842 and 1890 a sixty-volume series entitled *The New Pitaval*, named after Gayot de Pitaval and compiled initially by Julius Hitzig and Wilhelm Häring (also noted for fiction written under his pseudonym, Willibald Alexis), was published in Leipzig. Although the cases chosen were predominantly German, foreign cases, such as the murder trial of the Mannings in England and Galileo's miseries at the hands of the Inquisition, were interspersed. Between 1903 and 1913 the publication of German trials of current vintage was resumed in a seven-volume series entitled *The Pitaval of the Present Day*. More recent so-called "Pitavals," grouping German cases by region or period, have been created by authors including journalist Egon Erwin Kisch and lawyer Friedrich Kaul.

In 1910 court reporter Hugo Friedländer became the first German writer to undertake the singlehanded composition of a set of trial narratives. In his twelve-volume *Interesting Criminal Trials of Significance in Cultural History*, Friedländer represented that the accounts

19. See Albert Borowitz, "M. Tullius Cicero for the Defense," *Innocence and Arsenic: Studies in Crime and Literature* (New York: Harper & Row, 1977), 100–115.

20. Quintilian, *Institutio Oratoria*, with an English translation by H. E. Butler, 4 vols. (Cambridge, Mass.: Harvard Univ. Press, Loeb Library, 1921) 3:61.

21. A copy of this translation from the library of federal judge Harold Medina is in the Borowitz Collection.

were drawn from his own experiences in reporting courtroom proceedings. One of the most famous trials included in the set is the 1906 prosecution of the impostor Wilhelm Voigt, the "Captain from Köpenick," who, after donning a Prussian captain's uniform, arrested Köpenick's mayor and looted the town treasury. A celebrated 1931 stage comedy based on this incident was written by Carl Zuckmayer, and two filmed adaptations followed.

Another important author of true-crime studies was the Bavarian judge and criminal law reformer Anselm Ritter von Feuerbach, who in 1808 and 1811 published two volumes of *Notable Criminal Cases*, including a chapter on the serial poisoner Anna Maria Zwanziger. Another Feuerbach work is the famous account of his investigations regarding the enigmatic "wild child" Kaspar Hauser, of whom he became a friend and supporter. The mystery surrounding Kaspar Hauser's claim to have been imprisoned in childhood and his violent death remains Germany's favorite historical conundrum and has inspired literary works by Rainer Maria Rilke, Jakob Wassermann, and Peter Handke (author of the 1968 play *Kaspar*). See *Der Findling: Kaspar Hauser in der Literatur* [The Foundling: Kaspar Hauser in Literature], ed. Ulrich Struve (Stuttgart: J. B. Metzler, 1992). Some modern researchers have devised elaborate conspiracy theories of vast proportions, and the publisher Kaspar Hauser Verlag specializes in the case.

In the years before the Nazi takeover in 1933, significant crime nonfiction was written by authors famed in other literary fields. In 1923 journalist Maximilian Harden (born Felix Ernst Witkowski) published a volume of essays devoted to criminal trials, including chapters about his controversial attack on alleged homosexual activity of Wilhelm II's close friend and adviser Prince Eulenberg and Berlin commandant Count Kuno von Moltke. A year later novelist Alfred Döblin contributed the first book-length crime study in *Society's Outsiders: Crimes of the Present Day*, a multivolume set edited by expressionist Rudolf Leonhard; Döblin's book, *Two Girl Friends and their Poisoning-Murder*, is a fascinating study of *folie à deux* driving a pair of women to murder the husband of one of them.

The Nazi regime, which refused to acknowledge publicly that murder continued as a social ill in the Third Reich, buried the case of serial killer Bruno Lüdke arrested in 1943 and, after consolidating its power, generally did not permit publications about current crimes.[22] After World War II, however, interest in the crime field strongly rebounded in both Germany and Austria. Significant German nonfiction of the postwar era includes a 1974 documentary study of serial child-killer Peter Kürten, edited by Elisabeth Lenk and Roswitha Kaever (1974), and *Der Spiegel* journalist Gerhard Mauz's collection of articles on crimes in West Germany, *The Righteous and the Condemned* (1968). Many world-famous murder cases are skillfully related in the course of Jürgen Thorwald's two-volume history of scientific detection translated into English as *The Century of the Detective* (1965) and *Crime and Science* (1967). In Austria, there has been a profusion of books (dominated by the studies

---

22. At least two books in the Borowitz Collection include German criminal trials ended after the legislative confirmation of the Nazi dictatorship in March 1933: Paul Wiegler, *Schicksale und Verbrechen: Die grossen Prozesse der letzten hundert Jahre* [Misfortunes and Crimes: The Great Trials of the Last 100 Years] (Berlin: Ullstein, 1935); and E. Liebermann von Sonnenberg and O. Trettin, *Kriminal-Fälle* [Criminal Cases] (Berlin: Universitas, 1934).

of Brigitte Hamann) examining the 1889 love suicides of Crown Prince Rudolf and Maria Vetsera at Mayerling. Austrian writers have also explored recent cases in books such as prosecutor Werner Olscher's 1972 study of famous murder trials in Austria since World War II.

Early-nineteenth-century German drama and fiction, responding to the era's attraction to turbulent events and characters, often utilized crime history material. The salient works of this character include Schiller's youthful play *Die Räuber* [The Robbers] (1788); Heinrich von Kleist's novella "Michael Kohlhaas" (1808), recording the career of a sixteenth-century horse dealer, Hans Kohlhase, who turned to robbery and murder when he could not obtain legal redress from a nobleman who had wronged him; and Georg Büchner's fragmentary drama *Woyzeck*, written between 1835 and 1837 as a result of the author's interest in the German murder cases of defendants Johann Christian Woyzeck, Daniel Schmolling, and Johann Diess, in which insanity defenses had been raised. Although these authors and their contemporary E. T. A. Hoffmann (whose work also reflects a fascination with crime and obsession) often seem to give expression to extravagant imaginings, it is remarkable that in fact they all had professional or academic qualifications in law, medicine, science, or psychology. As is well known, *Pandora's Box* (1904), the second of Frank Wedekind's expressionistic Lulu plays, ends with Jack the Ripper's murder of the heroine. Film director Fritz Lang told film historian Sigmund Kracauer that the child murderer portrayed by Peter Lorre in *M* was inspired by the "Vampire of Düsseldorf," Peter Kürten.

One of the most important twentieth-century German authors of fact-based crime novels is Jakob Wassermann. His principal works in this genre are *Caspar Hauser* (1908) and *The Maurizius Case* (1928), drawn from a murder perpetrated by Karl Hau in Baden-Baden. The period since the end of World War II has produced many successful German fictional works based on true crime. The well-regarded psychological novelist Joachim Maass, in *The Gouffé Case* (1952), re-created a nineteenth-century French trunk murder. Erich Kuby's *Rosemarie* (1958), a wry look at the unlovely underside of the German "economic miracle" as revealed by the unsolved murder of prostitute Rosemarie Nitribitt, was a smash hit as a novel and a film in 1958. Journalist Hans Habe (born Hans Bekessy in Budapest), in addition to a collection of true-crime articles, wrote a 1962 novel based on Russian countess Marie Tarnowska, convicted in Italy of having procured the death of a count whose life she had persuaded him to insure for her benefit.

Italy

Italian writers have been more interested in organized crime, brigandage, and trials reflecting political corruption and antagonism than in criminal cases based on private misconduct. The preface to *Cronache Criminali Italiane* [Italian Criminal Chronicles] (1896), co-authored by Guglielmo Ferrero, son-in-law of biological determinist Cesare Lombroso, explains the origin of this literary preference for crimes against the public. Following Lombroso's teaching, the collaborators argue that "a night of love after an evening of gluttony or drunkenness explains the birth of a criminal degenerate," whereas brigandage is "a phenomenon for which the entire people, from the government down to the citizens, is directly responsible."

It cannot be concluded, however, that Italian literature scants the examination of aberrant individual behavior. Alessandro Manzoni's epic novel *The Betrothed* reflects both private and public misconduct from remote times: the scandalous life of the Nun of Monza, immured because of an illicit love affair with Gian Paolo Osio, a murderous neighbor of her convent; and the mass hysteria resulting from the Milanese plague of 1630. Manzoni later added a nonfictional pendant to the novel's treatment of the latter subject, *The History of the Column of Infamy*, which analyzes the unjust prosecution of "anointers" for intentionally spreading the plague germs.

One of the most famous Italian criminal biographies is Corrado Ricci's 1925 study of sixteenth-century parricide Beatrice Cenci. Ricci explodes two of the principal myths of the case, demonstrating that the incest defense was invented by Beatrice Cenci's lawyer and that Guido Reni's portrait of a sweet turbaned girl is not a death-cell painting of Beatrice. In 1999, however, documentation of an exhibition at Rome's Palazzo Barberini on Caravaggio and his followers suggested that his 1600 painting, *Judith and Holofernes* (Fig. 2), may have been inspired by the parricide for which Beatrice Cenci was executed the year before.[23] The Cenci case also inspired an 1851 novel by Francesco Dominico Guerrazzi, a patriot of the Risorgimento and enemy of the papal government of Rome. Guerrazzi converts Beatrice into a militant saint who continually exhorts her father to repent.

Many excellent crime biographies have appeared in Italy since World War II, including Mario Mazzucchelli's *The Nun of Monza* (1963) and journalist Giuseppe dall'Ongaro's well-documented biography of Italy's cherished outlaw Fra' Diavolo (Michele Pezza). Italians also continue to relish, as did their Roman forebears, collections of forensic speeches by eminent criminal advocates.

Modern Italian masters have used true-crime subject matter in a variety of literary modes. Novelist Alberto Moravia wrote the play *Beatrice Cenci* (1958), in which the parricide explains her revenge by a childhood "loss of innocence" caused by witnessing an amorous passage of her father. Moravia's novel *The Conformist* (1951), beautifully filmed by Bernardo Bertolucci, is based on the murder of Moravia's cousin, antifascist Carlo Rosselli, by French right-wing thugs hired by Mussolini. Sicilian novelist, historian, and commentator Leonardo Sciascia has often chosen the Mafia of his native island as his theme (for example, in the novel, *Mafia Vendetta* [1964]). In addition, his books deal with such diverse subjects as the Red Brigade's assassination and execution of Aldo Moro, the mysterious disappearance of Sicilian physicist Ettore Majorana in 1938, and an incident in the mob hysteria stemming from the Milanese plague of 1930 (a subject suggested by a passage in Manzoni's *The Betrothed*).

The 1997 Nobel Prize winner Dario Fo's hilarious comedy *Accidental Death of an Anarchist* is based on analogous incidents in the crime histories of the United States, drawing its plot from the mysterious fall of anarchist Andrea Salsedo from a window of New York City

---

23. See, to the same effect, Margarita Stocker, *Judith, Sexual Warrior: Women and Power in Western Culture* (New Haven: Yale, 1998), 110, citing M. Merini, *Michelangelo Merisi da Caravaggio* (1987), 418.

police headquarters in 1920 at the height of the Red Scare and the similar death of another anarchist, Pino Pinelli, in Milan in 1969.[24]

A highlight of Italian crime history is the still-controversial trial that followed the butchery of Count Francesco Bonmartini by his brother-in-law, lawyer Tullio Murri, in the count's Bologna apartment on September 2, 1902, apparently inspired by his mistreatment of his wife, Linda. As the case proceeded (resulting in a bizarre majority verdict convicting Linda of unpremeditated and nonessential "participation" in the crime), partisan journalists were swayed by the political allegiances of the tragedy's protagonists rather than by the evidence disclosed in the investigation; in right-wing columns Bonmartini's conservative views blotted out hints of sexual depravity, and Linda's brother Tullio and her father, an esteemed medical professor, Augusto Murri, were respectively attacked as socialist and freethinker. These ideological passions that may have distracted authorities in the pursuit of justice for Linda Murri are mirrored in Mauro Bolognini's memorable 1974 film *La grand bourgeoise*, starring Catherine Deneuve.

In a nonfictional study, *Isolina* (London: Peter Owen, 1993), Italian novelist Dacia Maraini reports another murder case from the dawn of the twentieth century in which she believes that the prosecution was frustrated by partiality to the military caste. In January 1900 pieces of the decapitated body of a pregnant woman were fished from Verona's River Adige, and her head turned up a year later, completing her identification as nineteen-year-old working-class woman Isolina Canuti. On the basis of personal investigations on the scene, Maraini concludes that the likely cause of death was a botched abortion. She shows how Isolina's lover, Lieutenant Carlo Trivulzio, and his comrades escaped persecution as the Verona community rallied around its military garrison. In a libel case that followed against socialist deputy Mario Todeschini, who had advocated Isolina's cause, the murdered woman was tarred as promiscuous. Trivulzio interrupted the proceedings by shouting: "But everybody had her. It's been proved."

Spain and Portugal

The criminal underbelly of Spain's Golden Age is exposed in the great picaresque or rogue novels that were a Spanish literary invention. Although this fiction is not based on the lives of identifiable criminals, Gerald Brenan observes that "the picaresque form had its root in social conditions."[25] He explains: "The ruin of the middle-income classes by inflation, the need so many people had of living by their wits, the hardships of the writer's life which threw him into low company were the things that prompted it. . . . These novels depict as a

---

24. See Carlo Ginzburg, *The Judge and the Historian: Marginal Notes on a Late–Twentieth Century Miscarriage of Justice*, trans. Anthony Shugar (London: Verso, 1999).

25. Alexander A. Parker, however, has noted that sixteenth-century Spain was not demonstrably richer in rogues than other European countries. *Literature and the Delinquent: The Picaresque Novel in Spain and Europe 1599– 1753* (Edinburgh: Edinburgh Univ. Press, 1967), 10.

rule a child growing up under sordid conditions and making his way through the world where everything is hostile and dangerous. He has no arms but his mother wit: by using it he becomes a criminal, but essentially he is innocent and well-intentioned and it is the wickedness of the world that corrupts him."[26] The leading examples of the picaresque genre are *The Life of Lazarillo de Tormes*, published anonymously in 1554; *Guzmán de Alfarache* (1599), written by Mateo Alemán, son of a prison doctor of Seville, and translated into English as *The Rogue* (1622) by James Mabbe; and Francisco de Quevedo's *La Vida del Buscón* [The Life of a Sharper], which was written between 1603 and 1608 and first appeared in 1626.

Scenes characteristic of picaresque fiction appear in Cervantes's *Don Quixote*. The Don, for example, is introduced to the reality of penal servitude when he encounters a dozen chained convicts on the road. Told that they have been condemned for their crimes to serve the king in his galleys, Don Quixote comments on their fate with surprising insight: "In short, however you put it, although these men are being led, they are going by force and not of their own free will." Cervantes's *Exemplary Novels* also reflect crime reality, including the organization of the thieves of Seville along the lines of a medieval guild; and the escapades of two well-born youths turned rogues (of whom a university record survives).

In 1837, the same Barcelona publisher that had issued a set of French trials in Spanish also released a similar series devoted to criminal cases of Spain, mingling public matters (for example, the death sentence of Don Carlos) with the intensely personal (such as a recent case of infanticide). The publication of crime collections has not always continued to be a feature of the Spanish literary scene, particularly during the Franco era when, true to totalitarian principles, the regime converted criminals into nonpersons. In his *Tribunal de muerte* [Death Court], originally released in 1963, novelist Carlos de Arce briefly reviews twenty-seven cases, from a counterfeiting of Spanish currency in 1331 to a murder case in 1928. It is de Arce's view that the typical "Iberian" murderer is more likely to kill on sudden impulse than to resemble the sadistic or split-personality killers found in other countries. A more interesting work is novelist Juan Madrid's *Malos tiempos* [Bad Times], which winds its way between fact and fiction in recounting contemporary Spanish cases, including the 1980 murder of the Marqués and Marquesa de Urquijo, one of Spain's great banking families.

Like their Italian counterparts, crime writers in Spain favor the lives of their brigands, of whom the most celebrated is Madrid's bandit Luis Candela. In 1927 journalist, biographer, and novelist Antonio Espina y García (born in Madrid in 1894) wrote a biography of Candelas in which the author displays his gifts for humor, irony, and word play. A two-volume collection of the lives of famous Spanish bandits by biographer F. Hernandez Girbal appeared in 1963 and 1973. Spanish authors have also produced works on crimes and acts of violence that were key events in their nation's history. A few examples are Antonio Pedrol Rius's clarification of the 1870 murder of General Juan Prim y Prats, who was struck down while attempting to introduce a new constitutional monarch; Leon-Ignacio's account of the 1640 reapers' uprising, "Corpus de Sangre," in Barcelona that triggered the disintegration of Spain; and Professor Juan Cantavella's study of nineteenth-century assassination plots against Spanish royalty.

26. Gerald Brenan, *The Literature of the Spanish People* (New York: Meridian, 1957), 174.

Latin America has also made significant contributions to fact-based crime literature. Among the outstanding works are Gabriel García Márquez's *News of a Kidnapping* (1997), a reportage of the 1990 kidnappings of ten Colombians (all but one of whom were journalists) by Medellín drug boss Pablo Escobar, and his novel *Chronicle of a Death Foretold*, based on the murder of a childhood friend of his in Sucre; Elena Poniatowski's *Massacre in Mexico* (1992), a collage of voices recalling the bloody repression of the peaceful protest by students in Mexico City in 1968; and Carlos Fuentes's novel *The Old Gringo*, retelling from the Mexican point of view the mysterious disappearance of American writer Ambrose Bierce in 1914.

An ambitious series of volumes, *A Gallery of Famous Criminals in Portugal* (1896–1908), originally edited by Antonio Palhares, chronicles Portuguese crimes "from the time when police services in our country were organized." Some of the more sensational cases in the collection, such as that of chloroform wife-murderer José Cardoso Vieira de Castro (1870), and Dr. Urbino de Freitas, who in 1890 mailed poisoned candy that took the life of his eleven-year-old relative Mario Sampaio, are the subject of contemporary pamphlets. Similar crime pamphlets appeared in the 1920s to document crimes that caught the public fancy, including the so-called crime of Serrazes tried in 1922: the two murderers José de Bettencourt and Fernando Novaes had unsuccessfully tried to defend themselves by claiming that they had acted to punish their victim Augusto Malafaia's attempts to rape a young woman who was the fiancée of one killer and sister of the other.[27] Another chronicler of historical crimes of Portugal is novelist Sousa Costa, whose works include *Great Crime Dramas (Portuguese Courts)* (1944).

Romania and Hungary

Fact-based crime literature in both Romania and Hungary is haunted by a serial killer from the distant past. Romania's favorite criminal is Vlad Tepes, the fifteenth-century Walachian prince who inspired Bram Stoker's *Dracula*. Modern nonfictional accounts of the prince sometimes view him as a patriot (for example, in Nicolae Stoicescu's *Vlad Tepes Prince of Walachia* [1978]) or as the proprietor of an exotic Transylvanian tourist attraction, Castle Dracula (in Radu Florescu's co-authored *In Search of Dracula* [1972]). Hungary's archcriminal, the early-sixteenth-century "bloody countess" Elisabeth Bathory, is often characterized as a female Dracula. A long succession of Hungarian biographies of the countess, who has also inspired novels and plays internationally, began in 1744. Elisabeth Bathory, however, by no means monopolizes her modern compatriots' interest in crime history. Marxist playwright Julius Hay, while in prison, wrote a drama (produced by Joan Littlewood in England in 1954 under the title *Have*) about the custom of early-twentieth-century peasant women poisoning their husbands to gain control of small landholdings. The false charges of Jewish ritual murder in the death of fourteen-year-old servant girl Eszter Solymosi in 1882 (the

---

27. Possibly the most famous of all Portuguese criminals, however, is not one of its murderers but the banknote counterfeiter Artur Virgilio Alves Reis.

subject of G. W. Pabst's 1948 film *The Trial*) also inspired a powerful Hungarian film, *The Raftsmen (Memoir of a River)* (1990).

Ödön von Horváth's German-language play *Sladek* (the original version written around 1927) is drawn from the author's participation in drafting a white paper on the failure of the German judicial system; it is based on the so-called Feme murders perpetrated by right-wing groups to silence persons suspected of disclosing illegal rearmament activities. See Ödön von Horváth, *Plays One, Sladek* and *A Sexual Congress*, trans. and intro. Penny Black (London: Oberon Books, 2000).[28]

Sweden

As in Romania and Hungary, Sweden's writers particularly favor a crime of the remote past, the eighteenth-century assassination of King Gustav III at a masked opera ball, which inspired Verdi's famous opera *Un Ballo in Maschera*. The murder is also the central event in *The Queen's Diadem* (1834), a novel by nineteenth-century Swedish romantic Carl Jonas Love Almqvist. A student of crime and penology, Almqvist was in 1851 found in absentia to be probably guilty of the attempted arsenic poisoning of a usurer.[29]

The master of twentieth-century true-crime writing in Sweden is Stockholm lawyer Yngve Lyttkens, who, beginning in 1946, wrote a fine series of monographs on famous Swedish murders. Lyttkens closely analyzes court proceedings but is equally adept at re-creating life in great manor houses, particularly when they shelter a secret poisoner. Firsthand accounts of criminal cases are provided by detective chief Gustaf Lidberg, including his spellbinding narrative of package bombings by engineer Martin Ekenberg between 1894 and 1909.

Russia

Dostoyevski leads the list of nineteenth-century Russian authors who incorporated true crime into imaginative works. In his letter to M. N. Katkov, Dostoyevski claimed that the realism of Raskolnikov's motivation to kill the old moneylender in *Crime and Punishment* was authenticated by newspaper accounts of crimes, including a seminary student's cold-blooded murder of a girl he had met by agreement in a shed. In his earlier work, *The House of the Dead*, Dostoyevski includes in a narrative of his four-year Siberian imprisonment the criminal biographies of fellow inmates, giving preference to those who had killed out of a sense

---

28. The name Feme derives from kangaroo courts that arose in the mid–thirteenth century in Westphalia during a period of imperial weakness. See John Heron Lepper, *Famous Secret Societies* (London: Sampson Low, Marston, n.d.), 66–67. Sir Walter Scott horrifically portrays the nocturnal proceedings of a Feme court in his novel *Anne of Geierstein* (1829).

29. See Albert Borowitz, "Innocence and Arsenic: The Literary and Criminal Careers of C. J. L. Almquist," *A Gallery of Sinister Perspectives: Ten Crimes and a Scandal* (Kent, Ohio: Kent State University Press, 1982), 21–33.

of lost honor. A similar bifurcated design is used in Chekhov's *Sakhalin Island*, an account of his three-month visit to the island prison colony (for reasons that remain obscure) in 1890; one of his inserted criminal portraits is of Yegor, who accepts without murmur a long imprisonment for a murder he did not commit. He tells Chekhov that he did not bring his wife and children to Sakhalin "because they're as well off at home."

Rare birds among Russia's great nineteenth-century writers, Turgenev and V. G. Korolenko held liberal views on legal and social issues. In his article "The Execution of Troppmann," Turgenev reported to readers back home how he witnessed, as an invited celebrity, the preparations in a Paris prison for the Alsatian mass murderer's execution, and then how he joined the throng assembled outside to watch the guillotine blade fall. As the crowd dispersed, "absolutely none of us looked like a man who recognized that he had been present at the accomplishment of an act of public justice."[30]

Korolenko was an even more unusual phenomenon among Russian writers in that he defended Jews against persecution. Attending Mendel Beiliss's 1913 ritual murder trial in Kiev, against the advice of his doctors, the ailing Korolenko wrote reports for three journals. In a euphoric mood when Beiliss was finally acquitted, the writer kissed a visiting friend and exclaimed tearfully: "You see, the truth is victorious. So don't think poorly of the Russian people!"

In the Soviet era unofficial comment on current prosecutions was suppressed, but writers were, of course, free to illuminate the defects of the tsarist justice system. Acting within these restraints, brothers Leonid and Victor Grossman wrote separate crime-history masterpieces reconstructing the nineteenth-century murder case of Alexander Sukhovo-Kobylin. Charged with the murder of his French mistress Louise Simon-Demanche, a fashionable red-haired milliner, Sukhovo-Kobylin was caught in the toils of corrupt Russian justice until his final release in 1857, probably as a result of family influence rather than overwhelming defense evidence. This terrible ordeal inspired the freed man to write a dramatic trilogy, of which the centerpiece, *The Case*, presents the Muromskys enmeshed in an endless criminal prosecution based in part on the false testimony of a servant and designed for the purpose of extorting bribes for the benefit of the officials overseeing the criminal courts. In 1928 Leonid Grossman, in *The Crime of Sukhovo-Kobylin*, a study of the merits of the murder charge, affirmed the dramatist's guilt, relying heavily on the unfavorable nineteenth-century public opinion. In 1936 a powerful rebuttal was made by Viktor Grossman in *The Case of Sukhovo-Kobylin*, where he arrived at the opposite conclusion, asserting (in the light of findings of a modern forensic scientist whose expertise he had invoked) that the famed playwright was innocent of the crime.[31]

Since the breakup of the Soviet Union, there has been a boom in true-crime publications, including accounts of corruption and organized crime in Russian cities and popular "encyclopedias" of world crime showing a bias against the West by an emphasis on its genocides, secret

30. Ivan Turgenev, "Kazn' Tropmana" [The Execution of Troppmann], *Sochineniya* [Writings] (Moscow: Naúka, 1983), xi, 150.

31. For a more detailed study of the Sukhovo-Kobylin affair, see Albert Borowitz, "The Eternal Suspect," in *Masterpieces of Murder*, ed. Jonathan Goodman (New York: Carroll & Graf, 1992), 123–40.

societies, and professional killers. Hope remains, however, for a more sober examination of crimes of the past, and a step in the right direction is historian S. A. Stepanov's *Puzzles in the Murder of Stolypin*, a study of the 1911 assassination of tsarist prime minister S. A. Stolypin.

India and Sri Lanka

One of the most ancient Indian works rooted in crime history is Vishakadatta's Sanskrit play *The Signet Ring of Rakshasa*, whose composition has been variously placed in the ninth century A.D. or centuries earlier. The plot concerns the successful scheme of an unscrupulous minister, Chanakya (or Kautilya), to win the allegiance of Rakshasa, who serves the rival dynasty of the Nandas. Among criminal means favored by Chanakya are "poison girls" (seductresses ordered to murder political enemies), forgery, employment of spies and double agents, and a faked execution.

From the nineteenth century on, Indian fact-based crime literature (much of it in English) has highlighted the activity of two hereditary groups of criminals: the ritual stranglers known as Thugs and the armed robber gangs called Dacoits. Among the numerous works on the Thugs in fiction and nonfiction are Captain P. Meadows Taylor's 1839 three-volume *Confessions of a Thug* and James L. Sleeman's *Thug, or a Million Murders* (ca. 1930), which celebrates the suppression of the cult in the nineteenth century by his grandfather, Major General Sir William Henry Sleeman. Neither the British nor Indian government has scored a final victory in their struggles against the Dacoits. A spectacular recent example of continuing Dacoit violence can be found in the career of Phoolan Devi. Kidnapped and raped by Dacoits, she became a gang leader herself and has been accused of fomenting a massacre to avenge her wrongs. After surrendering in return for immunity from capital punishment, she emerged from prison to become a member of India's Parliament and was recently murdered. Her life is recorded in Mala Sen's *India's Bandit Queen: The True Story of Phoolan Devi* (1991).

Fact-based crimes do not appear to figure prominently in the works of India's novelists. However, the assassination of Mahatma Gandhi casts its shadow over the love and political commitment of two young liberation workers in R. K. Narayan's *Waiting for the Mahatma* (1955).

In the neighboring island nation of Sri Lanka (formerly Ceylon), A. C. Alles, former solicitor general and judge of the Sri Lankan supreme court, has singlehandedly preserved the crime history of his country in an eleven-volume series entitled *Famous Criminal Cases of Sri Lanka*.

China and Japan

In Imperial China the district magistrate performed the functions of detective, prosecutor, and trial judge.[32] Despite the obvious potential for abuse of these manifold and conflictive duties, many magistrates became cherished superheroes of popular literature. Sung dynasty

---

32. See Albert Borowitz, "Strict Construction in Sung China: The Case of A Yün," *A Gallery of Sinister Perspectives*.

magistrate Pao Cheng[33] (A.D. 999–1062), first mentioned in an anthology of fact-based criminal cases published 150 years after his death, inspired fictional stories that began to appear
during the Ming dynasty (1368–1644). A selection of six of the Pao stories has been translated
and retold by Leon Comber in *The Strange Cases of Magistrate Pao* (1964). In these fanciful tales
of seduction, adultery, rape, and lascivious monks, Pao relies less on deduction than on ghosts
and apparitions; but he displays his mastery of disguise and a subtlety in the interpretation of
dreams, and he is consistently honest and persevering in bringing the guilty to justice.

Magistrate Pao also appears in drama, including two plays of the thirteenth-century
Yüan dynasty playwright Kuan Han-ching, *The Wife-Snatcher* and *The Butterfly Dream*. In
another play featuring Pao, *The Chalk Circle* by Li Hsing-tao, the magistrate proclaims his
honesty and enmity to wrongdoers regardless of social position: "I am honest, capable, pure
and upright, staunch and firm in my integrity. I am eager in service to my country and
scornful of devotion to money. I associate only with loyal and filial men and have nothing to
do with slanderers and flatterers. . . . The rich and powerful families therefore have only to
hear my name and they fold their hands. The cruel and wicked see my shadow and there is
none whose heart does not turn cold."[34] In the 1960s Magistrate Pao appeared as the hero
of a series of Hong Kong films based on the ancient stories of his exploits.

Another real Chinese detective-judge, more famous in the West because of the linguistic
and storytelling skills of R. H. van Gulik, is Judge Dee (Dee Jen-djieh) of the Tang dynasty.
In an anonymous eighteenth-century novel translated by van Gulik in 1949, *Dee Goong An*
[The Cases of Judge Dee], the author shows Judge Dee at work solving three cases simultaneously; the book reflects accurately the acumen and integrity of the historical magistrate
and the workings of the Chinese legal system, which remained essentially unchanged until
the fall of the Manchu dynasty in 1911. Van Gulik adapted the multiple plot structure of *Dee
Goong An* in his own modern detective novels featuring Judge Dee.

Other Chinese works are based more firmly on the foundation of actual crimes. Another
book translated by van Gulik is *T'ang-yin-pi-shih* [Parallel Cases from Under the Pear-Tree],
compiled around 1100 A.D. by Kuei Wan-jung, a scholar-official of the Southern Sung dynasty. Kuei's book presents summaries of 144 cases arranged in pairs selected to illustrate
parallels in evidentiary issues; for example, the case of a thief who twice feigned death is
juxtaposed with an anecdote of a wife-murderer who faked insanity. Van Gulik also refers
to an eighteenth-century crime story, entitled *Djing-foo-hsin-shoo*, which "describes a notorious nine-fold murder that actually occurred in Canton in about 1725."

The popularity of China's detective-judges is easily matched by that of the Sung dynasty
brigand chief, Sung Chiang, who established his band in the mountains of Shandong province from which he conducted far-ranging raids. Folk traditions gave him many of the attributes for which Robin Hood is famous in the West, such as kindness to the poor and

---

33. To avoid confusing non-Sinologists, I adopt transliterations of Chinese names and titles as they appear in the
works cited rather than using uniform current transliterations.

34. Ching-Hsi Perng, *Double Jeopardy: A Critique of Seven Yüan Courtroom Dramas* (Ann Arbor: Center for Chinese Studies, 1978), 105.

loyalty to the throne. Sung Chiang makes his most celebrated literary appearance as the hero of Lo Kuan Chung's fourteenth-century romance "Water Margin Novel," which Pearl Buck translated under the title, *All Men Are Brothers*.

Professor Jeffrey C. Kinkley, in *Chinese Justice, the Fiction: Law and Literature in Modern China* (Stanford: Stanford Univ. Press, 2000), chronicles a post-Mao resurgence of China's passion for crime narratives in many genres: "By the late 1980s, ancient cases, historical fiction, modern true crime, and modern crime fiction were all mixed together in anthologies of designated 'popular fiction.'"

In 1703, only a month after the tragic event described, Chikamatsu Monzaemon's first domestic tragedy, *The Love Suicides at Sonezaki,* premiered. Chikamatsu, whom critic and translator Donald Keene regards as Japan's greatest dramatist, wrote the play for the puppet theater, where it became so popular that it created a vogue for love suicides in life and on the stage (prompting the alarmed government to ban in 1722 the use of the word "suicide" in plays' titles). For the modern Western reader, however, the fatal love of Tokubei for a teenaged courtesan named Ohatsu is robbed of some of its romantic allure by the fact that the young hero is an employee of a dealer in soy sauce. Chikamatsu wrote other successful love-suicide plays and one murder drama, *The Woman-Killer*; in the Kabuki theater of his time murder was an engrossing subject.

Until the late nineteenth century, when translations of Western literature began to appear in great quantity, Japanese crime fiction was under strong Chinese influence. Saikaku Ihara's *Japanese Trials Under the Shade of a Cherry Tree*, a collection of forty-four very brief stories, was published in 1689. This book and other collections were based on accounts of Chinese court cases. Much of the fiction of Ryunosuke Akutagawa (1892–1927), including the stories "Rashomon" and "In a Grove" (which provided the basis for Akira Kurosawa's film *Rashomon*), interpret historical tales of Japan.

The Japanese tradition of basing works of imagination on recent crimes has reemerged in Yukio Mishima's novel *The Temple of the Golden Pavilion* (1959). This work is based on an arsonist's 1950 destruction of the ancient Zen temple of Kinkakuji in Kyoto. Newspaper accounts revealed a criminal destined for the pages of fiction: an ugly acolyte with a stammer who envied the beauty of the temple he served. In Mishima's enigmatic account, the arsonist Mizoguchi first plans to die in the fire but decides at the last minute to flee; he gazes at the scene of destruction as he puffs on a cigarette, feeling "like a man who settles down for a smoke after finishing a job of work." The arson that Mishima has immortalized will remind classically trained Western readers of the destruction of the Temple of Ephesus by Herostratus in a bid to win eternal fame. This striking parallel between two events far removed from each other in time and cultural setting epitomizes the universality of crime history and the literature that it has inspired.[35]

---

35. Soviet-era playwright Grigory Gorin presents Herostratus's arson as the antetype of the Reichstag fire in *Forget Herostratus!* included in *Stars in the Morning Sky: Five New Plays from the Soviet Union*, trans. Michael Glenny (London: Nick Hern Books, 1989). Jean-Paul Sartre had earlier ironically modernized the Herostratus legend in his short story "Erostratus," in *The Wall and Other Stories* (1939), trans. Lloyd Alexander (New York: New Directions, 1948).

Although much scholarly work remains to be done, *Blood and Ink* is a beginning in documenting the consensus of the world's writers and artists across the centuries that factual crime is worthy both of historical study and of transfiguration in works of imagination. The analysis of fact-based crime literature has been hampered too long by critical prejudice influenced by the annual bumper crops of mass-market crime journalism. My modest hope is to interest others in helping to separate true crime's wheat from its chaff.

Language barriers have made it impossible for me to attempt an exploration of African literature. A significant work available in English translation is Thomas Mofolo's *Chaka,* which was written in 1909 or 1910 in Sesuto and first translated into English by F. H. Dutton in 1931. In this novella, Chaka (or Shaka), founder of the Zulu nation, wades through blood like an African Macbeth until he is assassinated by his half-brothers Dingane and Mhlangana. See Stephen Taylor, *Shaka's Children: A History of the Zulu People* (London: HarperCollins, 1995).

Guide to

Fact-Based

Crime Literature

A

A.1 Ackland, Rodney *A Dead Secret.* London: Samuel French, 1958.

■ In 1912, insurance superintendent Frederick Henry Seddon was, on the basis of much-debated circumstantial evidence, convicted of the arsenic poisoning of his lodger Eliza Mary Barrow, whose property he had previously obtained in exchange for his grant of a life annuity. Seddon's wife Margaret was acquitted although the case against her was much the same. Although Ackland's play follows the case faithfully and buries Seddon's name in the initials of the principal character F. S. Dyson (created on the London stage by Paul Scofield), the text hints at—and the author's note in the acting edition explicitly proposes—another murderer: the Seddons' eccentric housemaid, named Mary Elizabeth Ellen Chater in real life but protectively called Henrietta Spicer in Ackland's drama. The possibility that Chater had a hand in the poisoning was suggested in defense counsel Edward Marshall Hall's cross-examination at the trial but not vigorously pursued; most commentators do not doubt the guilt of Seddon, whose miserliness was matched only by that of his victim.

A.2 Acton, Harold *The Pazzi Conspiracy: The Plot Against the Medici.* London: Thames & Hudson, 1979.

■ The Pazzi family concocted their plot to overthrow the Medicis "under the tolerant nose of Pope Sixtus VI" and in alliance with the Pope's ambitious nephew, Girolamo Riario. Acton, who lived in Florence, disentangles the intricate plot, which resulted in the wounding of Lorenzo de' Medici and the murder of his younger brother, Giuliano, on April 26, 1478, in the Duomo. The reaction of the Medici forces was swift and horrific: "Soon the windows of the palaces of the Signoria and of the Podestà, or chief of police, were festooned with dangling corpses." Bernardo Bandini, who had struck the first blow against Giuliano, was extradited from Constantinople and "hanged in his Turkish costume from a window of the Bargello, an exotic advertisement of the long arm of the law." Leonardo drew the hanged rebel, annotating his sketch with details of the rebel's outlandish attire. Sandro Botticelli was commissioned to paint frescos on the walls of the Signoria and the Bargello depicting executed and exiled Pazzi supporters.

For further discussion of the uses of art in the criminal punishments of Renaissance Italy, see Helen and Albert Borowitz, review of *Pictures and Punishment: Art and Criminal Prosecution during the Florentine Renaissance*, by Samuel Y. Edgerton Jr. (Ithaca: Cornell Univ. Press, 1985), in 45 *Maryland Law Review* 1066 (1986).

A.3 Ainsworth, William Harrison *Rookwood.* 1834. London: Everyman, 1931.

■ *Rookwood* is one of the first of the so-called Newgate novels, which glamorize criminals whose exploits were chronicled in the Newgate Calendar and other popular literature. See Keith Hollingsworth, *The Newgate Novel 1830–1847* (Detroit: Wayne State Univ. Press, 1963). In Ainsworth's Gothic novel, which turns on a struggle of half-brothers over an inheritance, the novelist intrudes the highwayman, horse thief, and smuggler Dick

Turpin. The most significant contribution of Ainsworth to the Turpin legend was his invention of the outlaw's headlong flight to York astride his loyal mount, Black Bess.

A.4 Akutagawa, Ryunosuke "Rashomon" and "In a Grove." *Rashomon: Akira Kirosawa, Director.* Ed. Donald Ritchie. New Brunswick: Rutgers Univ. Press, 1987.

■ The film *Rashomon* takes its setting and narrative, respectively, from two short stories by Ryunosuke Akutagawa, "Rashomon" and "In a Grove." According to commentator Tadao Sato, the latter story was in turn "based upon episodes in the tenth-century narrative, *Stories of the Past and Present (Konjaku Monogatari).* The original narrative is simple. A samurai traveling with his wife is tricked by a bandit who takes them to a grove, ties him up, and rapes the woman. After that the bandit goes away, the warrior and his wife continue their journey, although she blames him for not having prevented this occurrence." Akutagawa complicated the plot by inventing the violent death of the samurai and devising three different versions of the killing to be told by the bandit, a woman who has heard the wife's story, and a medium transmitting the account of the dead samurai. Director Kurosawa added a fourth variant, told by a woodcutter (perhaps a liar) who claims to have witnessed the fight between the bandit and the samurai.

A.5 Aleichem, Sholom [pseudonym of Solomon Rabinowitz] "Dreyfus in Kasrilevka." *Selected Stories of Sholom Aleichem.* Intro. Alfred Kazin. New York: Random House (Modern Library), 1956.

■ In Sholom Aleichem's Kasrilevka, which exemplifies the little Jewish towns of Eastern Europe, the people learn about the Dreyfus case from "Zeidel, Reb Shaye's son [who] was the only person in town who subscribed to a newspaper." As he reads the reports of the affair's turnabouts, the Jews of Kasrilevka interpret what they hear and become passionate champions of the disgraced captain. Their hopes rise when Dreyfus returns from Devil's Island for a fresh trial, which, however, results in another unjust verdict. Kasrilevka then raises a unanimous outcry—but "not against the judges who gave the wrong verdict, not at the generals who swore falsely, not at the French who showed themselves up so badly." Their voices, instead, condemn Zeidel as a liar, whom they would not believe if he "stood with one foot in heaven and the other on earth."

A.6 Alles, A[nthony] [Christopher] *Famous Criminal Cases of Sri Lanka.* Vol. 4 of 11 vols. Colombo: Published by the author, 1980.

■ A former solicitor general and judge of the supreme court of Sri Lanka (Ceylon), Alles has singlehandedly created a record of his country's famous criminal trials.

Volume 4 of the principal series of his essays is devoted to a group of disputed verdicts. The first study analyzes the trial of Mahadevan Sathasivam, a brilliant cricket batsman (whom the author calls a "wizard of the willow"), for the 1951 strangulation of his wife, whom he wanted to leave for another woman. The defendant's acquittal, which Alles regards as a "triumph for the administration of justice" in view of the conflicting evidence, may have been strongly influenced by the testimony of Sir Sydney Smith, a noted British forensic expert. Smith, with his usual assurance, placed the time of death at 11:30 A.M., two hours after a confessed accomplice in the crime, a new servant named William, claimed to have left the murder scene at the Sathasivams' home in a Colombo suburb.

Judge Alles observes that most cases of violent crime in Sri Lanka involve knifing (often with the country's "national weapon," the kris knife), clubbing, or firearms. Poisoning is rare, and the alleged use of arsenic as a murder weapon made its belated debut in the Kularatne poisoning case of 1967. At the trial, discussed by Alles in his second essay, the prosecution charged Dr. Daymon Kularatne, his mother Laura, and their cook Mavelege Sopia with murdering the doctor's estranged wife, Padmini, who was kept a virtual prisoner in an untended garret room of the family residence. After the jury convicted all three defendants, the Court of Criminal Appeal reversed, holding, inter alia, that two Crown scientific witnesses lacked sufficient expertise to support their testimony intended to show that the victim ingested potassium arsenite drawn from the doctor's dispensary. The local coloration of the tragedy is deepened by the prevailing belief of the parties in charms and talismans.

The much-debated murder conviction of twenty-year-old, convent-educated Pauline Ruth de Croos is the subject of another detailed study in this collection. A majority verdict found Pauline guilty of pushing an eleven-year-old schoolboy, Ramdas Gotabhaya ("Gota") Kirambakanda, the son of her married lover, into a well of St. Rita's Church in 1966. There was difficulty in establishing a motive; Judge Alles suspects that Pauline's lover, an unsavory brothel keeper, may have induced her to bring his child to the church and later to dispose of his school bag, two actions that were established clearly by the testimony of many witnesses. In Judge Alles's view, Pauline made a critical strategic mistake of attempting vainly to rely on the defense of mistaken identity, perhaps in an effort to conceal the role of her lover, who was acquitted. Pauline's death sentence was commuted to life imprisonment, and after serving several years she was released and was "reported to be usefully employed at a convent in the Southern Province."

A.7 **Almqvist, Carl Jonas Love** *The Queen's Diadem.* 1834. Trans. Yvonne L. Sandstroem. London: Skoob, 1992.

■ One of the towering figures of nineteenth-century Swedish literature, Almqvist chose as a recurrent theme the multiplex and fluid nature of personality. The most striking example in his fiction is the androgynous Tintomara, one of the principal characters in his novel *The Queen's Diadem*. Tintomara represents not the bisexual but rather the Platonic unification (and neutralization) of the male and female. She is the complete being free of the emotional and sexual cravings of either gender. Tintomara also symbolizes the transcendence of the human soul by what Almqvist referred to as the "celestial animal" soul, a soul that moves in graceful accord with the rhythm of nature and is indifferent to considerations of convention and morality. It is tempting to relate to Almqvist's preoccupation with duality and change in personality his delight (no doubt also partly linguistic and antiquarian in origin) with the alteration of names as an emblem of shifts in identity. Thus, the chimerical Tintomara was never baptized. She is identified first merely as "She" and then as "the girl." In subsequent pages of *The Queen's Diadem*, she bears a bewildering succession of names:

"Azouras," "Lazuli," "Tintomara," "Tourne-rose." The last name is particularly significant since it is a gallicized form of the name of the fourteen-volume work in which the bulk of Almqvist's writing appeared, the *Book of the Briar Rose*. This collection is itself a mirror of multiplicity and change in literary expression and form; its poems, essays, and dramatic and narrative forms jangle against each other, often within the same work, creating the impression of what Almqvist was to call a "fugue."

It is also striking that Almqvist's fiction tends to displace responsibility for murder from the murderer to outside influences—inheritance, society, or nature. Thus, in *Amorina* (written in 1822 and published in 1839), the crimes of Johannes, a mass murderer, are attributed to inherited bloodlust, to misuse of his criminal tendencies by corrupt nobles, and to rejection of his demand for absolution by a materialistic clergyman. Tintomara in *The Queen's Diadem* is completely indifferent to the fact that she was used by the assassins of King Gustav III to lure him to death at the famous masked ball celebrated by Verdi. To her, as a "celestial animal," all death is a part of nature. When she is asked whether she has seen how it looks when a person dies, she replies: "My mother died and I saw it."

Almqvist recognized that the mystery of crime is impenetrable. At least at times he must have recognized the ambiguity that marks not only external evidence of guilt and innocence but also the nature and origin of crime and the criminal impulse. Certainly, some of this ambiguity is expressed in the famous paradox that Tintomara's mother leaves her as a final bequest in a dramatic scene in *The Queen's Diadem*: "Tintomara," she cries, "two things are white: innocence and arsenic."

Ironically, the enigma of criminal responsibility is attached to Almqvist's life as well as his fiction. In 1851 he was charged with theft, fraud, and attempted arsenic poisoning but fled Sweden for America before he could be put on trial. See A. Hemmings-Sjöberg, *A Poet's Tragedy: The Trial of C. J. L. Almqvist*, trans. E. Classen (London: George Allen & Unwin, 1932).

A.8 Altick, Richard D[aniel] *Deadly Encounters: Two Victorian Sensations.* Philadelphia: Univ. of Pennsylvania Press, 1986.

■ A pendant to the author's *Victorian Studies in Scarlet* (1970), this work demonstrates how Victorian England's "Age of Sensation" in journalism, theater, and fiction was ushered in by two criminal cases of 1861, the Northumberland Street Tragedy and Baron de Vidil's assault on his stepson.

The first of these "deadly encounters" is by far the more interesting. A moneylender named William James Roberts lured Major William Murray to his dusty quarters in Northumberland Street near the Strand on the pretense of arranging a loan to a company of which Murray was a large shareholder. In reality, Roberts was obsessed with Murray's mistress, Anna Marie Moody (who called herself Mrs. Murray); he had invited Murray to his office with murder in his heart. As Murray sat at a table waiting for Roberts to produce his business card, the amorous moneylender fired a pistol at the back of his neck. Despite the surprise of the assault and his grievous wound, Murray mounted a furious counterattack with tongs and a glass bottle, reducing his opponent to "a mutilated creature, whose head was a mass of blood-stained pulp"; Roberts died in the hospital and Murray recovered. The coroner's jury found that Murray had acted in self-defense, and the press and public generally approved, although harboring some reservations about Murray's account of the incident and Anna Marie Moody's story that Roberts, who had lent her fifteen pounds, had been persecuting her with unwelcome attentions.

The second 1861 "sensation" was the assault by a dubious French "baron," Alfred Louis Pons de Vidil, on his son Alfred with a horsewhip in a Twickenham lane. Indicted for crimes including assault with intent to murder (a capital offense), Baron de Vidil was convicted only of unlawful wounding and sentenced to twelve months' hard labor. Because the victim had refused to testify against his father, the motive for the baron's attack remained unknown.

Altick believes that the sensation vogue in English popular literary culture "would not have had the same impetus, or taken the shape it did" without the "unconscious collaboration" of the two miscreants of 1861, the love-struck loan shark and the somewhat shady baron.

A.9 ———— *The Scholar Adventurers.* New York: Macmillan, 1950.

■ Altick, through this fascinating series of case studies, pays tribute to "unsung scholars" who "have adventures which are as exciting as any that have ever been told of their better publicized colleagues." One of the best known of these essays is "The Case of the Curious Bibliographers," recounting how, between 1932 and 1934, two young men in the London rare-book trade, John Carter and Graham Pollard, uncovered massive literary forgeries by a respected book collector and bibliographer, Thomas James Wise. The modus operandi of the forger was to fabricate ostensible prepublication pamphlet editions of genuine works of eminent Victorian authors such as the Brownings, George Eliot, Ruskin, Tennyson, Matthew Arnold, Swinburne, and Thackeray. Carter and Pollard traced the fabrications to an innocent printer and ultimately to Wise by subjecting the paper and typography of the pamphlets to searching analysis. Without explicitly proclaiming Wise's guilt, the literary detectives published their findings in a 1934 work, *An Enquiry into the Nature of Certain Nineteenth-Century Pamphlets.*

Altick believes that Wise's fraud originated in bibliomania. In his youth, his small salary as a clerk for a manufacturer of essential oils (ingredients of perfumes and soaps) did not permit him "to buy the books he craved." When he began to take a role in facsimile printing for the Browning and Shelley Societies, the road to crime opened before him. He could pass off the facsimiles for originals by removing the book societies' title pages. After this promising beginning, he turned to the forgery of Victorian pamphlets. Altick theorizes that, after Wise's affluence removed his original economic motive for fraud, he "kept playing with [the pamphlets] simply for the sardonic pleasure of gulling men who, in their absurd arrogance, prided themselves on knowing their way around the world of books."

A.10 ———— *Victorian Studies in Scarlet: Murders and Manners in the Age of Victoria.* New York: Norton, 1970.

■ Professor Altick is a distinguished pioneer in studying the impact of criminal cases on literature and popular culture. In this volume, he discusses the following murderers represented in the *Notable British Trials* series (see N.7): James Blomfield Rush, William Palmer, Thomas Smethurst, Edward Pritchard, Madeleine Smith, Jessie M'Lachlan, Franz Müller, Henry Wainwright, Kate Webster, Charles Peace, Adelaide Bartlett, Florence Maybrick, George Chapman, Samuel Dougal.

Altick, who consulted many other sources as well, gracefully acknowledges his debt to the *Notable British Trials* and to the crime essays of William Roughead.

Of particular value are five introductory chapters in which Altick establishes a rich setting for his exposition of the individual murder cases. In these early chapters, he discusses the origin of mass-media coverage of British murders, beginning with the Thurtell-Hunt case of 1823–24, William Corder the Red Barn murderer (1828), and the Scottish grave-robbers Burke and Hare; crime as a subject of street literature; popular crime novels; crime in stage melodramas; and the fascination that crime held for men and women of letters, such as Scott, Lamb, the Carlyles, Elizabeth Gaskell, Kingsley, Tennyson, Edward Fitzgerald, Dickens, and Charles Reade.

A.11 [American State Trials Series] *American State Trials: A Collection of the Important and Interesting Criminal Trials Which Have Taken Place in the United States, from the Beginning of Our Government to the Present Day.* Ed. John D. Lawson. 17 vols. St. Louis: Thomas Law Book Co., 1914–36.

■ John Davison Lawson, born in Hamilton, Ontario, in 1852, practiced law in St. Louis (1881–85) and later became a law professor and subsequently dean (1904–12) of the Law School of the University of Missouri. Recognizing the unavailability of collections of American criminal trials that would parallel the State Trials series in England and the successive French editions of *Causes célèbres,* Lawson conceived the project of assembling American criminal trials under the title *American State Trials.* For nearly a decade, with the financial support of William Keeney Bixby, he gathered one of the largest collections of American pamphlet reports of criminal trials and deposited them in what became known as the Lawson Library of Criminal Law and Criminology at the Law School of the University of Missouri.

Dean Lawson writes that judicial investigations seeking the discovery and punishment of crime "exhibit human nature in an infinite variety of positions, and show man as he is. Events and transactions, more wonderful than anything to be found in works of fiction become realities in the proceedings of criminal tribunals."

Following are the murder trials to be found in *American State Trials*. The city and year stated refer, unless otherwise indicated, to the place and date of the trial.

Vol. 1

• Levi Weeks acquitted of the murder of his lover Gulielma Sands, whose body was found in the Manhattan well; New York City, 1800. Weeks was defended by Alexander Hamilton and Aaron Burr.

- Samuel Tulley and John Dalton convicted of piracy of the American schooner *George Washington* and subsequent murder of a sailor; Boston, 1812. Tulley was hanged and after a black cap was placed over Dalton's head his presidential reprieve arrived, a real-life anticipation of the mock ending of *The Threepenny Opera*.
- George Bowen acquitted of murder in having successfully incited a fellow prisoner to commit suicide in order to cheat the gallows; Northampton, Massachusetts, 1816.
- Judge Edward C. Wilkinson, his brother Benjamin, and friend acquitted (on the basis of self-defense) in the killing of John Rothwell and Alexander H. Meeks; Harrodsburg, Kentucky, 1839. The victims were friends of a Louisville tailor whom Judge Wilkinson had struck with a poker in a scuffle over an ill-fitting coat.
- Alexander W. Holmes, a shipwrecked seaman, sentenced only to six months for manslaughter in throwing Frank Askin from an overloaded longboat; Philadelphia, 1842. Fourteen men (including Askin) and two women were jettisoned; the jury rejected the defense of self-preservation but recommended Askin to mercy.
- John C. Colt convicted of the hatchet murder of Samuel Adams; New York City, 1842. Colt, the brother of famous gun inventor Samuel Colt, tried to ship his victim's body in a box to New Orleans. Before he could be hanged, he stabbed himself to death in his cell.
- Joel Clough hanged for the murder of widow Mary W. Hamilton, who rejected his suit; Mount Holly, New Jersey, 1833.
- Christian Smith acquitted by a sympathetic jury of the murder of his neighbor Bornt Lake in a quarrel over property; Richmond, New York, 1817.
- Patrick Blake acquitted of the knife murder of his sleeping wife Margaret; New York City, 1816. The judge felt compelled to instruct the jury that the evidence was no stronger against Blake than against two women who slept in a bed nearby.

Vol. 2

- Bathsheba Spooner, her lover, and two hired soldiers convicted of the murder of her husband Joshua Spooner; Massachusetts, 1778. Mrs. Spooner was condemned to death in the first Massachusetts capital case under American jurisdictions.
- John Johnson convicted of the murder of his roommate James Murray for money; New York City, 1824.
- Thomas O. Selfridge tried and acquitted for the killing of Charles Austin, son of a political antagonist, on a public street; Boston, 1806.
- Dr. John W. Hughes convicted of murder for shooting to death his estranged beloved Tamzen Parsons; Cleveland, 1865.
- David F. Mayberry convicted of the murder of Andrew Alger to rob him of money while they rode horses on a Wisconsin road; Janesville, 1855. Mayberry was lynched before sentence could be imposed; Wisconsin had abolished the death penalty.
- Diana Sellick, liberated slave, tried for poisoning Betty Johnson, child of a free black woman with whom Sellick kept her own daughter; New York City, 1816.
- Elizabeth Southard, convicted of manslaughter in striking William P. Walker with a griddle in a boardinghouse quarrel; Richmond, 1851. The point of historical interest is that Southard, having less than one-fourth Negro blood, was tried as a white.

Vol. 3

- Matthew F. Ward acquitted of the murder of William H. G. Butler; Elizabethtown, Kentucky, 1854. Ward had shot Butler, principal of Louisville High School, for whipping Ward's younger brother and, even worse, calling the boy a liar.
- John Hanlon convicted of sex-murder of six-year-old Mary Mohrman; Philadelphia, 1870.
- Harris Seymour and ten others acquitted of kidnapping William Morgan, anti-Masonic polemicist, whose body was never recovered; Canandaigua, New York, 1827.
- William Dandridge Epes convicted of murder of his creditor, Francis Adolphus Muir; Petersburg, Virginia, 1848.
- Richard Lawrence acquitted and remanded to custody as insane in shooting wildly at President Andrew Jackson; Washington, 1835.
- Cyrus B. Dean convicted and hanged for murder of two revenue agents, Jonathan Ormsby and Asa March, who were trying to interdict potash smuggling into Canada; Burlington, Vermont, 1808.
- Noah Cherry, Robert Thompson, and Harris Atkinson, three black freedmen, convicted and hanged for the axe murder of poor white farmer James Worley and his wife; Goldsboro, North Carolina, 1873. The judge had instructed the jury to "look at the case just as if you were trying one of your respectable white neighbors."
- Dr. Valorus P. Coolidge convicted of the prussic-acid murder of reluctant lender Edward Mathews; Augusta, Maine, 1848. Like the more famous English poisoner, Dr. William Palmer, Dr. Coolidge had the distinction of performing an autopsy on his own victim.

Vol. 4

- Professor John W. Webster, Harvard chemistry professor, convicted and hanged for the murder of Dr. George Parkman, his pressing creditor; Boston, 1850. The so-called Harvard Murder Case marks an earlier forensic triumph of dentistry; Webster dismembered his victim but a set of false teeth found in his furnace identified Parkman.
- Thomas Lafon Jr., a wealthy physician's son, convicted of manslaughter in killing with a shovel a butcher boy, Joseph Hebring, who was fighting with Lafon's younger brother. The case became a class issue when it was revealed that Mrs. Lafon refused to allow the unconscious butcher boy to be carried into her house through the front door. The defendant was pardoned after a few months' imprisonment.
- John R. Kelly convicted of voluntary manslaughter for the accidental killing of David W. Oxford in an exchange of pistol shots with a ticket seller at a rural circus and sideshow; Dawson, Georgia, 1871. The circus owner, Colonel C. J. Ames, was also killed, and the mother of two exhibited Albino women and another spectator were wounded. Kelly and his brother Charles, previously convicted, escaped from jail.
- Thomas Ward, a carter, acquitted on the basis of self-defense in the killing of Albert Robinson, a pedestrian with whom he had a violent traffic dispute at a crossing; New York City, 1823. This is an early example of "road rage" in the Big Apple.

Vol. 5

- William Arrison, a medical student, convicted and hanged for murder of a lecturer and house surgeon at the Marine Hospital, Isaac Allison, and his wife, through the explosion of an "infernal machine"; Cincinnati, Ohio, 1854. The explosive device, composed of gunpowder, balls, and iron slugs, was encased in a box delivered to Mrs. Allison at the hospital. Dr. Allison and the murderer had quarreled over a book that the latter had borrowed and damaged. Bibliographer Thomas M. McDade observes that this may be the first bomb murder case in America.

- Emma Augusta Cunningham acquitted of stabbing murder of Dr. Harvey Burdell, of whom she claimed to be the secret wife; New York City, 1857.
- Anne K. Simpson acquitted of arsenic poisoning of her elderly husband; Fayetteville, North Carolina, 1850.
- Richard Smith convicted and hanged for shooting to death John Carson, his wife's first husband, who returned home after having been presumed dead; Philadelphia, 1816.
- Abraham Prescott, eighteen years old, convicted and hanged for beating Mrs. Sally Cochran to death with a stake; Concord, New Hampshire, 1834. Prescott had unsuccessfully pled insanity, claiming that he had attacked Mrs. Cochran during a fit of somnambulism.
- George Eaton convicted and hanged for the murder of Timothy Heenan during a quarrel among electioneering henchmen; Philadelphia, 1868. Unfortunately for the defendant, his victim was the brother of the popular boxing champion John C. Heenan.

Vol. 6

- George S. Twitchell Jr. convicted of murdering his wealthy mother-in-law, Mary E. Hill, whom he then threw out of a second-story window to fake an accident; Philadelphia, 1869. Twitchell poisoned himself to escape the gallows.
- Stephen and Jesse Boorn wrongly convicted of the murder of their weak-minded brother-in-law Russel Colvin; Bennington, Vermont, 1819. This case is one of America's object lessons in the unreliability of confessions and the infection of the justice system by community prejudice; Colvin returned home very much alive, in time to save Stephen Boorn from the gallows and Jesse from imprisonment.
- Lucretia Chapman acquitted of the arsenic poisoning of her schoolmaster husband William; Andalusia, Pennsylvania, 1832. In a separate trial, young Carolino Espos y Mina, more lover than lodger, whom she married less than two weeks after William Chapman's death, was convicted and hanged. (Except for its Spanish seasoning and nineteenth-century setting, the case will remind many of James Cain's *The Postman Always Rings Twice*.)
- David D. How convicted and hanged for the shooting murder of his neighbor, whom he called on at an early morning hour on the pretext of being a mail carrier; Angelica, New York, 1824. After the jury rendered its guilty verdict in reliance on an inescapable chain of circumstantial evidence, How confessed; he had frequently complained that Church had defrauded him of property and vowed revenge.

Vol. 7

- Brothers Israel, Isaac, and Nelson Thayer convicted of and hanged for murdering their money-lending lodger, seizing his cash, and simultaneously wiping out their debts to him; Buffalo, 1825. The murderers scheduled their crime (accomplished by gun and axe) for a day when they were to slaughter hogs, knowing there would be a good deal of blood about the house.

- Stephen M. Ballew, a Kentucky swindler, convicted and hanged for murdering James P. Golden while supposedly on an expedition to sell horses in behalf of the Golden family; McKinney, Texas, 1871. To make matters worse, the fast-talking Ballew married his victim's sister after the murder, claiming that he had left James behind in Texas to consummate their horse dealings.

- Brothers John Francis (Frank) Knapp and Joseph Jenkins Knapp Jr. convicted and hanged for their participation in the murder of wealthy octogenarian Joseph White, to whose grandniece Joseph Knapp was married; Salem, Massachusetts, 1830. Daniel Webster prosecuted Frank Knapp as a principal and, after the jury hung, obtained his conviction in a second trial of this renowned "Salem Murder Case." A confederate Richard Crowninshield, who actually wielded the lethal stiletto that took the old man's life, was acquitted, finding an alibi in his mistress's embraces.

- Burglars John Joyce and Peter Mathias convicted and hanged for strangling elderly widow Sarah Cross; Philadelphia, 1808.

- Ephraim Gilman convicted and sentenced to life imprisonment for strangling with his scarf farmer's widow Harriet Swan, who opposed Gilman's marriage to her daughter Abba; Paris, Maine, 1862. Gilman forged a suicide note, but forensic experts testified, not unreasonably, that the victim could not have strangled herself while lying in bed.

Vol. 8

- Josiah Burnham, imprisoned swindler and forger, convicted for stabbing to death his cell mate, insolvent debtor Captain Joseph Starkweather; Plymouth, New Hampshire, 1806. Hot-tempered Burnham had taken offense at allusions made by his fellow prisoners to his role as criminal co-respondent in a pending divorce case.

- Trials of the Lincoln assassination conspirators; Washington, D.C., 1865. In his commentary, editor Lawson is noncommittal concerning Mary Surratt's role but quotes her counsel's innocent explanation of her delivery of John Wilkes Booth's spyglass and revolver to Lloyd's tavern on Booth's escape route. The controversial conviction of Dr. Samuel Mudd, according to Lawson, "was based almost entirely on his own declarations; reason enough when they turned out to be false, for the judgment which the Court pronounced. Could it be possible that a professional man of experience could have in his house for a dozen hours a patient whose broken leg he sets, whom he provides with a crutch and whom he starts again on his journey, and this patient a man whom he had known for some months, had met socially several times and had business relations with more than once and who actually had been before this a guest in his own house?"

- Captain Henry Wirz, commandant of Andersonville prison, convicted and hanged for conspiracy to injure and destroy the health of Union prisoners and thirteen specifications of murder in violation of the laws and customs of war. Dean Lawson finds the conviction just because Wirz, in his view, was "a common murderer, directing his guards often against their will to inflict on the wretched prisoners cruel punishments and even death for trifling offenses and again and again with his own hands murdering his help-less victims."

Vol. 10

- Army deserter Edward D. Worrell convicted and hanged for the murder of Basil H. Gordon, a civil engineer whom he and a confederate, William H. Bruff, robbed of cash collections for the building of the North Missouri Railroad; Union, Missouri, 1857.

- Factory manager Leo M. Frank, wrongly convicted of the murder of one of his em-ployees, Mary Phagan; Atlanta, 1913. After the governor, doubting his guilt, commut-ed Frank's death sentence to life imprisonment, he was stabbed by a fellow inmate and subsequently lynched. Dean Lawson calls this famous case "a Tragedy of Errors in which Justice was the real victim."

- Boarder Orrin De Wolf convicted of strangling William Stiles, alcoholic husband of an unloving wife who was carrying on an affair with De Wolf; Worcester, Massachu-setts, 1845. De Wolf's death sentence was commuted to life imprisonment. The trial features a jury charge by famed Massachusetts chief justice Lemuel Shaw. "To err is human," Shaw told the jury reassuringly, "yet this should not deter us from acting under the weight of high responsibility."

- Robert McConaghy, convicted and hanged for the murder of his mother-in-law, Rosan-na Brown (wife of farmer John Brown), and five of her children, aged ten to twenty-one, by strangulation or with all weapons at hand (a flail, axe, and gun); Huntingdon, Penn-sylvania, 1840. Confessing after the executioner's first rope broke, McConaghy said: "I did not like Brown, and murdered them for their little bit of property." Yet McCon-aghy's apparent frenzy and the broad swath of his violence make this case a close kin of Pierre Rivière's family slaughter (see F.23).

Vol. 11

- Henrietta Robinson convicted and sentenced to death for the arsenic poisoning of her neighbor, grocer Timothy Lanagan; Troy, New York, 1854. The poison was adminis-tered in sugar added to tumblers of beer offered by the increasingly unstable Robin-son to Lanagan's family; both he and his brother's wife, Catherine Lubee, died within twenty-four hours. During the trial Robinson wore a heavy veil and became known as the "Veiled Murderess." Her insanity defense was rejected but her sentence was com-muted to life imprisonment; she died at age eighty-nine in the New York Hospital for the Insane.

- Frank James acquitted of the holdup of the Chicago, Rock Island & Pacific train at Winston, Missouri, on July 5, 1881, and the killing of passenger Frank McMillan. This is the most famous trial to emerge from the Wild West. It is an open question whether the verdict was actuated by hero-worship or fear of the James Gang's vengeance.

Vol. 12

- Trial of the Chicago Anarchists for conspiracy and murder in the Haymarket Riots; Chicago, 1886. Dean Lawson regards this trial as quintessentially American in its ap-plication of quick solutions: "With a speed unknown before or since to [Chicago's] criminal procedure and to a tribunal that could by no possibility be impartial, the eight men, none of whom had thrown the death-dealing bomb, were put on trial; for all sorts and conditions of men—wage earners as well as capitalists—first horrified at the tragedy, then in terror that the hand of the anarchist might yet reach their own homes, demanded that the prisoners should be sent to the gallows."

- Richard P. Robinson acquitted of the hatchet murder of prostitute Helen Jewett in a bordello followed by an attempt to burn her body; New York City, 1836. The evidence against nineteen-year-old clerk Robinson, who had been in love with Jewett, appeared overwhelming and the alibi he offered weak, but the jury may have been swayed by public support for the middle-class defendant. Rev. Mr. Brownlee of the Chatham street chapel, according to Dean Lawson, "openly supported the murder as a deed to be commended."

- Daniel E. Sickles, New York congressman and Civil War general and a hero at Gettysburg, acquitted of the murder of Philip Barton Key, son of the composer of America's national anthem; Washington, D.C., 1859. Sickles successfully pleaded justifiable homicide in taking delayed revenge on Key for his affair with Mrs. Sickles.

Vol. 13

- Benjamin F. Hunter, convicted and hanged for the murder of John M. Armstrong; Camden, New Jersey, 1878. The executioner had to chop a rope at the side of the gallows, releasing a weight that yanked Hunter off the ground. Hunter, an investor in Armstrong's failing music publishing business in Philadelphia, insured the publisher's life and then hired Thomas Graham to assist him in a hatchet attack. Armstrong, gravely wounded, managed to survive for a few days, and Hunter, taking no chances, opened his head bandages to speed his death.

- Dr. Thomas Thatcher Graves convicted of murdering wealthy widow Josephine A. Barnaby by mailing her as a New Year's gift a bottle of whiskey laced with arsenic; Denver, 1891. Graves had obtained control over Mrs. Barnaby's estate and finances after her husband's death. After the appellate court ordered a new trial on the basis of an erroneous jury instruction, Dr. Graves committed suicide. His crime can be regarded as one of the nineteenth-century forerunners of the Tylenol poisonings. For an account of the Graves murder by a great-grandson of Mrs. Barnaby, see Barnaby Conrad, *A Revolting Transaction* (New York: Arbor House, 1983).

- English solicitor Hugh M. Brooks (alias Walter Lennox-Maxwell, M.D.) convicted and hanged for the chloroform poisoning of traveling salesman Charles A. Preller; St. Louis, 1886. Having made an acquaintance on board a steamship from Liverpool to Boston, the two men met by agreement in St. Louis, where Brooks chloroformed Preller and absconded to New Zealand with his money, stuffing his victim's body in a trunk left in the St. Louis hotel room that Brooks had occupied.

Vol. 14

- Charles J. Guiteau convicted and hanged for the assassination of President James A. Garfield; Washington, D.C., 1881

- Leon F. Czolgosz convicted and hanged for the assassination of President William McKinley; Buffalo, New York, 1901.
- Crew member Thomas Bird convicted and hanged for piracy of a schooner and murder of its captain, William Connor; Portland, Maine (then a province of Massachusetts), 1790. Dean Lawson identifies this case as resulting in the first capital conviction in the U.S. courts.
- Schoolteacher Grace A. Lusk convicted and sentenced to nineteen years' imprisonment for murdering the wife of her lover, noted veterinarian Dr. David Roberts; Waukesha, Wisconsin, 1918. Lusk shot her rival after provoking a confrontation and then turned the gun on herself, missing the heart. A defense of insanity failed; when the verdict was announced, she assaulted the district attorney, but a commission appointed by the judge confirmed her sanity.
- John Ward convicted and hanged for the murder of Mrs. Ephraim Griswold with cutting and blunt instruments; Burlington, Vermont, 1866. In a written confession given to the prison chaplain the day before his execution, Ward declared that he and an accomplice had been hired by Charles H. Potter, whose wife was the victim's adopted daughter and heir-at-law; Potter, however, was acquitted.
- Albert Hicks, mate on the oysterman *E. A. Johnson*, convicted and executed for piracy and murder; New York City, 1860. More killer than pirate, Hicks murdered and robbed his captain and two shipmates in lower New York Bay. The execution was staged on Bedloe's Island before a fleet of excursion boats.

Vol. 15

- The trials of various criminals before the First and Second Vigilance Committees of San Francisco (1851–57) and related court trials are included in this volume.
- Laura D. Fair, convicted of murder for shooting her lover, the noted lawyer Alexander P. Crittenden, on a San Francisco ferry; San Francisco, 1871. On retrial, Fair, who had unsuccessfully sought to persuade Crittenden to divorce and become her fifth husband, was acquitted.
- William Henry Theodore Durrant convicted and hanged at St. Quentin prison for the lust murder of Blanche Lamont; San Francisco, 1895. In this famous "murder in the belfry," Durrant, a twenty-four-year-old medical student serving as assistant superintendent in the Sunday school of the Emanuel Baptist Church in the Mission District, strangled young church member Blanche Lamont and hid her nude body in the belfry tower. Nine days later he stabbed another girl, Minnie Williams, and left her body in a church closet. Durrant, who maintained his innocence to the last, was a master of nonchalance; when first informed that Blanche Lamont was missing, he expressed regret, since he had promised to lend her a copy of Thackeray's *The Newcomes*.

Vol. 16

- William P. Darnes, a politician who considered himself libeled by an article in a Democratic newspaper called *The Argus*, convicted only of manslaughter in the fourth degree for killing the paper's publisher, Andrew J. Davis, with blows of an iron cane; St.

Louis, 1840. Darnes was wise to choose the small Davis as his adversary, because Colonel William Gilpin, the editor, was known to be a fighting man.

- William Freeman convicted of the murder of John G. Van Nest; Auburn, New York, 1846. Freeman, an insane black man, axed to death Van Nest, his wife, and a child. Defended by William H. Seward, he received a death sentence that was reversed; he died before the execution could take place. In the first trial, Seward argued that the strongest evidence of insanity was "that idiotic smile which plays continually on the face of the maniac. . . . That chaotic smile is the external derangement which signifies that the strings of the harp are disordered and broken."

- Edward O. Coburn and Benjamin F. Dalton acquitted of manslaughter but convicted of assault and battery in the death of William Sumner; Boston, 1856. Sumner had been courting Dalton's wife and died shortly after the angered husband beat him in Coburn's presence; medical evidence was offered to show that Sumner had died of disease.

Vol. 17

- William H. Westervelt convicted and sentenced to seven years' imprisonment for conspiring with William Mosher and Joseph Douglass and others to kidnap the child Charles Brewster Ross; Philadelphia, 1875. Charley Ross, America's first famous victim of a kidnapping for ransom, was never found.

- Mary Harris, acquitted of murder in the shooting of her jilting fiancé Adoniram J. Burroughs on the steps of the Treasury Building; Washington, D.C., 1865. Harris successfully asserted a defense of temporary insanity. Mrs. Lincoln sent flowers to her in jail.

- Thomas J. Cluverius, rising young lawyer, convicted and hanged for the murder of his cousin, Fannie Lillian Madison, aged twenty-two, whose body was found floating in the city reservoir; Richmond, Virginia, 1885. Madison, seduced by Cluverius, was eight months pregnant and marks of blows belied the defense theory of suicide.

- Hannah Kinney acquitted of the poisoning of her husband, George T., with herb tea dosed with arsenic; Boston, 1840. There was no proof that Mrs. Kinney had any of the poison in her possession, and it was suggested that compounds prescribed by a quack physician might have contained arsenic.

- Henry G. Green convicted and hanged for the arsenic poisoning of his new bride, Mary Ann Green, member of a troupe of temperance performers; Troy, New York, 1845. It is possible that the crime was inspired by disapproval of the hasty marriage by Henry Green's mother.

A.12 Anderson, Maxwell The Sacco-Vanzetti plays: *Gods of the Lightning*. 1928. Co-written by Anderson with Harold Hickerson. In *Twenty-five Best Plays of the Modern American Theatre, Early Series*. Ed. and intro. John Gassner. New York: Crown, 1949. *Winterset*. 1935. In *Eleven Verse Plays 1929–1939*. New York: Harcourt Brace, n.d.

■ *Gods of the Lightning* is an angry prose play in which Macready, an IWW agitator, and Capraro, a nonviolent anarchist, are unjustly tried, convicted, and executed for the holdup murder of a paymaster. Macready, displaying in his testimony some of Sacco's aggressivity, voices the opinion that the U.S. Constitution "was made by a little group of hogs to protect their own trough." By contrast, the gentle, Vanzetti-like Capraro expresses feelings about America that reflect disillusionment rather than hostility: "I [honored the flag] before I came to this country. Now I know it is like all the other flags. They are all the same. When we are young boys we look on a flag and believe it is the flag of liberty and happy people—and now I know it is a flag to carry when the old men kill the young men for billions."

The verse tragedy *Winterset* imagines the destructive aftermath of a criminal case resembling the trial of Sacco and Vanzetti. The two anarchists are fused in Bartolomeo Romagna, who has been executed before the play's action begins, leaving behind his son Mio, whose mission is to establish the truth about the murder for which his father was erroneously convicted. The dramatist brings together the gangsters who were responsible for the famous crime: Trock Estrella, the gang boss who planned the payroll robbery, Shadow, the killer, and Garth Esdras, a gang member. Another character is Judge Gaunt, who presided over Romagna's trial and sent him to his death although aware of his innocence. Gaunt has "wandered perhaps in mind and body," a prey to guilt and rationalization. Trock, recently released from prison, is angry that a Professor Hobhouse has reopened the case of the paymaster killing; the gangster seeks to ensure that Garth and Judge Gaunt will remain silent. Mio, however, continues to press for the truth and obtains Trock's admission that Shadow (whom the boss has had killed) fired the shot for which Mio's father was executed. When the police arrive in search of the missing Judge Gaunt, Mio denounces Trock for both crimes, but Garth and his sister Miriamne have hidden Shadow's corpse, the only proof of Mio's allegations. Mio and Miriamne, who has fallen in love with him, are machine-gunned by Trock's gang as the drama comes to its close. Mio had briefly hoped that the young girl's love would cure his obsession with justice: "I've groped long enough through this everglades of old revenges."

A.13 André, Louis *La mystérieuse Baronne de Feuchères.* In series *Énigmes et drames judiciaires d'autrefois.* Paris: Perrin, 1925.

■ When the duc de Bourbon (Condé) met the adventuress Sophie Dawes from the Isle of Wight, he had already suffered enough for one lifetime, having lost his son the duc d'Enghien to Napoleon Bonaparte's firing squad at the Chateau de Vincennes in 1804. Completely bewitched by the young and audacious Sophie, the duc de Bourbon married her off to an infantry battalion chief Adrien-Victor Feuchères and installed his mistress (now the baronne de Feuchères) as informal "queen" of Chantilly, one of the Condé family's residences. As the duc doddered into old age, Sophie pressured him into making a will in favor of the duc d'Aumale, a child of the future Orleanist king Louis-Philippe; the baronne hoped thereby to secure the protection of the Orleanists for other property dispositions she induced her senile lover to make in her favor.

In August 1830 the duc de Bourbon was found hanging from looped handkerchiefs tied to a casement window fastener in his bedroom in the château de Saint-Leu. The investigative magistrate wrote a report recommending that the baronne de Feuchères be remanded for trial but intervention by the newly inaugurated Orleanist regime resulted in a finding of suicide. André, at the conclusion of his admirable account of this probable miscarriage of justice, cites later statements of two members of the duc de Bourbon's staff asserting that he was in fact smothered or strangled by Sophie and her lover (a junior officer of the gendarmerie).

A.14 Anouilh, Jean *Becket, or The Honor of God*. Trans. Lucienne Hill. New York: Coward-McCann, 1960.

■ According to his introduction, Anouilh found the inspiration for his play about Thomas Becket in a volume he purchased from a *bouquiniste* on the Seine, *The Conquest of England by the Normans*, by Augustin Thierry, "an historian of the Romantic school, forgotten today and scrapped; for history, too, has its fashions." In Thierry's time, it was believed that Becket was of Saxon origin, and Anouilh persisted in accepting this erroneous view even after a historian friend pointed out that the English saint was a "good Norman" from the vicinity of Rouen. In fact, the Saxon birth of Anouilh's Becket seems central to the play. Perhaps reflecting the shame of Vichy and suggesting the potential of the French for spiritual rebirth, Anouilh emphasizes the theme of "collaboration." Becket's parents "were able to keep their lands by agreeing to 'collaborate,' as they say," with the father of Henry II. Becket comments that his father, a very severe man, "managed by collaborating to amass a considerable fortune. As he was also a man of rigid principles, I imagine he contrived to do it in accordance with his conscience. That's a little piece of sleight of hand that men of principle are very skillful at in troubled times." Becket finds personal honor by undertaking to defend the honor of God against royal encroachment after Henry appoints him archbishop of Canterbury. Unlike his counterpart in Tennyson's *Becket* (see T.2), Anouilh's Henry is a sensual and malicious egoist disinclined to bother his head about politics; he twice beds his friend Becket's devoted mistress Gwendolen, on the second occasion driving her to suicide.

A.15 [Arden, Alice] Anon. *Arden of Faversham*. In *Three Elizabethan Domestic Tragedies*. Ed. Keith Sturgess. Harmondsworth, Middlesex: Penguin, 1969.

■ This is perhaps the earliest surviving example of an English play based on a true family murder without political overtones; editor Sturgess calls stage works of this character "domestic tragedies." Drawing realistic power from their journalistic sources, these works also belong to the genre of "warning literature," which, while satisfying the audience's appetite for murder and adultery, also provides the edifying example of divine retribution and repentance on the scaffold.

On February 15, 1551, Alice Arden (stepdaughter of Lord North), her lover Mosby, and confederates murdered her unwanted husband, Thomas, collector of customs and former mayor. The most remarkable feature of the case is the large number of botched attempts that preceded Thomas Arden's murder. An ingenious plan to have a painter poison Arden's soup had miscarried, and numerous ambushes had gone awry for such unpredictable reasons that the hand of God seemed to have shielded the intended victim. However, Thomas Arden's luck at last ran out during a card game in his own home. At a prearranged signal a ruffian named Black Will drew a towel around Arden's neck to strangle him, struck him with a fourteen-pound pressing iron, and then gashed his face when he seemed to revive; Alice added seven or eight knife thrusts in his breast.

An anonymous ballad, "The Complaint and Lamentation of Mistresse Arden," appeared when she was burned at the stake in Canterbury; the case was also related in Holinshed's *Chronicles*, which was the principal source of the play *Arden of Faversham*. The drama, often regarded as the finest of the early domestic tragedies, maintains the suspense of the murder conspiracy as long as possible; Arden is killed in scene 14 of the eighteen-scene piece. In an epilogue the author proclaims his loyalty to the unvarnished facts from which the drama sprung:

> Gentlemen, we hope you'll pardon this naked tragedy
> Wherein no filed points are foisted in
> To make it gracious to the ear or eye;
> For simple truth is gracious enough,
> And needs no other points of glozing stuff.

For an account of the Arden murder and the summary of the related documents, see Joseph H. Marshburn, *Murder and Witchcraft in England, 1550–1640* (Norman: Univ. of Oklahoma Press, 1971), 3–22. Twentieth-century works based on the Arden murder case include a novel by Diane Davidson, *Feversham* (New York: Crown, 1969), and an opera composed by Alexander Goehr in 1967 for the Hamburg State Opera, *Arden Muss Sterben* [Arden Must Die].

A.16 Arrabal, Fernando   *La vierge rouge* [The Red Virgin]. Paris: Acropole, 1986.
■ Born in Spanish-speaking Morocco in 1932, the absurdist playwright Arrabal moved to Paris in 1955 and thereafter wrote in French. *La vierge rouge*, a novel in the form of a prose poem of 124 chapters, each a little over a page long, is a surrealistic retelling of Aurora Rodríguez's murder of her daughter Hildegart in Madrid on June 9, 1933 (see H.3). In Arrabal's hands, the daughter (fancifully renamed) is just as precocious as in real life but is primarily set to work conducting experiments in alchemy at a basement stove specially constructed for her by her mother. Arrabal suggests that the daughter was murdered at her own request after finding that she could not make the painful choice between leading an independent but less ambitious life in England or continuing her scientific "mission" under her mother's domination.

A.17 Asbury, Herbert   *All Around the Town*. New York: Knopf, 1934.
■ Many of these articles drawn from New York City's history and personalities first appeared in the *New Yorker*. In selecting topics Asbury shows his predilection for crime, public disorder, and scandal. Only in the Big Apple could the Park Commission have mindlessly sold Oscar F. Spate the right to install green rocking chairs on public property and to charge for their use, leading to "rocking-chair riots." Asbury also portrays Madame

Adelaide Kleinschmidt, the social queen of Hackensack who is unmasked as a pickpocket; and Carry Nation appears as the "Big Wind from Kansas." Another of Asbury's colorful characters is John Allen, who, with his larcenous wife, Little Susy, robbed drunken sailors, worked the white-slavery racket with a procuress-kidnapper named Jane the Grabber, and operated *louche* dance-halls. The collection also pays tribute to a noted English immigrant, "Bristol Bill, the Burglar."

A.18 ———— *The Barbary Coast: An Informal History of the San Francisco Underworld*. New York: Knopf, 1933.

■ This sprightly history of San Francisco's fabled Barbary Coast begins with the California gold rush of 1849. According to Asbury, "gambling remained the principal diversion of the great mass of restless, turbulent, gold-hungry men who almost over night had transformed the once peaceful hamlet of San Francisco into a bawdy, bustling bedlam of mud-holes and shanties." After describing the city's early gambling houses, Asbury turns to subsequent chapters of the Barbary Coast's colorful history:

- An early vigilante group known as the Hounds and later as the San Francisco Society of Regulators, who first attacked Chileno shanties but later roamed the streets at will robbing pedestrians and stores
- California's most famous outlaw, Joaquín Murieta, who has been variously described as the Robin Hood of the Sierras or as a particularly bloodthirsty villain of the West
- Sydney-Town, a colony of arrivals from Australia whose criminal inhabitants were popularly called Sydney Ducks; this area, located along the waterfront at Broadway and Pacific Street and on the slopes of Telegraph Hill, later became known as the Barbary Coast
- The activities of San Francisco's Vigilance Committees
- The flourishing of the Barbary Coast's dives and music halls (including the Bella Union)
- Crime in Chinatown
- Murderers and thieves who preyed on sailors along the waterfront
- The Barbary Coast's commercialized prostitution, which, according to Asbury, had a semi-lawful status in San Francisco for more than sixty years
- Reformers' attacks on vice in the Barbary Coast beginning in 1912, after that district had become a "slummers' paradise"

A.19 ———— *Carry Nation*. New York: Knopf, 1929.

■ Asbury does not mince words about Carry Nation, America's temperance terrorist: "She followed the well-beaten trail of mental instability and extravagant religious zeal, and she was urged onward, and from her viewpoint upward, by a deep-rooted persecution mania and a highly developed scapegoat complex." Nation was immensely proud of her barroom destruction, which she referred to as "hatchetation." Asbury believes that her campaign against alcohol had its roots in the drunkenness of her first husband, whom she was compelled to leave after only a few months of marriage.

A.20 ────── *The French Quarter: An Informal History of the New Orleans Underworld.* New York: Knopf, 1936.

■ This longest and most entertaining of Asbury's underworld histories begins with the development of New Orleans during the administration of its French governor the Marquis de Vaudreuil (1743–53) and the period of Spanish domination that was initiated in 1769 when Don Alexander O'Reilly, an Irish soldier of fortune, took possession of Louisiana in the name of the King of Spain. Asbury warms to his principal theme of illicit urban activity when he turns to chapters of the city's history after the Louisiana Purchase of 1803. His subjects include:

- John A. Murrel, bandit, murderer, and slave-stealer of the Natchez Trace
- The invasion of the city by river criminals who stimulated the growth of its underworld
- Pirate Jean Lafitte and other swashbucklers
- Gambling on steamboat and shore
- Marie Laveau and other voodoo practitioners
- The occupation of the French Quarter by armed Vigilantes in 1858
- Prostitution in Basin Street and Storyville
- A series of fatal shootings in the 1880s involving men of some prominence in the state and city governments
- The gang of thieves captained by Yellow Henry Stewart
- The rise of the New Orleans mafia, which by 1885 numbered three hundred members under the presidency of Tony Matranga. The mob's murder of police chief David Hennessy led to a mass lynching of Italian prisoners in the Parish Prison at Congo Square.

A.21 ────── *The Gangs of New York.* New York: Knopf, 1928.

■ This is the first in the author's lively series of underworld histories of major American cities. Among the subjects included are:

- The Old Brewery at the heart of the Five Points, a breeding place of crime and gangs after its conversion into a dwelling in 1837
- The gangs of the Bowery such as the Bowery Boys and the Dead Rabbits
- Vice on the waterfront and river piracy
- A long-running feud between two gangster-bruisers, Lew Baker and Bill Poole ("Bill the Butcher"), which ended with Baker shooting Poole through the heart
- The Draft Riots of 1863
- Bank robber George Leonidas Leslie
- The Whyos, a gang that rose to prominence after the Civil War
- Edward "Monk" Eastman, a vicious gang leader whom Asbury describes as "a true moving picture gangster"
- The Chinese Tong Wars
- The murder of gambler Herman Rosenthal in 1912 on the orders of corrupt police lieutenant Charles Becker

A.22 ———— *Gem of the Prairie: An Informal History of the Chicago Underworld.* New York: Knopf, 1940.

■ Apologizing that limitations of space prevented the inclusion of a really comprehensive survey of the Chicago underworld during the prohibition epoch and accordingly devoting only his two last chapters to Al Capone and his contemporaries, Asbury devotes the bulk of this volume to highlights of the city's earlier crime history. Despite his lament that the Chicago underworld's "early growth was remarkably slow," the misdeeds of its citizenry produced an embarrassment of riches for the author:

- The 1855 mob that protested the application of the Sunday closing law to German beer gardens
- The anti-crime campaigns of Long John Wentworth, elected Chicago's mayor in 1857. Despite his efforts, Chicago acquired during the Civil War period worldwide renown as "the wickedest city in the United States."
- The rise of prostitution as the most profitable business of the Chicago underworld during the 1860s and the years immediately following the Chicago Fire of 1871
- Michael Cassius McDonald, who dominated gambling and confidence games until the middle 1890s
- The serial killings of Herman W. Mudgett, better known as H. H. Holmes, who butchered countless victims in his city "castle" until he was hanged in 1896 for the murder of Benjamin Pitezel. Mudgett had murdered Pitezel and set him afire in a scheme to collect life insurance proceeds.
- The crime wave that afflicted Chicago between 1890 and 1910. The Maxwell Street district, commonly known as Bloody Maxwell, was described by the *Chicago Tribune* in 1906 as "the wickedest police district in the world." Of the gangsters active in this period, the greatest notoriety was garnered by the trio of Gustave Marx, Harvey Van Dine, and Peter Neidermeyer, who called themselves the Automatic Trio but were known to police and public as the Car Barn Bandits. In 1903 the group embarked on a series of robberies of saloons, a station of the Northwestern Railroad, and the car barns of the Chicago City Railway. The men were hanged in 1904, and another gang member was sentenced to life imprisonment.
- Black Hand extortion gangs, which numbered between sixty and eighty during the first two decades of the twentieth century
- The notorious brothel-keepers Ada and Minna Everleigh, who offered their customers everything they could possibly want, including gold-plated spittoons

A.23 ———— *The Golden Flood: An Informal History of America's First Oil Field.* New York: Knopf, 1942.

■ Asbury's history of Pennsylvania's oil towns of the nineteenth century does full justice to what the author calls "sin among the derricks"; gambling, prostitution, and vigilantism (led by the Titusville Committee of Thirty) were features of the landscape. Separate chapters sketch the biography of Benedict Hagan, better known as Ben Hogan, bouncer, pugilist, brothel-keeper, thief, and ultimately gospel missionary, and describe the only major robbery in the history of the oil fields, the theft of $60,000 from John Benninghoff.

A.24 ———— *The Great Illusion: An Informal History of Prohibition.* Garden City: Doubleday, 1950.

■ Although there are many more detailed accounts of the Prohibition era, Asbury's book is of value in tracing the rise of American anti-alcohol sentiment from the early nineteenth century, when it was already evident in a pamphlet of Reverend Mason L. Weems (inventor of the George Washington myths) and in the attacks on drinking in the diary and correspondence of President John Adams.

A.25 ———— *Sucker's Progress: An Informal History of Gambling in America from the Colonies to Canfield.* New York: Dodd Mead, 1938.

■ Part 1 of this entertaining history is devoted to the development of the major gambling games and contrivances that won popularity in America: faro poker, craps, the lottery, and its illegitimate offspring, the policy or numbers game. In a chapter entitled "Small Fry," Asbury groups miscellaneous games and swindles, including roulette, three-card monte, and thimble-rig (the "shell game"). Part 2 of the book traces the expansion of American gambling from its fountainhead in New Orleans, whose early rivals were New York, Washington, and Mobile. Asbury also discusses gambling on the western rivers; the era of Mike McDonald, Chicago gambling house keeper; the westward movement of gamblers that began with the establishment of the Texas Republic and the California gold rush; John Morrissey, who developed gambling and horse racing at Saratoga Springs; and Richard A. Canfield of New York, Newport, and Saratoga, the last famous gambling house keeper of the nineteenth century. The happy conclusion of Asbury's chronicle is Henry Frick's purchase of three of the finest paintings in Canfield's collection for the Frick Museum, including Whistler's *Count Robert de Montesquiou.*

A.26 Atlay, J[ames] B[eresford] *Famous Trials of the [Nineteenth] Century.* London: Grant Richards, 1899.

■ J. B. Atlay's masterpiece is his 234-page study (later separately published) of the civil and criminal trials of the "Tichborne Claimant," who asserted that he was the long-missing Sir Roger Tichborne, heir of one of England's prominent Roman Catholic families. In 1854 the twenty-five-year-old Roger disappeared at sea, an apparent victim of the shipwreck of the English vessel *La Belle,* bound for London from Rio de Janeiro. Twelve years later a butcher in Wagga Wagga, Australia, wrote to Roger Tichborne's mother, asserting, with apologies for not having been a better correspondent, that he was her devoted son. When he arrived in England, hoping to reclaim his interest in the family property that had passed to the child of Roger's brother, the incongruities of his claim were apparent: in addition to his notable weakness in spelling and his deficient memory, the butcher from Australia was very stout, whereas the young Roger had been slight and pale. (Moreover, like the famous gloves in O. J. Simpson's trial, the military helmet of Roger Tichborne was too tight for the Australian.)

Atlay, who had no doubt that the Claimant was actuated by fraud in usurping a wealthy heir's identity, attributes the temporary success of his imposture to the unwillingness of Dowager Lady Henriette Félicité Tichborne to concede that her elder son Roger had been lost at sea; in 1863 she placed advertisements for news of him that came to the Claimant's attention. Lady Henriette was a native of France, a nation that had clasped Martin Guerre and many other audacious impostors to its bosom. Having mourned the deaths of her husband and her younger son, Alfred, the dowager was prepared to recognize the Claimant even before she received him. Atlay's account of their meeting in a Paris hotel is unforgettable: "It was a murky afternoon, the blinds were half down, the claimant was lying huddled on the bed with his clothes on, and his face turned to the wall. The mother bent over him and kissed him, saying, 'He looks like his father, and his ears are like his uncle's.'" In Lady Tichborne's campaign for her "son's" recognition, she was powerfully seconded by a long-time family solicitor, Edward Hopkins.

The longest legal proceedings in English history ensued. A civil suit brought by the Claimant to recover the Tichborne estates failed, despite the advocacy of Serjeant William Ballantine, in the face of evidence that he was Arthur Orton, son of a butcher from London's Wapping district. In a subsequent criminal prosecution for perjury, he was found guilty and imprisoned for ten years. The authenticity of the "confession" he sold after his release is disputed. The Claimant's erratic counsel, Dr. Edward Vaughan Kenealy, sought to prove that his client was in fact Roger Tichborne, whose injuries in the shipwreck were responsible for his eccentric conduct.

In a later work, *The Tichborne Claimant* (London: Hollis & Carter, 1957), Douglas Woodruff argues that while the Claimant failed to establish in the civil proceeding that he was Sir Roger Tichborne, the Crown's effort to show in the criminal trial that he was Arthur Orton should have been rejected by the jury as lacking in proof. Woodruff argues: "It was carrying effrontery beyond the bounds of sanity if Arthur Orton embarked with a wife and retinue and crossed the world, knowing they would all be destitute if he did not succeed in convincing a woman he had never seen and knew nothing whatever about at first hand, that he was her son. There is a vast improbability about the imposture being attempted, and a second improbability about it ever meeting with any success."

Most of the other articles in the collection study famous murder cases: those of John Thurtell; Burke and Hare; François Courvoisier, a Swiss valet who murdered his master Lord William Russell in 1840; Madeleine Smith; Constance Kent; and the poisoner Dr. Edward Pritchard. Less widely known is the ordeal of London solicitor William Henry Barbour ("A Miscarriage of Justice"), who was erroneously convicted of participating in a client's scheme to obtain fraudulent recoveries of unclaimed securities and dividends. Barbour, whom Atlay compares to Dumas's Edmond Dantès, served three years of a life sentence on Norfolk Island until influential sympathizers won his release.

The copy of Atlay's *Famous Trials* held by the Borowitz True Crime Collection belonged to Warden Lewis E. Lawes of Sing Sing prison. His bookplate shows the warden smoking at his desk as a recidivist runs up with a book in his hand, saying, "I'm in again Boss to return your book."

Barrister J. B. Atlay (1860–1912) wrote *The Trial of Lord Cochrane* (1897), *The Lives of the Victorian Chancellors* (1906–8), and other legal biographies. He also edited *The Trial of the Stauntons* (1911) in the *Notable British Trials* series.

A.27 **Atwood, Margaret** *Alias Grace.* New York: Doubleday, 1996.

■ The enigmatic central figure of this novel is the sixteen-year-old servant girl Grace Marks, convicted in 1843 of helping her fellow servant James McDermott in the brutal murder of their master, Thomas Kinnear, and his housekeeper and mistress, Nancy Montgomery, in the Canadian town of Richmond Hill. Because of her youth and supposed mental slowness, Grace's death sentence was commuted to life imprisonment following a period in a lunatic asylum. The uncertainty regarding her criminal responsibility persisted for about thirty years, some thinking her insane or possessed while others viewing her as innocent and still others as a vicious murderess. In 1872 she was granted a pardon and released from the Kingston penitentiary.

Atwood drew on inconclusive contemporary accounts, chiefly Susanna Moodie's *Life in the Clearings* (1853), as well as newspaper reports and the correspondence of Joseph Workman, medical director of the asylum to which Grace was committed. However, in large measure she relies on her own vital imagination, recreating through fictional characters the conflicting views held by criminologists, medical researchers, spiritualists, and charlatans. Dr. Simon Jordan, a fictional physician hired by Grace's petitioners, bases his speculations on nineteenth-century theories of hysteria, amnesia, and the dissociation of personality. In the end, overpowered by uncertainty, Dr. Jordan flees Kingston without writing his report on the puzzling Grace.

A.28 **Aubigné, Théodore-Agrippa d'** *Les tragiques* [Tragic Events]. 1616. Preface Albert-Marie Schmidt. Lausanne: Editions Rencontre, 1966.

■ At age sixteen Aubigné (1552–1635) joined the Protestant military forces in France's religious wars. Two years later he became engaged to Diane Salviati. Diane's father approved of the match, but Aubigné's enemies laid an ambush for the young man and wounded him severely. Believing that he was near death, Aubigné rode twenty-five leagues to catch a last glimpse of his fiancée at her home in Talcy. When he arrived, he lost consciousness and was left for dead. While he lay in a dreamlike state, Agrippa seemed to be transported to heaven, where he was granted a divine vision of France's sorrows. After his seemingly miraculous reawakening, Aubigné became a Huguenot champion in the military service of Henri IV, whom he ultimately abandoned as an apostate.

The literary fruit of Aubigné's narrow escape from assassination and of his espousal of the Protestant cause was the seven-part apocalyptic poem *Les tragiques*. In the poet's vision, his survival of his enemies' plot was a paradigm of the Huguenot experience:

I, who assemble in this fashion those who have escaped death,
To lend voices and hands in support of God,
Singing to the future age their fears and their sufferings,

And their eventual liberations, shall I be silent of my own?

In those harsh times, my mind, having left
To my assassins my body pierced in many places,
Although impure, was transported to the pure heavens,
By an angel comforting my grievous wounds.
For seven hours the heavenly abode opened
To show me the beautiful secrets and images that I now record.

The archvillain in Aubigné's portrayal of the late Valois monarchy is Catherine de Medici, who appears as a poisoner and sorceress who can raise the dead by compelling demons to reanimate their bones.

Aubigné's religious convictions were renounced by his progeny. His granddaughter Françoise, under the name of the marquise de Maintenon, persuaded Louis XIV to revoke the Edict of Nantes, which had decreed toleration of Protestant worship.

A.29 Avrich, Paul *The Haymarket Tragedy.* Princeton: Princeton Univ. Press, 1984.

■ Professor Avrich's magnificent work is a sympathetic but fair-minded study of the massacre in Chicago's Haymarket on May 4, 1886. Although the book admirably presents the development of American anarchism and labor activism in the decade preceding the tragedy, Avrich's chief concern is with "the human story—with the interest that adheres to men and women who have the courage to defy conventional standards of behavior and to withstand hardship and abuse for the sake of principles that they believe to be right." The book focuses on two anarchists who died on the scaffold after conviction of murder in the Haymarket trial. These leaders were Albert Parsons, scion of American Revolutionary War heroes and himself a Confederate veteran, and German-born August Spies, drawn to socialism, like Parsons, by "sympathy for the needy and disinherited."

Avrich persuasively shows that the Haymarket bloodbath was not a "riot," as it is often portrayed. The fatal May 4 rally was held a day after Chicago police fired at striking employees at the McCormick Reaper Works, killing at least two, and was both a response to that provocation and a show of strength in the anarchists' campaign for an eight-hour workday. The meeting proceeded peacefully and only about three hundred people remained in the square when intemperate police inspector John Bonfield marched his forces against the stragglers and ordered them to disperse. In response, an unknown person threw a bomb into police ranks. The final toll was seven policemen killed and sixty wounded, as well as seven or eight civilians dead and thirty to forty injured. Most of the casualties in the Haymarket were caused when the police opened fire indiscriminately, hitting their own forces as well as civilians.

Eight anarchist leaders were put on trial for the murder of officer Mathias J. Degan, the only policeman whose death was demonstrably caused exclusively by a bomb fragment. All defendants were convicted, although the bomber could not be identified and there was no evidence that any of the defendants had participated in the outrage. Judge Joseph E.

Gary permitted the jury to assume that the bomb thrower acted under the influence of exhortations to class violence in anarchist writings and speeches. Four defendants were hanged, one committed suicide in prison, and three were pardoned by Illinois's courageous governor, John Peter Altgeld, in 1893.

Alone among America's literary establishment, William Dean Howells denounced the execution of the anarchists. His private voice was equally eloquent. In a letter to his father he wrote, "The historical perspective is that this free Republic has killed five men for their opinions." In a letter written to the *New York Tribune*, but never sent, he portrayed the convictions as black humor:

> But perhaps the wildest of our humorists could not have conceived of a joke so monstrous as the conviction of seven men for a murderous conspiracy which they carried into effect while one was at home playing cards with his family, another was addressing a meeting five miles away, another was present with his wife and little children, two others had made pacific speeches, and not one, except on the testimony of a single, notoriously untruthful witness, was proven to have had anything to do with throwing the Haymarket bomb, or to have even remotely instigated the act.

In his book, Avrich does not identify the bomb thrower but hypothesizes that he probably came from a militant wing of the anarchist movement. He rejects the sensational invention by Frank Harris, in his 1908 novel *The Bomb*, of a deathbed confession by Rudolph Schnaubelt, who had fled from Chicago to Argentina to avoid arrest.

In 1985 Dr. Adah Maurer, a California psychologist, wrote to Avrich to express her belief that the bomber was her grandfather, George Meng, one of the Chicago delegates to the Pittsburgh congress of revolutionary socialists in 1883. Avrich stated that he "was inclined to believe Dr. Maurer's story," which had "the ring of truth" (*New York Times*, Nov. 12, 1985).

B

B.1 Bainbridge, Beryl *Watson's Apology.* New York: McGraw-Hill, 1984.

■ In *Watson's Apology* Beryl Bainbridge, using court documents and newspaper accounts, retells the shocking 1871 London murder of Anne Watson by her sixty-seven-year-old husband, John Selby Watson, a clergyman and schoolmaster. Besides exploring in horrific detail the disintegration of an ill-matched couple's marriage, Bainbridge recreates the thoughts and motives of the aging and seriously depressed classics scholar who had lost not only his teaching post but his publisher. His wife's indifference to his literary interests and her taunts about his publishing failures may have ignited Watson's murderous rage. Bainbridge shows special compassion for Watson's plight as a failed classicist as well as a joyless husband, emphasizing a Latin aphorism found among the clergyman's papers: "It is often harmful for one who has loved in the past to love forever." She also explores the sinister appearances, in Victorian eyes, of an order Watson placed on the day following the murder for the construction of a large trunk. After his conviction, and before his execution was commuted on the ground of insanity, Watson asked the prison chaplain to forward his written explanation of the trunk purchase to the London *Times*. This letter supports Bainbridge's idea that Watson's chief passion was literary activity: "I had it made of such capacity because I had . . . a great number of manuscripts and letters to put together."

B.2 Baldwin, James *Blues for Mister Charlie*. New York: Dell, 1964.

■ In August 1955 the body of fourteen-year-old Emmett Till, weighed down by a heavy fan, was fished out of the Tallahatchie River in rural Mississippi; the black youth had been pistol-whipped, and a bullet had been fired into his head. A few days before, Till, a visitor from Chicago, showed off for friends by asking a young white matron, Carolyn Bryant, who was operating a family grocery and meat market in her husband's absence, for a date. When she resisted his advances and went for a pistol, he emitted a "wolf whistle" in her direction. Carolyn's husband, Roy, and his half-brother, J. W. Milam, were tried for the killing and found not guilty.

On January 24, 1956, William Bradford Huie published in *Look* magazine an article based on paid interviews with Emmett Till's acquitted murderers (William Bradford Huie, *Wolf Whistle* [New York: Signet, 1959]). A subsequent scholarly account argues that other white men may also have been involved in the killing in defense of "Southern honor" (Stephen J. Whitfield, *A Death in the Delta* [New York: Free Press, 1988]).

James Baldwin has noted that his play *Blues for Mister Charlie* is based "very distantly, indeed" on the murder of Emmett Till. The action takes place in an unnamed Southern community that is sharply divided, as is the set, between Blacktown and Whitetown. The murder of Richard Henry, an angry young black man returned from New York with a sawed-off handgun, by Lyle Butler, a white bigot, appears to be predetermined by the community's history of sex-related racial violence. Richard's mother, a hotel worker, may have been pushed down the stairs of her workplace by a white lecher; and his adversary, Lyle, admittedly murdered the husband of a young black woman with whom he had been having an affair. After Richard taunts Lyle and his wife at their grocery store, Lyle demands an apology and, when none is offered, shoots Richard and drags his body into high weeds. After a nightmarish trial in which a key witness, liberal white newspaper editor Parnell James, is rendered ineffectual because of his conflicting attachments to the town's two ethnic groups, Lyle Butler is acquitted, and Parnell follows Juanita, a black student with whom he has long been in love, in the ranks of a civil rights protest.

Some critics misunderstood Baldwin's presentation of Richard Henry as a rejection of the notion that Emmett Till was an innocent child. Baldwin responded, "It was very important for me, you know, to have Richard Henry as offensive and brash and stupid as he is. Sure, he had no right to talk to anybody like that. But do you have the right to shoot him? That's the question" (Whitfield, *A Death in the Delta*, 123).

B.3 —— *The Evidence of Things Not Seen*. New York: Holt, 1995.

■ This essay on the conviction of Wayne Williams for the murders of two black men,

Jimmy Ray Payne and Nathaniel Cater, in Atlanta argues that the prosecution and community reactions were heavily influenced by America's tortured racial history. While unwilling to proclaim Williams innocent, Baldwin emphasizes the unfairness of the state having based its case on proof of an alleged pattern of conduct in connection with twenty-three other killings of black children in which Williams was not charged. The only pattern Baldwin could discern in the murders "was that the victims were young Black males—there were also two Black female children—living in the purgatory, or the eternity of poverty. To be poor and Black in a country so rich and White is to judge oneself very harshly and it means that one has nothing to lose. Why not get into the friendly car? What's the worst that can happen? For a poor child is, also, a very lonely child."

However, Baldwin rejected the defense claim that there never has been a black mass murderer; he found unanswerable the district attorney's reply that Idi Amin was a black mass murderer.

B.4 Balzac, Honoré de *A Harlot High and Low* [Splendeurs et misères des courtisanes]. 1839–47. Trans. and intro. Rayner Heppenstall. Harmondsworth: Penguin Classics, 1970. ■ This novel celebrates the conversion of Vautrin—who is depicted in former novels of the *Human Comedy* as the very embodiment of evil—into a champion of law and order. In Part 4 of *A Harlot High and Low*, entitled "The Last Incarnation of Vautrin," this protean character becomes chief of the Paris Sûreté. A similar transformation occurred in the life of Eugène-François Vidocq (see v.4), on whom Vautrin is patterned, but Vidocq did not possess Vautrin's dark soul. Balzac's convincing portrayal of prison life in this novel may have been enriched by information obtained from Vidocq, who became the novelist's friend.

B.5 —— "Lettre sur le procès de Peytel" [Letter about the Trial of Peytel]. *Oeuvres Complètes de Honoré de Balzac*. Vol. 40. Paris: Conard, 1911. 231–61. ■ When Balzac's former literary colleague, notary Sébastien Peytel, was convicted of murdering his new wife, Félicie, and a male domestic servant, Louis Rey, during a carriage journey on a country road, Balzac and the artist Gavarni visited him in prison. The novelist, following the precedents of Voltaire and Benjamin Constant (see v.9 and c.45), wrote his *Letter about the Trial of Peytel* as a memorandum in support of his friend's innocence.

Before putting pen to paper, Balzac visited the scene of the crime and experimented with gunshots to test how far the sound would carry. His central argument was that the crime did not reflect the premeditation that had been urged at the trial. If Peytel had wanted to murder his bride he would have done so at a time when an inconvenient third party, such as the servant, was not present. Moreover, Balzac had himself observed many places along the route where Peytel could have pitched the victims into six feet of water and ten feet of mud, instead of resorting to pistol and hammer. Unfortunately, the novelist did not observe that his argument could be turned around; if the servant (who Balzac believed was Félicie's lover) was the assailant, he also could have chosen a safer place for a planned attack.

In *L'Affaire Peytel* (Paris: Hachette, 1958), P. A. Perrod concludes that Peytel shot Félicie by accident after discovering her in Louis Rey's arms during the fatal journey; that he then pursued and killed the servant, his intended target. Perrod bases this theory on Gavarni's notes of a prison confession made to him by Peytel. According to Perrod, Peytel refused to tell the truth in court because he wanted to defend his dead wife's honor.

Perrod's speculation that Peytel shot Félicie by accident, intending to hit Rey, is similar to the theory advanced by Thackeray in his article on the case. See Albert Borowitz, "Why Thackeray Went to See a Man Hanged," *Innocence and Arsenic: Studies in Crime and Literature* (see B.28).

B.6 ———— *Old Goriot* [Le père Goriot]. 1834–35. Trans. Marion Ayton Crawford. Harmondsworth: Penguin Classics, 1951.

▪ Among the boarders at the Pension Vauquer, one of Balzac's greatest creations, Vautrin, makes his debut. This archcriminal is based on a friend of the author, the prodigious Eugène-François Vidocq, who founded the Paris Sûreté after many years on the run from the police as a minor offender and prison escapee (see V.4). Vautrin, when introduced in *Old Goriot*, has escaped from a prison camp, where he has been serving a sentence for forgery. The wily convict is attracted to Eugène de Rastignac, another of the boarders. He obtains Eugène's wavering assent to his scheme to have Frédéric Taillefer killed in a duel so that his sister, Victorine (another lodger in the pension), will become an heiress whom Eugène may profitably woo. Victorine's brother dies as planned, but before Eugène can be implicated, Vautrin is arrested by his old enemy, Bibi-Lupin, who has become chief of the Sûreté.

Vautrin appears in other novels in Balzac's *Human Comedy* (see, for example, B.4) and in the author's unsuccessful 1840 play *Vautrin*.

B.7 ———— *Une ténébreuse affaire* [A Mysterious Case]. *Oeuvres Complètes de Honorè de Balzac*. Vol. 21. Paris: Conard, 1914.

▪ This novel is based on the kidnapping of Senator Clément de Ris in 1800, which was probably an improvisation after a burglary attempt (see H.14). Balzac politicizes this occurrence, attributing a fictional abduction of Malin de Gondreville to a plot of Napoleon's Police Minister Fouché to destroy evidence of his own ties with Napoleon's enemies.

B.8 Bataille, Albert *Causes criminelles et mondaines 1880–1898.* [Criminal and Social Trials] 18 vols. Paris: Dentu, 1887–98.

▪ At age sixteen, Bataille came to Paris from Blois and joined the staff of *Le Figaro*, where he became the leading French trial reporter of the last two decades of the nineteenth century. His daily newspaper accounts of courtroom proceedings, often opinionated, are reproduced without significant editing in these volumes and accordingly preserve his dramatic rendering of unfolding events and his firsthand impressions of trial participants. Among the major cases reported are Caserio's assassination of President Carnot, the trial of the anarchist Ravachol, the Panama Canal scandals, and the Dreyfus case. Two collections of Bataille's reports have been translated into English and edited by Philip A. Wilkins: *Dramas of the French Courts* (London: Hutchinson, n.d.); *Inside the French Courts* (London: Hutchinson, n.d.)

B.9 Bedford, Sybille *The Trial of Dr. Adams.* New York: Simon & Schuster, 1959.
■ Novelist Bedford alertly attended the 1957 trial of Dr. John Bodkin Adams for the murder of one of his patients, the wealthy eighty-two-year-old Mrs. Alice Morrell, who had willed him a small legacy. After what was billed as the longest murder trial ever held at the Old Bailey, Adams was acquitted. Bedford regarded it as "admirable" that, "ungrudged, day after day is spent dispassionately thrashing out whether there has been an intent to kill in one man's mind, whether one woman's span was cut some weeks before its time." She is impelled, however, to qualify her praise for the judicial process: "But does it not strike us that our sense is intermittent and our conscience split? Can we not imagine that if our descendants were asked 150 years from now what struck them as most shocking and discrepant in our present time, they might point—provided they'll be there to tell the tale—to the hair-splitting niceties of this trial combined with the acceptance of the H-bomb as an example of our staggering schizophrenia" (157).

B.10 Behan, Brendan "The Quare Fellow." In Cóilín D. Owens and Joan N. Radner, eds. *Irish Drama 1900–1980.* Washington, D.C.: Catholic Univ. of America Press, 1990.
■ This drama of a Dublin prison hanging is inspired by the execution of pork butcher Bernard Kirwan for the gory murder of his younger brother, Lawrence. Brendan Behan (1923–1964) was in Mountjoy jail at the time and knew Kirwan. One of the prisoners in the play describes the crime: "He bled his brother into a crock, didn't he, that had been set aside for the pig-slaughtering and mangled the remains beyond all hope of identification."

The real-life murderer applied his professional skill in filleting his brother's body so expertly that identification was difficult. In 1936 Bernard Kirwan had received a seven-year sentence for armed robbery. While he was in prison, his mother died, leaving the small family farm in equal shares to her six children. Four of the beneficiaries had no interest in the property, but, with unlucky effect on his life expectancy, Lawrence Kirwan stayed on the farm. In November 1941, after Bernard was released from prison, Lawrence vanished. Six months later, his dismembered body was found in a bog a mile away from the farm.

When Kirwan went to the Mountjoy gallows, he balanced a cup of water on the back of his right hand to show that he was not nervous. What other prisoners considered bravery Brendan Behan took for madness. See Michael O'Sullivan, *Brendan Behan: A Life* (Boulder: Roberts Rinehart, 1999), 102–3.

The horrific nature of the condemned man's crime renders the play's attack on capital punishment absolute and uncompromising. The man who is to die is nameless and never appears onstage, but his doom is ever-present, as prisoners bet on his chances for a reprieve, his grave is dug in advance of the hanging, the executioner arrives, and prison life (if it can be called that) is resumed after the hanging. Behan's spokesman is the humane Warder Regan, who continually assaults the cruelty of the death penalty and of a complicit society that tolerates it. He sermonizes, for example, to the Chief Warder: "I was reared among people that drank at a death or prayed. Some did both. You think the law makes this man's death someway different, not like anyone else's. . . . [But] no one is going to jump on you in the morning and throttle the life out of you" (Act 3, scene 1).

B.11 Bell, Neal   *Two Small Bodies*. New York: Dramatists Play Service, 1980.
■ This two-character play is based on the controversial case of cocktail waitress Alice Crimmins, convicted of the 1965 murder of her two small children. See Albert Borowitz, "The Medea of Kew Gardens Hills," in Jonathan Goodman, ed., *The Lady Killers* (New York: Citadel Press, 1991), 55–73.

In Bell's strong drama, Lt. Brann, a police detective investigating the disappearance of two small children, becomes sexually obsessed with their mother, continuing his visits to her apartment even after the murders of the children have been confessed to by a male maniac. Perhaps Bell intends Brann to be motivated by the same prurient interest that Alice Crimmins's prosecutors showed in her highly active sex life, a preoccupation that led them to the dubious theory that she disposed of her children to make her home more accessible to male callers.

B.12 Belloc Lowndes, Marie   *The Chink in the Armour*. New York: Longmans Green, 1937.
■ Belloc Lowndes's novel adapts a Monte Carlo murder case of 1907. Marie ("Lady") Vere Goold and her third husband bludgeoned and stabbed to death the widow Emma Erika Levin when she inconveniently sought repayment of a loan she had made to them; they deposited her body in a trunk and departed for Marseilles with this interesting addition to their luggage. A goods clerk at the Marseilles station noticed blood oozing from the noisome trunk and alerted the police. After their conviction, the Vere Goolds were imprisoned at Cayenne, where Marie died of typhoid and her husband committed suicide.

The Chink in the Armour is set in a French gaming village, smaller than Monte Carlo, where murderers may move at ease among the odd assemblage of visitors. Madame Wachner and her husband, Fritz, serial killers, have a trunk awaiting their intended victim, Sylvia Bailey, but their murder plan is foiled by the widow's admirer, a French nobleman, Comte Paul de Virieu, who is suspicious of the couple after having observed them before at other casinos. The unsophisticated Bailey only begins to realize the danger when, upon looking into the Wachners' kitchen, "to her surprise she saw that a large trunk, corded and even labelled, stood in the middle of the floor. Close to the trunk was a large piece of sacking—and by it another coil of thick rope." Although previously warned of peril in a visit to a psychic, and repeatedly cautioned by several friends that the gambling resort attracted people willing to do anything for money, Bailey had trusted the Wachners as a sociable and harmless bourgeois couple.

Belloc Lowndes has created a setting where social life obscures danger. The novel's epigraph explains the title and the author's theme: "But there is one chink in the chain armour of civilized communities. Society is conducted on the assumption that murder will not be committed."

B.13 ———— *Letty Lynton*. New York: Jonathan Cape & Harrison Smith, 1931.

■ Belloc Lowndes freely bases her novel *Letty Lynton* on the Madeleine Smith poisoning case. She changes the period from mid-nineteenth century to early twentieth century, introducing a car breakdown as support for Letty's alibi. The French victim, Emile L'Angelier, becomes the Swedish Axel Ekebon, and the calculating Scottish Madeleine Smith appears as the impulsive and charming Letty Lynton. Instead of openly purchasing arsenic on three occasions, as Madeleine Smith did, Letty Lynton steals it from the laboratory of an ex-lover. Although Belloc Lowndes creates several minor characters, she follows the original case in portraying the motivation for the murder as being a desperate attempt to stop Letty/Madeleine's lover from showing her passionate letters to her father. Letty's fear of her strict parents was true to the original case, although in the novel the father stands by her in court, while in real life Madeleine Smith's parents never attended her trial.

The novel became embroiled—through no fault of its author—in copyright litigation resolved by a decision of U.S. Circuit Judge Learned Hand (*Sheldon v. Metro-Goldwyn Pictures Corp.*, 81 F.2d 49 [2d Cir. 1936]). Hand ruled that the motion picture play *Letty Lynton,* created by MGM after acquiring film rights to Belloc Lowndes's novel, infringed upon a successful Broadway play based even less faithfully on the Madeleine Smith case. Among the elements of the play borrowed by the film was the portrayal of the murderess's victim as a Latin American who woos her with a gaucho song.

B.14 ———— *Lizzie Borden: A Study in Conjecture.* New York: Longmans Green, 1939.

■ A great friend of Edmund Pearson, Belloc Lowndes differed with his theory that Lizzie Borden committed her axe murders because she was a "dissatisfied spinster daughter"; instead, the crime novelist was persuaded that the crimes were predominantly motivated by "the passion of love."

To elaborate on her vision of the tragedy, Belloc Lowndes invents a romance between Lizzie and Hiram Barrison, whom she meets on a French ship, *La Bretagne.* Lizzie's stepmother threatens to tell Mr. Borden about the lovers' rendezvous in the family barn and thereby seals her own doom. Lizzie dispatches her with a handleless axe, shielding herself from blood by pinning to her dress a movable window shade invented by a friend of her uncle. Before advancing on her sleeping father, she selects a new shield, a sheet of Parisian paper she had used in the interim to hide the murder weapon. She persuades family physician Doctor Bowen to burn the incriminating window shade.

At the end of the book, Lizzie promises to write to her lover Hiram. Belloc Lowndes adds: "But she never did."

B.15 ———— *The Lodger.* London: Methuen, 1913; reprint, New York: Scribner, 1913.

■ In this expansion of her 1911 short story of the same name, Belloc Lowndes freely recreates Jack the Ripper as a teetotaling religious maniac named "Mr. Sleuth" who preys on drunken women of dubious occupation. One of the finest fact-based crime novels in the English language, *The Lodger* focuses on the plight of Robert and Ellen Bunting, the murderer's landlords, who keep their suspicions to themselves because only Mr. Sleuth's rent money stands between them and starvation.

B.16 ———— *The Story of Ivy*. New York: Longmans Green. 1927.

■ *The Story of Ivy* is a novel freely based on the murder of James Maybrick. The beautiful young Ivy Lexton (Florence Maybrick) poisons her husband, Jervis (James Maybrick), with arsenic. The prosecution theory that Florence Maybrick administered arsenic obtained by soaking flypapers in water is discussed in the novel by Ivy and her lover, Dr. Roger Gretorex, in relation to the notorious Branksome case:

> He laughed. "Wonderful what people will do sometimes, isn't it? Steeping fly papers in water has long been a common way of ridding oneself of a tiresome husband. There's arsenic in almost everything we use—at least, that's what's said."
>
> "Arsenic?" Ivy pronounced the word very carefully. It was a new word in her limited vocabulary.
>
> ". . . There's plenty of the stuff in my surgery, at any rate. It's a splendid tonic, as well as a poison."

Ivy obtains the arsenic from his surgery, but it is Gretorex who is tried and convicted of murder. Only after his servant Mrs. Huntley, whom he had sworn to secrecy, reveals that she had observed Ivy alone with an arsenic bottle is Gretorex saved from execution. Ivy was willing to sacrifice her lover to the gallows, for she already has her sights on a much richer swain, Miles Rushworth. When Scotland Yard is on the point of charging Ivy with murder, it is Rushworth who tries to arrange her escape from England. As Gretorex said of the Branksome case: "The man will hang, and they'll let the woman off—though she ought to hang too!"

B.17 ———— *What Really Happened*. London: Longmans Green, 1926.

■ In her novel *What Really Happened*, Marie Belloc Lowndes invents variations on the theme of the Bravo murder case (see J.5). She apparently concurs with the popular rumor after the inquest that the murderer was the widow Jane Cox, whose possible motive in killing Charles Bravo was to secure her job as housekeeper and as Mrs. Bravo's companion after he had threatened her with dismissal. Belloc Lowndes moves the time from the 1870s to the 1920s and changes the lover of the beautiful, "scatter-brained" Eva Raydon (Florence Bravo) from the old Dr. James Gully to a young, handsome, and newly wealthy Jack Mintlaw. This romantic hero, who ended his service "as a colonel with every war decoration," had loved the war widow Eva Raydon but, lacking the financial security to propose marriage, had gone to Canada after the war, where with great luck he inherited a huge fortune. Hoping at last to marry Eva, he returned to England only to find the young widow remarried to Birtley Raydon (Charles Bravo), an upper-class lawyer, dominated by his mother, whose thrift and hypochondria produce tension in the marriage. It is Eva's extravagant wardrobe (rather than alcoholism, as in Florence Bravo's case) that enrages her husband and impels her to turn to Jack Mintlaw for money to pay her bills. Adelaide Strain (Mrs. Jane Cox), who had lived with Eva during the war and knew Mintlaw then, acts as a go-between for the lovers.

Unlike the real Mrs. Cox, who harmed Mrs. Bravo by her inquest testimony about Florence's relationship with Dr. Gully, Adelaide Strain saves Eva Raydon from conviction of murder by pointing her finger at a putative killer—the gardener's boy, Amos Purcell (conveniently already dead in a motorcycle accident). In her testimony, Mrs. Strain recalls: "Only a week before his death I was present at a most painful scene between him and Amos Purcell. . . . He accused the lad, in coarse and cruel language of being a thief, and Purcell said he would have the law on him." This episode she links with footsteps she heard in the hall on the night of the murder, suggesting that the dismissed servant had entered the foyer of the house where the beer and ginger beer for Raydon's nightcap of shandy-gaff were ready for her to mix. Thus she imputes her own genuine anger at dismissal by Birtley Raydon to the dead Purcell, whom she claims had enough time "to put a pinch of powder into either of the ingredients for the making of shandy-gaff." The author presents a sympathetic picture of Adelaide Strain, whose impulsive decision to poison her employer is generated by desperate fears for her child's welfare should she be cast out of the Raydon household.

B.18 Benét, Stephen Vincent *Western Star.* New York: Farrar & Rinehart, 1943.

■ The first killer among New England's settlers, John Billington figures prominently in this posthumously published Book 1 of Benét's projected narrative poem of American pioneers. Toward the end of the book, he is mourned as "a man who came with the first and should have thriven." In 1630 Billington shot John Newcomin to death after a quarrel of unknown cause.

B.19 Bennett, Alan *Single Spies: A Double Bill.* London: Faber & Faber, 1989.

■ A pair of witty and beautiful short plays are devoted to "Cambridge spies" Guy Burgess and Sir Anthony Blunt.

Originally a television script, "An Englishman Abroad" is based on the real-life visit of Australian actress Coral Browne (touring in *Hamlet* with Michael Redgrave) to Burgess's Moscow apartment. Gone to seed and guarded by a low-echelon Soviet policeman who plays the balalaika and also serves as his lover, Burgess persuades Browne to take his measurements (which have increased) to his discreet London tailor so that he can have a new suit to keep up an Englishman's appearance. Burgess's treason was facilitated by his inability to embrace an abstract notion of England: "You see, I can say I love London. I can say I love England. But I can't say I love my country. I don't know what that means."

The companion piece, "A Question of Attribution," shifts between two interrogations of Sir Anthony Blunt, distinguished art historian whose treason has not yet been revealed to the public. A British secret service agent named Chubb screens photographs of espionage suspects whom he hopes to have Blunt identify and interjects questions about art history, a subject in which he has taken increasing interest. A much subtler examiner is Her Majesty Queen Elizabeth II, whose questions about the disproven authenticity of the *Triple Portrait* formerly attributed to Titian suggest her own doubts of Blunt's loyalty: "So if one comes across a painting with the right background and pedigree, Sir Anthony, then it must be hard, I imagine—even inconceivable—to think that it is not what it claims to be." In a brilliant finale, Blunt lectures on the *Triple Portrait*, pointing out that not only did cleaning cause a third figure to emerge but that x-rays revealed the presence of a fourth and fifth man. Blunt dubs the false Titian "an Allegory of Supposition" that "is never-ending."

B.20 Berkeley, Anthony [pseudonym of Anthony Berkeley Cox]. SEE ALSO ILES, FRANCIS *The Poisoned Chocolates Case.* Garden City: Doubleday Doran (Crime Club), 1929.
■ Never has a detective novel of the Golden Age been so heavily bedecked with allusions to true crime. Under circumstances resembling those of the poisonings for which New Yorker Roland Molineux was tried and eventually acquitted, a secret killer sends a package of poisoned chocolates to Sir Eustace Pennefather at the Rainbow Club; he gives the box to fellow club member, Graham Bendix, whose wife dies after eating some of the candy. The baffling puzzle is submitted by Chief Inspector Moresby to the participants in a dinner meeting of the Crimes Circle, devoted to the solution of crimes. (The Circle's function more closely resembles that of London's famed Our Society, also known as the Crimes Club than the Detection Club, a crime fiction club of which Berkeley was a leading member.) The exclusive Circle's members, including Berkeley's series sleuth, Roger Sheringham, propose alternative solutions that hypothesize seriatim the various murder motives identified by F. Tennyson Jesse (see J.9) and draw analogies to famous real-life poisoning cases, including those of Marie Lafarge; Roland Molineux; Christiana Edmunds, who added strychnine to a Brighton confectioner's stock of chocolates to cover up an earlier poisoning attempt; Carlyle Harris; and English Quaker convert John Tawell, apprehended by use of the electric telegraph and hanged in 1845 (see B.30).
Berkeley's novel is expanded from his earlier short story, "The Avenging Chance" (1929), but it reaches a new solution so audacious that it will not be revealed in these pages. Berkeley also wrote crime novels and reviews of crime fiction under the name Francis Iles.

B.21 Berryman, John "It *was* a difficult crime to re-enact" [Dream Song 222]. In *His Toy, His Dream, His Rest: 308 Dream Songs.* New York: Farrar, Straus & Giroux, 1969.
■ Tried three times for manslaughter in the death of starlet Virginia Rappé, with whom he allegedly had rough sex during a wild party at a San Francisco hotel in 1921, film comic Roscoe "Fatty" Arbuckle was ultimately acquitted, only to find his life and career in ruins. See Andy Edmonds, *Frame-Up!: The Untold Story of Roscoe "Fatty" Arbuckle* (New York: William Morrow, 1991). In Dream Song 222, American poet John Berryman's protagonist opines that Fatty's crime was difficult to re-enact, "if crime it were." Still, the ambiguous

facts suggest a link between the male sex drive and the murderous impulse: ". . . both crimes lead into wails, at once or later."

B.22 Besnard, Marie *The Trial of Marie Besnard* [Mes mémoires]. Intro. Sybille Bedford. New York: Farrar Straus, 1963.

■ The prosecution of Marie Besnard of Loudun (southwest of Tours) for serial arsenic poisonings has been ranked among the most grievous failures of the French justice system since World War II. See Jean-Marc Théolleyre, *L'Accusée* [Justice Accused] (Paris: Laffont, 1991). After three trials in Poitiers and Bordeaux between 1952 and 1961, and five years in prison, Besnard was acquitted on charges of administering poison to eleven victims, including her mother and her second husband, Léon. Besnard's memoir of her ordeal, though probably the product of collaboration with a ghostwriter, reflects her own personality in its nonsequential recall of events and her understandable animus against town gossips, overzealous police, and fallible scientists who built the dubious case against her. Evidence introduced by the defense's forensic experts persuaded the jury that the poison found in the bodies exhumed by the police was due to contamination by arsenic in the cemetery soil. A detailed but rather lifeless account of the legal proceedings has been written by one of Marie's trial counsel with whom she formed a strong personal bond. See Jacqueline Favreau-Colombier, *Marie Besnard: La force de l'innocence* (Paris: Laffont,1985).

B.23 Bierstadt, Edward Hale *Satan Was a Man.* Garden City: Doubleday Doran, 1935.

■ An author of crime essays (*Curious Trials and Criminal Cases* [Garden City: Garden City Publishing, 1928] and *Enter Murderers!* [Garden City: Doubleday Doran, 1934]) turns against his own kind when he portrays a collector of true-crime books, Carroll Lindsey, as a homicidal maniac. Lindsey's murderous impulses are aroused through dreams of Lizzie Borden, Jack the Ripper, and Hawley Harvey Crippen. He poisons his hostile, alcoholic mother with a concoction of speakeasy gin (wood alcohol and gin flavoring) and rips the abdomen of her corpse. Later, he disposes of his unloved and sexually demanding wife, Lucille (whom, à la Crippen, he has replaced in his affections with a young mistress), by increasing the potency of the sodium dinitrophenol capsules she has been taking to reduce her weight. Both women had threatened Lindsey's fragile ego, his mother by ridiculing the failure of his literary aspirations and Lucille by taunting him with accusations of impotence.

Bierstadt acknowledged the sources of crime history on which he drew in the novel: Edwin H. Porter's *History of the Borden Murders* (1893) and Edmund Pearson's essay on the case; Filson Young's study of the Crippen case in the *Notable British Trials* series; and Leonard Matters's *The Mystery of Jack the Ripper* (London: Hutchinson, 1928), in which Jack is identified as "Doctor Stanley," who murders prostitutes to avenge his son's death from syphilis. Bierstadt's most interesting "take" on these true-crime materials is his view that Lizzie Borden hated her "sneering" father every bit as much as she despised her stepmother.

B.24 Billy, André *L'Assassinat d'Alain Guyader.* Paris: Flammarion, 1951.

■ The gang-authorized slaying of student Alain Guyader in 1948 near the Marne River in

France is an early example of the distressing high school murders that have afflicted the twentieth and twenty-first centuries. André Billy (1882–1971), prolific man of letters, journalist, and literary biographer, wrote this account of the case at the request of the victim's father, who believed that his son's reputation had been sullied by the flawed police investigation.

Alain Guyader, a seventeen-year-old student at a private secondary school in Paris, was among the brightest in his class, though he still felt the need to impress his schoolmates with purely imaginary exploits. He claimed to be engaged in arms traffic and espionage and to have fathered a child with his (invented) mistress. Bragging that he had become very wealthy, he exhibited a bundle of papers wrapped in an advertising leaflet that gave the appearance of a wad of banknotes. This turned out to be the most dangerous of his many hoaxes.

Among his school friends, he was particularly close to Claude Panconi, eighteen, who, though fancying himself a poet, displayed a greater talent in another literary genre: anonymous letters denouncing his fellow students. He was one of the founders of a secret gang of classmates who played hookey and threatened reprisals against outsiders who might be tempted to report their misbehavior. According to Billy, there was a social divide between the gang members and their enemies, on whom they maintained detailed files: Panconi and his associates were children of modestly paid government employees, and their targeted foes tended to come from families in "trade."

Despite his apparent friendship with Panconi, Guyader noted clear-eyed impressions of his schoolmate's defects: "Psychasthenia, obsessions, impulsiveness, tics. Periods of agitation together with anguish and anxiety each time a decision must be made. Absent-minded, solitary daydreams, intelligent, a subtle psychologist. Emotional, sometimes unbalanced. An artist's temperament, living in the past or in the future."

Another gang leader was Bernard Petit, who hated Guyader's academic superiority and vaunted adventures; moreover, Petit had incurred a debt to his schoolmate that he could not repay. In addition to his personal animus toward Guyader, Petit's obsession with the notion of the "perfect crime" turned his mind to murder.

On November 18, 1948, the Panconi-Petit gang met for the principal purpose of examining the measures to be taken for the organization of a resistance group in the event of an invasion of France by Stalin's army. Almost as an afterthought, the members in attendance also authorized the assassination and robbery of Guyader. On December 9 Panconi, having lured Guyader to the Marne countryside, shot him in the back with a gun supplied by Petit and then struck him on the head with the butt of the weapon. When the investigation of the murder began, the police made a persistent effort to exculpate Petit, the son of a policeman, and to support the defendants' ridiculous claim that the assassination of Guyader was a patriotic act taken to suppress his espionage. The cabal of the investigators was ultimately discredited, and the two principal malefactors, Panconi and Petit, were sentenced to prison terms of ten and five years, respectively.

Panconi's lawyer, Maître Gautrat (who later defended Marie Besnard (see B.22), briefly considered supporting his client's proffered defense that the crime had been inspired by his reading of French fiction describing "gratuitous" acts of crime, such as André Gide's novel *Les caves du Vatican* [Lafcadio's Adventures]; Jean-Paul Sartre's short story "Erostratus" [Herostratus] (see s.5); and Albert Camus's novel *The Stranger*.

B.25 Bleackley, Horace [William] *Some Distinguished Victims of the Scaffold.* London: Kegan Paul, Trench, Trübner, 1905.

■ Bleackley (1868–1931) edited the volumes on *Henry Fauntleroy* (1924) and, with S. M. Ellis, *Jack Sheppard* (1933) in the *Notable British Trials* series. His attractively produced collection, *Some Distinguished Victims of the Scaffold*, adorned with twenty-one illustrations, includes chapters on the eighteenth-century poisoner Mary Blandy; twins Daniel and Robert Perreau, hanged at Tyburn for counterfeiting and forgery in 1776; artist-criminal William Wynne Ryland, who engraved a portrait of George III and was executed for applying his skill to the forgery of bills of exchange; the execution (a judicial murder, in Bleackley's view) of Joseph Wall for bloody suppression of a mutiny when he was governor of the island of Goree in 1782; swindler John Hadfield (the "Keswick Impostor"), who married the beautiful Mary Robinson of Buttermere while posing as "Colonel Hope"; banker Henry Fauntleroy, who forged powers of attorney to facilitate embezzlement of clients' securities. The capital punishment theme of this collection is pursued in another fine volume by Bleackley, *The Hangmen of England* (1929).

B.26 Bolitho, William *Murder for Profit.* New York: Harper, 1926.

■ Despite his plethoric style, Bolitho, in his studies of five serial killers, created a durable monument of true-crime literature. The book begins with an insightful essay on William Burke and William Hare, who began as body snatchers and then murdered sixteen victims for delivery to Edinburgh's anotomists in 1828. Bolitho cites the curious phenomenon that serial murderers often have had dealings in secondhand goods, where fierce competition and shady practices are rampant. He sets out to demonstrate that the "heartless petty swindler . . . is the seed of the mass-murderer" and that body snatching was itself a "trade in the second-hand," where Burke had found his way. Bolitho also comments on the similarity of Burke's character to that of Doctor Knox, the man who, as a street ballad proclaims, "bought the beef." Both men were "fanatical self-admirers." It was, however, Burke's increasing thirst for blood and an attendant "contempt of punishment"—traits that Bolitho finds typical developments in the "hypertrophied" last stage of multiple slayings—that sealed the murderer's doom. Burke also spun a "day-dream universe" that "sustained him until his last choke."

Bolitho also places under his lens the Alsatian Jean-Baptiste Troppmann, who was executed in 1870 for his butchery of the eight members of the Kinck family in the Parisian suburb of Pantin (see B.68) in a scheme to despoil the Kincks of their fortune and to assume the identity of the paterfamilias, Jean Kinck. The son of an engineer-inventor, Troppmann developed more interest in the manufacture of prussic acid than machinery and initiated his murders by dispatching Jean Kinck with homemade poison. Bolitho identifies literary and political influences on Troppmann's development into a killer: obsessed with the vision of the underworld revealed by his favorite book, Eugène Sue's *The Wandering Jew*, Troppmann also embodied Emperor Napoleon III's ruthless drive to achieve power and wealth "through blood and perjury." According to Bolitho, public horror over Troppmann's crimes contributed to the disaster of Sedan and the fall of the Empire; the "hole at Pantin" where Troppmann buried his victims "was a hole in the regime."

George Joseph Smith, the brides-in-the-bath murderer, is the next object of Bolitho's examination. Beginning as a receiver of goods stolen by women under his thrall, he turned to the bathtub drowning of three lonely middle-class spinsters whom he had wed—the first for her money and the others for the life insurance proceeds. All the while he maintained a peaceful marital domicile with Edith Pegler in Bristol. Bolitho argues that the petty crook Smith was able to manage the repetitive scheme of his murders by regarding the killings as a kind of business, fussing over details of household budgets beforehand and afterward bargaining over the price of a coffin. Moreover, Smith was beset by the terrible egoism characteristic of the serial killer: "Besides their habit of living in a constructed lie, besides the lust of killing which is a mysterious but constant symptom, the damned class are invariably selfish to a degree of which the greatest actor can have no conception: passions that can be more justly compared with that of a mother for a sickly child than with any lesser love between the sexes."

Henri Désiré Landru, France's serial killer of thirteen generally middle-aged women whom he had married, crowded negotiations of the Versailles peace treaty out of the newspapers after the end of World War I. He shared many traits with England's G. J. Smith: beginning as a secondhand dealer and a petty swindler preying on women, he transformed himself (more quickly than Smith) into a killer of lonely women who were fascinated by his willpower and secret dreams. Bolitho, who attended Landru's trial, isolates an element of "poetry" in his appeal: to his scatter-brained mistress, Fernande, who managed not to end up in the furnace that probably incinerated Landru's other loves, he penned love letters that, despite their banality, operated in his milieu as "expressions of real feeling." Landru's case has left a rich heritage in nonfiction, novels, and films. See, for example, F. A. Mackenzie, *Landru*, in the *Famous Trials* series (New York: Scribner, 1928); Henri Béraud, Emmanuel Bourcier, and André Salmon, *L'Affaire Landru* (Paris: Albin Michel, 1924); René Masson, *Landru* [novel], trans. Gillian Tindall (Garden City: Doubleday, 1965); William Wiser, *Disappearances* [novel] (New York: Atheneum, 1980). In Charles Chaplin's comic film *Monsieur Verdoux* (1947), the serial killings are small potatoes when compared with munitions making. Claude Chabrol's screenplay, cowritten with François Sagan for his 1962 release *Landru*, is more realistic but less memorable.

Mercifully unaware of what the later twentieth century would wreak, Bolitho regards Fritz Haarmann of Hanover as the worst of mass murderers. With a background of crimes against male children, theft, burglary, and fraud, Haarmann emerged from an insane asylum and prison to fit nicely into the corrupt world of the Weimar Republic. Becoming a butcher by trade as well as a police spy, he, with the help of his younger lover, Hans Grans, murdered upward of forty male victims, mainly homeless teenagers he had "philanthropically" picked up, favoring those he found attractive. Haarmann chopped up his victims' remains (some of which were found in Hanover's River Leine), and sold their clothes (once again Bolitho's theme of secondhand dealing reappears). Haarmann was suspected of including flesh of his victims in his meat sales, but the prosecution took pains to disprove this rumor.

In a peroration written in prose as exalted as Thomas Carlyle's, Bolitho proclaims that all his serial killers, monsters at first sight, shrink into homunculi when layers of societal complicity in their crimes are stripped away.

B.27 Borowitz, Albert *A Gallery of Sinister Perspectives: Ten Crimes and a Scandal.* Kent, Ohio: Kent State Univ. Press, 1982.

■ This is a series of studies of writers, intellectuals, and musicians who directly confronted crime in their own lives or were inspired by actual criminal cases to create significant works of the imagination. Subjects included are:

- Robert Browning's *The Ring and the Book*
- Beatrice Cenci's parricide in literature and opera
- The literary and criminal careers of C. J. L. Almqvist
- A Sung Dynasty case of attempted murder (A Yün)
- Emlyn Williams's drama *Night Must Fall*
- The legend of opera composer Jean-Baptiste Lully's murder of his rival, Robert Cambert
- The trial of Nicolas Fouquet as reflected in the letters of Madame de Sévigné
- The murder of Dr. George Parkman by Professor John Webster (the Harvard Murder Case of 1849)
- The larceny trial of Jane Leigh Perrot, Jane Austen's aunt
- The influence of the Panama Canal scandals on W. S. Gilbert's *Utopia, Limited*
- The Garrick Club controversy, which set Dickens and Thackeray at odds
- Literary views on capital punishment.

B.28 ——— *Innocence and Arsenic: Studies in Crime and Literature.* New York: Harper, 1977.
■ The author's first collection on crime and literature consists of essays on:

- The views of C. P. Snow and his wife, Pamela Hansford Johnson, on the Moors Murder Case (the trial of Myra Hindley and Ian Brady)
- The origins of Dr. Jekyll and Mr. Hyde
- William Makepeace Thackeray's attendance at a public hanging
- Charles Dickens's *The Mystery of Edwin Drood*
- Salieri and the "murder" of Mozart
- Theories of the identity of Jack the Ripper

- Cicero's defense of the poisoning trial of Aulus Cluentius Habitus
- The 1968 trial of Aldo Braibanti in Rome for "psychological kidnapping" of two young men
- Henri de Latouche's authorship of the so-called memoirs of Clarisse Manson, volatile witness in the Fualdès murder case

Ross Macdonald opined that this collection "places Albert Borowitz among the widest-ranging scholars and most rigorous stylists in the true crime field."

B.29 ——— *The Thurtell-Hunt Murder Case: Dark Mirror to Regency England.* Baton Rouge: Louisiana State Univ. Press, 1987.

■ Called England's "most literary murder case," the 1823 ambush killing of crooked gambler William Weare in Hertfordshire by John Thurtell and two accomplices has inspired more fiction and drama than any other English murder before Jack the Ripper's spree. Set in the gaudy milieu of boxing and gambling from which the case arose, this account details the Hogarthian descent of Thurtell, son of a Norfolk mayor, into loose living and crime. The book retraces the routes followed by Thurtell and his confederates to the site of the ambush (to which Borowitz was guided by a local Thurtell aficionado). A final chapter presents the rich literary aftermath of the case.

B.30 ——— *The Woman Who Murdered Black Satin: The Bermondsey Horror.* Columbus: Ohio State Univ. Press, 1981.

■ This is the first book-length study of an important early Victorian criminal case, the murder of Patrick O'Connor in Bermondsey (South London) by his mistress, Marie (or Maria) Manning (Fig. 12), and her husband. Notable among students of the case was Charles Dickens, who based his characterization of Mlle. Hortense, the murderess in *Bleak House*, on the personality of Mrs. Manning; he was so moved by the brutish behavior of the crowd at the Mannings' double execution that he advocated an end to public hangings. Principal themes of the book are commercialization of the public's interest in murder cases and the beginning of the English campaign for the abolition of capital punishment.

B.31 Borrow, George *Celebrated Trials, and Remarkable Cases of Criminal Jurisprudence from the Earliest Records to the Year 1825.* 6 vols. London: Knight & Lacey, 1825.

■ Borrow's early work, a compilation of criminal trials in the tradition of the Newgate Calendar, included in the final volume the murder case of John Thurtell, whom the author, as a child, had greatly admired. Thurtell was hanged in 1824 (one year before the appearance of Borrow's trial series) for the murder of a crooked gambler, William Weare (see B.29.).

B.32 ——— *The Zincali: or, An Account of the Gypsies of Spain* [1841]; *Lavengro* [1851]; *Romany Rye* [1857]. In *The Works of George Borrow.* Norwich ed. 16 vols. (vols. 10, 3–4,5–6, respectively). Ed. Clement Shorter. New York: Wells, 1923–24.

■ The personality of murderer John Thurtell (see B.29)—sometimes viewed as sinister and repellent, occasionally as engaging, but always as masterful—dominates much of the work of Norwich-bred George Borrow. As a child, Borrow was strongly attracted to boxing, his enthusiasm probably fired by his father's recurrent boast of having fought the formidable Big Ben Brain. George, following in Captain Borrow's footsteps, prided himself on his acquaintance with Thurtell, nine years his senior; not only did he claim that John taught him how to box, but it has even been stated that Alderman Thurtell's house on Ipswich Road near Harford Bridge became a favorite resort of Norwich's fight crowd.

In light of his pretensions to friendship, there has been a good deal of speculation as to whether Borrow attended Thurtell's trial and execution. According to one of the contemporary accounts of the hanging, Thurtell, on the scaffold, "fixed his eyes on a young gentleman in the crowd, whom he had frequently seen as a spectator at the commencement of the proceedings against him. Seeing that the individual was affected by the circumstance, he removed them to another quarter." Some commentators have identified George Borrow as the sensitive "young gentleman" in the crowd. The evidence on the question to be drawn from his own work is inconclusive but does not appear to support this theory. Within a year after the execution, Borrow was to write of Thurtell's last moments in his anonymous six-volume compilation *Celebrated Trials* (1825). His account of Thurtell's case was, like the balance of this series, primarily culled from other published sources; it contains nothing that appears to reflect firsthand knowledge or experience. Indeed, he describes the hanging in three brief paragraphs, which draw heavily on Edward Herbert's article in *London Magazine*; Borrow does not name Herbert but refers to him simply as an "eye-witness."

Whatever the strength of Borrow's personal bond with Thurtell may have been in their Norwich years, the recurrent appearances of Thurtell in Borrow's major works confirm the fascination that the author felt for his former acquaintance after he was revealed to be a murderer. In the introduction to *The Zincali: or, An Account of the Gypsies of Spain* (1841), Borrow recalls that at age fourteen he attended a prizefight near Norwich that Thurtell had promoted: "The terrible Thurtell was present, lord of the concourse; for wherever he moved he was master, and whenever he spoke, even when in chains, every other voice was silent. He stood on the mead, grim and pale as usual, with his bruisers around." A more menacing Thurtell (now unnamed but identified beyond all doubt) is encountered by the hero of the semiautobiographical novel *Lavengro* (1851); Borrow has left a memorable portrait of the fearsome promoter as he unsuccessfully attempts to bully a country magistrate into making an enclosed farm field available for a prizefight:

> He was a man somewhat under thirty, and nearly six feet in height. . . . he wore neither whiskers nor moustache and appeared not to delight in hair, which was of a light brown, being closely cropped; the forehead was rather high, but somewhat narrow; the face neither broad nor sharp, the nose almost delicate; the eyes were grey, with an expression in which there was sternness blended with something approaching to feline; his complexion was exceedingly pale, relieved, however, by certain pock-marks, which here

and there studded his countenance; his form was athletic but lean; his arms long. In the whole appearance of the man there was a blending of the bluff and the sharp. You might have supposed him a bruiser; his dress was that of one in all its minutiae; something was wanting, however, in his manner—the quietness of the professional man; he rather looked like one performing the part—well—very well—but still performing a part.

Undaunted by the magistrate's refusal, Thurtell stages the fight "in the precincts of the old town, near the field of the chapel." A thunderstorm bursts out during the match, and a gypsy friend of the protagonist Lavengro (Borrow) calls his attention to a cloud that resembles a "stream of blood." The gypsy reveals to Lavengro that the cloud foretells a "bloody fortune" for Thurtell, to whom he points, as the promoter, accompanied by the victorious bruiser, drives away from the field with a "smile of triumph."

Dramatic as the scene may be, there is no reason to believe that the incident of the gypsy's fortune-telling is factual; throughout his works Borrow often described meetings with men who were later to be hanged, including the celebrated Scottish jail breaker and murderer David Haggart; and on each occasion he delights in his retrospective knowledge of their destinies.

The last lines of the chapter of the gypsy's prophecy introduce a strain of Borrow's sympathy for Thurtell. Anticipating that his reader will judge that Thurtell merited the predicted doom as "a bad, violent man," Borrow cautions, "Softly, friend; when thou wouldst speak harshly of the dead, remember that thou hast not yet fulfilled thy own [fortune]!" However, even this word of compassion hardly prepares us for the eulogy for Thurtell that Borrow puts in the mouth of a jockey in *Romany Rye* (1857), the sequel to *Lavengro*. The jockey tells Lavengro how Thurtell, now referred to only as "Jack," lent him two hundred pounds when he was down on his luck. When he was repaid, Jack refused the jockey's gift of a horse and asked him instead to "come and see him hanged when the time was come." The jockey agreed to the request, not knowing that one day he would keep his word, standing up in his gig before Hertford Gaol, removing his hat, and shouting, "God Almighty bless you, Jack!" Some men are born to be hanged and some are not, the jockey muses. Accepting the stories of Thurtell's gallantry in war, the jockey contrasts him favorably with a cowardly nobleman he calls Whitefeather, who intentionally fell off his horse at Waterloo on the day before the battle: "Jack was hanged because, along with his bad qualities, he had courage and generosity; this fellow [Whitefeather] is not, because with all Jack's bad qualities, and many more, amongst which is cunning, he has neither their courage nor generosity."

B.33 Bossard, Abbé Eùgene *Gilles de Rais maréchal de France dit Barbe Bleue.* 1886. Grenoble: Jérome Millon, 1992.

■ Reputed to be France's most prolific serial killer, Gilles de Rais, marshal of France and valiant comrade-in-arms of Joan of Arc, was hanged and burned alive at Nantes in 1440. In separate ecclesiastical and secular trials, Gilles was convicted of the evocation of demons, sodomy, and the torture-killing of 140 children and young adults of both sexes.

Abbé Bossard's controversial work, based on his doctoral thesis of 1886, was the first scholarly study of Gilles's trials and is the fountainhead of all later analyses by writers who have either supported or opposed his conclusions. Given his career in the church, it is not surprising that Bossard finds that the investigation and trials of Gilles, spearheaded by Jean de Malestroit, bishop of Nantes, were models of fairness, even when assessed under nineteenth-century standards. The abbé accepts the truth of Gilles's detailed confessions and views his descent from military heroism into unspeakable crimes as the result of boundless ambition to achieve esoteric knowledge (including experimentation in alchemy, not regarded by medieval French authorities as a criminal enterprise), wealth, and power.

Two of Bossard's principal conclusions have stirred ongoing disputes among historians. The abbé's persuasion of Gilles's guilt and the justness of his condemnation, while shared by many (see, for example, Emile Gabory, *Alias Bluebeard: The Life and Death of Gilles de Raiz* [New York: Brewer & Warren, 1930]), was hotly contested by other commentators, including Voltaire and Salomon Reinach. A modern advocate of Gilles's innocence is the novelist Gilbert Prouteau, who argues that the marshal was the victim of persecution by Bishop Malestroit, a traitorous ally of the English during the Hundred Years' War whom Gilles had favored hanging (Gilbert Prouteau, *Gilles de Rais, ou la gueule du loup* [Monaco: Éditions du Rocher, 1992]). Prouteau also contends that both the bishop and Jean V, Duke of Brittany, wanted to eliminate Gilles so that they could seize the balance of his vast estates. In 1992, Prouteau arranged for his case seeking posthumous vindication of Gilles to be heard by an unofficial "arbitration court." According to an article in the *New York Times*, November 22, 1992, the court earlier that week concluded that the marshal's execution was unjust. The reporter commented: "In a country that still harbors resentment over its numerous drubbings during the Hundred Years' War, perhaps the most convincing argument was that Bishop Malestroit was in league with the English."

Numerous scholars have also parted company with Abbé Bossard in his conclusions regarding the influence of Gilles de Rais on the myths and stories of Bluebeard. Bossard concludes that Gilles's crimes inspired many competing versions of the Bluebeard legend, particularly among the Breton population, and that seventeenth-century author Charles Perrault selected one of these as the source for his celebrated tale. More recent commentators, including Emile Gabory, doubt the suggested link between Gilles and Perrault's Bluebeard, pointing out that, whatever his other excesses may have been, Gilles was a firm monogamist.

B.34 Boswell, James *Boswell for the Defence: 1769–1774.* Ed. William K. Wimsatt Jr. and Frederick A. Pottle. New York: McGraw-Hill, 1959.

■ The humanity of Boswell often overrode his professional judgment in his zealous defense of John Reid on a capital charge of sheep stealing in 1774. Reid, Boswell's first criminal client, by court appointment, had been acquitted on a similar charge in 1766 due to Boswell's advocacy, and an important Scots judge, Lord Justice-Clerk Thomas Miller, had bitterly attacked that verdict. In 1774, Reid was charged with stealing nineteen sheep, some of which were found in his possession. His defense—that he had purchased the animals in good faith from the actual thief, cattle dealer William Gardner—failed to impress the jury, and he was sentenced to death.

In the pages of his journal (1769–74 in this edition), Boswell reflected on his growing obsession with his campaign to save Reid's life. Recognizing the pathological extent of his emotional commitment, he wrote, "I had by sympathy sucked the dismal ideas of John Reid's situation, and as spirits or strong substance of any kind, when transferred to another body of a more delicate nature, will have much more influence than on the body from which it is transferred, so I suffered much more than John did."

A fourteen-day reprieve gave Reid brief hope, but, in the light of Lord Justice-Clerk Miller's continued hostility, an application for a further reprieve (to provide time to obtain a confession from Gardner, who had been transported to America) was denied. Before Reid's execution, Boswell briefly plotted with a surgeon and others to attempt the resuscitation of the hanged man. When he stood near the gallows and saw how "effectually" Reid was hanged, "the rope having fixed upon his neck very firmly," and his body left dangling nearly three-quarters of an hour, Boswell concluded that "any attempt to recover him would have been in vain." He recorded a sense of relief: "I comforted myself in thinking that by giving up the scheme I had avoided much anxiety and uneasiness."

B.35 ———— *The Life of Samuel Johnson L.L.D.* New York: Random House (Modern Library), n.d. [intervention of Dr. Johnson on behalf of Rev. William Dodd, clergyman condemned for forgery]

■ In 1777, Dr. Johnson generously fought to save the life of the Reverend Dr. William Dodd, a popular and high-living forty-eight-year-old London preacher sentenced to the gallows for forging a bond to raise money to meet pressing debts. In the course of his unsuccessful campaign for Dodd, summarized by Boswell in considerable detail, Johnson wrote (in Dodd's name) letters to the Lord Chancellor, Henry Bathurst, and to Lord Mansfield, the Chief Justice, Dodd's speech to the Recorder of London before sentencing and the prisoner's sermon "to his unhappy brethren" in the chapel of Newgate prison. To Dodd's letter of fervent thanks, Johnson replied with a request that the condemned man include in his devotions a petition for his benefactor's "eternal welfare."

When, after Dodd's execution, a man expressed doubt that the doomed man had written his prison sermon, Johnson produced his famous quip: "Why should you think so? Depend upon it, Sir, when a man knows that he is to be hanged in a fortnight, it concentrates his mind wonderfully." In 1783 Johnson made his final comment on Dodd's case: "I was very willing to have him pardoned, that is, to have the sentence changed to transportation; but, when he was once hanged, I did not wish he should be made a saint."

Among the holdings of the Borowitz True Crime Collection relating to the Dodd tragedy is Percy Fitzgerald, *A Famous Forgery, Being the Story of "the Unfortunate" Doctor Dodd* (London: Chapman & Hall, 1865).

B.36 Bouchardon, Pierre *L'Abbé Delacollonge*. Paris: Alphonse Lemerre, 1931.

■ In 1835 Abbé Jean-Baptiste Delacollonge, vicar of a village near Beaune, strangled his mistress, Fanny Besson, so he said, to test how much pain she would feel if he were to carry out a murder-suicide pact. The jury that tried him found he had acted without pre-meditation but was appalled by what he did to hide his crime: he dismembered Fanny with a billhook, deposited her entrails in a latrine, and dumped her body parts in a pond, where they were found floating. The prosecutor, and Bouchardon as well, compared the case to rector Antoine Mingrat's 1882 murder of a virtuous young married woman, Marie Gérin. The Mingrat crime elicited a diatribe by Paul-Louis Courier, a famed polemicist, against the temptations that arise from permitting young priests to come into close contact with female parishioners through the confessional.

Pierre Bouchardon (1870–1950), a French magistrate, gained initial prominence as an investigator for the Council of War inquiry into the espionage of Mata Hari and after World War II was called on to consider evidence regarding the charges against Marshal Pétain before the High Court (*Haute Cour*). Despite his busy professional career, Bou-chardon wrote more than thirty-five books devoted to criminal cases. Unlike G. Lenotre, who is primarily remembered as a historian of crime episodes during the French Revolution, Bouchardon generally preferred to deal with "common-law" cases, in which criminal conduct, devoid of historical overtones, was actuated by personal motives.

Immersed early in life in the works of Balzac, Bouchardon generally drew the epigraphs of his works and their chapters from the *Comédie humaine*, and he wrote studies of criminal cases in which Balzac took particular interest (for example, the murder trial of Sébastien-Benoît Peytel [see B.69]). Bouchardon's books are well planned with an eye to orderly narrative development and elements of surprise; devoid of excessive detail, a fault of many crime historians, these works rarely exceed 250 pages printed in a small format and are wonderfully readable.

B.37 ———— *L'Affaire Lafarge.* Paris: Albin Michel, 1924.
■ In 1840 young Parisian newlywed Marie-Fortunée Cappelle Lafarge (see L.4 and L.5) was convicted in a controversial trial at Tulle (southeast of Limoges) of the arsenic poisoning of her husband, Charles, an unattractive provincial ironmaster whose sexual advances disgusted her. Marie's poisoning campaign allegedly began with a tainted cake she mailed him in Paris, where he was attempting to secure an iron-making patent. He became ill after taking a bite out of pastry crust he was sampling at midnight in a "symbolic tea party" arranged by Marie by letter (back home at the depressing family chateau in Le Glandier she was supposed to partake of a similar sweet at precisely the same moment). Lafarge's agonies increased on his return to Le Glandier, and he died under his wife's ministrations (she having purchased arsenic to "kill rats"). Marie was convicted of his murder, although several expert witnesses could find no arsenic in the body of the deceased, and the renowned toxicologist Mathieu Orfila, summoned to perform new tests during the course of the trial, could only detect a quantity of the poison that did not exceed a half of a milligram.

Bouchardon, in the course of his service as a presiding trial judge, was able to study the original records of the Lafarge murder investigation and based his book on the results of his documentary review rather than attempting a biography of Marie or a detailed account of her trial. Nevertheless, he cannot resist delineating the principal traits of Marie's personality that made her a darling of France's romantic writers. A dreamer lost in the pages of Walter Scott, Chateaubriand, and George Sand, she may have been a source of Madame Bovary's personality, and Bouchardon also suggests that her power of seduction may have inspired Alexandre Dumas's *père* (whom Marie claimed to have met in her childhood) to create Milady de Winter in *The Three Musketeers*. Bouchardon, in his own analysis of Marie Lafarge's personality, emphasizes compulsions suggestive of instability: mythomania, kleptomania (in a separate trial she was convicted of stealing the diamonds of her friend Marie de Léautaud), and graphorrhea. Bouchardon castigates writers who have sought to vindicate Madame Lafarge by citing the absence of a rational motive; he places her alongside other celebrated female poisoners as a "hysterical degenerate." He comments further in his final chapter that Balzac probably understood the mechanism of her crime as well as anyone, implying in a passage of *Little Miseries of Conjugal Life* that Marie was driven over the brink by physical repulsion.

Other writers do not share Bouchardon's unruffled confidence of Marie Lafarge's guilt. For example, Henri Ramet, retired first presiding judge of the court of appeals of Toulouse, and his collaborator, Paul Voivenel, a forensic expert serving the same court, point to the insufficient proof of significant traces of arsenic in Charles Lafarge's body, but they fail to account for the undoubted presence of the poison in beverages at Le Glandier (Ramet and Voivenel, *La madone de l'arsenic: L'Affaire Lafarge* [Paris: Librairie des Champs-Élysées, 1936]). The authors speculate that Lafarge may have died of acute appendicitis. More recently, a feminist writer has proclaimed Marie Lafarge a victim of prejudice against rebellious women but still does not definitively acquit her as a poisoner, asserting that she "continues to haunt our collective imagination" (Laure Adler, *L'Amour à l'arsenic: Histoire de Marie Lafarge* [Paris: Denoël, 1985]).

Edith Saunders, who has written a nonfictional account of the case in English, concludes that the widespread belief in Marie Lafarge's innocence "was based on her manner, her obvious conviction of her own innocence, her unwavering assertions of innocence," but opines that given her possession of arsenic "her word means nothing" (Saunders, *The Mystery of Marie Lafarge* [New York: Morrow, 1952], 238).

B.38 ——— *L'Affaire Pranzini.* Paris: Albin Michel, 1934.

■ In the early morning of March 17, 1887, Henri Pranzini, who had been sleeping with courtesan Claudine-Marie Regnault (known to the trade as Régine de Montille), awakened on schedule in her bedroom on rue Montaigne in Paris and slit her throat. With similar brutality, he dispatched her chambermaid, Annette Gremeret, and Annette's little daughter, Marie-Louise (whom he came close to decapitating).

While the Paris press jeered at the Sûreté and its hapless Chief Taylor for their inability to find the killer, Pranzini was arrested by the Marseille police on a tip given by prostitutes to whom he had passed jewelry stolen from Marie Regnault's apartment. After Pranzini was arrested during a performance of *The Barber of Seville* and turned over to the Paris police, the criminal's checkered past came to light. Born in Alexandria, Egypt, in 1856, Pranzini spoke several languages, all with a foreign accent. Willing to pursue any calling that would lend itself to theft, swindling, or easy money, Pranzini had been a tour organizer, guide, courier, interpreter, and Pullman car employee. His principal asset, however, was his sexual prowess, which he sold to both women and men. Police speculated that the motive of the robbery of Marie Regnault's apartment and the triple murder that accompanied it was to defray the cost of a projected trip to America, where a bride-to-be passionately awaited him.

Although bestial, and fearless in perpetrating the slaughter of the rue Montaigne, Pranzini immediately lost his self-possession, scattering damning clues around the apartment and leaving a well-marked trail as he made ineffectual efforts to dispose of his booty. Bouchardon draws the following lesson: "A criminal is rarely complete. Although he be bold, bent on any outrage, possessing a fertile imagination so that he leaves nothing to chance and keeps his full presence of mind in the midst of the scene of carnage, and is able to find the means of escaping as he has broken in, without being encountered, he passes, often immediately, through a period of unimaginable depression, when he piles imprudence upon folly and loses even the most elementary instinct of self-preservation." (For H. B. Irving's essay on the Pranzini case, see 1.6.)

B.39 ———— *L'Assassin X: Affaire Prado.* Paris: Albin Michel, 1935.

■ Louis Prado was called by a contemporary balladeer a "pale follower of Pranzini" because of the strong resemblance between the crimes perpetrated by the two murderers. During the night of January 14, 1886, Prado murdered courtesan Camille-Marie Aguétant in her apartment on the rue Caumartin and stole jewelry and other valuables. Almost two years later the "gentleman-burglar," as Bouchardon dubs him, was arrested for an unrelated jewelry theft and for wounding a pursuing police officer. Tried for the Aguétant murder and the attempt to kill the policeman, Prado faced courtroom opposition from his two most current mistresses, who were charged with receiving stolen goods: the opulent brunette Eugénie Forestier and the ethereal blonde Mauricette Couronneau, who had given birth to a daughter. Foiling Prado's hope that she would furnish an alibi, Forestier testified that Prado had confessed to killing Aguétant.

The Prado trial drew comments from many journalists and men of letters, including novelist-critic Jules-Amédée Barbey d'Aurevilly. Famed as a dandy, Barbey d'Aurevilly lampooned a question by the prosecutor as to whether Prado, during a visit to Spain, had dressed as a Spanish grandee. Barbey commented: "I have met only one Spanish grandee; he wasn't dressed as well as I."

After Prado's execution, Sûreté chief Goron received unfavorable press attention as had already been his lot in the Pranzini case. Previously savaged for accepting a card case made of Pranzini's skin, Goron was now attacked for acceding to Prado's last wish that his body not be given to the Paris medical school.

Bouchardon calls Prado "murderer X" because of his uncertain nationality and the be-wildering array of names the criminal used; at times he claimed to be Count Louis-Frédéric de Linska de Castillon, or Haro de Mendozza. In an epilogue Bouchardon cites an interview in which a doctor claimed that Prado was the murderer's real name and that he was the son of a former Peruvian chief of state. (For H. B. Irving's essay on the Prado case, see I.6.)

B.40 ———— *L'Auberge de la tête noire* [The Black Head Inn]. Paris: Perrin, 1926.
■ The title essay is devoted to Dr. Edme-Samuel Castaing tried at Paris in 1823 for successive poisonings of two wealthy brothers, Hippolyte and Auguste Ballet, whom he was allegedly despoiling. The same poison, acetate of morphine, was implicated in both cases, and Castaing produced an ingenious explanation for purchasing the lethal substance while his friend Auguste lay ill at a county inn: the poison was intended to dispose of cats and dogs who were making a racket and depriving Auguste of much-needed sleep. Castaing was convicted of Auguste's murder only, and even this judgment required the votes of judges to be added to those of the sharply divided jurors. Bouchardon recalls that Alexandre Dumas *père*, observing the trial, was strongly moved by Castaing's invitation to the young spectators to witness his execution. Dumas, concerned about the possibility that justice had miscarried, took an oath to oppose capital punishment.

Another article in the volume, "My First Crime," discharges a nostalgic obligation of the author to his maternal grandfather, who had told him in childhood of the 1846 trial of an intruder, Jean-François Roudier, for the murder of a little boy and an elderly governess in a house near Aubusson. In the process of investigating the trial records, Bouchardon also appeased one of his recurring infantile fears, satisfying himself that the murdered child had died under the assailant's hammer while in a deep sleep.

Rounding out this collection are essays on Dumollard (to whom Bouchardon later devoted a monograph; see B.52), the murderer and robber of maids whom he escorted to imaginary domestic positions; and the brothers Antoine and Louis Verse, who were saved from wrongful execution in 1819 by the last-minute confession of François Ponsy, who preceded them on the scaffold to expiate an unrelated murder.

B.41 ———— *L'Auberge de Peyrebeille, suivi de la véridique histoire du roman de Stendhal* Le rouge et le noir [The Peyreville Inn, Followed by the True History of Stendhal's novel The Red and the Black]. Paris: Albin Michel, 1924.
■ Among France's most blood-curdling murder legends are those attached to the Red Inn of Peyrebeille, in the Ardèche, whose proprietors Pierre Martin and his wife Marie Breysse, with the help of their Languedocien servant Jean Rochette, reputedly robbed and brutally murdered innumerable guests. Bouchardon, after cursorily recounting the legends, plunges into the surviving records of the homicidal trio's 1833 trial and execution; he observes that the only crimes of which they were convicted (rightly, in his opinion) were the murder of Jean-Antoine Enjolras and the theft of a hundred francs from another of the notorious inn's guest.

The other essay in this volume is devoted to Antoine-Marie Berthet (the original of

Julien Sorel, antihero of Stendhal's *The Red and the Black*). Berthet, a deranged tutor, was guillotined in 1828 for attempting to murder Madame Michoud de la Tour in the course of a mass celebrated at the church in Brangues. Berthet fell in love with the lady during his service in her household and fancied that she had replaced him with another lover after vows of eternal fidelity.

B.42 ——— "Autres procès burlesques" [Other Comical Trials]. In *Énigmes et drames judiciaires d'autrefois* [second series]. Paris: Perrin, 1930.

■ The humorous trials promised by the title often adjudicated gruesome crimes. Pierre Sarda (nicknamed Tragine), like the Count of Monte Cristo but with far less justification, set out to avenge himself on the family and laborers of a man who he believed had wrongly condemned him. At his 1841 trial, the unrepentent Tragine bullied adverse witnesses and judges alike but was saved from the guillotine only because his two principal victims had not died of their grievous wounds.

In 1819 and 1820 Claude Terrier, a habitual criminal, murdered and robbed seven people near Montluçon and set fire to their homes to cover up his crimes. He aided his identification and arrest by proudly displaying to a cutler and truss-maker named Trébardoux the truss he wore for a double hernia. A third murder trial is that of the alchemist Joseph Salvator, who unsuccessfully tried to persuade his jury in 1837 that he could not be guilty of passing counterfeit coins and a related murder and assault; he offered to demonstrate in court his ability to turn base metal into gold, a talent that made it inconceivable for him to have wasted his time in petty counterfeiting. In his accounts of the Sarda and Salvator cases, Bouchardon illustrates the fair-mindedness of prosecutor Pierre-Ambroise Plougoulm, who made it a point of honor to shore up inadequate arguments made by opposing counsel for the defense.

In other pieces in the collection, the judicial issues are less substantial, enabling Bouchardon to give freer play to burlesque elements. He gives us the delicious Belgian trial of the French "sibyl" Marie-Anne-Adelaide Lenormand for prohibited fortune-telling and fraud; the unsuccessful defamation suit brought against a journalist by a sensitive executioner who objected to the defendant's use of the popular term for a practitioner of his profession (*bourreau*); and the failed appeal by two provincial barristers to the French Supreme Court protesting a trial court ban against the wearing of moustaches. Finally, Bouchardon retells an unsuccessful attempt to prosecute a reckless driving incident near the Tuileries as an assault on the royal person of Louis-Philippe, who was passing along on foot when the defendant's carriage hurtled by. Bouchardon notes ironically that the monarch was later to survive almost as many real assassination attempts as there were years in his reign.

B.43 ——— *Le banquier de Pontoise*. In series *Crime et Chatiment*. Paris: Éditions des Portiques, 1929.

■ The title piece in this series depicts a true locked-room murder mystery of January 15,

1844, in which banker André Donon-Cadot was bludgeoned to death in his residential office. For Monsieur Allart, head of the Sûreté, the solution to the puzzle lay elsewhere in the banker's house: the killer Pierre Rousselet had been hired by the banker's son Edouard, who shared the favors of his father's mistress. Edouard clumsily spruced up the crime scene after the escape of Rousselet and locked the office door from the outside. Bouchardon, summarizing the trial, fashioned an epigram capable of suggesting to the modern reader that Kato Kaelin is of ancient lineage: "Every *cause célèbre* has its buffoon."

The second essay recalls an 1838 murder and theft in the rue du Temple, Paris, by an underworld gang that inspired principal characters in Eugène Sue's *The Mysteries of Paris*.

B.44 ———— *Célestine Doudet institutrice.* Paris: Albin Michel. 1928.

■ Bouchardon's account of the international "nanny murder case" that shocked nineteenth-century Paris is masterly and discriminating. Flore-Marguerite-Célestine Doudet, former lady of the wardrobe to Queen Victoria, was engaged in 1852 by Dr. James Loftus Marsden of Great Malvern as governess for his five daughters. After she established her young charges at a lodging house in Paris to pursue their education, neighbors, visitors, and even Célestine's sister Zéphyrine complained of her harsh regimen and her physical and mental abuse of the children. Célestine, however, attributed the children's inadequate diet and corporal punishment to their father's instructions and blamed their deteriorating condition on whooping cough and their penchant for masturbation, a vice that she trumpeted to all and sundry. In July 1853, two months after suffering unexplained injuries, Mary Ann Marsden died, and her sister Lucy followed her in death after her father had brought her and her surviving sisters back to Great Malvern.

Following the advice of the eminent French barrister Chaix d'Est-Ange, Dr. Marsden filed a criminal complaint against the governess. The prosecution was bifurcated; Célestine was tried first in the criminal trial court of the Seine for involuntary manslaughter in the death of Mary Ann and subsequently in the correctional court for violence against her sisters. The first trial resulted in an acquittal and the second in a guilty verdict. Doudet's counsel Berryer imprudently delayed the appeal of the latter verdict until publication of a scandalous investigation he had conducted in England to demonstrate the truth of the governess's allegations about the sexual habits of the Marsden girls and the harsh treatment they had suffered at their father's hands. The defamatory nature of the defense's "findings" lent new force to the prosecution's stance on appeal, and the appellate court increased the prison sentence from two to five years. Despite the efforts of ardent supporters, including the romantic painter Ary Scheffer, Doudet served more than four years before being released because of poor health. After recovering in England, she won many new offers of professional employment.

Bouchardon thinks that the French courts got this mysterious case just about right. The causes of the deaths of Mary Ann and Lucy were not clearly established, especially in light of the substantial time elapsed after the last traumas attributable to Doudet; Bouchardon, however, does not doubt that the governess treated all the Marsden girls sadistically and believes that she invented the masturbation charges to justify her cruel treatment.

B.45 ———— *Le cocher de Monsieur Armand: Les amours funestes d'Angélina* [Monsieur Armand's Coachman: Angelina's Fatal Love Affair]. In series *Crime et Chatiment*. Paris: Éditions des Portiques, 1930.

■ When Bette Davis uttered her immortal words "What a dump," she was unwittingly echoing key testimony in an 1863 criminal case. Maurice Roux, coachman-valet of Montpellier flour merchant André Armand, told fellow servants that his master didn't "know the difference between a house and a dump." Roux claimed that, in revenge for these frank words, Armand trailed him to the wood cellar where he struck him with a log at the nape of his neck, bound his limbs, and attempted to strangle him with an unknotted cord. The trial of Armand for attempted murder inspired public interest sharpened by class antagonisms; the jury, persuaded that Armand had faked the strangulation, voted acquittal. (Bouchardon notes that it became a modish parlor game for guests to attempt to tie their own wrists behind their backs in the shortest time possible.)

Bouchardon pairs the Armand trial with another case involving a coachman. In 1859 lovely teenager Angélina Lemoine gave birth to a baby son, the fruit of her Carson McCullers–like liaison with her family's ugly, illiterate coachman, Jean Fétis. Her proud mother, Victoire, promptly placed the newborn on the fire and attempted unsuccessfully to conceal his ashes. Both women were tried for infanticide; despite weak medical evidence that the child was born alive, Victoire was convicted of murder with extenuating circumstances. Sentenced to twenty years' imprisonment, she followed a family tradition by going mad. Angélina, who walked out of court a free woman, attributed the loss of her virginity to her having read novels by George Sand.

B.46 ———— *Le crime de Vouziers.* In series *Énigmes et drames judiciaires d'autrefois.* Paris: Perrin, 1926.

■ In 1836 Frédéric Benoît, the delicate-looking youngest son of a justice of the peace, was executed for two related murders: after stealing some of his father's hidden gold pieces, he cut the throat of his mother in their home in Vouziers (near Reims) as she slept; and he later dispatched a former homosexual lover in a Versailles hotel with a razor to prevent his threatened disclosure of the first crime. Suspicions in the Vouziers murder investigation first fell on Frédéric's disreputable brother, Auguste, and, following his establishment of an alibi, on a compulsive and self-accusatory anonymous letter writer, a butcher named Antoine-Auguste Labauve. When Frédéric was identified as the real killer after the Versailles murder, he seemed to satisfy crime fiction's predilection for incriminating the "least likely suspect," for his dissolute behavior was not widely known.

Benoît's trial was held in Paris during the 1832 cholera epidemic and was one of the first to be governed by new legislation reforming the criminal code. One of the jurors was the humane and patriotic doctor Poumiès de la Siboutie, who included his recollections of the trial in his memoirs. Bouchardon pays tribute to the doctor and also to the impassioned closing argument of Chaix d'Est-Ange, "one of the purest gems of nineteenth-century forensic eloquence." Chaix d'Est-Ange, then thirty-two years old, appeared for the private interests (*partie civile*) of the family of the Versailles victim, Joseph Formage, and of

Labauve, who had been erroneously prosecuted for the Vouziers murder. Bouchardon describes Chaix d'Est-Ange's dramatic style in words that could equally be applied to Thomas De Quincey: "He followed the murderer step by step. Though the night was black, precautions well taken and the bolts shot, he followed him into the room of the crime. He recounted everything as if he had seen it happen, and his avenging words shook the audience with a long shiver of horror. He created emotion."

B.47 ———— *Le crime du château de Bitremont.* Paris: Albin Michel, 1925.

■ Any lingering doubt that nicotine is a deadly poison would be routed by this account of the 1850 murder of Gustave Fougnies by his nefarious brother-in-law Count Hippolyte de Boccarmé with the apparent complicity of his wife. De Boccarmé, alarmed by the marriage of the lame and sickly Gustave, on whose estate he was counting to shore up his tottering fortunes, invited his brother-in-law to his chateau near Mons, Belgium, and, under mysterious circumstances, forced liquid nicotine of his own manufacture down the young man's throat. The crime was exposed when Professor Jean-Servais Stas's experiments identified the poison, and de Boccarmé's distillation apparatus were discovered within a false ceiling built into the chateau. Though born under good auspices, on a ship rounding the Cape of Good Hope, de Boccarmé ended his days under the guillotine's blade; his wife was acquitted, despite strong evidence against her. If this was justice, Shakespeare should have spared Lady Macbeth!

It is rare for Bouchardon to have treated a crime beyond the borders of France, but he may have been tempted by the appearance of the formidable Charles Lachaud as one of the defense counsel for the count. Lachaud's conversational wit seems to have rivaled his courtroom dazzle. Bouchardon cites his reply to a woman's question regarding the respective functions of the royal prosecutor and the prosecutor general: "Madame, it's quite simple. If you deceive your husband, it's the former who will prosecute you. If you kill him, it's the latter."

Unlike France, Belgium permitted the investigative magistrate to testify at the trial. Bouchardon's reservations about this procedure are pertinent to the appearance of Kenneth Starr before the House Judiciary Committee hearing on President Clinton's impeachment: "The drawback is to make too much of the written investigative report of which its author can be no more than a reflection—a too-brilliant reflection—while the legislature intended that the trial should be essentially oral. Also, and above all, this procedure brings into the arena a magistrate whose functions and dignity ought to keep him outside the combat zone. If he defends his report with predictable pride of authorship, he is vulnerable to refutations or sharp recriminations on the part of the accused; and does this not cause justice to suffer?"

B.48 ———— *Crimes d'autrefois* [Crimes of the Past]. In series *Énigmes et drames judiciaires d'autrefois.* Paris: Perrin, 1926.

■ This collection includes an essay on Jacques Collignon, whose surname passed into generic Parisian usage as a shorthand description of abusive coachmen. Reported to the prefect of police in late 1834 for having overcharged two passengers, Monsieur and Madame Juge, and ordered to make restitution, Collignon called on the complainants and shot them to death. At his trial, which resulted in a sentence to the guillotine, Collignon maintained that his victims were the real murderers; they had intended to destroy his livelihood.

In two other articles dealing, respectively, with the peasant bread revolt in Buzançais (1847) and the mutiny and murders aboard the *Foederis-Arca* (1864), Bouchardon illustrates the ability of nineteenth-century French courts and juries to determine degrees of individual responsibility in the midst of acts of mass violence.

A chapter entitled "The Walker in the Vincennes Woods" recounts Louis-Auguste Papavoine's random knife murder of two children on a Sunday outing. After abandoning his initial assertion that the killings were patriotic acts committed under the delusion that the victims were royal heirs, Papavoine blamed the crimes on his "sufferings and continual insomnia." His impossible defense was brilliantly handled by twenty-eight-year-old newcomer Alphonse-Gabriel-Victor Paillet, who was to become head of the Paris bar and would win fame as defender of the poisoner Madame Lafarge. In his unsuccessful argument for Papavoine, Paillet urged that the very motiveless character of the murders supported the conclusion that the crime was not premeditated and was born of Papavoine's derangement.

The collection also includes studies of two famous criminals, the murderer and poet Lacenaire and the serial poisoner Hélène Jégado, the latter of whom is the subject of an extended monograph by Bouchardon (see B.57).

B.49 ———— *Les dames de Jeufosse.* Paris: Albin Michel, 1928.

▪ In Bouchardon's retelling, the 1857 drama in the park of the Jeufosse family manor in Normandy begins like a variant of the first scene of *Don Giovanni*. The Jeufosse's guard Jean-Baptiste Leufroy-Crépel killed with buckshot fired from one of his rifle barrels a nocturnal intruder who, after depositing a love letter, failed to respond to the guard's order to halt his flight. As Crépel well knew, the dead man (who had been accompanied by a Leporello-like servant) was a notorious local womanizer, the Jeufosses' neighbor and friend, Emile Guillot. Guillot had been relentlessly pursuing young Blanche de Jeufosse and her flirtatious teacher-companion Laurance-Caroline Thouzery with his gallantries, enjoying a degree of success that remains mysterious in each case. Crépel, Blanche's mother, and two brothers were charged with premeditated murder but acquitted on the ground of their right to defend the sanctity of their domicile against trespassers. The Jeufosses, however, were condemned to pay civil damages to the victim's family. The most famous of the defense counsel was the aging Maître Berryer, whose argument won a thunderous ovation from lawyers observing the trial from the galleries. Berryer's prediction that even acquittal would not restore the Jeufosse family's happiness was fulfilled; the once-vivacious Blanche died a lonely old maid in 1918.

B.50 ———— *Le Docteur Couty de la Pommerais.* Paris: Albin Michel, 1929.

▪ Dr. Désiré-Edmond Couty de la Pommerais was executed in 1864 outside Paris's Grande Roquette prison for poisoning his deluded mistress, Madame Julie-Françoise de Pauw, with digitalin in 1863. The prosecution dropped as insufficiently proved a second count charging the defendant with having disposed of his mother-in-law by similar means in 1861, shortly after his marriage. Among other difficulties encountered by famed defense counsel Charles Lachaud at the trial was how to explain why his client, as a homeopath schooled in the administration of small doses, was in possession of an enormous supply of lethal digitalin. The evidence of Couty de Pommerais's financial motive was also patent; he had insured Julie de Pauw's life for 500,000 francs after persuading her that he planned to help her fake a serious illness in the hope of frightening the insurance companies into paying a handsome settlement for the cancellation of their policies. The malady he induced by poison was only too real.

Twenty years after Couty de la Pommerais's execution, decadent author Villiers de l'Isle Adam perpetrated a hoax in the pages of the *Figaro*. He wrote that Dr. Velpeau, desiring to test whether the severed head of a decapitated man retains brief consciousness, obtained his colleague Couty de la Pommerais's agreement to blink three times with his right eye after the blade fell. According to Villiers de l'Isle Adam's fictitious report, the guillotined man managed only one blink.

B.51 ———— *Le duel du chemin de la favorite.* Paris: Albin Michel, 1927.

■ This account of a pistol duel that ended in tragedy in the Bois de Boulogne in 1845 is a literary and theater name-dropper's delight. The quarrel between two Parisian journalists, the expert marksman Rosemond de Beauvallon of the *Globe* and Alexandre-Henri Dujarier, co-owner of the *Presse*, arose from a trivial gambling quarrel that masked bitter professional rivalry. Hopeless with any weapons, Dujarier fired at random and threw away his pistol; his adversary, however, took careful aim and shot him through the head. At Beauvallon's murder trial, novelist Alexandre Dumas and dancer Lola Montès testified about collateral matters but garnered much of the spectators' attention. Dumas's response to the court's inquiry as to his profession caused hilarity among reporters: "I would say that I am a dramatic author, if I were not in the nation of the great Corneille."

The trial ended in a popular acquittal; France's Supreme Court had only rendered dueling subject to murder prosecution in 1837, and defense counsel Maître Berryer had been able to persuade the jury that Beauvallon had followed punctiliously the old code of honor.

Bouchardon's suspenseful narrative carries a sting in its tail. A new witness, François-Auguste de Meynard, appeared with startling evidence that, contrary to the French dueling principles, the combat had been rigged in the victor's favor. The pistols used belonged to Beauvallon's brother-in-law, and in the early morning of the day fixed for the duel, the journalist had practiced firing the weapons in a private garden in Chaillot before meeting his opponent in the woods. In separate trials attendant on these disclosures, Beauvallon and one of his dueling seconds were convicted of perjury but were irregularly released from the Conciergerie prison during the disorders of 1848.

B.52 ———— *Dumollard le tueur de bonnes* [Dumollard, the Killer of Housemaids]. Paris: Albin Michel, 1936.

■ In this superb monograph, Bouchardon returns to the serial "maid killer" Martin Dumollard, to whom he had devoted a shorter study a decade earlier. Dumollard's modus operandi was so rigidly established and so free of camouflage that France's Supreme Court apportioned the blame for his long reign of terror between the savage killer and negligent police authorities. Between 1855 and 1861, Dumollard would lure unemployed or poorly paid young women from Lyon to the countryside lying to the northeast, on the strength of a fictitious job offer and would then attempt to rob them of their meagre possessions; he murdered at least four women (burying one alive) and stripped their bodies, not to facilitate a sexual assault but to add their clothing to his booty. Some of the women, alarmed to find themselves with him at nightfall on a deserted country byway, fled unharmed, and his final targeted victim, Marie Pichon (who identified him upon his arrest, recognizing the scar and swelling that deformed his upper lip), successfully resisted a strangulation attempt with a lasso.

A strange feature of this case was that Dumollard enjoyed the complicity of his wife, who, at his instruction, washed bloodstains from the victims' clothing, altered the garments to her own size, and removed identifying labels. Among the large inventory of stolen property maintained by the Dumollards in their home, two items plainly damned them both: equally illiterate, they had no explanation to offer for their possession of a writing case and a pen holder. Dumollard was guillotined after a trial in which he showed little interest while stuffing himself with food, and his wife was sentenced to twenty years of hard labor.

In his last chapter, Bouchardon attacks the levity of the *Figaro*, which repeatedly published Dumollard jokes after the execution; most of them were dreadful puns based on the double meaning of the word *bonne* in French—"maid" or "good."

When Jean-François Millet's famous painting *The Man with the Hoe* was completed in 1862, some viewers saw in the impassive peasant the artist's impression of Dumollard. In 1863, Paul de Saint-Victor expressed his horror in more general terms: "Imagine a monster without brow, dim-eyed and with an idiotic grin, planted in the middle of a field like a scarecrow. No trace of intelligence humanizes this brute at rest. Has he just been working, or murdering? Does he dig the land or hollow out the grave?" (see Gerd Muehsam, *French Painters and Paintings from the 14th Century to Post-Impressionism* [New York: Ungar, 1970], 382).

B.53 ———— *L'Enfant de la Villette*. In series *Le sphinx*. Paris: Éditions de la Nouvelle Revue Critique, 1930.

■ The title essay in this outstanding collection explores the motivation for three related murders that appear to reflect an odd blend of spontaneity and premeditation. In 1840 the body of a boy of twelve or thirteen was found in a drainage ditch in the Parisian suburb of La Villette; his skull had been shattered and his throat savagely cut. Although the authorities took the unusual step of embalming the corpse in the hope that public viewing would produce an identification, the mystery remained intractable until bodies of a woman and a ten-year-old girl, bearing similar injuries, were discovered in a stream in

Artigues near Bordeaux. As a result of a hotel keeper's suspicions, Pierre-Vincent Eliçabide was arrested and eventually charged with the three murders.

After abandoning plans to become a priest, Eliçabide had turned to teaching with little success. From Paris he wrote to his fiancée, Marie Anizat, requesting that she send her son, Joseph, to him so that he could undertake his education. When she complied, unaware of the failure of Eliçabide's career as an instructor, he murdered the youth and then lured Marie and her daughter, Mathilde, to Artigues where he butchered them to prevent them from discovering Joseph's violent death.

After all three killings, Eliçabide pocketed modest funds and adornments that the victims had on their persons, but the crimes do not seem to have been committed for profit. While Marie and her daughter seem clearly to have been eliminated with pre-meditation to remove damning witnesses, the principal enigma of the case surrounds the motive for the first murder. Eliçabide horrified jurors and trial spectators by claiming that he had "philanthropically" decided to end Joseph's life at one of its happiest moments, as he was being introduced to the splendors of Paris and was unaware of the disappointments that life might later hold in store for him. Bouchardon, on the contrary, argues that the failed teacher was motivated by "pride," that, if he had not killed the youth, he would have had to return him to his mother: "But then, he must confess to her that after four months of vain efforts and chimerical illusions, he was reduced to the most fearful distress, a distress of which there would now be a witness."

Although a resolute opponent of revisionist attacks on criminal convictions, Bouchardon includes two examples of justice gone astray. In one case ("The Woman Poisoner Who Was Poisoned"), tavern keeper Pauline Druaux was found guilty of poisoning her husband and brother in 1887 by unknown means. She was later freed when the cause of the deaths was identified as carbon monoxide that had escaped from a stovepipe. In "Baroness Dupuytren's Cook," Pierre-Augustin Gillard, a discharged cook, was freed from prison after having been erroneously found to have furnished the household key to his friend Louis-François-Théophile Lemoine, who entered the Paris apartment of the widowed Baroness Dupuytren in 1833, murdered an elderly maid, and carried off jewelry, silver, and other valuables. Dissatisfied with his release and a payment from Louis-Philippe, Gillard, who fancied himself a gifted poet, showered his execrable verses on the throne, seeking expungement of his conviction and more generous compensation.

The remaining essay in the collection, "The Drama of the Rue des Hirondelles," tells of the 1842 death of Jean-Alexis-Aimé Sirey (son of a famous compiler of French law reports and statutes) during a violent quarrel with promising Paris barrister Edouard Caumartin over the favors of an opera soprano. Both Sirey and Caumartin appeared to be dissolute and hot tempered, so that Bouchardon has little quarrel with the jury's verdict of acquittal, which seemed to reflect acceptance of the defense theory that Sirey had impaled himself on the blade of his antagonist's sword cane drawn in self-defense.

B.54 ———— *L'Énigme du Cimitière Saint-Aubin (procès du Frère Léotade)*. Paris: Albin Michel, 1926.

■ One of France's most puzzling causes célèbres is the 1847 rape-murder of fifteen-year-old bookbinder's assistant Cécile-Anne Combettes, whose corpse was found in the cemetery of Saint-Aubin, in Toulouse, adjacent to the walled garden of a monastery belonging to the Brothers of the Christian Doctrine. Cécile had helped her employer, Jean Bertrand Conte, deliver books to the monastery, but, having been told to wait in the vestibule while Conte conferred with the director of the novitiate, disappeared from view until her violated corpse, with its head smashed, was discovered in the cemetery.

Brother Léotade, a purchasing agent for the monastery, was charged with the crime after Conte, himself not above suspicion because of his seduction of a sister-in-law some years in the past, claimed to have seen the monk in the vestibule when he had arrived with Cécile. The friars rallied around their accused brother even to the point of encouraging or rehearsing false testimony indicating that the outrage had been committed outside the monastery walls. The prosecution, for its part, was not averse to stirring antireligious sentiment among the jurors by arguing that the monks were engaged in a conspiracy to hide the truth that one of their own had committed the double crime in a burst of suppressed lust.

Brother Léotade's first trial was interrupted by the outbreak of the Revolution of 1848; but on retrial, the defendant was convicted by a majority of jurors under a compromise verdict finding him guilty of a "rape attempt" and murder, with extenuating circumstances. Léotade died a model prisoner after serving nineteen months of his life sentence in Toulon.

Bouchardon believes that Léotade should have been acquitted with benefit of doubt. He believes that the defense erred by attempting to prove that the crime was committed outside the monastery. Instead, he finds it more likely that the killer was an unknown friar other than Léotade and that the shady Conte had arranged to bring Cécile to a private interview with her assassin with no idea, however, that a brutal crime would result from the improper rendezvous.

B.55 ———— *La faute de l'Abbé Auriol.* In series *Le sphinx.* Paris: Éditions de la Nouvelle Revue Critique, 1933.

■ "The Sin of Abbé Auriol," the principal essay in this excellent collection, recalls the poisoning of two elderly sisters in the village of Nohèdes near Prades in 1881. The murderer, Abbé Joseph Auriol, who ministered to the souls of Nohèdes, dispatched his landladies, Marie and Rose Fonda-Salvadoure, with generous doses of hellebore and prussic acid in order to succeed to their property as Rose's legatee under a will drawn after Marie's death. The abbé's purpose was to finance his liaison with the local schoolteacher, Alexandrine V., who also roomed with the Fondas. Bouchardon emphasizes the short-comings of the forensic scientists, who could not establish presence of the poisons in the victims' bodies. When he learned of the laboratory failures, Auriol cannily withdrew his previous confession. The jury found him guilty with extenuating circumstances; a few years later he died in a prison colony.

"Men of the Robe on the Bench of the Accused" revives a nightmare visited on the bar of Chambon-sur-Voueize (near Montluçon) in 1841. Five jurists stood on trial for complicity in a fatal duel: two trial-court judges (including a bar association president), a barrister, a solicitor, and a *notaire* (family affairs lawyer). The victim, a solicitor named Alphonse-Etienne Ranjon, had declared professional war on his dueling antagonist, Périgault de Grandchamp, whom he accused of infringing on the solicitors' traditional monopoly over pleadings and pretrial procedure. In return, Grandchamp was outraged by Ranjon's insolence in making a court argument when the barrister he had briefed left gaps in his presentation. With so many lawyers and judges of Chambon on trial, it is small wonder that the case had to be moved to nearby Guéret. Grandchamp and his fellow defendants were acquitted and the public applauded; a dead lawyer rarely inspires tears.

The amusing essay "In the Name of the Law" illustrates the usefulness of public hysteria to inventive criminals. In 1893, at the height of the Panama Canal fraud scandal, a gang pulled off a burglary by posing as a team of canal investigators.

The last article, "The Calais Castaways," shows Napoleon in one of his generous moments as First Consul. Emigrés, who had foresworn enmity to the French Republic and entered the India service of the British Crown, were shipwrecked on the French coast en route to Calcutta. Facing capital charges as "returned exiles bearing weapons," the shipwreck survivors, led by the duc de Choiseul-Stainville (the failed rescuer of the French royal family at Varennes), endured barbaric imprisonment and tortuous legal proceedings until freed by Napoleon's understanding that escapees of the sea's wrath were not their country's foes.

B.56 ——— *La femme à l'ombrelle.* Paris: Albin Michel, 1930.

■ This once famous case began like a Maupassant tale gone wrong. In May 1867, the body of a woman was found in the forest of Fontainebleau, shielded from the road by her open umbrella. It was the theory of the prosecutor, and accepted by a jury in Melun, that the beautiful victim, Madame Sidonie-Marguerite Mertens, a part-time courtesan, had been pounced on and suffocated by her puny hunchbacked friend and procuress Mathilde-Louise-Alexandrine Frigard. The ever-smiling defendant's crime was apparently inspired by her scheme to divert her friend's small fortune through forgeries of her signature and perhaps also by a threat posed by Madame Mertens's new male lover to their lesbian relationship (discreetly veiled from the jury). The ultimate victims were the forensic scientists who had testified with such assurance in support of the unlikely suffocation; after the verdict, which went unappealed, tiny Madame Frigard confessed to having caused her sturdier companion to inhale prussic acid. Bouchardon's account of the case is shapely and suspenseful.

B.57 ——— *Hélène Jégado l'empoisonneuse bretonne.* Paris: Albin Michel, 1937.

■ What psychological traits characterize the serial poisoner? A useful source book for examining this issue is Bouchardon's well-documented portrayal of cook Hélène Jégado, whose arsenic (obtained from sources never identified) claimed the lives of more than thirty of her employers, their relatives, and her fellow servants between 1833 and 1851. Jégado found in poison a means of avenging real or fancied wounds to her self-love and ambition that she suffered as a household servant. The legal and medical professionals who studied her case observed an extraordinary disproportion between the wrongs she sensed and the crimes with which she responded. In many instances, she selected victims, including children and the elderly, against whom even she, in her distorted thought processes, could not fashion any grievances. In these instances she revealed in the clearest light her drive to translate into action the principle of evil that dominated her character and to demonstrate her power to decree life or death; she took particular delight in predicting the death of her prey. When a poisoning had begun, Jégado tended the dying victim with a mixture of hypocrisy and sadism, even pressing a crucifix to the lips of the last housemaid she murdered.

Before her execution in 1852, Jégado confessed to a priest all the murders of which she was accused, except three among her first seven poisonings, which she falsely attributed to an innocent fellow servant. Bouchardon notes that the guillotine only hastened nature's death sentence, since Jégado went to the scaffold with a painful breast cancer.

B.58 ———— *L'Homme aux oreilles percées* [The Man with Pierced Ears]. In series *Le sphinx*. Paris: Éditions de là Nouvelle Revue Critique, n.d.

■ In 1892, Mathias Hadelt, a thief and impostor who preyed on monasteries, was guillotined at Valence for murdering Father Ildefonse, the elderly treasurer of the Trappist monastery of Aigueville near Montélimar. Hadelt, who was residing in the monastery in the guise of the novice Brother Eugène, cleverly sandwiched the murder (probably committed with a shoemaker's paring knife) and thefts from the monastery's strongbox around attendance at the compline service. One of the damning physical clues was the observation that Hadelt's ears had once been pierced, the sign of a refractory prisoner. Bouchardon traces Hadelt's criminal career through a series of disguises and identities, concluding that he might well have escaped suspicion if he had not been obligated by rules of the monastery to deposit trivial pieces of jewelry with its treasury, thereby becoming involved in the police inquiry as an apparent "victim" of the murderer's theft.

The second priestly murder case included in this volume is much more famous: the 1857 murder of the Archbishop of Paris Marie-Dominique-Auguste Sibour by the quarrelsome Abbé Jean-Louis Verger during church services in honor of Saint Genevieve, patroness of Paris. The trial, which Verger did his best to disrupt, proceeded at a near-record pace, and Verger was guillotined only twenty-eight days after the assassination. Two appeals and a petition to Napoleon III had failed; Verger's counsel offered a half-hearted insanity defense, and there was little in the murderer's past to recommend him to mercy. In addition to thwarted ambition and persecution mania, doctrinal fanaticism played a role in the crime: as he struck the archbishop with a hidden knife, Verger shouted, "Down with the goddesses!" voicing his opposition to the doctrine of the Immaculate Conception and to the worship of the Virgin Mary and Saint Genevieve. Nevertheless, as Bouchardon notes with exasperation, there were many who lamented the fate of the abbé. After his execution, the journal *Droit* intoned, "Verger belongs to history."

B.59 ———— *Madame de Vaucrose, suivi de la fragilité de l'aveu* [Madame de Vaucrose, Followed by The Fragility of Confession]. Paris: Albin Michel, 1947.

■ Bouchardon juxtaposes two cases that demonstrate how police and magistrates may go astray by assuming too readily that a murder in a residence has been committed by a member of the household. In 1898, tyrannical and parsimonious widow Ursule-Antonine Vaucrose, age seventy-six, was strangled and suffocated in her bedroom in a large gloomy country house near Uzès in Provence, and valuables were missing. Her pathetically subservient younger son, Fernand, age fifty-two, was unjustly accused by a housemaid, Marie Bastide, who later retracted her charges and identified day laborer Joachim Audibert as the killer. There is reason to believe that Marie, who took a fatal dose of absinthe, was involved in the crime. After Fernand de Vaucrose suffered preventive detention and his name was arbitrarily blackened by the investigative magistrate in the order granting his release, a recidivist thief named Barthélemy-Auguste Gayte was convicted of acting as a receiver of goods stolen in the burglary of Madame de Vaucrose's house with knowledge that her murder had preceded the theft. The murderer was never identified, but the prosecution admitted in open court that Fernand de Vaucrose had not participated in the crime. Bouchardon believes that the intruder, Gayte, was in fact the strangler and that the maid, Marie Bastide, whose bedroom commanded the entrance in the murder room, lent him her assistance.

In a shorter concluding essay, Bouchardon illustrates the truth of its title, *La fragilité de l'aveu* [The Fragility of Confessions], by recounting the narrow escape of Rosalie-Pauline Gardin from the guillotine. In the light of her bitter and violent inheritance-related quarrels with her father, Martin Doise, who owned a small farm near Lille, she was an obvious suspect when he was beaten to death and robbed in his home in 1861. Although four months pregnant, she was confined incommunicado in a small cell she called the "black hole" until she confessed the murder. In her trial at Douai, the jury found her guilty with extenuating circumstances. Subsequently, she was vindicated when a professional criminal and his accomplice confessed to carrying out the crime in the hope of carrying off the hoard that Doise was reputed to have; their disappointing booty was no more than a watch and three knives.

B.60 ———— *La malle mystérieuse: Affaire Eyraud-Gabrielle Bompard* [The Mysterious Trunk: The Eyraud-Gabrielle Bompard Murder Case]. Paris: Albin Michel, 1933.

■ Bouchardon paints unsparing portraits of the September and May lovers who became France's famous trunk murderers. Michel Eyraud, a forty-six-year-old deserter, swindler, and fraudulent bankrupt is introduced: "With his torso set on short bow legs, a lumbering gait, flat feet, a large nose, a chinless face, one eye smaller than the other constantly blinking, an enflamed and swollen lower lip, a bump on the left of his forehead, sparse hair on the top of his head, decayed teeth, hands of a strangler, Eyraud had an unpleasant look and hardly made a winning impression." And his twenty-one-year-old mistress, Gabrielle Bompard, fares little better: "She was whimsical, lazy, voluble, hardly respectable in her words, always moved by the need to make an impression; above all, she was profoundly deceitful without the most rudimentary sense of morality. She had an immoderate taste for finery, loved nobody and drove her father (who, widowed early, was responsible for raising her) to despair."

The victim of this dangerous couple, the prominent debt collector and process server Toussaint-Augustin Gouffé, disappeared from his Paris office on Friday, July 26, 1889. A widower, Gouffé was accustomed to devoting his Friday evenings to ladies of the town but returned home in time for breakfast with his daughters on Saturday morning. But this time he did not return. His corpse, enclosed in a sack and bearing signs of strangulation, was found near Lyon, and the shattered remains of a trunk in which he had been transported were shortly thereafter discovered and reassembled. The search for Gouffé had been led by M. Goron, head of the Paris Sûreté, and the identification of the corpse was made by the eminent forensic scientist Dr. Alexandre Lacassagne.

Eyraud and Bompard fled abroad after the crime. Gabrielle returned to Paris and gave herself up, claiming that she had only been a passive witness of the murder, which she fully attributed to her lover. Eyraud, extradited from Havana, told a very different story, which Bouchardon accepts as essentially true. In desperate need of funds, Eyraud had arranged for Bompard to lure the amorous Gouffé to a rented apartment. In preparation for the rendezvous, he had rigged rope and pulleys to the ceiling and attached an end of the rope to the red and white cord of Gabrielle's dressing gown. While Gouffé was embracing her on a chaise longue, Gabrielle, in a feigned show of playfulness, slipped the noose of the cord around his neck, and Eyraud, hidden in a curtained alcove, pulled on the rope that ran through the pulleys. Gouffé was hanged and may have died instantly, but Eyraud, to make sure, strung him up once again.

The fruits of the crime proved to be disappointing, because Gouffé carried little money in his pockets when he set forth on his night wanderings. Immediately after the murder, Eyraud used the dead man's keys to invade his business office; but once there, he was struck by sudden panic and fled without finding anything of value. Returning to the murder scene, he called on Gabrielle's assistance to pack the corpse in a large and specially reinforced trunk they had recently purchased, and they carried the victim to Lyon.

The trial of Eyraud and Bompard could not match the strangeness of the crime or the excitement of the police investigation. The dramatic highlight was the attempt of Bompard's defense counsel, the youthful Henri-Robert, to persuade the jury that his client's free will had been disabled by the hynotic influence of her lover. Eyraud was executed and Bompard was sentenced to twenty years' hard labor.

The Museum of the Paris Police Prefecture exhibits what purports to be the red and white cord of Bompard's bathrobe that was used to hang Gouffé, but Eyraud claimed to have disposed of this incriminating piece of evidence during his overseas flight from justice.

B.61 ——— *Le mystère du château de Chamblas*. Paris: Albin Michel, 1922.

■ During the night of September 1, 1840, a timely rifle shot fired through a kitchen window of the chateau of Chamblas near Le Puy-en-Velay, southwest of Lyon, ended the life of the unhappy Louis-Jean-Marie Vilhardin de Marcellange. The fatal bullet was timely from the point of view of the victim's estranged wife, Theodora, and her mother, the countess de Larochenégly de Chamblas, because the next day Monsieur de Marcellange planned, much to the ladies' displeasure, to lease away the chateau and its appurtenant land. In a second trial held at Lyon, the ladies' trusted servant, Jacques Besson, was convicted of the killing and sentenced to death, but his employers wisely dropped out of sight and were never brought to justice for having commissioned the crime. The Lyon trial was highlighted by the forensic duel between two gifted French barristers, Charles Lachaud, appearing for the defendant, and the young Théodore Bac, representing the victim's siblings as *partie civile*. At the conclusion of his impartial account of the case, Bouchardon musters overwhelming evidence in support of Besson's guilt: 1) on the murder night two reliable witnesses, Monsieur and Madame Pugin, heard the door close at the hôtel de Chamblas in Le Puy, a sound that, according to Besson's accusers, evidenced his return to his mistresses' home after completing his homicidal mission; 2) Besson clearly lied in denying possession of olive-colored velvet trousers, which several witnesses agreed had been worn by a prowler near the chateau before the murder; 3) a key witness, Claude Reynaud, had recognized Besson in the vicinity of the chateau, and the variations in his successive statements on the identification were explainable on the basis of timidity. As a last gift to the reader Bouchardon sets out the full text of a long-lost popular ballad celebrating the case. The anonymous author of the verses comments on the suspicious failure of Besson's two mistresses to attend his Lyon trial: "O widow de Marcellange! O countess de Chamblas! Your absence is very strange in such a tragic case!"

B.62 ———— *Un précurseur de Landru: L'Horloger Pel.* Grenoble: Arthaud, 1934.

■ The title of the principal essay, "A Precursor of Landru: The Watchmaker Pel," and a chapter heading referring to Bluebeard, suggest that Bouchardon believed in the guilt of Albert Pel, convicted at a second trial of poisoning, dismembering, and incinerating his servant and lover Elise Boehmer at Montreuil in 1884. The jury, sitting in Melun, spared Pel's life by a finding of extenuating circumstances—unlike the jury at the first trial in Paris, which had condemned him to death. Although a series of mysterious deaths, illnesses, and disappearances of women in Pel's life seem to proclaim him a serial poisoner, the case is not without its mysteries, not to say absurdities.

The first jury acquitted the jeweler and self-styled inventor and chemist of murdering his first spouse, Eugénie Buffereau, although significant amounts of arsenic were found in the abdomen, liver, and kidneys of her exhumed body. This verdict could not be reexamined at the retrial. Bouchardon quotes an article by contemporary journalist Henri Rochefort attributing the Melun finding of extenuating circumstances to the jury's doubt that the murder of Elise Boehmer had been sufficiently established. What can one say, Rochefort asked, of a justice system that considered a woman's disappearance without a trace to be stronger evidence of poisoning than discovery of arsenic in an exhumed corpse? The answer to this query that can be gleaned from this intriguing study of the case is that jurors were less impressed by scientific evidence than by neighbors' testimony about a glowing furnace and an intolerable smell.

A short appended essay, "Chance, the King of Policemen," collects a number of examples of criminal investigations aided or led astray by pure accident. Among the most famous cases mentioned is that of Joseph Lesurques, executed as a participant in the Lyon Mail murders because he happened to accompany a friend to a police station where he was erroneously identified as one of the mail robbers. A criminal beneficiary of accident was Bolo Pasha, investigated during World War I by Bouchardon, then a French intelligence officer, for receiving pay from the enemy. The proof of Bolo's treason was long delayed by the inability of French police to confirm reports that a check on a Milan bank had been cashed for Bolo's account; it turned out that the informer had meant to say "Turin" instead of "Milan."

B.63 ———— *Les procès burlesques* [Comical Trials]. In series *Énigmes et drames judiciaires d'autrefois*. Paris: Perrin, 1929.

■ Although the title of this collection promises burlesques, the leading essay deals with the trial of Euphémie Lacoste for the 1843 arsenic poisoning of her elderly and unpleasant husband, Henri. The young widow was acquitted, much to the pleasure of Marie Lafarge, who had been convicted in an earlier poisoning to which the Lacoste case was compared. Bouchardon abstains from his own conclusions, opining that Madame Lacoste could only have been acquitted with the benefit of doubt.

A comic highlight of the book is Bouchardon's account ("Le collectionneur ingénu") of the rise and fall of Denis Vrain-Lucas, who forged correspondence between historical luminaries for sale to gullible academician Michel Chasles. Among Vrain-Lucas's masterpieces, all in impeccable French transcriptions dating from centuries past, were letters of Cleopatra to Julius Caesar, Alexander the Great to Aristotle, and Mary Magdalen to Lazarus; 194 supposedly original pieces emanated from the busy pen of Joan of Arc.

B.64 ———— *Le puits du presbytère d'Entrammes (affaire de l'Abbé Bruneau)* [The Well of the Entrammes Parish House (The Case of Abbé Bruneau)]. Paris: Albin Michel, 1942.

■ In *The Well of the Entrammes Parish House*, Bouchardon argues persuasively that the guilt of Abbé Bruneau, popularly regarded as one of France's cruelest murderers, was far from clear. In 1894, Bruneau, a thief and womanizer who had served as assistant to Abbé Fricot, parish priest at Entrammes near the famous cheesemaking monastery of Port Salut in eastern Brittany, faced multiple charges before the trial court of the Mayenne: arsons in 1891 and 1892 after overinsuring property; embezzlement of funds intended for the repair of his church; murder (on July 15, 1893) of an elderly flower seller of Laval, the widow Bourdais, with forty strokes of a table knife, and theft of her money and securities; murder of Abbé Fricot, whose body was found in the well on the Entrammes church garden on the morning of January 3, 1894, battered by logs that covered it from view. The jury acquitted Bruneau of all charges, except those relating to Abbé Fricot's murder, for which he was guillotined.

Bruneau admitted only sexual transgressions, which were well established by prostitutes who testified at the trial. In Bouchardon's view, "he was judged more on the sordidness of his life than on charges related to a particular crime." In addition, the hair-raising details of the murder of Fricot must have inflamed the jury, especially the suggestion that, to stifle the cries of the dying priest, Bruneau had trailed his bloodstained fingers across the keyboard of the church harmonium. This Grand Guignol scenario helped the prosecution overcome the apparent lack of a motive for the killing; the best hypothesis it could offer was that Fricot, hatless and without an overcoat, had led Bruneau into the church garden on a bitterly cold winter evening to rebuke him for thefts he was suspected of having made.

One of Bouchardon's subtlest achievements is his reexamination of the damning testimony of Sister Bouvier, who belatedly claimed to remember an absurd statement by Bruneau that the appearance of Abbé Fricot's murder must have been faked to cover up his suicide leap into the well. Bouchardon renders Bruneau's observation more credible by the transposition or suppression of a few of the words that the nun recalled: "We feared at first that he had committed suicide. But, happily for the reputation of our poor *curé*, it was murder. The proof of this is that logs were thrown on top of his body."

B.65 ———— *Ravachol et cie* [Ravchol and Company]. Paris: Hachette, 1931.

■ Ravachol (who discarded his original name, François-Claudius Koeningstein, in favor of his mother's family name) claimed to be taking revenge for the earlier conviction of a fellow anarchist, Henri-Louis-Charles Decamps, when in 1892 he bombed the Paris apartment houses where Decamps's judge and prosecutor resided. As Bouchardon shows, however, Ravachol's credentials as an anarchist humanitarian are dubious, since, between 1886 and 1891, he had established an appalling record as a violent common criminal with no respect for life. Preying on elderly, defenseless hoarders in the Loire region, he murdered five victims and stole their possessions; adding sacrilege to crime, he rifled the tomb of a baroness and tore a necklace from her corpse. Bouchardon's judgment of Ravachol is unsparing: "Born too late, he would have been more at home in those remote ages, when, to live well, many criminals, half-savage, burned, pillaged, and cut throats, indifferent to the cries and death rattles of their victims. An avenger of wrongs, Ravachol? No, a wild beast."

Still, the Paris jury that considered his bombings (which did not result in any deaths) made a finding of extenuating circumstances, perhaps fearing that more reprisal attacks would follow a restaurant bombing on the eve of trial. The Loire jury that considered Ravachol's previous murders was more resolute, convicting him, without any recommendation to mercy, of the killing and robbery of a hermit.

Bouchardon also writes of Auguste Vaillant's 1893 terror bombing of the Palais Bourbon while the National Assembly was in session. Miraculously, no lives were lost despite the heavy-studded nails sprayed by the exploding device. Bouchardon appears to have greater sympathy for Vaillant than his predecessor, Ravachol, whom the new outrage was intended to avenge. Vaillant, abandoned in his childhood by both parents, had drifted into a life of petty crime and international wandering. Despite a superficial attraction to the philosophical foundations of anarchism, Vaillant seemed motivated in large part by a desire for self-glorification, best illustrated by the alacrity with which he confessed.

B.66 ———— *Souvenirs.* Paris: Albin Michel, 1953.

■ Oddly, Bouchardon's memoirs make no mention of his prodigious output of crime histories. He does confide, though, that his literary taste was formed by immersion in Balzac and that his interest in criminal law was sharpened when he read the memoirs of poisoner Marie Lafarge and listened to his maternal grandfather's meticulous account of the 1845 murder of a five-year-old child and his governess by a pharmacist named Jean-François Roudier (Bouchardon was later to write an essay on the case under the name "My First Crime"; see B.40). Reviewing his own career in the French magistracy, Bouchardon gives principal attention to his investigations of chief personages of espionage and treason affairs during World War I: Mata Hari, "Bolo Pacha," and Joseph Caillaux. Never doubting for a moment the guilt of any of his investigations' targets, Bouchardon was nonetheless frank in recalling with pleasure the sway of Mata Hari's hips.

B.67 ———— *La tragique histoire de l'instituteur Lesnier (1847–1855)* [The Tragic History of Schoolteacher Lesnier]. In series *Énigmes et drames judiciaires d'autrefois.* Paris: Perrin, 1928.

■ In his preface, Bouchardon denounces the fad for revisionism in the study of classic crimes, but he admits readily that judicial errors are often induced by "coincidences and illusions," as well as by weaknesses of testimony, sometimes worked on by passion, partiality, or corruption. In support of his thesis he reviews two rural cases. The first is the unjust prosecution of schoolmaster Jean-François-Dieudonné Lesnier for the 1847 murder of elderly recluse Claude Gay. In 1855 Lesnier was replaced in prison by the real killer. The other, shorter article concerns the errors of justice in the investigation of a violent burglary of the house of the Grigourès couple in Castel-Coudec. Two local residents (whose innocent explanation of soot on their faces was disbelieved) were immediately suspected, Auguste-Pierre-Prosper Baffet and Yves Louarn (Le Louarn). Ultimately, an unrelated gang was found to be responsible, but by then the innocent pair were already dead.

B.68 ———— *Troppmann.* Paris: Albin Michel, 1932.

■ In one of the most atrocious crimes of nineteenth-century France, Jean-Baptiste Troppmann, a twenty-year old Alsatian mechanic, during the night of September 19, 1869, used knife, pick, and strangler's hands to dispatch Madame Jean Kinck and five minor children on a deserted plain of Pantin on the outskirts of Paris. Previously Troppman had poisoned Monsieur Kinck on the way back from a trip they had made together to Alsace, and he also knifed his eldest son, Gustave, to death near the site of the later butchery of the rest of the family. Bouchardon, modestly claiming that the merit of his book lay in its reliance on records rather than popular legend, addresses the two principal enigmas of the case: 1) what was the purpose of Kinck's traveling to Alsace with Troppmann; and 2) could Troppmann, acting alone, have murdered Madame Kinck and five children without resistance, flight, or effective calls for help? Regarding the fatal Alsatian voyage, Bouchar-don hypothesizes that Troppmann had dangled before the hardworking brush manufacturer Kinck some get-rich-quick scheme, perhaps in the nature of a mythical mining venture. The gullible Kinck, who was a fellow Alsatian, brought along check forms that Troppmann probably intended for him to deliver with a substantial amount filled in as an "investment." But the checks remained blank at Kinck's death, and Troppmann's later attempt to forge and cash the instruments failed. On the second principal point in issue, Bouchardon accepts the view of the forensic scientists that the element of surprise, the young ages of the Kinck children, and the murderer's division of his six victims into two groups of three enabled the agile Troppmann to slaughter them all singlehanded, without the assistance of the three confederates he subsequently invented in the vain hope of postponing his date with the scaffold. The trial and guillotining of Troppmann were heavily attended by French luminaries; Turgenev wrote an account of the execution (see T.15).

B.69 ————— *La tuerie du pont d'Andert (1838)*. In series *Énigmes et drames judiciaires d'autrefois*. Paris: Perrin, 1928.

■ The case of Sébastien-Benoît Peytel, executed in 1839 for the murder of his wife, Félicie, and servant Louis Rey, attracted the passionate attention of writers and artists. Peytel, a *notaire* (family affairs lawyer) at Belley, was supported by Balzac and Gavarni, with whom they had worked on the Parisian journal *Le Voleur*. Thackeray wrote an article protesting his execution. Bouchardon describes the trial and its attendant furor but stays above the fray. He even puts in a good word for King Louis-Philippe, who examined the file closely before denying clemency; the king, notes Bouchardon, had every reason to appear unbiased, for Peytel in his journalistic days had lampooned the potbellied monarch in "The Physiology of the Pear."

B.70 ————— *Vacher l'éventreur*. Paris: Albin Michel, 1939.

■ If Jack the Ripper had been caught and brought to justice, his trial might have resembled that of France's Joseph Vacher. Dubbed "Jack the Ripper of the Southeast," Vacher, between 1894 and 1897, slashed the throats of at least eleven victims, including young male and female animal herders, and often proceeded to disembowel and sexually abuse their bodies. At his trial, the killer attempted to demonstrate his mental illness by citing a number of causes: the bite of a rabid dog and a harmful medicine administered as its cure; a gunshot wound to his head self-inflicted after a young woman rejected his suit; and abusive treatment in an asylum from which he claimed to have been released before he had recovered his sanity. At other moments, he professed himself to be an involuntary agent of God and compared his sufferings to those of Joan of Arc. Due to a jurisdictional tangle, Vacher was prosecuted for only a single murder. A panel of medical experts, headed by eminent Alexandre Lacassagne (see L.1), found him mentally competent, and the trial judge charged him repeatedly with simulating madness to impress the jury. Bouchardon believes that Vacher was abnormal rather than clinically insane and opines that "if abnormal murderers of the Vacher type were always guillotined, there would be fewer murderers." Vacher was put to death in Bourg, the last "patient" of executioner Anatole Deibler.

B.71 Boucicault, Dion[ysius Lardner] *The Colleen Bawn.* 1860. In *Nineteenth Century Plays.* Ed. George Rowell. 2d ed. Oxford: Oxford Univ. Press, 1972.

■ Dion Boucicault's lively melodrama is ultimately derived from reality: John Scanlan's murder of his wife, Ellen (with the help of his servant Sullivan), in the course of a boating excursion on the river Shannon in 1819. The motive was Scanlan's desire to remove an obstacle to a more profitable marriage. The immediate literary source of the play was Gerald Griffin's novel *The Collegians* (1829). Departing from history and Griffin's narrative, Boucicault provides a happy outcome in a "sensation" scene that became a hallmark of stage melodrama and the silent films that followed: moonshiner Myles-na-Coppaleen (played by Boucicault) saves the "Colleen Bawn," Eily O'Connor (played by Agnes Robertson, the dramatist's wife), from the waters of the river. The responsibility of the victim's husband is progressively reduced in the novel and the play. In Griffin's account, Hardress Cregan (Scanlan) orders his servant Danny Mann (Sullivan) to abduct his unwanted wife, Eily (Ellen), to America, but to "harm not a hair of the poor wretch's head." Mann, however, finds that murder is a more reliable silencer. In Boucicault's reworking, it is Hardress's financially pressed mother who, unbeknownst to her son, instructs Mann to kill Eily.

In real life, Boucicault may not have been so tenderhearted a husband as his Hardress Cregan. In July 1845 the playwright married a French widow, Anne Guiot, and later that summer the couple took a wedding trip to the Continent. Stephen Fiske, a journalist, repeated malicious gossip that arose when Anne did not return: "They took a tour through Switzerland. Boucicault went up the Alps with a wife, and came down with a black hatband. How did the wife die? Nobody knows; but Boucicault must have inherited her money, for he returned to London and drove a pair of gray ponies in Hyde Park, and resumed his semi-fashionable, semi-Bohemian life."

The Scanlan murder also inspired Sir Julius Benedict's light opera *The Lily of Killarney* (1862).

B.72 Bourget, Paul *André Cornélis.* Paris: Alphonse Lemerre, 1887.

■ Léon Peltzer's world-famous crime repaid his elder brother Armand's kindness of a decade before when he had saved Léon from the specter of prosecution for fraudulent bankruptcy with the assistance of Antwerp lawyer Guillaume Bernays. In the years that followed Léon's financial crisis, Armand Peltzer fell in love with Bernays's wife, Julie, and rumors (apparently false) of a romance caused the lawyer to break relations with Armand. In 1882, at his brother's instigation, Léon, disguised as bewigged English entrepreneur Henry Vaughan, arranged a "business" rendezvous with Bernays at a Brussels apartment and shot him at short range in the back of the neck. Léon and Armand were imprisoned for premeditated and intentional murder, respectively; Armand died in prison three years later, and Léon, freed after thirty years with the help of writer Gérard Harry, threw himself into the North Sea at age seventy-five (see Gérard Harry, *The Peltzer Case,* in the *Famous Trials* series [New York: Scribner, 1928]).

In his novel *André Cornélis*, published five years after the murder, Paul Bourget shifts the scene of the crime to Paris and adopts the premise that the murderers were never brought to trial. The victim's widow, Madame Cornélis, innocently marries Jacques Termonde (Armand Peltzer), the man who arranged for his brother Édouard (Léon Peltzer) to murder her husband. Reenacting Hamlet's dilemma, her son André sets about investigating the family mystery and discovers the dreadful truth. He must then decide whether to allow his stepfather's crime to go unavenged or to ruin his mother's life. All ends in irony and disappointment. André wrests from Édouard letters incriminating Jacques and confronts his stepfather with the evidence, hoping to compel him to commit suicide rather than have his crime disclosed to his adoring wife. Jacques, however, rebuffs the threat, pleading to be spared for the six months it will take for his terminal illness to run its course. Enraged, André stabs him, but before he dies, Jacques has time to scrawl a note to this wife, absolving André by pretending he has killed himself. André is forced to live with his great enemy's generosity and to realize that he has failed to kill him in his mother's heart.

B.73 Brand, Christianna   *Heaven Knows Who.* New York: Scribner, 1960.

■ South African–born mystery novelist Christianna Brand, in *Heaven Knows Who*, analyzes the Jessie M'Lachlan case, which William Roughead, who edited the trial for the *Notable British Trials* series, called "the ideal murder." Though she uncovered some additional facts and provides more detail than Roughead could in his more restrictive format, she uses her title as her last line, leaving readers to decide this difficult case for themselves. However, in the course of the book Brand appears to be taking the side of Jessie M'Lachlan, as did the Scottish public, partly due to the prejudicial behavior of the judge during the trial.

M'Lachlan was prosecuted for the murder on July 4, 1862, of Jess M'Pherson, servant of John Fleming, a prosperous Glasgow accountant who was away for the weekend. On his return, his father James (who claimed to be eighty-seven or seventy-eight, depending on the circumstances) told him that the servant had gone away and that he had not checked her locked bedroom, although he had heard screams coming from it on the night of July 4. When the room was opened, the murder victim was discovered, nude from the waist down. The police, after checking the kitchen, where both a meat cleaver and a bloody hammer were found, surmised that the murderer dragged his victim into the bedroom after killing her in the kitchen. James Fleming was taken into custody but released after a pawnbroker reported that Jessie M'Lachlan, a friend of the victim, had pawned silver belonging to the Fleming household, where she had earlier worked. Jessie, of delicate build and allegedly suffering from a weak heart, did not seem capable of murdering the larger and stronger M'Pherson. James Fleming was also an unlikely suspect due to his advanced age. However, a decade before he had admitted to his church that he had impregnated a servant girl, a fact that Jessie's lawyer tried without success to enter into evidence during the trial. To the police the unlikely pair of suspects appeared to fit their observation that the victim's wounds indicated the murderer was weak.

The most dramatic part of the book is Brand's discussion of the trial before the hostile Lord Deas during the Glasgow Autumn Circuit in September 1862. She states: "British justice blushes for the conduct both before and during the trial." Besides his frequent interventions against the prisoner, he also saw himself as the protector of the "innocent" and kept any evidence of bad character from being introduced against James Fleming. His charge to the jury Brand characterizes as "the second speech for the prosecution, as delivered from the judicial bench by Lord Death." The judge did not stop at biased words but used a most significant visual aid: "When he came into court on the Friday he carried the black cap openly in his hand and laid it on the desk before him . . . to give the jury a broad hint" that he was prepared to pronounce the death sentence. It took only nineteen minutes for the jury to reach the verdict of guilty. After the verdict and before sentence was passed, the prisoner insisted that a statement she had given to her lawyers before the trial be read in open court. This statement, which asserted that old Fleming had given Jessie the household silver and the victim's clothes to simulate a burglary, tallied so well with much of the evidence that after its reading the jury looked shaken, and a policeman burst into tears. Roughead wrote that it "fitted the proven facts so perfectly as to render its fabrication incredible." Lord Deas, however, called it "a tissue of as wicked falsehoods as any to which I have ever listened" and pronounced the sentence of death.

A week before the execution was to take place, the date was postponed due to strong public feeling that the trial had been unfair. The case was reviewed by a Crown Commissioner, George Young, whose findings led the Home Secretary to commute the sentence to penal servitude. After fifteen years, Jessie was released and emigrated to Port Huron, Michigan, where her son, three years old at the time of the trial, had preceded her. She died there in 1899. Fleming was never brought to trial; but due to the public's anger, he and his family left Glasgow.

In a mystery novel based on the case, *The Dear Old Gentleman*, by George Goodchild and Bechhofer Roberts (New York: Macmillan, 1954), Jessie M'Lachlan (Margaret Sampson) is released by a majority verdict of not proven. The dear old gentleman, Angus Aitken, who is the novelists' recreation of James Fleming, writes a written confession in a nursing home when he believes he is near death. He admits to having killed the victim (renamed Bessie McIntosh). The amorous geezer had been carrying on an affair with Sampson (of which a dead child had been born), and she had "obliged" him since while her husband was at sea. McIntosh became jealous and threatened to inform Mr. Sampson; therefore, the old man had silenced her.

B.74 Bredin, Jean-Denis   *The Affair: The Case of Alfred Dreyfus.* New York: Braziller, 1986.
■ This book, written by a prominent French trial lawyer, is the most definitive modern account of one of the greatest miscarriages of justice in French history, the conviction of army captain Alfred Dreyfus of treasonously supplying secret information to Germany. Although much emphasis has been placed on the divisiveness of "the Affair," Bredin observes that the battle of values between the two camps was fought only within the ruling class. The farmers seem to have been indifferent to a conflict that they viewed as middle class, urban, or, even worse, Parisian. The workers also kept their distance.

Among the publications of Dreyfus's contemporaries, Joseph Reinach's *Histoire de l'affaire Dreyfus* (Paris: Éditions de la Revue Blanche [vol. 1] and Charpentier and Fasquelle (vols. 2–6), 1901–8) remains an indispensable source.

B.75 Bridie, James [pseudonym of Osborne Mavor] *The Anatomist: A Lamentable Comedy of Knox, Burke and Hare and the West Port Murders.* In A Sleeping Clergyman *and Other Plays.* London: Constable, 1934.

■ The central issue posed by the dramatist is the extent to which Edinburgh anatomist Dr. Robert Knox had guilty knowledge that the dissecting subjects furnished to him by Burke and Hare had been murdered. The most severe judgment is that made by Mary Dishart: "I think you are a vain, hysterical, talented, stupid man. I think that you are wickedly blind and careless when your mind is fixed on something. But all men are like that. There is nothing very uncommon about you, Dr. Knox."

B.76 ———— *Dr. Angelus.* In *John Knox and Other Plays.* London: Constable, 1949.

■ The play is a paraphrase of the infamous career of Glasgow's Dr. Edward William Pritchard, who was hanged in July 1865 for poisoning his mother-in-law, Jane Taylor, and his wife, Mary Jane, with antimony and aconite (see R.22). In an Act 3 soliloquy, Dr. Cyril Angelus (Dr. Pritchard) explains that, believing self-realization to be the "aim and object of existence," he turned to murder when he became "frustrated, hog-tied, hemmed in on every side in such a manner as to prevent the fulfillment of his destiny." Bridie enriches his plot by inventing Dr. Angelus's inexperienced partner, George Johnson, whom the murderer persuades, against the young man's better judgment, to certify both poisoning deaths as due to natural causes. Johnson, though lacerated by guilt, attacks a self-important consultant, Sir Gregory Butt, for relying on professional etiquette as an excuse for not acting on evidence of foul play: "you're an old tin idol and a pompous old quack. Angelus may be a murderer and I may be a bloody coward but you're not fit to black our boots."

The production of the play at the Phoenix Theatre in 1947 was undertaken by Alastair Sim, who also performed the title role.

B.77 ———— *Mary Read.* In *Moral Plays.* London: Constable, 1936.

■ This play, written by Bridie with Claud Gurney and starring Flora Robson in the title role at its London premiere in 1934, suggests that the only respectable profession for an "unprotected" woman to enter in the eighteenth century was piracy. Before becoming a buccaneer, the historical Mary had considerable experience as a cross-dresser, first impersonating her dead half-brother to claim his grandmother's financial support and then volunteering for naval and military service. Bridie's Mary Read expresses a feeling of liberation in first donning male attire, telling her mother, "I have legs and arms now. I can swing my arms. I can walk a full pace. I can breathe . . . I'm myself at last." In the final act of the play, Bridie adopts the legend reported by Daniel Defoe that Mary killed a violent pirate in a duel that she had arranged to save the life of her lover, who had quarreled with her adversary but lacked her fighting skills.

The historical Mary Read is discussed in Daniel Defoe's *A General History of the Pyrates*

(1724), edited by Manuel Schonhorn (Columbia: Univ. of South Carolina Press, 1972), 153–59; and in a fictionalized biography by Frank Shay, *Mary Read: Pirate Wench* (London: Hurst & Blackett, n.d.).

B.78 Broad, Lewis *The Innocence of Edith Thompson.* New York: Roy, n.d.
■ Edith Thompson, age thirty, and her lover, a ship's steward named Frederick Bywaters, age twenty-one, were hanged in 1923 for the murder of Edith's husband, Percy, a shipping clerk. Bywaters stabbed Percy Thompson to death within a hundred yards of his home when he and his wife were returning from the theater. Edith's murder conviction was based on the theory that she had incited Bywaters to commit the crime through correspondence that referred to her attempts to kill her husband (who suffered from a heart ailment) through the administration of poison and ground glass. Examining the circumstances of the killing (which left no possibility of escape for the assailant), Broad reasons that the crime could not have been premeditated. The author also concludes that Edith's letters to Bywaters did not support her conviction; her accounts of poisoning attempts, he argues, were games of make-believe designed to maintain a hold over her lover, and her final letter suggesting that she and Bywaters might have to continue a clandestine affair contains no hint that a murder was imminent. To Broad "the jealousy of love" incited Thompson's crime; he observes that "if every woman who plays upon her lover's jealousy exposes herself to the peril of a charge of murder, then being in love must be ranked as a dangerous occupation."

A remarkable feature of the trial noted by Broad is that Mr. Justice Shearman, in his summation, referred to a passage in Edith Thompson's correspondence relating to a popular novel she had been reading, *Bella Donna* by Robert Hichens. The judge noted darkly, "It is the case, admitted on oath by herself, that there is at the end of the book somebody poisoning her husband or trying to poison her husband." Broad points out that Thompson's comments on the fictional poisoner were disapproving.

B.79 Browning, Robert *The Inn Album.* 1875. In *The Poems and Plays of Robert Browning.* Intro. Saxe Cummins. New York: Modern Library, 1934.
■ Written in verse, *The Inn Album* combines narrative and dialogue to offer a sensationalized version of an incident in the life of a disreputable gambler, Henry William FitzGerald (1793–1839), nineteenth Baron de Ros. A statement in *Notes and Queries* of March 25, 1876, summarizes the true-life scandal: "The original story was, of course, too repulsive to be adhered to in all its details, of, first, the gambling lord producing the portrait of the lady he had seduced and abandoned, and offering his expected dupe . . . an introduction to the lady, as a bribe to induce him to wait for payment of the money he had won; secondly, the eager acceptance of the bribe by the young gambler, and the suicide of the lady from horror at the base proposal of her seducer."

In Browning's adaptation, four characters assemble at a country inn: a dissolute elder man; a younger man, his gambling protégé, who has won 10,000 pounds from his financially embarrassed master; a married lady whom both men, unbeknownst to each other, had wooed in the past with varying degrees of success (the elder man had seduced her and the young man's marriage proposal had been rejected because of her secret affair); and a girl to whom the young man was now engaged. Browning added elements of violence and melodrama to the episode from Baron de Ros's life. In order to compel his former mistress to sleep with his protégé, the elder man in *The Inn Album* threatens to blackmail her by revealing their past liaison to her clergyman husband and enters his menace on a page of the inn's guestbook (the "inn album"), where visitors customarily noted their banal words of admiration for the country setting and climate (such as "Hail, calm ac-clivity, salubrious spot!"). Outraged by this act of betrayal, the younger man strangles his mentor, but his intervention has come too late: the lady he once loved has already taken poison. The drama ends on a jarringly light note as the young fiancée arrives at the inn, hoping to receive the married lady's appraisal of her intended bridegroom:

> And then, to give herself a countenance,
> Before she comes upon the pair inside,
> Loud—the oft-quoted, long-laughed-over line—
> "'Hail, calm acclivity, salubrious spot!'
> Open the door!"

Literary critic John Hitner believes that elements of Browning's plot were drawn from the two trials of the "Tichborne impostor" (Arthur Orton), of which the poet attended several sessions (Hitner, *Browning's Analysis of a Murder: A Case for* The Inn Album [Marquette: Northern Michigan Univ. Press, 1969]). One coincidence noted by Hitner was "the testimony of Lady Radcliffe which refuted the charges made against her by Tichborne, who stated under oath that he had once seduced her."

B.80 ———— *Red Cotton Night-Cap Country, or Turf and Towers*. London: Smith Elder, 1873.
■ This long narrative poem deals not with crime but with scandal, mental aberration, and violent impulses resulting in self-mutilation and suicide; nevertheless, its detailed use of trial records places it very close in method and subject matter to the author's more famous *The Ring and the Book*. In 1870, Antonio Mellerio, a Parisian jeweler, lept to his death from the belvedere on the roof of his chateau at Tailleville near St. Aubin-sur-Mer, Normandy. Mellerio's affair with Mme. Debacker, a milliner, had scandalized his mother, who died of a broken heart. In remorse, Mellerio burnt his hands off to the wrists. Some attributed his subsequent suicide to guilt, but Browning cites the possibility that he acted out of religious faith, expecting that the Virgin would miraculously enable him to fly unharmed from the chateau to her church nearby:

> A sublime spring from the balustrade
> About the tower so often talked about,
> A flash in middle air, and stone-dead lay
> Monsieur Léonce Miranda [Mellerio] on the turf.

Browning would not call Mellerio mad:

> No! sane, I say,
> Such being the conditions of his life,
> Such end of life was not irrational,
> Hold a belief, you only half-believe,
> With all-momentous issues either way,—
> And I advise you imitate this leap,
> Put faith to proof, be cured or killed at once!

After Mellerio's death, litigation over the disposition of his estate ended with a determination by the court that there was no evidence of suicide and that, despite his eccentricity, Mellerio had been competent to conduct his affairs. See Mark Siegchrist, *Rough in Brutal Print: The Legal Sources of Browning's* Red Cotton Night-Cap Country (Columbus: Ohio State Univ. Press, 1981).

B.81 ———— *The Ring and the Book.* 1868–69. In *The Poems and Plays of Robert Browning.* Intro. Saxe Cummins. New York: Modern Library, 1934.

■ *The Ring and the Book* is a long narrative poem that follows, for the most part, with scrupulous accuracy the events of a triple murder committed by Count Guido Franceschini and four henchmen in Rome in 1698. The principal defendant, Guido, was a poor nobleman from Arezzo, Tuscany. He had gone to Rome to seek his fortune and served as secretary to a cardinal. But he had entered his forties without having obtained either distinction or financial success. Then he married Pompilia Comparini, the thirteen-year-old daughter of a well-to-do Roman middle-class couple. Guido's motives for entering this marriage may be a subject for controversy, but there is no doubt that it turned out to be an unsuccessful venture. He brought his child-bride and her parents home to his family mansion. Soon dissension developed between Guido and Pompilia's parents, and they returned to Rome leaving their daughter behind. Whatever the rights and wrongs of this family dispute may have been, Pompilia's parents, once back at home, took a step that was certainly not designed to charm their son-in-law. They publicly announced that Pompilia was not their daughter after all, but the offspring of a Roman prostitute. On the basis of this claim they instituted legal proceedings against Count Guido to recover their dowry.

Meanwhile, Pompilia was very unhappy with her husband. Under circumstances that were later to be the subject of considerable legal dispute, she arranged to flee to Rome in the company of Guiseppe Caponsacchi, a young nobleman of Arezzo who held the ecclesiastical office of canon. Count Guido intercepted the two fugitives en route. A prosecution was then instituted in Rome against Pompilia and Caponsacchi for elopement and adultery. It is not clear what the court's conclusion was as to the more interesting of the two charges, but the two defendants were punished very lightly, Caponsacchi being confined to a small town near Rome for three years and Pompilia being placed, perhaps without any formal judgment, in an institution for penitent women.

About one month later, Pompilia was released to the custody of her parents and shortly thereafter, on December 18, 1697, gave birth to a son. The news of the birth appears to have enraged Count Guido further. On the evening of January 2, 1698, Guido and four armed accomplices went to the house of Pompilia's parents and murdered them together with the young mother. The five assailants were tried, convicted, and executed for their crime in February 1698.

One of the most fascinating aspects of *The Ring and the Book* is the poet's insistence that the truth about human behavior does not consist of a single accurate statement from which all inconsistencies are sifted out and excluded. In Browning's view, to render a mature judgment on a human dispute one must first allow the actors in the drama to place their own widely varying interpretations on the actions and motives of themselves and their enemies, and one must also listen to the highly partisan arguments of the professional and lay adherents to the parties in the dispute. In order, in the words of G. K. Chesterton, to "depict the various strange ways in which a fact gets itself presented to the world," Browning tells the story of Guido's crime from the points of view of nine narrators: the pro-Guido man in the street ("Half-Rome"); the anti-Guido man in the street (the "Other Half-Rome"); the sophisticated newsreader ("Tertium Quid") who knows the issues but leaves the decisions to the professionals; Count Guido himself; Caponsacchi; Pompilia; counsel for the defense; counsel for the prosecution; and the Pope, who considered and rejected Guido's appeal.

Browning appears to find Guido guilty. He is not concerned with Guido's legal guilt, however, but with what G. K. Chesterton, in his essay on the poem, has called "spiritual guilt." To Browning, Guido was guilty of renouncing the power to feel or inspire love in favor of an empty pursuit of a career and of wealth; he was guilty in his assumption that his noble birth guaranteed him certain rewards withheld from common men and exempted him from their moral code.

Works regarding the legal sources of *The Ring and the Book* include John Marshall Gest, *The Old Yellow Book: Source of Browning's* The Ring and the Book (Philadelphia: Univ. of Pennsylvania Press, 1927); Beatrice Corrigan, *Curious Annals* (Toronto: Univ. of Toronto Press, 1956); Richard D. Altick and James F. Loucks II, *Browning's Roman Murder Story: A Reading of "The Ring and the Book"* (Chicago: Univ. of Chicago Press, 1968); Albert Borowitz, "The Ring and the Book and the Murder," in *A Gallery of Sinister Perspectives: Ten Crimes and a Scandal* (see B.27).

B.82 Büchner, Georg *Woyzeck.* In *Georg Büchner: The Complete Collected Works.* Trans. and commentary Henry J. Schmidt. New York: Avon, 1977.

■ This fragmentary drama, written between 1835 and 1837, was inspired by three murder cases in which the defendant's sanity was in dispute. The principal source was the trial of forty-one-year-old unemployed barber and former soldier Johann Christian Woyzeck, executed in 1824 for the stabbing death of his once-in-a-while mistress, the forty-six-year-old widow Johanna Christiane Woost, in Leipzig. Woyzeck, whose mental state is faithfully reflected in Büchner's play and its operatic setting in Alban Berg's *Wozzeck*, had a past history of unhappy and violent love affairs and was afflicted by supernatural apparitions and voices and by paranoid dreams of Masonic conspiracy. Increasingly disturbed by Woost's attentions to a rival, Woyzeck bought a knife. He met her by chance and took her home, putting his criminal plan out of his mind. However, when they entered the hallway and she refused him entrance, his murderous thoughts returned, and he stabbed her to death.

Medical experts battled over Woyzeck's sanity for three years before he was put to death. Most influential in supporting the defendant's criminal responsibility was the opinion of Councillor Johann Christian Clarus, physician of the city of Leipzig, who combined moralizing with scientific expertise. The rising youth, he opined, would learn from Woyzeck's example that "disinclination to work, gambling, drunkenness, illicit satisfaction of sexual lust and bad company" could lead to a similar fate. Clarus's views were opposed by Bamberg physician Carl Moritz Marc, who believed that Woyzeck suffered from insanity induced by physical illness. Büchner, who had himself received medical training, probably had as a teenager read reports of the Woyzeck case in a professional journal to which his father was a contributor.

The Schmolling and Diess cases have been identified as supplementary sources of Büchner's drama. In 1817 near Berlin, thirty-eight-year-old tobacco roller Daniel Schmolling murdered Henriette Lehne. His death sentence having been commuted to life imprisonment, he killed a fellow inmate in 1825. When the appeal of Schmolling on his insanity plea in the Lehne murder was heard by the Berlin court of appeals, a report was issued by E. T. A. Hoffmann, then serving as a judge on the court, who opined that a criminal could not escape the force of the law merely "because the motive for the crime could not be ascertained, and the otherwise mentally and physically healthy criminal simply says that a blind, irresistible impulse drove him to his action."

In the third murder case on which Büchner may have drawn, Johann Diess murdered his thirty-seven-year-old sweetheart, linen weaver Elisabetha Reuter, near Darmstadt in 1836. Diess died in prison four years later after having been determined to be sane. As in Büchner's *Woyzeck*, a child was born of Diess's love affair with his victim.

B.83 Bulwer Lytton, Edward *Pelham: or, The Adventures of a Gentleman.* 3 vols. London: Henry Colburn, 1828.

▪ Bulwer's novel is inspired by the 1823 ambush murder of crooked gambler William Weare by John Thurtell and his confederates in Hertfordshire. In 1824, the year of Thurtell's hanging, Bulwer Lytton claimed to have had two narrow escapes from would-be murderers with robbery on their minds; the first was a poor cottager with whom he lodged overnight on the way to Keswick, and the other a fellow pedestrian on a Scottish road who, after affronting him with rude remarks, ultimately pulled out a murderous-looking "life-preserver" (a sling shot) behind his back. These hair-raising experiences must have reinforced Bulwer-Lytton's interest in the fate of Weare in a lonely country lane. *Pelham*, however, was itself a hybrid creation that drew on a number of literary antecedents. It is regarded as one of the first of the so-called silver fork novels, portraying scenes of English high society, and it inspired the later works of Disraeli in the same genre. However, the murder narrative Bulwer Lytton interpolates in the action seems at odds with the book's prevailing light tone. With its dominant themes of revenge, pursuit, and detection, the subplot owes a heavy debt to William Godwin's *Caleb Williams* (1794). It is no accident that the murder victim in *Pelham*, Sir John Tyrrell, a dissolute nobleman addicted to gambling, has the same last name (with a slight variation in spelling) as Barnabas Tyrrel, the victim in Godwin's novel, though Bulwer Lytton, perhaps to disguise his borrowing, invokes in a chapter epigraph the example of still another Tyrrell, the assassin of the young princes in *Richard III*. In addition to reflecting Godwin's influence, Bulwer Lytton capitalized heavily on the popularity of Pierce Egan's *Life in London* by ending his narrative with a scene in the murderer's underground hideout, which Pelham penetrates in disguise after being given a lesson in criminal slang.

Within this familiar literary framework, Bulwer Lytton introduces characters and events from John Thurtell's murder. His readers would have identified the villainous Sir John Tyrrell, despite his high birth, with Weare, and the murderer, Tom Thornton, a boxing enthusiast and crooked gambler, with Thurtell. Thornton preys on English expatriates in Paris, pickings that will never run short, a friend of Pelham predicts, "because rogues are like spiders, and eat each other, when there is nothing else to catch." This prophecy is fulfilled when Thornton murders Tyrrell with the help of his accomplice Dawson (Hunt or Probert). The passage describing Pelham's discovery of the body would have reminded any English reader of the Thurtell-Hunt news stories of four years before:

> The ground over which [the horseman] passed was steeped in the moonshine, and I saw the long and disguising cloak in which he was enveloped, as clearly as by the light of day. I paused; and as I was following him with my looks, my eye fell upon some obscure object by the left side of the pool. I threw my horse's rein over the hedge, and firmly grasping my stick, hastened to the spot. As I approached the object, I perceived that it was a human figure; it was lying still and motionless; the limbs were half immersed in the water; the face was turned upwards; the side and throat were wet with a deep red stain,—it was of blood; the thin, dark hairs of the head were clotted together over a frightful and disfiguring contusion. I bent over the face in a shuddering and freezing silence. It was the countenance of Sir John Tyrrell.

Pelham brings Thornton to justice by securing the confession of Dawson, in which Thurtell's rumored vampirism takes on an added horror by being transformed into a calculating scheme to dispose of evidence: "Thornton's linen and hands were stained with blood. The former he took off, locked up carefully, and burned at the first opportunity; the latter he washed; and, that the water might not lead to detection, *drank it*."

B.84 Burke, Thomas *Murder at Elstree: or, Mr. Thurtell and His Gig.* London: Longmans, 1936.
■ This novella of the Thurtell-Hunt murder of 1823 begins with a description of a crooked fight near Norwich promoted by John Thurtell, in which a verbatim quotation of the gypsy

fortune-telling passage from George Borrow's *Lavengro* (see B.32) is incorporated, and ends as Thurtell on the scaffold has the "fleeting satisfaction" of recognizing Borrow in the crowd. Although marred by a heavily doom-laden style favored by the "had-he-but-known" school of crime writing, *Murder at Elstree* for the most part follows the reported facts with reasonable accuracy and provides plausible answers for some of the eternal riddles of the case. According to Burke, it was Joseph Hunt who originally suggested to Thurtell both that he murder gambler William Weare and that the crime be committed somewhere along the Elstree road. Thurtell is credited with fixing the precise murder locale at Phillimore Lodge and with recalling the "useful ponds" in the neighborhood. He is also freed of the stigma of having murdered without profit, for Burke hypothesizes that Thurtell found Weare's well-filled moneybag on his body and hid it before he brought his confederates to Gill's Hill Lane. Burke blames the failed rendezvous squarely on Hunt, "whose zest for the affair had passed out with the planning of it." While drinking at the White Lion in Edgware, Hunt sees Thurtell's gig pass by but does not tell Probert. Burke renders a lenient judgment on Thurtell's character. Before coming to London, Thurtell, a mixture of the bluffer and the gullible, was not a bad man but was drifting to bad: "The kind of life which appealed to him—the life of which the Prince Regent had been the examplar—had its being on a bad road; a road which only the man of positive good force can safely ride. Under good management Thurtell might have been a negatively decent man. Riding this road, he became, by stages imperceptible to himself, a desperate, but still not a positive, bad man." See Albert Borowitz, *The Thurtell-Hunt Murder Case: Dark Mirror to Regency England* (see B.29).

C

c.1 Cabanès, Augustin [Docteur Cabanès] *Les morts mystérieuses de l'histoire.* 2 series. Paris: Albin Michel, n.d.

■ The highlight of this examination into the medical causes of the deaths of France's rulers is an extended consideration of the fate of Louis XVII. Without choosing among any of the pretenders, Cabanès contented himself with the conclusion that the Dauphin did not die in the Temple. Why, otherwise, had the authorities failed to have the dead child's body identified by his sister, who occupied a neighboring cell and whose testimony would have been decisive?

c.2 Cable, George W[ashington] *Strange True Stories of Louisiana.* New York: Scribners, 1901.

■ Cable, a New Orleans novelist, authenticates the historicity of his accounts by including an introductory chapter explaining how he obtained the court records and autobiographical manuscripts on which his narratives are based; he also reproduces four photographs of his documentation among the illustrations of the work. Despite striving for historical accuracy, Cable acknowledges at the outset that "true stories are not often good art" and that the role of art in rendering history is "not so much to transcend nature as to make nature transcend herself."

Two linked tales in the book arise out of the American South's practice of slavery, which Cable indicts as ultimately responsible for the personal tragedies he recounts: "The two stories teach the same truth: that a public practice is answerable for whatever can happen easier with it than without it, no matter whether it must, or only may, happen."

In "Salome Müller, the White Slave," Cable revives the New Orleans trial of 1844 in which an olive-skinned Alsatian woman, sold into slavery as a child by a dealer who fraudulently represented that she was black, brought suit to recover her freedom. By chance, she had been recognized by relatives while working in her master's coffeehouse. Although her family identified Salome by birthmarks on her thighs, the slaveowner and his vendor prevailed at trial, arguing that the plaintiff's relatives were "imaginative and enthusiastic" Germans and referring to famous European impostures, such as that of the false Martin Guerre. On appeal, the Louisiana Supreme Court reversed, holding that Salome benefited from the presumption in favor of free birth. No evidence had been put forward that she was born of an African mother, and the evidence of her birthmarks was unimpeached: Salome went free after twenty-five years of servitude.

"The 'Haunted House' in Royal Street" tells of Madame Lalaurie, darling of New Orleans society who chained and abused her slaves in a wing of the Royal Street house that she acquired in 1831. When a young slave girl, whom Madame Lalaurie pursued with a whip, fell to her death from the roof of the house, the authorities imposed only a small fine. Madame Lalaurie's social triumphs continued, without her guests' "suspicion that she kept her cook in the kitchen by means of a twenty-four-foot chain fastened to her person and to the wall or floor." In 1834 the cook, chained as she was, intentionally set the house on fire. A crowd rushing in to help save Madame Lalaurie and her possessions came upon the maltreated and shackled slaves, whom she had seemed content to abandon to their fates. As news of the discovery spread, an angry mob gathered, but Madame Lalaurie fled the city in her coach, driven by the one black servant she had not abused.

Cable rounds out this tale of horror with an autobiographical and historical epilogue that enhances the significance of the story by relating Madame Lalaurie's brutality to the communal racism of the Old South. One day during the Reconstruction years, Cable sat in the lofty drawing room of Madame Lalaurie's house, which had been converted into a racially integrated girls' high school, despite the tradition that the building was haunted by the ghosts of tormented slaves. As he listened to the classes engaging in their annual examinations, Cable observed the rainbow of the students' complexions. In 1874 the White League made an abortive attempt to evict "colored" girls from the school, but three years later New Orleans schools were overhauled to achieve the separation of the races.

c.3 Cain, James M. *The Postman Always Rings Twice.* New York: Knopf, 1934.

■ Screenwriter Vincent Lawrence preached to James Cain that a strong narrative must turn on the "love rack," the magical moment when a couple falls in love. Cain asked Lawrence: "Why couldn't *the whole thing* be a love rack; why such attention to the one episode where they fall in love?" Lawrence agreed that Cain's idea was fruitful, and their later conversation about the murder of Albert Snyder by his wife Ruth and her lover Judd Gray (see G.38) served as the creative spark that Cain needed (see Roy Hoopes, *Cain* [New York: Holt, Rinehart & Winston, 1982], 231–33). Ironically, the version of the Snyder-Gray murder that Lawrence related to Cain was more fancy than fact: "I heard that when Ruth Snyder packed Gray off to Syracuse where he was to stay the night she murdered her husband, she gave him a bottle of wine, which he desperately wanted on the train. But he had no corkscrew with him and dared not ask the porter for one, for fear it would be the one thing they'd remember him by. When the police lab analyzed it, they found enough arsenic to kill a regiment of men. Did you ever hear that, Cain?"

This information, however inaccurate, "jelled" Cain's story line for his classic *roman noir*, *The Postman Always Rings Twice*. In the novel, drifter Frank Chambers arrives at a gas station and lunchroom in the San Fernando Valley that is run by middle-aged Nick Papadakis and his young wife, Cora. Frank and Cora fall in love and murder Nick in a successfully arranged automobile "accident." The postman, Death, rings a second time for each of the lovers: Cora is killed in a genuine automobile accident, and Frank is erroneously convicted of her murder.

c.4 Calvi, François de [F. D. C. Lyonnois] *Histoire générale des larrons* [General History of Thieves]. Rouen: Jacques Caillové, 1636.

■ In this early-seventeenth-century "general history of thieves," author de Calvi found it necessary to apologize for dealing with what appeared at first glance to be a repellent subject. In his preface, he insisted on the cautionary value of his work; readers would find reenforcement for the doctrine that idleness, guided by the Devil, led to criminal acts. The book is divided into three sections dealing, respectively, with the cruelty and malice of thieves, the tricks of cutpurses, and the stratagems of crooks. De Calvi's history includes many criminal narratives, including the murder of the Parisian Melander and the discovery of his assassins and the career of the cutpurse Maillard.

c.5 Calvino, Italo "A Beautiful March Day." In *Numbers in the Dark, and Other Stories*. Trans. Tim Parks. New York: Random House (Vintage Books), 1996.

■ Italo Calvino (1923–1985) was a member of the partisans during the German occupation of northern Italy in World War II. His short work "A Beautiful March Day" is the interior monologue of an unnamed conspirator awaiting the arrival of Caesar at the Roman Senate on March 15 (the Ides), 44 B.C. The narrator fears that the political significance of striking a blow against tyranny will be diminished because of the republicans' procrastination and the extinction of their bloody deed by the beauty of the Roman spring. As the assassin withdraws the dagger he thrust into the dictator's body, he is "overcome by a short of vertigo, a feeling of emptiness, of being alone, not here in Rome, today, but alone forever after, in the centuries to come, the fear that people won't understand what we did here today, that they won't be able to do it again, that they will remain indifferent as this beautiful calm morning in March." Thornton Wilder's novel *The Ides of March* is discussed at w.21.

c.6 Campbell, Marjorie Freeman *A Century of Crime: The Development of Crime Detection Methods in Canada.* Toronto: McClelland and Stewart, 1970.

■ A poet as well as a crime historian, Campbell emphasizes the human element in detection as well as the growth of forensic science and police administration. Dominant in the first half of the book, devoted to the nineteenth century, is the figure of Scottish-born American John Wilson Murray, who became one of Canada's most celebrated and self-laudatory detectives. After claiming principal credit for foiling a Confederate plot to capture Johnson Island in Lake Erie's Sandusky Bay and to burn Detroit, Cleveland, and Buffalo, Murray rose to the peak of Canada's Department of Criminal Investigation. Campbell illustrates his acumen by narrating some dazzling successes: the discovery and preservation of a footprint in a swamp convicting hired hand James B. Allison of murdering farm wife Emma Orr; the capture of master counterfeiter Edwin Johnson; and, his masterpiece, the assembling of damning evidence against Reginald Birchall, who fatally shot Frederick Cornwallis Benwell in Ontario's Blenheim Swamp after luring him there from their native England to inspect an illusory farming property (see w.2).

Each of Campbell's twentieth-century studies turns on application of a branch of forensic science. The 1962 conviction of flax grower Arthur Kendall for the decade-old murder of his wife, Helen, in the presence of their children was clinched by evidence of stubborn bloodstains on the floor of a cabin on Lake Huron. Equally unlucky was bank robber–murderer Joseph Herbert McAuliffe, identified by a fingerprint on a thumbnail-sized metal piece attached to a pocket of a blue suit coat he had abandoned in his flight. Ballistics tripped up Victor Ernest Hoffman, who senselessly shot eight victims at the Petersons' Saskatchewan farm in 1967. Hoffman's insanity did not dull his interest in firearms detection: he had tried unsuccessfully to disguise the rifling of his 22-caliber Browning weapon "by putting grinding compound in the barrel of the gun and firing a couple of boxes of shells through it. He also put sand in the barrel."

c.7 Camus, Albert *The Stranger.* Trans. Stuart Gilbert. New York: Knopf, 1946.

■ In his essay opposing capital punishment, "Réflexions sur la guillotine" (1957), Camus (1913–1960) attributes to his mother a story about the author's father, Lucien Auguste Camus, who died in the Battle of the Marne. When the murderer of a farm family was sentenced to death, Lucien Camus got up in the middle of the night so that he could reach the place of execution on time. Although he had been full of hatred for the condemned man, he returned home in distress and could not speak of his experience, and he suddenly began to vomit.

Meursault, the murderer in Albert Camus's novel *The Stranger*, relates a similar episode as he awaits his own execution: "I remembered a story Mother used to tell me about my father. I never set eyes on him. Perhaps the only things I really knew about him were what Mother had told me. One of these was that he'd gone to see a murderer executed. The mere thought of it turned his stomach. But he'd seen it through and, on coming home, was violently sick. At the time, I found my father's conduct rather disgusting. But now I understood; it was so natural. How had I failed to recognize that nothing was more important than an execution; that, viewed from one angle, it's the only thing that can genuinely interest a man?"

c.8 Canler, Louis *Mémoires de Canler, ancien chef de Sûreté*. 1862. Ed. and annotated Jacques Brenner. Paris: Mercure de France, 1968.
▪ Although he served as chief of the Paris Sûreté between 1849 and 1851, Canler is most justly famous for his four decades as detective, which are recorded in these memoirs (also available in an abridged English-language edition, *Autobiography of a French Detective from 1818 to 1858* [London: Ward & Lock, 1962]). Highlights of his reminiscences include his interrogation of Lacenaire (see L.3); his search for Fieschi and his accomplices, who had attempted to assassinate Louis Philippe; and Orsini's attack on Napoleon III.

c.9 Capote, Truman *Answered Prayers*. New York: Random House, 1987.
▪ In "La Côte Basque," the third and final section of this unfinished novel, Capote introduces among the restaurant's decadent patrons a "jazzy little carrot-top killer" whom he names Ann Hopkins. Ann is a thinly veiled portrait of parvenue Ann Woodward, who on an October night in 1955 killed her wealthy husband, William, with two shotgun blasts at their palatial Long Island home, claiming to have mistaken him for a prowler. Capote moves the shooting to Newport and invents a brief first marriage for his femme fatale. He had no doubt that the killing was a premeditated scheme to forestall a financially calamitous divorce and credits Ann Woodward with propagating the legend of the prowler in advance. Yet, a subsequent nonfictional account of the case absolves Ann (Susan Braudy, *This Crazy Thing Called Love: The Golden World and Fatal Marriage of Ann and Billy Woodward* [New York: Knopf, 1992]).

c.10 ———— "Handcarved Coffins: A Nonfiction Account of an American Crime." In *Music for Chameleons*. New York: Random House, 1980.
▪ The idea for this work had been proposed to Capote by Alvin Dewey of the Kansas Bureau of Investigation, with whom the author had become friendly during his researches for *In Cold Blood*. Dewey told him about a series of bizarre murders in Nebraska, including one instance in which the killer had used rattlesnakes as his murder weapon. Although Capote's subtitle calls the work nonfiction, and while he may have conducted interviews, "Handcarved Coffins," in which long dialogues alternate with descriptive passages, is mainly fictional. In interviews Capote declined to identify the murderer, who, he claimed, "was never accused of anything."
In 1978 a similar case was reported in Los Angeles. Paul Morantz, a lawyer who had won a judgment against the cultlike group Synanon on behalf of some defectors, was bitten by a four-foot rattlesnake found in his mailbox; Morantz survived the bite and later charged Synanon members with carrying out a "reign of terror." In 1980 Synanon founder Charles Dederich and two others pleaded no contest to charges that they had solicited an assault and conspired to murder Morantz. As a part of a plea bargain that did not require him to serve jail time, Dederich agreed to give up control of Synanon. He died in 1997.

C.11 ———— *In Cold Blood.* New York: Random House, 1966.

▪ Capote's true-crime masterpiece is a compelling narrative of two events that, in the author's view, equally constituted the taking of lives "in cold blood": the 1959 murder of Kansas farmer Herbert Clutter, his wife, Bonnie, and their two children, Nancy and Kenyon, by Richard Hickock and Perry Smith in the cheated hope of finding a hoard of cash in the farmhouse; and the 1965 hangings of Hickock and Smith. When Capote first proposed his book project to the *New Yorker,* the killers were still unknown, and he proposed to sketch the portrait of "a small, strange town, a town in the grip of an unsolved mass murder." The author's famous charm ultimately seduced the townspeople into becoming his willing collaborators, and after the murderers were arrested, he established a close relationship with them as well, particularly with the diminutive Perry Smith, whose fondness for uncommon words may have struck a responsive chord.

Capote stirred controversy by claiming that in his account of the Clutter murders, he had invented a new literary genre, the "nonfiction novel." What Capote suggested by this term was "a narrative form that employed all the techniques of fictional art, but was nevertheless immaculately factual"; in order to do narrative reporting properly, the writer "must be able to empathize with personalities outside his usual imaginative range, mentalities unlike his own, kinds of people he would never have written about had he not been forced to by encountering them inside the journalistic situation." To the extent that Capote's method rests on empathetic recreation of emotions and on invention or extension of conversations or events that neither he nor his informants could have witnessed, the so-called "nonfiction novel" is a logical outgrowth of the pioneering nineteenth-century crime studies of Thomas De Quincey and Celia Thaxter.

Capote's technique has inspired a recent best-selling French nonfiction novel, Emmanuel Carrère's *The Adversary: A True Story of Monstrous Deception,* trans. Linda Coverdale (New York: Metropolitan Books, 2001).

c.12 Carlyle, Thomas *The Diamond Necklace.* Boston: Houghton Mifflin, 1913.

▪ Arguing that the Age of Romance never appears romantic to itself but is in fact unceasing, Carlyle cites the example of the Diamond Necklace Affair that disgraced Marie Antoinette on the eve of the French Revolution. The central figure was the swindler Jeanne de la Motte, whose genius, according to Carlyle, lay in uniting two fixed ideas: the need of court jeweler Boehmer to dispose of the diamond necklace he had made as a speculation, and the obsessive desire of worldly Cardinal Louis de Rohan to win the favor of the queen. "Countess" de la Motte and her confederates persuaded Boehmer and Rohan that Marie Antoinette wanted the necklace, the cardinal signed a purchase contract in her behalf, and the countess made off with the priceless jewelry. Carlyle is grudging in his estimate of Jeanne de la Motte; while conceding her dramaturgic and histrionic talent, he sees in her no "strength of transcendent audacity, amounting to the bastard-heroic."

c.13 Carr, John Dickson *The Burning Court.* New York: Harper, 1937.

▪ This is one of the masterpieces of Golden Age mystery fiction in which the author keeps the reader in suspense as to whether the arsenic poisoning of Miles Despard and the disappearance of his body from a sealed granite crypt can be explained rationally or only by supernatural agency. Evidence accumulates that Ted Stevens's wife, Marie, is a witch who recurrently comes back as the "nondead." She bears an uncanny resemblance to a nineteenth-century poisoner as well as to the Marquise de Brinvilliers, who was executed for serial killings in France's "Age of Arsenic" during the reign of Louis XIV. Sanity appears to triumph in the end, for crime expert Gaudan Cross provides persuasive explanations for the mysteries surrounding the death of Despard and his vanishing corpse. In the Epilogue, however, another plot twist awaits: Marie Stevens, Connecticut housewife, is revealed to be a revenant witch who killed Despard and stole his body by supernatural means, as her poor husband, Ted, had feared.

c.14 ———— *The Murder of Sir Edmund Godfrey.* New York: Harper, 1936.

■ In 1678, Sir Edmund Berry Godfrey, an English Protestant magistrate who had heard testimony from Titus Oates revealing the "Papist Plot" to overthrow the government, was found strangled and stabbed with his own sword on Primrose Hill south of London. Carr casts his narrative of the unsolved crime into the form of a detective story. "Let the evidence not all be thrown at us in a lump," he proclaimed in explaining his approach, "but let it grow up as the story unfolds, so that each new turn is a surprise to us as it was to those who saw it happen." Adopting the conclusion of J. G. Muddiman in his article "The Mystery of Sir E. B. Godfrey" (*National Review* [Sept. 1924]), Carr identifies the killer as a brutal nobleman who had committed many acts of murder and violence, Philip Herbert, seventh Earl of Pembroke. The so-called Mad Peer had been indicted for a murder earlier in 1678 by a grand jury on which Sir Edmund Godfrey had served as foreman.

Stephen Knight, in *The Killing of Justice Godfrey* (London: Granada, 1984), concurs with Muddiman and Carr about Pembroke's guilt but provides a political motive for the assassination of Godfrey. He theorizes that Pembroke was the "hit man" of a group of extremist republican conspirators who punished Godfrey, a member of their group, for his "betrayal" of their cause.

c.15 Carter, Dan T. *Scottsboro: A Tragedy of the American South.* Rev. ed. Baton Rouge: Louisiana State Univ. Press, 1979.

■ This is an authoritative history of the "Scottsboro Boys." In 1931 nine black youths were charged by fellow hoboes, Victoria Price and Ruby Bates, white women of dubious reputation, with having raped them on a moving freight train near Scottsboro, Alabama. Although Price's testimony was contradictory, Bates recanted her accusations, and the medical evidence supported the defense position that no sexual attack had occurred, most Alabamians rallied behind the prosecution. This strident majority considered the defendants' execution as necessary to protect the white womanhood of the South against an inferior and dangerous race. Carter, however, demonstrates that other factors complicated the legal representation of the Scottsboro defendants. For a long time the Communist Party (and its International Labor Defense) engaged in a bitter struggle with the NAACP for control of the defense and stoked the fears of Southerners that the Scottsboro trials were being used as a pretext for red agitation. When Samuel Leibowitz served as chief defense counsel, he became the focus of courtroom argument and rabid journalism that appealed to prejudices against Jews and New Yorkers who were seen as intruding into Alabama's affairs. Leibowitz added thunder to the atmosphere by public attacks on the primitivism of Alabama's citizenry.

Carter follows the tortuous path of the Scottsboro cases through the courts and recounts the heartbreaking efforts of the defendants' lawyers and advocates to win their freedom. Even a personal appeal by President Franklin D. Roosevelt to Georgia's governor Bibb Graves failed to win paroles, and the last prisoner, Andy Wright (who had violated an earlier parole), was not freed until 1950.

In his original edition, Carter reported that the Scottsboro Boys' accusers had died in 1961. His information turned out to be erroneous. In 1977, Victoria Price (then Mrs. Street) failed in her suit alleging that the telecast of "Judge Horton and the Scottsboro Boys," based on Carter's book, had caused her to suffer "grave and lasting damage by having her privacy invaded and her peace of mind disturbed" and did "falsely and without foundation make plaintiff out to be guilty of committing perjury."

As his epigraph, Carter quotes from Kay Boyle's 1937 poem "A Communication to Nancy Cunard" (*Collected Poems of Kay Boyle* [Port Townsend, Wash.: Copper Canyon Press, n.d.], 66–70), which portrays the Scottsboro Boys and their accusers as secret sharers:

Not girls or men, Negroes or white, but
people with this in common:
People that no one had use for, had nothing
to give to, no place to offer
But the cars of a freight-train . . .

c.16 Casselari, René *Dramas of French Crime: Being the Exploits of the Celebrated Detective René Casselari.* London: Hutchinson, n.d.

■ Casselari was for twenty years a detective commissary of the Sûreté. His most celebrated cases included the theft of the Mona Lisa and the pursuit of the Bonnot bank robbers. One of his glamorous assignments was to enlist apache queen Casque d'Or's help in the investigation of her old flame Hannier, an antique dealer suspected of complicity in the robbery of the Amiens museum.

c.17 Castelot, André *Destins hors-série de l'histoire.* Paris: Perrin, 1963.

■ This collection of thirty-five historical sketches includes short pieces on Charlotte Corday, Dr. Ignace Guillotin, Mata Hari, the Mayerling suicides, and Madame Steinheil.

c.18 —— *Drames et tragédies de l'histoire.* Paris: Perrin, 1966.

■ Castelot continues his investigation of historical mysteries, including the assassination of Henri IV, the Calas case, the Lindbergh kidnapping, and the Anastasia mystery.

c.19 [Celebrated Trials Series] *Celebrated Trials.* 6 vols. Gen. ed. Jonathan Goodman. Newton Abbot: David & Charles, 1973–76.

■ This unhappily short-lived series of British trials, under the general editorship of crime historian and novelist Jonathan Goodman, established high standards from the outset by selecting extremely distinguished authors to introduce and edit each volume. The subjects of the trials and their respective editors are as follows:

- Trial of Ian Brady and Myra Hindley (the Moors Murder Case). Ed. Jonathan Goodman.
- Trial of Ruth Ellis, who murdered her lover, race car driver David Blakely in 1955 and became the last woman to be hanged in Great Britain. Her case inspired the film *Dance with a Stranger* (1985). Ed. Jonathan Goodman and Patrick Pringle.
- Trial of George Archer-Shee, a Royal Naval College cadet accused in 1908 of the theft and forgery of a five-shilling postal order. George's father brought suit against the Crown for his son's vindication, but before any verdict, the Admiralty accepted George's claim of innocence. This is the case on which Terence Rattigan based his play *The Winslow Boy* (1946). Ed. Ewen Montagu.
- Trial of Walter Graham Rowland, hanged for hammering Olive Balchin to death in 1946. Cecil concludes that he was plainly guilty, although David John Ware confessed to the crime after Rowland's death sentence was imposed (only to withdraw the confession shortly thereafter). Ed. Henry Cecil.
- Two murder trials of Brian Donald Hume (see w.14). Ed. Ivan Butler.
- Trial of Elvira Barney, daughter of Sir John and Lady Mullens, acquitted of murdering her lover in her Belgravia flat in 1932. Ed. Peter Cotes (original director of Agatha Christie's *The Mousetrap*).

c.20 Cellini, Benvenuto *The Life of Benvenuto Cellini.* [An autobiography begun in 1558.] Trans. John Addington Symonds. 2 vols. London: John C. Nimmo, 1888.

■ Florentine goldsmith and sculptor Cellini (1500–1571) committed many acts of violence, including two murders that he describes cold-bloodedly in his memoirs: the ambush stabbing of a corporal of the Roman city guard who had killed Cellini's brother, Cecchino, in a street affray; and the lethal dagger attack on goldsmith Pompeo, who had insulted him. Cellini calmly recalls the latter assault: "I drew a little dagger with a sharpened edge, and breaking the line of his defenders, laid my hands upon his breast so quickly and coolly, that none of them were able to prevent me. Then I aimed to strike him in the face; but fright made him turn his head round; and I stabbed him just beneath the ear."

When sculptor Bandinelli reproached Cellini for his murders, he responded haughtily: "At any rate, the men I have killed do not shame me so much as your bad statues shame you; for the earth covers my victims, whereas yours are exposed to the view of the world."

American playwright and film writer Edwin Justus Mayer evoked Cellini's hot temper in the 1924 stage comedy *The Firebrand* (New York: Boni & Liveright). In Act I Mayer's vainglorious Cellini, in successive versions of a brawl in which he left two men dead, progressively exaggerates the odds he faced. Mayer later adapted his script for the book of

The Firebrand of Florence, a 1945 operetta-like musical comedy, with music and lyrics by Kurt Weill and Ira Gershwin.

c.21 Cendrars, Blaise [pseudonym of Frédéric Sauser] *Moravagine.* Paris: Bernard Grasset, 1926.

▪ Blaise Cendrars's serial killer and revolutionary destroyer, Moravagine, originated in a chance encounter made by the author in a workers' restaurant in Berne, Switzerland, in 1907: "Seated crosswise on a bench, he wolfed down his plate of potatoes and a large cup of coffee with milk. Since he had no bread, I paid for a round loaf. As he didn't know where to go to sleep, I took him home with me. He was a sorry specimen who had just been released from prison. He had raped two young girls. He had been sentenced to twenty-five years. He was a poor devil who was completely stupefied. And who was ashamed. . . . His name was Meunier or Ménier. It was especially his appearance that stuck in my mind."

The novel's narrator, a physician, frees Prince Moravagine from an asylum where he was committed after stabbing his wife to death. The madman and his liberator become inseparable friends and engage in increasingly violent adventures on three continents, capped by a failed terrorist plot in support of the Russian Revolution of 1905. Along the way, Moravagine's homicidal life intersects with Europe's crimes, contemporary and past. Moravagine disembowels women in Berlin and is compared to Jack the Ripper; he arrives in Paris when the city is gripped by fear of the Bonnot Gang; and he dies during World War I as a military hospital patient in a cell once occupied by the Man in the Iron Mask on the Ile Sainte-Marguérite.

The narrator wonders at Maravagine's indifference to his victims' sufferings and speculates that he is unconscious of their separate identity, regarding them instead as doubles of his own masochistic self. The novel's rebelliousness, and the prominence it gives to utilitarian objects and soulless science from which emotional associations are stripped away, amply justify the remark of Cendrars critic J.-H. Lévesque that "all of Dadaism is present in *Moravagine*."

c.22 Champagnac, J.-B. J. *Causes célèbres anciennes et nouvelles.* 8 vols. Paris: Ménard, 1833.

▪ The compiler justifies his work by referring to the growth of readers' taste for the "horrible" after the fall of the First Empire. Organizing crime narratives in chronological order beginning with the early seventh century, the series draws on general histories of France and its regions as sources for the earlier periods when writers, obsessed with lives of the high and mighty, considered crime only tangentially. Starting with the seventeenth century, it utilizes collections of causes célèbres, such as those of Gayot de Pitaval, Richer and des Essarts; and some nineteenth-century accounts rely on the *Gazette des Tribunaux*. A list of the principal works consulted is included in an index.

c.23 Chikamatsu Monzaemon *Four Major Plays of Chikamatsu.* Trans. Donald Keene. New York: Columbia Univ. Press, 1998.

■ This collection includes three domestic puppet plays by Chikamatsu Monzaemon (1653–1725), including two love-suicide tragedies. The first of these, *The Love Suicides at Sonezaki* (1703), inspired a vogue for such suicides in life as well as on the stage, a parallel to the West's Werther mania. Also in the volume is Chikamatsu's *The Love Suicides at Amijima* (1721), which is often acclaimed as the dramatist's masterpiece; traditional sources (which Keene regards as unreliable) relate that the suicides occurred on November 1720, two months before the premiere. The hero Jihei loves both a prostitute Koharu and his wife, Osan, and can preserve his moral purity only by suicide. Koharu decides to join him in death, enunciating a noble religious motive: "If I can save living creatures at will when once I mount a lotus calyx in Paradise and become a Buddha, I want to protect women of my profession, so that never again will there be love suicides."

c.24 **Christie, Agatha** *By the Pricking of My Thumbs*. London: Crime Club, 1968.

■ This is a rare example of a Christie whodunit in which crime history is expressly invoked. Tommy Beresford, searching for his wife, Tuppence, interviews Dr. Murray, who advises him of the death of Mrs. Moody of a morphine overdose and recalls poisoners of the past, mostly under fictitious names. An English killer to whom the doctor gives his correct name is the well-known Herbert Rowse Armstrong of Hay-on-Wye (see F.21): "You remember in the case of Armstrong, anyone who had in any way offended him or insulted him or, indeed, if he even thought anyone had insulted him, that person was quickly asked to tea and given arsenic sandwiches. A sort of intensified touchiness. His first crimes were obviously mere crimes for personal advantage. Inheriting of money. The removal of a wife so that he could marry another woman."

Christie's knowledge of crime history comes to the fore in a famous short story "Philomel Cottage," which appeared in her collection *The Listerdale Mystery* (London: Collins, 1934). The heroine of the story, Alix Martin, foils the murderous designs of her new husband, Gerald, in their rustic cottage. Displaying, like her creator Christie, a gift for inventing crime fiction, Alix induces Gerald's fatal heart attack by persuading him that she has murdered two previous spouses and has now poisoned his coffee. In her narrative of imagined crimes, Alix fabricates an autobiographical detail drawn from Christie's own life: "During the war I worked for a time in a hospital dispensary. There I had the handling of all kinds of rare drugs and poisons."

The character and crimes of Gerald Martin are reminiscent of two serial bride-killers, George Joseph Smith and Henri Désiré Landru (the latter name may be the source of Gerald's previous Gallic nom de guerre, Charles Lemaitre). (See B.26.) Gerald's habit of recording the progress of his crime in a diary may have been inspired by the Moat Farm murderer, Samuel Herbert Dougal (see w.15). (The Borowitz True Crime Collection owns a leaf of this revealing diary.) Gerald's predilection for burying his victim in the cellar and his American past echo the career of Dr. Hawley Harvey Crippen. In the course of telling her fictitious crimes, Alix claims to have administered a fatal dose of hyoscine, the drug that Crippen used to dispose of his wife.

In a 1936 stage version, *Love from a Stranger*, by actor Frank Vosper (revived in the 2001 season of the Shaw Festival at Niagara-on-the-Lake, Ontario), the serial murderer (renamed Bruce Lovell) and a country physician, Dr. Gribble, share a passion for the *Notable British Trials* series (N.7); a fictitious volume in the series turns out to be devoted to Lovell's past crimes. Vosper played the role of Lovell in the premiere of the play. In 1937 his naked and bruised body washed ashore near Eastbourne after he had gone missing at an end-of-voyage party on an ocean liner from New York.

c.25 Churchill, Caryl, with Orlando Gough and Ian Spink *Lives of the Great Poisoners.* London: Methuen, 1993.

■ This comedy of poison divides roles among actors, singers, and dancers. The first section portrays Dr. Hawley Harvey Crippen's murder of his wife, Cora, and his shipboard arrest. Cora is then transformed into Medea, who takes revenge on her faithless lover Jason and his new bride Creusa. In the final sequence of scenes, Medea is reincarnated as Mme. de Brinvilliers, the central figure in France's seventeenth-century Age of Arsenic. Throughout the play, a Chorus of Poisons dances its accompaniment to the kaleidoscopic events. Churchill also introduces an "industrial chemist," Midgley, who, by the invention of leaded petrol and freon, is responsible for atmospheric pollution that outdoes the poisonings of the play's celebrated criminals.

Perhaps the most amusing lines are given to Brinvilliers and her lover and partner in murder, Sainte-Croix. Each would dearly like to kill the other but the task is daunting, for while commanding a vast inventory of poisons, they both know the antidotes.

c.26 Cicero, Marcus Tullius *Murder Trials.* Trans. and intro. Michael Grant. New York: Dorset, 1986.

■ Cicero's speeches as defense counsel are entitled to be regarded as literature, however narrowly defined, because they were undoubtedly polished and elaborated with an eye to publication. The four orations included in this volume are the Roman advocate's defenses of:

- Sextus Roscius the Younger, of Ameria in southern Umbria, acquitted of murdering his father. In this early triumph of his legal career, Cicero argued that Sextus Roscius the Elder had been murdered at the behest of an influential freedman, Chrysonus (a favorite of the right-wing dictator Sulla), with the objective of obtaining control of the dead man's estate.
- Aulus Cluentius Habitus, apparently acquitted of two criminal charges: bribing a jury to find his hated stepfather, Oppianicus, guilty of an attempt to poison him; and plotting to poison Oppianicus. Despite Cicero's professional lapse (viewed from the standpoint of modern ethics) in changing sides in the tortuous course of this family dispute, his defense of the rule of law remains stirring: "Law is the bond which secures these our privileges in the commonwealth, the foundation of our liberty, the fountain-

head of justice. Within the law are reposed the mind and heart, the judgment and the conviction of the state. The state without law would be like the human body without mind—unable to employ the parts which are to it as sinews, blood and limbs. The magistrates who administer the law, the jurors who interpret it—all of us in short—obey the law to the end that we may be free" (see Albert Borowitz, "M. Tullius Cicero for the Defense," in *Innocence and Arsenic: Studies in Crime and Literature*, 100–115 [see B.28]).

- Gaius Rabirius, tried inconclusively thirty-seven years after the fact (perhaps at the instance of Julius Caesar) for complicity in the assassination of tribune Lucius Appuleius Saturninus in 100 B.C.
- Deiotarus, a prince in central Asia Minor whom Cicero defended against an allegation of plotting the ambush killing of Julius Caesar, then dictator. Cicero's speech was made before Caesar in the dictator's own house, but no ruling was ever made.

c.27 Claretie, Georges   *Drames et comédies judiciaires: Chroniques du palais.* Paris: Berger-Levrault, 1911.

■ In a warm preface, Maître Charles Chenu, former head of the Paris Bar, praises *Le Figaro*'s trial reporter Georges Claretie's ability to present in several hundred lines a long hearing of four or five hours and to turn the court transcript into a "personal work, where light is cast in the right places, unnecessary details are lost in shadow, the soul of each character is revealed and his elusive secrets fathomed."

Highlights of 1910 cases reported by Claretie include:

- The condemnation of Jean Liabeuf, an apache who wore armbands with pointed iron spikes. Liabeuf murdered a policeman and wounded five others when they confronted him during his pursuit of two officers against whom he sought revenge for sending him to prison. In a related case, radical journalist Gustave Hervé was sentenced to four years' imprisonment under France's press laws for praising Liabeuf's action as not lacking "a certain beauty, a certain grandeur."
- The conviction of two soldiers, Graby and Michel, for the train murder of Mme. Gouin that netted them five francs. Michel was ordered to serve twenty years of hard labor, and Graby's death sentence was commuted. No military man had been shot since 1874, according to Claretie, who notes wryly, "When one commits a murder, there is every advantage to be a soldier."
- The massacre of five members of a farm household by a pair of teenagers, Richard Jacquiard, age sixteen, and Charles Vienny, age fifteen. Jacquiard's death penalty was commuted to life imprisonment, and Vienny was sentenced to serve twenty years in a correctional facility. At the trial, lawyers wrangled about "the influence of reading on these young malleable brains," but Claretie quotes Victor Hugo: "Don't cut off this head; educate it."
- The bizarre strangulation of three patients in an insane asylum by a male nurse,

Thabuis. The defense pled doubt, partly on the basis of the fact that four mental patients served as witnesses, and a sentence of seven years' imprisonment was imposed.

c.28 Claude, Antoine François *Mémoires de M. Claude.* 10 vols. Paris: Rouff, 1881–83.

■ When Monsieur Claude first met the young Prince Louis Napoleon (who would one day appoint him chief of the Sûreté under the Second Empire, 1859–75), he was unfavorably impressed. Disguised as a workman, the prince was paying a visit to his mistress at her father's underworld tavern, the *Lapin Blanc*, just as the girl was ordering a murderous attack on Claude in retribution for an earlier investigation. From this moment on, Claude had "always felt convinced that Prince Louis was the original of Prince Rodolphe, the hero of [Eugène Sue's] *Mystères de Paris*."

Highlights of Claude's police recollections include:

- Felice Orsini's bombing assassination attempt on the life of Napoleon III, of which Claude claimed to have had advance warning from a palace spy he calls Madame X.
- The fruitless pursuit of an Alsatian named Jud, the railroad assassin of Judge Poinsot of the Imperial Court.
- Jean-Baptiste Troppmann's murders of the Kincks. Claude believes that Troppmann did not act alone, and he hints darkly that "political causes were concerned in these murders." There is no doubt that he suspected Germany's involvement, for he asserts: "Ever since the Jud affair, I knew from what quarter blew the wind of assassination."
- Prince Pierre Bonaparte's murder of liberal reporter Victor Noir, who had called on him with a companion to present his editor's challenge to a duel because of a journalistic dispute concerning Corsican politics. The ubiquitous Madame X informed Claude that Noir's visit was intended to entice the fiery prince into a violent affray in which he would be outnumbered.

There is an abridged English translation of Claude's memoirs, *Memoirs of Monsieur Claude, Chief of Police under the Second Empire*, trans. Katherine Prescott Wormeley (Boston: Houghton Mifflin, 1907).

c.29 Clouston, J. Storer *His First Offense.* London: Philip Allan, 1934.

■ First published in 1911, this is a merciless and delightful sendup of the Crippen case, crime journalism, and amateur detectives. The imbroglio begins harmlessly when Irwin Molyneux, scholarly essayist and covert thriller writer, and his imperious wife, Harriet, lose their cook just before they are to give a dinner for Irwin's demanding cousin, the Bishop of Bedford. Harriet competently prepares the meal but vanishes from sight so that her demeaning culinary activity will not become known to the bishop. Scotland Yard, private sleuths, and the press jump to the conclusion that Molyneux has murdered his wife, buried her dismembered body in his garden, and fled with the parlormaid to America. Marcel Carné converted the novel into the 1937 film *Drôle de drame* (also called

Bizarre, Bizarre) with a script by Jacques Prévert that introduces a topsy-turvy Jack the Ripper—an animal lover who murders butchers.

c.30 Clune, Frank   *The Kelly Hunters: The Authentic, Impartial History of the Life and Times of Edward Kelly, the Ironclad Outlaw.* Sydney: Angus & Robertson, 1955.

■ This study of outlaw Ned Kelly, perhaps the most famous Australian in whatever walk of life, is the fruit of the author's two decades of research, documented by an extensive bibliography. The title refers both to the forces of law and order that tracked Ned to a climactic shootout at Glenrowan and to authors, like Clune, who have searched for grains of truth in mountains of legend.

Although Clune has no doubt that Kelly was wrong to become an enemy of society and that his capture and hanging were inevitable, he has much to say in the outlaw's defense. Out of respect for the bravery of its famous "bushranger" (an outlaw who roams the "bush"), Australians have a saying, "as game as Ned Kelly." Ned's father was John "Red" Kelly of County Tipperary, and his paternal grandmother came from the Cody clan that gave America Buffalo Bill. After his transportation to Australia for stealing two pigs, Red tried to live quietly, but police persecution of the Kellys and of the Quinns (the family of Red's wife, Ellen) resulted in jail time and bitterness for the youthful Ned. After he turned to horse stealing, the police, on the basis of perjured testimony, charged Ned, his brother, Dan, and his mother, Ellen, with conspiring to murder Constable Fitzpatrick and imposed a three-year jail sentence on Mrs. Kelly. A police hunt for Ned and Dan Kelly and two comrades ensued under orders to shoot to kill. The result was a catastrophe for the Kelly hunters; at the "battle" of Stringybark Creek, three policemen were shot to death by the Kellys. The Australian authorities responded by "outlawing" the gang members, whom anyone could now shoot on sight as if they were predatory beasts.

From this fatal shoot-out dates the so-called Kelly War, during which Ned and his three gang members staged a pair of startling bank robberies to procure funds for their survival on the run and for aid to their indigent families. Expecting a showdown with the police, Ned reversed a biblical injunction: he beat into suits of armor the moldplates that he removed from stolen plowshares. The gang wore the armor only once, when they were besieged by overwhelming police forces at Glenrowan in 1880, in an encounter the Kellys intentionally provoked by assassinating a police spy who had betrayed them. Ned was wounded and taken alive; one comrade was shot dead, and two others apparently swallowed poison. Before his execution at age twenty-five, Ned's mother admonished him: "Mind you die like a Kelly."

Unlike Jesse James, whom many Americans admire, Ned Kelly never killed civilians who had done him no harm. Perhaps this fact, together with the suffering of his family at the hands of the corrupt police and the strange armor he fashioned for his Armageddon, contributed to his immortality.

Ned Kelly appears in a series of paintings and drawings by the twentieth-century Australian artist Sidney Nolan.

c.31 Cohen, Patricia Cline *The Murder of Helen Jewett: The Life and Death of a Prostitute in Nineteenth-Century New York.* New York: Knopf, 1998.

■ Patricia Cline Cohen succeeds in restoring the rich interior life of a victim commonly dismissed as a generic prostitute. The sensational 1836 axe and arson murder in a New York City brothel was immediately taken up by a massive press campaign waged in penny papers, crime pamphlets, and urban newspapers. The rivalrous journalists presented different views of the victim that ranged from "degraded wretch" to "an American [Madame] de Staël" whose literary taste and romantic epistolary style set her apart from other "girls of the town." Cohen points out that Jewett used letters partly "to fashion herself as a literary romantic" and a woman of refinement and cultivation; at the same time, she designed her correspondence to flatter and manipulate her clients and to control the course of their relationships.

To the reform press the literary prostitute was a warning to girls against the evils of reading novels. Jewett had read "the pernicious works of Bulwer," and Byron's portrait "hung conspicuously in her chamber." *The Journal of Public Morals* admonished readers in the month following the murder: "Avoid the perusal of novels . . . it is impossible to read them without injury."

Young men, too, were cautioned at evening meetings against licentiousness and the temptation that lurked in the city. The reformers blamed the corruption of young men on their employers, who introduced them to theaters and brothels to entertain customers, and on the police, who protected the city's red light districts. Cohen states, "The Men's Moral Reform group basically sided with the unfortunate young men of New York, sucked into temptations sanctioned by the police and the mercantile elite."

Jewett's client, the nineteen-year-old clerk Richard P. Robinson, was arrested for her murder. To all appearances Robinson fit the reformers' description of an innocent in the big city. This image began to dissipate after the discovery of his diary revealing his profligacy and sexual depravity.

Despite strong evidence linking him to the weapon and the scene of the crime, Robinson was acquitted after fifteen minutes of jury deliberation. The outcome angered the public, and a week after the verdict a joke circulated that Robinson had had the services of six lawyers—the three defense counsel, two prosecutors, and the trial judge.

Cohen speculates about two possible murder motives. In a letter to Robinson, Jewett had threatened to reveal some wrongdoing on his part, perhaps embezzlement from his employer. A second impulse to murder may have arisen from Robinson's inability to endure the surprising emotional intensity of his relationship with Jewett. Cohen suggests that he may have found the solution to his Jewett problem on the stage of the Bowery Theater, which presented a dramatization of Theodore Fay's novel *Norman Leslie*, based on the trial of Levi Weeks for the 1799 New York murder of his fiancée, Juliana (Gulielma) Sands, which resulted in Weeks's acquittal.

Nathaniel Hawthorne, who took a great interest in the trial of Robinson, admired the beauty of Helen Jewett's wax figure in a Boston exhibit.

c.32 Collins, Wilkie *The Moonstone*. 1868. Intro. Vincent Starrett. New York: Limited Editions Club, 1959.

■ This tale of the peregrinations of the Moonstone, a diamond stolen from a Hindu temple, is the first English detective novel. Collins's plot is an ingenious invention. In a somnambulistic spell induced by laudanum, Franklin Blake takes the Moonstone from a cabinet of his cousin Rachel Verinder, who has inherited the gem. Still unconscious, Blake entrusts the diamond for safekeeping to Godfrey Ablewhite, who retains the jewel for himself, only to suffer death as a consequence of his dishonesty.

This fanciful story is deeply rooted in crime history. From G. C. King's *Natural History of Precious Stones* (London, 1865), Collins, in preparation for his novel, "copied out passages about crimes committed for Indian diamonds and about bad-luck superstitions surrounding such large ones as the Kohinoor and the Orloff in the Czar of Russia's scepter" (see Nuel Pharr Davis, *The Life of Wilkie Collins* [Urbana: Univ. of Illinois Press, 1956], 250).

Other important elements in *The Moonstone* derive from Victorian crimes. In 1860 little Francis Kent was stabbed and almost decapitated in the family mansion outside the village of Road, near Trowbridge. His half-sister Constance was arrested for the crime. At a preliminary hearing, it was learned that one of Constance's three nightdresses was missing. Inspector Whicher, who had taken over the case, suspected that the missing garment was bloodstained and had been destroyed by Constance to conceal her guilt. The evidence against the young girl, however, was insufficient to support prosecution. In 1865 the case returned to the headlines with the news that Constance, who had entered a convent in France, had confessed the murder to the Bow Street magistrates.

In Collins's novel, Inspector Whicher (who in 1850 had appeared in thin disguise as Sergeant Witchem in a series on London's detective police in *Household Words*, edited by Charles Dickens), becomes Sergeant Cuff, called on to investigate the disappearance of the Moonstone. Like Whicher, he suspects the daughter of the house (Rachel Verinder) of the crime and speculates that she has disposed of an incriminating nightgown stained not with blood, as in the Kent murder, but with fresh varnish.

Richard Altick, in *Deadly Encounters* (1986; see A.8) has identified the Northumberland Street tragedy of 1861 as the source of another episode in *The Moonstone*. In the Northumberland Street case, Major William Murray was lured to a deathtrap by his unknown love rival, moneylender William Roberts, but was able to save his life by a counterattack on his assailant. Collins adapts this melodramatic encounter by having Godfrey Ablewhite induced to enter a Northumberland Street apartment, where he is blindfolded, gagged, and searched.

c.33 —— *The Woman in White*. 3 vols. London: Sampson Low, 1860.

■ The imprisonment of Laura Fairlie in an asylum as part of a plot to seize her fortune was inspired by the case of the Marquise Marie de Douhault (see L.19). Collins read an account of the case in Maurice Méjean's *Recueil des causes célèbres et des arrêts qui les ont décidées* (1808).

c.34 Colombani, Roger   *L'affaire Weidmann.* Paris: Albin Michel, 1989.

■ Beginning with the botched kidnapping of an American tourist, the aspiring dancer Jean de Koven, Eugen Weidmann murdered two women and four men in the Paris area in 1937. His other victims included a woman lured by the false offer of a position as governess, a chauffeur, a publicity agent, a real estate broker, and a man Weidmann had met as an inmate in a German prison. On the surface, his crimes seemed in most cases to have a profit motive, but they generally brought him very small winnings. Born in Frankfurt-am-Main in 1908, Weidmann early showed himself to be an incorrigible criminal; he had been sent to a juvenile detention facility and then served prison terms for theft and burglary in Canada and Germany prior to his arrival in Paris in 1937.

Colombani, a leading reporter for *France-Soir*, places his narrative in the context of the rise of Nazism and of turbulent French politics on the eve of World War II. The principal mystery of the case related to Weidmann's state of mind. The court-appointed experts pronounced the defendants sane, but the most eminent of the defense counsel, Vincent de Moro Giafferi, argued that Weidmann was sufficiently abnormal to be spared capital punishment and had also suffered psychological damage because of the violent atmosphere of Nazi Germany. The star-studded courtroom observers (including novelist Colette) awaited the imposition of the death penalty as a foregone conclusion.

After Weidmann's execution outside Versailles prison, women awaited the departure of police to dip their handkerchieves in Weidmann's blood, which stained the sidewalk. Prime Minister Edouard Daladier immediately called for an end to public executions.

Like Bruno Richard Hauptmann in the United States, Weidmann was execrated by the public as the embodiment of the Nazi spirit. Even individuals of more moderate temperament, including the investigative magistrate Berry, speculated that Weidmann might have been dispatched to France by the Nazi regime for the purpose of committing brutal crimes calculated to destabilize the French government. How else, he wondered, could the Gestapo, which vetted released German prisoners, have allowed him to slip across the border? When the Nazis occupied Paris, they did their utmost to locate and seize records relating to the Weidmann case, perhaps to suppress historical traces of the atrocities of which an Aryan was capable.

c.35 Conan Doyle, Sir Arthur   *The Case of Oscar Slater.* New York: George H. Doran, 1912.

■ After his failed intervention on behalf of George Edalji (see c.38), Sir Arthur Conan Doyle had more success—although at the expense of many years of efforts and considerable sums of money—in obtaining the release of Oscar Slater, wrongly convicted of murdering elderly Miss Marion Gilchrist in her Glasgow flat on a December night in 1908. Born a German Jew named Leschziner, Slater was arrested after it was learned that he had been trying to sell a pawn ticket for a diamond brooch that police thought might match a piece of jewelry stolen at the time of Miss Gilchrist's murder. The police found that the two brooches did not match; but once they had Slater in their hands they built a case against him on the basis of shaky eyewitness testimony and the erroneous theory that he had arranged after the crime to flee to America (in fact, his travel arrangements had been made much earlier). Slater was convicted by a majority verdict, and he received a death sentence that was commuted to life imprisonment only twenty-four hours before the scheduled time of his hanging.

After Slater's conviction, Doyle joined William Roughead (who had edited a *Notable British Trials* volume on the case), newspaper reporter William Park, and others in a campaign to secure his freedom. One of Conan Doyle's first actions was to publish *The Case of Oscar Slater* (1912), in which he attacked the inconsistencies in the eyewitness testimony and deficiencies in the police inquiry. Doyle theorized that the actual murderer had obtained a key to Miss Gilchrist's flat and had some superficial familiarity with its internal arrangements, knowing, for example, that she kept her jewels in a spare bedroom but unaware of the precise location of her extensive jewelry hoard within that room.

After eighteen and a half years, Slater was finally released from prison. He sent Conan Doyle a letter thanking him as his liberator; his gratitude, however, had its limits, because he rejected Conan Doyle's suggestion that he reimburse the legal costs that the author had incurred in his behalf.

c.36 ———— "J. Habakuk Jephson's Statement." In *The Conan Doyle Stories*. London: John Murray, 1929.

■ In November 1872, a Canadian-built brigantine renamed the *Mary Celeste* by her American owners set sail from New York City, bound for Genoa with a cargo of alcohol. The ship's captain, Benjamin Briggs, was accompanied by his wife, Sarah, and his two-year-old daughter, Sophia Matilda, and commanded a crew of seven. On December 5, the vessel, in seaworthy condition, was encountered by another ship, the *Dei Gratia*, "totally abandoned and derelict, at a point about midway between the Azores and Cape Roca [Cabo da Roca] on the Portuguese coast" (George S. Bryan, *Mystery Ship: The* Mary Celeste *in Fancy and in Fact* [Philadelphia: Lippincott, 1942]). From the time the *Mary Celeste* was brought into Gibraltar for an English salvage hearing, wild theories of the ship's fate created an eerie maritime legend perhaps unequaled since the myth of the *Flying Dutchman*.

The first and best-known fictional account of the *Mary Celeste* enigma, "J. Habakuk Jephson's Statement," was published by twenty-five-year-old Arthur Conan Doyle in the *Cornhill Magazine* in 1884, a few years before the first appearance of Sherlock Holmes. This tale is mainly narrated through a journal of the fatal voyage that was kept by an invented passenger, Dr. Jephson, a wounded Civil War physician who studied at Harvard and became a noted abolitionist. Jephson recalls in hair-raising detail how the captain and his family, together with other whites aboard, were murdered in a black conspiracy led by a mulatto passenger from New Orleans, Septimius Goring, who hated the white race because of the mistreatment of his mother while in slavery and the mutilation of one of his hands by a white man. Jephson is spared after the mutineers lead him ashore to a black-ruled town in North Africa; his life is held sacred because a talisman given him by a black servant in America proves to be the missing ear of a statue worshiped by the townspeople.

Other yarns published in the years that followed by authors or purported "survivors" of the sea tragedy were equally exotic. It was suggested, for example, that a "homicidal religious maniac" had murdered the ship's company one by one, or that the ship had been attacked by a giant octopus. More soberly, George S. Bryan, in his *Mystery Ship*, explores the possibility that the *Mary Celeste* was prematurely abandoned and that its lone lifeboat sank without survivors. Possible causes of abandonment might have been fear of explosion because of leakage of alcoholic vapors from the cargo or concern that strong winds would run the ship aground.

C.37 ———— "The Leather Funnel." In *The Conan Doyle Stories*. London: John Murray, 1929.
■ In this Poe-like ghost story, Lionel Dacre, collector of occult literature and objects, entertains the narrator in his house near the Arc de Triomphe. He shows his guest a large leather funnel with initials and a heraldic crown etched at the wide end and its narrow neck "all haggled and scored, as if someone had notched it round with a blunt knife." A professed believer in the power of antique curios to evoke dreams of their history, Dacre persuades his friend to place the funnel at the side of his pillow. In his sleep, the guest dreams of a horrifying scene in which a woman is to be subjected to torture by water poured into her throat through the funnel. After he awakes in terror, Dacre explains that the funnel was used in the questioning of the Marquise de Brinvilliers, serial poisoner during seventeenth-century France's "Affair of Poisons." Answering his friend's question about the marks on the funnel's neck, he proposes a chilling theory: "She was a cruel tigress. . . . I think it is evident that like other tigresses her teeth were both strong and sharp."

C.38 ———— *The Story of Mr. George Edalji*. 1907. London: Grey House Books, 1985.
■ Young solicitor George Edalji, son of the Reverend Shapurj Edalji (an Anglican vicar who had been reared as a Parsee in his native India) and an English mother, served three of the seven years imprisonment to which he was sentenced for killing a mining pit pony in a Staffordshire colliery field. The crime was one of a series of similar crimes over a period of seven months of 1903 during which five horses, three cows, and several sheep were mutilated. The suspicion of the Staffordshire police focused on Edalji because they already believed him responsible for a series of vicious anonymous letters and hoaxes of which the Edaljis had been targets between 1892 and 1895 and once again in 1903, when the outrages against animals were in progress.

When Sir Arthur Conan Doyle first met George Edalji, he followed the methods of his fictional sleuth Sherlock Holmes by observing him silently and immediately found the young man incapable of committing the barbarous crimes. Edalji, as Conan Doyle recalled in the first of his 1907 columns on the case in the *Daily Telegraph*, was reading and "held the paper close to his eyes and rather sideways, proving not only a high degree of myopia, but marked astigmatism. The idea of such a man scouring fields at night and assaulting cattle while avoiding the watching police was ludicrous to anyone." Believing that the prosecution was founded on color prejudice, Conan Doyle steadfastly advocated Edalji's cause but was unable to secure either pardon or compensation for him after his early release from prison.

In their introduction to this collection of Conan Doyle's Edalji articles, the Whittington-Egans criticize Sherlock Holmes's creator for overstating Edalji's blindness and for his conclusion that the police were acting solely out of prejudice. In their view, police captain Anson was not a "rustic simpleton," and "his fixed belief in the guilt of the parson's son must have had some solid bedrock, something other than wildfire gossip and calumny." Still, they believe that Conan Doyle "was never seen in a more noble light, fighting and suffering, not infallible, but unimpeachable and adamant in his cause."

In his entry on George Edalji in his charming dictionary of the unknown famous, *Who He?* (London: Buchan & Enright, 1984), Jonathan Goodman suggests that the Edalji case is perhaps the historical source of Peter Shaffer's play *Equus*, first produced by the English National Theatre at the Old Vic in 1973. In a "Note on the Play," printed in the London playbills, Shaffer attributes the crime plot to an "alarming crime which [a friend] had heard about . . . at a dinner party in London." Asserting, however, that every person and incident in *Equus* were of his own invention, Shaffer pronounced himself grateful that he had "never received confirmed details of the 'real' story."

c.39 ───── *Strange Studies from Life and Other Narratives: The Complete True Crime Writings of Sir Arthur Conan Doyle.* Comp. and ed. Jack Tracy. Intro. Peter Rubin. Illus. Sidney Paget. Bloomington, Ind.: Gaslight Publications, 1988.

■ The principal crime essays included are three of a projected set of twelve "Strange Studies from Life" for *Strand* magazine; Doyle broke off the series after May 1901 to write *The Hound of the Baskervilles*. Doyle's talent for fast-paced narrative is in evidence here, and each of the cases has remarkable features:

- In 1860 William Godfrey Youngman attempted clumsily to disguise his murder of Mary Wells Streeter, whose life he had insured, by dispatching at the same time his two brothers and his mother. He blamed his mother for the massacre and claimed to have killed her in an effort to wrest away her knife. In Doyle's view, "impulsiveness, jealousy, vindictiveness are the fruitful parents of crime, but the insanity of selfishness is the most dangerous and also the most unlovely of them all."
- George Victor Townley (whom Doyle renames George Vincent Parker) stabbed Bessie Goodwin (renamed Mary Groves) to death in a country lane after she broke off their engagement but then, in distress, sent for help to staunch her bleeding (see s.36).
- On the basis of doubtful circumstantial evidence, plasterer and occasional rent collector George Mullins was hanged for the 1860 murder of elderly Mary Emsley, a wealthy real estate owner. Doyle comments that "it is better that ninety-nine guilty should escape than that one innocent man should suffer."

Other pieces collected in the volume concern an 1827 gang murder to silence an inconvenient witness in the country town of Market-Drayton; the 1863 mutiny aboard the ship *Flowery Land;* dueling in France; and psychic phenomena that revealed crimes or the location of corpses (such as the three dreams of Mrs. Marten that revealed the burial place of her daughter Maria murdered by her faithless lover, William Corder, at the Red Barn in 1827).

c.40 ——— *The Valley of Fear*. In *The Annotated Sherlock Holmes*. 2 vols. Ed. William S. Baring-Gould. New York: Clarkson N. Potter, 1967.

■ The editor comments that Sir Arthur Conan Doyle "never tried to keep it a secret" that he had based the "Scowrers" in Part 2 of *The Valley of Fear*, on "Allan J. Pinkerton's book, *The Molly Maguires and the Detectives*, published in 1877 in New York by G.W. Carleton and Company." Hyman Parker argues that because of fears of libel, Doyle substituted the name Scowrers for that of the Molly Maguires, terrorists among Irish immigrant coal miners in nineteenth-century Pennsylvania. Allan Pinkerton's controversial young operative, James McParland, infiltrated the Mollys and testified at their trials. See Wayne G. Broehl Jr., *The Molly Maguires* (Cambridge: Harvard Univ. Press, 1964).

Allan Pinkerton's detective business methods and his highly fictionalized narratives were burlesqued by Mark Twain in his unfinished novel *Simon Wheeler, Detective* (New York: New York Public Library, 1963).

c.41 ——— Peter Costello. *The Real World of Sherlock Holmes: The True Crimes Investigated by Arthur Conan Doyle.* New York: Carroll & Graf, 1991.

■ The subtitle of this book indulges in overstatement, because most of the chapters deal with cases in which the author believes—often on the basis of hearsay report or supposition—that Conan Doyle may have taken an interest. Sir Arthur's interventions in behalf of unjustly convicted Oscar Slater and George Edalji are well known, and Costello also devotes a chapter to the treason prosecution of Sir Roger Casement, whom Conan Doyle ardently defended. Sir Arthur was strongly moved by the plight of his mother's second cousin, Sir Arthur Vicars, from whose custody the Irish Crown Jewels were stolen in 1907, and he used the theft as the basis for a Sherlock Holmes story, "The Bruce-Partington Plans," which appeared in the *Strand* magazine in 1908. The unsolved 1908 murder of a general's wife, Caroline Luard, also inspired a Holmes adventure, "The Problem of Thor Bridge" (1922).

Sometimes Conan Doyle's study of a true crime appears to qualify as an in-depth investigation; such was the case when he proposed theories for the solution of the murder of Irene Kanthack near the Zoo Park in Johannesburg and the killing of traveling salesman Job Winter at Umtali, Rhodesia (Zimbabwe). According to Costello, Conan Doyle also suggested that police search the moat where they found the body of Samuel Herbert Dougal's victim, Camille Cecile Holland. Late in his life, Conan Doyle's sleuthing acumen was likely to take second place to his interest in spiritualism. When Agatha Christie made her famous disappearance in 1926, Conan Doyle obtained one of her gloves and submitted it for examination by Horace Leaf, whom Costello calls "a well-known medium and psychometrist."

Among other famous criminals in whom Conan Doyle expressed interest were Jack the Ripper, Dr. Crippen, and George Joseph Smith (the "brides-in-the-bath" killer). Costello also relates a story (originating with France's criminologist Edmond Locard) that the famed anarchist motor bandit, Jules Bonnot, had once served as Conan Doyle's chauffeur in England.

c.42 Conrad, Earl *Mr. Seward for the Defense.* New York: Rinehart, 1956.

■ In 1846 Seward, twice governor of New York and a leader of the Whig Party, braved the wrath of party members and people of his hometown of Auburn by successively defending on grounds of insanity two men charged with murder. The first defendant, Henry Wyatt, a prisoner in Auburn Prison, one of the town's principal industries, had murdered an inmate named James Gordon, who had falsely accused him of having killed a man in Ohio. After he denied the charge, prison officials beat him unmercifully and put him into a small dungeon cell. When he emerged, he attacked Gordon with a blade from a large pair of shears.

The second case, of which Conrad provides a stirring account, upset the townsfolk even more profoundly. William Freeman (well named because he was a black freeman with Native American blood) had massacred four members of the wealthy and well-respected Van Nest family after serving a term in prison for a horse stealing, which he had denied committing. While incarcerated, he had been deafened by blows to the head with a board. After his release his formerly sociable personality had darkened; he obsessively demanded "wages" for his false imprisonment and forced labor. When he failed to obtain arrest warrants against those he saw as his oppressors, he deliberately went about purchasing and grinding a knife. As a first act of a projected campaign of revenge, he massacred the Van Nests (including a two-year-old child), against whom he had no grievance, having targeted them, apparently, because their house was in a remote location.

In addition to the unpopularity of the defense among Auburn's citizens, who came close to lynching Freeman after he was captured, Seward confronted a serious personal problem in agreeing to act as the killer's lawyer. Without justification, it was charged that Freeman had attended the Wyatt trial at which Seward had urged (unsuccessfully) an insanity defense; and that Freeman had concluded, though close to deaf, that he was accordingly free to commit murder with impunity. At the trial, townspeople's testimony about the defendant's mental state vied with expert opinion. Freeman was convicted after jury deliberations that lasted an hour only for the sake of maintaining an appearance of propriety. The court of appeals, however, reversed on the ground that the trial judge had unduly restricted the defense's proffered evidence of Freeman's insanity after his capture. Freeman was never retried because the trial judge, after visiting him in prison, was belatedly persuaded that he was hopelessly demented.

In his dramatic narrative of the Seward trial, Conrad brilliantly succeeds in humanizing abstract legal principles and in linking Seward's defense to his opposition to slavery, racial stereotypes, and neglect of the education of black children, as well as to his respect for scientific theory that was groping its way toward a better understanding of mental disorders. The author, who is greatly interested in African American history, also wrote *Scottsboro Boy* (New York: Doubleday, 1950) with Haywood Patterson, one of the Scottsboro defendants (see c.15).

c.43 Conrad, Joseph *Nostromo.* 1904. *Complete Works of Joseph Conrad.* Vol. 9. New York: Doubleday Page, 1926.

■ In the Author's Note to his masterpiece *Nostromo*, Conrad attributed the principal plot element to a story he had heard when very young "of some man who was supposed to have stolen single-handed a whole lighter-full of silver, somewhere on the Tierra Firme seaboard during the troubles of a revolution." About twenty-six or twenty-seven years later, this tale was confirmed by an anecdote in a shabby volume that he picked up outside a secondhand bookshop (modern literary detection has identified this book as *On Many Seas: The Life and Exploits of a Yankee Sailor* by Frederick Benton Williams [pseudonym of Herbert Eliot Hamblen], 1897). Williams's thief Nicolo becomes Conrad's Nostromo, who innocently comes into possession of a cargo of silver bullion after a maritime collision. When an associate takes four silver bars from the cache to weight his body in preparation for a suicide at sea, Nostromo is compelled to forestall an accusation of theft by disposing of the balance of the silver hoard in small quantities. Thus, the guileless Nostromo becomes a prisoner of the silver that chance brought under his control.

C.44 ——— *The Secret Agent*. 1907. *Complete Works of Joseph Conrad*. Vol. 13. New York: Doubleday Page, 1926.

■ The idea of this ironic novel of futile London anarchists originated in Conrad's conversation with Ford Madox Ford in which they "recalled the already old story of the attempt to blow up the Greenwich Observatory [in 1894]; a blood-stained inanity of so fatuous a kind that it was impossible to fathom its origin by any reasonable or even unreasonable process of thought. For perverse unreason has its own logical processes. But that outrage could not be laid hold of mentally in any sort of way, so that one remained faced by the fact of a man [Martial Bourdin] blown to bits for nothing even most remotely resembling an idea, anarchistic or other. As to the outer wall of the Observatory it did not show as much as the faintest crack."

In his poem, "Animula," T. S. Eliot offers a sarcastic prayer for the dead terrorist:

Pray for Guiterriez, avid of speed and power,
For Boudin, blown to pieces,
For this one who made a great fortune,
And that one who made his own way.

Alfred Hitchcock freely adapted the plot of *The Secret Agent* for his film *Sabotage* (1936).

c.45 Constant, Benjamin *L'Affaire Regnault*. Grenoble: University of Grenoble, 1979.

■ Benjamin Constant's intervention on behalf of Wilfred Regnault, unjustly convicted of murder in 1817, places the novelist in the humanitarian company of Voltaire, champion of Jean Calas (see v.9), and Zola, defender of Captain Alfred Dreyfus. Regnault, a grocer in the little Norman town of Amfreville, was sentenced to death for the stabbing and strangulation of the widow Jouvin, a domestic servant of lumber dealer Jean Enoult, in her master's storeroom. In the first of two publications taking the form of letters to Regnault's appellate counsel Odilon Barrot, Constant showed how the investigation and trial were infected by the false rumor (propagated by the right-wing mayor of Amfreville) that Regnault, staunch liberal supporter of the property rights of farmers, had participated in the September massacres of 1792. In his second letter, Constant demonstrated convincingly the unreliability of the prosecutor's star witness, as well as the lack of a motive (the victim was Regnault's debtor and had undertaken to discharge debts far exceeding the amount stolen from the scene of the crime). The chronology presented by the prosecution did not work either. For example, a dog barked long before the time Regnault was alleged to have entered Jean Enoult's property; Constant asks whether the animal is supposed to have acted "by premonition."

Regnault's death sentence was commuted, but his innocence was not officially recognized; he was imprisoned for twelve years.

c.46 Cozzens, James Gould *A Rope for Dr. Webster.* Bloomfield Hills, Mich.: Bruccoli Clark, 1976.

■ This edition of Cozzens's article on the Harvard murder case of 1849, limited to 350 numbered and signed copies, is all that remains of a volume of essays on classic trials that he and his friend George Bradshaw had planned while they were in the Air Force (Matthew J. Bruccoli, *James Gould Cozzens: A Life Apart* [San Diego: Harcourt Brace Jovanovich, 1983], 271–72). Professor John White Webster was hanged for the murder of his insistent creditor, Dr. George Parkman, a benefactor of the Harvard Medical College. Webster's conviction was based in part on the identification of Parkman's false teeth among human remains found in the professor's assay furnace. In Cozzens's view, Webster was "duly hanged for a crime that, in the law's defining, he almost certainly never committed." The author is inclined to accept as true the ostensible confession of Webster filed in support of an unsuccessful petition for commutation of his death sentence, namely, that, overcome by anger, he had killed Parkman by accident. Cozzens remarks: "Looked at with the detachment of a century passed it can only be said that, unlike premeditated murder, such a misadventure is wholly in character."

c.47 Crabbe, George "The Poor of the Borough: Peter Grimes." In *George Crabbe, Tales, 1812, and Other Selected Poems*. Ed. Howard Mills. Cambridge: Cambridge Univ. Press, 1967.

■ Peter Grimes, the misanthropic fisherman of Benjamin Britten's 1945 opera, made his first appearance in Crabbe's suite of twenty-four poems *The Borough* (1810). In Crabbe's verse narrative, Grimes mistreats and strikes his father, supplements his fishing with thefts ashore, and is suspected of causing the deaths of three poor apprentices, whom he has sadistically abused, enjoying the sensation of having "a feeling creature subject to his power." Although he escapes punishment, Grimes becomes an outcast and is driven mad by avenging spirits of his father and two of his young victims.

E. M. Forster explained how Crabbe's "sombre masterpiece" originated: "[Crabbe] came across an old fisherman who had had a succession of apprentices from London and a sum of money with each. The apprentices tended to disappear and the fisherman was warned he would be charged with murder next time. . . . According to Edward FitzGerald . . . the fisherman's name was Tom Brown" ("George Crabbe and Peter Grimes," in *Two Cheers for Democracy* [New York: Harcourt Brace, 1951], 175–76).

c.48 Crane, Stephen *Maggie: Girl of the Streets.* 1893. In *Twenty Stories.* Comp. and intro. Carl Van Doren. Cleveland: World, 1945.

■ Crane's short novel *Maggie*, is a tale of a girl, seduced and abandoned, who becomes a prostitute in a New York slum and throws herself into the river. The work was influenced by police reporter Jacob Riis's writings on slums and the impoverished Crane's own explorations of the Bowery. After corrupt police lieutenant Charles Becker was implicated in the murder of gambler Herman Rosenthal, "it was often said that it had been the sight of Charles Becker manhandling a young prostitute that had driven Stephen Crane to write *Maggie: A Girl of the Streets.* In fact, *Maggie* was published nine months before Becker put on the uniform" (see Andy Logan, *Against the Evidence: The Becker-Rosenthal Affair* [New York: McCall, 1970], 108).

Crane's encounter with patrolman Becker actually occurred when Crane gallantly but, as events proved, misguidedly defended Dora Clark against the police officer's street arrest for prostitution. Becker was exonerated after a lengthy police court hearing on the charges that Clark had brought against him. The outcome was humiliating for Crane, who had testified on behalf of the young woman and refused to answer the cross-examiner's questions about his sex life. In 1915, a decade and a half after Crane's death, Becker was electrocuted for his role in the Rosenthal murder plot.

c.49 Cullen, Countee "Not Sacco and Vanzetti" and "Scottsboro, Too, Is Worth Its Song." In *My Soul's High Song: The Collected Writings of Countee Cullen, Voice of the Harlem Renaissance.* Ed. and intro. Gerald Early. New York: Doubleday (Anchor), 1991.

■ In the mind of African American poet Cullen (1903–46), the trials of Sacco and Vanzetti and of the Scottsboro Boys were paired as miscarriages of justice based on ethnic and racial prejudice. In his poem "Not Sacco and Vanzetti," Cullen speaks unenvyingly of the plight of the Italian anarchists' judges when they must face the Last Judgment: "These men who do not die, but death decree– / These are the men I should not care to be."

It is to "American poets" that he addresses "Scottsboro, Too, Is Worth Its Song." He had expected to hear their voices once again raised in outrage, "Remembering their sharp and pretty / tunes for Sacco and Vanzetti." His hopes, however, were disappointed by his fellow poets' silence: "But they have raised no cry. / I wonder why."

D

D.1 Daudet, Alphonse *The Immortal.* New York: Alden, 1889.

■ In this novel, Denis Vrain-Lucas, the audacious forger of centuries-old French correspondence and transcriptions, becomes the hunchbacked bookbinder Albin Fage, who sells his invented documents to plodding historian Léonard Astier-Réhu, member of the Acádemie Française. The title is both an ironic reference to the sobriquet given to Acádemie members, whom Daudet depicts as untalented courtiers, and to their dean, Jean Réhu (Madame Léonard Astier-Réhu's grandfather), who at age ninety-five seems quite literally "immortal." Unlike Léonard, who writes histories based on documentation of doubtful authenticity, Jean Réhu can say of the chief events of the past century, "I've seen that, too, myself."

D.2 Davis, Natalie Zemon   *The Return of Martin Guerre.* Cambridge: Harvard Univ. Press, 1983.

■ Professor Davis served as a consultant in the filming of *The Return of Martin Guerre* (1982), starring Gérard Depardieu in the title role. She "was prompted to dig deeper into the case, to make historical sense of it," and her book on the case is the fruit of her researches. An admirer of historian Emmanuel Le Roy Ladurie, who encouraged her investigation, Davis sets out to recreate the economic, social, and religious setting of the famous imposture. She notes, for example, that the affluent de Rols may have agreed to the childhood marriage of their daughter Bertrande to the unprepossessing Martin because of their interest in the Guerre tileworks. Davis also stresses the impact of the Protestantism of the de Rols family, which may have dissuaded the Catholic clergy from taking an interest in the imposture prosecution of Arnaud du Tilh, the "false Martin Guerre."

Still, the central mystery of the case lies hidden in Bertrande's acceptance of du Tilh as a substitute for her long-missing husband. Davis regards her as a willing participant in the fraud rather than a dupe, agreeing in this respect with Janet Lewis, who wrote an engaging fictional account of the case (see L.23). Contemporaries found an uncanny element in the imposture. One of du Tilh's judges, Jean de Coras, who published a narrative of the case, suspected that du Tilh must have practiced magic, and Michel de Montaigne, in his essay "The Lame," opined that judgment should have been withheld in the light of the puzzling trial record.

D.3 Decaux, Alain   *Les assassins.* Paris: Perrin, 1986.

■ The collection is divided between political assassinations (the murders of Archduke Ferdinand, French socialist leader Jean Jaurès, and King Alexander I of Yugoslavia) and killings for gain (the Bonnot bank robbers, Madame Steinheil, Landru, the kidnapping of the Lindbergh baby, Dr. Petiot, and Pierrot le Fou).

D.4 ———   *Les grands mystères du passé.* Paris: Perrin, 1971.

■ The subjects of the essays include the Man in the Iron Mask, the sexually ambiguous chevalier d'Eon, the fate of Louis XVII (see L.17), Kaspar Hauser, the Mayerling murdersuicide, and Anastasia.

D.5 ———   *Grands secrets, grands enigmes.* Paris: Perrin, 1970.

■ Twenty-five short articles ask such questions as whether Joan of Arc was burned, whether Robespierre committed suicide, whether Joseph Lesurques was guilty of the Lyons Mail (Courrier de Lyon) killings, who killed Henri IV, and what became of Louis XVII.

D.6 ———— *Nouveaux dossiers secrets de l'histoire.* Paris: Perrin, 1967.

■ In this volume of his series of modern historical mysteries, Decaux addresses, among other questions, the responsibility for the fate of Jean Chiappe, who served as prefect of police in Paris between 1927 and 1934. The plane carrying Chiappe (newly appointed Vichy's high commissioner for Syria and Lebanon) from Marseilles to Tunis was shot down on November 27, 1940, during a fierce air and naval engagement between British and Italian forces near Sardinia. Pierre Laval, for political purposes, blamed the British for the downing of the unarmed Air France craft. Decaux tends to assign responsibility to Italian air gunners.

D.7 [Dee, Judge] *Dee Goong An: Three Murder Cases Solved by Judge Dee.* Intro. and notes R. H. van Gulik. New York: Arno, 1976.

■ This reprint of the 1949 Tokyo edition of van Gulik's translation presents an anonymous eighteenth-century Chinese detective novel based on the personality of an actual district magistrate (A.D. 630–700) of the Tang Dynasty, who ended his days as a minister of state. Famous across the centuries for his acumen and integrity as detective and judge, Dee is shown in this novel to be grappling simultaneously with three cases that span the social classes and the categories of murder motives: a killing for gain in the silk trade; a murder accusation against a woman in a small village; and suspicion that a prefect's son poisoned his bride on their wedding night. Van Gulik borrowed the multiple plot structure of *Dee Goong An* when he embarked on his successful series of modern Judge Dee mystery novels.

D.8 Defoe, Daniel *A General History of the Pyrates.* 1724. Ed. Manuel Schonhorn. Columbia: Univ. of South Carolina Press, 1972.

■ Only in 1932 did Professor John Robert Moore proclaim this two-volume history published under the name of "Captain Charles Johnson" to be the work of Daniel Defoe. Moore cited in support of his attribution the style and idiom typical of Defoe, and reflections of his interest in foreign trade, storms at sea, colonial projects, and other subjects treated in his recognized writings. To these topics may be added Defoe's abiding fascination with lawbreakers and adventurers. The luminaries whose careers are retold in Defoe's history include Captains Henry Avery, Edward Teach (Blackbeard), and William Kidd, as well as the female pirates and friends Mary Read and Ann Bonny.

D.9 ———— *The King of Pirates Being an Account of the Famous Enterprises of Captain Avery with Lives of Other Pirates and Robbers.* In *Romances and Narratives by Daniel Defoe.* Vol. 16. Ed. George A. Aitken. London: Dent, 1895.

■ In addition to tracts on the pirate captains Avery and Gow, this collection offers five others on the exploits of criminal landlubbers. A pioneer of the true-crime essay, Defoe in

1724 published an extended narrative of the murder of six English travelers by brutal French highwaymen near Calais in September 1723. The sole survivor of the massacre, servant Richard Spindelow, who had been left for dead, was able to identify Joseph Bizeau (a former member of Cartouche's gang) and Pierre Le Febvre as the robber chieftains. Comparing the murderers' bloody crime with the less violent rule of Cartouche over the Paris underworld, Defoe declared that the new atrocity was "a fact so cruel, and so outrageously vile, that nothing like it had ever been committed but in France."

Also included in the volume are Defoe's two pamphlets on the brief career of the burglar and prison-breaker Jack Sheppard, who made two spectacular escapes from Newgate Prison in 1724 before his final capture and hanging. The second narrative is told by Jack in the first person; Defoe advertised such publications as autobiographies delivered to him in manuscript by the criminal either in his death cell or even at the foot of the scaffold.

The best constructed of the included crime narratives relates the life of the insidious Jonathan Wild, who presided over London's network of thieves and claimed "rewards" from owners to whom he arranged to restore stolen goods (see F.10). Defoe includes two dialogues between Wild and clients seeking the recovery of their property from thieves; one of these scenes, told in the first person, appears to suggest that Defoe had personal experience with Wild's machinations.

The final essay is on the professional methods of six notorious robbers; Defoe teaches in exquisite detail how to filch a sword from a pedestrian's belt.

D.10 ———— *Moll Flanders: The Fortunes and Misfortunes of the Famous*. 1722. New York: Heritage Press, 1942.

▪ The novel's famous heroine, after a life of prostitution, incest, and thievery, rediscovers virtue after being transported to the American colonies. Defoe describes scenes in the London underworld with particular gusto and shows a connoisseur's knowledge of shoplifting techniques. The Defoe critic, John Robert Moore, notes that Moll Flanders's larcenous exploits were drawn from the career of a female criminal, Moll King, whom Defoe described in the following news report he later wrote for Nathanial Mist's *Weekly Journal*: "A most notorious Offender, famous for stealing Gold Watches from the Ladies' Sides in the Churches, for which she has been several times convicted, being lately return'd from Transportation, has been taken, and is committed in Newgate." Moll King is also mentioned (with the middle letters of her name left blank) in one of Defoe's tracts on archcriminal Jonathan Wild (see D.9).

D.11 ———— *Roxana (The Fortunate Mistress)*. 1724. In *Romances and Narratives by Daniel Defoe*. Vols. 12 and 13. Ed. George A. Aitken. London: Dent, 1895.

▪ Roxana, a beautiful Frenchwoman, did not find marriage to her liking after her first husband abandoned her and their five children. She therefore captivated a succession of wealthy protectors before she found wedded bliss with a devoted merchant. Defoe scholar John Robert Moore writes in his biography of the author, "One of Defoe's originals for her character was the notorious Mrs. Mary Butler, the former mistress of the second Duke of

Buckingham, who was convicted of forging bonds for very large amounts in the name of Sir Robert Clayton, the trustee of Buckingham's estate." In his preface, Defoe was more discreet about his "beautiful lady's" true identity, claiming, however, that "he was particularly acquainted with this lady's first husband, the brewer, and with his father, and also with his bad circumstances, and knows that first part of the story to be true."

D.12 deFord, Miriam Allen   *Murderers Sane and Mad: Case Histories in the Motivation and Rationale of Murder.* London: Abelard-Schuman, 1966.

■ The publication of a collection of deFord's fact-crime articles had long been advocated by Anthony Boucher and other crime authors and critics. Among the issues considered by deFord is "whether such a person exists as a sane, normal murderer." This problem is exemplified by the case of a fiftyish quack chiropractor, or "naturopath," Hjalmar Groneman, acquitted in San Francisco of manslaughter and criminal negligence in the 1935 death of Ella May Clemmons. Shortly before her death, Groneman had married Ella May, in a dubious ceremony, to finance his cohabitation with Charlotte Enberg, whom he installed as his wife's nurse.

In her article on Burton Abbott, executed for the 1955 murder of fourteen-year-old Stephanie Bryan in Berkeley, deFord avows a "faint, infinitesimal, yet lingering doubt." Apart from the difficulty of reconciling conflicting psychological profiles of Abbott, how likely was it, she asks, that a 130-pound tubercular war veteran, who had had one lung and five ribs removed, could have carried the victim's body uphill to the grave where it was found in an advanced state of decomposition?

The portrait of teenager Roman Rodriguez, convicted of the 1952 second-degree murder of San Francisco high schooler Hilda Pagan, embodies deFord's resistance to ethnic stereotypes. Inhibited by a strong attachment to his mother, Rodriguez could not fulfill Hilda's expectation of passion on demand and killed her in frenzied panic. He stripped her body to simulate a rape of which he was incapable.

In deFord's words, Barbara Graham, controversially gassed in 1955 for battering sixty-three-year-old Mabel Monohan to death in a gang's fruitless search for a rumored cache of her son-in-law's gambling casino hoard, was "weak, malleable, self-indulgent and foolish" but "as sane as the next stupid little girl with bad heredity and worse upbringing." Although deFord regards the 1958 film of the case, *I Want to Live* with Susan Hayward, as "evasive and falsified," she does not believe that Barbara, who almost certainly participated in the break-in at the Monohan house, was capable of the extreme violence of which the elderly woman was the victim.

Sane but "abysmally stupid"—that is deFord's appraisal of Louise Peete, who, a quarter-century apart, committed two murders for gain that "were almost completely copies of each other." The end results, however, were different. For the killing of Jacob Denton, buried in a cellar, Peete served a term in prison; the murder of Margaret Logan, shot through the back of the head like Denton and interred under an avocado tree, brought Peete to San Quentin's gas chamber, still protesting her innocence and respectability.

The compulsive burglar and triple murderer William Heirens does not fall into the category of legal insanity, deFord argues, but "might serve as a case history of sexual abnormality as a symptom of profound mental disturbance." He achieved orgasms by entering the windows of apartments he planned to rob (sometimes of war bonds and often of women's clothing). Of his three murder victims, Jacqueline Alice Ross, age forty-three, and Frances Brown, age thirty-three, surprised him during a burglary, and only six-year-old Suzanne Degnan seems to have been killed with premeditation. At times Heirens experienced guilt and remorse, inventing an alter ego, George Merman, on whom he blamed the crimes, and leaving his famous lipsticked message on Frances Brown's mirror: "For heaven's sake catch me before I kill more. I cannot control myself." Still, Heirens unsuccessfully pursued remedies seeking reversal of his 1947 sentence to three life terms when he was eighteen. In deFord's view, "Heirens is unfit to live a normal life among normal people. It is his inescapable tragedy to know, for some of the time at least, that this is so."

The volume also includes deFord's articles on Leopold and Loeb and on John Christie, the 10 Rillington Place murderer.

For thirty-seven years a labor journalist, Miriam Allen deFord (1888–1975) was also a noted true-crime author, dubbed by critic Anthony Boucher "the Tennyson Jesse of America." In his 1962 anthology *The Quality of Murder*, Boucher expressed the wish that a "sensible publisher" would issue a collection of her crime essays, a desire fulfilled four years later by the appearance of *Murderers Sane and Mad*.

D.13 ———— *The Overbury Affair.* New York: Chilton, 1960.
■ Winner of the Mystery Writers of America "Edgar" Award for true crime, deFord's work briskly explores the tangled thicket of Sir Thomas Overbury's mysterious death in the Tower of London on September 15, 1613. Sir Thomas, brilliant and ambitious secretary of Robert Carr, Earl of Somerset (a favorite of James I), was imprisoned to silence his acid tongue and pen during the pendency of annulment proceedings that cleared the way for amoral Frances Howard to marry Carr. DeFord believes Howard was justly convicted of ordering the poisoning of Overbury but that Carr, also convicted, knew nothing of his countess's plot until after Overbury's death. Unlike Robert Carr, Frances confessed her crime in court, winning praise for contrition in some quarters but striking others as a hypocrite. DeFord, however, has her own interpretation: "There were those present who hated her, who sneered at her humility as hypocrisy, which indeed it may have been— though one may murder and then be sorry, if only for oneself."

In her book, deFord notes reflections of the Overbury affair in poetry and drama at the time of the case and afterward: Richard Niccols's contemporary verse "Sir Thomas Overbury's Vision," and poet Richard Savage's play *Sir Thomas Overbury* (1721).

D.14 ———— *The Real Bonnie and Clyde.* New York: Ace Books, 1968.
■ Demythifying Bonnie Parker and Clyde Barrow after the appearance of the popular 1967 film with Faye Dunaway and Warren Beatty, deFord calls the bandits "a sorry pair on whom to base a legend." Their earnings from robbing stores, filling stations, and banks were small, and John Dillinger commented on their lack of professionalism: "They were

kill-crazy punks and clodhoppers—bad news to decent bank robbers. They gave us a bad name." Still deFord finds some redeeming traits in them: a genuine attachment to each other that survived Bonnie's infidelities and Clyde's enigmatic sexual orientation and the devotion of both to their mothers. In her concluding remarks, deFord suggests that Bonnie may not have committed a single murder and wonders what life might have held for her had she not entered into her strange union with a man whose real passions were cars and guns. Two of Bonnie's "poems" appear to indicate that her daydreams were "derived from movies and radio soap operas and Sunday supplement reading, in which Bonnie Parker actually lived, and to whose standards, as she understood them, she conformed."

D.15 De la Torre, Lillian *Elizabeth Is Missing.* New York: Knopf, 1945.

■ De La Torre's solution to the mysterious month-long disappearance of Elizabeth Canning in 1753 near London is a blend of medical hypothesis and fictive invention. Canning was found to have perjured herself when she returned home with her tale of imprisonment in an attic after refusing to join the staff of a bordello. Kindly Henry Fielding, who interviewed her, had believed her unreservedly (see F.8). De La Torre regards Elizabeth Canning's statements as a mixture of truth and lies. She essentially accepts the young woman's account of her abduction on January 1 and of her escape on January 29, but she believes that she filled the gap between those dates with "made-up stories." The reason for Canning's fabrications, according to de La Torre, was that Elizabeth was the victim of hysterical amnesia. Her abduction was carried out at the order of alehouse keeper John Wintlebury, whom she had served as a domestic for eighteen months; it was probably he who had her carried off to Mother Wells's bordello so that he could seduce her there. Because of her hysterical fit, de La Torre theorizes, the girl can't have proved very entertaining, so Wintlebury must have abandoned his addresses after a few days, and the folks at Mother Wells's thanked their lucky stars when Elizabeth finally found an exit from the disreputable premises. See Fig. 5.

D.16 ——— *Goodbye, Miss Lizzie Borden.* In *Murder: Plain and Fanciful.* Ed. James Sandoe. New York: Sheridan House, 1948.

■ In this gripping one-act play, Lizzie Borden's sister, Emma, about to leave the Fall River house forever, is revealed to be the killer of their father and stepmother. She tells Lizzie that her crimes were directed by divine guidance. Emma makes her confession after Lizzie confronts her with the axe and bloody apron, which Lizzie, ever protective, had secreted in her father's "hidey hole" behind a projecting brick in the fireplace. In her anger over Lizzie's possession of the damning evidence, Emma raises the axe against her sister; only the untimely return of a prying reporter prevents a new murder, and Emma rushes out to catch her train, leaving Lizzie to cover up for her once again.

D.17 ——— *The Truth About Belle Gunness.* New York: Fawcett (Gold Medal), 1955.

■ On the basis of interviews with fourteen elderly Hoosiers with firsthand knowledge, de la Torre retells the case of Norwegian-born serial killer Belle Gunness and proposes a solution to the mystery of her disappearance. In 1908 the Gunness farm in La Porte, Indiana, burned to the ground, and the charred bodies of a headless woman and three children were found in the ashes. The authorities identified the victims as Belle Gunness and her three foster children: Myrtle, age eleven; Lucy, age nine; and Philip, age five. In the case of Belle, the match seemed doubtful at first, unless her 280-pound frame had been strangely diminished by the blaze to the corpse (weighing an estimated 150 pounds with head restored) that was retrieved from the ruins. A dentist, however, buttressed the identification of the woman by recognizing as his work upper and lower bridges, imbedded in fragments of live teeth, that were belatedly found in the debris.

Further excavations made in Belle Gunness's hog lot revealed that, if she was a victim of foul play in the fire, her demise was not to be mourned. Remains of at least ten bodies were unearthed, including those of Belle's teenage daughter, Jennie, a hired hand, and several men who had unluckily responded to her matrimonial advertisements. Belle may have previously dispatched two husbands, one by poison and the second by a drubbing with a sausage grinder. Her favored modus operandi, however, appears to have been a dose of arsenic and/or strychnine followed by a hammer blow to the head.

Ray Lamphere, Belle Gunness's former employee and lover, was tried for murdering Belle and the three children but was convicted only of arson in a compromise verdict. Before dying in prison of consumption in 1909, Lamphere reportedly confessed to a fellow inmate that he had set fire to the farmhouse at Belle's instruction and that the headless woman was a substitute for Belle, who had escaped from La Porte with the aid of Ray and a corrupt sheriff.

De la Torre proposes an ingenious alternative solution, drawn from investigations in the 1950s by Charles F. Pahrman. She theorizes that after her flight, Belle was murdered and robbed by an accomplice, who wrenched her dental plates and live teeth from her mouth and "planted" them in the farm's ashes.

In 1952 de la Torre wrote, directed, and played Belle Gunness in a play called *The Coffee Cup*, in which Belle survives the La Porte fire and lives under the name Brunhilde Larson in an Indiana farmhouse. The text of the play appears in *Butcher, Baker, Murder Maker: Stories by Members of the Mystery Writers of America, Inc.* (New York: Borzoi, 1954). The legends and folk literature of the Gunness case are studied in Janet L. Langlois, *Belle Gunness: The Lady Bluebeard* (Bloomington: Indiana Univ. Press, 1985).

D.18 Delayen, Gaston *L'Affaire du courrier de Lyon: Les procès Lesurques, Durochat, Vidal, Dubosq, et Béroldy.* 5th ed. Paris: Librairie d'Education Nationale, 1905.

■ In 1796 the Paris-Lyon mail coach, carrying valuables, including funds destined for Napoleon's army in Italy, was attacked and robbed on a road in the brigand-infested countryside near Melun southeast of Paris. The courier, Jean-Joseph Excoffon, suffered three lethal stab wounds in the chest and belly, and his neck was slashed by a sabre; the postilion-driver Etienne Audebert was unspeakably butchered. Five trials resulted in the execution of seven defendants convicted of participation in the crime: Joseph Lesurques, Etienne Couriol, David Bernard, Joseph Durochat (a passenger on the Lyon coach), Vidal-Dufour, André Dubosq, and Louis Béroldy (or Roussy). For three-quarters of a century, the family of

Lesurques, supported by public opinion, vainly petitioned for his rehabilitation, claiming that witnesses placing him near the scene of the crime had been misled by the blond Lesurques's resemblance to Dubosq, who wore a blond wig. After a consideration of trial records released to him by the French Minister of Justices Delayen weighed the factors respectively supporting Lesurques's innocence or guilt. Strongly in his favor was that he was first identified by country witnesses only after he voluntarily accompanied a friend to police offices where the Lyon mail case was being investigated. Moreover, many of the eyewitnesses at his trial were mistaken or self-contradictory: Couriol and Durochat, after their convictions, proclaimed Lesurques's innocence; and one witness, Madame Alfroy, retracted her identification of Lesurques after she confronted the bewigged Dubosq at the latter's trial. In the scales weighing against Lesurques, Delayen placed evidence of his acquaintance with members of the criminal gang that attacked the coach; the refusal of most eyewitnesses to swerve from their identification of Lesurques even when Dubosq was forced to don his wig in court; and the alteration of the date in jeweler Legrand's register in an apparent effort to establish an alibi for Lesurques. Although impressed by the strength of the prosecution's case, Delayen would not have voted to convict Lesurques, "because doubt, however slight, should benefit the accused." However, the author does not believe that such doubt provided a sufficient basis for the posthumous rehabilitation of the executed man.

D.19 ———— *L'Inavouable secret du lieutenant de la Roncière.* Paris: Albin Michel, 1925.

■ In 1834, the household of Baron Charles Robert de Morell, commandant of the Cavalry School in Saumur, France, was afflicted by a campaign of poison-pen letters. The likely author, who signed early missives as "An Officer" or "R," appeared to be a womanizing and rebellious lieutenant stationed in Saumur, Emile de la Roncière. Addressees included the Morells' high-strung sixteen-year-old daughter Marie, her mother, and an English governess, Miss Allen. The mysterious correspondent insulted Marie and expressed an ardent passion for Madame de Morell. Another target of abusive letters was cavalry officer Octave-Charles-Marie d'Estouilly, whose slow-paced wooing of Marie the writer claimed to have disrupted. On the night of September 23, Marie aroused her family with the story that she had been attacked and bitten by an intruder whom she identified as La Roncière. This melodramatic incident by no means put an end to the stream of hostile letters, which continued even after the lieutenant was imprisoned and under close watch. In some of the last letters, the wielder of the poison pen claimed that he had raped Marie in the hope that her parents would compel her to marry him.

In an 1835 trial, Roncière was convicted of attempted rape and intentional infliction of wounds under "attenuating circumstances." He served eight years in prison, and the last two years of his sentence were remitted. The harsh verdict was rendered in the face of expert testimony that the anonymous letters were in Marie de Morell's hand and that the stationery closely resembled hers.

The accepted wisdom concerning the La Roncière case is that the lieutenant was the victim of an impressionable young woman's vengeance spurred by her feeling that he was cold to her budding charms. Delayen, however, relates a contrarian version that assigns considerable blame to La Roncière. The story he weaves is double hearsay based on a confidence imparted by La Roncière's trial judge, Placide Isidore Férey, to Eugène Carré, a barrister whose chambers author Delayen joined as a legal neophyte. According to Carré, La Roncière, after suffering from Marie's letter hoax, made a drunken boast to two fellow officers that he could seduce her, trumping his earlier success with the governess. Without explaining his purpose, he persuaded Miss Allen to admit him to the Morells' house on the night of September 23, threw himself on Marie, and cut off a lock of her pubic hair to show as a trophy of conquest to the officers before whom he made his infamous wager.

La Roncière's case is a source of John Fowles's novel *The French Lieutenant's Woman* (F.26) and is also the subject of an essay of H. B. Irving (I.4).

D.20 ——— *La passion de la Marquise Diane de Ganges*. In series *Énigmes et drames judiciaires d'autrefois*. Paris: Perrin, 1927.

■ Delayen was a member of the French crime club of the 1920s known as the Dinner of the Eleven. In his account of the persecution and murder of Marquise Diane de Ganges by her two brothers-in-law with the support of her husband, this leading French crime historian tempers his obvious emotional attachment to his pathetic heroine by admirable scholarship. The case in Delayen's hands is an object lesson in the helplessness of French noblewomen in the seventeenth century once their male defenders departed from the scene. Formerly the darling of the royal court nicknamed "la belle Provençale" and the target of Louis XIV's youthful gallantries, the marquise, after the death of her wealthy grandfather who made her his heir, had nobody to protect her from the greed, lechery, and murderous designs of her husband's family. All her oppressors escaped the hand of justice.

D.21 De Quincey, Thomas "On Murder Considered as One of the Fine Arts." In *Selected Writings of Thomas De Quincey*. New York: Random House, 1937.

■ Biographer Horace Ainsworth Eaton traces De Quincey's interest in crime to 1818, when he assumed editorship of *The Westmorland Gazette* (*Thomas De Quincey* [New York: Oxford Univ. Press, 1936]). During his tenure at the *Gazette*, trial reports occupied a large portion of available space. Eaton asserts that De Quincey selected "peculiarly mysterious and revolting cases" and that "his prepossession necessitated frequent apologies for the omission of really important news and communications."

De Quincey's essay "On Murder Considered as One of the Fine Arts," which appeared in three parts in 1827, 1839, and 1854, exploited his true-crime obsession with literary virtuosity (see the Introduction to this Guide). The first two sections (published in *Blackwood's Magazine*) apply mock-aesthetic standards to the appraisal of murderers' achievements. The 1827 paper is cast in the form of the "Williams Lecture on Murder Considered as One of the Fine Arts" as delivered to the "Society of Connoisseurs of Murder." Written in a similar ironic tone, the second paper, published in 1839, focuses on the gloomy misanthropy of "Toad-in-the-hole," a particularly exacting member of the murder connoisseurs' club who was given to "constant disparagements of all modern murders as vicious abortions, belonging to no authentic school of art."

The final paper, a postscript entitled "Three Memorable Murders," turns from humor to suspenseful and psychologically acute crime narratives. De Quincey relates the murders committed by John Williams (the so-called Ratcliffe Highway murderer who introduced London to the horrors of serial killing) and the M'Kean brothers, who killed a maidservant in an inn but were foiled in their robbery attempt when a boy, twelve or fourteen years old, performed a surprising athletic feat by vaulting over a balustrade and making good his escape.

Biographer Eaton puzzles, as have many others, over the "singularly gentle" De Quincey's preoccupation with violence, concluding that "the very fact of murder had by the law of contraries a fascination for him." From another angle, "the murders had an evident appeal, in that they offered him an opportunity to reconstruct motives and circumstances with all the delight which comes from the solving of puzzles."

D.22 Des Essarts, Nicolas-Toussaint Le Moyne, *dit*   *Causes célèbres, curieuses et intéressantes de toutes les cours souveraines du royaume, avec les jugements qui les ont décidées* [Curious and Interesting Cases from All the Sovereign Courts of the Realm, with the Judgments Rendered]. Paris, 1784–86.

■ An edition of 196 volumes appeared between 1773 and 1789; the Borowitz True Crime Collection includes a partial group of 108 volumes beginning with Volume 2 (1784) and ending with Volume 124 (1786).

D.23 Dickens, Charles   *Barnaby Rudge.* 1841. In *The Works of Charles Dickens.* Vols. 3 and 4. London: Chapman & Hall, 1881–82.

■ Dickens's brilliant study of mob psychology imaginatively recreates the anti-Catholic riots instigated in London by Lord George Gordon in 1780. A high point of the novel is the description of the rioters' storming of Newgate prison, which far surpasses in expressive power the taking of the Bastille in *A Tale of Two Cities.* The historical Lord Gordon was acquitted of high treason on the ground that he had no treasonous intentions. Later he was imprisoned for five years in Newgate after being convicted of defaming the queen of France, the French ambassador, and the administration of English justice. Dickens's factual and fictional writings about crime are reviewed in Philip Collins's *Dickens and Crime* (London: Macmillan, 1962).

D.24 ——   *Bleak House.* 1852–53. In *The Works of Charles Dickens.* Vols. 26 and 27. London: Chapman & Hall, 1882–83.

■ In 1849, in the midst of a raging cholera epidemic, Maria Manning and her husband, Frederick, murdered her lover, Patrick O'Connor, in the Bermondsey district of South London. Dickens attended their hanging; his horror at the unruly behavior of the crowd led him to advocate an immediate end to public hanging (see Albert Borowitz, *The Woman Who Murdered Black Satin: The Bermondsey Horror* [1981]; B.30). In his novel *Bleak House* Dickens incorporated traits and gestures of Maria Manning in his characterization of Mlle. Hortense, Lady Dedlock's French maid who murders lawyer Tulkinghorn. The feline maid is introduced ominously: "There is something indefinably keen and wan about her anatomy; and she has a watchful way of looking out of the corners of her eyes without turning her head, which could be pleasantly dispensed with—especially when she is in an ill humour and near knives."

Though dressed elegantly (as was Maria Manning, who favored black satin), Hortense seemed "to go about like a very neat She-Wolf imperfectly tamed."

When Lady Dedlock demonstrates a preference for her pretty young maid Rose, Hortense cools her passionate resentment by walking off barefoot through the rain-soaked grass. The park-keeper's wife suggested that Hortense fancied that the wet grass was saturated with blood: "She'd as soon walk through that as anything else, I think, when her own's up!"

Hortense kills Tulkinghorn in revenge for his refusal to meet her demands to be paid more money for her brief part in his inquiries into Lady Dedlock's scandalous past.

D.25 ——— "Hunted Down." 1859. In *The Works of Charles Dickens*. Vol. 30. London: Chapman & Hall, 1881–82.

■ Julius Slinkton, the serial killer tracked in this story by the insurance actuary Mr. Meltham, is Dickens's fictional portrait of Thomas Griffiths Wainewright, artist, critic, and poisoner. Dickens caught sight of Wainewright in Newgate in 1837 when he visited the prison with the actor William Charles Macready. Philip Collins believes that in the characterization of Slinkton, Dickens also recalled William Palmer, the notorious serial poisoner from Rugeley.

D.26 ——— *Little Dorrit*. 1855–57. In *The Works of Charles Dickens*. Vols. 13 and 14. London: Chapman & Hall, 1881–82.

■ Dickens's Mr. Merdle is based on the crooked financier John Sadleir, whose suicide caused a sensation in 1856. For a summary of Sadleir's career and its literary echoes see T.14.

D.27 ——— *Martin Chuzzlewit, The Life and Adventures of*. 1843–44. In *The Works of Charles Dickens*. Vols. 17 and 18. London: Chapman & Hall, 1881–82.

■ Dickens's portrayal of the murder of the swindler Montague Tigg by Jonas Chuzzlewit was strongly influenced by John Thurtell's 1823 killing of crooked gambler William Weare in a Hertfordshire ambush. (See Albert Borowitz, *The Thurtell-Hunt Murder Case: Dark Mirror to Regency England* [1987]). Tigg, in the company of Jonas, takes a fearful carriage ride into the country under storming skies; the episode would have stirred Victorian memories of Thurtell's gig and white-faced horse that carried William Weare to a death-trap.

D.28 ——— *Oliver Twist*. 1837–38. In *The Works of Charles Dickens*. Vol. 6. London: Chapman & Hall, 1881–82.

■ In 1810, Isaac (Ikey) Solomons was sentenced to transportation for life as a pickpocket. He was not sent out of the country, and after his release following six years' imprisonment, he became one of London's leading fences. Arrested in 1827, Solomons escaped from custody and joined his wife (a convict on unrelated charges) in Van Diemen's Land (Tasmania). He was recognized there as an escaped criminal and shipped back to London, where he was convicted on two of thirteen charges of theft and receiving stolen goods. Solomons returned to Van Diemen's Land as a convict in 1831.

Many writers have assumed or declared that Ikey Solomons inspired the character of Fagin in *Oliver Twist*. This was apparently the view of Thackeray, who adopted the pen name of Ikey Solomons, Esq., Junior in writing his comic novel *Catherine* (see T.5), in which he lampooned the "Newgate novels" that glamorized criminals. Edwin Pugh, in *The Charles Dickens Originals* (1912), identified Solomons as Fagin's original, asserting that "no other Dickens commentator seems to have discovered the identity of this gentleman." Several modern critics, including Philip Collins in his *Dickens and Crime* (1962), accept this identification. However, Solomons's biographer, J. J. Tobias, in *Prince of Fences* (1974), disagrees, noting that Dickens did not utilize any of the incidents of Solomons's colorful career and did not refer to the well-known fence as a source when Eliza Davis charged the author with antisemitism because of Fagin's stereotypical Jewish traits.

D.29 ———— *A Tale of Two Cities*. 1859. In *The Works of Charles Dickens*. Vol. 11. London: Chapman & Hall, 1881–82.

■ The origins of Dickens's Dr. Manette are to be found in documents of the French Revolution and in Thomas Carlyle's history, which Dickens proudly claimed to have read nine times before embarking on the writing of *A Tale of Two Cities*. In addition to his exercise of direct influence on Dickens through the pages of his history, Carlyle, according to Dickens, sent him "two cartloads" of books on the French Revolution and its prelude, which apparently included Louis Sebastien Mercier's *Le tableau de Paris*, published in Amsterdam in 1782. The Mercier volume describes movingly a prisoner released from the Bastille on the accession of Louis XVI:

> [He is] an old man, who has for forty-seven years groaned under detention within four thick, cold walls. The low door of his tomb turns on terrible hinges, opens not halfway as ordinarily, and an unknown voice tells him that he can leave. He believes that it is a dream. He hesitates, gets up and walks with trembling steps, astonished by the space that he is traversing. He stops as if bewildered and lost; his eyes can hardly bear the light of day; he looks at the sky like a newfound object; his eyes stare; and he cannot cry. Stupefied by his freedom of movement, his legs, in spite of himself, remain as immobile as his tongue.

When he is brought back to the street where he had lived, his house is gone, the whole neighborhood is changed, and nobody knows him. An old family servant is found who tells him that his children are scattered abroad and that all his friends are gone. Overwhelmed with grief, he calls on the minister who released him from prison and begs to be returned to his cell.

The original version of a significant passage in Dickens's portrayal of Dr. Manette is easily identified in the pages of Carlyle's *French Revolution*. Carlyle writes that, when the Bastille was stormed, a letter was found that had been written years before by a prisoner begging for news of his wife. The lines quoted by Carlyle from this letter are the source of the conclusion of Dr. Manette's narrative that was read into evidence at Charles Darnay's second trial in Paris: "If for my consolation Monseigneur would grant me, for the sake of God and the Most Blessed Trinity, that I could have news of my dear wife; were it only her name on a card, to show that she is alive! It were the greatest consolation I could receive; and I should forever bless the greatness of Monseigneur."

The scene in which Dr. Manette attends to a dying woman in the Evremondes' chateau may well be based on a local tradition of Wiltshire. A ballad in Sir Walter Scott's *Rokeby*, which describes a similar occurrence, was founded on a story in John Aubrey's correspondence. In the Aubrey anecdote, Dr. Manette's role in the drama was played by a midwife: "Sir . . . Dayrell of Littlecote in Corn, Wilts, having got his lady's waiting woman with child, when her travail came, sent a servant with a horse for a midwife, whom he was to bring hoodwinked. She was brought, and layd the woman, but as soon as the child was born, she sawe the knight take the child and murder it, and burn it in the fire in the chamber. She having done her business was extraordinarily rewarded for her paines, and sent blindfolded away." Dr. Manette was less lucky, being compensated for his professional attentions by eighteen years in the Bastille.

D.30 Döblin, Alfred *Die beiden Freundinnen und ihr Giftmord* [The Two Girlfriends and Their Poisoning Murder]. In series *Aussenseiter der Gesellschaft: Die Verbrechen der Gegenwart* [Society's Outsiders: The Crimes of the Present]. Ed. Rudolf Leonhard. Vol. 1. Berlin: Verlag die Schmiede, 1924.

■ A practicing physician later to win fame as author of the novel *Berlin Alexanderplatz*, Döblin applies psychological insight and method in unraveling the complex relationship between two young women, Elli Link and Margarete Bende, who stood trial in Berlin for the poisoning of Link's abusive husband in 1922. Elli and Margarete turned to each other for consolation and support in dealing with their unhappy marriages and drifted into a lesbian relationship. Although Elli assumed the male sexual role, their correspondence indicated that she fell under the influence of the passionate Margarete, who encouraged her to persist in her ultimately successful effort to dispose of her husband, Link, by arsenic. Elli was sentenced to five years in prison for murder without deliberation, and Margarete served a year and a half in the penitentiary for abetting the poisoning. The victim's behavior was considered an extenuating circumstance. After bringing to bear a detailed interpretation of the women's correspondence (which Elli retained, perhaps, through compulsion to be punished) and of their prison dreams, Döblin stands in awe of the ultimate mystery of criminal motivation. Beyond heredity, he cites a "dark parapsychic influence or a group of such influences," and "a complex of the way of the world."

The series of which Döblin's study was the first volume was projected to include contributions by major literary figures, including Thomas Mann and Jakob Wasserman, but it was not completed. The fourteen volumes in the Borowitz True Crime Collection feature works by journalist Egon Erwin Kisch, expressionist novelist Ernst Weiss, poet Iwan Goll, and dramatist Franz Theodor Csokor.

D.31 Doctorow, E. L.   *Ragtime.* New York: Random House, 1975.

▪ This novel is a collage in which fictional characters are brought arbitrarily into relationships with historical figures of the ragtime era (in a manner more amusingly utilized by Woody Allen in his 1983 film *Zelig*). Doctorow's narrative draws substantially on two events in crime history. The trials of demented millionaire Harry K. Thaw for the murder of New York architect Stanford White dominate the background of *Ragtime*'s first third. The balance of the novel relates the rise and fall of the fictional African American terrorist Coalhouse Walker Jr., whose violence is unleashed after racist volunteer firemen vandalize and desecrate his automobile. Walker is based on sixteenth-century German firebrand Hans Kohlhase, who sought revenge after a Junker's henchmen seized and abused his horses. Kohlhase had made an earlier appearance in literature as the title character of Heinrich von Kleist's novella "Michael Kohlhaas" (1810), which Doctorow has identified as his source. In this instance Doctorow's use of historical analogy to further his plot plays him false, leading to an apparent defamation of Booker T. Washington. To end Hans Kohlhase's rebellion, Martin Luther brokered a conditional amnesty that failed to prevent Kohlhase's ultimate execution. In the denouement of *Ragtime*, Doctorow substitutes Booker T. Washington for Luther; Washington and others persuade Coalhouse Walker to abandon his scheme to blow up the Morgan Library, only to lead him unwittingly into a fatal volley of police fire.

D.32 Dostoyevsky, Fyodor   *The Brothers Karamazov.* Trans. Constance Garnett. New York: Modern Library, n.d.

▪ Biographer Ernest Simmons suggests that, in the design of Dostoyevsky's unwritten novel *The Life of a Great Sinner*, discussed in his notebooks for 1869–70, the murder of the hero's father by his serfs is similar to the murder of Dostoyevsky's own father, Mikhail (*Dostoevski: The Making of a Novelist* [London: University Press, 1940], 245). Many critics find a variant of this theme in the murder of Fyodor Karamazov by the servant Smerdyakov. However, Dostoyevski biographer Geir Kjetsaa has argued that the author's father was not murdered but died of one of his apoplectic attacks brought on by anger at his peasants' work and by the heat of the day (*Fyodor Dostoyevsky: A Writer's Life,* trans. Siri Hustvedt and David McDuff [New York: Viking, 1987], 29–36). Kjetsa also rejects the notion that Dostoyevski believed his father to have been a murder victim.

D.33 ——   *Crime and Punishment.* Trans. Constance Garnett. New York: Illustrated Modern Library, 1944.

▪ In a draft of his letter to M. N. Katkov outlining his first thoughts on *Crime and Punishment*, Dostoyevski identified current events persuading him that his plan for Raskolnikov's murder of an old moneylender was realistic:

Certain events, which have happened in the most recent past, have convinced me that my subject is not at all eccentric, (precisely because the murderer is an educated and even a well-disposed man). I was told last year of a student in Moscow, who had been expelled from the university after some trouble in school, who decided to rob the post and to kill the mailman. There are still many traces in our newspapers of extraordinary instability in our ideas, which inspires horrible deeds. [That seminary student, for example, who met the girl, by agreement with her in a shed, and killed her and whom they arrested within an hour eating his breakfast, etc.] In short I am convinced that my subject matter is in part justified by our times.

See *The Notebooks for* Crime and Punishment, ed. and trans. Edward Wasiolek (Chicago: Univ. of Chicago Press, 1967), 173.

Critic Ernest J. Simmons has noted that while abroad, Dostoyevsky "read every Russian newspaper he could get his hands on" and "particularly devoured the domestic tragedies, police records, and criminal processes which seemed to him more real than the commonplace happenings of every-day life" (*Dostoevsky: The Making of a Novelist* [London: Oxford Univ. Press, 1940], 200). In *The Idiot*, elements are borrowed from several criminal trials, including the case of fifteen-year-old Olga Umetskaya, accused of repeatedly trying to burn down the family house to avenge parental abuse. See V. S. Dorovatovskaya-Liubimov, "*Idiot* Dostoevskogo i ugolovnaya khronika ego vremeni [Dostoevski's *Idiot* and the Criminal Chronicles of His Time]," *Pechat' i revoliutsiya* 3:31–53 (1928). Dostoyevsky's later masterpiece, *The Possessed*, was inspired by nihilist Sergei G. Nechaev's 1869 murder of student Ivan Ivanov, a comrade he suspected of disloyalty to their group. See Philip Pomper, *Sergei Nechaev* (New Brunswick, N.J.: Rutgers Univ. Press, 1979).

Katerina Nikolaevna Akhmatova, the femme fatale of Dostoyevsky's *A Raw Youth*, (trans. Constance Garnett [New York: Dial Press, 1947]), may express the author's own enthusiasm for true crime when she reminds the novel's young hero how they used to scan the news together: "We reckoned up the murders and serious crimes and set them off against the cheering items" (276–77).

D.34 ———— *The House of the Dead*. Trans. and intro. David McDuff. London: Penguin, 1985. ■ This narrative is based on Dostoyevsky's four-year imprisonment at Omsk, Siberia, for his part in the Petrashevist conspiracy. Imbedded in his recollections of fellow convicts are several extended accounts of the crimes that brought them to the Omsk prison fortress:

- Luka Kuzmich, a thin little Ukrainian convict who murdered an arrogant commanding officer fond of asserting that he was the "Tsar and God as well."
- Baklushin, a simple soldier who shot a wealthy German whose marriage proposal had been accepted by Baklushin's mistress Louise. The convict commented bitterly that shooting a German was not reason enough to deport a man.
- Shishkov, who murdered his wife Akulka after she publicly declared her unwavering

love for Filka Morosov, despite the fact that Morosov had defamed her virtue before her marriage.

Even though Dostoyevsky's prison comrades included criminals far more desperate than these, it is striking that he took most interest in the men who had killed out of a sense of lost honor.

Doyle, Sir Arthur Conan. *See Conan Doyle, Sir Arthur*

D.35 Dreiser, Theodore *An American Tragedy.* New York: Boni & Liveright, 1925.

■ At least from 1914 on, Dreiser looked into a number of American murder cases as possible subjects for a novel, believing that these crimes were often impelled by a drive to rise in a society dominated by materialism. Among the murders he considered were three poisoning trials: the case of Roland Molineux, who poisoned Katherine Adams with an adulterated bottle of Bromo-Seltzer intended for Harry Cornish, athletic director of the Knickerbocker Club, of which Molineux was a member; the 1891 murder of Helen Potts by her lover, a young medical student named Carlyle Harris, who found their socially ill-assorted match an obstacle to his professional aspirations; and the Reverend Clarence Richeson's 1911 killing of a young parishioner, Avis Linnell, whose pregnancy threatened his plans to marry a wealthy woman. After writing six chapters based on the Richeson murder, he abandoned the project in favor of the Gillette-Brown case of 1906. In that year Chester Gillette, a supervisor in his uncle's skirt factory, drowned his pregnant sweetheart, an employee of that factory, Grace "Billy" Brown, in Big Moose Lake in the Adirondacks after battering her with a tennis racket. In preparation of the sprawling realist novel that, in support of its author's attack on materialistic standards of the good life, was to be titled *An American Tragedy*, Dreiser toured the murder scene and visited Sing Sing prison, where he interviewed a condemned inmate, Anthony Pantano. To lend authenticity to the courtroom scenes in the powerful second volume of his work, Dreiser, according to his biographer W. A. Swanberg "clung to fact when he could, lifting some 30 pages verbatim from old New York newspaper accounts of the court proceedings and the letters between the ill-fated lovers" (*Dreiser* [New York: Scribner, 1965], 294).

Despite his extensive borrowings from reports of the Gillette case, some of the most memorable elements of Dreiser's novel are pure invention. It has been pointed out that the early life of Clyde Griffiths (the fictional name Dreiser chose to preserve Chester Gillette's initials) bears a closer resemblance to the author's own experience than to Gillette's (see Craig Brandon, *Murder in the Adirondacks: "An American Tragedy" Revisited* [Utica: North Country Books, 1986], 338).

Dreiser makes more significant alterations of reality in his portrayal of the murder of Grace Brown (renamed Roberta "Bobbie" Alden in the novel). As Chester Gillette probably did, Clyde Griffiths makes careful plans for the drowning. When the critical moment arrives, however, he could not go through with the planned assault, and Grace's death is at least initially an accident. While Clyde is distracted by thoughts of the intended murder, Roberta startles him, and he unintentionally strikes her with his camera tripod (an innocent replacement for Chester Gillette's murderous tennis racket), knocking her out of the boat. Clyde's crime is his decision not to rescue Roberta from the waters of the lake.

Another critical variance between fact and fiction relates to the motive for the killing. Dreiser invented a romance between Clyde Griffiths and the wealthy Sondra Finchley, who embodies Clyde's hope to rise in society. In reality, Chester Gillette saw several women during his affair with Grace Brown. District Attorney George W. Ward and some of the newspapers tried to exaggerate the relationship between Gillette and Harriet Benedict, the daughter of a lawyer, in order to fabricate a love triangle. In his account of the Gillette case, Craig Brandon discounts the role of Harriet Benedict: "The reason Harriet was singled out . . . was because it was her misfortune to have her photograph on the film that was found in Chester's camera when he was arrested. Ward used the other woman idea in his presentation at the trial." See Fig. 17.

D.36 ———— *The Cowperwood Trilogy.* Consisting of *The Financier* (New York: Harper, 1912); *The Titan* (New York: John Lane, 1914); *The Stoic* (New York: Doubleday, 1947).
■ In 1871, the year of the Great Chicago Fire, Charles Tyson Yerkes, faced a related disaster in his native city of Philadelphia: caught short because of the impact of the Chicago fire on investment values, he was convicted of embezzlement in the sale of municipal bonds for Philadelphia. After serving seven months of a sentence of two years and nine months, Yerkes was never able to restore his hometown reputation, and he moved in 1882 to Chicago. There, by corrupt means, including bribery of aldermen (the so-called Grey Wolves), he obtained control of the street railway system and financed the construction of the Downtown Union Loop (elevated railway). Yerkes's contempt for the streetcar riders is revealed in his alleged remark when criticized for providing inadequate service: "Let the strap-holders pay the dividends." After failing to obtain legislation that would have assured him a long-term traction monopoly, Yerkes left Chicago for London, where he headed the syndicate that built the Underground electric train system. Shining fitfully through his cloudy reputation is a memorable act of philanthropy, Yerkes's 1892 gift of an observatory to the University of Chicago.

Ever fascinated by the struggle for power and survival, Dreiser modelled Frank Cowperwood, protagonist of *The Financier, The Titan,* and *The Stoic,* after the unscrupulous Yerkes. Purporting to admire predatory capitalists like his Cowperwood, Dreiser attacked urban reformers in a 1914 interview reported in the *Chicago Journal*: "A big city is not a teacup to be seasoned by old maids. It is a big city where men must fight and think for themselves, where the weak must go down and the strong remain."

The three novels of Dreiser's Cowperwood series are respectively based on Yerkes's activities in Philadelphia, Chicago, and London. In *The Financier* (1912) Cowperwood's romance with Aileen Butler, daughter of Philadelphia contractor and politician Edward Butler, leads to his undoing. When an anonymous note informs Butler of the affair, he and his cronies arrange to have Cowperwood indicted for embezzlement.

The sequel, *The Titan* (1914), closely adapts the facts of Yerkes's rise and fall as street and elevated railway king of Chicago. In Dreiser's interpretation, the gift of a telescope and observatory to the city's university was a calculated step intended to restore Cowperwood/Yerkes's reputation. The tale of Cowperwood's financial coups and shady political intrigues shows the business titan distinctly unluckier in love; both his second wife, Aileen Butler (whom he married after release from prison in Philadelphia), and a mistress prove unfaithful, and by the novel's end he plans to leave for Europe with his new girlfriend, Berenice Fleming.

The final volume of the trilogy, *The Stoic*, was completed with the assistance of Dreiser's wife, Helen, and published posthumously in 1947. In this weakest of the novels, Cowperwood manages to achieve control over the London Underground despite the growing complexity of his sex life. A key to Cowperwood's London success was his relationship with London financier Lord Stane, who patiently explained to the American robber baron the English style of doing business: "In England, you see, one progresses more through favor and the friendship of financial as well as social groups than through particular individuals, however gifted they may be. And if you are not well and favorably known to certain groups and accepted by them, it may be difficult to proceed."

D.37 Dryden, John, and Nathaniel Lee *The Duke of Guise*. 1683. In *The Works of John Dryden*. Vol. 14. Berkeley: Univ. of California Press, 1992.

■ Dryden's first work for the stage, written in 1661, was a tragedy of Henry, Duke of Guise. More than twenty years later, the poet returned to the same theme in a play on which he collaborated with Nathaniel Lee; he incorporated a scene from the earlier version, in which the duke returns to Paris against King Henry III's express command. The avowed purpose of Dryden in the later play was to suggest a parallel between two political conflicts of past and present: the opposition of the Catholic "Holy League" (under Guise's leadership) to the planned succession of Henry of Navarre; and the strife in late-seventeenth-century England over the selection of James as the heir of his brother Charles II. Because of the stormy political climate, the English chancellor banned production of the play for a while but, with the king's apparent approval, the prohibition was subsequently lifted. Still, pamphleteers denounced Dryden, accusing him of suggesting resemblances between Henry III and Charles II and between the Duke of Guise and Charles's seditious illegitimate son, the Duke of Monmouth. In a lengthy response, entitled *The Vindication: or, The Parallel of the French Holy-League, and the English League and Covenant, Turn'd into a Seditious Libell against the King and His Royal Highness* (1683), Dryden vituperatively rebuts these charges.

In their play, Dryden and Lee soften the character of Guise by dwelling on his apparently chaste love affair with a court lady, Marmoutier, who tries unsuccessfully to reconcile him with King Henry III, also smitten with her beauty. Some of Guise's followers do not fare as well in the authors' hands; indeed, one supporter, Malicorne, has sold his soul to the Devil and was gulled by his tempter into misreading the term of his bond. Among Henry's partisans, the old soldier Grillon, though hot tempered, is on the side of the angels. He refuses the king's command to participate in Guise's assassination at Blois: "Sir, I have eaten and drunk in my own defence, when I was hungry and thirsty. I have plunder'd, when you have not paid me—I have been content with a Farmer's Daughter, when a better Whore was not to be had. As for Cutting off a Traytor, I'le execute him lawfully in my own Function, when I meet him in the Field; but for your Chamber-practice [the intended murder ambush in the Blois Chateau], that's not my Talent."

D.38 Duke, Winifred *Bastard Verdict.* New York: Knopf, 1934.

■ Winifred Duke, who edited for *Notable British Trials* the 1920 trial of Harold Greenwood, a solicitor acquitted of poisoning his wife, based the novel *Bastard Verdict* on the case and also discussed it in the essay "The Riddle of Rumsey House," in *Six Trials* (see D.40). According to Duke's essay, Greenwood appears to have been an "easy-going, rather stupid, irresponsible, philandering, and comfort-loving man," whose behavior kept the village gossips busy. His wife, Mabel, though, a churchgoing, charitable, and gracious woman, was very popular in the village of Kidwelly, South Wales. It was Mrs. Greenwood's private income, not her husband's earnings, that made it possible for them to live with their four children in a large mansion, Rumsey House.

In the novel Muriel Fieldend (Mabel Greenwood) suffers from a variety of ailments, supposedly brought on by a bad heart, and is addicted to patent medicines and to consultations with Dr. Morgan (Dr. Griffiths), who lives conveniently across the street with his unmarried sister. Miss Morgan is one of several women with whom Harold Fieldend (Harold Greenwood) carries on a flirtation, much to the annoyance of his wife. When Mrs. Fieldend dies suddenly after an attack of indigestion, which her husband attributes to a gooseberry tart, Dr. Morgan, who attends her in her last illness, certifies that death was caused by heart disease. Though gossip about Fieldend's unseemly behavior begins immediately after his wife's death, tongues wag with renewed fury when in less than four months the widower marries a young woman, Gwyn Powell (Gwyn Jones), whose family, residing in the neighboring village where Fieldend practices, have been his friends and lunch companions for twenty years. The sinister rumors are greeted with scorn by the defiant Fieldend, who threatens legal action against the gossips. But it is not long before an inquest reveals a small amount of arsenic in the exhumed body; Fieldend is charged with having put weed killer in the bottle of burgundy that his wife drank at lunch. The Crown's theory is demolished by Fieldend's daughter, Hermione (Irene Greenwood), who testifies that both at lunch and dinner she had drunk burgundy from the bottle the Crown claimed was poisoned. Fieldend's lawyer, Sir Richard Whitley-Arkinglaze (Sir Edward Marshall Hall), contends that Fieldend had not administered the poison. The famous lawyer obtains a verdict of not guilty but never receives so much as a thank-you from his client.

In Duke's novel, Gwyn's brother expresses the attitude of the community regarding the jury's action when he says: "Not guilty of killing her by putting weed killer in the wine she drank. That's a very different thing from saying he never gave her poison at all. It was the only possible verdict on the evidence." This comment reflects an amplification of the Greenwood jury's verdict that was made by its foreman but not read in court; it was published only in 1930, after the deaths of the judge and of Greenwood. In her essay in *Six Trials*, Duke quotes the amplification: "We are satisfied on the evidence in this case that a dangerous dose of arsenic was administered to Mabel Greenwood on Sunday, 15th June,

1919, but we are not satisfied that this was the immediate cause of death. The evidence before us is insufficient, and does not conclusively satisfy us as to how, or by whom, the arsenic was administered. We therefore return a verdict of Not Guilty."

Duke concludes in her essay: "Such a finding was tatamount [*sic*] to the invidious Scots verdict of 'Not Proven,' which has been explained as meaning: 'Not Guilty, but don't do it again.'" On the title page of the novel she quotes Sir Walter Scott, who called his country's unique verdict "that bastard verdict Not Proven."

It is what happens to Fieldend after such a bastard verdict has been handed down that Duke explores in the second half of her novel: "His real punishment began from the moment he stepped out of the dock, a free man." She also focuses on the plight of his second wife, Gwyn, who shares the opprobrium cast on the acquitted murderer by an unforgiving public. She would endure with him "a life-sentence, in place of a death-sentence."

Winifred Duke (1890–1962), the daughter of a vicar, was born in Liverpool and lived her adult years in Edinburgh, where she benefited by the encouragement and friendship of eminent crime historian William Roughead. She wrote mystery fiction as well as novels based on Scottish history; was a master of the crime essay; and edited three volumes in the *Notable British Trials* series: the *Trial of Harold Greenwood* (1930), the subject of her novel, *Bastard Verdict*; the *Trial of Field and Gray* (1939); and the *Trial of Frederick Nodder* (1950).

D.39 ———— *Madeleine Smith: A Tragi-Comedy in Two Acts.* Edinburgh: William Hodge, 1928.
▪ Madeleine Smith was freed on the so-called Scottish verdict of "Not Proven" when tried in Edinburgh in 1857 for the arsenic poisoning of her lover, Pierre Emile L'Angelier (see s.32). As characterized by crime historian Winifred Duke in this play, Madeleine is a tough and cynical survivor. Asked by her young brother James what "Not Proven" means, she replies, "Not Guilty, but don't do it again." In her final monologue, Madeleine correctly foresees a long life in which the murder trial will seem like a dream; she attributes her release to her pretty ankles, of which she gave the exclusively male jury an "excellent view."

D.40 ———— *Six Trials.* London: Gollancz, 1934.
▪ Dedicating this collection to William Roughead, Duke includes mostly celebrated murder cases that have been studied by other masters of true crime: Philip Cross, the medical poisoner of Shandy Hall, County Cork, Ireland ("A Medical Miscreant"); the murder of Julia Wallace ("The Perfect Murder"); the acquittal of Harold Greenwood, charged with poisoning his wife ("The Riddle of Rumsey House"), the case that Duke fictionalized in her *Bastard Verdict*; the Gorse Hall murder of 1909 ("The Double Acquittal"; see G.27); and the acquittal of Robert Wood in the murder of Phyllis Dimmock ("Rex *versus* Robert Wood").

Perhaps out of fear of exposure to a libel action, Duke deals cautiously with the acquittal of Sarah Ann Hearn, defended by Norman Birkett in the 1930 arsenic poisoning of her neighbor and friend, Mrs. Alice Thomas, in Cornwall ("The Farmer's Wife"). According to the prosecution, the poison had been administered, at least in an initial dose, in salmon sandwiches prepared by Mrs. Hearn for a jaunt with the Thomases to Bude.

Only Mrs. Thomas took ill, and the jury, which took only fifty-four minutes to reach its verdict, may have wondered how Mrs. Hearn could have steered the poisoned sandwich into her alleged victim's hands. The absence of apparent motive was another problem, and the jury was unswayed by evidence that Mrs. Hearn's sister, Lydia (Minnie) Everard, had also died of arsenic poisoning earlier in 1930 while under her care.

D.41 ———— *Skin for Skin.* Boston: Little, Brown, 1935.

■ Basing this novel on the famous trial of insurance salesman William Herbert Wallace for the 1931 bludgeoning murder of his wife, Julia, in their Liverpool home, Duke takes her title from Job 2:4: "Skin for skin, yea, all that a man hath will he give for his life." Duke assumes that Wallace was guilty and tells the story of the plotting and commission of the crime from the point of view of her fictional alter ego, whom she names Mr. Bruce of Salchester. She documents the dreary lower-middle-class lives of the Bruces, contrasting the wife's contentment with the husband's frustration over their "Darby and Joan" existence. After Mr. Bruce's conviction, as in real life, is reversed, and he returns to the community, the anger of the public engulfs "the man they didn't hang," and his life becomes even bleaker. In the final chapter, Mr. Bruce confesses his guilt to a compassionate housekeeper.

D.42 ———— *The Stroke of Murder.* London: Robert Hale, 1937.

■ One of Duke's best works is this collection of four extended studies of murder cases. The first, "The Hand-Cart Horror," relates the most famous Liverpool murder case between the poisoning of James Maybrick and the killing of Julia Wallace. In 1913 Catherine Bradfield, a single woman of about forty, was battered to death with a marline spike in a rope and twine shop that she managed for her brother, a tarpaulin manufacturer. Strangely, the products and implements of the family business and its employees' regular work assignments combined to carry out the grisly crime. George Ball (alias Sumner), age twenty-two, a packer who used the spike in his daily work to splice rope, murdered Bradfield and, with the help of the shop's handcart boy, Samuel Eltoft, sewed the corpse into a sack weighted with bits of iron and wheeled it in a tarpaulin-covered cart to the city's canal. The motive for the crime was not established; although Ball was found to possess pornographic photographs of trussed women, there was no evidence that Catherine Bradfield had been sexually assaulted. More likely, Ball had murdered his kind manager for the few pounds of current receipts. Ball was hanged for the killing, and Eltoft was sentenced to four years in prison as accessory after the fact. Duke expresses relief that this was "one of those too rare cases where the victim's memory received sympathy and regret, and her destroyer a whole-hearted revulsion and contempt."

The epigraph of Duke's article on the "Agra double murders" ("Edith Thompson of Meerut") is Swedish author C. J. L. Almqvist's encapsulation of crime's ambiguities: "Two things are white: innocence and arsenic" (see A.7). Augusta Fulham, wife of Edward Fulham, a deputy examiner of military accounts, and her lover, Lieutenant Harry Clark, an army medical officer, were convicted in Allahabad, India, of jointly poisoning their unwanted spouses in 1911: Fulham died after months-long administration of arsenic and other toxic drugs in Meerut and Agra, and Mrs. Clark was subsequently butchered in the latter city by a group of hired Indian assassins. The title of this essay, which minutely examines the evidence in the High Court trial and the earlier proceedings before a magistrate, is explained by the fact that, like Edith Thompson, Augusta Fulham was condemned in large part because of a voluminous correspondence detailing her failed attempts to murder her husband with poison supplied by her lover (including a drug intended to mimic heat stroke). Unlike Thompson, Fulham, however, was not recording wild imaginings but rather the details of merciless assaults against her husband's body and mind. Clark admitted his guilt, claiming that he had put Fulham out of his misery after first intending only to weaken his health. The jury summarily rejected Augusta's assertion that she was acting under her lover's hypnotic influence. Clark was hanged, and Augusta, because of her pregnancy, won a commutation of her death sentence to life imprisonment. Duke notes a final twist of fate: ten months after giving birth to a son (fathered by her lover?), she died suddenly "from the same illness which she had endeavoured to bring upon her unfortunate husband—heat stroke." An excellent full-length account of the case is provided by Molly Whittington-Egan, *Khaki Mischief: The Agra Murder Case* (London: Souvenir, 1990).

The unsolved 1914 strangulation of five-year-old Willie Starchfield ("The Clue of the Coconut Cake"), whose body was found under the seat of a third-class carriage of the North London Railway, is, in Duke's understated retelling, a poignant tragedy of the urban poor. On the basis of eyewitness testimony so weak that the prosecutor and the trial judge did not permit the case to go to the jury, Willie's father, John, was tried for the crime. The sadness of the affair is multiplied by the fact that John, a newspaper seller who had lost his two other children to illness before Willie's death, was an authentic hero: in 1912 he had tackled a mad gunman, Stephen Titus, in Tottenham Court Road. Two years after Willie's murder, John Starchfield died of wounds he had sustained in overpowering Titus.

The final essay in this volume ("She Died Young") concerns a crime Duke treated in a volume she edited in the *Notable British Trials* series, the trial of Jack Alfred Field and William Thomas Gray for the 1920 murder of Irene Munro, whose body was found buried in the shingle of the "Crumbles" near Eastbourne.

D.43 Dumas, Alexandre, *père* *Celebrated Crimes* [Crimes célèbres]. Trans. I. G. Burnham. 8 vols. Philadelphia: Barrie, 1895.

■ The crimes and mysteries treated in this series originally published in Paris in 1839–40 include: the Borgia poisonings; the murder of Francesco Cenci (1598) by his daughter, Beatrice, and confederates; the poisoning of Marie de La Motte and her son Édouard by habitual criminal Antoine-François Desrues; the Man in the Iron Mask; the assassination (1819) of German playwright August von Kotzebue, a political informant to Tsar Alexander I, by a German nationalist student, Karl Ludwig Sand; the sixteenth-century impersonation of Martin Guerre by Arnaud Du Tilh.

In this early work written with several collaborators, Dumas relies on traditional sources and breaks no new ground. In his account of the Cenci affair, for example, he accepts the dubious argument of Beatrice's counsel that she was the victim of incestuous rape. In his piece on the Iron Mask, Dumas recounts alternative theories of the mysterious prisoner's identity without weaving his own narrative. In his Three Musketeers novel of 1848–50, *Le vicomte de Bragelonne*, however, he introduced the Iron Mask as a major character and identified him as a twin brother of Louis XIV (see D.46).

D.44 ———— *Le chevalier de Maison-Rouge*. 1846. New York: Thomas Nelson, n.d.
■ This novel is a highly fictionalized account of the efforts of historical "Chevalier de Maison-Rouge" (Alexandre-Dominique-Joseph Gonsse, marquis de Rougeville [1761–1814]) to rescue Marie Antoinette from prison during the Terror. At the end of the novel, the chevalier commits suicide at the foot of Marie Antoinette's scaffold, whereas in real life he was executed in 1814 for assistance to invading Russian forces (see L.18).

D.45 ———— *The Count of Monte Cristo*. 1844–48. 2 vols. New York: Thomas Nelson, n.d.
■ Dumas's Edmond Dantès, the Count of Monte Cristo, was based on the principal figure in what the French like to call a *fait divers*, a human interest story often featuring crime or violence. Dumas found the roots of his novel in an 1838 work by a lawyer Jacques Peuchet, entitled *Historical Memoirs Drawn from the Archives of the Police of Paris*. Peuchet's work tells of a young shoemaker, François Picaud, who was falsely denounced as a traitor in 1807 and imprisoned—not in the Chateau d'If, the fortress that held the future Count of Monte Cristo, but in the Chateau de Fenestrelle. From this prison Picaud emerged in 1814 to avenge himself serially on his enemies. Even the Abbé de Faria, who taught Edmond Dantès and led him to the treasure of Monte Cristo, has been identified as a historical personage; the real Faria was an adept in the doctrines of Swedenborg and Mesmer and became a pioneer of the techniques of psychological suggestion.

D.46 ———— *The Man in the Iron Mask*. Intro. André Maurois. New York: Limited Editions Club, 1965.
■ In his *Celebrated Crimes*, first published in France in 1839–40, Alexandre Dumas included an article summarizing the various theories concerning the identity of the Man in the Iron Mask, the "unknown prisoner" who haunts seventeenth-century French history. When he created a fictional account of this historical enigma in the concluding portion of his Three Musketeers novel, *The Viscount de Bragelonne: or, Ten Years After* (1848–50), Dumas adopted the historical theory identifying the Man in the Iron Mask as the sequestered twin of the reigning king Louis XIV. In the novel, Aramis, one of the Three Musketeers, rescues the prisoner and schemes to place him on the throne. The plot is foiled, however, when the twins are brought face to face in the presence of their mother, Anne of Austria, who recognizes the true king. The pretender is sent to the island prison of Sainte-Marguerite, and his face will never again be unmasked.

Dumas returned to the same subject in *The Princess of Monaco: or, Life and Adventures of Catherine Charlotte de Gramont de Grimaldi* (1854). In this narrative, which purports to be the edited memoirs of Charlotte de Gramont, princess of Monaco, Dumas refers to a mysterious night of love that Charlotte spent with "Jules-Philippe," the Man in the Iron Mask, in his prison at Pignerol in Savoy.

D.47 ———— *Marguerite de Valois (La reine Margot)*. 1845–47. New York: Thomas Nelson, n.d.
■ Sexual intrigue at the Valois court at the time of the marriage of Henri of Navarre (who would become Henri IV of France) with Marguerite (Margot) de Valois plays in counterpoint with the bloody massacre of Huguenots on St. Bartholomew's Day 1572. Dumas spices his tale with mysterious potions, sorcery, and ingenious royal poisonings.

The contemporary sixteenth-century interpretations of the St. Bartholomew's Day massacre are studied in Robert M. Kingdon, *Myths about the St. Bartholomew's Day Massacres 1572–1576* (Cambridge: Harvard Univ. Press, 1988).

D.48 ———— *The Queen's Necklace*. 1849–50. Intro. Henri Peyre. New York: Limited Editions Club, 1973.
■ In this novel, Dumas brilliantly reconstructs the theft of the diamond necklace produced for Queen Marie Antoinette by court jeweler Boehmer (see c.12). The novel ends with the branding of the thief Jeanne de la Motte on the scaffold; in real life, she later escaped from prison and wrote her memoirs in England.

D.49 Dumas, Alexandre, *fils* *Les femmes qui tuent et les femmes qui votent* [Women Who Kill and Women Who Vote]. Paris: Calmann Lévy, 1880.
■ In this book advocating reform of women's social, legal, and political status, Dumas takes as his starting point three sensational trials of female defendants in 1880 (see Albert Bataille, *Causes criminelles et mondaines 1880–1898* [Paris: Dentu, 1887]):

- Marie Bière, abandoned by an "elegant and worldly" Parisian, Robert Gentien, to whom she bore a child who died at six months, was acquitted after shooting and seriously wounding him.
- Hélène Dumaire was sentenced to ten years' imprisonment for the murder of her former lover, Dr. Picart of Laon, who had posted banns for his marriage to another woman.
- Madame Marie de Tilly, who threw vitriol in the face of her husband's young mistress, Marie Maréchal, a milliner's assistant, blinding her in one eye and disfiguring her, was acquitted to resounding applause.

In Dumas's estimation, all three crimes were inspired by women's inability to find legal remedies and, what was more important, socially approved courses of action in confronting sexual and family issues. Among the restrictions he deplored were the inadequacy of divorce and paternity laws; society's condemnation of women who sought love outside marriage; the limitations on the rights of unwed women to pass property to their children; and the denial of voting rights to women. Repeatedly Dumas emphasizes his view that women suffered more grievously as a result of hostile custom and social prejudice than because of refusal of the legislature to grant equal rights.

D.50 Dunlap, William *André.* In *Early American Drama*. Ed. Jeffrey H. Richards. Harmondsworth: Penguin Classics, 1997.

■ In 1780 young British major John André negotiated with General Benedict Arnold for the transfer of the American fort at West Point to British control. In disguise and carrying a forged pass in the name of "John Anderson," André was caught while trying to return to British-held territory; after pleading in vain for a firing squad, he was hanged as a spy. William Dunlap (1766–1839), America's first professional playwright, staged *André* in 1798 when the political wounds of the Revolution were still fresh. The son of a Tory, Dunlap created a highly sympathetic portrait of André, and it is no surprise that the play's run did not survive its third performance. The hostility of the opening night's audience was sharpened by a scene in which a fictional American officer named Bland pleads with George Washington (identified only as "the General") for the life of André, who previously saved Bland from a British prison. Outraged by Washington's refusal, the young officer tears a patriotic cockade from his helmet. When the audience hissed, Dunlap understood that the play was in trouble and overnight tried to repair the damage by writing a new scene in which Bland regrets his rashness and restores the cockade. This gesture was too little and too late; the play was doomed.

When the work was published shortly after the production closed, Dunlap buttressed its claim to historicity by appending "authentic documents," including the proceedings of Major André's court martial. The prologue of the play itself contains an eloquent defense of the poet's right to build his work on a foundation of facts even where recency can excite the audience's passions:

Our Poet builds upon a fact tonight;
Yet claims, in building, every Poet's right;
To choose, embellish, lop, or add, or blend,
Fiction with truth, as best may suit his end;
Which, he avows, is pleasure to impart,
And move the passions but to mend the heart.

D.51 Dunne, Dominick *Justice: Crimes, Trials, and Punishments*. New York: Crown, 2001.

■ This collection of *Vanity Fair* articles bears the ironic title of an essay that marked the author's debut in crime writing, a reportage of a case in which justice was *not* done: John Sweeney, former lover of Dunne's daughter, Dominique, served only two and a half years for her murder. Sweeney's stangulation assault on Dominique five weeks before the murderous attack left such clearly visible marks on her neck that the young actress needed no cosmetics to portray an abuse victim in an episode of *Hill Street Blues*. The trial judge infuriated the grieving Dunne by excluding evidence of attacks by Sweeney on a previous girl friend.

Unlike the studies in Calvin Trillin's 1984 collection *Killings*, which concern crimes on the back pages (see Albert Borowitz, Book Review, *Criminal Law Review* [July–Aug. 1984], 396–400), the rest of Dunne's articles examine murders among the rich and famous:

- Marvin Pancoast's slaying of Alfred Bloomingdale's mistress, Vicki Morgan, who was supposedly penning a tell-all and tell-who memoir. Her life and death inspired Dunne's 1990 novel and a television miniseries, both titled *An Inconvenient Woman*.
- The "fatally charming" Claus von Bülow's ultimate acquittal on charges of attempted arsenic poisoning of his wife, Sunny, in her Newport mansion
- The trials of Lyle and Erik Menendez for the ferocious murders of their parents. In the first trial, a sexual abuse defense was successful, but a retrial resulted in life imprisonment without parole.
- The killing of du Pont family member Dean MacGuigan's lover, an "occasional hooker" named Pati Margello
- The famous 1943 New York City murder of heiress Patricia Burton, battered with candlesticks by her estranged bisexual husband, Canadian airman Wayne Lonergan
- The mysterious fate of banker Edmond J. Safra, who died in Monte Carlo in 1999 of "asphyxiation in a locked, bunker-like bathroom in a conflagration that engulfed his magnificent duplex penthouse, atop a building housing the Republic National Bank, which he had made final arrangements to sell a few days previously"
- The golf-club bludgeoning of Martha Moxley in 1975, for which Michael Skakel was indicted a quarter-century later. Dunne, whose 1993 novel *A Season in Purgatory* turned the fatal golf club into a baseball bat, was instrumental in reawakening police interest in the crime.

The centerpiece of Dunne's eminently readable book is a series of ten articles detailing his impressions of O. J. Simpson's criminal and civil trials for the murders and wrongful deaths of Nicole Brown Simpson and Ron Goldman. Even in such familiar territory, Dunne's relentless interviewing and schmoozing are fruitful. He records, for example, a possible explanation of the prosecution's puzzling decision not to introduce the slow-motion Bronco flight to show O.J.'s consciousness of guilt: police helicopter recordings, available to the defense, might have caught a persuasively weeping Simpson lamenting that he had fallen prey to a police conspiracy.

Time and again Dunne is able to induce celebrities to make offguard revelations simply because his own celebrity, growing over the years, opens doors . . . and mouths. Although he relishes his reportorial triumphs, his view of justice is disillusioned: "From hanging out at murder trials, as I do, I have grown despondent about the goodness of people. Truth has taken an ignominious decline in importance. Truth is what you get the jury to believe" (214).

D.52 Dunne, Finley Peter *Mr. Dooley and the Chicago Irish: The Autobiography of a Nineteenth-Century Ethnic Group.* Ed. and intro. Charles Fanning. Washington, D.C.: Catholic Univ. of America Press, 1987.

■ This volume collects the Chicago pieces of Dunne's immortal "Mr. Dooley." An Irish immigrant speaking a brogue and a mind that were very much his own, Martin J. Dooley tended bar on "Archey Road" (Archer Avenue) in the working-class neighborhood of

Bridgeport on Chicago's South Side. Mr. Dooley's trenchant comments on his city's affairs included highly original views on local crimes of his era. In "Hanging Aldermen: How Boodle Is Dispensed," the bartender appraises rumors that streetcar magnate, Charles T. Yerkes (the original of Theodore Dreiser's Frank Cowperwood, see D.36), bribed aldermen to approve a fifty-year street-railway franchise. In Mr. Dooley's opinion, the corruptible politicians are not so culpable as the "widdies and orphans," who are shareholders in the streetcar companies for which Yerkes acts. "A New Verdict in the Cronin Murder Case" elicits Mr. Dooley's brilliant analysis of a late-nineteenth-century murder that was dubbed the "crime of the century." Dr. Patrick Henry Cronin, a Chicago physician associated with the Irish nationalist group, Clan na Gael Camp 96, was killed in 1889 after accusing fellow members of embezzling funds. The 1894 acquittal of police sergeant Daniel Coughlin divided Mr. Dooley's customers into hostile factions, but the wily barkeeper, so as not to lose their patronage, agreed with every opinion they expressed in turn. When one habitué, John McKenna, pressed him for details about his own membership in the Clan na Gael, Mr. Dooley, after exhausting all other dodges, accused his questioner of being a "British spoy."

Mr. Dooley had little patience for the impenetrable testimony of forensic scientists in the trial of Adolph Luetgert, arrested in 1897 for murdering his wife and grinding up her remains as raw material for his sausage factory ("Expert Testimony at the Luetgert Trial"). Under Mr. Dooley's more practical approach to criminal law, "[Lootgert] ought to be hanged on gin'ral principles; f'r a man must keep his wife around th' house, an' whin she isn't there, it shows he's a poor provider."

D.53 Dylan, Bob [pseudonym of Robert Allen Zimmerman], and Jacques Levy "Hurricane." On LP *Desire* (1976).

■ Stronger in protest than in rhyme, the lyrics to this song proclaiming the innocence of middleweight boxer Rubin "Hurricane" Carter in a barroom shooting introduce the narrative:

Here comes the story of the Hurricane
The man the authorities came to blame
For somethin' that he never done.

E

E.1 Eliot, T[homas] S[tearns] *Murder in the Cathedral.* New York: Harcourt Brace, 1935.
■ Written for production at the Canterbury Festival in 1935, the poetic drama brings into conflict many views regarding the meaning of Archbishop Thomas Becket's life and his assassination in Canterbury Cathedral in 1170. Returning to England after a seven-year absence due to estrangement from King Henry II, Becket is met by Four Tempters. The first three offer him temporal prizes: a return to his early life of pleasure; resumption of

political authority as the King's Chancellor; and alliance with the barons in opposition to Henry. A final Tempter exhorts Thomas to continue on his spiritual course for the glory of achieving sainthood after death, but the Archbishop spurns his counsel: "The last temptation is the greatest treason: / To do the right deed for the wrong reason."

In Becket's view, which he expresses in a sermon preached in the cathedral on Christmas morning, Christian martyrdom is not "the effect of a man's will to become a saint" but is "always the design of God."

Four Knights appear to charge Becket with insurrection against King Henry; when he refuses to bow to the throne's ultimatum that would have required rescission of certain steps he had taken as England's supreme spiritual authority, they kill him. After the chorus of Canterbury women laments the defilement of the entire world by the act of sacrilegious violence, the murderers address the audience and prosily justify their bloody deed. The Second Knight, for example, urges a long historical perspective: "But, if you have now arrived at a just subordination of the pretensions of the Church to the welfare of the State, remember that it is we who took the first step."

E.2 Ellroy, James *Black Dahlia.* New York: Mysterious Press, 1987.

■ In January 1947, the mutilated and bisected body of a young woman was found in a weedy vacant lot in Los Angeles. Soon identified as Elizabeth Short, a pursuer of both men and a career in film, Elizabeth became known as the "Black Dahlia" because of the tight-fitting black dresses she favored when she was on the prowl. The nickname was drawn from the title of *The Blue Dahlia*, a 1946 film scripted by Raymond Chandler and starring Alan Ladd.

The Dahlia's murder has never been solved. The case may have had a personal appeal to James Ellroy, who lost his mother, Jean Ellroy, to an unknown killer in 1958. See James Ellroy, *My Dark Places: An L.A. Crime Memoir* (New York: Knopf, 1996). The narrator of his novel *Black Dahlia*, Los Angeles policeman and former boxer Dwight (Bucky) Bleichert, is impressed to observe how strongly people he interviews about the murder link the Dahlia's story to their own lives: "The longer I listened the more they talked about themselves, interweaving their sad tales with the story of the Black Dahlia, who they actually believed to be a glamorous siren headed for Hollywood stardom."

Many of the novel's principal characters share this Dahlia obsession. Bleichert fantasizes about Elizabeth Short when he makes love. Madeleine Sprague, a Dahlia look-alike, adopts her characteristic dress when she picks up men at bars, hoping that her resemblance to the dead girl will stoke Bleichert's passion. Bucky's police partner, a retired prizefighter named Lee Blanchard, is emotionally stirred by the torture-murder of the Dahlia because of the burden of guilt he bears in having failed to prevent the murder of his younger sister.

As Bleichert and Blanchard investigate the Dahlia mystery, they reveal layer upon layer of urban evils—prostitution, pornography, sadism, police brutality and corruption, and unsafe housing construction by contractors with gangster ties. After Blanchard is murdered, Bleichert discovers that a pair of perverted lovers killed and mutilated Elizabeth Short, but he does not reveal their names to the authorities, preferring to mete out his own brand of secret justice.

Ellroy's noir vision of Los Angeles in his novel influenced producer/saxophonist Bob Belden's composition of a jazz suite, *Black Dahlia,* released in 2001 on the Blue Note label.

In John Gregory Dunne's 1997 novel *True Confessions,* Los Angeles police detective, and formerly vice squad bagman, Tom Spellacy investigates the Dahlia-like torso murder of Lois Fazenda, whom he casually dubs "the Virgin Tramp," igniting a media frenzy. The "web of circumstances" spun by the crime ruins the career of Tom's brother and alter ego, Des, an ambitious priest. Des had had the misfortune of meeting the Virgin Tramp when she hitched a ride with a prominent Catholic layman who became one of her countless lovers.

E.3 Enfield, D. E. *L.E.L.: A Mystery of the Thirties.* London: Published by Leonard and Virginia Woolf at the Hogarth Press, 1928.

■ This account of the life and literary career of Letitia E. Landon begins with the death of Lord Byron in 1824. From 1821 to 1830 her facile pen produced five volumes of poetry on the theme of love and death with touches of Byronic disillusionment. Her books, signed mysteriously L.E.L., quickly became best sellers in "an England . . . which had ignored Keats and Shelley, deified Byron, . . . where the novels of Bulwer Lytton were on every table and Shakespeare was acted in the version of Colley Cibber." Famous as a poet before she was twenty-five, by 1830 she turned to novels and criticism to sustain herself financially and to accommodate the public's changing taste. It may well have been her sharp criticism that made enemies, or perhaps it was her flirtatious and indiscreet manner at her salons. Whether the motive was literary or marital jealousy, someone began sending anonymous letters spreading rumors of L.E.L.'s scandalous behavior. Though most likely false, the accusations aroused suspicions that caused a suitor to break his engagement, and to be cast off at the age of thirty-two was a disaster to any single woman at the time. L.E.L. was quick, however, to find a substitute fiancé in the unlikely figure of Captain George Maclean, governor of Cape Castle, West Africa.

Perhaps the captain revived her childhood impressions of Africa from tales told by her father of his trip there and novels she had read. Her friends were surprised and relieved that L.E.L. was finally betrothed. Disraeli wrote to his sister: "L.E.L. is at last going to be married, but to an obscure man you never heard of. He has some foreign appointment where he will take her."

In Africa she tried to make the best of an unhappy situation, but her letters revealed trouble. Her husband neglected her, drank heavily, and, in her words, was "the most unliveable with person you can imagine." She also confided ominously, "He says he will never leave off correcting me till he has broken my temper, which you know was never bad." To her correspondents in London, the news of her death from an overdose of prussic acid just a few months after her arrival at her husband's post raised suspicions of murder. Maclean had buried her within twelve hours of her death without an autopsy and after an inadequate investigation.

Furthermore, he had destroyed letters she was sending by her maid back to England. L.E.L.'s London physician denied in the press that he had prescribed the poison. When the maid returned to London, she recalled for the first time that an African servant had brought a cup of coffee to her mistress just before her death; her statement cast suspicion on the governor, whom she disliked. Several newspapers covered the story, and Letitia's brother wrote to the Colonial Office asking for an official inquiry. A year later, after a second letter, he received the response that there were too many difficulties for a "proper investigation" and that "the papers to which you allude . . . are at present mislaid."

The Borowitz True Crime Collection holds Lytton Strachey's signed copy of Enfield's *L.E.L.*

E.4 Erlanger, Philippe *L'Étrange mort de Henri IV*. Preface Frédéric Pottecher. In series *Les causes célèbres*. Geneva: Photo-Service, 1972.

■ In *The Strange Death of Henri IV*, Erlanger seeks to overthrow the traditional view that the assassination of King Henri IV by François Ravaillac in 1610 was the work of a semi-madman acting alone. The historian argues that the pro-Spanish, ultra-Catholic faction manipulated the assassin as its tool and suggests that the Reichstag fire of 1933 provides a modern analogy.

E.5 Espina y García, Antonio *Luis Candelas, el bandido de Madrid*. 1929. 6th ed. Madrid: Collection Austral, 1996.

■ Candelas, Spain's favorite nineteenth-century thief and highwayman, would not have approved of his nickname, the "Bandit" of Madrid. In his understanding, a bandit was a violent robber who gave little thought about taking human life, and he often said that he would not shake the hand of such a villain. His own talents, like those of his French contemporary, Cartouche, ran to organizing a gang of urban criminals, corruption of strategically placed servants, and formulation of exquisitely subtle capers. The burglary of the Lonja del Ginovés utilized a chimney, a woman's chemise, a safe, and the jealousy of a wife.

One day a wife found a little box containing a chemise together with an invoice addressed to her husband. This incriminating evidence had, of course, been planted by the Candelas gang. When the injured spouse broke into tears, she was consoled by her maid (fiancée of one of Candelas's henchmen), who suggested she seek further confirmation of her husband's infidelity by examining his safe when he was out on the town. The wife filched her husband's key, and when she opened the safe at night, she was confronted by a masked man who looted the contents and escaped through the chimney by which he had entered.

Although Candelas baffled the forces of law and order in a series of jail breaks, he ended his life on the gallows in 1837. Espina's account of the outlaw's career is in the form of a "novelized" biography, one of his favorite genres. Like French writers such as G. Lenotre, he favored "little history," which focuses on everyday life. In the prologue to his *Six Spanish Lives* (1967), he explained his interest in this source of literature: "'Little history' is a lode extremely rich in action, plot, character and anecdote. In reality, more than a mine, it is a grotto that is enchanted or full of enchantment. From it the writer can extract an infinity of themes and subjects, settings and characters intimately united with a biographical narrative." Espina's storytelling is spiced with wordplay, euphuisms, and a generous admixture of slang.

Fig. 1. Théodore Géricault. This drawing (ca. 1816–17) probably depicts the assassination of
Tiberius Gracchus by a Roman mob in 133 B.C. *Promised gift, Cleveland Museum of Art.* See P.15.

Fig. 2. *Judith and Holofernes*, Michelangelo Merisi da Caravaggio. Galleria Nazionale d'Arte Antica, Palazzo Barberini-Corsini, Rome. This 1600 painting may have been inspired by the parricide for which Beatrice Cenci was executed the year before (see the Introduction's discussion of Italian true-crime literature). *Scala/Art Resource, New York.*

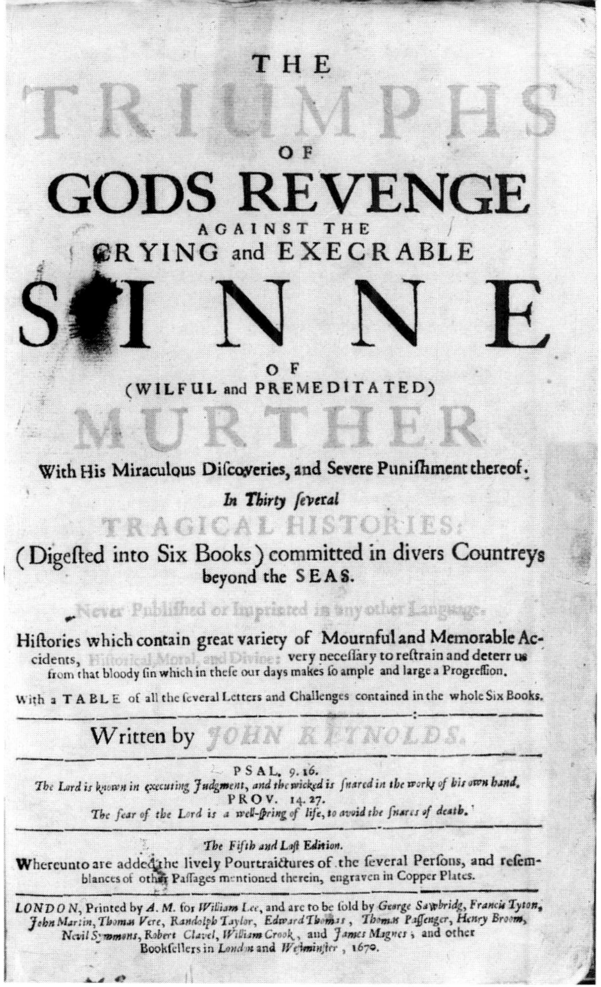

THE
TRIUMPHS
OF
GODS REVENGE
AGAINST THE
CRYING and EXECRABLE
SINNE
OF
(WILFUL and PREMEDITATED)
MURTHER

With His Miraculous Discoveries, and Severe Punishment thereof.

In Thirty several

TRAGICAL HISTORIES;

(Digested into Six Books) committed in divers Countreys
beyond the SEAS.

Never Published or Imprinted in any other Language.

Histories which contain great variety of Mournful and Memorable Accidents,
.... very necessary to restrain and deter us
from that bloody sin which in these our days makes so ample and large a Progression.

With a TABLE of all the several Letters and Challenges contained in the whole Six Books.

Written by JOHN REYNOLDS.

PSAL. 9. 16.
The Lord is known in executing Judgment, and the wicked is snared in the works of his own hand.
PROV. 14. 27.
The fear of the Lord is a well-spring of life, to avoid the snares of death.

The Fifth and Last Edition.

Whereunto are added the lively Pourtraictures of the several Persons, and resemblances of other Passages mentioned therein, engraven in Copper Plates.

LONDON, Printed by A. M. for William Lee, and are to be sold by George Sawbridge, Francis Tyton, John Martin, Thomas Vere, Randolph Taylor, Edward Thomas, Thomas Passenger, Henry Brome, Nevil Symmons, Robert Clavel, William Crook, and James Magnes, and other Booksellers in London and Westminster, 1670.

Fiat Justitia

Via Homicide

THE TRIVMPHS
OF GODS REVENGE
against the
Crying & Execrable
Sinne of (Willfull and
Premeditated) Murther
Expressd In Thirtye
Severall Tragicall Historyes
Digested into Six Bookes
& co[m]mon great variety of
Mournefull and memorable incidents
Amorous Mirull & tyme
The whole Worke now
Corrected and purified
Written By John Reynolds

LONDON Printed
for & by ... and are To
be sould by the Booke
sellers of London.

Fig. 3a&b. Title pages from John Reynolds's *The Triumphs of God's Revenge Against . . . Murther* (London, 1670). Borowitz True Crime Collection, Kent State University Libraries. See R.11.

An Exact Representation of ye Holes Shepherd made in ye Chimney and of ye Locks Bolts & Doors he broke open in making his wonderfull Escape out of Newgate Oct ye 15th 1724 between ye in ye morning & in ye evening.

AA Shepherds Hand cuff
B ye Iron Staple Screw which he Wrote to which the Shandals were Padlock'd
C ye Iron Staple in the floor to which his Shandals were Padlock'd

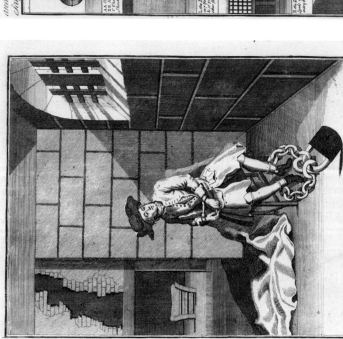

JACK SHEPHERD.
Drawn from the Life.

A. The Hole he made in ye Chimney when he got loose

Fig. 4a&b. Jack
Shepherd (Sheppard)
drawn from the life
(London print, 1724).
The print includes a
representation of the
holes Sheppard made
in a chimney and of
locks, bolts, and doors
he broke in escaping
from London's
Newgate prison.
*Borowitz True Crime
Collection, Kent State
University Libraries.* See
H.23.

Fig. 5. A caricature of gypsy Mary Squires as a witch. Squires was exculpated from complicity in the alleged 1753 "kidnapping" of Elizabeth Canning near London. *Borowitz True Crime Collection, Kent State University Libraries.* See D.15.

Fig. 6. Nineteenth-century French medallions. *Left*: French School portrait of Jean-Paul Marat. *Right*: Elshoecht (Jean-Jacques-Marie-Carl Vital), portrait of Marat's 1793 assassin, Charlotte Corday. *Author's collection.* See w.11.

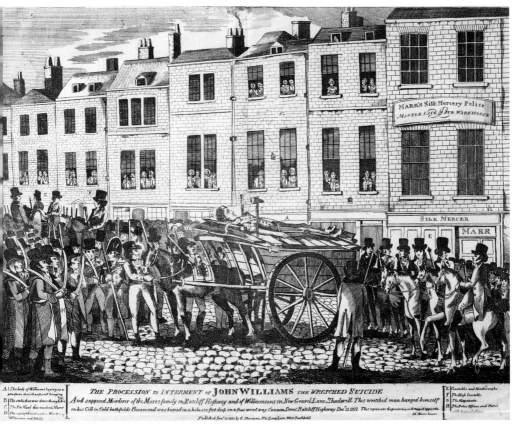

Fig. 7. The procession to interment of John Williams "the wretched suicide," the so-called Ratcliffe Highway murderer (London print, 1813). *Borowitz True Crime Collection, Kent State University Libraries.* See D.21.

MEMOIRS

OF

VIDOCQ.

VIDOCQ ARRESTING PONS.—*Page* 569.

PHILADELPHIA:

T. B. PETERSON & BROTHERS.

306 CHESTNUT STREET.

Fig. 8. The title page of *Memoirs of [Eugène-François] Vidocq* (Philadelphia: T. B. Peterson, 1859). The first French edition appeared in 1828. *Borowitz True Crime Collection, Kent State University Libraries.* See v.6.

Fig. 9. A nineteenth-century English child's plate depicting a young London street entertainer, Carlo Ferrari, known as the "Poor Italian Boy." Carlo was murdered in 1831 by John Bishop and Thomas Williams, who offered his body as a dissecting subject. The plate may have been intended to caution children against running away from home. *Borowitz True Crime Collection, Kent State University Libraries.* See s.35.

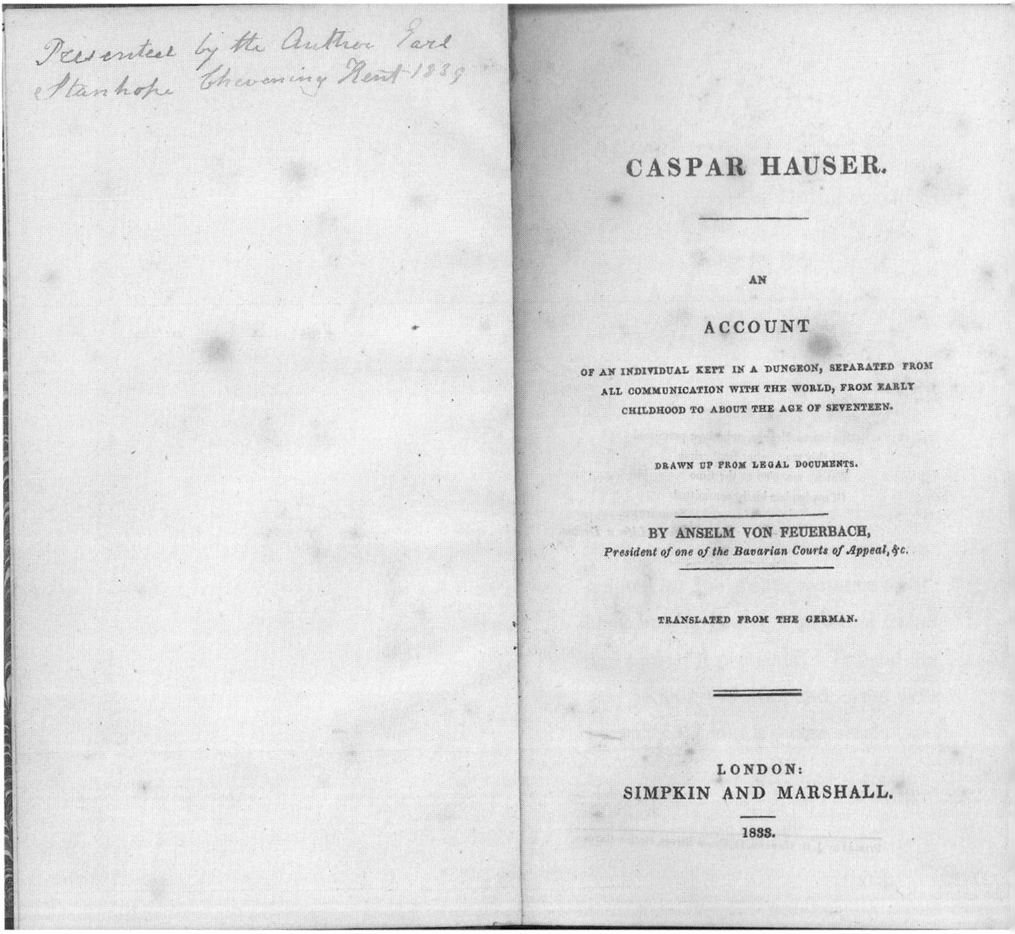

Presented by the Author Earl Stanhope Chevening Kent 1839

CASPAR HAUSER.

AN

ACCOUNT

OF AN INDIVIDUAL KEPT IN A DUNGEON, SEPARATED FROM ALL COMMUNICATION WITH THE WORLD, FROM EARLY CHILDHOOD TO ABOUT THE AGE OF SEVENTEEN.

DRAWN UP FROM LEGAL DOCUMENTS.

BY ANSELM VON FEUERBACH,
President of one of the Bavarian Courts of Appeal, &c.

TRANSLATED FROM THE GERMAN.

LONDON:
SIMPKIN AND MARSHALL.

1833.

Fig. 10. The title page of Paul Johann Anselm Ritter von Feuerbach, *Caspar Hauser* (London , 1833). This rare copy was presented by Earl Stanhope to a recipient in 1839, six years after the death of Hauser, in which Stanhope has often been implicated. *Borowitz True Crime Collection, Kent State University Libraries.* See w.7.

Fig. 11. In this hand-colored print of Mary Cecilia Rogers (the original of Edgar Allan Poe's Marie Roget), the caption describes Mary as "Known as the beautiful Cigar Girl Murder'd at Hoboken on Sunday July 25 1841. Aged 21 Years." The portrait was drawn "by the direction of Mr. J. Anderson her late Employer No. 2 Wall Street 321 Broadway N.Y." *Borowitz True Crime Collection, Kent State University Libraries.* See P.16.

Fig. 12. Maria Manning. This print from a daguerreotype was taken during the murder investigation of the Southwark (South London) Police Court, 1849. *Borowitz True Crime Collection, Kent State University Libraries.* See B.30.

Fig. 14. This piece of Staffordshire pottery represents English serial poisoner William Palmer and his house. In 1856 Palmer was executed in front of the Stafford jail. *Borowitz True Crime Collection, Kent State University Libraries.* See G.37.

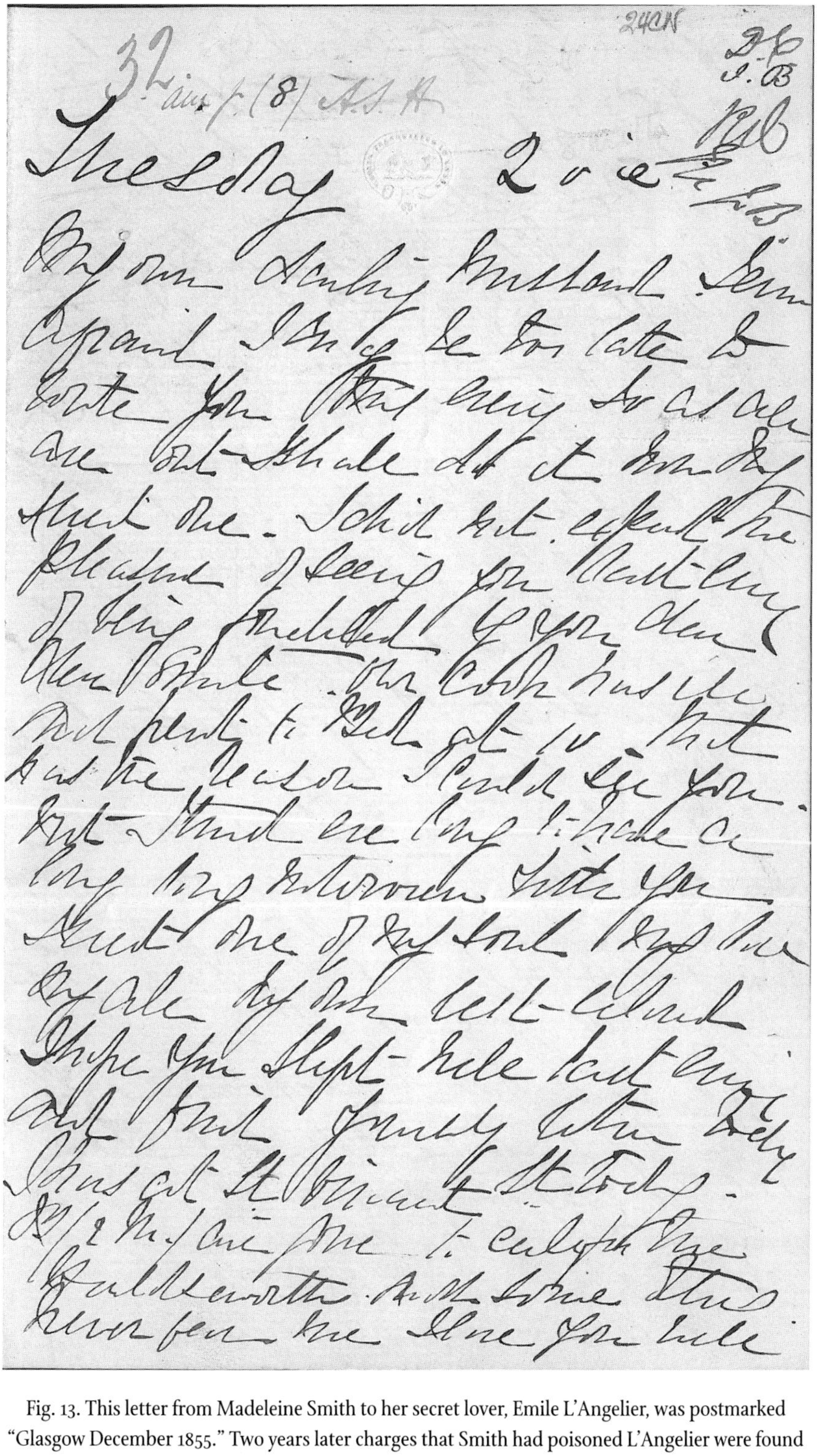

Fig. 13. This letter from Madeleine Smith to her secret lover, Emile L'Angelier, was postmarked "Glasgow December 1855." Two years later charges that Smith had poisoned L'Angelier were found "not proven." *Borowitz True Crime Collection, Kent State University Libraries.* See s.32.

Fig. 15. A broadside (1864) of the trial and execution of Franz Müller at the Old Bailey for the murder of Mr. Briggs on the North London Railway. *Borowitz True Crime Collection, Kent State University Libraries.* See N.7.

Fig. 16. Memorial plate of Prince Albert Victor, Duke of Clarence, who died in 1892. A grandson of Queen Victoria, Clarence is one of the myriad Jack the Ripper suspects. See Michael Harrison, *Clarence: Was He Jack the Ripper?* (New York: Drake, 1974). *Borowitz True Crime Collection, Kent State University Libraries.*

Fig. 17. "Entreating," a song sheet in memory of Grace Brown, victim in the "American Tragedy" (Chester Gillette) murder case of 1906. *Borowitz True Crime Collection, Kent State University Libraries.* See D.35.

Fig. 18. Contemporary publications relating to three famous American murder trials: Harry Thaw, Professor John W. Webster (the "Harvard Murder Case"), and Leopold and Loeb. *Borowitz True Crime Collection, Kent State University Libraries.*

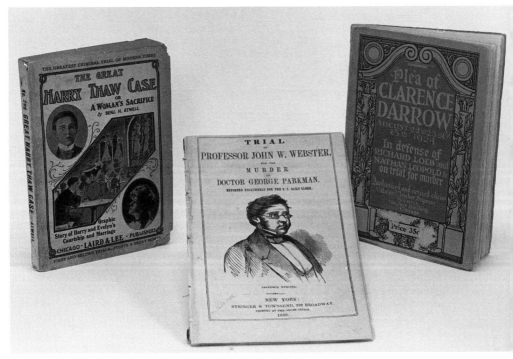

F

F.1 [Famous Trials Series] *Famous Trials*. 16 vols. Gen. ed. George Dilnot. London: Geoffrey Bles, 1928–31.

■ By contrast with the *Notable British Trials*, most of these volumes, rather than presenting edited trial transcripts, are narratives that include extensive quotations from the courtroom record. The editors, who vary in skill, include mystery writers Edgar Wallace and John Rhode. A list of the cases in the series (mostly British) and their respective editors follows:

- Trial of Patrick Mahon, the "Crumbles" murderer. Ed. Edgar Wallace.
- Trial of Harry K. Thaw, murderer of architect Stanford White in New York City. Ed. F. A. MacKenzie.
- Trial of the Peltzer brothers, Armand and Léon, convicted in Brussels of the 1882 murder of Guillaume Bernays, whose wife Armand amorously pursued. Ed. Gérard Harry.
- Trial of Harvard Professor John W. Webster, hanged for the 1849 murder of his pressing creditor Dr. George Parkman. Ed. George Dilnot.
- Trial of William Corder's murder of Maria Marten in the "Red Barn" (a reprint of a contemporary account of 1828). Ed. J. Curtis.
- Trial of Scotland Yard inspectors for conspiracy with swindler Harry Benson, who carried on fraudulent billing agencies (the "Trial of the Detectives"). Ed. George Dilnot.
- Trial of Constance Kent's 1860 murder of her little brother, the "Road Murder," which is a source of Wilkie Collins's novel *The Moonstone*. Ed. John Rhode.
- Trial of Henri Désiré Landru, French serial killer and incinerator of women. Ed. F. A. MacKenzie.
- Trial of Norman Thorne, who murdered, dismembered and buried Elsie Cameron in 1924 at his chicken farm in Crowborough, Sussex. Ed. Helena Normanton.
- Trial of Thomas Henry Allaway, hanged for the 1922 murder of Irene May Wilkins at Bournemouth. Ed. W. Lloyd Woodland.
- Trial of Jim the Penman (James Townsend Saward), a forger sentenced in 1857 to transportation for life. Ed. George Dilnot.
- Trial of American swindlers George and Austin Bidwell, who perpetrated the "Bank of England Forgery" of 1873 by issuing and cashing fictitious bills of exchange totaling more than £102,000. Ed. George Dilnot.
- Trial of Alexander Campbell Mason, burglary convict sentenced to prison for the 1923 murder of a taxi driver primarily on the basis of a criminal associate's evidence. Ed. H. Fletcher Moulton.
- Trial of Herbert John Bennett, hanged for murdering his wife, Mary, on Yarmouth Beach in 1900. Ed. Edgar Wallace.
- Trial of William Henry Podmore, oil company salesman, hanged for the 1929 hammer slaying of Vivian Messiter, a representative of Podmore's employer who discovered his fictitious sales orders. Ed. H. Fletcher Moulton and W. Lloyd Woodland.

• Trial of Alfred Arthur Rouse, the "burning car" murderer, whose case is also the subject of a volume in *Notable British Trials* (see N.7). Ed. Sydney Tremaine.

F.2 Faralicq, René *The French Police from Within*. London: Cassell, 1933.

■ Former police commissioner Faralicq, who here recounts his adventures, headed the Special Brigade from 1919 to 1925. This was a detective with a rare taste for literature: in 1908 he was awarded the Sully Prudhomme prize for poetry, and he also achieved some fame as a commentator on Dante.

F.3 Faulkner, William *Intruder in the Dust*. New York: Random House, 1948.

■ This novel originated in Faulkner's idea of "a mystery story, original in that the solver is a negro in jail for the murder and is about to be lynched, solves murder in self defense." According to biographer Joseph Blotner, a lynching had occurred in the author's hometown: "Little more than a dozen years before, it had happened in Oxford. Elwood Higginbotham had confessed to killing a white man, Glen Roberts, with a shotgun. At 8:30 P.M., while the jury was still out, a mob of about seventy-five white men with dirt-smudged faces took the prisoner from the county jail a block from where the jurors sat. A half-hour later his body hung from a tree on a country road" (*Faulkner: A Biography* [New York: Random House, 1974] 2:1245–46).

F.4 Feuchtwanger, Lion *Paris Gazette*. [Originally titled *Exil*]. London: Hutchinson, 1940.

■ In March 1935 undercover agents of the Nazis kidnapped dissident journalist Berthold Jakob in Switzerland and drove him, perhaps drugged, across the German border. The chief kidnapper, acting purely for money, was a German journalist, Dr. Hans Wesemann, who had lured Jakob to the Swiss town of Riehen with promises of issuing a forged passport and furnishing him with information that he could communicate to the English press once he was safely abroad.

The Swiss government and public were outraged by the Gestapo's incursion. After exhausting diplomatic channels, Switzerland initiated arbitration proceedings in the Hague, and the German government responded to this step by returning Jakob to Switzerland in September 1935. Kidnapper Wesemann had imprudently reentered Switzerland shortly after the crime; he was put on trial before a cantonal court in Basel and was sentenced to three years' imprisonment dating from the time of his arrest.

The happy turn in émigré Jakob's fortunes did not prove to be long lasting. In 1941 Nazi henchmen snatched him in Portugal, and three years later he died in Gestapo custody in Berlin. The story of Jakob's kidnapping is told in Frank Arnau, *Menschenraub* [Kidnapping] (Munich: Kurt Desch, 1968), 49–77. A firsthand account of Wesemann's trial is included in Geo London, *Les grands procès de l'année—1936* (Paris: Editions de France, 1937), 119–33.

In his novel *Paris Gazette* (the third in his tetralogy entitled *The Waiting Room*) Feuchtwanger interweaves two motifs of Nazi assaults on dissident journalism: the kidnapping of Jakob (renamed Friedrich Benjamin) and the Nazi purchase and neutralization of *Westland*, an opposition newspaper in Saarbrücken (which becomes the *Paris Gazette* in the novel). Feuchtwanger's Friedrich Benjamin draws the moral of his experience of war and recent imprisonment in Germany in nondoctrinaire terms: "I know quite well, of course, that people think a man is a fool when he sees the source of all evil in humanity's aggressive instincts and thinks that the first thing to do is to change human nature. . . . But for my part I am convinced that the thing to do is to change the people who live in the social fabric rather than the fabric itself" (586).

F.5 ———— *Power.* [Originally titled *The Jew Süss*]. 1925. Trans. Willa Muir and Edwin Muir. New York: Viking, 1927.

▪ The rise and fall of Josef Süss Oppenheimer inspired this novel as well as an infamous 1940 film by Nazi director Veidt Harlan. In 1733 Oppenheimer was appointed financial agent ("Court Jew") to Duke Karl Alexander of Württemberg, and in that post he managed to enrich himself and live a profligate personal life while appeasing his master's need for vast funds to satisfy his mania for building castles. After the Duke died in 1737, Oppenheimer was convicted of treason and other crimes and was hanged before a jubilant crowd in a cage hoisted above the gallows to mock the heights from which the financier had fallen. The internationalization of the antisemitism blatantly served in Oppenheimer's humiliation and execution was documented in the Jewish Museum's 1996–97 exhibition on Court Jews by the prints of the hanging that appeared in many countries. See *From Court Jews to the Rothschilds: Art, Patronage and Power, 1600–1800.* [Exhibition at the Jewish Museum, New York City, Sept. 8, 1996–Jan. 19, 1997.] Ed. Vivian B. Mann and Richard I. Cohen (New York: Prestel, 1996). More recently, a sympathetic German biography of Oppenheimer has appeared, Hellmut G. Haasis, *Joseph Süss Oppenheimer, genannt Jud Süss, Finanzier, Freidenker, Justizopfer* (Reinbek: Rowohlt, 1998).

Feuchtwanger introduces a Rigoletto-like motif to explain Oppenheimer's disillusionment with the German prince to whose passions he had catered. He arranges to convey Magdalen Sibylle, daughter of a politician named Weissensee, to the bedchamber of Duke Karl Alexander. In revenge, Weissensee takes the duke to the residence of Oppenheimer's daughter, Noemi, who falls to her death from the roof of the house while attempting to escape. At the end of the novel, Oppenheimer declines the offer of the old Prince Thurn and Taxis to have the condemned man's life saved through conversion to Christianity. In the gallows cage, Oppenheimer calls on the Hebrew name of the Lord.

F.6 Feuerbach, Anselm Ritter von *Narratives of Remarkable Criminal Trials.* Trans. Lady (Lucie) Duff Gordon. New York: Harper, 1846.

▪ Judge Feuerbach, father of philosopher Ludwig Feuerbach, was a historian of criminal cases of his native Bavaria as well as a judge and reformer of his country's criminal code. A selection of his crime studies is beautifully translated, in somewhat abridged form, by Lady Lucie Duff Gordon, eminent in her day as a woman of letters, *saloniste,* and friend of George Meredith (who commented after her house was closed that "a light has gone out in our country").

By far the most famous criminal examined in Feuerbach's book is Anna Maria Zwanziger, a serial poisoner whom the judge dubbed "the German Brinvilliers." Despite her advanced age and faded looks, housekeeper and nursemaid Zwanziger, when she found new domestic employment, often conceived the ambition to marry the head of the household, particularly, it seems, if he had the misfortune to belong to the judicial profession. In pursuit of her chimerical dream of wedded bliss, she poisoned the wives of Justice Glaser and Magistrate Gebhard and dispatched by similar means Justice Grohmann, who intended to take a much younger bride. In addition, Zwanziger poisoned (nonlethally in most cases) a large number of other persons, sometimes because they had irritated her but more often out of sadistic delight in their ensuing illnesses or because of the secret power that arsenic gave her.

Other criminals who figure in Feuerbach's collection deserve to be better known: for example, John Paul Forster, who insinuated himself into the shop of Nuremberg corn chandler Christopher Bäumler and used exquisite timing in accomplishing the successive murders of Bäumler and his maid when each was alone in the premises; and the amorous cleric Francis Salesius Riembauer ("The Tartuffe of Real Life"), who murdered a discarded mistress and administered last rites while she lay dying. The essay "The Unknown Murderer" relates the unsolved 1817 murder of goldsmith Christopher Rupprecht. While he lay fatally wounded, he was heard to identify his assailant as "Schmidt the woodcutter." Since the scene of the attack was a small Bavarian town, it was small wonder that this description fit three people; but none of them proved to be guilty.

The Borowitz True Crime Collection holds the first volume of Feuerbach's work in a German edition, *Aktenmässige Darstellung merkwürdiger Verbrechen* [Documentary Presentation of Notable Crimes] (Giessen, 1828). See also M.14 and W.7.

F.7 Field, Rachel *All This, and Heaven Too.* New York: Macmillan, 1938.
■ Field, grandniece of Henriette Deluzy, wrote this fictionalized account of the Duc de Praslin's murder of his wife (Paris, 1847), allegedly for love of Governess Deluzy. The Field novel was the basis of the 1940 film of the same name starring Bette Davis and Charles Boyer.

F.8 Fielding, Henry *A Clear State of the Case of Elizabeth Canning.* London: A. Millar, 1753.
■ An eighteenth-century English forerunner of America's Tawana Brawley, a servant girl named Elizabeth Canning disappeared on the night of January 1, 1753, while returning to her home in London from a visit to her aunt near Houndsditch. On January 29, four weeks later, the eighteen-year-old Canning returned in rags, emaciated, cold, and weak.

She told a story that stirred one of the greatest legal controversies in London history. Near the gate of Bethlehem Hospital in Moorsfield, she said, she had been assaulted and robbed and then kept prisoner in an attic on a ration of bread and water when she refused to become a prostitute. The place of her captivity was identified by friends who heard her tale as "Mother" Susannah Wells's brothel at Enfield Wash, although the house did not match Canning's description in all respects. Wells, together with an old gypsy who called herself

Mary Squires and others, was tried at the Old Bailey; Mary Squires was sentenced to be hanged, and Susannah Wells to be branded on the thumb and imprisoned for six months.

Public sentiment immediately turned and, on the basis of new evidence supporting Mary Squires's alibi, the king pardoned her. Canning was convicted of perjury and transported to America, where she joined the household of a former rector of Yale University; she married in 1756 and died in 1773, still clinging to her kidnapping story.

Henry Fielding, who served as a London magistrate at the time of the case, was requested by Canning's solicitor to receive her sworn deposition after her charges of abduction became public and to counsel her representatives on the best means to bring the wrongdoers to justice. The highly susceptible Fielding was moved by the youth of the girl, and he ignored the conflict of responsibilities that was involved in his acting simultaneously as a private adviser and a public official. After he was persuaded of Canning's veracity, he also heard the evidence of Virtue Hall, a young woman who, despite her name, had been identified as present at Mother Wells's brothel when Canning was brought in. After receiving this apparent confirmation of Canning's story, Fielding ordered the detention of Wells and Squires.

After the kidnapping trial that ensued, Fielding's actions were called into question; in his own defense he wrote a shilling pamphlet, *A Clear State of the Case of Elizabeth Canning*. He begins by acknowledging that Canning's story is "a very extraordinary narrative . . . , consisting of many strange particulars resembling rather a wild dream than a real fact." Still, Fielding would have found it more improbable that she was lying than telling the truth, for he could not believe that a young girl, without motive, would swear lives away or would be "witty enough to invent a . . . story full of variety of strange incidents, and worthy the invention of some writer of romances." Fielding was prepared to concede that he might have been guilty of honest error in his appraisal of Canning's veracity. He asked only the public's recognition that he had discharged his duty with the same integrity demonstrated by his principal antagonist in the Canning controversy, Sir Crisp Gascoyne, lord mayor of London.

F.9 ———— *An Enquiry into the Causes and the Late Increase of Robbers, with Some Proposals for Remedying This Growing Evil.* London: A. Millar, 1751.

■ Henry Fielding is remembered in the history of criminal law as a tough-minded and compassionate justice of the peace of Middlesex County and in Westminster (greater London). Regarded as a founder, with his blind brother, John, of London's police force, Fielding was faced with a terrible conflict between his recognition of the inhumanity of the frequent executions under the "Bloody Code" and his abiding faith that capital punishment, properly applied, could have a deterrent effect on the rising crime rate.

Fielding set down his thoughts on criminal punishment in his treatise *An Enquiry into the Causes of the Late Increase of Robbers* (1751). Quoting Lord Hale, he postulated that the principal end of all punishment was less to punish for past offenses than to "deter men from the breach of laws, so that they may not offend and so not suffer at all." The humane goal of punishment then was to make punishment unnecessary at some point in the utopian future. Only with that hope in his heart could Fielding be reconciled to the infliction of capital punishment for petty thefts, for "no man indeed of common humanity or common sense can think the life of a man and a few shillings to be of an equal consideration, or that the law in punishing theft with death proceeds (as perhaps a private person sometimes may) with any view to vengeance. The terror of the example is the only thing proposed, and one man is sacrificed to the preservation of thousands."

And so the kindly Fielding set about the task of proposing how the terror of punishment could be maximized. First, the sovereign must renounce his prerogative of mercy and decline to pardon criminals under death sentence, for "pardons have brought many more men to the gallows than they have saved." Second, reforms must be introduced into the manner of execution, since a convicted thief, far from fearing death, often viewed his execution as a source of glory rather than shame, and the procession to the gallows at Tyburn (the site of the modern Marble Arch) as a triumph.

The greatest cause of the convict's bravado Fielding found in the very frequency of executions in the city—"the thief who is hanged to-day hath learned his intrepidity from the example of his hanged predecessors." The design of those who made executions public had been to add the punishment of shame to that of death, but experience had been contrary: the mob found diversion and the convict an easy heroism. One way of preventing frequency of executions was to attack the roots of crime, and Fielding in his treatise suggested a broad store of remedies: restraint of the passion for luxury, drunkenness, and gambling; improvement of provision for the poor; stricter punishment of receivers of stolen goods; and improved administration of criminal justice.

While these goals were being pursued, the performance of executions should be modified. Executions should not be delayed so long that public resentment of the crime cooled and that the punishment itself became the sole subject of contemplation. "No good mind," Fielding wrote, "can avoid compassionating a set of wretches who are put to death we know not why, unless, as it almost appears, to make a holiday for, and to entertain, the mob." He also proposed that executions be to "some degree private" so that, taking added intensity from the imaginations of the excluded public, they could assume the terror of the off-stage murders of classical drama. Terror should also be heightened, Fielding wrote, by giving execution the highest degree of solemnity. He suggested that at the end of the trials the Court of Old Bailey be adjourned for four days; that a gallows be erected in the area before the court; and that all the convicted criminals be brought down together to receive sentence and be executed forthwith in the presence of their judges. Fielding had little room for appellate courts in his scheme of things.

F.10 ———— *The Life of Mr. Jonathan Wild the Great.* London: A. Millar, 1743.

■ This satirical novel likens Jonathan Wild (see D.9), prince of London's thieves and trafficker in stolen goods (hanged in 1725), to Sir Robert Walpole, who had fallen from power as prime minister in February 1742. The fictional Wild is ironically presented as a "great man" on the basis of the fake values that Fielding believed had also supported Walpole. Among the maxims attributed by Fielding to Wild as the basis for success in roguery are: to forgive no enemy but be cautious and often dilatory in revenge; to shun poverty and distress but to ally himself as close as possible to power and riches; to maintain a constant gravity in his countenance and behavior and to affect wisdom on all occasions; to foment eternal jealousies in his gang.

F.11 —— *A True State of the Case of Bosavern Penlez, Who Suffered on Account of the Late Riot in the Strand.* London: A. Millar, 1749.

■ Fielding wrote this pamphlet to defend the government's role in suppressing the "July Riots" in London in 1749 and in executing one of the rioters, Bosavern Penlez, a clergyman's son from Exeter who worked as a wigmaker.

The trouble arose on Saturday afternoon when sailors of HMS *Grafton* were robbed at a brothel on the Strand. Rioting and arson broke out on the two nights that followed. On Monday morning, magistrate Fielding, returning to town, took measures to prevent further disorders. He charged six men with rioting. One, Bosavern Penlez, was hanged amid an outpouring of public sympathy.

In his pamphlet Fielding reviews the long history of English legal measures against rioting to refute the common misunderstanding that the Riot Act introduced under George I was a novel infringement of free expression. After citing verbatim the reports of several peace officers regarding the excesses of the mob, Fielding attacks the central premise of Penlez's sympathizers that the mob's action was based on a laudable antipathy to brothels: "Are these then the people to redress the evil? Play-houses have been in a former age reputed a grievance; but did the players rise in a body to demolish them? Gaming houses are still thought a nuisance; but no man, I believe, hath ever seen a body of gamesters assembled to break them open, and burn their goods."

In a concluding footnote, Fielding added a further element to support the hanging of Penlez: the rioter had also been arraigned on a capital charge of looting, but the judge did not permit trial on this count since he was already capitally convicted of participation in the riot.

For the pains he had taken to restore public order, Fielding was the subject of unjustified innuendo that he was receiving protection money from London's brothels.

F.12 Figerou, Pierre   *La belle Madame Lescombat, son amant et son mari.* In series *Énigmes et drames judiciaires d'autrefois.* Preface Pierre de Pressac. Paris: Perrin, 1927.

■ Figerou and de Pressac were members of the Parisian crime-history dinner club called the Dinner of the Eleven. In this posthumous work, Figerou, with meticulous attention to trial records and to the Ancien Régime's criminal procedures, discusses one of the great causes célèbres of eighteenth-century Paris, the murder of architect Louis-Alexandre Lescombat by Jean-Louis Demougeot, the lover of the victim's wife, Marie-Catherine. Both Demougeot and Madame Lescombat were executed in what was believed to be a murder conspiracy. Figerou argues that under modern court procedures Madame Lescombat would have been acquitted.

F.13 Fitere, Jean-Marie   *Violette Nozière.* In series *N'Avouez jamais.* Paris: Presses de le Cité, 1975.

■ On August 24, 1933, eighteen-year-old Violette Nozière (sometimes spelled Nozières), who was leading a secret life as syphilitic streetwalker and bar-hopper, poisoned both her parents. Her father died and her mother survived, first to testify against her and ultimately to forgive her. Taking a leaf from the book of Beatrice Cenci, Violette urged unpersuasively that her father had sexually abused her but never offered an excuse for trying for a clean sweep of parents.

Nevertheless, before the trial began, Violette became the muse of the surrealist poets and artists, who published a little book in her honor (see N.8), but her more prosaic jury found her guilty. Sentenced to death she was spared as a matter of course, for no Frenchwoman had been guillotined in half a century. Violette found favor with three very different administrations. In 1942 Marshal Pétain reduced her life sentence at hard labor to twelve years; as head of the provisional government, General de Gaulle cancelled the order that had barred her from Paris and other regions for twenty years; and finally in 1963 the Rouen court granted her final rehabilitation by ordering the expungement of her criminal record, the first time such action had been taken in a nonpolitical murder case.

Author Fitère, though dedicating his book to Maitre de Vésinne-Larue, who battled for thirty years on behalf of Violette Nozière, maintains an admirable balance in his account of this still-controversial case.

F.14 Fitzgerald, F. Scott   *The Great Gatsby.* 1925. In *The Portable F. Scott Fitzgerald.* New York: Viking, 1945.

■ The externals of Jay Gatsby (born Gatz) were based on Max Fleischman, a Long Island "gentleman" bootlegger whose house Fitzgerald had visited. According to Edmund Wilson, Fitzgerald tired of Fleischman's "bragging about how much his tapestries were worth and how much his bath-room was worth and how he never wore a shirt twice—and he had a revolver studded with diamonds." The exasperated Fitzgerald told Fleischman, "he was nothing but a bootlegger, no matter how much money he made . . . . I told him I never would have come into his damn house if it hadn't been to be polite and that it was a torture to stay in a place where everything was in such terrible taste." Biographer Matthew J. Bruccoli, in *Some Sort of Epic Grandeur: The Life of F. Scott Fitzgerald* (New York: Harcourt Brace, 1981), refers to the bootlegger as Max Gerlach, quoting Zelda Fitzgerald's comment near the end of her life that Gatsby's character was based on "a neighbor named Von Guerlach or something who was said to be General Pershing's nephew and was in trouble over bootlegging" (183).

Gambling overlord Arnold Rothstein also makes an appearance in the novel, assuming the guise of Meyer Wolfsheim, whom Gatsby introduces to his friend Nick Carroway over lunch at a 42nd Street cellar restaurant. The repellent Wolfsheim, who wears cuff buttons made of human molars, nostalgically recalls the night he saw gambler Herman Rosenthal gunned down at the orders of crooked police lieutenant Charles Becker. When he leaves, Gatsby tells Carroway that Wolfsheim fixed the "Black Sox" World Series in 1919.

In *The Slaying of Joseph Bowne Elwell* (London: Harrap, 1987; see G.26), Jonathan Goodman suggests that "bits and pieces of Gatsby were derived, not from Joseph Bowne

Elwell himself, but from the impression of him as a fascinatingly shady egotist that was created by reporters of the Elwell case" (213–14)

In 1999, an operatic setting of *The Great Gatsby*, with music (incorporating pastiches of Jazz Age songs) and lyrics by John Harbison, premiered at the Metropolitan Opera with Dawn Powell as Daisy Buchanan and Jerry Hadley as Gatsby.

In Fitzgerald's late story "Pat Hobby's Christmas Wish," feckless scriptwriter Hobby misreads his boss's letter as confessing involvement in the unsolved 1922 murder of Hollywood director William Desmond Taylor.

F.15 Flanner, Janet ["Genet" of the *New Yorker*]   *An American in Paris.* New York: Simon & Schuster, 1940.

■ A section on crime and punishment includes reportages on Marthe Hanau's financial swindles; the brutal murders (1933) of Mme. and Mlle. Lancelin of Le Mans by their cook and housemaid Christine and Léa Papin; the trial of Violette Nozière for poisoning her parents (1934; see F.13); and the death of executioner Anatole-Joseph-François Deibler. An elegant practitioner of the classic *New Yorker* essay style, Flanner combines trenchant wit with valuable insight into French social and criminal behavior.

F.16 Flaubert, Gustave   *Bibliomania.* 1836. London: Rodale Press, 1954.

■ In 1836, Don Vincente, a Spanish monk, was executed for a murder caused by an extreme affliction of bibliomania. Don Vincente strangled a rival book collector, stole what he believed to be the only existing copy of a book published in 1482 by the first Spanish printer, and burned down his victim's house in a vain effort to hide the crime (see Andrew Lang, *The Library* [London: Macmillan, 1881], 54–56). At his trial, Don Vincente was thunderstruck when he learned that there was another copy of the treasured book in the Louvre.

The fifteen-year old Flaubert's fictionalized account was his first published work and appeared in the year of the mad collector's execution. Flaubert gives the criminous tragi-comedy a turn of the screw by having the condemned murderer destroy the second copy of the rare edition in order to restore his claim to possession of a unique book.

F.17 Floriot, René   *Les erreurs judiciaires.* Paris: Flammarion, 1968.

■ Trial lawyer Floriot divides his discussion of judicial errors into seven principal categories:

- Condemnations in cases where no crime has been committed
- False reasoning from true evidence
- Logical conclusions drawn from false premises
- False confessions
- Forgery
- False or erroneous testimony (which Floriot blames for most judicial errors)
- Errors of forensic experts

Among the famous cases discussed are those of Joseph Lesurques, erroneously identified as the Lyon mail murderer (see D.18); Lieutenant Emile de la Roncière (see D. 19); Alfred Dreyfus; and Gaston Dominici.

F.18 Fo, Dario *Accidental Death of an Anarchist*. In *Plays of Dario Fo*. Vol. 1. London: Methuen, 1997.

■ This comic play purports to be based on the controversial 1969 death of anarchist Pino Pinelli, who fell from the window of Milan police headquarters during an interrogation. In his prologue Fo purports to have based his farce on documents in the Pinelli case: "We wish to make it clear that the dialogue in this play is based on a reconstruction of authentic documents in the Pinelli case. There was no need to invent any of the situations that you will find represented here."

In fact, however, this claim obscures an artifice that the playwright employed in developing his plot. The events presented were drawn from the mysterious death of anarchist Andrea Salsedo, who fell from a window of New York City police headquarters in 1920 at the height of the Red Scare. Fo transported this American police scandal to Milan and conflated Salsedo's violent end with the death of Pinelli under similar circumstances.

Explaining his choice of farce as the vehicle for the play's grim subject, Fo explains: "In laughter you are left with a sediment of rage; in laughter you cannot achieve catharsis."

F.19 Ford, Ford Madox *Great Trade Route*. New York: Oxford Univ. Press, 1937.

■ In a chapter ironically titled "Fiat Justitia" (Let Justice Be Done), Ford records his impressions of the Lindbergh kidnapping trial, which he attended in Flemington, New Jersey. Almost all local residents whom he met (including his barber) shared Ford's opinion that Hauptmann's guilt had not been proved. In his view, the trial was unsatisfactory because of "the undue vindictiveness of the prosecution and the moral cowardice of the defence"; the prosecutor, in his closing argument, "expressed personal hatred for the prisoner . . . and his conviction that the prisoner would sizzle in hell."

Ford does not condemn the passionate interest in the trial. It was not that many could even have suspected a capacity to commit a similar crime, but "almost any man could imagine himself in circumstances in which he might incur trial for a capital offence . . . if merely unjustly." The deterrence theory urged to support the imposition of capital punishment is unsubstantiated, Ford argues, but oddly he concedes one exception to his position: there is nothing like shootings at dawn to put a stop to desertions.

F.20 Ford, John *Perkin Warbeck*. 1634. In *John Ford, Five Plays*. Ed. Havelock Ellis. New York: Hill & Wang (Mermaid Dramabook), 1957.

■ Before the Tichborne Claimant, the most famous impostor in England was Perkin Warbeck. Born in Flanders, reputedly the son of a converted Jew, Warbeck was a protean aspirant to the English throne, successively claiming to be the son of the Duke of Clarence or of Richard III before settling into the role of Richard, Duke of York, the purported survivor of the two princes Richard III was believed to have murdered in the Tower of London. War-beck's rebellion against Henry VII, abetted by Margaret of Burgundy,

Edward IV's sister, was a resounding failure, and he was captured by royal forces. After escaping from the Tower, Warbeck was executed.

Ford's play is oddly sympathetic to the brazen impersonator. Many of the characters, generally to suit their own political advantage, dismiss Warbeck's claim to the throne as rank imposture. To Henry VII he is "Duke Perkin," an "eager whelp" nursed by Margaret of Burgundy. James IV of Scotland, even as he decides to ally himself with Warbeck in a campaign against the English foe, addresses him as "Duke of York, for such thou sayst thou art." Warbeck's future father-in-law, in an aside, calls him "no Plantagenet . . . [B]y red rose or white," and the Earl of Crawford murmurs:

> . . . my reason cannot answer
> Such argument of fine imposture, couched
> In witchcraft of persuasion, that it fashions
> Impossibilities, as if appearance
> Could cozen truth itself; this dukeling mushroom
> Hath doubtless charmed the king.

Perhaps the victim of his own powers of deception, Warbeck never confesses his fraud. In her 1830 novel *The Fortunes of Perkin Warbeck*, Mary Shelley depicts Warbeck as the genuine Duke Richard.

F.21 Forester, C[ecil] S[cott]   *Payment Deferred*. London: Lane, 1926.

■ The novel *Payment Deferred* by C. S. Forester (author of the *Horatio Hornblower* series) tells the story of William Marble, an impecunious bank employee who impulsively poisons a wealthy nephew and steals his money, hastily burying the body in the garden of his suburban house, only to spend the rest of his days obsessively guarding the flower bed where his victim lies. In desperation, Marble becomes an aficionado of books on crime, first borrowing from the public library a volume on criminal trials and later building a collection of his own on the subject. In his reading he learns that "two out of every three of the criminals mentioned came to grief through inability to dispose of the body. There was a tale of a woman [Mary Pearcey] who had walked for miles through London streets with a body in a perambulator; there was an account of Crippen's life in London with the body of his murdered wife buried in his cellar; but the police laid hold of them all in time." In the ironic denouement, the police do not discover the buried body but suspect Marble of murdering his wife, Annie, who, ill with influenza, unimaginatively used her husband's remaining supply of poison (cyanide) to commit suicide after learning that Marble had carried on an affair with a neighbor. The book concludes: "Marble went down through history as an extraordinarily clumsy murderer."

Forester's novel appeared four years after the execution of Herbert Rowse Armstrong, a solicitor in Hay-on-Wye, for the arsenic poisoning of his ailing (and probably hypochondriacal) wife, Katherine. The case for Armstrong's guilt is argued in Robin Odell, *Exhumation of a Murder: The Life and Trial of Major Armstrong* (London: Harrap, 1975), on the basis of researches by J. H. H. Gaute and H. B. Trumper. Subsequently, a solicitor who acquired Armstrong's house and law office quarters, has attempted unpersuasively to establish his innocence (Martin Beales, *Dead Not Buried* [London: Hale, 1995]).

Bushnell Dimond, who, in the middle of the twentieth century, contributed to the identification of fiction based on true crime, believed that the Armstrong case "was useful" to Forester, noting that "defense counsel at the trial contended that Mrs. Armstrong, perhaps aware of her husband's infidelity and half-crazy anyhow, committed suicide."

The novel was adapted for the stage under the same title by Jeffrey Dell. The play, which ran on Broadway in 1931, starred Charles Laughton as Marble and his wife, Elsa Lanchester, as Marble's daughter, Winnie. Laughton re-created his role in the film version of the following year.

F.22 Forster, Joseph   *Studies in Black and Red.* London: Ward & Downey, 1896.

■ This is a collection of thirty brief British, Irish, and French crime narratives. Included are:

- Two impostors, the Tichborne claimant and the false Martin Guerre
- Madeleine Smith, freed of a poisoning charge under the Scottish verdict of not proven
- Charles Peace, who led a double life as fiddle-playing householder and burglar-murderer
- John Bellingham's assassination of Prime Minister Spencer Percival
- James Blomfield Rush, who massacred the Jermy family at Stanfield Hall
- Frederick and Maria Manning's murder of her lover Patrick O'Connor
- David Haggart, jail-breaker and murderer
- Catherine Hayes, who conspired to murder her husband and became the "heroine" of Thackeray's comic novel *Catherine* (see T.5).
- John Williams, the Ratcliffe Highway murderer immortalized by Thomas De Quincey
- William Burke and William Hare, Edinburgh body snatchers and murderers, and their English counterparts, John Bishop and Thomas Williams
- Murderous domestic servant Kate Webster
- The first famous Victorian murderer, James Greenacre, who killed and dismembered his mistress Sarah Gale
- Dumollard, French serial killer of servant girls he engaged for fictitious employment
- Scottish poisoner Dr. E. W. Pritchard
- Jean Calas, French Huguenot wrongly convicted of the murder of his son

Two other murderers studied by Forster are less well known but worthy of note. In 1845 Thomas Henry Hocker killed music master James Delarue near Hampstead, striking his head repeatedly with a stick and kicking his face. While a policeman inspected the body, Hocker coolly returned to the scene of his crime and took his victim's pulse. Another strange feature of the case was a letter found in Delarue's coat pocket: forged by Hocker, it was addressed to James Cooper (Hocker's private name for Delarue in their correspondence) and purported to be written by an abandoned girlfriend of the victim named Caroline. The motive for this odd forgery was never established.

Forster also includes a short account of John Scanlan's murder of his wife, Ellen (with the assistance of his devoted servant Sullivan), in the course of a boating excursion on the river Shannon in 1819. At Sullivan's suggestion, Scanlan had an excommunicated priest perform the marriage ceremony, falsely believing that under the law of Ireland the union would be null and void. When a more profitable marital opportunity cropped up, murder dissolved the Scanlans' bond.

This tragedy was given a happier ending in Dion Boucicault's play *The Colleen Bawn* (1860; see B.71), based on a novel by Gerald Griffin. Later the same plot furnished the libretto for Sir Julius Benedict's light opera *The Lily of Killarney*, which premiered at Covent Garden in 1862.

F.23 Foucault, Michel *I, Pierre Rivière, Having Slaughtered My Mother, My Sister, and My Brother...: A Case of Parricide in the 19th Century.* Ed. Michel Foucault. Trans. Frank Jellinek. New York: Pantheon, 1975.

■ This book results from collective work undertaken by Michel Foucault and ten colleagues in a seminar at the Collège de France on issues in criminality and criminal law. The focus of inquiry is the 1835 billhook massacre by twenty-year old farmer Pierre Rivière of his mother, Marie-Anne, his eighteen-year old sister, Marguerite, and his seven-year old brother, Jules. The death penalty imposed after trial was ultimately commuted by King Louis-Philippe on the basis of Rivière's apparent insanity; the murderer later committed suicide in prison.

Accompanying the assembled records of the case are commentaries by Foucault and his collaborators on such issues as criminal insanity, the political implications of parricide, and the presentation of murder in popular narratives.

Foucault's own commentary, which examines Rivière's memoir of the reasons for his crimes, is particularly illuminating. Perhaps in no other case is a murderer's narrative so elaborately interlaced with his crime. Rivière asserted that he murdered his mother to protect his father against her oppression and killed his sister to avenge the support she had lent their mother's malice. His little brother Jules, his father's darling, Pierre dispatched for the strangest reason of all: to make it impossible for his father to grieve for Pierre after his likely execution.

As Foucault notes, Rivière originally intended to "surround" the murder with his memoir. The young semi-literate farmer was to begin by writing the narrative that would announce at the outset the crime to follow; then he would detail his parents' contentious marriage and his reasons for taking violent action in his father's behalf. At this point the murder was to have been committed, and, then the completed memoir was to be posted to the authorities. Foucault refers to Rivière with some justification as a "double *auteur*," inventor of both the crime and the narrative of which it was an indispensable part.

F.24 Fouquier, Armand *Causes célèbres de tous les peuples.* 7 vols. Paris: Lebrun, 1858–67.

■ Fouquier's collection of causes célèbres, attractively illustrated, won international popularity. A Spanish translation was published, and in America Edmund Pearson drew on

Fou-quier's accounts as sources for brief studies of French murders. Among the criminal cases included in Fouquier's series are: the assassinations and assassination attempts by François Ravaillac, Robert-François Damiens, Charlotte Corday, Jean-Pierre Louvel, Giuseppe Maria Fieschi, and Felice Orsini; poisoners, including the Marquise de Brinvilliers, Marie Lafarge, and Euphémie Lacoste; other murderers, such as Louis-Auguste Papavoine, Pierre-François Lacenaire, the Duc de Praslin, and the murderers of Joseph-Bernardin Fualdès.

F.25 Fourquet, Émile *Vacher.* Paris: Gallimard, 1931.

■ Fourquet, as investigating magistrate, was responsible for the identification of Joseph Vacher as the sadistic ripper who claimed at least eleven victims between 1894 and 1897 (see B.70). Having jurisdiction over only a single crime (Vacher's murder and rape of fourteen-year-old animal herder Victor Portalier), Fourquet, through inquiries in other districts, was able to tie the killer (then in jail for a foiled assault on a farmer's wife) to similar attacks elsewhere. By his own account, the magistrate beguiled Vacher into confessing to eleven murders by suggesting to his prisoner that a high number of avowed outrages would increase his chances of successfully pleading insanity. Judge Fourquet was himself convinced that Vacher was abnormal but not insane, citing several factors in support of his thesis: the choice of young victims unable to defend themselves, the interruption of his attack when adult rescuers appeared on the scene, the use of disguises, the hiding of his victims' bodies, and the mouthing of anarchist slogans to justify his crimes. However, his attempt to establish Vacher's sanity led him to doubtful attributions of other murders where theft rather than sexual gratification was the motive.

For his triumph in identifying and securing the conviction and execution of one of France's worst criminals, Fourquet was poorly rewarded. Denied advancement or his coveted admission to the Legion of Honor, Fourquet in 1912 resigned from the magistracy because of a new "base action" on the part of the Ministry of Justice. The judge suffered a posthumous indignity when French director Bertrand Tavernier made him the villain of the 1975 film *The Judge and the Assassin*. In the muddled film, Fourquet (renamed Rousseau) ensures the execution of Vacher (only thinly disguised as Bouvier, since both his real and transformed names mean "cowhand"). By his ardor in the investigation, the judge seeks to advance his own judicial career and the anti-Dreyfusard cause, although aware of the murderer's insanity. The movie ends with a hymn to the Communards and a postscript suggesting that Vacher was a small-scale killer compared with the mines and factories of France, which, according to Tavernier, took the lives of 2,500 children during the period of the murders.

F.26 Fowles, John *The French Lieutenant's Woman.* London: Jonathan Cape, 1969.

■ Charles Smithson encounters Sarah Woodruff as a romantic figure looking out to sea from Lyme Regis as she yearns for French naval lieutenant Varguennes, who has seduced (so she says) and abandoned her. In a vain attempt to cure Charles of his obsession with Sarah, Dr. Grogan acquaints him with the true story of Marie de Morell, a nineteenth-century Frenchwoman who inflicted great pain on herself and others to assuage her feelings of rejection by a young man to whom she was strongly attracted. Marie falsely accused Lieutenant Emile de La Roncière (who served under her father at a cavalry school in the Loire Valley) of sending poison-pen letters and attempting to rape her. La Roncière was convicted in 1835 and sentenced to imprisonment for many years before his exoneration and rehabilitation (see D.19).

F.27 France, Anatole [pseudonym of Jacques-Anatole-François Thibault] *Penguin Island.* 1908. Intro. H. R. Steeves. New York: Random House (Modern Library), 1933.

■ The eponymous birds of Penguin Island are baptized and transformed into humans. Their island is towed to the Breton coast where they are condemned to live through the horrors of European history as citizens of Penguinia. In a famous section, France satirizes the unjust treason prosecution of Captain Alfred Dreyfus, which he converts into the ridiculous "Affair of the Eighty Thousand Trusses of Hay." A middle-class Jew named Pyrot is falsely charged with having stolen the hay from military stores for resale to Penguinia's bitter enemies the Porpoises. The real villain is Count de Maubec (Esterhazy), who defrauded the state by receiving the price of nonexistent hay.

No party or personality of the Dreyfus case emerges unscathed from France's merciless caricatures. Pyrot is the victim of an unholy union of Church, royalists, and the military led by Greatauk, Minister of Justice, who, told that there is no evidence against the accused, orders, "Let it be found." On the other side of the battle, wealthy Jewish financiers are depicted as reluctant to support a poor coreligionist, and socialists are split by internecine disputes. Not even Pyrot's most ardent supporters are allowed to survive the civil broils with their dignity intact. Colomban (a sendup of myopic Emile Zola) is menaced by a crowd when he posts wall placards in favor of Pyrot; the mob "threw at him threatening looks which he received with the calm that comes from courage and short-sightedness."

Another passionate Dreyfusard writer, Octave Mirbeau, was so moved by the affair's revelation of "the passion for murder and the joy of the manhunt" that he created in 1898 a terrifying novel of cruelty, transposed to an Asian setting, *Torture Garden* (trans. Alvah C. Bessie [New York: Berkeley, 1955]). The Dreyfus case also figures prominently in Roger Martin du Gard's 1913 novel *Jean Barois* (trans. Stuart Gilbert [New York: Viking, 1949]) and in *Jean Santeuil*, an early version of Marcel Proust's *Remembrance of Things Past* (see P.21).

F.28 Freeman, Kathleen *The Murder of Herodes, and Other Trials from the Athenian Law Courts.* London: Macdonald, 1946.

■ This volume of Freeman's translations of Athenian legal arguments includes four that relate to murder cases. Athenian procedure in the fifth century B.C. did not permit lawyers to appear in court, and it became customary for experts in rhetoric and legal principles to draft courtroom speeches for the private parties who acted as prosecutor or defendant. The gem of Freeman's collection is Antiphon's brilliant argument (written ca. 419 B.C.) in defense of Helos, a young man from Mytilene on the island of Lesbos, charged with the murder of Herodes, a fellow passenger on a ship bound for the Thracian coast. The facts are murky, for Herodes had disappeared mysteriously at night in a port where the two travelers had been compelled by a storm to change ships.

Other legal orations included are:

- A speech written by Lysias between 400 and 380 B.C. in defense of Euphiletus, who entered a claim of justifiable homicide when charged with killing Eratosthenes, his wife's seducer, when he finally caught the pair in flagrante delicto.
- Lysias's only speech in his own behalf as prosecutor, delivered in 403 B.C. Lysias accused the defendant, Eratosthenes (no kin to the seducer), a member of the short-lived government of the Thirty Tyrants, of having illegally arrested Lysias's brother and put him to death without trial.
- A speech of Antiphon for the prosecution (written between 450 and 411 B.C.). The prosecutor charged his stepmother with having commissioned the poisoning of his father; the defendant asserted that she had believed the lethal drink to have been a love potion.

A tantalizing mystery clings to all these ancient cases, since the orations were published without any indication of the jury verdict. When the full text survives, the forensic argument reveals a beautiful form, including an orderly presentation of the facts and an extended section of persuasion in which the speech writer attempts to demonstrate that his reconstruction of the parties' actions and motives is more probable than that offered by his adversary.

F.29 Friedländer, Hugo *Interessante Kriminal-Prozesse von Kulturhistorischer Bedeutung: Darstellung Merkwürdiger Strafrechtsfälle aus Gegenwart und Jüngsvergangenheit* [Interesting Criminal Trials of Significance in Cultural History: Accounts of Notable Criminal Cases from the Present and Recent Past]. Intro. Justizrat Dr. Erich Sello of Berlin. Berlin-Grunewald: Verlag Berliner Buchversand, 1910.

■ Court reporter Friedländer described this important series, which began to appear in 1910, as based on his own experiences. In his introduction to the first volume, eminent Berlin advocate Erich Sello (who debuts in the pages of the work as a thirty-one-year-old lawyer in the Neustettin synagogue arson trial) lauds Friedländer's opus for renewing the lapsed tradition of Germany's "Pitaval" criminal trial accounts. Friedländer can, in fact, be seen as playing a role similar to that of the French reporters Albert Bataille and Geo London, whose annual trial volumes document their country's trials from the last quarter of the nineteenth century up to the eve of World War II. Friedländer's scope, however, is incomparably broader, for he takes his readers out of the courtroom and immerses them in the historical-cultural ambiance of the events that set criminal proceedings in motion.

Among the noteworthy trials in Friedländer's twelve volumes are:

- *In Vol. 1:* Wilhelm Voigt, a swindler who impersonated the "Captain from Köpenick." See z.1.

- *In Vol. 2:* Karl Hau, the Baden-Baden murderer. See H.1.
- *In Vol. 3:* Countess Marie Tarnowska, convicted at Venice of conspiring to murder her lover, Count Kamarovski. See Horace Wyndham, *Crime on the Continent* (Boston: Little Brown, 1928), 251–80.
- *In Vols. 4 and 11:* Parties to proceedings arising from charges of Maximilian Harden and others that a homosexual clique surrounded Kaiser Wilhelm II. See H.12.
- *In Vol. 6:* Art history professor Richard Mather, sentenced to pay 300 marks and to serve thirty days in jail for falsely accusing Carlo Böcklin of passing off certain of his paintings as works of his famous father, Heinrich Böcklin.
- *In Vol. 9:* Antisemites acquitted of burning the Neustattin synagogue in 1881.
- *In Vol. 12:* The robber-murderer August Sternickel.

F.30 **Fuentes, Carlos**   *The Old Gringo.* Trans. Margaret Sayers Peden and the author. New York: Farrar, Straus & Giroux, 1985.

■ Carlos Fuentes, an important Mexican novelist and his country's ambassador to France in 1975–77, based *The Old Gringo* on the disappearance during the Mexican civil war of Ambrose Bierce, whose writings Fuentes greatly admired. Bierce published short stories, poetry, and satire and was extremely popular as a journalist for the *San Francisco Examiner*, where his weekly column "Prattle" created and destroyed literary and political reputations. In 1913, at the age of seventy-one, Bierce traveled to Mexico "with a pretty definite purpose, which, however, is not at present disclosable." That statement, followed by the disappearance of Bierce, led many to believe that he sought death in Mexico and that he found it at the hands of the revolutionaries.

Fuentes's novel recreates the last days of Bierce, focusing on a triangular love-hate relationship among the writer; a young American woman, Harriet Winslow, who has come to Mexico to teach; and revolutionary Mexican general Tomás Arroyo, who served under Villa. The conflicting American and Mexican values systems and the struggles for political power during this period are symbolized by the interactions of these three characters. In the end, Bierce is shot in the back by Arroyo, who delivers the body to Villa only to be killed himself by the revolutionary leader. Villa, concerned about the negative American reaction to finding Bierce's body with wounds in the back, "reexecutes" the corpse from the front in a more traditional military style. At the end of the novel, Harriet brings home the body of Bierce, which she buries as her father's corpse in Arlington Cemetery, thereby ensuring the complete disappearance of the old Gringo under the Winslow tombstone. Confronting reporters from American newspapers, Harriet tells them that their battle cry "save Mexico for progress and democracy" is meaningless: "What mattered was to live with Mexico in spite of progress and democracy, that each of us carries his Mexico and his United States within him, a dark and bloody frontier we dare to cross only at night: that's what the old gringo had said" (187).

While Fuentes develops variations on the theme of the execution of Bierce by Mexican revolutionaries, Edward H. Smith in his essay "The Ambrose Bierce Irony"(in *Mysteries of the Missing* [New York: Lincoln MacVeigh, 1927], 257–72), notes that Bierce had written three stories on the subject of "vanishment." As a writer, Smith notes, Bierce "reveled in the mysterious, the dark, the terrible and the bizarre." The mysterious description he offered of his purpose in going to Mexico led to all kinds of legends. Some saw his trip as a reversion to his early days as a volunteer in the Union Army during the American Civil War. In that conflict Bierce had demonstrated bravery for which he was breveted as a major; perhaps in old age he sought to redeem his past sins by death in combat. Fuentes has the old gringo say: "I came here to die . . . to be a gringo in Mexico is one way of dying."

Choosing Mexico was a reflection, according to Fuentes, of Bierce's disenchantment with his career as the tool of the Hearst press. In the novel, the old Gringo explains to Harriet, "You must understand the defeat of a man who believed he was master of his fate, who even believed he could shape the destinies of others through a journalism of accusation and satire . . . while my lord and master of the press cannibalized my anger for the greater glory of his political interests and his massive circulation." Fuentes's fictional explanation of the death of Bierce reflects the rumors of a military execution based on the last letter Bierce wrote from Chihuahua in January 1914, where he described himself as a military adviser to Villa. Smith rejects the execution rumors, which he finds were based on tales told by a Mexican officer, and presents his less romantic view of Bierce's final days: "My own guess is that he started out to fight battles and shoulder hardships as he had done when a boy. . . . Wounded or stricken with disease, he probably lay down in some pesthouse of a hospital, some troop train filled with other stricken men; or he may have crawled off to some water hole and died, with nothing more articulate than the winds and the stars for witness."

F.31 Funck-Brentano, Frantz *Les brigands.* 1904. Paris: Tallandier, 1978.
■ This lively survey of French brigands and highwaymen features separate chapters on the Guilleri robber gang, whose chief was hanged at La Rochelle in 1608; eighteenth-century Parisian archgangster Cartouche; and smuggler-guerrilla Mandrin. There is also discussion of Schinderhannes, the Rhine bandit, and of famous groups of organized criminals, such as the chauffeurs ("heaters"), who held victims' feet to the fire until they revealed the hiding places of their valuables.

F.32 ───── *Legends of the Bastille* [Légendes et archives de la Bastille]. Intro. Victorien Sardou. Trans. George Maidment. London: Downey, 1899.
■ This absorbing history of the Bastille sketches its history as well as life in the prison; theories of the identity of its most enigmatic inmate, the Man in the Iron Mask; men of letters in the Bastille, including Voltaire, incarcerated twice for defaming the Regent and brawling with a nobleman; Masers de Latude, celebrated prison breaker, who delivered an explosive device to the marquise de Pompadour; and the fall of the Bastille.

As his candidate for the Iron Mask, Funck-Brentano selects Count Hercules Antony Mattioli, the double-dealing secretary of state to Charles IV, Duke of Mantua. After arranging to sell the Mantuan dependency of Casal to Louis XIV for a costly diamond and the sum of 100 double louis, Mattioli undercut the corrupt deal by tipping off the courts of

Vienna, Madrid, Turin, and the Venetian Republic. In a gross violation of international law, Louis XIV had Mattioli abducted and secretly jailed at Pignerol. According to Funck-Brentano, the prisoner's velvet mask was not devised as added punishment but "in reality constituted a relief to his captivity, for it permitted the prisoner to leave his room, while the other state prisoners were rigorously mewed up in theirs."

The various theories of the Iron Mask's identity are ably discussed in John Noone, *The Man Behind the Iron Mask* (New York: St. Martin's, 1988). Noone believes that the prisoner was a valet, Eustache Danger (whom he distinguishes from Eustache *Dauger* de Cavoye, identified by many earlier writers. In Noone's view, "The secret prisoner was 'only a valet.' His importance lay not in anything he was, but in something he knew." Noone cites a 1687 letter (disclosed at a Cannes conference in 1987) that confirms that the wearing of a steel mask (later exchanged for velvet) was not a myth. A briefer survey of opinion is provided in Rupert Furneaux, *The Man Behind the Mask* (London: Cassell, 1954).

F.33 ———— *Mandrin, capitaine des contrebandiers* [Mandarin, Smugglers' Captain]. In series *La vivante histoire*. Paris: Hachette, 1936.

■ The eighteenth-century smuggler Louis Mandrin came to embody the popular hatred of the tax-farming system that was the principal target of his depredations. Born near Grenoble in 1725, Mandrin organized a virtual army of smugglers who invaded France in six campaigns from their Savoyard base during 1754. The troops mustered by the tax farmers were generally no match for his forces, but Mandrin was finally captured in a stealthy assault on his chateau in Savoy and executed at Valence in May 1755. The King of France apologized for the intrusion that his army had made into Savoy to seize the bandit chief, but Mandrin had the last (though posthumous) laugh, passing into legend as the Robin Hood of the French. Funck-Brentano, in his classic account of Mandrin's exploits, avoids idolatry but praises the smuggler's dignity and self-possession in confronting death: "He responded with grace and vivacity to the questions that were put to him, when they were not indiscreet. His conversation was full of 'sentiment'; but, occasionally, he bluntly told off the louts who treated him like a curious animal or jeered at his misery."

F.34 Furneaux, Rupert *Famous Criminal Cases*. 7 vols. New York: Roy, 1955–62.

■ This useful set provides contemporary accounts of British murder cases from 1953 to 1962. The highlights include:

- *Vol. 1:* John Reginald Halliday Christie (the "Monster of Rillington Place");
- Christopher Craig and Derek Bentley, boy bandits who shot a policeman;
- Louisa Merrifield, murderer of a Blackpole widow, Mrs. Sarah Ricketts; and
- Ronald John Chesney, murderer who had formerly been acquitted of matricide under the name John Donald Merrett
- *Vol. 2:* Juliet Hulme and Pauline Parker, the New Zealand murderers of Pauline's mother in 1954; and Gaston Dominici, convicted of having murdered the vacationing Drummond family near the defendant's farm in Lurs, France, in 1952

- *Vol. 3:* Ruth Ellis, who was condemned in 1955 for shooting her lover, David Blakely, and was the last woman hanged in England
- *Vol. 4:* Dr. John Bodkin Adams, acquitted in 1957 of the murder in 1950 of his eighty-one-year-old patient, Mrs. Alice Morrell
- *Vol. 5:* Kenneth Barlow, a male nurse, convicted of the 1957 murder of his wife, Elizabeth, by injection of insulin
- *Vol. 6:* Brian Donald Hume, who confessed in 1958 to the stabbing murder of Stanley Setty in 1950 (having been convicted only as an accessory after the fact by disposing of Setty's body); and Guenther Podola, who shot and killed an unarmed policeman in the execution of his duty
- *Vol. 7:* James Hanratty, who was, amid great controversy, found guilty of shooting Michael John Gregsten in the "A6 Murder"

One of the cases treated by Furneaux, the 1954 Parker-Hulme murder trial, had dramatic reverberations in the 1990s. In the New Zealand city of Christchurch, Pauline Yvonne Parker, age sixteen, and Juliet Marion Hulme, age fifteen, were convicted of killing Pauline's mother, Honora Mary Parker. The girls had developed such an intense friendship that their parents became alarmed. When Juliet's father, a distinguished British scientist, ended his service as rector of Christchurch University College and planned to take his family to South Africa, Pauline wanted to go with them so as not to be parted from Juliet. She regarded her mother Honora as the principal obstacle to the fulfillment of this wish. Pauline's diary, found by the police, reveals that she coolly planned to put her mother out of the way: "Next time I write in this diary, Mother will be dead. How odd—yet how pleasing."

The two girls took turns battering Mrs. Parker to death with a brick stuffed in a stocking. Both of them were convicted of murder and, because of their youth, were sentenced to be detained "until Her Majesty's Pleasure be made known."

In 1990, it was revealed that Juliet Hulme, after her release from prison, won success as the mystery writer who calls herself Anne Perry. Perry explains her youthful decision to join in the murder: "I was afraid (Pauline) would die if she didn't come with us. I had a dramatic turn of the mind. It was pretty stupid and very wrong but I did not want to let down the one friend who had stood by me." Perry has also pointed out that she was taking a medicine for a respiratory ailment that was eventually taken off the market because of its "judgment-altering qualities."

The discovery of Perry's identity was made by a New Zealand reporter in connection with the appearance of the brilliant 1994 film *Heavenly Creatures,* based on the Parker-Hulme murder. Directed by Peter Jackson and presenting Kate Winslet as Juliet Hulme, the film explores the dream world jointly created by Pauline and Juliet to indulge their fantasies that they were "heavenly creatures" worthy of royal adventures. The dream sequences are peopled by figures in full-size latex costumes whose movements were digitally controlled.

G

G.1 Gailly, Gerard *Le Lieutenant-Criminel Tardieu et sa femme.* Paris: Editions du Lys, 1945.
■ The sprightly title essay sketches the lives and sudden deaths of seventeenth-century Paris's renowned miser, Lieutenant-Criminel (police chief) Jean Tardieu and his wife, Marie, who were murdered by a pair of house-breakers in 1665. The killers, René and François Touchet (who may have been brothers), claimed that they had come to the Tardieu house seeking alms, a thankless quest given the householders' reputation for niggardliness; the murders occurred, the Touchets claimed, only when the Tardieus called for help, causing the inexperienced trespassers to lose their composure.

Gailly dashes cold water on this defense (which the jury rejected), showing how the Touchets had likely committed two previous armed robberies. Jean Tardieu apparently was one of the sources for Harpagon, Molière's immortal miser (see M.34).

G.2 Galtier-Boissière, Jean *Mysteries of the French Secret Police.* Trans. Ronald Leslie-Melville. London: Stanley Paul, 1938.
■ Galtier-Boissiére, founder and editor of the French illustrated magazine *Le Crapouillot*, reviews the history of the French police from the Ancien Régime to the campaign against the Cagoulards, a hooded right-wing terrorist group, on the eve of World War II.

G.3 García Márquez, Gabriel *Chronicle of a Death Foretold* [Crónica de una muerte anunciada]. Trans. Gregory Rabassa. New York: Knopf, 1982.
■ The narrator of this short novel returns to his hometown to chronicle the murder of Santiago Nasar committed there twenty-seven years earlier by twin brothers Pablo and Pedro Vicario while the townspeople stood silently by. The title of the work seems to be inaccurately rendered in the English version: the murder is announced by the Vicarios in advance to a dozen neighbors (very much in the style of Agatha Christie's thriller, *A Murder Is Announced* (1950) rather than "foretold" by a third person or an oracular agency. Santiago's mother, Plácida Linero, a town resident with "a well-earned reputation" for elucidating the prophetic meaning of dreams, fails to notice any "ominous augury" in two of her son's dreams described to her on the mornings preceding his death.

The Vicario twins stab Santiago to death after their sister Angela's bridegroom discovers that she is not a virgin and returns her to her home. Interrogated by her brothers, she falsely identifies Santiago Nasar as the seducer, because she desires to shield her lover and believes that Santiago is too formidable an adversary for the twins to confront. In the latter calculation, she was probably right, because the twins' repeated announcements of their planned revenge appears to have intended to cause their neighbors to prevent the crime.

The reasons for failure of the townspeople to intervene as the Vicarios had hoped are manifold. Some lapsed into passivity or the role of spectators. Many thought that the twins were merely indulging in drunken bravado. The mother of Prudencia Cotes, Pablo Vicario's fiancée, backed the twins' cause, remarking as they hurried from her door, "Honor doesn't wait."

Men in authority dithered at vital moments. The mayor, Colonel Lázaro Aponte, took the lurking twins' knives away, but when he was told that they had obtained substitute weapons, missed the fatal encounter when "he went into the social club to check on a date for dominoes that night." The priest, Father Amador, thought first that the Vicarios' threat was a matter for the civil authorities, but after he briefly considered speaking to Plácida Linero, forgot about the entire matter in his excitement over the imminent visit of his bishop. Santiago Nasar's close friend, Cristo Bedoya, broke off his pursuit of Santiago to ascertain a sick man's condition.

Only rarely could it be said that the failure to give a timely warning to Santiago was motivated by personal animosity. One exception was Victoria Guzmán, the cook in Santiago's household. Seduced by his father and outraged by Santiago's advances to her adolescent daughter, Divina Flor, Victoria remained silent, her daughter later speculated, "because in the depths of her heart she wanted them to kill him."

Failed by all the bystanders who could have saved him, Santiago is unable to escape his reluctant killers. When, too late, he realized that they were waiting for him, "his reaction was not one of panic as has so often been said, but rather the bewilderment of innocence."

Colombian novelist García Márquez, winner of the 1982 Nobel Prize for Literature, closely patterned *Chronicle of a Death Foretold* after the murder of his friend Cayetano Gentile Chimento in Sucre on January 22, 1951. The crime was fostered by a pestilential local custom of scribbling disgraceful lampoons on the town's walls. One of the most inflammatory of these graffiti appeared below the door of Miguel Palencia, advising him that his bride-to-be, Margarita Chica Salas, was not a virgin. When Margarita identified Cayetano as her seducer, very few accepted her version, because, in the words of García Márquez's biographer, "the whole town knew that he had not been the only man to drink from her virginal waters" (see Dasso Saldívar, *García Márquez: El viaje a la semilla* [Madrid: Alfaquara, 1997], 266). Although they were good friends of Cayetano, the bride's brothers felt compelled to avenge their family's honor, and one of them, José Joaquín Chica Salas, stabbed him to death. As he died, Cayetano counseled his mother to be patient, resigned, and serene but told his brothers to continue the cycle of violence. García Márquez brooded on the tragedy for thirty years before converting it into a masterly novella of what he called a town's "collective responsibility."

In 1987 *Chronicle of a Death Foretold* was released as a film directed by Francesco Rosi, and theatrical versions were mounted in New York City in a 1995 dance-drama staged by Lincoln Center and a later production by Colombian director and adaptor Jorge Ali Triana for the Repertorio Español.

G.4 ——— *News of a Kidnapping.* Trans. Edith Grossman. New York: Knopf, 1997.
■ This magnificent account of the 1990 kidnapping of ten Colombians at the command of Medellín drug boss Pedro Escobar is often heartbreaking but ultimately a celebration of human endurance and liberation in the tradition of Beethoven's *Fidelio*.

Escobar took his hostages, all but one of whom were journalists and some related to prominent politicians, in order to ensure that he would not be extradited to the United

States and could, instead, negotiate a surrender that would put him beyond the reach of his enemies. García Márquez portrays Escobar as an almost supernaturally serene man unable to distinguish between good and evil but a master of the craft of deal making. "This is a negotiation," he once exploded in anger at the government's foot dragging, "not a game to find out who is clever and who is stupid." In the reaction of Medellín to Escobar's reign of terror, García Márquez found a mirror of his nation's character: "Perhaps the most Colombian aspect of the situation was the astonishing capacity of the people of Medellín to accustom themselves to everything, good and bad, with a resiliency that may be the cruelest form courage can take."

There were many heroes among the hostages, including two women who did not survive: the indomitable Marina Montoya, cruelly executed to pressure the government; and Diana Turbay, a famous television journalist and magazine editor, shot (perhaps accidentally) in the crossfire of a military sweep in the area where she was imprisoned. The final triumph belongs to Maruja Pachón and Pacho Santos, whose release heralded Escobar's surrender.

G.5 Gaskell, Elizabeth *Mary Barton.* 1848. London: Penguin, 1994.

■ In this working-class novel, Mary Barton's unemployed unionist father, John, vents his anger against a wealthy mill owner Carson by murdering Carson's son Harry, who has been secretly wooing Mary. After James Wilson, Mary's beloved, is tried for the crime and acquitted, John Barton comes to see the error of his class hatred:

> To intimidate a class of men, known only to those below them as desirous to obtain the greatest quantity of work for the lowest wages,—at most to remove an overbearing partner from an obnoxious firm, who stood in the way of those who struggled as well as they were able to obtain their rights,—this was the light in which John Barton had viewed this deed; . . . But now he knew that he had killed a man, and a brother,— now he knew that no good thing could come out of this evil, even to the sufferers whose cause he had so blindly espoused.

Several years before the appearance of the novel, a mill owner, Thomas Ashton of Pole Bank, had been murdered in a dispute with a trade union. His brother, James, had gone to a dance and Thomas went to the mill in his place. The last person who spoke to him was his twelve-year-old sister, Mary. In 1849, the now-adult Mary started reading *Mary Barton* and fainted when she came to a description of the murder. Her husband, Thomas Potter, and his brother, Sir John Potter, blamed Mrs. Gaskell for reopening family wounds. In an explanatory letter to Sir John, the author explained that "if the circumstances were present to my mind at the time of my writing 'Mary Barton' it was so unconsciously, although its occurrence, and that of one or two similar cases at Glasgow at the time of a strike, were, I have no doubt, suggestive of the plot, as having shown me to what lengths the animosity of irritated workmen would go" (see Elizabeth Haldane, *Mrs. Gaskell and Her Friends* [New York: Appleton, 1931], 38–42).

G.6 Gay, John   *The Beggar's Opera.* 1728. Intro. Oswald Doughty. London: Daniel O'Connor, 1922.

■ Gay's ballad opera was inspired by Jonathan Swift's remark eleven years earlier: "What an odd, pretty sort of thing a Newgate Pastoral might make." Patrick Pringle, in his *Stand and Deliver* (see P.20), comments that Gay's hero, Captain Macheath, "although of exaggerated virtue and certainly not typical, could be identified with more than one gallant highwayman of the Commonwealth period."

G.7 Gayot de Pitaval, François   *Causes célèbres et intéressantes, avec les jugements qui les ont décidées.* 22 vols. The Hague: Neaulme, 1738–46.

■ Gayot de Pitaval (1673–1743), a member of the bar of the Parlement de Paris, is the author of the first significant French-language collection of causes célèbres. Although criticized for disorderly narrative presentation, this work established a precedent for many other collections of French criminal cases and, in translation, had a major influence on the development of a similar literary genre in Germany. Among the cases included in Pitaval's series are those of the impersonator of Martin Guerre, the seventeenth-century serial poisoner Marquise de Brinvilliers, and the murder of the marquise de Ganges (1757) by her brothers-in-law who, rebuffed in their amorous advances, wished to share her riches with the indifferent marquis.

In a preface, Gayot de Pitaval explains why he turned to crime history, a category of which he must be regarded as one of the principal inventors:

> The strange and surprising facts in the agreeable stories that are works of the imagination cause us a poisoned pleasure, so to speak, because of the falsity of the events. This feigned beauty is not a true beauty; it astonishes us at first, but the illusion dissipates, and the natural repugnance that we feel for the false revolts us, at the bottom of our heart, against the most beautiful of fictions.
>
> But when the true combines with the wonderful, and when nature offers them to us in a fabric of facts, where it seems to have borrowed from a happy genius for embellishment, then our mind and our heart enjoy a pleasure that is pure and exquisite.

G.8 Genet, Jean   *The Maids.* In *The Maids and Deathwatch: Two Plays.* Intro. Jean-Paul Sartre. Trans. Bernard Frechtman. New York: Grove, 1954.

■ *The Maids* is based on the two murderous housemaids of Le Mans, Christine and Léa Papin (see F.15). In Jean Genet's play, the two maids, sisters named Solange and Claire, are bound by a love-hate relationship with their employer (referred to only as "Madame") and with each other. They have vented their spite against Madame by sending anonymous letters charging Madame's lover ("Monsieur") with theft, an accusation that has resulted in his being jailed.

Solange and Claire engage in repeated game-playing ceremonies that involve an interchange of personalities; as the curtain rises Claire impersonates Madame and

Solange becomes Claire, whom she ordinarily dominates as the stronger-willed older sister. An alarm clock warns them to break off the ritual before Madame's return, and Solange regrets that, as usual, they have been interrupted before she can act out the murder of Madame. "The same thing happens every time," she complains to Claire. "And it's all your fault, you're never ready. I can't finish you off."

In real life the maids are no greater successes at homicide. Solange could not bring herself to strangle the sleeping Madame, and Claire's attempt to serve her poisoned tea miscarries when Madame rushes out to free her lover, who has been bailed. Solange, in an extended soliloquy, assumes the identity and prestige that would have come to her as her employer's killer: "Madame may call me Mademoiselle Solange. . . . Exactly. It's because of what I've done. Madame and Monsieur will call me Mademoiselle Solange Lemercier . . . . What? Oh! Madame needn't feel sorry for me. I'm Madame's equal and I hold my head high."

Claire, play-acting again in her role as Madame, drinks the tea that was intended for her employer and dies. Solange exults in imagining Madame's reaction when she will learn of the death that has liberated both servants from her oppression: "She enters her apartment— but Madame is dead. Her two maids are alive: they've just risen up, free, from Madame's icy form."

G.9 **Gherardini, Giovanni** *The Thieving Magpie* [La gazza ladra]. Music by Gioacchino Rossini. First performed at Milan, Teatro alla Scala, May 31, 1817.

■ Gherardini based his libretto on a popular French "historical melodrama" presented away from the center of Paris in one of the new "boulevard" theaters devoted to spectacular melodrama. Written by Jean-Marie-Théodore Baudouin d'Aubigny and Louis-Charles Caigniez, the stage work was first performed in 1815 under the title *The Thieving Magpie: or, The Serving-Girl of Palaiseau*, and played to full houses well into the 1830s. In the theatrical version and Rossini's opera, a maid is falsely accused of stealing silverware that has actually been filched by a magpie; proof of the bird's theft saves the girl from execution.

In a historical note that precedes the published text of their play, d'Aubigny and Caigniez state:

> Everyone knows that a Magpie Mass used to be celebrated in Paris, in reparation of the error of the judges who had condemned to death an unfortunate female servant, unjustly accused of thefts made by a magpie. Although there are different versions of the period and circumstances of this famous trial, it is nonetheless certain that it took place; for it cannot be assumed that the Magpie Mass would have been established without reason. The most widely disseminated tradition is that the theft consisted of spoons, forks and silver coins that were found, but too late, in a gutter, where the bird successively hid them. It is this last version that we have chosen.

Local historians have found no evidence that the miscarriage of justice actually occurred at Palaiseau, but they do confirm that the Magpie Mass was celebrated at Paris's famous left-bank church of St.-Germain-des-Prés and, at the beginning of the nineteenth century, in one of the parishes of Rouen (see F. Cossonnet, *Recherches historiques sur Palaiseau* [1895], 229; Gabriel Dauphin, *Palaiseau d'hier et d'aujourd'hui* [1970], 403).

An early-nineteenth-century English pamphlet owned by the Borowitz True Crime Collection summarizes the plot of the French play; it asserts that the story is "founded on a trial in France, of a maid servant, who was accused of robbing her master of jewels, etc. to a considerable amount, and who was convicted and executed on PRESUMPTIVE EVIDENCE" (*The Maid and Magpie: or, The Real Thief Detected: Containing the True Story of an Unfortunate Female Who Was Sentenced to be Executed on Strong Presumptive Evidence. . . .* [Bath: H. Gye, ca. 1815–20?]).

Although Rossini ordinarily exercised strong control over his opera librettos, he gave the legally trained Gherardini free rein in conceiving the trial scene in *The Thieving Magpie*: "Because of your wide experience at the bar, I leave you entirely free to deal as you see fit with the courtroom scene. But I want you to follow my suggestions as to the rest." The Magpie Mass and the trial from which it sprang furnish the basis of a Belgian comic strip drawn by [Juan Manuel] Cicuendez, with text by O[ctave] Joly, in the series "Les belles histoires de l'Oncle Paul," published in the *Journal de Spirou*, no. 1674 (May 14, 1970). The strip, entitled "La messe de la pie," tells a variant of the story's ending: "[The servants'] employers, in despair because they had caused an innocent girl to be condemned, founded a mass for the repose of her soul in the church Saint-Jean de la Grève [presumably located on the Palaiseau square where she had been executed]."

G.10 Gide, Andre *L'Affaire Redureau, suivie de faits divers.* Comp. Andre Gide. Paris: Gallimard, 1930.

■ In this volume, Gide pursues real-life manifestations of the *acte gratuit* (gratuitous and often dangerous action), which he had previously explored in his novel *Les caves du Vatican* [Lafcadio's Adventures] (1914), where Lafcadio impulsively murders Amédée. Gide concedes, in his preface to the nonfiction collection, that "no human action is truly unmotivated; there is no *acte gratuit*, except in appearance," and he is forced to admit that "the present knowledge of psychology does not permit us to understand everything, and that there are, on the map of the human soul, many unexplored regions, *terrae incognitae*."

The principal essay is devoted to the slaughter of seven members of a farm household in 1913 by fifteen-year-old Marcel Redureau, whose rage was apparently triggered by his master's criticism of his work at a wine press. Gide also appears to implicate among the springs of the massacre the emotional volatility of adolescence and Marcel's unusual timorousness that was capable of sudden conversion into reckless action, much as a coward could become a valiant soldier on the field of battle.

The balance of the volume (published in the crime series *Ne Jugez Pas*, directed by Gide) consists primarily of human interest stories (*faits divers*) solicited by Gide from readers of *La nouvelle revue française* to illustrate his theme of psychological enigmas. The themes of the submissions he accepted include bizarre suicides, child criminals, and cannibalism.

G.11 ————— *The Counterfeiters* [1925], trans. Dorothy Bussy; and *Journal of "The Counter-feiters,"* trans. and annotated Justin O'Brien. New York: Random House (Vintage Books), 1973.

■ The schoolroom "suicide" of Boris at the end of Gide's novel was based on the horrifying death of young Nény in the middle of a class at the Lycée Blaise-Pascal at Clermont-Ferrand in 1909. According to the local newspaper, the schoolboy had been raised in a violent family and in fact was obliged to seek refuge with neighbors on the eve of his death. Another sinister influence, according to the paper, was Nény's "assiduous and uncontrolled reading of German philosophers."

At the school an "evil society of youngsters" had been formed to force its members to commit suicide. Nény drew a lot requiring him to kill himself first, and his comrades egged him on by accusing him of cowardice. On the day before the tragedy, his two comrades "made him go through a complete rehearsal of this heinous act, marking with a chalk X on the floor the place where he was to blow out his brains the next day." At the time arranged, "the victim got up, stood at the spot marked with the chalk, took out his revolver, and fired it into his right temple.... [W]hen he fell, one of the conspirators had the horrible presence of mind to leap for the revolver and spirit it away."

Gide reproduces these details faithfully in *The Counterfeiters*. Three schoolboys organize the "Brotherhood of Strong Men" for the pleasure of keeping Boris out of it, but the ringleader Ghéridanisol then decides that "it would be far more perversely effective to let him in" so that "he might gradually be led on to the performance of some monstrous act." True to the brotherhood's motto that "the strong man cares nothing for life," the trio of conspirators rigs a drawing of lots that will require Boris to frighten their classmates by going through the motions of firing a pistol at his temple; Ghéridanisol gives his false assurance that the gun is not loaded. When he sees Boris's dead body being carried away, his fit of trembling is mistaken for a sign of excessive emotion; Gide comments that "one prefers to suppose anything rather than the inhumanity of so young a creature."

In the May 10, 1999, issue of the *New Yorker,* Philip Gourevitch pointed out the eerie similarity of this passage of *The Counterfeiters*, and of the crime on which it was based, to the Littleton, Colorado, school shootings of 1999.

G.12 ————— *Recollections of the Assize Court.* Trans. Philip A. Wilkins. London: Hutchinson, n.d.

■ Gide's recollections of his service on a provincial jury gleam with insight and rueful comprehension of shortcomings in French criminal trials. "The simplest story," Gide argues, "is the one which always has the best chance of being believed, usually it corresponds least to the facts." A chronic problem on which he seizes is the tendency of jurors to vote guilty in doubtful circumstances and to compensate for their indefensible conclusion by finding "extenuating circumstances." Gide took a personal interest in the fate of one defendant, Yves Cordier, whose sentence for participation in robbery of a sailor he found unduly harsh. Interviewing Cordier's family to glean a better understanding of the young man's past, he was successful in obtaining a reduction in the term of his imprisonment.

G.13 Gilbert, Sir William Schwenk *Utopia, Limited: or, The Flowers of Progress.* 1893. In *Plays and Poems of W. S. Gilbert.* New York: Random House, 1932.

■ One of the principal targets of satire in the late Gilbert and Sullivan operetta *Utopia, Limited* is the abuse by unscrupulous promoters of the limited-liability shield provided by business corporations. The assertion of limited liability as a refuge from personal responsibility becomes the basic constitutional principle of the dream realm known as Utopia, Limited. In his Act I patter song, Mr. Goldbury, a "Company Promoter" and afterward "Comptroller of the Utopian Household," praises the advantages of undercapitalized companies:

> They [the incorporators] then proceed to
> trade with all who'll trust 'em
> Quite irrespective of their capital
> (It's shady, but it's sanctified by custom;)
> Bank, Railway, Loan, or Panama Canal.

The last of Mr. Goldbury's quoted lines refers to recent financial scandals, including the welter of criminal charges growing out of the Panama Canal construction program by the French-controlled Panama Company. In February 1893, eight months prior to the opening of *Utopia*, the aged Ferdinand de Lesseps (hero of the building of the Suez Canal), his son, and two others were found guilty of fraud in an 1888 bond issue to raise funds for the canal project in Panama, of attempted fraud in another aborted bond issue, and the misappropriation of company funds (see Albert Borowitz, "Gilbert and Sullivan on Corporation Law: 'Utopia Limited' and the Panama Canal Frauds," in *A Gallery of Sinister Perspectives: Ten Crimes and a Scandal,* 11–26 [B.27]).

The study of criminal cases was one of Gilbert's hobbies. In 1911, after his death, his crime library was purchased by Sir Arthur Conan Doyle.

G.14 Ginzburg, Carlo *The Judge and the Historian: Marginal Notes on a Late-Twentieth-Century Miscarriage of Justice.* Trans. Antony Shugaar. London: Verso, 1999.

■ On December 12, 1969, a bomb blast at the Banca dell'Agricultura in Milan killed seventeen people. Three days later, an anarchist and railway employee named Giuseppe (Pino) Pinelli, suspected of involvement in the explosion, fell to his death under disputed circumstances while being interrogated on the fifth floor of Milan police headquarters by Superintendent Luigi Calabresi. (This incident inspired Dario Fo's farce, *Accidental Death of an Anarchist*; see F.18). Calabresi was murdered in front of his residence in 1972; sixteen years afterward, Leonardo Marino confessed that he drove the car used in the killing and implicated three members of an anarchist group calling itself Lotta Continua (Continuous Struggle): Adriano Sofri, Giorgio Pietrostefani, and, the alleged gunman, Ovidio Bompressi.

A friend of Adriano Sofri for more than thirty years, Ginzburg, a well-known historian of the witch cult, was morally certain of Sofri's innocence and sprang to his defense in the present work, which updates a book that was originally published in Italy in 1991. The Milan court of appeals handed down what Ginzburg terms "three radically different verdicts," of which the most recent reviewed in the book resulted in sentencing Sofri, Pietrostefani, and Bompressi to twenty-two years and acquitting Marino because of expiration of the statute of limitations.

Ginzburg ornaments a devastating analysis of judicial errors by brief comments on divergences between the functions of the historian and the judge. Both professions share the belief that it is possible to prove that the protagonist of a historical event or the subject of a criminal proceeding took a given action. However, the historian examines contextual sources from the period in question for the modest purpose of shedding light, as Natalie Zemon Davis has written, on "the world [individuals of the time] would have seen and the reactions they might have had" (*The Return of Martin Guerre;* see D.2). Judges, by contrast, fail to perform their duty when they seek to transform contextual possibilities into the required evidence of guilt beyond a reasonable doubt. Such a failing, Ginzburg argues, underlies the abysmal performance by the bench in the Sofri case.

Although the asserted divergence between judge and historian gives the book its title and academic savor, the heart of Ginzburg's argument for Sofri's innocence is a remorseless exposé of evidentiary miscues that would be egregious in the practice of either profession. The prosecution stood or fell on the testimony of Marino, who was unreliable in many significant respects. He was wrong about the color of the car he allegedly drove to the scene of the crime; the getaway route; and his claim to have met Pietrosanti in Pisa following a rally. His version of the details of the shooting was contradicted by eyewitnesses. Of most importance was the fact that the circumstances of his belated confession and the date of his first interrogations by *carabinieri* "are shrouded in mystery."

G.15 Giono, Jean *Notes sur l'affaire Dominici suivies d'un essai sur le caractères des personnages.* Paris: Gallimard, 1955.

■ On August 5, 1952, British nutrition expert Sir Jack Drummond and his wife, Ann, were shot to death near a highway in Lurs, France, and their ten-year-old daughter, Elizabeth, was fatally clubbed with a rifle butt, perhaps hours after the deaths of her parents. Gaston Dominici, a seventy-seven-year-old farmer whose property was located 150 meters from the scene of the crimes, was condemned to death for the murders before commutation of his sentence by French president René Coty and then pardon by General de Gaulle in 1960.

Novelist Jean Giono, who attended almost all the trial sessions but avoided the closing arguments as mere "eloquence," published notes of his impressions. Unpersuaded that the guilty verdict was adequately supported by evidence, Giono believed that he had observed "a trial of words." Gaston Dominici often could not understand the standard French in which the proceedings were conducted, and his own courtroom vocabulary was limited, according to Giono's count, to about thirty or thirty-five words. In an appended essay on the character of the Dominici family members, Giono sketches the small communities of Haute Provence where Dominici lived his long life but tourists rarely come. In the course of the trial, the defendant won the novelist's respect (if not a belief in his innocence) when, like a provincial Virgil, he unexpectedly burst out with six perfectly constructed sentences in praise of his bucolic life.

The guilt of Dominici remains hotly debated to this day. In his book *Dominici non coupable, les assassins retrouvés* [Dominici Not Guilty, the Murderers Rediscovered] (Paris: Flammarion, 1997), William Reymond has argued that Sir Jack Drummond was a long-time member of the British secret service and was the victim of a Cold War assassination staged from Germany. Elaborating this theory, Lionel Dumarcet, in *L'Affaire Dominici* (Paris: De Vecchi, 1999), theorizes that after Sir Jack was killed, unknown local inhabitants arrived at the site of the assassination to steal the Drummonds' possessions and, in the course of their plunder, may have administered the coup de grace to the dying Lady Ann and then murdered the child to eliminate her as a witness.

G.16 Gisquet, M. *Mémoires de M. Gisquet, ancien préfet de police.* 6 vols. Brussels: Jamar, 1841.
■ Gisquet served as prefect of police in Paris between 1831 and 1836. The *Encyclopédie nationale de la police*, published after World War II, credited him with "the official creation of the Service of the Sûreté, which until then had constituted only a semi-unofficial group of investigators and informers under the direction of the famous Vidocq." Police historian Philip John Stead describes Gisquet, a banker by profession, as "a somewhat equivocal character" who was involved in "a cloudy business of buying muskets for the army in which speculation and peculation do not appear entirely to have been strangers" (*The Police of Paris* [London: Staples, 1957]).

Gisquet notified readers that the purpose of his memoirs was "to make known the acts of my administration; to combat ill-founded prejudices against the police; and to enlighten the country concerning the cause and nature of the troublesome charges of which the police have been the target since 1830." After some historical background, Gisquet begins his narrative with the creation of the police prefecture in 1800. In the course of the book he relates his participation in the July Revolution of 1830 and defends his conduct in the purchase of muskets that sullied his reputation. Among the public and criminal matters discussed are political disturbances and plots; the cholera epidemic of 1832; the uprising of 1832; actions against the "false Dauphins" claiming to be Louis XVII; censorship of republican journals and suppression of hawkers of street literature; the attempt of Fieschi and his comrades to assassinate Louis Philippe with an "infernal machine" (vol. 5); the assassination attempt on the king by Alibaud (vol. 6); the suppression of Victor Hugo's play *The Man Who Laughs*; prostitution; and crime and prisons in Paris.

G.17 Glaspell, Susan *Trifles.* In *Plays by Susan Glaspell.* New York: Dodd Mead, 1920.
■ In the one-act play *Trifles*, and her short story "A Jury of Her Peers," Glaspell draws upon the murder trial of an Iowa farm woman who hatcheted her husband in bed; the author had reported the trial as a journalist.

In the play, county attorney Henderson questions farmer Hale and his wife about the murder of their neighbor, John Wright, who was found in his bed strangled with a rope.

The victim's wife, Minnie, is under suspicion. Glaspell tellingly accumulates the details ("trifles") of Mrs. Wright's married life that establish her husband's tyranny. The most horrifying discovery is made by the wife of Sheriff Peters, who finds Minnie Wright's pet canary with its neck wrung. Mrs. Hale and Mrs. Peters, sharing female understanding of Minnie's marital suffering, suppress the evidence of the dead bird.

G.18 Glass, Alan *Love in a Thirsty Land.* A play first performed at the Jewish Repertory Theatre, New York City, March 2000.

■ In 1875, Pasach Rubenstein cut the throat of cousin Sarah Alexander, his pregnant sweetheart, near a farmhouse in rural New Lots, Long Island, neighboring a thickly settled section of Brooklyn called East New York. The motive was not fear over the immigration of Pasach's wife, which had often been postponed. More likely, the murderer, even for the brief period of life that his pulmonary tuberculosis would spare him, could not "face the religious guilt and communal shame that would have followed the birth of Sarah's child" (Albert Borowitz, "The Frozen Footprints," in Jonathan Goodman, ed., *The Country House Murders* [London: Alison & Busby, 1987]).

In Glass's play, the two principal figures in the case (whose first names are spelled "Pesach" and "Sara" in the typescript) are not related. They are locked in a tragic dialectic concerning the place of Jewish newcomers in nineteenth-century America. Pesach, perhaps without genuine faith, continues to follow traditional religious observances, but Sara has turned to socialism and assimilation. He chokes her accidentally when she taunts him about his decision to delay their marriage until he can offer an explanation to his first wife, who is finally on her way to New York. Two other characters, Pesach's aunt and his third cousin, are the author's inventions, and the defense attorney (who, in actuality, was a distinguished advocate, William Augustus Beach) is a well-meaning lawyer who knows more about real estate than criminal law. The play ends with Rubenstein's death of tuberculosis before the case is submitted to the jury. In fact, the trial concluded with a finding of murder in the first degree after a jury deliberation of an hour and twenty minutes. The *Brooklyn Eagle*, which reported the case with bemused compassion, wrote of the defendant's then pending appeal, that "a Higher Court has cognizance of the case, and the appeal to human ears will avail nothing."

G.19 [Gold Medal Murder Series] *Gold Medal Series of Classic Murder Trials.* 12 vols. New York: Fawcett (Gold Medal), 1951–57.

■ This is the finest set of paperback original editions devoted primarily to the book-length presentation of famous American murder cases. Each volume is written by an experienced true-crime author, and the Gold Medal paperback often is the first extended study of the crime in question. The following books in the series are in order of publication (note that the word "girl" always appears in the titles):

- *The Girl in the Stateroom,* Charles Boswell and Lewis Thompson: Ship steward James Camb's murder of passenger Gay Gibson (the "Porthole Murder")

- *The Girl in the Red Velvet Swing,* Charles Samuels: Harry K. Thaw's murder of architect Stanford White
- *The Girl in the Death Cell,* Fred J. Cook: Ruth Snyder and Judd Gray, lovers who collaborated in murder of Snyder's husband (inspiring Sophie Treadwell's play *Machinal*)
- *The Girl in Lover's Lane,*Charles Boswell: The Hall-Mills case, involving the unsolved New Jersey murders of a minister and his beloved choir singer
- *The Girl in Poison Cottage,* Richard H. Hoffman and Jim Bishop: The Creighton-Appelgate murder case, in which Everett Appelgate and serial poisoner Mary Frances Creighton were electrocuted for the arsenic murder of Mrs. Appelgate
- *The Girl in the House of Hate,* Charles and Louise Samuels: Lizzie Borden
- *The Girl with the Scarlet Brand,* Charles Boswell and Louis Thompson: Florence Maybrick, convicted of poisoning her husband James, whom some now identify as Jack the Ripper
- *The Girl on the Gallows,* Q. Patrick: Edith Thompson and Frederick Bywaters, both hanged for the murder of Thompson's husband
- *The Girl on the Lonely Beach,* Fred J. Cook: Starr Faithfull, whose unsolved death at the seashore inspired John O'Hara's novel *Butterfield 8*
- *The Girl in the Murder Flat,* Mel Heimer: Wayne Lonergan, sentenced to thirty years' imprisonment (of which he served twenty-one) for the murder of his heiress girlfriend Patricia Burton
- *The Girls in Nightmare House,* Charles Boswell and Lewis Thompson: H. H. Holmes (Herman Mudgett), Chicago serial killer who inhabited the "Murder Castle" and was executed for the murder of Benjamin Pitezel
- *The Girl in the Belfry,* Joseph Henry Jackson and Lenore Glen Offord: Theodore Durrant, who murdered two young women in a San Francisco church, carrying one of the bodies into the belfry

Another Gold Medal volume, which fits the series format except for its title, is Charles Samuels's *Death Was the Bridegroom* (1955), a study of Chester Gillette's murder of his pregnant girlfriend Grace Brown, the case on which Theodore Dreiser based *An American Tragedy*.

G.20 Goodman, Alice *The Death of Klinghoffer.* Music by John Adams. First performed in Brussels, Belgium, March 19, 1991.

■ After the success of their 1987 opera *Nixon in China*, "minimalist" composer Adams, librettist Goodman, and director Peter Sellars reassembled their principal singers in another work based on an event in recent history, the 1985 hijacking of Italian cruise liner *Achille Lauro* by Arab terrorists and their murder of a Jewish American passenger, wheelchair-bound Leon Klinghoffer.

In Goodman's libretto, the stark depravity shown by the killers in taking the life of a defenseless civilian, whose only relation to the Arab-Israeli dispute lay in his religion and ethnicity, is blurred by a number of devices, literary and ideological. The setting of the crime is aestheticized by lyrical invocations of the sea in passages including an Ocean Chorus and the reflections of the ship's captain, whose figure, according to John Adams, is "heavily indebted to Joseph Conrad" and is reminiscent of "Marlow (the Conradian mouthpiece in *Lord Jim* and several other tales) in the way he likes to spin out a good yarn and intertwine events with his own psychological and philosophical musing."

An even more problematical aspect of the libretto is its portrayal of the political conflict out of which the murder arose. The opera's prologue seeks to establish a formal evenhandedness by presenting a Chorus of Exiled Palestinians followed immediately by a Chorus of Exiled Jews. The Palestinian grievance, however, is stated with an immediacy that is unmatched in the Jewish chorus:

My father's house was razed
In nineteen forty-eight
When the Israelis passed
Over our street.

The Palestinians vow to "take the stones [the Israeli] broke / And break his teeth." In their choral commentary, the exiled Jews returning to Israel with "no money left" refer, presumably in a muted allusion to the Holocaust, to "all we endured since we parted" and carp about inconvenient features of the Israeli scene, "the movie houses picketed by Hasidim," and "the military barracks." At the beginning of Act 2, Goodman further tips the choral balance in favor of the Arab cause by introducing a "Hagar Chorus," which concludes the tale of the exile of Hagar and Ishmael with the prophesy that the expelled son "will die as a free man / on his own land." As the tense days of the hijacking unfold, Arab terrorists regard themselves as more heroic than the prosperous and hedonistic tourists whom they confront. Even the fear understandably experienced by the hostages becomes the butt of contempt when viewed in relation to the hazards of seafaring. The hijacker Molqi sings:

Every sound
That you can hear
Is a passenger
Afraid for his life.
The sea is stiff
With men who died
Unafraid.

In the opera's concluding scene, Adams and Goodman put Middle East politics aside and give the stage to the cancer-stricken Marilyn Klinghoffer, who movingly laments the brave husband in whose place she would have wanted to die.

G.21 Goodman, Jonathan *Acts of Murder.* New York: Carol Publishing Group, 1993.
▪ With his theatrical background, Goodman is perfectly cast as the chronicler of murders

associated with the stage and the screen. The first essay, by far the longest, deals with the 1897 stabbing death of popular matinee idol William Terriss as he was entering his private stage door to the Adelphi Theatre, London, where he was starring in *Secret Service*, a melodrama by William Gillette (the original stage Sherlock Holmes). The murderer, an unsuccessful actor named Richard Archer Prince, having become obsessed with the notion that West End stars were determined to keep him out of the limelight for fear of being outshone, had focused his hatred on Terriss (upon whom, incidentally, Bernard Shaw had modeled the part of Dick Dudgeon in *The Devil's Disciple*).

Among the seven other essays are accounts of how Roscoe "Fatty" Arbuckle's film career was ruined by the sudden death of a young actress during a party in his suite at the St. Francis Hotel, San Francisco, in 1921; the case of Philip Yale Drew, one-time star of cowboy films, who in 1929 was suspected of the murder of a tobacconist in Reading, west of London, while he was in the town with a touring production of a thriller called *The Monster*; and the unsolved 1922 murder of the Hollywood director William Desmond Taylor, which created unwelcome publicity for several female stars.

After National Service in the Royal Air Force, Jonathan Goodman (1931–) went into the theater, at first as a stage manager and then as a director, working in the West End, on touring productions, and in repertory companies. (It was during his four years at Liverpool Playhouse, the longest-established English repertory theater, that he became interested in the local Wallace murder case, the subject of his first true-crime book.) After working as a television producer, he became managing editor of a specialist publishing company, writing books in his spare time. But since 1982 he has been a freelance writer. He has published some forty books, most of them in the true-crime genre, but also novels, poetry, and an edition of the journals of his friend Rayner Heppenstall. He is Honorary Secretary of Our Society (sometimes referred to as the Crimes Club), a dining club of true-crime aficionados that has flourished in London since 1903.

Remarkable among crime writers for his ability to disentangle fact from hoary misconceptions that other researchers have failed to expose, Goodman has pithily stated a problem faced by all historians: "Legend is more pliable, and therefore more durable, than truth."

G.22 ——— *The Burning of Evelyn Foster*. New York: Scribner, 1977.

■ Late on Twelfth Night 1931, twenty-seven-year-old Evelyn Foster, a self-employed taxi driver whose father operated a bus company from the village of Otterburn, Northumberland, was found by one of her father's drivers at Wolf's Nick, the most desolate part of the moors between Newcastle-upon-Tyne and Otterburn; she was lying, dreadfully burned, close to her burnt-out car. She was driven to the family home, and, in periods of consciousness before she died the following morning, she told how she had been flagged down by a dapper, bowler-hatted man who got out of an occupied private car near Otterburn and how she had agreed to drive him to Ponteland, close to Newcastle, where he could catch a bus into the city. When they were within a few miles of Ponteland, the man had become threatening, insisting that she turn back, and on the return journey he had assaulted and "interfered" with her. Having forced her to stop the car at Wolf's Nick, he had poured fluid over her from a container he had in his pocket, set fire to the car, and sent it free-wheeling onto the moorland, where she, only partially conscious, had rolled free. Her last words, to her mother, were, "I have been murdered." But, following a fruitless search for the bowler-hatted man, the retired army officer who had been appointed chief constable of Northumberland made it clear that he disbelieved Evelyn Foster's account. Even after a coroner's inquest, held in Otterburn's War Memorial Hall, had returned a verdict of wilful murder, he refused to take action. The investigation, already ended, was not reopened.

In the shortest of Goodman's monographs (accurately described by the *New York Times* as "a small gem of a book"), he seeks to unravel a whatwasit—accident, suicide, or murder?—rather than a whodunit. However, after revealing evidence that Evelyn Foster *was* murdered, he discusses tantalizing connections and similarities between the "Wolf's Nick mystery" and a contemporary murder, simply solved, that was committed by a horse groom named Ernest Brown.

G.23 ———— *The Killing of Julia Wallace.* New York: Scribner, 1969.

■ On a Monday night in 1931, a telephone message was left at the City Café, in the center of Liverpool, for William Herbert Wallace, a Prudential insurance agent who belonged to the chess club that met at the café on Mondays. The message, given to Wallace when he arrived, was from a man calling himself R. M. Qualtrough, asking Wallace to be at 25 Menlove Gardens East the following evening, as "I have my girl's twenty-first birthday on, and I want to do something for her in the way of his business." On the Tuesday evening, Wallace traveled from his home in the suburb of Anfield to the Menlove Gardens district, only to be told by a number of local people that, though there were Menlove Gardens North, South, and West, there was no such place as Menlove Gardens East. He returned to Anfield and, in the presence of next-door neighbors, entered his small house; he emerged moments later, having found his wife Julia lying battered to death in the front parlor. The detectives on the case eventually concluded that Wallace was the murderer; that it was he who had made the R. M. Qualtrough phone call, so as to provide himself with a sort of alibi; that he had killed his wife shortly before setting off for the Menlove Gardens district. Despite the equivocal nature of each component of the prosecution case, he was found guilty and was sentenced to death. The case made history in three ways: by being the first in which the defense costs of a person accused of a "non-trade crime" were guaranteed by his union; because, on the eve of the appeal, special prayers, described as "intercessions extraordinary," which sought "true judgment" from the Judges of Appeal, were offered at services in Liverpool Cathedral; and because, for the first time since the Court of Criminal Appeal was set up in 1907, the three judges quashed a verdict of guilty in a murder case on the grounds that it "was not proved with that certainty which is necessary."

Goodman's account—based on long and intensive research and made particularly compelling by its scene-painting and characterization of the dramatis personae—is followed by lucid argument that Wallace was innocent. Many of his points are persuasive, but the one that seems to clinch the argument relates to some bent spokes on a milkboy's bicycle. He outlines facts suggestive of the guilt of another insurance agent; the man is disguised as "Mr. X" in this first edition, but in subsequent editions, published after the man's death, he is identified as Richard Gordon Parry.

In 1978, Goodman published a whodunit, *The Last Sentence* (New York: St. Martin's), which is, in many respects, strongly reminiscent of the Wallace case (as are several other novels). The period is up-to-date, the setting changed to London; even so, as the fictional culprit bore similarities to a person involved innocently in the real case, Goodman elicited a written assurance from the latter that the literary misrepresentation would not result in a libel action.

G.24——— *Murder in High Places* (London: Piatkus, 1986). *Murder in Low Places* (London: Piatkus, 1988).

■ The respective titles seem self-explanatory, but (as he always does in his collections and anthologies) Goodman includes certain cases that are at the very edge of, or even slightly overlap, each title's circumference. In the first book, the major essay examines the case of Marguerite Fahmy, a beautiful Frenchwoman who in 1923, while staying with her husband, an Egyptian prince, and his entourage at the Savoy Hotel, shot him to death during the worst thunderstorm over London in memory. The second book, longer and covering more cases than the first, contains an illuminating account of the Burke and Hare case (Edinburgh, 1827), with a postscript on the similarly motivated murder by Bishop, Williams, and May (London, 1831), which led to the passing of the Anatomy Act, effectively making dead bodies valueless.

G.25 ——— *The Passing of Starr Faithfull.* Kent, Ohio: Kent State Univ. Press, 1996.

■ On a summer morning in 1931, the body of a beautiful young woman, Starr Faithfull, was found on a Long Island beach. Apart from formalities associated with sudden death, that might have been the end of the matter; but, chiefly as a result of comments made by the stepfather, law officers and newspaper reporters unearthed lurid facts about her life which kept her name on front pages in Britain as well as America for many weeks. Stories about her love affairs with artists in London and Manhattan, and with a Scottish surgeon on a Cunard liner, seemed tame compared with the revelation that, as a child, she had been sexually abused by a leading Boston politician. At times, details about Starr Faithfull's past took second place to details about her stepfather's murky business affairs and involvement in legal cases, one of murder. When the case file was eventually closed, the question remained: had Starr Faithfull committed suicide, died by accident, or been murdered?

Described by a *New Yorker* essayist as "this mystery with the wonderful name," the Starr Faithfull case has inspired a number of novels, notably John O'Hara's *Butterfield 8.* Surprisingly, though, Goodman's is the first full-length factual account. The only author to have been granted full access to the massive police dossier, he uses that source, along with countless others, to answer the "whatwasit" question; and in the penultimate chapter (as usual, he devotes the last chapter to the postcase lives of the protagonists), he puts forward a convincing argument that Starr Faithfull was murdered and then assembles evidence that strongly suggests both the motive for the murder and the identity of the murderer. The book was first published in Great Britain, where it won the Crime Writers' Association's Gold Dagger award.

G.26 ———— *The Slaying of Joseph Bowne Elwell.* New York: St. Martin's, 1988.

■ On a June morning in 1920, someone somehow managed to gain access to Joseph Bowne Elwell's art-filled, well-protected house on West 70th Street in Manhattan, shoot him neatly through the head while he was sitting in a thronelike chair (at a moment when he, extremely vain about his appearance, was not wearing one of his collection of specially ordered wigs or his complicated set of dentures), and then escape, as if into thin air.

Elwell was almost as mysterious as his murderer: as well as being the greatest bridge player of his time, the leading tutor of the game (to, among others, the king of England and the millionaire Vanderbilts), and the author of best-selling bridge textbooks, he was an unofficial "spy-catcher," a heavy gambler on the stock exchange, the owner of a string of race horses, a developer of Florida real estate, a dealer in bootleg liquor, and, following separation from his wife (who was related to the presidential Roosevelts), a most industrious philanderer.

Chiefly because of the locked-house nature of the crime, there seemed no doubt that he had been killed by an intimate acquaintance; but no one was ever charged, let alone convicted.

The Elwell case has been used as the basis of crime novels (including one of the most famous, S. S. Van Dine's *The Benson Murder Case* [1926], the first of far too many starring the foppish amateur detective Philo Vance); indirectly, it resulted in the formation of the writing partnership known as Ellery Queen; and Goodman suggests, persuasively, that Elwell may have been one of the inspirations for *The Great Gatsby*. He believes that if only the various groups of investigators had worked together, rather than in opposition, the mystery would have been solved. In the light of his startling discoveries about Elwell's rich crony, the mentally disturbed Walter Lewisohn, one tends to agree.

G.27 ———— *The Stabbing of George Harry Storrs.* Columbus: Ohio State Univ. Press, 1983.

■ The opening sentences of Goodman's book read: "In all but a few murder cases, the crime comes as a complete surprise to the victim: confident of dying naturally, he has made no effort to prevent the criminal quietus, has not augmented any preparation for a possible meeting with his Maker. In the Gorse Hall case, however, the victim, a man called George Harry Storrs, seems to have been warned of the fatal attack and to have taken some notice of the warning."

In September 1909, after Storrs, a Cheshire tycoon, claimed that an intruder had fired shots through the window of his mansion, Gorse Hall, overlooking the cotton town of Stalybridge, he erected an alarm-bell on the roof of the telephone-less building and arranged for policemen to patrol the grounds at night. However, as municipal elections on November 1 stretched the resources of the local police force, there was no patrol that night.

A young man entered the house, stabbed Storrs several times, leaving him dying, and then escaped. There were many indications that Storrs had known the assailant's identity—or, at least, the reason for the attack. The case made legal history by being the first in which two men were separately charged with, and acquitted of, a murder.

In examining the evidence, Goodman concludes that if Cornelius Howard (who may have been Storrs's illegitimate son) had not been acquitted before another local man, Mark Wilde, was charged with the crime, then the latter might well have been convicted. Wilde's counsel was able to stress to the jury that one man had been wrongly charged and that the same could be true of Wilde. But Goodman argues, on the basis of impressive research, that a third man may have had a stronger motive for the murder than either Howard or Wilde. As in his other monographs, there is a strong evocation of place and period.

G.28 Gorin, Grigory [pseudonym of Grigory Ofshtein] *Forget Herostratus!* In *Stars in the Morning Sky: Five New Plays from the Soviet Union.* Trans. Michael Glenny. London: Nick Hern Books, 1989.

■ In the fourth century b.c., an arsonist hoping to acquire eternal fame burned down one of the seven wonders of the ancient world, the temple of the goddess Artemis (Diana) at Ephesus. Tradition calls the criminal Herostratus, but the name merely describes his misdeed, for it means "destroyer of the shrine." The customary date assigned to the fire, 356 b.c., would indicate that the glory desired by the arsonist was to be eclipsed: that is the year that witnessed the birth of Alexander the Great.

Introducing a twentieth-century "man of the theatre" into his cast of characters, playwright Gorin suggests a parallel between Herostratus and Hitler. The razing of the temple becomes the antetype of the Reichstag fire, and Herostratus's crime memoirs are invented as an urtext of *Mein Kampf.* Unlike Brecht's Hitler in *The Resistible Rise of Arturo Ui* (1941), Gorin's villain is destroyed before he can do more harm, by the intervention of a courageous judge who declares his independence of a collaborationist satrap.

A modern arson with overtones of Herostatus's crime is the destruction of the Temple of the Golden Pavilion in Kyoto. See Yukio Mishima, *The Temple of the Golden Pavilion* (M.33).

G.29 Goron, Marie-François *L'Amour à Paris: Nouveaux mémoires.* 3 vols. [*L'Amour criminel; Les industries de l'amour; Les parias de l'amour.*] Paris: Flammarion, n.d.

■ This series, written by a detective and (from 1887) Sûreté chief, is devoted to love and crime in Paris. Most of the first volume, *Criminal Love,* is devoted to the trunk murder of Toussaint-Augustin Gouffé by lovers Michel Eyraud and Gabrielle Bompard, whom Goron helped to bring to justice (see B.60).

The sequel, *Love's Industries,* deals primarily with prostitution; Goron sees little chance for the adoption of an English proposal to punish the customer rather than the prostitute since "it is the customers who make the laws and police regulations." He also describes other love criminals, such as the fraudulent "Miss Ellen," who bilked aspiring bridegrooms by misrepresenting herself as a lonely widow; unscrupulous matrimonial agencies; collusive divorces based on staged scenes of adultery; crimes of vengeance inspired by infidelity; and blackmail by knowing servants.

The series finale, *The Pariahs of Love*, addresses the "disinherited of society or nature; all those crazies who know nothing of love but its bitterness and resentment; all those unhinged characters whom morbid sensitivities render incapable of tenderness." Included in his gallery are blackmailed homosexuals, sadists, murderers of children, women in love with priests, morphine addicts and alcoholics, and polygamists.

For a biography of Goron, see Jean-Emile Néaumet, *Un flic* [A Cop] *à la Belle Epoque* (Paris: Albin Michel, 1998).

G.30 ———— *Behind the French C.I.D.: Leaves from the Memoirs of Goron, Former Detective Chief.* Trans. and ed. Philip A. Wilkins. London: Hutchinson, n.d.
■ Presenting highlights from the memoirs of Goron, who had served as head of the French Sûreté, Wilkins translated accounts of Louis Prado's razor-slaying of Marie Aguétant (1886) and the triple murder committed by Henri Pranzini in the course of a burglary (1887).

G.31 ———— *Les mémoires de M. Goron ancien chef de la Sûreté.* 2 vols. Paris: Rouff, n.d. [Originally published in 4 vols., Paris, 1897.]
■ The copiously illustrated edition, issued in 253 installments totaling 2,024 pages, is studded with detective and Sûreté chief Goron's detailed reminiscences of many of France's best-known late-nineteenth-century crimes, including those of Jean-Baptiste Troppmann; Henri Pranzini; Louis Prado; Eugène Allmayer, swindler who escaped from Mazas prison; the inventive thief Renard, who made a great haul at the home of the marquis de Panisse-Passis by posing as an investigator of the Panama Canal frauds; and practitioners of anarchist terror, including Clément Duval, Ravachol, Auguste Vaillant, Émile Henry, and Caserio (the assassin of the president of the republic, Sadi Carnot).

In the second volume, Goron comments on detective work of foreign police with whom he had contact as chief of the Sûreté, devoting chapters to England, Belgium, Switzerland, Holland, Portugal, Turkey, Germany, Italy, and Spain. He also discusses various issues in policing, including forgeries; criminals using chloroform to perpetrate robberies; mothers who kill; suburban gangs; thieves and their techniques; government employees who murder; the repression of crime and the death penalty (Goron favored the guillotine as the "most human" mode of execution, which he had never seen misfunction).

G.32 ———— *The Truth About the Case: The Experiences of M.F. Goron.* Ed. Albert Keyser. Philadelphia: Lippincott, 1907.
■ This author, who claims to have met Goron some years before this publication, further asserts that this book draws upon the detective's previously unpublished "diary." In one adventure, Goron serves an English client falsely accused of cheating at cards by disguising himself as a boot manufacturer from Limoges.

G.33 Gorsse, Pierre de   *La justice égarée par les femmes.* Paris: Société Privée d'Imprimerie et d'Édition, 1946.

■ These studies of justice "led astray" by women include essays on Clarisse Manson, hysterical witness in the Fualdès case; Marie de Morell, false accuser of Lieutenant La Roncière (see D.19); Marie Lafarge; and Marguerite Steinheil.

G.34 Graeme, Bruce [pseudonym of Graham Montague Jeffries]   *Passion, Murder and Mystery.* London: Hutchinson, n.d.

■ A British thriller writer, Graeme provides his public a well-selected menu of classic French murder trials, which he regards as "so rich in dramatic material, so full of successive mysteries, so teeming with sensations, that stories of fiction cannot compare in interest with them." The cases include those of serial poisoner Jeanne Weber; Mata Hari; the trunk murder of M. Gouffé by Gabrielle Bompard and Michel Eyraud; Mme. Bessarabo, jointly charged with her daughter for murder; Madame de Feuchères (Sophie Dawes); and Madame Marguerite Steinheil.

G.35 Grant, Douglas   *The Cock Lane Ghost.* London: Macmillan, 1965.

■ In 1762 all London was in the thrall of the invisible Cock Lane Ghost, nicknamed "Scratching Fanny," who afflicted twelve-year-old Elizabeth Parsons with mysterious knockings and scratchings. To questions put to her, the revenant answered with one rap for yes and two for no. By such rudimentary means of communication, the ghost revealed that she was the unquiet spirit of Frances Lynes. Frances and her lover, William Kent, had been tenants of the Parsonses at their Cock Lane home. "Scratching Fanny" claimed that Kent had poisoned her while she was suffering from smallpox.

As skeptics began to look into the ghost's assertions, it became clear that the Parsonses had a grudge against Kent arising out of a financial dispute and therefore ample motive to raise the accusing ghost by persuading their daughter to act as a false medium. Still, the claim of supernatural agency was not dismissed out of hand, and an informal committee including Dr. Samuel Johnson was assembled to test Elizabeth Parsons's honesty. In his entertaining account of the case, Douglas Grant points out that Johnson, appalled by the notion of physical annihilation in death, took a strong interest in searching for reliable evidence of ghost sightings or other occult occurrences suggesting the reality of an afterlife. Grant, however, believes that Johnson's predominant motive in joining the committee was to save Kent from a possibly unjust accusation: "If superstition was marked in his character, charity ran deeper, and Kent's predicament as a man would have moved him to action sooner than the lure of a ghost."

The Committee of Gentlemen on which Johnson served met at the Parsons house to test the reality of the visitations that the young Elizabeth claimed to have received and then adjourned to the church vault where the ghost had promised it would rap on the coffin of Frances Lynes. The results of these inquiries persuaded the committee that Elizabeth was shamming. Johnson's written report detailed their experience:

On this night many Gentlemen, eminent for their rank and character, were, by the invitation of the Rev. Mr. Aldrich of Clerkenwell, assembled at his house, for the examination of the noises supposed to be made by a departed spirit, for the detection of some enormous crime.

About ten at night, the gentlemen met in the chamber, in which the girl, supposed to be disturbed by a spirit, had, with proper caution, been put to bed by several ladies. They sat rather more than an hour, and hearing nothing went downstairs, when they interrogated the father of the girl, who denied, in the strongest terms, any knowledge or belief of fraud.

The supposed spirit had before publicly promised, by an affirmative knock, that it would attend one of the gentlemen into the vault, under the church of St. John, Clerkenwell, where the body is deposited, and give a token of her presence there by a knock upon her coffin: It was therefore determined to make this trial of the existence or veracity of the supposed spirit.

While they were enquiring and deliberating, they were summoned into the girl's chamber by some Ladies, who were near her bed, and who had heard knocks and scratches. When the gentlemen entered, the girl declared that she felt the spirit like a mouse, upon her back, and was required to hold her hands out of bed. From that time, though the spirit was very solemnly required to manifest its existence, by appearance, by impression, on the hand or body of any present, by scratches, knocks, or any other agency, no evidence of any preternatural power was exhibited.

The spirit was then very seriously advertised, that the person to whom the promise was made, of striking the coffin, was then about to visit the vault, and that the performance of the promise was then claimed. The company, at once, went into the church, and the gentleman, to whom the promise was made, went, with one more, into the vault. The spirit was solemnly required to perform its promise, but nothing more than silence ensued; the person supposed to be accused by the spirit, then went down, with several others, but no effect was perceived. Upon their return, they examined the girl, but could draw no confession from her. Between two and three she desired, and was permitted, to go home with her father.

It is therefore the opinion of the whole assembly, that the child has some art of making or counterfeiting particular noises, and that there is no agency of any higher cause.

After these revelations, Elizabeth Parsons's parents and certain of their supporters were convicted of criminal conspiracy after a trial before Lord Mansfield. Richard Parsons was sentenced to two years' imprisonment and his wife to one year. Elizabeth Parsons was not prosecuted, but she suffered the indignity of frequent comparison with the perjured Elizabeth Canning (see D.15).

The case has left a rich legacy in literature, the theater, and art. Oliver Goldsmith has been credited with the authorship of a pamphlet, *The Mystery Revealed: Containing a Series of Transactions and Authentic Testimonials Respecting the Supposed Cock-Lane Ghost; Which*

Have Been Concealed from the Public (republished in 1928 in an edition of seventy-five copies by Richard W. Ellis at the Georgian Press, Westport). Charles Churchill lampooned Dr. Johnson as "Pomposo" in his three-part satirical poem "The Ghost." London's obsession with the Cock Lane sensation was ridiculed on the stage by David Garrick as the Farmer in *The Farmer's Return from London* (a role in which he is portrayed in a painting by the young Johann Zoffany); and in a print by William Hogarth, captioned "Credulity, Superstition, and Fanaticism: A Medley," which juxtaposes Elizabeth Parsons with another famous hoaxer, Mary Tofts, who claimed to have given birth to rabbits.

In the late nineteenth century, Andrew Lang included a short narrative of the case as the title essay in a volume concerning human evidence of the supernatural, *Cock-Lane and Common-Sense* (London: Longmans Green, 1894); the Borowitz True Crime Collection owns a copy of the large-paper edition limited to sixty copies.

The Cock Lane affair is the starting point for Lillian de la Torre's fictional account of another ghost-busting investigation by Dr. Johnson, "The Manifestations in Mincing Lane," in her brilliant set of Boswell pastiches, *Dr. Sam: Johnson, Detector* (New York: Knopf, 1946). In this story, the phantom turns out to be a half-hanged robber determined (in collaboration with an anatomist who has revived him) to frighten away tenants so that he can reclaim a hidden treasure.

G.36 Grasilier, Léonce   *L'Affaire Petit du Petit-Val.* In series *Énigmes et drames judiciaires d'autrefois.* Paris: Perrin, 1927.

■ Blaming theft and falsification of official records for obscuring the facts, Grasilier claims to have solved the mysterious slaughter of François-Gaspard-Philippe Petit du Petit-Val together with his mother-in-law and her sister, his sister-in-law, and the three ladies' chambermaids in the park of Petit-Val's chateau at Vitry-sur-Seine on the night of April 2, 1796. The author rejects both legends favored by tradition: that the killings were related to the cover-up of the escape of the young Louis XVII from the Temple Prison (see L.17); or that the Michel brothers, fraudulent businessmen, committed the murders to retrieve evidence of their indebtedness to Petit-Val. Instead, Grasilier concludes that the killings were instigated by the violent *sans-culotte* Frédéric-Joseph Dupont du Chambon, a cousin of Petit-Val's deceased wife, in an effort to ensure the family estate for the maternal line. Unfortunately, the proposed solution presents improbabilities of its own, including the fact that one of the victims was Dupont du Chambon's own mother. A point of literary interest noted by Grasilier is the nineteenth-century investigation of the Petit-Val mystery pursued by the Duchesse d'Abrantès, memoirist of the Empire and the Restoration.

G.37 Graves, Robert   *They Hanged My Saintly Billy.* New York: Doubleday, 1957.

■ Graves's last novel takes its title from the exclamation of serial poisoner William Palmer's mother on learning that her beloved son had been hanged for the murder of gambler John Parsons Cook. Palmer was in fact a killer that only his mother could acquit. Nevertheless, Graves, perhaps with tongue well imbedded in cheek, undertook to demonstrate Palmer's innocence. If he fails in this quixotic attempt, he still has created one of his liveliest novels, which, in his words, was "full of sex, drink, incest, suicide, dope, horse-racing, murder, scandalous legal procedure, cross-examinations, inquests and ends with a good public hanging—attended by 30,000."

G.38 Gray, Judd *Doomed Ship.* New York: Horace Liveright, 1928.

■ A publisher's note guarantees the authenticity of this memoir finished by Judd Gray on January 11, 1928, less than an hour before his execution at Sing Sing for collaborating with his lover, Ruth Snyder, in the murder of her husband Albert whom they battered with a window sash weight and strangled with picture wire. Liveright's note concludes, "The work is a unique document, and very likely the only one of its kind known in the annals of English or American criminal history." (The final manuscript was prepared for publication by Gray's sister, Margaret.)

The book is divided into three main parts: an affectionate remembrance of scenes from Gray's childhood; an account of his love affair with Ruth Snyder, ending with their murder of Albert Snyder and Gray's arrest; impressions of the trial and lessons of Gray's religious conversion. A brief addendum, "The Pilgrims of the Night," sketches the last hours before electrocution.

Even as he faced death, Gray, who had been a corset salesman, recalled the spell Ruth Snyder cast during their first meeting, "a sort of dazzling loveliness and that lilac perfume." Later, however, as his "ideal" vision faded, he saw her as a Jekyll and Hyde, sexually promiscuous, manipulative, and leading him on to the murder of her husband after preliminary experiments with poisons. At the trial the two lovers turned against each other in their testimony. Gray admitted wielding the sash weight but attributed the strangulation to Ruth. In his memoir, he adopts a more gallant stance, asserting that she was not motivated by her husband's life insurance and that the alcoholic haze in which he acted did not permit him to define their respective roles in the murder. Gray's title epitomizes his relationship with Ruth Snyder by referring to line in Oscar Wilde's "The Ballad of Reading Gaol": "Like two doomed ships that pass in storm / We had crossed each other's way."

G.39 Greene, Graham *England Made Me.* Garden City: Doubleday Doran, 1935.

■ In 1935 Ivar Kreuger, Swedish "Match King" and international financier, shot himself in Paris. At the time of his suicide, his business empire was on the verge of collapse, riddled by looting of assets, fraudulent accounting, and Kreuger's forgery of an Italian government bond issue.

Graham Greene's early novel *England Made Me*, published only three years after Kreuger's death, is dominated by a Swedish magnate and financier with a similar name, Erik Krogh, whose "intricate network" of companies "was knitted together by his personal credit. Honesty was a word which had never troubled him: a man was honest so long as his credit was good." When Krogh is introduced by Greene, the unscrupulous tycoon is brooding about Kreuger's suicide: "A man of his [Krogh's] credit did not go to prison. Kreuger, lying shot in the Paris hotel, was his example. He questioned his courage for the final act as little as he questioned his honesty."

For the time being Krogh staves off disaster by twin coups: he has stemmed panic selling of shares of an Amsterdam operation by illegally siphoning off funds of an affiliate to prop up the market, and he has also succeeded in the flotation of an American stock issue. Less fortunate are Krogh's English secretary and mistress, Kate Farrant, and her raffish twin brother, Tony. After she persuades Krogh to give her charming but rudderless brother a job, Tony learns compromising secrets about Krogh's defalcations and is murdered by the financier's henchman Hall.

Nine months after Ivar Kreuger's suicide, *The Match King*, a Warner Brothers film based on his rise and fall, was rushed into distribution. Warren Williams, as the dishonest magnate renamed Paul Kroll, repeatedly voices his anthem: "Don't worry till it happens and I'll take care of it then."

G.40 Gregory, Augusta, Lady   *The Gaol Gate*. 1906. In *Irish Drama 1900–1980*. Ed. Cóilín D. Owens and Joan N. Radner. Washington, D.C.: Catholic Univ. of America Press, 1990.

■ First produced at Dublin's Abbey Theatre in 1906, this one-act play was Lady Gregory's first tragedy. She recalls that it was inspired by incidents of law, crime, and punishment that occurred within three months. She heard of "a man who had gone to welcome his brother coming out of gaol, and heard he had died there before the gates had been opened for him." Another event involved a young carpenter from Lady Gregory's "old home" who was falsely accused of informing against a man for firing on a landlord's agent.

In the play, Mary Cahel and her daughter-in-law wait at the gaol gate for the release of Denis Cahel, their son and husband. Neighbors have spread the rumor that Denis, while in prison, informed against their boys, Terry Fury and Pat Ruane. The gatekeeper tells the women that Denis is "dead since the dawn of yesterday" and that Fury and Ruane have been released. Exulting that her son was not an informer after all, Mary Cahel proclaims: "I to stoop on a stick through half a hundred years, I will never be tired with praising. Come hither, Mary Cushin, till we shout it through the roads, Denis Cahel died for his neighbour!"

G.41 Grinnell-Milne, Duncan   *The Killing of William Rufus: An Investigation in the New Forest*. New York: Augustus M. Kelley, 1968.

■ Grinnell-Milne conducted an on-the-scene investigation of the mysterious death of King William Rufus (second son of William the Conqueror), shot to death by an arrow in the New Forest during an early summer evening deer hunt. An impressive array of evidence contributes to the author's persuasive solution: topography, ordnance maps corrected by the author's own sketch map, contemporary chronicles, oral tradition, hunting practices, even the tendency of deer to run away from perceived danger. The book concludes that skilled French archer Walter Tirel, a guest at the hunt, was wrongly accused of accidentally shooting the king after his arrow grazed a deer's back. In fact, Grinnell-Milne contends, it was a case of premeditated murder to clear the path for the victim's younger brother, Henry I, to seize the throne. The deadly arrow was probably shot from the bow of the chief hunter, who stood twenty yards away from William Rufus. Gilbert Clare, Earl of Tunbridge, is identified as the probable orchestrator of the assassination. Perhaps the most impressive proof of premeditated killing is the speed and efficiency with which Henry took the steps necessary to his coronation in London a little over two and a half days after William Rufus was felled in the woods.

G.42 Guare, John *Six Degrees of Separation*. New York: Vintage, 1994.

■ Guare's play came out of a publicly inspired hoax perpetrated by petty criminal and con man David Hampton, who impersonated the son of film star Sidney Poitier. He persuaded several prominent New Yorkers that he was a friend of their children and that he had been mugged and needed a place to stay for a night until his father arrived the next day to work on a movie he was directing. In each case he obtained spending money from his hosts and also stole property from their homes. Reportedly, two pairs of victims were Jay Iselin, subsequently president of Cooper Union, and his wife, Lea, a lawyer; and Osborn Elliott, a former editor of *Newsweek*, and his wife, Inger (Jeanie Kasindorf, "Six Degrees of Impersonation," *New York Magazine* [Mar. 25, 1991]). Arrested after these impostures, Hampton settled a string of accumulated criminal charges by pleading guilty to attempted burglary. And when he committed further offenses, he was incarcerated in Dannemora state prison between January 1985 and October 1986.

Despite undergoing a punishment that was intended to be chastening, Hampton was outraged when *Six Degrees of Separation* was staged and sued Guare for violation of his statutory right of privacy. His claim was dismissed on the ground that the character of Paul, the Poitier impostor in the play, did not use Hampton's "name, portrait or picture" (*Hampton v. Guare*, 20 Med. L. Rptr. 1160 [New York Supreme Court New York County 1992]).

In Guare's play, Ouisa, the middle-class white wife defrauded by Paul, comes to feel more warmth for the young man than for her own children: "We were hardly taken in. We believed him—for a few hours. He did more for us in a few hours than our children ever did. He wanted to be your child."

G.43 Guernes de Pont-Sainte-Maxence *La vie de Saint Thomas Becket*. Ed. Emmanuel Walberg. Paris: Honoré Champion, 1936.

■ Guernes, a "wandering cleric," was born in the small town of Pont-Sainte-Maxence, in the north of the Ile de France. He began this long narrative poem in honor of Saint Thomas Becket in 1172, only two years after his assassination. Unwilling to rely solely on earlier works in Latin, Guernes crossed the Channel and visited Canterbury. There, warmly received by the monks of the Holy Trinity, he consulted friends and lifelong servants of the saint and asserts in his poem that from these private sources he "heard, culled and learned the truth." It is likely that Guernes knew Becket personally.

According to Guernes, the saint's assassins took action after Henry II bitterly lamented to his courtiers that nobody had avenged the wrongs to his lineage and realm committed by a man "who has eaten my bread and come to my court as a pauper and whom I have greatly exalted."

G.44 Gunnarsson, Gunnar   *The Black Cliffs.* [Originally titled *Black Birds* (Svartfugl)]. 1929. Trans. Cecil Wood. Intro. Richard N. Ringler. Madison: Univ. of Wisconsin Press, 1967.

■ In 1802, Iceland, a nation famous for its law-abiding people, was shocked by a double murder on the farm Syvendeaa near the rocky shoreline of the Northwestern Peninsula. Over a century later, Icelandic novelist Gunnar Gunnarsson, writing in Danish, turned the case into a probing psychological novel, which he named "Black Birds" after the black-and-white diving birds (*alcidae*) that lent their coloration to the cliffs near the murder scene. In a key passage, Gunnarsson invokes the ever-renewing bird life on the cliffs as a symbol of the natural element in man as well as beast and mirrors the ambiguity of moral judgments in the "white-shining, black-sparkling cloud of sea birds."

In the novel, farmer Bjarni Bjarnason and his mistress, Steinun Sveinsdottir, are convicted and executed for successive murders of their unwanted spouses, Jon Thorgrimsson and Gudrun Egilsdottir. At their trials, the lovers cannot bring their stories into accord. Bjarni claims that he struck Jon in self-defense before throwing him into the sea; but, according to Steinun, he had described his murder as unprovoked. She also attempted to minimize her own role in the subsequent unsuccessful attempt to poison Gudrun and in Bjarni's ultimate strangulation of his wife.

The principal focus of the novel (more than half of which is devoted to the murderers' trial) is on varying reactions to the crimes within the remote community. The vindictive judge Gudmund Scheving believes that "even more horrible that what has been done are the fantasies which the suspicions about it have awakened. The black thoughts and dreams that have been aroused can be washed away by only one thing. The two must die. I almost said: whether they killed or not."

The senior minister of the local church, the Reverend Jon Ormsson, preferred to look the other way when marital discord on the Syvendeaa farm was brought to his attention. Ormsson's young curate, Eiulv Kolbeinsson, who narrates the story, is impelled by his belief in God's grace to extend his pastoral care to the despised murderers. Even his identification with their plight, however, may not be free of alloyed motives, for he has taken the girl he married away from his younger brother.

H

H.1 Habe, Hans [pseudonym of Hans Bekessy] *Gentlemen of the Jury* [Meine Herren Geschworenen]. Trans. Frances Hogarth-Gaute. London: Harrap, 1967.

■ Born in Budapest in 1911, Habe became a police and court reporter in Vienna and later a highly successful novelist. *Gentlemen of the Jury*, a collection of seven studies of European crimes, is concerned, Habe states in his introduction, with "the characters of the criminals and the nature of their crimes." The scope of his examination was, however, widened by his having learned "to read criminal cases as an integral part of history" and to regard a lawbreaker, if only in a negative sense, as "a representative of his period."

A highlight of the volume is provided by Habe's suspenseful reminiscences of the first important murder case that he covered as a young reporter for a Viennese newspaper ("The Lainz Zoo Murder"). In the second trial, the verdict fell one vote short of the eight required of the twelve-juror panel to convict pencil company salesman Gustav Bauer of shooting his lover, prostitute Katharina Fellner, to death in 1928 in the Lainz Zoo grounds near Vienna. Habe may have influenced the result when he confounded an eyewitness by introducing a café manager who was a remarkable "double" of Bauer. When he visited the defendant after his acquittal, Habe's confidence in his innocence was shaken: Bauer performed a song he had written in prison, ending with the chorus: "And then he strangled her, strangled her, strangled her."

Habe believes that the guilt of Peter Grupen, hanged in 1922 for the murder of Dorothea Rohrbeck and her stepdaughter, Ursula Schade, was probable ("The Death of the Heiress"), but he would have rendered a verdict of not guilty.

In "The Man Who Played with Trains," Habe admits an early professional embarrassment. As a young Viennese reporter, he interviewed survivors of a deadly train bombing at a Hungarian bridge on the line to Budapest. A man who claimed to be a passenger gave Habe a great story but turned out to be the sadistic Hungarian train wrecker, Sylvester Matuska, who draped his perversion in messianic pretension: he had "decided to construct a Communist party of a religious nature" by "mak[ing] mankind aware of universal suffering."

Lieutenant Adolf Hofrichter is the subject of the essay "Was the Lieutenant a Poisoner?" Dismissed from the Austrian general staff, Lieutenant Hofrichter was convicted by a military tribunal of poisoning Captain Richard Mader in 1909 with cyanide disguised as "potency pills" mailed to him and eleven other general staff officers who had graduated with Hofrichter in the 1905 class of the military academy. Hofrichter made and later retracted a confession. In 1935, Habe met Hofrichter (who had long before been released from prison and pardoned) and reviewed trial records in connection with the production of a play, *Hofrichter*, by famous Viennese lawyer Dr. Flandrak, which asserted the lieutenant's innocence. Habe helped arrange the staging of the play across the Czech border beyond the reach of Austrian fascist censorship. It is his own conclusion that Hofrichter's guilt "was not as certainly established as Anglo-Saxon law demands." Lieutenant Hofrichter's case is fictionalized in M. Fagyas, *The Devil's Lieutenant* (New York: Putnam, 1970).

"The Baden-Baden Murder" relates the 1906 shooting of Frau Molitor by her son-in-law, Karl Hau, a profligate American lawyer of German extraction who hobnobbed with celebrities as far afield as Washington and Constantinople. The crime was bizarrely preluded by stratagems never satisfactorily explained: Hau's dispatch of a bogus telegram from his wife, Lina, to Frau Molitor advising that Lina's younger sister, Olga, had fallen ill in Paris; his subsequent visit to Baden-Baden disguised in a wig and beard; and his impersonation of a postmaster in a telephone call to his mother-in-law on the day of the murder advising that the original of the fake telegram had been traced and requesting her to proceed to the post office at once. On her way to the post office in the company of Olga, Frau Molitor was shot.

At his trial, Hau refused to answer most questions put to him, apparently hoping to create the impression that he was shielding Olga. The device did not succeed. Hau was imprisoned until his pardon in 1924. He committed suicide two years later by taking poison at Hadrian's Villa. Relying on the opinion of a modern American psychiatrist Joseph E. Mencken, Habe speculates that Hau may have suffered from a schizophrenic condition evidenced by his habit of wearing disguises and that "he had not identified with 'that man' who had [committed the crime]."

The Baden-Baden slaying inspired Jakob Wassermann's 1928 novel *The Maurizius Case* (New York: Liveright, 1929), in which Leonhart Maurizius, an art historian, has been imprisoned for eighteen years after his erroneous conviction for shooting his wife at the gate of their villa. Sixteen-year-old Etzel Andergast, son of Attorney General Baron Wolf von Andergast, who prosecuted Maurizius, is spurred by a thirst for justice and rebellion against his cold father to seek the truth. At last he wrests from a perjured eyewitness, Herr Waremme, the fact that the shot was fired by Leonhart Maurizius's young sister-in-law, Anna Jahn, enraged by her unfulfilled passion for Leonhart. When Etzel confronts his father with his findings, the Baron replies dismissively that Maurizius has already been pardoned but that he will not seek official vindication of the prisoner's innocence. Etzel, in anger, accuses his father of earlier knowledge of the real killer's identity, and the Baron's reason crumbles under this accusation of injustice.

Gentlemen of the Jury also includes chapters on the murder trials of Marguerite Steinheil and Henriette Caillaux (see H.20).

H.2 Hachette, Alfred *L'Affaire Mique (1745–1794)*. In *Énigmes et drames judiciaires d'autrefois*. Paris: Perrin, 1928.

■ The clumsy imposture of stonecutter Charles-François Mougenot, claiming to be Claude-Nicolas Mique, who was killed in a 1745 naval battle, ended ingloriously with Mougenot's death in Bicêtre prison. The triumph of the false claimant's targets, royal architect Richard Mique and his son, Simon, was, however, short lived, for the daughter and son-in-law of Mougenot were awarded damages in Republican civil courts for the impostor's "false imprisonment" and ultimately procured the execution of the two Miques as participants in the "conspiracy of the prisons" fabricated by Terror prosecutor Fouquier-Tinville in 1794. Substituting responsible hypotheses for frequent gaps in surviving documentation, Alfred Hachette picks his way through the maze of legal and political conflicts that led to the tragic downfall of the Mique family.

H.3 Hackl, Erich *Aurora's Motive*. Trans. Edna McCown. New York: Knopf, 1989.

■ The daughter of a provincial Spanish lawyer and reformist dreamer, Aurora Rodríguez decided to produce a brilliant child who would lead the way to a new society. Advertising for a man to perform the procreative act without subsequent entanglements, she chose a lapsed priest in the merchant marine. The fruit of this briefest of encounters was a daughter, Hildegart, who was to become a precocious wonder of Spain, campaigning for republicanism, sexual liberation, and socialism. Dubbed the "Red Virgin," Hildegart, at age seventeen, attracted the attention of H. G. Wells and Havelock Ellis, who in 1933 invited her to London to collaborate in eugenics undertakings. Shortly before Hildegart's planned departure, Aurora shot Hildegart in her sleep. According to Hackl's account, Aurora, on the evening preceding the killing, confessed to her mother that "she was too weak, too exhausted, too burned out, to fulfill the mission that her mother had destined her for"; Aurora had created Hildegart and "it was up to her now to sacrifice her work that had failed" (97–98).

Hackl based his short account on Hildegart's press articles, on Aurora's prison conversations with a journalist, and on court reports. He enriches the narrative with imagined emotions of the principal characters, but for the most part he distances himself from the tragic events in a manner introduced into nineteenth-century German literature by Heinrich von Kleist.

H.4 Hadas, Pamela White *Beside Herself: Pocahontas to Patty Hearst.* New York: Knopf, 1983.
■ Poet Hadas speaks in the voices of women associated with memorable chapters of the American experience, including celebrated crimes. In the longest poem, "Patty Hearst: Versions of Her Story," the narrative of the protagonist's transformation from kidnap victim to Tania, Symbionese Liberation Army bank robber, is related as a fable ineptly devised by Fabula Grunt, a fairy godmother. Others speaking their minds are Patty's mother (the "Queen"), an SLA comrade, Emily Harris, who lapses into obscene street speech when she assumes her alternative persona as the terrorist Yolanda; and the Reporter, who blasts out daily coverage on his "electrified tripewriter." Two other female characters identify closely with Patty's fate, her girlfriend, referred to as "Tania-in-Waiting," and a housewife who serves on Patty's jury. The trial reunites Patty with her girlhood friend, who reflects:

> She made me
> see what matters. Once more
> close, we do not lie.
>   Either we are not guilty
>   or both of us are.

(For a comparison of Patty Hearst's "abrupt sloughing of the past" to the Western pioneer experience, see Joan Didion, "Girl of the Golden West," in *After Henry* [New York: Simon & Schuster, 1992].)

In her four brief monologues, "Madeira's Headmistress," Hadas expresses Jean Harris's grievances against her faithless lover and against a society that demanded conformity to external norms but took no interest in the woman within:

> Nobody
> seems to notice I am not here, in tears,
> at all. The woman in a pretty dress
> is nowhere; headmistress and mistress though
> I've acted, I'm not here, and never was.

Other poems are narrated by Wild West bandit queen Belle Starr ("The Bandit Queen Remembers"); temperance vigilante Carry Nation; and the "Wives of Watergate."

H.5 ———— "The Terrible Memory of Lizzie Borden." In *Self-Evidence: A Selection of Verse 1977–1997*. Evanston: Northwestern Univ. Press (Triquarterly Books), 1998.

■ According to the poet's footnote, these nine brief interior monologues contain a "reiteration of unfathomable alibis" that "indicate pretty clearly that, murderess or not, Lizzie Borden had a terrible memory." Lizzie does her woeful best to remember her discovery of her father's body; her conversation with him when he came home shortly before; her domestic activities on the fatal morning; her laughter at the top of the stairs; her eating pears that "were dropping one by one;" her arrest and trial; and her conversion into a legend. In defense of her many failures of recollection, Lizzie proposes an explanation that comes too close for comfort: "It's kind of hard to split hairs with an ax."

H.6 Hall, Sir John   *The Bravo Mystery, and Other Cases*. London: John Lane, 1923.

■ The title essay maintains that from the moment Charles Bravo took ill from tartar emetic poisoning, the behavior of his wife, Florence, "bore all the appearances of innocence." Hall explains: "Unlike other persons who have been strongly suspected of administering poison she made no attempt to keep away the doctors or the sick man's relations and, more important still, no charge of procuring a noxious drug, under some palpably false pretext, can be made against her."

Nevertheless, it seemed suspicious to Hall that she spoke of a "coppery" saucepan or a riding accident as possible causes of her husband's illness even after Dr. Johnson had said in her presence that Mr. Bravo was suffering from poison.

Without identifying the guilty party, Hall finds it "impossible to dissociate" Mrs. Bravo and her companion, Mrs. Jane Cox, in the mysterious case: "If one be guilty, the other cannot be innocent and, without question, some of their proceedings are terribly suspicious." See J.5.

Other chapters include accounts of the "Northumberland Street Tragedy" (see A.8); and M. Rosamond de Beauvallon's killing of Alexandre Henri Dujarier in a rigged duel ("An Affair of Honour"; see B.51). The final study exculpates the Prince Regent (later George IV) of involvement in his jockey's deliberate loss (in collusion with a bookmaker) of a Newmarket race on the prince's horse Escape in 1791.

Colonel Sir John Richard Hall, ninth baronet (1865–1928), edited two trials in the *Notable British Trials* series, those of Abraham Thornton (1926) and Adelaide Bartlett (1927). The Borowitz True Crime Library owns many *Notable British Trials* volumes from Hall's library, including some bearing his bookplate.

H.7 ———— *Four Famous Mysteries*. London: Nisbet, 1922.

■ In "The Mystery of Tilsit," Hall identifies the Comte d'Antraigues, a double-dealing secret agent to several European courts, as involved in informing British Foreign Minister

George Canning in 1807 of negotiations between Napoleon and Tsar Alexander I on a raft in the Niemen River, in which the rulers agreed that the Dutch fleet would be put at Napoleon's disposition.

Hall tackles another mystery of the Napoleonic era in "The Strange Story of Mr. Bathurst." In 1809, Benjamin Bathurst, recalled British envoy to the Court of Vienna, disappeared in the small Prussian town of Perleberg en route to London. While speculating that Bathurst's mind may have been disturbed, Hall concludes that he was probably killed by a clique of Prussian officers concerned that he might reveal their plans to throw off Napoleon's yoke.

After summarizing the facts and theories relating to the murder of Protestant magistrate Sir Edmund Berry Godfrey in the course of the "Popish Plot" fever ("The Murder of Sir Edmund Berry Godfrey"), Hall proposes his own thesis: perhaps Godfrey, in league with Edward Coleman, former secretary of the Duchess of York, was in the pay of the French. Hall speculates: "After Coleman's arrest, [Godfrey] may have been called upon, and have refused, to fulfill some promise or to redeem some pledge. Coleman's friends may have threatened him or he may have threatened them: In either case, a furious altercation, followed by a murderous assault, may have taken place."

The keystone of the collection is a long essay on the 1825 murder of liberal polemicist Paul-Louis Courier, shot through the back in a forest on his Touraine property by a group of peasants. The crime was probably instigated by his wife, who had been having an affair with one of the conspirators, Pierre Dubois, whom her cuckolded husband had fired from his position as their carter. In two trials, Dubois and three other men were acquitted. Hall notes a bizarre twist in Courier's destiny: "In his lifetime, Courier had constantly inveighed against the vices of Courts, while loudly extolling the virtues of the country labourer. It was a strange irony of fate that he should be the victim of a conspiracy of peasants, whose plans were laid as craftily as any conceived in the most corrupt of Courts."

H.8 Hamann, Brigitte *Rudolf: Kronprinz und Rebell.* Munich: Piper, 1987.
■ In her coolheaded biography of Crown Prince Rudolf of Austria-Hungary, Hamann does not dignify by more than passing references the wild theories that have accreted around the shooting deaths of the prince and his pregnant seventeen-year-old mistress, Mary Vetsera, at the Mayerling hunting lodge in the Vienna Woods on the well-remembered morning of January 30, 1889.

Other writers more avid for sensation have repeated murder rumors concerning foresters' wives seduced by Rudolf and their bloodthirsty husbands; soldiers of Rudolf's father, Emperor Franz Joseph; assassins in the pay of Bismarck; or those usual suspects, the Masons and the Jesuits. Hamann, while noting the insufficiency of reliable firsthand sources, favors the traditional theory of a suicide pact but strips the deaths of romance. She cites medical evidence that Rudolf shot Mary hours before he took his own life, belatedly converting the murder of a "euphoric" and star-struck girl into a "joint suicide." For Rudolf the idea of dying with an attractive woman was nothing new. He had earlier floated the project with another mistress, Mizzi Caspar, who had laughed it off as a joke in bad taste. Hamann believes, however, that by the time he came to Mayerling, Rudolf's suicidal intention was fixed and that Mary, whom he had planned to send to England to deliver their child, persuaded him only with difficulty to let her join him in death.

Rather than seeking to identify a dominant motive for the prince's suicide, Hamann calls attention to cumulative pressures that undermined his mental and physical health: the deterioration of his marriage without the possibility of divorce; his inability to confront his father, whose pro-German policies Rudolf saw as threatening the breakup of the Austrian empire and war with France under the *revanchiste* leadership of General Boulanger. The point of no return may have been reached on Rudolf's last evening in Vienna, when Franz Josef required him to appear in Prussian uniform at a German embassy party in honor of Kaiser Wilhelm II, whom the liberal and patriotic crown prince detested.

Among novels inspired by the deaths of Prince Rudolf and his lover are Claude Anet's *Mayerling* (1930), which inspired the memorable 1935 film with Charles Boyer and Danielle Darrieux.

H.9 Hamilton, Patrick *The Gorse Trilogy.* [*The West Pier; Mr. Stimpson and Mr. Gorse; Unknown Assailant.*] London: Constable, 1951–55.

■ In naming his anti-hero Ernest Ralph Gorse, Hamilton signaled his kinship with con man and sadistic murderer Neville George Clevely Heath (*gorse*, like *heath*, being a wasteland shrub). Heath was executed in 1946 for the mutilation killing of Margery Gardiner in a Notting Hill hotel in late June of that year; in early July, Heath brutally slaughtered Doreen Marshall and concealed her body under a rhododendron bush in Bournemouth. Before turning to these violent crimes, the handsome Heath had compiled an unenviable record of fraud and imposture. He was dismissed from short-lived RAF service in 1937 after appropriating a noncommissioned officer's car. In 1938 he was sentenced to three years' Borstal treatment after housebreaking, theft of jewelry, and forgery. During service in World War II he was court-martialed for fraudulently obtaining a second pay book and for issuing bad checks. In 1945 Heath faced another court-martial for wearing military decorations without authority.

In the three completed volumes of Hamilton's projected four-volume series, Gorse appears as a charming con man, but murder remains in his future. In *The West Pier*, which reflects Hamilton's childhood in the Brighton area, Gorse swindles Esther Downes, a naive shopgirl, of her savings of sixty-eight pounds. In the sequel, *Mr. Stimpson and Mrs. Gorse*, the target of his larcenous attentions is the foolish suburbanite Mrs. Plumleigh-Bruce, who incautiously pays a large sum into a joint account on the strength of his marriage proposal. In the third novel Gorse once again chooses a working-class victim of his fraudulent designs: a pub barmaid, Ivy Barton, whom he relieves of a paltry sum. In *Unseen Assailant*, the darker impulses of Gorse become more apparent. The book begins with a *News of the World* account of a working girl robbed and tied to a tractor in Norfolk by an "unknown assailant" and concludes with Gorse subjecting Ivy to similar abuse.

A successful British television miniseries, *The Charmer*, starring Nigel Havers, showed

Gorse's villainy in full bloom, as Hamilton would have done had he lived to write his fourth volume.

H.10 ———— *Rope: A Play*. London: Constable, 1929.

■ Wyndham Brandon and Charles Granillo, apparently lovers, strangle twenty-year-old Ronald Kentley with a rope and place his body in a chest as the curtain rises. They lay out sandwiches on the chest lid, and party guests, including the victim's father, Sir Johnstone Kentley, arrive. Among the other guests is Rupert Cadell, the lame mentor of Brandon and Granillo who shares their enthusiasm for Nietzsche. Brandon teases Sir Johnstone, asking how Ronald is getting on. The guests depart, but Cadell returns on the pretext that he left his cigarette case behind. In fact, he had spotted a damning piece of evidence—Ronald's ticket to the Coliseum—in Granillo's waistcoat pocket and deftly snatched it. Confronting the murderers with his discovery, he forces them to open the lid of the chest. He is horrified by beholding "the staring and futile remains of something that four hours ago lived, and laughed, and ran, and found it good." Rejecting Brandon's appeal for his silence, Cadell whistles for the police.

Patrick Hamilton denied to the end of his life that *Rope* had been influenced by Leopold and Loeb's murder of Bobby Franks in 1924. However, his biographer, Nigel Jones, opines that "the circumstances of the play are too similar to those of the *cause célèbre* to leave room for much doubt that, consciously or unconsciously, murder case and murder play are intimately connected" (Nigel Jones, *Through a Glass Darkly: The Life of Patrick Hamilton* [London: Abacus, 1993], 154).

In 1948 Alfred Hitchcock preserved the stage-thriller character of *Rope* by converting it into a monoset film, telling a story in real time beginning at 7:30 P.M. and ending at 9:15 P.M. Francois Truffaut comments, "In the history of cinema this is the only instance in which an entire film has been shot with no interruption for the different camera setups" (*Hitchcock* [New York: Simon & Schuster (Touchstone), 1967], 131).

H.11 Hanchett, William *The Lincoln Murder Conspiracies*. Urbana: Univ. of Illinois Press, 1983.

■ To the historically minded, Professor Hanchett's work brought welcome news that the practice of conspiracy theory was a favorite American pastime long before the assassination of President Kennedy. Hanchett examines and refutes the many unfounded and often fraudulent explanations that have been given for John Wilkes Booth's assassination of Abraham Lincoln:

- An alleged grand conspiracy on the part of the Confederacy and the antiwar Democrats
- Author Otto Eisenschiml's fingering of Secretary of War Edwin M. Stanton as the mastermind of the assassination in support of a Radical plot to continue the war
- The assertion that Lafayette C. Baker, chief of the War Department's National Detective Police, fomented the murder plot to preserve his extraordinary power
- A conspiracy directed by the Catholic Church.

Hanchett supports the traditional view that the assassination resulted from a "simple conspiracy" on the part of John Wilkes Booth and his small band of like-minded friends. One of the peculiarities of many conspiratorial thinkers about the Kennedy assassination is that, in brooding about the second marksman on the "grassy knoll," they make a conjectural leap to conclude that the possible collaboration of two or more killers must entail a vast political or institutional conspiracy.

Beginning in 1988, however, a new version of the Confederate "grand conspiracy" theory of the Lincoln assassination has emerged, the brainchild of Brigadier General William A. Tidwell, who served in the Central Intelligence Agency for twenty-three years. General Tidwell constructs his hypothesis along the following lines: After several false starts, Confederate agents "settled on" John Wilkes Booth as the man to capture President Lincoln. The kidnapping failed, as did a later plot to infiltrate a munitions expert, Thomas F. Harney, into Washington to blow up the White House. Booth, failing to understand that Lee's surrender had effectively ended the war, then decided to assassinate the president as an alternative means of disrupting Union command and control. In a supplementary study in 1995, Tidwell suggests that most of the sum of $1,500 in gold withdrawn by Judah P. Benjamin on April 1, 1865, defrayed the expenses of Harney's sabotage mission. (See William A. Tidwell, with James O. Hall and David Winfred Gaddy, *Come Retribution: The Confederate Secret Service and the Assassination of Lincoln* (Jackson: Univ. of Mississippi Press, 1988); William A. Tidwell, *April '65: Confederate Covert Action in the American Civil War* (Kent, Ohio: Kent State Univ. Press, 1995). Professor Hanchett has guardedly supported Tidwell's conclusions, stating that when Harney did not arrive in Washington, Booth "apparently believed that the fate of the Confederate States now rested in his hands alone" (Hanchett, "Shooting the President as a Military Necessity," in Charles Hubbard, ed., *Lincoln and His Contemporaries* [Macon, Ga.: Mercer Univ. Press, 1999], 139–48).

It is a solace to turn from wrangling over conspiracy theories of Lincoln's death to contemporary testimony of the nation's grief and confusion. Although his threnodies, "O Captain! My Captain!" and "When Lilacs Last in the Dooryard Bloom'd" are far better known, Walt Whitman also wrote a brief prose impression of President Lincoln's assassination, which is included in John Carey, ed., *Eyewitness to History* (New York: Avon, 1990). Whitman begins by explaining his association of lilacs with the tragedy: "I remember where I was stopping at the time, the season being advanced, there were many lilacs in full bloom. By one of those caprices that enter and give tinge to events without being at all a part of them, I find myself always reminded of the great tragedy of that day by the sight and odour of those blossoms. It never fails."

Among the events Whitman swiftly describes at Ford's Theater, one he found "especially exciting," was the narrow escape of an innocent man from a second assassination: "The infuriated crowd, through some chance, got started against one man, either for words he uttered, or perhaps without any cause at all, and were proceeding at once to actually hang him on a neighbouring lamp-post, when he was rescued by a few heroic policemen, who placed him in their midst and fought their way slowly and amid great peril toward the Station House."

H.12 Harden, Maximilian [pseudonym of Felix Ernst Witkowski] *Köpfe (Prozesse)* [Trials]. 1913. Vol. 3. Berlin: Erich Reiss, 1923.

■ Harden, a polemical journalist and editor of *Zukunft* [The Future], is best known for his charges in 1906 that Kaiser Wilhelm II was surrounded by a kitchen cabinet (camarilla) of homosexuals. His principal targets were Prince Philipp zu Eulenburg, German ambassador to Austria, and Count Kuno von Moltke, military commandant of Berlin. In the view of the independent conservative journal, the *Post*, Harden was a "disciple of Herostratus," who was willing to bring Germany to ruin in the interest of personal notoriety. See John C. G. Röhl, *Kaiser, Hof, und Staat: Wilhelm II und die deutsche Politik* (Munich: C. H. Beck, 1988); Maximilian Jacta, *Accusé levez-vous: Procès célèbres d'Allemagne*, trans. Denis Simon (Verviers, Belgium: Editions Gerard, 1967). Moltke's defamation suit, after the government intervened as prosecutor, resulted in the imposition of a four-month jail sentence on Harden. However, the journalist emerged victorious, winning a settlement in which criminal charges against him were dropped, and the prosecution acknowledged his patriotic motives. Eulenburg was less fortunate. His testimony that he had committed neither punishable homosexual acts nor any other "obscene actions" led to his prosecution for perjury, a charge that led to periodic trial postponements for reasons of his poor health until his death in 1921.

The two longest chapters in *Prozesse* are devoted to Harden's campaign against Eulenburg and Moltke. The journalist maintains that it was Prince Otto von Bismarck who first alerted him to Eulenburg's sexual proclivities.

Subjects of other essays include Pontius Pilate; French swindler Thérèse Humbert; and Baden-Baden murderer Karl Hau, whose crime inspired Jakob Wassermann's masterpiece *The Maurizius Case* (see H.1).

H.13 Hare, David *Knuckle.* In *The History Plays*. London: Faber & Faber, 1984.

■ In 1924 Patrick Herbert Mahon, a married sales manager with past convictions for embezzlement and violent bank burglary, invited his pregnant mistress, typist Emily Kaye, to a bungalow he had rented on the "Crumbles" beach near Eastbourne. Their relationship was fraying, and she had suggested a quiet getaway together as a "love experiment." The outcome was tragic; Mahon murdered Kaye in the cottage and dismembered her body. Despite his claim that Kaye had accidentally hit her head on a coal caldron during a scuffle, he was convicted and hanged. Even after he confessed his guilt to prison officials, Mahon asked them not to make his statement public for fear of the "bad impression it might make" (see *The Trial of Patrick Herbert Mahon*, intro. Edgar Wallace, in *Famous Trials* series [New York: Scribner's, 1928]).

In Hare's *Knuckle*, produced in 1974, an idealistic nurse, Sarah Delafield, learns that her father, Patrick, a merchant banker, has provided financing for unscrupulous developers who have used violent means to rout an elderly owner from a house that they mean to acquire. Horrified by her discovery, Sarah either drowns or pretends to drown herself at the Crumbles. She had decided to embarrass her father by choosing "a place famous for a ghastly murder." To her gun-running brother, Curly, who investigates her disappearance, the story of her staged suicide at the Mahon murder scene rings true: "The story has just the right amount of quiet. She slipped obligingly into the sea. An English murder. Who needs ropes or guns or daggers? We can trust our victims to pass quietly in the night. . . . Just fall away with barely the crack of the knuckle as they go."

H.14 Hauterive, Ernest d' *L'Enlèvement du Sénateur Clément de Ris.* In series *Énigmes et drames judiciaires d'autrefois.* Paris: Perrin, 1927.

▪ Hauterive (born 1861), the son-in-law of Alexandre Dumas *fils* and a member of the literary circle of G. Lenôtre (see L.14), specialized in the history of the French police under the First Empire. In his account of the kidnapping of Senator Clément de Ris (1800), he attributes the enigmatic crime to a band of six former Chouan rebels who spirited the senator away as an improvisation after a disappointing burglary attempt. The book is a study in the duplicity of the Police Minister Joseph Fouché, who secretly granted immunity to three captors, as a bargain for de Ris's safe return, while allowing their confederates to be executed. Hauterive comments aptly concerning Fouché's double game and de Ris's unwillingness to affront the minister by testifying: "Since Pontius Pilate how many people have washed their hands without making them any cleaner!" (192). The de Ris kidnapping and accreted legends inspired Balzac's novel *Une ténébreuse affaire* (see B.7).

H.15 Hawthorne, Nathaniel *The Marble Faun.* 1860. 2 vols. Boston: Houghton Mifflin, 1891.

▪ Both of the principal female characters of *The Marble Faun* are associated by Hawthorne with Beatrice Cenci, who conspired to murder her father, Francesco, supposedly in revenge for incestuous rape (see S.28). The dove-pure painter Hilda, viewing the Guido Reni painting traditionally accepted as the portrait of Beatrice, speculates as to whether she herself is "stained with guilt" (see Frederick Crews, *The Sins of the Fathers: Hawthorne's Psychological Themes* [London: Oxford Univ. Press, 1966], 217).

Miriam, another painter whose work often depicts scenes of violence by women (Jael, Judith, Salome), is destined, like Beatrice Cenci, to inspire a man (Donatello, the "Faun") to murder her male oppressor. Hawthorne also suggests that Miriam was innocently involved in a scandalous criminal case of the recent past. It has been convincingly argued that the woman Hawthorne had in the mind was Henriette Deluzy, governess in the household of the Praslins (see F.7). Hawthorne may have known Henriette as the wife of a neighbor's son in Massachusetts (see Nathalia Wright, "Hawthorne and the Praslin Murder," *New England Quarterly* [Sept. 1942]: 5–14).

H.16 —— *The Scarlet Letter.* 1850. Ed. Sculley Bradley, Richmond Croom Beatty, E. Hudson Long, and Seymour Gross. 2nd ed. New York: Norton, 1978.

▪ James T. Fields, the publisher of *The Scarlet Letter*, was struck by Hawthorne's fondness for the English *State Trials*:

Hearing him [Hawthorne] say once that the old English State Trials were enchanting reading, and knowing that he did not possess a copy of those heavy folios, I picked up a set one day in a book-shop and sent them to him. He often told me that he spent more hours over them and got more delectation out of them that tongue could tell, and he said, if five lives were vouchsafed to him, he could employ them all in writing stories out of those books. He had sketched, in his mind, several romances founded on the remarkable trials reported in the ancient volumes; and one day, I remember, he made my blood tingle by relating some of the situations he intended, if his life was spared, to weave into future romances.

In two related works, Professor Alfred S. Reid persuasively argued that one of the principal sources of *The Scarlet Letter* was the trial of the murderers of Sir Thomas Overbury in the Tower of London in 1613, which was included in the *State Trials* and was also the subject of other works to which Hawthorne had access, including the 1616 poem by Richard Niccols, "Sir Thomas Overbury's Vision" (see Alfred S. Reid, *The Yellow Ruff and the Scarlet Letter: A Source of Hawthorne's Novel* (Gainesville: Univ. Press of Florida, 1955); *Sir Thomas Overbury's Vision (1916) by Richard Niccols and Other English Sources of Nathaniel Hawthorne's "The Scarlet Letter,"* facsimile reproductions with an introduction by Alfred S. Reid (Gainesville: Scholars' Facsimiles and Reprints, 1957).

Sir Thomas Overbury's imprisonment in the Tower was treacherously arranged by his former friend, Robert Carr (who was to become the Earl of Somerset), because of Overbury's opposition to Carr's plan to marry his adulterous mistress, Lady Frances, Countess of Essex. Carr and Lady Frances then procured the slow poisoning of their enemy. Among the co-conspirators in the murder plot were Mrs. Anne Turner, a disreputable friend of the Countess; a quack doctor and necromancer, Simon Forman; and the Lieutenant of the Tower, Jervase Helwyse, who facilitated the importation of the poisons. See D.13.

Reid cites two extensive allusions to the Overbury murder in the pages of *The Scarlet Letter*. In chapter 9, describing the sinister doctor Roger Chillingworth, Hester Prynne's husband, the narrator refers to gossip that Chillingworth was an associate of Simon Forman: "There was an aged handscraftsman, it is true, who had been a citizen of London at the period of Sir Thomas Overbury's murder, now some thirty years agone; he testified to having seen the physician [Chillingworth], under some other name, which the narrator of the story had now forgotten, in company with Doctor Forman, the famous old conjurer, who was implicated in the affair of Overbury."

A second reference to the Overbury murder links the fictional Mistress Hibbins, a "reputed witch-lady," to Anne Turner, one of Sir Thomas's poisoners. The historical Anne Turner had introduced the starched yellow ruff to the world of fashion and had been condemned to wear her creation on the scaffold. In chapter 20 Hawthorne gives Mistress Hibbins a similar adornment: "She made a very grand appearance; having on a high head-dress, a rich gown of velvet, and a ruff done up with the famous yellow starch, of which Ann [*sic*] Turner, her especial friend, had taught her the secret, before this last good lady had been hanged for Sir Thomas Overbury's murder."

Beginning with these textual hints, Reid draws many suggestive parallels between the Overbury murder and the plot, characters, and meaning of Hawthorne's novel:

- The yellow ruff is likened to the scarlet letter that Hester Prynne is condemned to wear.
- The blisters that Sir Thomas Overbury's poisoning caused to appear on his body are analogous to the scarlet letter that some bystanders believe they saw imprinted in minister Arthur Dimmesdale's breast as a stigma of the remorse he feels for his secret adultery with Hester.
- Hester, like Lady Frances, commits adultery, gives birth to a child in prison, and is fated to live in isolation from society.
- Roger Chillingworth's plot against Dimmesdale's physical and psychological health recalls the poisoning plot and the aura of witchcraft by which it was deemed to have been surrounded.

In addition to noting many details of resemblance between the old English trial and Hawthorne's novel, Reid identifies fundamental thematic affinities between the fiction and its historical source: "In their broad outlines of adultery, witchcraft, isolation, revenge, violation of a human soul, concealed sin, dying confession, and divine judgment upon sinners, *The Scarlet Letter* and the Overbury affair share common motifs."

H.17 Hay, Julius *Have.* 1936. Vancouver: Talonbooks, 1976.

■ Communist and patriotic Hungarian, Hay was jailed after the Revolution of 1956. International protests won him amnesty in 1960. *Have*, one of his first major plays, was inspired by widespread poisoning of Hungarian farmers by their wives in the early decades of the twentieth century for the purpose of inheriting small parcels of land.

Mrs. Kepes, a midwife who distributes arsenic to land-hungry wives, states the play's theme that the old regime has worked a separation of women and the poor from the land: "The land is ice, when it's not your land. Your foot steps, your body freezes. Not to have is to freeze to death. Do you want to freeze to death? The women of the village don't. What is yours keeps you warm. God gives the warmth. God gives the land. But stretch your hand for it yourself."

Police corporal Dani Ballo and his pregnant sweetheart, Mari Arva, work at cross-purposes to build a secure life together. After she marries a prosperous farmer, Neighbor David, Mari poisons him and his sickly daughter with arsenic supplied by Mrs. Kepes so that the child she will bear can inherit David's property. Dani, however, hopes to advance his police career by an "independent investigation" and believes that David's daughter poisoned him. After Mari confesses to the two murders, he calmly arranges the evidence on a table before him and begins to interrogate her.

H.18 Hecht, Ben *Gaily, Gaily.* Garden City: Doubleday, 1963.

■ The noted novelist and playwright, with little evident regard for literal truth, re-creates his five years as a cub reporter on the *Chicago Journal*, 1910–15. Although confessing that his frequent inability to recall the actual names of personnages did not check the flow of his narrative, Hecht introduces sketches of historical luminaries on both sides of the law, including mobster Big Jim Colosimo and Al Capone and lawyers Clarence Darrow and

Charles Erbstein. The stories (originally separately published) included in this volume evoke the journalistic swashbuckling that gave birth to the play *The Front Page*, co-authored by Hecht with Charles MacArthur.

H.19 Hellman, Lillian   *The Children's Hour.* New York: Knopf 1934.

■ Dashiell Hammett, to whom this play is dedicated, called Hellman's attention to William Roughead's essay "Closed Doors; or, The Great Drumsheugh Case" (in *Bad Companions* [Edinburgh: Green, 1930]; see R.16). This study focuses on an Edinburgh scandal that arose in 1810 when a boarding student falsely accused two teachers, Marianne Woods and Jane Pirie, of lesbianism. In Hellman's version, the two victims, Karen Wright and Martha Dobie, suffer the far-reaching and subtle consequences of defamation and rumor. Karen breaks off her engagement to Dr. Joseph Cardin, because, despite his loyalty, she suspects he believes that "there might be just a little truth in it all." Then the two women part after Martha confesses to Karen that the child's lies caused her to recognize that she was in love with Karen and resented her engagement.

Lillian Faderman has written a book-length study of the defamation case that the Scottish teachers brought against Dame Helen Cumming Gordon, who had destroyed their teaching careers by spreading the false report of sexual impropriety (Lillian Faderman, *Scotch Verdict* [London: Quartet, 1985]). After prevailing in the House of Lords in 1819, almost a decade after the trouble began, the plaintiffs ultimately settled their claims for 3,500 pounds, less the costs of appeal.

H.20 Heppenstall, Rayner   *A Little Pattern of French Crime.* London: Hamish Hamilton, 1969.

■ Despite the author's quirky and intrusive style, there is considerable charm and some instruction in this impressionistic vision of crime during France's Belle Epoque. Heppenstall focuses on the trials of two women that resulted in debatable acquittals. The fortunate defendants were Marguerite Steinheil, who had been charged with murdering her artist husband, Adolphe, and her mother in the Steinheil apartment in Paris; and Henriette Caillaux, who had indisputably shot *Le Figaro*'s editor Gaston Calmette out of fear that he was about to publish correspondence from her husband, former Prime Minister Joseph Caillaux, at a time they were carrying on a premarital affair. Interwoven in the narrative are brief references to other murders of the era, including anarchist outrages. Whenever possible Heppenstall emphasizes associations of men of letters with figures in the principal cases, such as Marcel Proust's friendship with Calmette and Paul Bourget's presence at the *Figaro* offices at the moment of Madame Caillaux's fatal interview with the editor.

H.21 Hesse, Raymond   *Les criminels peints par eux-mêmes.* Paris: Bernard Grasset, 1912.

■ Hesse, a fabulist whom Anatole France dubbed "the French Aesop," turns to another genre in this work, *Criminals Painted by Themselves*. He takes as his subject the literature, mainly autobiographical, that French criminals have created either as caricatures that exaggerate their personality defects or as idealized masks to conceal their insensitivity and egoism. Hesse traces the literary impulse of the criminal to the ancient Greek Herostratus, who burned the Temple of Ephesus to ensure eternal fame (see G.28). In his study of criminal autobiographies Hesse takes particular interest in the authors' revelation of their motives. Although acknowledging that the roots of crime may be intertangled, Hesse recognizes six categories of motivation. Four roughly correspond to classifications established in F. Tennyson Jesse's seminal work (see J.9): money, sadism, political conviction (such as anarchism), and revenge. Two other motives identified by Hesse appear at first glance to be distinctively French: the influence of women on their passionate lovers (Hesse cites the murder of Gouffé; see B.60) and the deleterious effect of certain literature (such as the baleful influence of James Fenimore Cooper's Sioux chieftains on cousins Clément and Henri Marchembled, who in 1885 murdered a childhood friend Maria Lebent with seventeen knife thrusts). We might now regard the latter example as illustrative of copycat crime.

H.22 Heyward, DuBose *Porgy.* New York: George H. Doran, 1925.

■ Heyward drew the title character of his novel *Porgy* (which later was converted into a play on which he collaborated with his wife, Dorothy, and then into the opera *Porgy and Bess*, by George and Ira Gershwin) from a police news item in the *Charleston News and Courier*:

> Samuel Smalls, who is a cripple and, with his goat cart, is familiar to King Street, was held for the June term of Court of Sessions on an aggravated assault charge. It is alleged that on Saturday night he attempted to shoot Maggie Barnes at 4 Romney Street. His shots went wide of the mark. Smalls was up on a similar charge some months ago and was given a suspended sentence; he had attempted to escape in his wagon and was run down and captured by the police patrol.

Although Smalls's disability and goat cart suggest attributes of Porgy, the pattern of recurrent violence in the life of the Charleston peddler bears a closer resemblance to the conduct of the novel's powerful villain, Crown. See Hollis Alpert, *The Life and Times of Porgy and Bess: The Story of an American Classic* (New York: Nick Hern [Walker], 1990), 16–20.

H.23 Hibbert, Christopher *The Road to Tyburn: The Story of Jack Sheppard and the Eighteenth Century Underworld.* Cleveland: World Publishing, 1957.

■ As he stepped into the cart that led him to execution at Tyburn (now Marble Arch) in London in 1724, there was nothing in the demeanor of diminutive twenty-two-year-old thief and jail breaker Jack Sheppard or in his behavior to suggest the "brutal scoundrel" described by William Makepeace Thackeray. Yet Sheppard, particularly after his celebrated 1,724 escapes from Newgate prison, became a creature of English crime legend, inspiring a "Newgate novel" of William Harrison Ainsworth bearing his name, countless stage works, and street literature. Hibbert's lively account of Jack's swashbuckling career is the centerpiece of a broader portrait of the eighteenth-century English underworld that was mirrored in John Gay's *The Beggar's Opera.*

The Borowitz True Crime Collection holds a contemporary print of "Jack Shepherd [*sic*] Drawn from the Life" showing the fettered prisoner in his cell, and "An Exact Representation of the Holes Shepherd made in the Chimney and of the Locks Bolts & Doors he broke Open in makeing [*sic*] his wonderfull escape out of Newgate October 15, 1724, between 4 in the afternoon & 1 in the morning." See Fig. 4 a & b.

The story of Jack Sheppard has also reached the silver screen. In 1969, English pop singer Tommy Steele took the title role in *Where's Jack?*

H.24 Higdon, Hal *Crime of the Century: The Leopold and Loeb Case.* New York: Putnam, 1976.
■ Strangely there are few nonfiction works on the Leopold-Loeb case, and this workmanlike, demythifying account is the most useful. Higdon concludes that it was Loeb who wielded the fatal chisel and was more prone to crime than was Leopold, whose love for Loeb led him to join the murder plot as well as earlier arsons and burglaries. Leopold, however, admitted to having been the aggressor in their apparently limited sexual relations.

It is ironic that Higdon's narrative of the so-called "perfect crime" reveals it to have been a series of bungles; the only detail reflecting any ingenuity—the plan to have the ransom money thrown from a moving train by Bobby Franks's father—was not carried out.

H.25 Hobsbawm, E[ric] J. *Bandits.* London: Weidenfeld & Nicolson, 1969.
■ In this imaginative and wide-ranging study drawing on the experience and traditions of many peoples in Europe, Asia, and America, Hobsbawm analyzes the phenomenon he calls "social banditry." In his definition, social bandits are "peasant outlaws whom the lord and state regard as criminals, but who remain within peasant society, and are considered by their people as heroes, as champions, avengers, fighters for justice, perhaps even leaders of liberation, and in any case as men to be admired, helped and supported."

Hobsbawm divides social banditry into three principal forms, which he discusses in separate chapters:

- The "noble robber," or Robin Hood, who lives in freedom and, more often in legend than reality, robs the rich to give to the poor. This category includes France's smuggler, Louis Mandrin; Diego Corrientes (1757–81), an Andalusian robber whom popular opinion compared to Christ; and Jesse James, who supposedly lent a widow funds to pay her banker and then held up the banker to retrieve the cash.
- The avengers, whose cruel actions are often inspired by personal traumas inflicted by feuds or injustices. "Their appeal," writes Hobsbawm, "is not that of the agents of justice, but of men who prove that even the poor and weak can be terrible." As examples, he cites Ferreira da Silva (?1898–1938), *cangaçeiro* or bandit of northeastern Brazil, and the "ghastly phenomenon of the Colombian *violencia* in the years after 1948."
- Primitive resistance fighters or guerrilla units, including tsarist Russia's Cossacks and Balkan bands that Hobsbawm groups under the term "haiduk." These bandit-warriors sometimes defended frontiers in exchange for recognition of their status as free men. In Hobsbawm's vision, the haiduks, whose "permanent existence went with formal

structure and organization," had affinities with "the great brigand republic which is the subject of the Chinese Water Margin novel [*All Men Are Brothers*]."

In subsequent chapters, Hobsbawm extends his inquiry to the roles of social bandits in larger upheavals: participation in armed revolutions; and activity as "expropriators"—or, more simply stated, bank robbers—to raise funds for political propaganda. A narrative highlight of the study of "expropriators" is the adventurous career of Francisco Sabaté Llopart "Quico," an insurrectionist against the Franco regime after World War II. In unexpected confrontations, Sabaté always walked toward the police, "not only a sound psychological tactic but the hero's way."

H.26 Hoffmann, Ernst Theodor Amadeus "Die Marquise de la Pivardière" (nach Richers *Causes célèbres*). *Dictungen und Schriften*. Vol. 11. Weimar: Erich Lichtenstein, 1924. 305–49.
■ Hoffmann's tale of the bizarre eighteenth-century trial of the Marquise de la Pivardière for the alleged murder of her cheating husband, who in fact remained very much alive, draws upon François Richer's reworking of a cause célèbre by Gayot de Pitaval. In Hoffmann's version, the marquise did not commit adultery with her chaplain, Sylvain-François Charost, but cherished a virtuous attachment to him as a former admirer whose youthful suit had been frustrated by her domineering father. Hoffmann also supports the dismissal of the murder charges against the marquise and Charost, finding that the man who intervened in the proceedings with the claim that he was the real Marquis de la Pivardière had strongly established his identity. At the end of the tale, Hoffmann explains away the most damning eyewitness testimony to the murder: the nine-year old daughter of the Pivardières, who stated that she had seen bloodstains in her father's bedroom, had been pressured by neighbors; and two housemaids had based their so-called firsthand observations of the murder on misinterpretations of hearsay accounts, and they also suffered abusive questioning by investigative authorities. See S.40.

Hoffmann also drew on the causes célèbres of Pitaval and Richer as sources of information regarding the Marquise Brinvilliers, a seventeenth-century poisoner who appears in his famous tale "Das Fräulein von Scudery."

H.27 Holbrook, Stewart H. *Murder Out Yonder: An Informal Study of Certain Classic Crimes in Back-Country America*. New York: Macmillan, 1941.
■ "Informal" is not the best word for Holbrook's style; "flippant" would serve better. Still, these appealing accounts of crimes in remote American locales have the merit of rescuing half-forgotten cases as well as reviving classics. Holbrook considers:

- Franz Edmund Creffield, who, as Prophet Joshua the Second, established a cult of adoring females in an Oregon Garden of Eden. To outsiders it seemed that he was mating promiscuously with his followers, but his Church of the Bride of a Second Christ believed that the prophet was engaged in selecting "the Mother of a Second Christ." In 1906 Joshua claimed that the San Francisco earthquake and fire resulted from the curse he laid upon the city. Prophet Joshua soon afterward was shot to death in Seattle by George Mitchell, brother of a young girl whom the cult leader had seduced. After his acquittal, Mitchell was murdered in retribution by his sister and the prophet's widow.

- Norman Williams, hanged at the Dalles, Oregon, in 1905 for the murder of his neighboring homesteader and secret wife, Alma Nesbitt. The conviction was based on the analysis by a female forensic scientist (a rarity in her day) of a bloody burlap sack, with gray hairs adhering, unearthed at Williams's abandoned farm.

- Harry Orchard, who confessed the 1905 bombing murder of Frank Steunenberg, who as governor of Idaho had called in federal troops during the Coeur d'Alene mining labor riots. Holbrook accepts without reservation Orchard's story that the killing was commissioned by "Big Bill" Haywood of the Western Federation of Miners (see L.40).

- Tinhorn gambler Harry Hayward, hanged in Minneapolis in 1895 for the elaborately planned shooting murder of a fashionable dressmaker, Kitty Ging, as she rode in a buggy along Lake Calhoun with Claus Blixt, a dimwitted apartment building engineer whom Hayward had terrorized into committing the crime. The thirty-year-old Ging, in love with the calculating Hayward, had taken out life insurance in his favor and had signed promissory notes in a similar amount evidencing fictitious borrowings from him. On the night of the shooting, Hayward established an alibi by taking a young woman to a performance of a musical comedy, Hoyt's *A Trip to Chinatown*, at the Grand Opera House.

- The 1910 siege of Cameron Dam in Sawyer County, Wisconsin. John F. Dietz, who resisted a "small army of deputies" (of whom one died before Dietz surrendered), had barred the use of a dam by a neighboring lumber company in a long-standing dispute over his asserted right to collect a toll. Dietz was sentenced to life imprisonment and was pardoned after ten years; his case seems to prefigure Randy Weaver's.

- Dr. John MacGregor, convicted in 1912 of the arsenic poisoning of young Scyrel Sparling, whose father and two elder brothers had previously died under similar circumstances on their farm near Bad Axe, Michigan. MacGregor, the family physician to whom Mrs. Sparling had assigned proceeds of her dead son's life insurance, was pardoned by Michigan's governor Ferris in 1916 on the ground that his imprisonment had been a "terrible mistake." His decision leaves Holbrook and the reader bewildered.

- Belle Gunness, serial killer who buried her victims on her farm in La Porte, Indiana (see D.17).

- Edward Rulloff, linguist and murderer (see P.5).

- A New England burglar of respectable upbringing, George Abbott (who took the name Frank Almy after escaping from prison in Windsor, Vermont), hanged in 1892 for the murder of a farmer's daughter, Christie Warden. Abbott attacked and shot Christie in the Vale of Tempe in Hanover, New Hampshire, after she rejected his suit. He was captured in the Wardens's barn, where he hid out after the crime.

- The murder of Sarah Meservey in Tenants Habor, Maine (see P.4).

H.28 Holiday, Billie, and Alex Meeropol "Strange Fruit." A song introduced at Café Society, New York City, 1939.

■ First published in 1937, in a magazine of the New York teachers' union, as a poem by Alex Meeropol (who later adopted the sons of Ethel and Julius Rosenberg, executed atomic bomb spies), its devastating attack on lynching of Southern blacks is powered by the central image of the gallows tree:

> Southern trees bear a strange fruit,
> Blood on the leaves and blood at the root,
> Black body swinging in the Southern breeze,
> Strange fruit hanging from the poplar trees.

Poet Meeropol (known professionally as Lewis Allan) initially set the words to music of his own, but the immortality of the work was ensured when Billie Holiday introduced her own version of the song at New York City's Café Society in 1939. See David Margolick, *Strange Fruit: Billie Holiday, Café Society and an Early Cry for Civil Rights* (Philadelphia: Running Press, 2000).

The title of the Holiday-Meeropol song has been adopted by an anthology of anti-lynching plays by female authors (*Strange Fruit: Plays on Lynching by American Women*, ed. Kathy A. Perkins and Judith L. Stephens [Bloomington: Indiana Univ. Press 1998]).

Another of the immortal lynching protest songs of the 1930s is Irving Berlin's "Supper Time," performed by Ethel Waters in the topical revue, *As Thousands Cheer* (1933). Under a headline reading "Unknown Negro Lynched by Frenzied Mob," Waters "delivered the magnificently understated lament of the wife of the victim, who must tell her children that they will never see their father again" (Laurence Bergreen, *As Thousands Cheer: The Life of Irving Berlin* [New York: Viking, 1990], 321).

H.29 Holmes, Richard   *Dr. Johnson and Mr. Savage.* New York: Pantheon, 1993.
■ Between 1737 and 1739, the young Samuel Johnson was guided through London's nocturnal haunts by Richard Savage, proto-romantic poet and convicted murderer. Holmes's book is a study of the friendship between the two men and is also, in the author's words, "the biography of a biography," a close analysis of Johnson's *Life of Savage* (London, 1744).

Savage's self-image as a social outcast was based in large part on his claim that he was the illegitimate son of Lady Macclesfield and Earl Rivers. Although Holmes cites evidence tending to disprove this noble parentage, he does not believe that the poet was a conscious impostor: "Much of the evidence, documentary and otherwise, is reconciled if we assume that through the disrupted, unhappy circumstances of his childhood, Savage was genuinely deluded about his identity."

Holmes links Savage's persuasion of his high rank to the murder for which he was sentenced to death, only to be spared by a pardon granted through the intercession of Queen Caroline. In 1727 Savage and two cronies became involved in a brawl at Robinson's Coffee-House (a tavern and brothel), in which the poet made a lethal sword thrust into the belly of James Sinclair, one of their antagonists. Holmes believes that although it was William Merchant, one of the poet's drinking companions, who had initiated the affray,

Savage's sense of noblesse oblige caused him to draw his sword in defense of his other friend, James Gregory, whose sword had shattered.

Holmes demonstrates how Johnson, in his account of the trial, consistently interprets the evidence in a light favorable to Savage. In making this tribute of friendship, and in writing a biography predominantly favorable to his raffish subject, Johnson did not blind himself to Savage's failings. Holmes summarizes Johnson's position as Savage's biographer: "If [Savage] was frequently a vain and self-deluded man, and an untrustworthy friend, yet the hardships he suffered should make us forgive him."

H.30 Holt, J[ames] C. *Robin Hood.* Rev. ed. London: Thames & Hudson, 1989.

■ Holt's work is an outstanding example of the considerable body of scholarship that has been devoted to uncovering the origins of the Robin Hood legends and to the search for an historical figure that may have originally inspired them. Impressed by discoveries that, on several occasions in the thirteenth century, the surname "Robinhood" was attributed to criminals, Holt argues that the Robin Hood legend was well known as early as 1261–62. This dating, in his view, strengthens the possibility that the original Robin Hood was a fugitive against whom penalties were assessed in the York assizes of 1225. It is not easy to disentangle fact and fiction in the Robin Hood legends, though, for Holt examines their many similarities to other early outlaw traditions, including those related to three real-life figures, Hereward the Wake, Eustace the Monk, and Fulk fitz Warin. Further, Holt acknowledges the possibility that "there was not just one original Robin Hood, real or fictional, but many. Each one acknowledged the legend by adopting the surname or by accepting it from others. Each one contributed to it and thereby became difficult to distinguish from the legend itself. Each one was real, committing real crimes, engaged in real adventures; but each one was moulded by the legend he adopted or had imposed upon him with the name."

H.31 Hood, Thomas "The Dream of Eugene Aram." In *The Poetical Works of Thomas Hood.* Vol. 1. Boston: Little, Brown, 1860. 118–24.

■ Yorkshireman Eugene Aram, schoolmaster and linguistic theorist, was hanged in 1759 for the murder of Daniel Clark in 1745. Aram and a weaver named Richard Houseman had murdered Daniel Clark, a shoemaker, and stolen his valuables; they hid his body in St. Robert's Cave, outside the town of Knaresborough where the murderers and their victim had resided. Shortly after the crime, Aram, under suspicion as one of the last to have seen Clark alive, secretly left Knaresborough, abandoning his abused wife, Anna. In 1758, when lime diggers discovered a human skeleton on Thistle Hill near Knaresborough, Houseman told authorities that it was not Clark's body but, thoroughly terrified, led them to St. Robert's Cave, where he identified the murdered man's remains. Houseman testified for the Crown against Aram, who unsuccessfully attempted suicide after his conviction.

In Thomas Hood's poem "The Dream of Eugene Aram" (1829), the first literary work in which Aram appears as the principal figure, the fugitive schoolmaster tells one of his pupils at Lynn of a dream in which the corpse of his murder victim cannot be hidden from view:

For I knew my secret then was one
  That earth refused to keep:
Or land or sea, though he should be
  Ten thousand fathoms deep.

A sympathetic portrayal of Aram as a high-souled murderer appears in Edward Bulwer Lytton's novel *Eugene Aram*, which was published in 1832, partly under the influence of Hood's poem. In 1873 Sir Henry Irving enjoyed great success in the title role of William Gorman Wills's play *Eugene Aram*.

Professor Nancy Jane Tyson has shown how Eugene Aram became a literary prototype of the scholar-criminal. Nancy Jane Tyson, *Eugene Aram: The Literary History and Typology of the Scholar-Criminal* (Hamden, Conn.: Archon, 1983). This book originated as a dissertation under the direction of Richard D. Altick.

H.32 Hopkins, Tighe   *The Romance of Escapes: Studies of Some Historic Flights with a Personal Commentary.* Illus. ed. London: John Murray, 1920.

▪ After an introductory section on the "art and mystery of escape," touching on such famous prison-breakers as Jack Sheppard, Henri Masers de Latude, and Baron Trenck, Hopkins studies in more detail eleven notable escapes. In the most stunning of Hopkins's revelations, Casanova is shown to have fabricated the adventurous details of his escape from the Leads prison in Venice; most likely, the swashbuckling memoirist bribed a jailer named Lorenzo. Other chapters of the books include the escape of Prince Louis Napoleon (the future Napoleon III) from the Fortress of Ham disguised as a workman bearing a wooden plank on his shoulder; the flight of Irish rebel John Mitchel from Tasmanian exile; and the self-styled Abbé Count de Buquoit, whom Hopkins describes as the first prisoner to have escaped from the Bastille.

H.33 ———   *The Romance of Fraud.* New York: Dutton, 1914.

▪ This mistitled collection addresses varied topics in the history of crime and punishment, including:

- Exotic counterfeits ("The Tailless Hippo")
- The author's visit to the condemned cell of Newgate on the eve of the London prison's demolition
- Physical clues in criminal investigations ("The Trail")
- Prison literature, secret codes, and other recreations of prisoners
- The Australian prison colony ("The Paradise and Hell of Felons")
- The history of piracy
- The escape of Union soldiers from Richmond's Libby Prison
- The tattooing of criminals
- The criminal procedure of the Inquisition
- The master thief's employment of scouts and accomplices

- The history of police in England and India
- Proposals for development of a parole system in England
- Antoine Quentin Fouquier-Tinville, public prosecutor under the French Terror
- The links between the criminal impulse and superstition
- Hopkins's rejection of A. S. Barnes's thesis that the Man in the Iron Mask was Charles II's illegitimate son, James Stuart, alias James de la Cloche, alias Henry de Rohan (see Monsignor A. S. Barnes, *The Man of the Mask* [London: Smith Elder, 1908])

H.34 Hughes, [James] Langston   *Scottsboro, Limited: A One-Act Play.* 1931. In *The Political Plays of Langston Hughes*. Intro. and analyses Susan Duffy. Carbondale: Southern Illinois Univ. Press, 2000.

■ During the period of his allegiance to the American Communist Party, Hughes (1902–1967) wrote this agit-prop play about the rape trial of the Scottsboro Boys (see C.15) and their rescue from the electric chair by black and white workers united under the Red flag. A single white actor plays the roles of many oppressors, including sheriff, judge, prison keeper, and preacher. Plants in the audience represent members of the racist mob as well as the "Red voices" that take up the defendants' cause. At the end a chorus in unison urges workers to rise and fight, and the audience responds unanimously. At a performance in Los Angeles in 1932, the play was preceded by "A Chant for Tom Mooney," a poem predicting eternal fame for a labor leader imprisoned for a 1916 Preparedness Day bombing in San Francisco and pardoned in 1939.

H.35 Hugo, Victor   "Claude Gueux." 1834. In *The Last Day of a Condemned Man, and Other Prison Writings*. Trans. Geoff Woollen. Oxford: Oxford Univ. Press (World's Classics), 1992.

■ Translator Woollen describes the historical Gueux, born in Burgundy's Côte d'Or in 1804, as "a violent, habitual petty criminal, who by the age of fourteen had already tasted imprisonment." He had served almost six years in Clairvaux prison, 1823–29, including six months added for an attack on the guards. A theft returned him in 1830 to Clairvaux, where his father was also doing time for a similar offense. The elder Gueux died in detention in March 1831. Later that year his son murdered the head warden, perhaps motivated by torment suffered at his hands or acting to avenge his injustices to fellow inmates as well.

Hugo's short story, although written in a spare documentary style, includes fictional elements that create a sympathetic portrait of Claude Gueux. No mention is made of the elder Gueux's criminal record, and the son's long imprisonment is due to a minor theft that "resulted in three days of bread and warmth" for his mistress and child. He kills a stubbornly malevolent workshop superintendent who has separated him from his devoted friend Albin Legrand and has refused to countermand his decision despite Claude's frequent entreaties. After sentencing the superintendent to death in the formulaic language of a French judicial decision and winning the assent of his inmates, Claude butchers his oppressor with an axe.

The execution of Claude Gueux becomes, in Hugo's telling, a powerful sermon against inhumane prison regimes and capital punishment. For the guillotine Hugo would substitute improved education: "Take the common man's head, cultivate it, weed it, water it, sow it, enlighten it, moralize it, and put it to good use; then you will have no need to cut it off."

H.36 Huie, William Bradford   *Ruby McCollum: Woman in the Suwannee Jail.* Rev. ed. New York: Signet Books, 1964.

■ On Florida's Suwannee River (which Stephen Foster never visited), 1952 was not a good year. On Sunday morning, August 3, Ruby McCollum, the wealthiest black woman in Live Oak, fired four bullets into the back of Dr. Clifford LeRoy Adams Jr., popular physician to the "poor folks" and recently elected as state senator. With the help of restrictive evidentiary rulings from Judge Hal W. Adams (no kin to the victim), Mrs. McCollum, whose husband, Sam, ran a profitable numbers racket, was convicted of having murdered Dr. Adams in a quarrel over a medical bill. In fact, as the townspeople knew, she had given birth to the doctor's daughter, Loretta, and at the time of the murder she was pregnant again but faced rejection by her white lover who aspired to be Florida's governor. After the conviction, while Ruby McCollum was held incommunicado in the county jail, Alabama-born journalist William Bradford Huie investigated the case, amassing evidence that Dr. Adams had led a secret criminal life behind his facade of public and professional service. The doctor was prosecuted (unsuccessfully) for submitting fraudulent medical service claims for third-party reimbursement, and he had also tried his hand at arson and forgery. The Florida Supreme Court quashed Ruby's conviction on the basis of a procedural irregularity; but before the second trial could begin, the defendant was found to be suffering from a "prison psychosis" rendering her incompetent to mount a defense. She was confined for twenty years in a Florida mental institution.

Although Huie showed unwavering personal devotion to Ruby McCollum's cause, his book suffers from a self-centered narrative style. Ultimately, Ruby, whom he never met, recedes into the background as Huie turns with relish to an account of his own defense against Judge Adams's charge that he had committed criminal contempt by making disparaging remarks about the judge in an out-of-court interview with a prospective witness.

In 1999 Thulani Davis's play *Everybody's Ruby,* based on the McCollum case, was presented by the Public Theater in New York City. In this effective drama, Ruby McCollum's tragedy is developed in counterpoint with another African American woman's misfortune: Zora Neale Hurston's abandonment of her career as an author. Hurston enacts her withdrawal from the world of literature by selling her typewriter to a secondhand goods dealer and surrendering to her friend William Bradford Huie (whom she had brought to Live Oak) the notes she had been making for a book on Ruby's trial.

H.37 Huxley, Aldous   *The Devils of Loudun.* 1952. New York: Harper Torchbooks, 1959.

■ In 1634 the French priest Urbain Grandier was burned at the stake in Loudun for having practiced sorcery and induced the diabolic possession of nuns of the Ursuline convent.

Grandier's penchant for making enemies contributed to his downfall. In 1618, for example, he insisted that as canon of the local church of Sainte-Croix he had a right to walk in a procession ahead of the prior of Coussay, who happened to be the Bishop of Luçon,

Armand-Jean du Plessis (later Cardinal) de Richelieu. Jeanne des Anges, dwarfish and slightly deformed prioress of the house of Ursuline nuns established in Loudun in 1626, resented Grandier's romance with Madeleine de Brou. She became one of the most spectacularly possessed nuns, revealed by exorcism to have been invaded by three hawthorn prickles and a bunch of roses.

Huxley's narrative is enriched by his discussion of religious beliefs of Grandier's era, but he avows a personal willingness to suspend disbelief before the supernatural: "Do devils exist? And, if so, were they present in the bodies of Soeur Jeanne and her fellow nuns? As with the notion of possession, I can see nothing intrinsically absurd or self-contradictory in the notion that there may be nonhuman spirits, good, bad and indifferent."

In an epilogue, however, he attacks manipulation of what he calls "herd-intoxication" in behalf of theology or ideology. He thunders: "Every idol, however exalted, turns out, in the long run, to be a Moloch, hungry for human sacrifice."

In 1961 the Royal Shakespeare Company premiered John Whiting's play *The Devils*, based on Huxley's book. Ken Russell's unbridled film version, with Vanessa Redgrave, was released in 1971.

H.38 ———— "The Gioconda Smile." In *Mortal Coils*. London: Chatto & Windus, 1922.
▪ Although there is critical controversy on the point, this story appears to have been at least partly inspired by the trial of Herbert Rowse Armstrong for the arsenic poisoning of his wife, Katherine, in Hay-on-Wye in 1921. Huxley invents a new killer: a jealous woman serving as the ailing victim's companion.

I

I.1 Ihara Saikaku   *Tales of Japanese Justice*. [Previously translated as *Japanese Trials Under the Shade of a Cherry Tree*, 1689.] Trans. Thomas M. Kondo and Alfred H. Marks. Honolulu: Univ. Press of Hawaii, 1980.
▪ Ihara Saikaku's collection of cases is a variant of Kuei Wan-jung's thirteenth-century classic *Parallel Cases from Under the Pear-Tree* (see K.13). Unlike its Chinese model, however, these forty-four tales are not presented in a series of related pairs. The judge-detective is a Kyoto official known as the Shoshidai, who is referred to in the stories only as "His Lordship." The decisions that he rendered in cases of murder, theft, and fraud as well as civil controversies over real estate, commercial transactions, and inheritances, reflect the jurisprudence of two Shoshidai ministers, Itakura Katsushige and his son, Itakura Shigemune.

Some of the issues faced by Ihara Saikaku's judge seem remarkably close to those of the present day. In "Two Choices: One Good, One Bad," the judge must determine the criminal responsibility of a seven-year-old child who stabbed a nine-year-old companion to death in a street parade. His Lordship announces his intention to have the child choose between a doll and a gold coin; if he selects the coin, he will be proved to have "adult understanding." As the judge had intended, the child's relatives coach him a hundred times to pick the doll. Still, when the critical question is posed to him in court, he takes the coin. His Lordship reaches a surprising but wise decision. Although the youngster had been warned that his life was at stake, he "naively" took the gold coin: "This clearly proves that he is too young to distinguish anything. Is there anything more important than life? The child will be spared."

A form of a lie-detection test is applied in the story "Pulse-Taking Priest Thumps a Thief." A priest feels the pulses of twelve apprentices as they testify about a theft. The guilty person "seemed perfectly calm and his testimony above suspicion, but his pulse was nevertheless unusually rapid, in fact, nearly unable to bear the strain."

Best known as a novelist, Ihara Saikaku (1641–93) included in his masterpiece *Five Women Who Loved Love* (1686) the story of a young girl, Yaoya Osichi, who was burned at the stake for setting a blaze that consumed a large portion of the city of Edo. His tale of Ishikawa Goemon, a notorious robber boiled in a caldron in 1594, appears in *Twenty Cases of Unfilial Children in Japan* (1686).

I.2 Iles, Francis [*See also* Berkeley, Anthony] *Malice Aforethought: The Story of a Commonplace Crime.* New York: Harper, 1931.

■ Iles bases his novel on the 1922 murder trial of Hay-on-Wye solicitor Herbert Rowse Armstrong for the arsenic poisoning of his wife, changing the profession of the killer to physician and the poison to morphia. However, the character of Dr. Edmund Bickleigh (Armstrong) as a meek husband henpecked by his dominant wife, Julia (Katherine Mary Armstrong), follows the tradition surrounding the case.

The novel opens with a tennis party during which Julia humiliates Bickleigh before the assembled neighbors, including several of the flirtatious doctor's lady friends. Iles suggests that the doctor's "wormhood" had its roots in a feeling of inferiority derived from two sources: his small physique and his lowly position as the son of a chemist. To quote Iles: "What stature and upbringing had begun, marriage perfected." Subject to glorious visions to compensate for his daily indignities, the doctor, after the tennis party, begins to dream of "his life without Julia: the freedom, the expansion, the regained self-respect, the losing of that continual dread of what she might say in front of other people."

The grandiosity of Bickleigh's dreams becomes a part of his life when he poisons Julia apparently without detection and decides that he is capable of committing further "perfect murders" in the artistic manner described in Thomas De Quincey's essay, "On Murder Considered as One of the Fine Arts." Dr. Bickleigh muses: "Murder could be a fine art: but it was not for everyone. Murder was a fine art for the superman." Thinking himself capable of homicidal brilliance, the doctor proceeds to plan the death of Madeleine Cranmere Bourne (a lady friend who opted to marry another suitor, Dennis Bourne, even after Julia's death had freed Bickleigh to marry her) and the solicitor William Chatford, who, motivated by retroactive jealousy of Bickleigh's seduction of a woman who later became Chatford's wife, had brought Julia's murder to the attention of Scotland Yard. The doctor's plan to poison the two at a tea party backfires when Madeleine recovers quickly and Chatford does not die. Bickleigh pursues Chatford to his sickbed in an attempt to administer another dose and manages to blunder into the arms of the alerted Scotland Yard detectives. The novel ends ironically with Bickleigh being acquitted of Julia's murder, despite a strong case against him, and then rearrested for the death of Dennis Bourne, who has contracted typhoid fever through no fault of Bickleigh. It was, in fact, Madeleine's "repeated and mean refusals to improve the sanitation" at her residence that caused Dennis to contract the fatal disease, but Bickleigh's blunders as a bacteriologist in the attempted tea-party murders enabled the police to attribute Dennis's death to his "malice aforethought."

I.3 Irving, H[enry] B[rodribb] *A Book of Remarkable Criminals*. London: Cassell, 1918.

■ The twenty-eight-page introduction to this work gives us Irving's most detailed commentary on the allure of criminal cases. He begins with an anecdote he heard from his father, actor Sir Henry Irving. One night Alfred, Lord Tennyson and the philosopher Benjamin Jowett "had talked together well into the small hours of the morning. [Sir Henry Irving] asked Tennyson what was the subject of conversation that had so engrossed them. 'Murders,' replied Tennyson." H. B. Irving adds his own gloss: "It would have been interesting to have heard Tennyson and Jowett discussing such a theme. The fact is a tribute to the interest that crime has for many men of intellect and imagination. Indeed, how could it be otherwise? Rob history and fiction of crime, how tame and colourless would be the residue!"

Reflecting on World War I, "one of the greatest crimes on record," Irving contends that such world leaders as Frederick the Great or Napoleon were in essence no different from private wrongdoers such as Jack Sheppard or Charley Peace. From this premise Irving draws the conclusion: "If this war is to mean anything to posterity, the crime against humanity must be judged in the future by the same rigid standard as the crime against the person."

Irving did not believe that ordinary people differ much from convicted criminals. Pleased that the "comforting theory of the Lombroso school has been exploded," he was persuaded that "the ordinary inmate of our prisons [has been] shown to be only in a very slight degree below the average in mental and physical fitness of the normal man, a difference easily explained by the environment and conditions in which the ordinary criminal is bred." In all our natures, however, he recognizes the existence of an "instinct to destroy which finds comparatively harmless expression in certain forms of taking life, which is at its worst when we fall to taking each other's."

In the investigation of crime, especially on the broader lines of inquiry permitted by Continental procedure, Irving argues that "we can track to the source the springs of conduct and character, and come near to solving as far as is humanly possible the mystery of human motive."

The first of the seven sections of the book is devoted to a leisurely biography of Charles Peace, a nineteenth-century burglar. "In Charley Peace alone," Irving gushes, "is revived that good-humoured popularity which in the seventeenth and eighteenth centuries fell to the lot of Claude Duval, Dick Turpin and Jack Sheppard. But Peace has one grievance against posterity; he has endured one humiliation which these heroes have been spared. His name has been omitted from the pages of the 'Dictionary of National Biography.'"

Peace's favored place in English crime lore probably is due to his late years in London where, like Jekyll and Hyde, he lived a double life. By day he was a church-going, violin-playing seller of musical instruments and an inventor; but when night fell, he returned to his lifelong profession of burglary, for which he had served several prison terms. There is a dark side to this romantic life of crime, for Peace killed two people, Constable Cock, who confronted him at the scene of a burglary, and later a neighbor named Dyson, whose wife Peace had been pursuing. Irving believes that, before his execution for the Dyson murder, Peace sincerely repented; one of the external signs of his reformation was the burglar's intervention on behalf of a man who had been erroneously convicted and transported for the killing of Constable Cock. Irving concludes: "The only interesting criminals are those worthy of something better. Peace was one of these. If his life may be said to point a moral, it is the very simple one that crime is no career for a man of brains."

Irish-born Robert Butler, who was hanged in Brisbane, Australia, in 1905 for the murder of William Munday in the course of a nocturnal street robbery ("The Career of Robert Butler"), struck Irving as possessing some points of resemblance to Charley Peace. Like Peace, Butler was a loner, used a revolver to compensate for his insignificant physique, was something of a musician, and viewed his fellow men with contempt. Irving, however, noted important differences: "Butler was an intellectual, inferior as a craftsman to Peace, the essential practical, unread, naturally gifted artist. Butler was a man of books. He had been schoolmaster, journalist. He had studied the lives of great men, and, as a criminal, had devoted especial attention to those of Frederick the Great and Napoleon."

Butler spent much of his life in prison for burglaries often disguised by arson. He had successfully defended himself on a charge of murdering the Dewar family in Dunedin, New Zealand, and setting their house on fire. Unlike many criminals whose last dying moments are recorded, Butler did not undergo a religious conversion. To a Freethought advocate who visited him in his condemned cell, Butler wrote: "I shall have to find my way across the harbour bar without the aid of any pilot."

In his narrative "M. Derues," Irving suggests that the cunning, snobbish eighteenth-century French grocer who bore that name (more accurately spelled Desrues) may have been the first murderer to have disposed of a victim in a trunk. Aspiring to purchase a provincial estate from a nobleman, Etienne Saint-Faust de Lamotte and his wife, Derues misrepresented himself as high born and well heeled. When he could not pay the amount due under his purchase contract, Derues lured Madame de Lamotte and her young son to Paris. There he orchestrated a hoax to make it appear that he had paid his purchase obligation to the lady and that she had thereupon absconded with a lover. In reality, he had poisoned Madame de Lamotte and transported her body in a trunk to a vacant cellar in a Paris house, where he buried her; he then administered a fatal dose of poison to her son in Versailles. Despite a bold attempt at covering up his crimes, including his impersonation of the deceased Madame de Lamotte at a notary's office in Lyon, Derues saw his scheme quickly unravel. Convicted of the two murders, he was broken on the wheel and thrown alive onto a fire. His wife was imprisoned for participation in his fraud and died in the September massacres during the French Revolution.

A concluding group of articles illustrates what Irving calls "dual crime," in which two persons combine to commit a murder. Irving undertook these studies in the light of a monograph by the Italian advocate Scipio Sighele, translated into French as *Le crime à deux* (Lyon, 1893). Irving observes that the power relationships between the criminal collaborators and their relative commitment to evil may vary. In the case of Michel Eyraud and Gabrielle Bompard, France's famous trunk murderers (see B.60), who are the subject of one of Irving's essays, he concludes that "both man and woman are idle, vicious criminals by instinct. They come together, lead an abandoned life, sinking lower and lower in moral degradation." The young Natalis Gaudry, induced by Jenny Amenaide Brécourt (the "Widow Gras") to ensure a generous admirer's continued enslavement by blinding him with vitriol (Paris, 1877), is not a man of criminal inclinations: "Here a man, brave, honest, of hitherto irreproachable character, is tempted by a woman to commit the most cruel and infamous of crimes. At first he repels the suggestion; at last, when his senses have been excited, his passion inflamed by the cunning of the woman, . . . he yields to the repeated solicitation and does a deed in every way repugnant to his normal character."

Despite the attempt of her famed defender, Charles Lachaud, to throw sole blame on Gaudry, the Widow Gras drew the heavier sentence, fifteen years' imprisonment.

In another 1877 French murder trial recounted by Irving, Léon Vitalis was sentenced to death for stabbing to death with a cheese knife his former mistress, Madame Boyer, after transferring his affections to the seventeen-year-old daughter of the house, convent-educated Marie, who had inherited the family fortune. Marie was sentenced to life imprisonment for her role in the crime, which was followed by dismemberment of Madame Boyer and the burial of her remains near Marseille.

Irving also includes among his studies of "dual crime" the murder of chemist Louis Aubert by Marin Fenayrou and his wife, Gabrielle, the victim's former mistress. Aubert was dispatched with a hammer and sword-stick; his body was found floating in a river, though wrapped in lead piping. The motive remains unclear, since there is a surfeit of choices: the revenge of Marin's marital dishonor or his envy of Aubert's greater business success; the victim's refusal to return Gabrielle's letters; and the possibility that Aubert was privy to dark secrets about the Fenayrou chemist's shop, where Aubert had been employed before going into the trade for his own account. Both of the Fenayrous were sentenced to penal servitude, and Marin's brother, Lucien, who assisted them in the murder, was acquitted.

Irving comments on the women in the last two cases: "There are some women, such as Marie Boyer and Gabrielle Fenayrou, who may be described as passively criminal, chameleon-like, taking colour from their surroundings. By the force of a man's influence they commit a dreadful crime—in the one instance it is matricide, in the other the murder of a former lover—but neither of the women is profoundly vicious or criminal in her instincts.

Henry Brodribb Irving (1870–1919) was the son of the famous actor, Sir Henry Irving. He was educated for the law because his father did his best to discourage Harry (as Henry Brodribb was called) and his younger brother, Laurence, from entering the acting profession. Nevertheless, after his admission to the Bar of the Inner Temple in 1894, Harry gave up law for the stage and ultimately formed his own theater company. He re-created several of his father's melodramas, scoring a notable success in Charles Reade's adaptation of the French true-crime-based thriller *The Lyons Mail*. Hesketh Pearson, in his book *The Last Actor-Managers* (London: Methuen, 1950), is predominantly negative in his appraisal of H. B. Irving's acting career.

Perhaps Irving's more memorable achievements were his essays on criminal cases of England, France, and America. His work profoundly influenced his Scottish successor, William Roughead, but is stylistically far superior. He seasons his straightforward narrative with moderate helpings of witty comment but, unlike Roughead, never lapses into intrusive jocularity.

Irving's biographer, Austin Brereton, in his *"H. B." and Laurence Irving* (Boston: Small Maynard, 1923), expresses strong reservations about H. B.'s devotion to criminology. While impressed by "the immense amount of research" and "his grasp of detail, his ready condensation of facts and his lucid style," Brereton questioned whether anyone benefited from the works and even suggested that Irving's interest in crime might have contributed to his early death: "'H.B'" outwore his physical strength ere he was fifty. Would it have been otherwise if he had not so thoroughly and so constantly pursued such a morbid hobby as the study of murder?"

Irving was the founder of "Our Society," also known as the "Crimes Club," which still meets regularly to hear and discuss papers on famous criminal cases. I had the pleasure of paying a visit to his daughter, Elizabeth, Lady Brunner, at her house, Greys Court, which she and her late husband, Sir Felix, decided to give to the National Trust in 1968. Lady Brunner was happy to learn from our conversation that her father's literary work is not forgotten.

I.4 ——— *Last Studies in Criminology.* London: Collins, 1921.

■ The four essays in this indispensable collection all consider judicial errors. The first three concern famous martyrs of injustice: Adolf Beck, the victim of faulty eyewitness testimony; Joseph Lesurques, often thought to have been mistakenly guillotined because of his fatal resemblance to Dubosc, one of the Lyons mail (Courrier de Lyon) murderers; and Lieutenant Emile Clément de la Roncière, falsely accused by love-struck Marie de Morell of sending her obscene letters and attempting to rape her.

"The Calvary of Peter Vaux" is a poignant review of a less familiar judicial crime, the transportation of a patently innocent man to the prison colony of Cayenne for life. Vaux, a high-principled republican, rose to become mayor of the small village of Longepierre near Verdun. He incurred the wrath of the reactionary party of well-to-do landowners (the "notables") and attracted the political rivalry of a tavern keeper named Gallemard. Truckling to the notables and angered by their rejection of his political and social overtures, Gallemard took his revenge by burning houses belonging to the conservatives and their friends. At the same time he settled his scores against Vaux by procuring his conviction for the arsons. Eventually, Gallemard was arrested and hanged himself in prison. Still, successive French governments refused to review the conviction of Vaux, who died in Cayenne at age fifty-three in 1875. It was not until 1897 that France's Court of

Cassation, which had been granted broader authority to revise criminal judgments, proclaimed his innocence. In Irving's masterly hands, Vaux's ordeal resembles the tale of the Count of Monte Cristo shorn of revenge and a happy ending.

I.5 ———— *Occasional Papers, Dramatic and Historical.* London: Bickers, 1906.
■ This collection of eight essays is divided equally between those relating to the stage and others dealing with crime and law.

In "The True Story of Eugene Aram," Irving succeeds in demythologizing Eugene Aram, Yorkshire schoolmaster and linguistic theorist who murdered a partner in fraud, shoemaker Daniel Clarke (also spelled Clark), in 1744, buried his body in a cave, and was hanged in 1759 after the hiding place of the corpse was belatedly revealed by a confederate. In a manner reminiscent of Oscar Wilde's in "Pen, Pencil and Poison," Irving separates Aram's murder from his academic career rather than presenting him in the romantic guise of scholar-criminal:

> To record as distinct and yet present in the one man the attributes of the thoughtful and gifted scholar and those of the sordid and deliberate murderer must surely yield a more profitable and singular result than the endeavor to blend the two into a sympathetic whole by melting together in the crucible of lachrymose heroism those discrepancies that lie at the very root of character, and everlastingly mock the efforts of the methodical biographer to force consistency upon the inconsistent.

Unlike Thomas Hood and Edward Bulwer Lytton, who created romantic images of Aram (see H.31), Irving rejects the notion that the schoolmaster was "a good man struggling against adversity." He condemns instead the coldness Aram displayed in going to the gallows without a word of apology. "One would be grateful," Irving remarks, "for just some little acknowledgment of human weakness from this consciously irreproachable assassin."

Irving's essay, "The Fall of the House of Goodere," describes a murder worthy of the Grand Guignol. In 1741, spurred by a feud over succession to the family fortune, British naval captain Samuel Goodere abducted his eccentric elder brother Sir John on the streets of Bristol and had him conveyed by barge to the man-of-war *Ruby*, which Samuel commanded. There the captain ordered two crew members, Mahony and White, to strangle him in the purser's cabin. Through a thin partition, Jones, the ship's cooper, heard the death struggle and saw a person's hand on the dead victim's throat. The hand, which Jones described as "whiter than that of a common sailor," belonged to Captain Goodere, who was hanged after trial at Bristol.

In "The Fualdès Case," Irving tackles France's mysterious cause célèbre of 1817, the murder of magistrate Joseph-Bernardin Fualdès at a house of ill repute in Rodez (see B.28). Despite "the intimidation of witnesses, which was practiced to such an outrageous extent by the relatives of the principal criminals" and the "protracted lying" of Clarisse Manson, who sometimes stated that she had been accidentally present at the scene of the crime, Irving accepts the guilt of the convicted leaders of the murder conspiracy, Fualdès's broker

Joseph Jausion and Jausion's brother-in-law, Bernard-Charles Bastide-Gramont, who was the victim's godson.

I.6 ———— *Studies of French Criminals of the Nineteenth Century.* London: Heinemann, 1901.
■ In the preface to this first volume of his crime studies, Irving quotes Edmund Burke's expression of enthusiasm for the study of criminal trials: "The annals of criminal juris-prudence exhibit human nature in a variety of positions, at once the most striking, interesting, and affecting. They present tragedies of real life, often heightened in their effect by the grossness of the injustice, and the malignity of the prejudices which accompanied them. At the same time, real culprits, as original characters, stand forward on the canvas of humanity as prominent objects for our special study."

Irving adds his own comment on the merit of examining French criminal records: "As studies of character, and as examples of the administration of criminal justice in France, they may be of some interest or value to those who look to the human document for speci-mens of human character as it actually is, or for suggestions on which to build some work of fiction."

From the point of view of the student of character, the French system of criminal pro-cedure, in Irving's estimation, possessed one supreme advantage: "At the cost of much that is to our notions trivial and irrelevant, it tells in every trial not only the bare details of the actual crime that is the object of inquiry, but the story of the life of the accused person. By inquisitorial methods, often startling to us, that story is dragged into the light of day, and the criminal confronted in the most poignant fashion, with the whole record of his past."

The criminals considered by Irving include:

- The sociopath Lacenaire, stigmatized by Théophile Gautier as a false poet but a genu-ine murderer (see L.3)
- Jean Baptiste Troppmann, who slaughtered the Kinck family (see B.68)
- Aimé Thomas Barré, failed stock market plunger and shady business broker, and his friend, Paul Lebiez, medical student with a grim interpretation of the Darwinian strug-gle for existence, both guillotined for the murder and robbery of an old woman who sold milk and hoarded her earnings. The murderers were arrested after depositing two parcels, each containing an arm and thigh of their victim, in the cupboard of a rented room; they stuffed the rest of the body (which Lebiez had dismembered) in a port-manteau that they sent out of Paris by train. Irving notes a resemblance of their crime to Raskolnikov's murder of an elderly pawnbroker in *Crime and Punishment* but re-gards their actions as more cold blooded. Lebiez's "extreme application of the Dar-winian hypothesis stood him in good stead as a criminal; it made him coldly insensible to [the] horror of murder." Barré, by contrast, "clutched at crime merely as an expedi-ent for mending his shattered fortunes."
- Three "criminous" abbés: Auriol (see B.55); Boudes; and Bruneau (see B.64). Boudes's case, less well known than the others, is not the least astounding. By the time he stood trial at age sixty, his catalog of crime was long and varied. In 1860 he attempted to murder a priest by poisoning sacred vessels of the church he served as curate. Fifteen

years later, he fatally stabbed a parish priest in his bed. He committed numerous sex offenses against children of both genders and was guilty of thefts, embezzlements, and arsons. For a decade (1876–86) he feigned madness in an asylum, hoping that when he was released his crimes would be barred by limitations periods. In 1889 he was belatedly sentenced to penal servitude for life.

- Three killers whom Irving groups as "adventurers": Michel Campi, Henri Pranzini (see B.38), and the mysterious man who called himself Prado (see B.39). Campi was executed for the 1883 murder of a retired lawyer in his Paris apartment. Although robbery was the apparent motive, the pretrial procedure was delayed by prolonged investigation into the irrelevant question of the killer's identity; Campi had posed as the great "Unknown." In prison he confessed to a priest that there was no terrible secret attaching to his past. Irving concludes with a literary sigh: "And so after all Campi was not a son of Napoleon III, nor a brother of General Boulanger, nor any of the interesting individuals that baffled journalism or fantastic gossip had tried to make him."

- Jeanne Daniloff Weiss, who swallowed a lethal dose of strychnine after being convicted of attempting to poison her husband, an ex-captain in the army, at Ain-Fezza, near Oran, Algeria, in 1890, at the insistence of her lover, engineer Felix Roques. Irving studied the case as an example of crime à deux, concluding that "though Roques was the instigator or chief promoter of the crime, it was the passion which this strange creature [Jeanne] fed in him, the absolute abandonment to him of her body and soul, the entire merging of her independent existence in his, the abdication of her own free will, that made his overwhelming motive and most appropriate instrument for a cruel murder."

- Albert Pel, whose case Irving pairs with that of Euphrasie Mercier, because they both undertook to destroy their victims' bodies by fire. Watchmaker and serial arsenic poisoner, Pel was, in Irving's unforgettable words: "Murderer certainly, thief no less clearly, a man vain and passionate, fond of music and chemistry, with pronounced goitre and tendency to consumption; his face that of a Mephistopheles with the light of hell gone out of it, or of a Don Quixote of the laboratory seeking the philosopher's stone in gold spectacles" (see B.62).

  Charged originally with having administered arsenic to seven women for profit, Pel was convicted, at a second trial, of poisoning, dismembering, and cremating his second wife, Elsie Boehmer, in 1884. The generous jury found extenuating circumstances.

  Euphrasie Mercier installed her brother and two sisters, all afflicted by a religious mania, in the newly acquired residence of Elodie Ménétret, who had hired her as companion and housekeeper. Euphrasie's blackmailing nephew led police to Mlle. Ménétret's charred bones, which lay buried beneath a bed of dahlias. A jury found Euphrasie guilty of murder and of theft of her victim's property but, like Pel's panel, saved her from the guillotine by a finding of extenuating circumstances. Irving comments wryly that "if Pel had chosen as his third wife Euphrasie Mercier, no one could have declared the couple ill-assorted." Euphrasie's murder, reset in England, is the subject of the stage thriller *Ladies in Retirement*, by Reginald Denham and Edward Percy (New York: Random House, 1940).

- Three of France's late-nineteenth-century anarchists: Ravachol, Vaillant, and Emile Henri. The first two have also been studied by Pierre Bouchardon (see B.65).

J

J.1 Jackson, Joseph Henry *The Portable Murder Book.* Ed. Joseph Henry Jackson. New York: Viking, 1945.

■ Jackson culls from the works of eminent crime essayists, including Edmund Pearson, Alexander Woollcott, Celia Thaxter, William Roughead, F. Tennyson Jesse, and H. B. Irving. The governing criterion for selection was the editor's view that "in every good murder, there must be suggested the conflict between good and evil which is at once the final ingredient of effective tragedy and of life itself."

Celia Thaxter's "A Memorable Murder," an imaginative reconstruction, in the manner of Thomas De Quincey, of Louis Wagner's 1873 murder of the Christensens at the Isles of Shoals, blazed the trail for American masters of the true-crime genre. Dorothy Sayers's article, "The Murder of Julia Wallace," also included, pointed the way for Jonathan Goodman's ultimate exculpation of William Herbert Wallace in his wife's murder (see G.23). She suggests that someone "tell the story again, identifying . . . the unknown man whom Wallace himself named as a murderer."

J.2 Jacob, Madeleine *À vous de juger* [For You to Judge]. Paris: Editions Les Yeux Ouverts, 1962.

■ Five studies are included: Gaston Dominici; Pauline Dubuisson, who kept her lovers and her ratings in a "little black book" and who inspired Brigitte Bardot's role in the film *La Verité;* Sylvie Paul, who participated in the 1951 murder of a hotel keeper in the fifteenth arrondissement; Abbé Desnoyers, *curé* of Uruffe, who put a bullet into the back of the neck of his pregnant young mistress (1956); Maître Pierre Jaccoud, head of the Genevan Bar, whose 1960 murder conviction scandalized the Swiss city.

J.3 James, P[hyllis] D[orothy], and T. A. Critchley *The Maul and The Pear Tree: The Ratcliffe Highway Murders 1811.* New York: Mysterious Press, 1986.

■ In this study of London's infamous Ratcliffe Highway murders, crime novelist P. D. James, turning to nonfiction for the first time, joined forces with T. A. Critchley, a police historian with whom she had worked in England's Home Office. Parting company with Thomas De Quincey (see D.21), the authors believe that John Williams "was virtually condemned and his memory vilified on evidence so inadequate, circumstantial and irrelevant that no competent court of law would commit him for trial."

In December 1811 a mysterious assassin, acting alone or with one or more accomplices, butchered seven members of the Dockland households of Timothy Marr, linen draper, and John Williamson, keeper of a pub called the King's Arms. Blunt weapons covered with blood were found on the murder sites, a ship carpenter's mallet (maul) in the Marrs' bedroom, and an iron chisel or bar at the pub; the knife or razor used to cut the victims' throats appeared to have been carried away. John Williams, a sailor whom London prejudices assumed to be Irish, became a prime suspect when the maul was traced to the Pear

Tree, a lodging house where Williams stayed when ashore. While awaiting interrogation by magistrates, Williams hanged himself in his jail cell.

The evidence against the suspect was of dubious strength. All the residents of the Pear Tree had access to the maul, which belonged to the tool collection of an absent German seaman named John Peterson. The authorities and the public comforted themselves that Williams's suicide was itself evidence of guilt, but an earlier suspect named Bailey, a bricklayer's laborer from Norfolk, had hanged himself without a like inference being drawn.

James and Critchley are on firmest ground in demonstrating the inefficiency of the investigation and in arguing that, as far as the case had progressed when Williams took his own life, he could not have been successfully prosecuted. Less persuasive, however, are the authors' efforts to propose an alternative solution to the murder mystery. They argue, without factual support, that further evidence incriminating Williams discovered at the Pear Tree after his death was fabricated and that a sailor, William Ablass, or a carpenter named Cornelius Hart, may have been the Ratcliffe Highway killer. Ablass had been a moving spirit in a mutiny aboard the *Roxburgh Castle* in which Williams had participated, and Hart was working on alterations in the Marrs' shop window immediately prior to the massacres. Whoever is proposed to fit the profile of London's first serial killer, the brutality, scale, and motivelessness of the slayings remain baffling.

Although he had not been tried for the murders, Williams was buried at crossroads like a convict who had "cheated the gallows," and a stake had been driven through his heart.

The Borowitz True Crime Collection owns a print published on January 11, 1812, "The Procession to Interment of John Williams the Wretched Suicide" (Fig. 7).

J.4 Jay, Felix *Sin, Crimes and Retribution in Early Latin America: A Translation and Critique of Sources — Lope de Aguirre, Francisco de Carvajal, Juan Rodriguez Freyle.* Lewiston, N.Y.: Edwin Mellen Press, 1999.

■ The sixteenth- and seventeenth-century Spanish sources assembled and translated by Jay document, often in the words of eyewitnesses, serial killings and other appalling crimes among the conquistadores. Most celebrated among the villains was Lope de Aguirre, the self-styled Wrath of God, who made a bloodbath of Governor Pedro de Ursúa's 1559 Amazonian expedition in search of the golden cities of El Dorado. Aguirre ordered the assassinations of Ursúa and of his successor, Don Fernando Guzmán, and slaughtered soldiers whom he suspected of disaffection or of tepid enthusiasm for his barbarities. When he took command of the expedition, Aguirre declared his rebellion against the Spanish throne and wrote an incredibly insolent letter to King Philip II. After reaching the ocean, he seized the Venezuelan island of Margarita, where his forces plundered the treasury and murdered the governor. After returning to the mainland, Aguirre saw his soldiers melt away. His last crime was the killing of his daughter to prevent her from falling into the hands of captors. Aguirre was executed in 1561. The best of the contemporary accounts of his cruelties was rendered by one of his soldiers, Gonzalo de Zúñiga (born in Seville in 1530), who believed that Aguirre's crimes were partly inspired by class hatred: "Aguirre hated gentlemen and noblemen generally. And so he started to kill them all, but picking out always just one at a time, for he did not dare to kill them all at once."

Lope de Aguirre is the subject of Robert Southey's *Expedition of Orsua, and the Crimes of Aguirre* (1821), and a stunning film directed by Werner Herzog with Klaus Kinski in the title role, *Aguirre: The Wrath of God* (1972).

The second section of Felix Jay's volume, "The Demon of the Andes," is devoted to Francisco de Carvajal, who, in Felix Jay's opinion, "shares with Lope de Aguirre the doubtful privilege of being the most atrocious killer in Peru"; his butcheries in the service of a usurper, Gonzalo Pizarro, claimed him the name "Demon of the Andes." Both he and his master were executed in 1548. His treacherous nature is illuminated by his treatment of a friend, Francisco Hurtado. He released Hurtado from jail in fulfillment of the obligations of friendship and then ordered his execution in performance of his duties as a servant of Gonzalo Pizarro.

The concluding portion of the collection is a group of stories of murder, witchcraft, and theft from Juan Rodriguez Freyle's seventeenth-century chronicles of Bogotá, Colombia.

J.5 Jenkins, Elizabeth *Dr. Gully's Story*. New York: Coward, McCann & Geoghegan, 1972. ■ Novelist and biographer Jenkins acquired an unsurpassed familiarity with the details of the puzzling 1876 death of Charles Bravo at Balham (near London) of antimony poisoning. An inquest concluded that the death was due to intentional poisoning rather than suicide, but nobody was brought to trial. Crime historians have proposed three candidates for the murderer's mantle: Florence Ricardo Bravo, the victim's bride of several months, who might have wished to rid herself of an unwanted husband; Mrs. Jane Cox, Florence's enigmatic companion and overseer of the household staff; and Dr. James Manby Gully, eminent neuropath and physician to such luminaries as Tennyson and Carlyle. While Florence (then twenty-five) was still the wife of her first husband, alcoholic and abusive Captain Alexander Ricardo, Gully, at age sixty-two, embarked on an affair with her after she initially consulted him to cure her dependence on chloral to overcome insomnia.

Jenkins recounts the case from the viewpoint of Dr. Gully, whom she absolves from responsibility for the death of Charles Bravo, Florence's second husband. The theory espoused in the novel is that Florence added antimony to the water bottle on her husband's washstand; that her purpose was to render him sufficiently ill to interrupt, at least temporarily, his demand that she return to his bed after two recent miscarriages; and that, under the influence of her excessive drinking, she had unintentionally given him a lethal dose of the poison.

Jenkins has convincingly re-created the social background of the Bravo murder case, imagining with particular vividness the oppressive atmosphere of the wealthy Victorian household. Sympathetic to the romance of Florence Ricardo Bravo with Dr. Gully, the novelist demonstrates the complications in carrying on such an affair under the eyes of a large and Argus-eyed domestic staff. In Jenkins's view, the ill-starred lovers became estranged due to Florence's alcoholism, their ostracism by society, her pregnancy and abortion, the difference in their ages and interests, and the intrusion of Mrs. Cox.

At the inquest, Mrs. Bravo's attempt to maintain the facade of respectability was thwarted by the testimony of Mrs. Cox and other servants. The inquest scandalized the public and ruined the reputations of the three principal figures involved, but particularly that of Dr. Gully, who had the most to lose because of the high esteem in which he had been held.

J.6 ———— *Harriet.* Garden City: Doubleday Doran, 1934.

■ This probing novel studies the 1876 murder of Harriet Staunton (here renamed Harriet Oman) in Penge, England, as it slowly developed from neglect to abuse, starvation, and attempted cover-up. She analyzes the motives of four attractive young people, the Staunton brothers, Louis and Patrick (whom Jenkins calls Lewis and Patrick Oman); Patrick's wife, Elizabeth; and her sister, Alice (whose family name, actually Rhodes, is altered by Jenkins to Hoppner). Perhaps, the novelist suggests, none of the malefactors had a criminal design at the outset.

Lewis, the dashing adventurer who married the mentally retarded Harriet for her money, exiled his wife and their young child to the household of his adoring brother Patrick on the payment of a pound a week for room and board. Patrick's wife, Elizabeth, who found it difficult to manage the family's meager finances, was eager to have the payment. It was her sister, Alice, who lived with Lewis as his "wife" after Harriet and child had moved to Patrick's house. Elizabeth began to look forward to her sister's legitimizing her relationship with Lewis, an event that could only occur with the death of Harriet. As time went on, Patrick and Elizabeth became more abusive to Harriet, whom they imprisoned and starved to death. Alice was of like mind with Elizabeth, looking forward to the inheritance that would be secured once Lewis was free to marry her as Harriet's widower; but, less directly involved in the mistreatment of their weak-minded prey, she escaped the law's reckoning. Jenkins, however, is less merciful than the Crown in her assessment of Alice's role. She describes Alice's despair when her suitor Lewis chooses to marry Harriet and her immediate acquiescence in becoming his mistress. Jenkins points to Alice's love of clothing and suggests that she stole Harriet's finery and jewels left in Lewis's house after Harriet was moved with only inadequate possessions to Patrick's residence.

J.7 ———— *Six Criminal Women.* London: Sampson Low Marston, 1949.

■ Elizabeth Jenkins's *Six Criminal Women* treats a variety of female criminals: Madame Rachel, the nefarious victorian cosmetologist; Alice Perrers, a greedy mistress of Edward III; the seventeenth-century forger Lady Ivie; the beautiful poisoner Lady Frances Howard, later Countess of Somerset, who murdered Sir Thomas Overbury in the Tower of London; the eighteenth-century pickpocket Jane Webb; and the mysterious Florence Bravo, who escaped prosecution for the poisoning of her husband, Charles.

Although all these malefactors, except Lady Ivie, have been studied at length in earlier works acknowledged in her Foreword, Jenkins brings original perceptions to bear on these astounding women. She focuses, for example, on Madame Rachel's methods of advertising cosmetics, quoting from *Beautiful for Ever*, the 1863 pamphlet she calls "one of the earliest masterpieces of modern advertising." She also describes Madame Rachel's "Arabian bath," a beauty treatment that featured the costly "Jordan water" from the distant East, which turned out, like her other preparations, to come "from the pump in the back yard." Madame Rachel's heartless exploitation of the aging beauty Mrs. Borrodaile reveals her skill in perpetrating a confidence racket. Jenkins likens the pathetic victim, whom the London *Times* called a "senescent Sappho," to "the deluded elderly woman who pursued men . . . in W. S. Gilbert's operas."

In her charming essay on Jane Webb, the eighteenth-century English pickpocket better known as Jenny Diver, the nickname that she sports in *The Three Penny Opera*, Jenkins highlights the fact that her criminal dexterity was forecast in childhood when, at the age of ten, she was "reckoned an extraordinary workwoman with her needle." Jenkins remarks, "In Jenny's case it was an accomplishment that boded ill for the rest of society."

Unlike her novel *Dr. Gully's Story*, which attributes the murder of Charles Bravo to his wife, Florence, Jenkins's earlier study of the case in this volume follows Sir John Hall's identification of Jane Cox, the housekeeper, as the probable poisoner. The murder motive suggested here was "to maintain her [Mrs. Cox's] own security and that of her children." She seemed to face a serious threat to her position in the household, since Charles Bravo, keen on retrenchment, had estimated that Mrs. Cox was costing him 400 pounds, the total expense of keeping a pair of horses.

J.8 Jesse, F[ryniwyd] Tennyson *Comments on Cain.* London: William Heinnemann, 1948.
■ This volume presents a trio of murder trials Jesse attended in the United States, England, and France. In a preface devoted to the divergent histories of the criminal justice systems in these countries, Jesse sometimes displays a coarsening of sensibility, remarking, for example, that "though a great many women would be the better for being raped, and a great many people would be better dead, nobody can be allowed to go round raping and killing, even from the most altruistic motives." Fortunately, however, the essays that follow are much better.

Jesse was overwhelmed by contrasts and surprises in Pasadena, California, where the city housing the Huntington Library was also the scene of a sordid "penthouse" shooting above a florist's shop. The defendant was the shop's proprietary, drink-sodden Harold Wolcott (whom the defense called the "Boy Harold" and the prosecution preferred to name the "Man Wolcott"); and the victim was Wolcott's long-time mistress, Helen Bendowski. All the participants in the trial defeated Jesse's expectations. The prosecutor was fairer than her prejudices led her to anticipate. The judge scandalized the Englishwoman when, at the moment when the jury was to return with its verdict, he entered the no-smoking courtroom with a lighted cigar in his mouth, "stopped at counsels' table and stood there for a moment or two talking with counsel for the defense." The greatest shock, however, was registered by the jury, which, in finding Wolcott guilty of manslaughter, rendered what in Jesse's view was "the only verdict which the circumstances did not warrant."

Jesse's account of the 1933 murder of senile James Pullen, of Bath, by his impatient son-in-law, Reginald Ivor Hinks, is one of the author's most scintillating. Hinks, first known to law enforcement as a petty thief who victimized susceptible women, set the stage for Pullen's death on November 30 when he called the fire brigade to his home, falsely claiming that his father-in-law had collapsed in a bathtub. On the following evening he cried emergency once again, reporting that Pullen had committed suicide by placing his head inside a gas stove. Hinks's scheme was exploded by evidence that a bruise on the back of the old man's head must have been caused before death, because the blood in the bruise did not show the symptoms of carbon-gas poisoning as did the blood in the rest of the body. A strange feature of the case was that the murder had long been foreseen by the people and police of Bath, but that they could do nothing to prevent it. Jesse comments: "At least twice, and probably more often, Reginald Ivor had attempted the death of his father-in-law. It was the crime that everyone foresaw but which under English law no one could prevent. It is not criminal to dress an old man and send him to wander out in the highways and byways, although naturally in a very old man suffering from senile decay it may be a dangerous proceeding." In keeping with "his vanity and his egotistical optimism," Hinks maintained his innocence until hanged.

The final essay is Jesse's eyewitness account of the Versailles trial of serial killer Eugene Weidmann, which Jesse covered for the *Daily Mail* (see c.34).

Fryn Tennyson Jesse (1881–1958) was a grandniece of Alfred, Lord Tennyson (himself a great fancier of criminal annals). She took up journalism and, during World War I, reported from France's battle areas. Becoming a versatile author, she wrote novels (including *The Lacquer Lady* [1929] and *A Pin to See the Peepshow* [1934]), short stories (for example, *The Solange Stories* [1931]), and poems and essays, and her plays were produced in the West End. She became the first woman to edit a volume (*Madeleine Smith* [1927]) for the *Notable British Trials* and, in all, edited six trials in that series (her final work being *Evans and Christie* [1957]). She also published two collections of essays on murder, *Murder and Its Motives* (1924) and *Comments on Cain* (1948).

See Joanna Colenbrander, *A Portrait of Fryn: A Biography of F. Tennyson Jesse* (London: André Deutsch, 1984).

J.9 ———— *Murder and Its Motives.* New York: Knopf, 1924.
■ Following an Introduction, "The Classification of Motives," Jesse studies six criminals in separate chapters exemplifying the workings of the respective motives she has identified:

- Murder for Gain: William Palmer
- Murder for Revenge: Constance Kent
- Murder for Elimination: the De Quérangals
- Murder for Jealousy: Mrs. Pearcey
- Murder for Lust of Killing: Neill Cream
- Murder from Conviction: Orsini

Jesse's introduction remains a discerning overview of the lessons to be learned from crime studies. She begins by justly appraising the frequent unreasonableness of the murderer's calculations: "Murder is the most curious of all the phenomena, because it is the one which shows the most distorted point of view in the perpetrator. There are many crimes which can be said to be worth while, in which the gamble is not out of all proportion, just as there are many vices in which the devotee is at least repaid with a pleasure which he can find commensurate to the risks. But even apart from the fact that in murder a man is staking all he has to throw, he generally stakes it for a ridiculously small reward."

However, some of Jesse's observations, once piquant, may appear merely quaint when judged in light of the rise in multiple and random killings. For example, little credibility now attaches to Jesse's concept of the "murderee," a term she coined to describe "a race of human beings who lay themselves out to be murdered." When she considered trunk murders, Jesse speculated about the traits that made one "trunkable" and quoted her hairdresser's remark: "What I always say is: *You'll never find a nice girl in a trunk.*" As our generation is more likely than hers to repeat the bromide, "We are all murderers," so we are inclined to believe that we are all "trunkable."

The six classes of Jesse's murder motives no longer seem to account for all modern killings. Without pretension to comprehensiveness, at least five other categories can be proposed:

- Murder for self-aggrandizement or self-glorification. This grouping would include killers obsessed with the notion of the "perfect crime," such as Leopold and Loeb and the French high-school killers of schoolmate Alain Guyader (see B.24). Their ancient Greek paradigm is Herostratus, who burned the Temple of Ephesus to gain eternal fame (see S.5).
- The copycat crime
- Murders out of hatred directed against an individual or group
- Murder committed out of a desire for arrest and punishment, a motive recognized by Charles Dickens (see B.30)
- *Folie à deux*, the pathological interaction of two personalities, neither of which would likely have spawned a murder in isolation

J.10 ———— *A Pin to See the Peepshow.* Garden City: Doubleday, Doran, 1934.

■ This novel, woven from the tragic Thompson-Bywaters murder case (see B.78), suggests that Edith Thompson was a victim of her own imagination and of her need to sustain her love affair with Bywaters as an escape from a failed marriage and a dreary middle-class life. The title refers to a fateful encounter between domineering, fantasy-prone Julia Almond (Thompson), then sixteen, with a nine-year old student Leonard Carr (Bywaters), whom she was minding as a stand-in for her teacher. Leonard demanded a pin as the price for her looking into his peepshow box in which he had created an "amazingly real and utterly unearthly" winter scene. Many years later, Julia (then married to the incompatible Herbert Starling) carries on a romance with Leonard Carr that is a similar mixture of reality and dream. Prior to her execution the prison's medical officer, Dr. Ogilvie, muses on Julia's fate, seeing her as a woman "at the mercy of her imagination and her body"; few people realized that "body and mind were two separate entities that had to be reconciled, enemies that had to learn how to come to terms, lovers that could not exist without the other." Doubtless speaking for Jesse, Dr. Ogilvie also speculates that Julia's romance would not have had a tragic outcome had she been either higher or lower in the social scale; the age difference between her and her lover also told against her.

J.11 Johnston, Denis *Murder Hath No Tongue.* [Alternatively titled *The Glass Murder.*] In *The Dramatic Works of Denis Johnston.* Vol. 3. Gerrards Cross, Buckinghamshire: Colin Smythe, 1992.

■ This television play, reflecting 1963 broadcast revisions by producer Peter Collinson to Johnston's script, is based on the murder of bank clerk William Glass in Newtownstewart, County Tyrone, in 1871. Anticipating the coup of Agatha Christie in a famous stage work, the real-life killer (who struck his victim on bank premises in the heart of a busy town) was a police inspector assigned to the case. Collinson's deft retouchings heighten the suspense of this courtroom drama: until the last few pages the identity of the defendant, T. H. Montgomery (who ultimately confesses his crime inspired by desperate financial straits), is visually and verbally withheld. In his original version, Johnston had placed his dramatic emphasis elsewhere, showing how a guilty man was convicted on the basis of erroneous evidence. For an account of the Montgomery case, see Charles Kingston, "Inspector Montgomery's Crime," in *Rogues and Adventuresses* (London: John Lane Bodley Head, 1928), 194–216.

J.12 —— *Strange Occurrence on Ireland's Eye.* In *Collected Plays of Denis Johnston.* Vol. 2. London: Jonathan Cape, 1960.

■ In 1852, artist William Burke Kirwan was convicted of murdering his wife while she was swimming off Ireland's Eye, an island lying off the coast of County Dublin near Howth. The cause of death was far from clear; the prosecution speculated about death by smothering or forcible drowning while the defense theorized that Mrs. Kirwan had suffered an epileptic fit. The verdict was probably based, to a significant extent, on defendant Kirwan's personal character and behavior: he had fathered seven children with his mistress, Teresa Kenny, whom he maintained in a separate domicile in Sandymount. He had been heard to quarrel with Mrs. Kirwan shortly before her demise and did not seem unduly concerned about her disappearance when a boat came to Ireland's Eye to return them to the mainland after their day's expedition. Johnston stacks the deck in favor of Kirwan by moving the action to 1937, when focusing on adultery as an automatic motive for murder might seem less reasonable. He also weakens the inference of guilt by reducing the scope of Kirwan's marital betrayal; in the play Teresa had only one pregnancy, terminated two years in the past at Mrs. Kirwan's insistence.

In William Roughead's classic account of the Kirwan case, one suspects that the author, while professing neutrality, believed in the justice of the verdict (see William Roughead, "The Secret of Ireland's Eye: A Detective Story," in *The Fatal Countess and Other Studies* [Edinburgh: Green, 1924], 185–224). Kirwan's death sentence was commuted to imprisonment on Spike Island in Queenstown harbor; after twenty-four years' penal servitude, he ended his days in America.

J.13 Jones, Ann   *Women Who Kill.* New York: Holt, Rinehart & Winston, 1980.

■ This often-illuminating work shows how the legal issues faced by women on trial for murder have been distorted, either in favor of their defense or to its detriment, by irrelevant gender considerations. Of Lizzie Borden's acquittal, Jones writes: "That a woman should kill her father, to whom she was attached even in a pre-Freudian era by so many Freudian strings, was simply *unthinkable.*"

Yet Alice Crimmins, estranged housewife convicted of manslaughter and then of murder in two successive trials for the killing of her two small children in 1965, was, in Jones's view, a "prisoner of sexual politics." The women's movement was just coming into existence, and Crimmins's energetic sexuality presented a threatening image of a housewife out of control.

J.14 Joyce, James   *Ulysses.* New York: Random House, 1934.

■ In her soliloquy, Molly Bloom ponders the controversial Victorian murder case of American Florence Maybrick (see s.21), imprisoned after being convicted of poisoning her British husband James, an arsenic addict:

> take that Mrs. Maybrick that poisoned her husband for what I wonder in love with some other man yes it was found out on her wasnt she the downright villian to go and do a thing like that of course some men can be dreadfully aggravating drive you mad and always the worst word in the world what do they ask us to marry them for if were so bad as all that comes to yes because they cant get on without us white Arsenic she put in his tea off flypaper wasnt it I wonder why they call it that if I asked him hed say its from the Greek leave us as wise as we were before she must have been madly in love with the other fellow to run the chance of being hanged O she didnt care if that was her nature what could she do besides theyre not brutes enough to go and hang a woman surely are they

K

K.1 Kasserman, David Richard   *Fall River Outrage: Life, Murder, and Justice in Early Industrial New England.* Philadelphia: Univ. of Pennsylvania Press, 1986.

■ On December 21, 1832, the corpse of Sarah Maria Cornell was found hanging from a cord attached to a pole supporting the roof of a haystack on a farm in Tiverton, Rhode Island, near Fall River, Massachusetts; the cord was knotted around the victim's neck by a clove hitch. A pregnant cotton mill worker from Fall River, Cornell had left her home on the day before for a rendezvous, placing in a band box the note: "If I should be missing enquire of the Rev. Mr. Avery of Bristol he will know where I am." Ephraim K. Avery, a minister of the

Methodist Episcopal Church in Bristol, Rhode Island, had secured her expulsion from the Methodist "meeting" of Lowell, Massachusetts, in 1830 after her confession of sexual improprieties, but he had seen her more recently at a camp meeting at Thompson, Connecticut, where Cornell claimed he had seduced and impregnated her. In a sensational trial, Avery was acquitted of Cornell's murder. Disgraced and hounded by an unforgiving public, the minister gave up his pulpit and fled to Lorain County, Ohio, where he found a more tranquil life as a farmer.

Professor Kasserman's interest in the Avery case grew out of his research on the American cotton industry. His book views the trial as a struggle between the cotton mill interests of Fall River and the Methodist Church. The mill entrepreneurs rallied to the cause of Cornell, one of their employees, but battled even more ardently in their own behalf, anxious to show that women laborers were safe in mill towns and that "factory life did not impede their workers' moral development." With equal fervor, the Methodist leadership defended their brother Avery and, in so doing, stirred the prejudices of other denominations that viewed Methodism as antidemocratic, unhealthily emotional, and a close kin of Masonry. Both the mill owners (who aided the prosecution through a vigilante group called the Fall River Committee) and their Methodist adversaries accused the other side of manipulating and intimidating witnesses.

Although Kasserman does not express an opinion on Avery's guilt or innocence, he is clearly impressed by the weight of circumstantial evidence that linked Avery to the correspondence establishing the rendezvous at which Cornell met her death and that placed him in the vicinity of Fall River at the time of the murder. The theory espoused by the defense that Cornell committed suicide in revenge for Avery's persecution does not appear persuasive.

Popular theater works of 1833 did not disguise their authors' views that Avery was guilty. Kasserman cites two examples in his final chapter, "Public Justice": *The Factory Girl: or, The Fall River Murder* (Newport); and *The Fall River Murder* (Richmond Hill, N.Y.). However, Raymond Paul's novel *The Tragedy at Tiverton* (1984) names a different murderer.

K.2 Kaufman, Moises *Gross Indecency: The Three Trials of Oscar Wilde.* New York: Vintage, 1998.

■ This play brilliantly renders the mixture of sublime and sordid to be found in the three trials of Oscar Wilde (his prosecution of the Marquess of Queensberry for criminal libel followed by Wilde's two trials for sexual indecency, the latter resulting in the playwright's conviction and imprisonment). The trials and contemporary responses are presented through the voices of barristers, witnesses, and many other men, including Lord Alfred Douglas, Frank Harris, and George Bernard Shaw; Queen Victoria, in a brief appearance, is gratuitously ridiculed. A highlight of the drama is an interview with Wilde scholar Marvin Taylor at the beginning of Act 2. Speaking in a hesitant academic manner, Taylor propounds the fascinating, if debatable, thesis that Wilde may not have considered himself a homosexual because it was only after his trials that "people began identifying themselves as a specific type of person based on their attraction to people of the same sex."

K.3 Kennedy, Ludovic *Ten Rillington Place.* New York: Simon & Schuster, 1961.

■ At this infamous address in Notting Hill lived two men whose names would be forever linked in crime history: feeble-minded Timothy Evans; John Reginald Halliday Christie, a World War II reserve policeman with a record of prison sentences for theft, fraud, and battery. In 1949 the strangled bodies of Evans's wife, Beryl, and his fourteen-month-old daughter, Geraldine, were found in the Rillington Place wash house. Evans confessed to both murders but was tried only for killing Geraldine; he was convicted, partly on the basis of Christie's testimony, and hanged in 1950.

In 1953, a tenant of the ground-floor apartment previously occupied by Christie discovered three female bodies in a kitchen closet that had been covered by wallpaper. The police found the body of Christie's wife, Ethel, also strangled, under the floor of the front room of the flat and two more female corpses buried in the garden. The five victims apart from Ethel were identified as three prostitutes—Rita Nelson, Kathleen Maloney, and Hectorina McLennan, all found in the kitchen closet—and interred in the garden were Ruth Fuerst, an Austrian girl, and Muriel Eady, a fellow employee of Christie. In a statement, Christie admitted that his standard procedure in the killing of the prostitutes was to lure them to his apartment, where he gassed them from a concealed pipe before strangling and raping them. Christie was hanged for the murder of his wife in 1953.

Ludovic Kennedy, who has a strong penchant for revisionism, argued in *Ten Rillington Place* that it is beyond belief for a single London house to shelter two stranglers and that Christie was responsible for the two murders with which Evans had been charged. Kennedy theorizes that Beryl Evans wanted to terminate her pregnancy and that Christie offered to abort the fetus as a pretext for a sexual assault and strangulation. Kennedy is highly critical of the police and of John Scott Henderson QC, the Recorder of Portsmouth, who reported to Parliament on the day of Christie's hanging that Evans had murdered both his wife and daughter. A second inquiry, headed by a High Court judge, Sir Daniel Brabin QC, was launched in 1965, four years after the appearance of Kennedy's book; Brabin concluded that Evans had probably strangled his wife but that Christie was the more likely of the two to have killed little Geraldine. Since Evans had been convicted only of murdering his daughter, he received a posthumous pardon.

John Eddowes, in *The Two Killers of Rillington Place* (London: Little Brown, 1994), attacked Kennedy in unusually blunt terms for factual inaccuracies and for slanting his presentation of the case in a direction supporting his thesis. Eddowes is persuaded that the police investigators who believed Evans guilty of killing both wife and child were fully justified in taking that view. Remarkably, John Eddowes, in reaching this conclusion, rejects the position taken by his father, Michael Eddowes, in *The Man on Your Conscience* (London: Cassell, 1955).

K.4 Kertzer, David I. *The Kidnapping of Edgardo Mortara.* New York: Knopf, 1997.

■ American historian Kertzer's study of the 1858 kidnapping of Edgardo Mortara and its aftermath is powerful and impeccably researched. On the orders of the Inquisitor, Papal police forcibly took six-year-old Edgardo from his Jewish parents in Bologna because their

Christian maid, fearing the child would die of an illness, had clandestinely baptized him. The Inquisitor had ruled that the boy had become a Catholic and could not be raised in a Jewish household. Despite the family's appeal to Pope Pius IX and international controversy, Edgardo was never returned to his family. He became a Catholic priest under the name Father Pio Edgardo; in 1940 he died in Belgium at age eighty-eight.

Law professor Steven Lubet, in his favorable review of Kertzer's book, argues that the Mortara kidnapping is a cautionary tale that should be considered by those who advocate exclusive reliance on the "child's best interest" standard in adoption and custody cases ("Judicial Kidnapping, Then and Now: The Case of Edgardo Mortara," 93 *Northwestern University Law Review* [1999], 961–75).

K.5 Kessel, Joseph *Stavisky: L'Homme que j'ai connu* [Stavisky: The Man I Knew]. Paris: Gallimard, 1974.

■ In 1934, novelist, travel writer, and journalist Joseph Kessel sketched his recollections of Serge Stavisky, whom he met shortly before the archswindler's downfall and apparent suicide (see M.37). Kessel portrays his notorious friend as capable of acts of disinterested friendship, recalling his willingness to invest in a magazine that the author and his brother Georges had briefly planned to found. It appears, however, that the young writer failed to consider that he may have been caught in the vast web Stavisky was spinning to catch personalities with actual or potential power or influence. In Kessel's view, Stavisky (then masquerading as M. Alexandre) was living out a self-deluding dream that, while his feet were firmly planted in the underworld, he would usher in a new order as Europe's financial savior.

A touching detail in Kessel's reminiscences is the absolute assurance of the Hotel Claridge's staff that their popular guest Stavisky would not return after his sudden departure in December 1933: they noted that he had packed photographs of his children, to whom he was strongly attached.

K.6 Kesselman, Wendy *My Sister in This House.* Garden City: Nelson Doubleday, 1982.

■ This play is based on the 1933 murder of Madame Lancelin and her daughter in Le Mans, France, by their cook and housemaid, Christine Papin, and her younger sister Léa (see F.15). Unlike Jean Genet's more surrealistic rendering of this crime, *The Maids* (see G.8), Kesselman's drama reproduces from the trial record many details of Madame Lancelin's domestic tyranny. The demanding employer (renamed Madame Danzard by Kesselman) used a pair of white gloves to detect traces of dust overlooked by the maids and forced Léa to her knees to pick up a scrap of paper (which, in the play, becomes a chocolate wrapper discarded by Madame Danzard's idle daughter, Isabelle, and flicked onto the rug by Madame to humiliate her servant). Denied any recognition of their humanity and huddled together in a single attic bed, Kesselman's maids become increasingly dependent on each other for emotional support and initiate a lesbian relationship. As Christine Papin maintained in her defense, the external circumstance triggering the murders in the play is the short-circuiting of an electric iron for which Christine feared she and her sister would be blamed. Kesselman, however, probes for a more devastating threat to the maids' fragile universe. In her recreation of the final catastrophe, Madame Danzard and Isabelle, angered by the "ruined" iron, allude to the girls' lesbianism and vow that the sisters will never again find employment together. The murderous attacks follow.

In 1995 Kesselman's play was adapted as a film entitled *Sister My Sister*.

K.7 Kingsley, Charles *Hypatia: or, New Foes with an Old Face*. London: Dent, n.d.

■ Hypatia, a neo-Platonic philopher and teacher in Alexandria, Egypt, was stripped naked and murdered with oyster shells by a Christian mob in 415 A.D. because of her relationship with Orestes, the pagan prefect of the city. Kingsley's first historical novel, devoted to the life and death of this eminent female intellectual, weaves an exotic tale of an ancient city torn by strife among Christians, Jews, and pagans. In his final chapter, Kingsley sermonizes that, from the violence that encompassed Hypatia's death, "the Church of Alexandria received a deadly wound." Philosophers, according to the author, fared no better: "Twenty years after Hypatia's death, philosophy was flickering down to the very socket. Hypatia's murder was its deathblow. In language tremendous and unmistakable, philosophers had been informed that mankind had done with them; that they had been weighed in the balances, and found wanting; that if they had no better gospel than that to preach, they must make way for those who had."

Tennyson objected that he "really was hurt at having Hypatia stripd at her death," but he should have addressed this complaint not to Kingsley but to history, which had visited this indignity on the real Hypatia (see Susan Chitty, *The Beast and the Monk: A Life of Charles Kingsley* [New York: Mason/Charter, 1974], 154).

K.8 Kleist, Henrich von "Michael Kohlhaas." 1810. In *The Marquise of O, and Other Stories*. Trans. Martin Greenberg. Preface by Thomas Mann. New York: Criterion, 1960.

■ Regarded as Kleist's prose masterpiece, this novella is based on the criminal career of sixteenth-century German rebel Hans Kohlhase, executed for a campaign of terror motivated by outrage over his failure to obtain justice for a nobleman's seizure and mistreatment of his horses. Kleist moves the reader by economical and objective narration of horrifying events; he minimizes the use of direct discourse and eschews authorial intervention or other overt appeals for emotional response. Michael Kohlhaas is the pattern for Coalhouse Walker in E. L. Doctorow's *Ragtime* (see D.31).

K.9 Koltès, Bernard-Marie *Roberto Zucco*. In *Bernard-Marie Koltès, Plays: I*. Ed. David Bradby. London: Methuen Drama, 1997.

■ The character of French playwright Koltès's antihero is based on a serial killer, Roberto Succo, who was given a life sentence in Italy in 1981 for the murder of both his parents. After five years he was paroled and committed other crimes, including the murder of a police inspector. As the result of a tip from a woman, he was recaptured. While in a Treviso prison, Succo managed to escape to the roof from which he threw tiles at a crowd assembled below until he was overpowered. Shortly after being returned to custody, he committed suicide.

Koltès became interested in Succo in 1998 after seeing a "wanted" poster of the fugitive criminal on a metro. The dramatist was struck by the fact that the poster showed many portraits of Succo, each of which "was so different from the others that you had to look several times before you could be sure that it was the same person." This firsthand impression of the "transparency" of the serial killer is reflected in Scene 6 of the play, in which an Old Gentleman sitting next to Zucco on a bench in a metro station fails to recognize him, even though a wanted poster of the criminal is pasted on the wall above them. The forces of the law are themselves baffled by the causes of apparently motiveless killing. In Scene 1, one prison officer attributes the phenomenon to "sheer evil," while another locates the aggressive impulse in male sexuality. Zucco, though, explains his actions by an inability to perceive the victims' reality: "I don't have enemies and I never attack. If I crush other living creatures it's not because I'm evil but because I step on them without seeing them."

K.10 Kraus, Karl *Sittlichkeit und Kriminalität* [Morality and Criminality]. 1908. Vienna: Press of "Die Fackel" [The Torch], 1923.

■ The Austrian satirist and critic Karl Kraus (1874–1936) was encouraged by his friend, Ludwig Ritter von Janikowsky, to collect in this volume the best of Kraus's social commentaries from the pages of his periodical, *Die Fackel*. A central theme of the book, announced in the title essay, is that criminal justice should not intrude into matters of personal and, more specifically, sexual morality. Illustrating the essay's argument by reference to a sensational prosecution for adultery, Kraus asserts: "In the eternal realm of sex drives, which are older than the impulse towards hypocrisy, the lawgiver will always bungle to no avail."

In trenchant commentaries on criminal cases in the first years of the twentieth century, Kraus reflects examples of what he calls "sexual justice" and other inequities of the Austrian courts, which favored male over female, libertine over prostitute, old over young, Christian over Jew, and officials over just about anyone else. Among the victims of inhumane prosecutions attacked by Kraus are:

- Twenty-three-year-old Anton Krafft, sentenced to life imprisonment because poverty and drink impelled him to attempt snatching a woman's purse on the Ringstrasse
- Frau Hervay, a Jewish woman despised by a public that believed she was responsible for the suicide of her husband, a district's chief officer, because she had failed to disclose her immoral past. To appease the community's outrage, a flimsy prosecution for bigamy (which Kraus likens to a witch trial) was mounted against Frau Hervay.
- Franziska Klein, charged with murder in the course of robbery. In the absence of strong proof to support its case, the prosecution introduced evidence of Frau Klein's penchant for lovers and money. Kraus comments wryly: "It is the lot of women to 'fall,' and the lot of prosecutors to make their careers."
- Frau Rutthofer, whose claim of self-defense in the murder of her abusive husband, a regional councillor, was treated with derision in court and by the press. The prosecution

accused her of having led a life "not free from reproach" and of having written spicy verses. After a parade of officials testified to the dead man's respectability, the accused cried out, "I am sorry that nobody saw him when he lost his temper. At nightime we never had any witnesses."

In the course of the book, Kraus is critical of Maximilian Harden (see H.12), a writer he had once admired but now regarded as a polemicist insufficiently respectful of his opponents' rights to privacy. In an essay on Harden included in his 1910 collection, *The Wall of China*, Kraus concurred with Oscar Wilde's aphorism, "That a man's a poisoner is nothing against his prose." Unwilling to concede that the converse of Wilde's proposition held true, Kraus added: "A man's prose, however, can prove that he is a murderer."

K.11 Kuan Han-ching *Selected Plays of Kuan Han-ching.* Peking: Foreign Languages Press, 1958.

▪ Courtroom dramas were much in vogue during the Yüan dynasty of the thirteenth and fourteenth centuries. Kuan Han-ching, one of the most prolific dramatists of the period, devoted two plays to the famous district magistrate of the Sung dynasty, Pao Ch'eng. In each work, Pao Ch'eng, acting in his judicial capacity, achieves a just and merciful outcome, but only after engaging in trickery. At the end of *The Wife-Snatcher*, Pao secures by artful forgery the emperor's consent to the execution of a violent nobleman who specializes in the abduction of married women. In the second Pao play, *The Butterfly Dream*, the judge more openly persuades the emperor to spare the lives of three sons of farmer Wang who have killed a noble bully to avenge his murder of their father for accidentally blocking his horse's way. Still, to preserve the appearance of judicial propriety and to provide a surprise ending, Judge Pao orders the corpse of an executed horse thief to be masqueraded as the body of the youngest Wang, whom, alone of the three brothers, he had earlier ordered to be hanged to expiate the revenge killing. The emperor's order sparing all the Wang sons makes the reason for his clemency plain: "For the court sets store by virtuous wives and mothers, and values those who are good sons to their parents."

K.12 Kuby, Erich *Rosemarie.* New York: Knopf, 1959.

▪ The still unsolved strangulation of a Frankfurt call girl, Rosemarie Nitribitt, in 1957 exposed the unlovely side of West Germany's "Economic Miracle." In the Author's Note to his *roman noir* based on the case, Kuby explains the furor caused by the murder: "What produced such an avalanche of publicity and aroused such excitement was the social aspects of the case—the fact that the girl's customers were drawn from the top level of German industry, and the fact that during the last phase of her life she enjoyed such an enormous income."

Kuby's Rosemarie, operating (as did Nitribitt) under the code name Rebecca, becomes the favored plaything and agent of the Insulation Batting Cartel, and she finds herself caught in a web of major-league prostitution, industrial espionage, and sexual blackmail. Each business secret or cry of passion coaxed by Rosemarie from visitors to her apartment is recorded on listening devices installed by the police and two of the cartel's industrialists. It was tycoon Schmitt who hired a prince to introduce business rivals targeted for recording: "Only a special combination of biological and commercial factors made it possible or worth while to have Prince Karl Heinrich send a business acquaintance to Rosemarie, and have her turn on the recording."

Although he seems to point a novelist's finger at his fictional industrialist Konrad Hartog, whom Rosemarie seeks to blackmail into marriage, and Hartog's sister, Marga, Kuby wisely does not attempt an explicit solution of Rosemarie's murder. There were too many clients and employers who had reason to put her out of the way.

A 1958 German film version of *Rosemarie* starred Nadja Tiller.

K.13 Kuei Wan-jung *Parallel Cases from Under the Pear-Tree* [T'ang-yin-pi-shih]. Trans. R.H. van Gulik. Leiden: E. J. Brill, 1956.

■ The author was a Chinese magistrate of the Southern Sung Dynasty who earlier in his career had served as a police inspector. In this work, dating from 1211 A.D., Kuei compiled summaries of 144 criminal and civil cases tried over a period of about fourteen centuries, ca. 300 B.C.–1100 A.D. The cases are presented in pairs to illustrate parallels in evidence. The editor of a Yüan Dynasty reissue of the *Parallel Cases* in 1303 emphasized its value to the justice system: "Contemplating its knowledge of redressing wrongs, discerning falsehood, discovering evil, disclosing what is hidden, and also of searching and probing concealed wickedness and its methods for tracing criminals and for enticing criminals, it seemed to me like a good physician who diagnoses life and death by the condition of the pulse, or like a brilliant mirror that shows the difference between beauty and ugliness by its reflected images, so that everything becomes clear at a glance."

L

L.1 Lacassagne, Alexandre *Vacher l'eventreur* [Vacher the Ripper] *et les crimes sadiques.* Lyon: Storck, 1899.

■ Leader of the team of forensic scientists who pronounced serial killer Joseph Vacher (see B.70 and F.25) to be sane, Dr. Lacassagne promptly published this work in anticipation of the professional and public outcry against his verdict. The book reflects a study that he and colleagues made of sadism, intending to assemble "everything of the greatest importance that medical-legal science knows about that subject." Lacassagne includes his medical report on Vacher and other documents of the case, drawing parallels to such infamous forerunners as Gilles de Rais ("Bluebeard"), the Marquis de Sade, and Jack the Ripper. Central to his finding that Vacher was criminally responsible for his serial killings is Lacassagne's view that sadists are not necessarily insane. In a chapter on Vacher's state of mind, Lacassagne asserts: "Abnormal people of [the sadistic] type are not always insane. The bizarre and strange manifestations of sexual pleasure are as varied as those employed to appease hunger or thirst. That in no way involves madness."

L.2 Lacenaire, Pierre-François *Mémoires, avec ses poèmes et ses lettres.* Paris: Albin Michel, 1968.

■ According to Théophile Gautier, Lacenaire was a "true murderer and a false poet." There is little memorable in either Lacenaire's surviving poetic oeuvre or in his two crimes committed in late 1834 with unreliable and ultimately treacherous confederates: the murder and robbery of Chardon and his mother and the failed attack on a bank messenger. What preserves Lacenaire's reputation as a romantic antihero is his memoirs penned in the Conciergerie in the weeks before his execution. A true disciple of Rousseau, Lacenaire, in his self-pitying recollections, attributed his evil fate to rejection by his mother, mistreatment by teachers and schoolmates in the religious schools favored by his devout father, and the thwarting of his career and literary aspirations. It was all these experiences that led Lacenaire to despise his fellow man and to undertake what he called a "duel with society." Lacenaire attributes his strategy for embarking on a life of crime to a reading of the descriptions of the underworld in Vidocq's memoirs (see V.6): he arranged to be arrested for a minor theft in the hope that his imprisonment for the offense would introduce him to hardened criminals who could help advance his grander felonious schemes.

**L.3 ——— ** *The Memoirs of Lacenaire.* Trans. and ed. Philip John Stead. London: Staples, 1952.

■ This translation of Lacenaire's memoirs (see L.2) is preceded by Stead's introduction summarizing the murderer's life and trial. The author, a historian of the Paris police, credits Chief Inspector Louis Canler, "a born police-officer, patient, unshakeable and possessed of the professional instinct," for the successful tracking of Lacenaire through a maze of false identities. In his assessment of Lacenaire's popularity, he points to the criminal's middle-class origins, his poetic pose, and his compelling Byronic appearance in court: "An eagle profile, an intellectual brow, a sardonic upper lip bracketed by a thin cruel moustache, dark, brooding eyes. Yet the face, inauspicious in repose, could lighten to radiance as he spoke."

L.4 Lafarge, Marie-Fortunée Cappelle *Heures de prison.* 3 vols. Paris: Librairie Nouvelle, 1853–54.

■ This prison memoir of Marie Lafarge begins with her transfer to prison in Montpellier after her murder conviction (see B.37). Hostile crowds gathered along the route, and one of the onlookers favored her with a performance of the newly minted street ballad of her crime. The memoir, which breaks off in 1837 because of the deterioration of her health, reflects Marie's gratitude to her uncle Maurice Collet and his family (particularly cousin Adèle) for their visits and support as well as vicissitudes in her relations with the prison's administrators and staff. At first given favorable treatment, Marie saw her personal furniture removed and visits restricted because of her communications with "Lafargistes" who petitioned the French government on her behalf. Marie also suffered a period of close confinement following a gatekeeper's false report of an escape conspiracy.

Through the pages of the journal can be traced the development of Marie's tubercular disease, at first misdiagnosed as a nervous disorder and a bad case of homesickness. After transfer to a hospital at St. Rémy, Marie was released by Louis-Napoleon in 1852; she died in September of that year.

A gratifying news item recorded by Marie Lafarge in her journal was the acquittal of Euphémie Lacoste on arsenic poisoning charges, largely because of the doubts left by the Lafarge trial.

L.5 ———— *Memoirs of Madame Lafarge.* Philadelphia: Carey & Hart, 1841.

■ With a change of gender, one can apply to Madame Lafarge (assuming that she was actually the author of her memoirs) the famous dictum of Oscar Wilde regarding Thomas Griffiths Wainewright: "That a man's a poisoner is nothing against her prose." This autobiography, which ends on Marie Lafarge's imprisonment prior to her trials for theft and murder, is filled with scintillating observations on social life in Paris and the provinces. (A plain woman who was obsessed with cosmetic aids is described, for example, as ugly enough to be good but not good enough to be ugly.) However, as the narrative approaches the events that culminate in Charles Lafarge's death, Marie's recollections do not always do her great honor. She admits having invented a lover as a pretext for warding off the consummation of her marriage; nevertheless, she maintains, her mother-in-law's remarks about her expanding waistline persuaded her that she had "been elevated to the dignity of motherhood by the grace of God." She directs in many quarters her suspicions of responsibility for her husband's death, noting a rumor that Charles's first wife was murdered and remarking as well that Denis Barbier, her husband's unsavory agent, had free access to his sickbed. Even the medical profession is not spared from her aspersions. Marie claims that it was Dr. Bardon who advised her to purchase arsenic to kill the rats that were disturbing Charles Lafarge's rest.

L.6 Lambton, Arthur   *"Thou Shalt Do No Murder."* London: Hurst & Blackett, n.d.

■ This collection of the author's previously published brief sketches of famous crimes (including the cases of Jean Pierre Vaquier, Edith Thompson and Frederick Bywater, Herbert Armstrong, George Joseph Smith, Thomas Neill Cream, and Florence Maybrick) is amusing because of the author's opinionated style, refreshing lack of sympathy for criminals, and attachment to fellow members of London's Crimes Club ("Our Society"). Typical of Lambton's lack of reserve in expressing his views is his comment on the Maybrick case: "In all my acquaintance I have only met one man *with brains* who believed Mrs. Maybrick to be innocent. He, too, was a member of the Crimes Club."

L.7 Lane, Roger   *Policing the City: Boston 1822–1885.* Cambridge: Harvard Univ. Press, 1967.

■ This groundbreaking scholarly study of an American police force follows the development of the Boston police from the incorporation of the city in 1822 to the passage of the metropolitan police measure of 1885, when control of the police passed to the Commonwealth. It was in 1846, during the administration of City Marshal Francis Tukey (dubbed "our Vidocq") that the first three detectives were added to the public payroll. Lane assesses the influence of the memoirs of French detective and Sûreté chief Eugène-François Vidocq on American crime journalism and detective memoirs. According to Lane, American detective memoirs, like Vidocq's, were "heavily inclined to romance, to disguises, deduction, lost heiresses, and missing jewels" (153).

Lane sees the "creation of a professional, preventive police" as "both a result and a cause of the inability of citizens to deal with [the business of maintaining order] on their own." Among problems dramatizing the need for a strong police function were riots, felonious crimes (including sophisticated crimes for profit), and drunkenness.

L.8 Lang, Andrew *Historical Mysteries*. London: Smith Elder, 1904.

■ This is a superb collection of essays on historical mysteries, a genre of which Andrew Lang was a master. The titles and subjects of the chapters dealing with crime or fraud are as follows:

- "The Case of Elizabeth Canning": Lang agrees with Henry Fielding (see F.8) that Canning told the truth when she explained her mysterious disappearance on New Year's Day 1753 by a story of imprisonment by a gang attempting to force her into prostitution. He explains the rejection of her account: "In my opinion Elizabeth Canning was a victim of the common sense of the eighteenth century. She told a very strange tale, and common-sense holds that what is strange cannot be true."
- "The Murder of Escovedo": Lang is unable to propose a motive for Philip II's order to assassinate Juan de Escovedo, the secretary of the king's illegitimate brother, the famous Don John of Austria.
- " The Campden Mystery": Lang suggests that there is only one rational explanation for the "Campden wonder," the execution of Joan Perry and her two sons for the murder of Will Harrison, who had disappeared from Chipping Campden in 1660. After the Perrys' hangings, Harrison returned home, very much alive, with an exotic tale of being attacked and kidnapped (see M.13). It is Lang's thesis that Harrison's two-year absence was due to his knowledge of "some secret of the troubled times: he was a witness better out of the way." He "may conceivably have held a secret that bore on the case of one of the Regicides." See also *The Campden Wonder*, ed. Sir George Clark (London: Oxford Univ. Press, 1959).
- "The Case of Allan Breck": Lang returns to the so-called Appin Murder, which Robert Louis Stevenson wove into the narrative of *Kidnapped* (see S.52). At the beginning of his article, he refers to reports from two descendants of the Stewart faction that the hated victim nicknamed the "Red Fox," a pro-English factor seeking to evict loyal Scots tenants of forfeited estates, was shot with the participation of Allan Breck and an accomplice whose name Lang declines to repeat. His reticence was dictated by loyalty to his sources and by doubt as to whether Allan in fact had an accessory.
- "The Cardinal's Necklace": This article recounts briefly the theft of the diamond necklace that Cardinal Louis de Rohan intended to present to Marie Antoinette (C.12). Lang

rejects the line of speculation that Rohan was in love with the queen, believing instead that his gift was proposed "in obedience to his dominating idea–the recovery of the Queen's good graces."

- "The Mystery of Kaspar Hauser: The Child of Europe": The saga of Kaspar Hauser, the "Child of Europe," arose when "a boy, apparently idiotic, . . . appeared, as if from the clouds, in Nuremberg (1828), divided Germany into hostile parties, and caused legal proceedings as late as 1883." According to the romantic theory of the case, the mysterious youth "was the Crown Prince of Baden, stolen as an infant in the interests of a junior branch of the House, reduced to imbecility by systematic ill-treatment, turned loose on the world at the age of sixteen, and finally murdered, lest his secret origin might be discovered."

   Lang regards Kaspar as a humbug and believes it likely that the young man inflicted the fatal knife wound to ensure continued attention, but that the weapon pierced more deeply than he had intended. See also M.14.

- "The Gowrie Conspiracy": It is Lang's conclusion that the slaughter of the Earl of Gowrie and his brother at Perth, Scotland, by the forces of their guest, King James VI, arose from the victims' plot against the throne, "as the King could not possibly invented and carried out the affair." Lang had earlier discussed the matter at full length in his *King James and the Gowrie Mystery* (London: Longmans, 1902).

- "The Strange Case of Daniel Dunglas Home": Lang describes the great lengths to which Victorian scientists went in unsuccessful efforts to prove that Scottish spiritualist Home was a fraud. Robert Browning, who, with his wife, had attended a séance with Home, presented him as an American impostor in his narrative poem *Mr. Sludge, the Medium*. For full-length studies of Home, see Elizabeth Jenkins, *The Shadow and the Light: A Defence of Daniel Dunglas Home the Medium* (London: Hamish Hamilton, 1982); and Horace Wyndham, *Mr. Sludge, the Medium: Being the Life and Adventures of Daniel Dunglas Home* (London: Geoffrey Bles, 1937), of which the Borowitz True Crime Collection owns the author's corrected page proof.

- "The Chevalier d'Éon": Lang states that the mystery of this transvestite secret agent was not his sex (he was clearly a man) but why he assumed feminine attire at age forty-two and continued to wear it for forty years. Lang's answer: "he was obliged to clutch at some mode of keeping himself in the public eye."

- "Saint-Germain the Deathless": A remarkable charlatan, Comte de Saint Germain, sometimes claimed to have lived many centuries before he became the intimate and secret emissary of Louis XV. He peddled an elixir that restored youth and purported to remove the flaw from a diamond. Nobody knows when he died, and, if we are to credit his wildest assertions of longevity, he never did! Lang states, perhaps figuratively, that Saint-Germain may be the historic original of the romantic characters who pass through the ages in Bulwer Lytton's *The Haunters and the Haunted* and Thackeray's "The Notch on the Axe" in *Roundabout Papers*.

- "The End of Jeanne de la Motte": This brief concluding piece compares conflicting accounts of the escape from the Salpétrière prison by Jeanne de la Motte, the central figure in the theft of a diamond necklace intended for Marie Antoinette. The mode of Jeanne's death seems less open to dispute: in 1791 she succumbed to serious injuries suffered when she jumped out of a window to escape from creditors.

The literary career of Andrew Lang (1844–1912) is astounding both for accomplishment and versatility. He studied folklore and produced a dozen fairy-tale books; translated Homer; composed a four-volume history of his native Scotland; and wrote books on subjects as diverse as the identity of Pickle the Spy (who kept the English informed on the activities of the defeated Bonnie Prince Charlie), Joan of Arc, Mary Stuart, Dickens's *The Mystery of Edwin Drood*, the history of the St. Andrews golf course, and the eighteenth-century London furor over the Cock Lane Ghost. He devoted other volumes to historical mysteries of Britain and continental Europe that influenced the writings of William Roughead. Unlike Roughead, who savored domestic murders, Lang preferred to study crime and intrigue that were intertwined with political events or circumstances.

L.9 ———— *The Valet's Tragedy, and Other Studies.* London: Longmans Green, 1903.
■ In the title essay and its companion piece, "The Valet's Master," Lang argues persuasively that the Man in the Iron Mask was Martin (who became known in his prisons as Eustache Dauger), the valet of Roux de Marsilly. Dauger's master was broken on the wheel by the French after his capture on Swiss soil; his alleged crime of plotting to assassinate Louis XIV was trumped up, but he seems to have attempted to draw England into a Protestant league against France. Lang believes that Dauger may not have known what dark secret he was supposed to harbor and that his jailers over time may well have forgotten, if they ever understood, why he was to be kept masked.

In his scrupulous consideration of the murder of Protestant magistrate Sir Edmund Berry Godfrey in the course of the "Popish Plot" madness, Lang does not "propose to unriddle the mystery," contenting himself with the remarks: "We cannot deny that Godfrey may have been murdered to conceal Catholic secrets, of which, thanks to his inexplicable familiarity with Coleman [secretary of the Duchess of York], he may have had many. But we have tried to prove that we do not *know* him to have had any such Catholic secrets, or much beyond [Titus] Oates's fables; and we have probably succeeded in showing that against the Jesuits, as Sir Edmund's destroyers, there is no evidence at all."

Among the subjects of his other studies are the tennis-playing impostor who successfully impersonated Joan of Arc after her death, apparently persuading St. Joan's own brothers of her asserted survival; and Amy Robsart, whose mysterious death from a fall, according to Lang, was not compassed by either her husband, Lord Robert Dudley, or Queen Elizabeth I: "It might be a mere half-sportive attempt by rustics to enter a house known to be, at the moment, untenanted by the servants, and may have caused to Amy an alarm, so that, rushing downstairs in terror, she fell and broke her neck. . . . Or a partisan of Dudley's, finding poison difficult or impossible, may have, in his zeal, murdered Amy, under the disguise of an accident."

L.10 Lang, Fritz, and Thea von Harbou *M.* Dir. Fritz Lang. Released by Nero-Film, Berlin, May 11, 1931.

▣ Despite Lang's strong statements to the contrary, he and von Harbou, his wife, probably were influenced by the case of Peter Kürten, arrested in May 1930 for serial murders in and around Düsseldorf. Unlike Franz Becker, the murderer in Lang's classic film who preyed only on children, Kürten made no distinction of age or gender in his eight murders and eleven murder attempts in 1929 and 1930 alone; he even claimed the life of a swan in an attack in a park. Kürten was also versatile in his murder methods and weapons. In addition to strangulation he favored knife, shears, stiletto, and hammer.

A bizarre detail appears to relate the investigation of Kürten's reign of terror to a famous twist in the plot of *M.* In Frederick W. Ott, *The Films of Fritz Lang* (Secaucus: Citadel, 1979), the author states: "According to a press account of the period, the underworld of Düsseldorf had pursued the killer because he had disrupted their 'legitimate' criminal activity, a situation which parallels the fiction of Lang's *M*" (155).

See Margaret Seaton Wagner, *The Monster of Düsseldorf: The Life and Trial of Peter Kürten* (New York: Dutton, 1933); Elisabeth Lenk and Roswitha Kaever, *Leben und Wirken des Peter Kürten, genannt der Vampir von Düsseldorf* (Munich: Rogner & Bernhard, 1974).

L.11 Latouche, Henri de [pseudonym of Hyacinthe-Joseph-Alexandre Thabaud]
Memoirs of Madame Manson, Explanatory of Her Conduct, on the Trial for the Assassination of M. Fualdès. London: Baldwin Cradock & Joy, 1818.

▣ The Fualdès murder came to light on March 20, 1817, when a woman walking by the banks of the Aveyron River outside the town of Rodez in southern France saw a body floating in the water near a mill. When the corpse was retrieved, the victim, whose throat had been cut, was identified as a well-known citizen of Rodez, the recently retired magistrate Joseph-Bernardin Fualdès. During the Revolution Fualdès had served as a juryman of the Revolutionary Tribunal and was on the jury that condemned Charlotte Corday. However, Fualdès was not a radical and had briefly served as royal procurer under the Restoration. Nevertheless, many persisted in seeing the death of Fualdès as the retributive work of the White Terror, which was still active in other parts of France.

The murder of Fualdès, though its solution remains in controversy to this day, probably had a more prosaic motivation. The police inquiry disclosed that on the evening before the discovery of his body, Fualdès had left his house for an appointment, carrying with him a bulky package. There was speculation that he was meeting to arrange for the negotiation of a considerable amount of securities that he had received as proceeds of real estate he had sold to provide for his retirement. However, Fualdès's trail led to a strange place for the transaction of such business. Investigators determined that he was murdered in the kitchen of the town's only brothel and house of assignation, operated by a couple named Bancal. Witnesses indicated that a crowd of murderers and accomplices took part in the crime and later formed a macabre cortege that brought the body to the river. (This procession was depicted in a series of drawings of Théodore Géricault.) M. Bancal was arrested, and a number of other arrests followed. Among the principal suspects taken into custody were Bernard Charles Bastide-Gramont, Fualdès's godson, and Joseph Jausion, Bastide's brother-in-law, who acted as Fualdès's agent and securities broker. Despite the White Terror rumors, the police theorized that the magistrate was murdered either to obtain valuable securities or to cover up maladministration of his financial affairs.

The principal witness in the murder trials that ensued was the maddening Clarisse Manson (daughter of a judge of Rodez), who gave at least six different versions of her story that never resolved the central mysteries of her testimony: whether she was present at the Bancal house, and, if so, whether she had seen the murder being committed. Two days after Bastide, Jausion, and others were found guilty of premeditated murder at their first trial, Mme. Manson was arrested and charged with false testimony. While in jail she agreed to have her memoirs ghostwritten by Henri de Latouche, who is better known in literary history for his encouragement of Balzac's career than for his own awkward novels.

Latouche had been reporting the Fualdès murder trial for the *Gazette de France* under the nom de plume *le sténographe parisienne*. In the *Memoirs of Madame Manson*, which became an international bestseller, he painted, none too subtly, an unflattering portrait of the shifty witness as vain, flirtatious, and a stranger to logic. In Latouche's rendering, Clarisse, who bore the first name of novelist Samuel Richardson's tragic heroine, often speaks in language that might have suited Richardson's other famous creation, Pamela: "From that dreadful night I date all my misfortunes! What have been the sorrows of a whole life, when put in competition with those that have overwhelmed me for the last few months! How many bitter tears have I shed! O my father, mother, brothers, my son! ties ever dear and sacred, that alone reconciled me to life! without you, without the consolations of religion, I had made an attempt upon my life!"

After the release of her memoirs, Clarisse insisted that they had been prepared solely for her mother's eyes, and she criticized Latouche's faulty composition, the negligence of the style, and the "detailed description of acts which were quite inconsequential."

Following a second trial, at which Clarisse produced a new version of her testimony, the jury convicted most of the defendants; Bastide, Jausion, and a third defendant were executed in June 1818, and all charges against Mme. Manson were dropped. In his work *Le magistrat assassiné (Affaire Fualdès)*, published in 1954, the distinguished police criminologist Edmond Locard stated that an analysis of the handwriting of one of the threatening letters Clarisse Manson claimed to have received from those who wanted her to remain silent showed that the letter was forged by Clarisse herself. A more recent work on the case asserts that in 1833, during her final illness, she told her son and the Abbé de Villiers that she had seen nothing and knew nothing of the murder of Monsieur Fualdès (Peter Shankland and Michael Havers QC, *Murder with a Double Tongue: The Enigma of Clarissa Manson* [London: William Kimber, 1978]; see also Albert I. Borowitz, "Henri de Latouche and the Murder Memoirs of Clarisse Manson," in *Innocence and Arsenic: Studies in Crime and Literature*, 132–62 [B.28]).

L.12 Le Corbeiller, Armand *Le long martyre de Françoise Salmon*. In series *Énigmes et drames judiciaires d'autrefois*. Paris: Perrin, 1927.

■ With simplicity and clarity, Armand Le Corbeiller narrates the sufferings of Françoise Salmon, whose erroneous conviction was compared to that of Jean Calas (see v.9). In August 1781, after only five days of domestic service to the Huet-Duparc family in Caen, Françoise found herself accused of poisoning the eighty-eight-year-old grandfather Paysant de Beaulieu and attempted poisoning of seven other members of the household. Only the humanity and love of justice showed by Louis XVI and his ministers, as well as the skill and self-sacrifice of Salmon's lawyer Pierre-Noël Le Cauchois, saved the innocent young woman from torture and death at the stake to which she was destined by a negligent and possibly corrupt police investigation. After her acquittal, Salmon became the protégée of Madame Stéphanie-Félicité de Genlis, teacher of the children of the Duke d'Orléans and author of moral tales and works on education.

In his detailed summaries of the arguments that saved Salmon's life, Le Corbeiller emphasizes the contention of Le Cauchois and his colleagues that key evidence was planted on Salmon by unknown guilty persons within the Huet-Duparc family. How could Salmon have been the source of grains of arsenic found in her left pocket, the lawyers asked, when her left hand was withered and useless?

L.13 Leiber, Jerry, and Mike Stoller "Tango." 1975. On *Other Songs by Leiber and Stoller*. Nonesuch Records, 1978.

■ Lyricist Leiber and his composer partner Stoller have said that "Tango" was "provoked" by the *Los Angeles Times* obituary of Ramon Navarro, a retired film actor best known for his "Latin lover" image. On Halloween 1968, two brothers, Paul Robert Ferguson and Thomas Scott Ferguson, tortured Navarro in his Hollywood home, hoping to find $5,000 in cash that they had heard (from other male hustlers) the actor kept hidden. Navarro choked to death on his own blood after the Fergusons thrust a dildo (a jocular gift of another screen lover, Rudolf Valentino) down his throat.

The Leiber-Stoller song begins by introducing the tango motif, a reference to Navarro's exotic film persona:

Oh, the Tango is done with a thin black mustache
A wide scarlet sash, black boots and a whip

A phonograph plays a broken record, as the lyrics suggest the lonely Navarro's willingness to consort with dangerous men whom he does not know:

He was a collector of beautiful strangers
And life was a party right up to the end
The door always open to love and love's dangers
Who did it? A lover? A stranger? A friend?

After the murder, the old broken tango record continues to turn, and six times the refrain "Over it plays" is repeated in a room now fallen silent.

L.14 Lenotre, G. [pseudonym of Louis-Léon-Théodore Gosselin] *Babet l'empoisonneuse ou l'empoisonée*. In series *Énigmes et drames judiciaires d'autrefois*. Paris: Perrin, 1927.

■ This little masterpiece, one of Lenotre's few monographs on a criminal case largely independent of its historical setting, focuses on a hellish ménage à trois: Françoise Leverd (also known as Madame de Mellertz), a hotel keeper's daughter risen to become first the mistress and subsequently estate manager of the count de Normont; Charles, the count's spineless eldest son, who may have been the lover of Madame de Mellertz; and Elisabeth ("Babet") Leverd, Françoise's niece, who marries Charles against her aunt's wishes. A decade passes during which Babet claims to have suffered grievous abuse at the hands of her aunt (including assaults by hired bravos and the poisoning of an infant daughter). A climax was reached during the night of April 1, 1813, when Babet was found in her country home at Choisy apparently poisoned by a draft forced down her throat from a cup; after a prolonged illness she recovered. A subsequent criminal trial, however, remained inconclusive, and Lenotre leaves the reader, as he is himself, in doubt whether Babet was actually poisoned at the instance of her husband and aunt or whether she faked the crime to triumph over her family enemies.

Théodore Gosselin (1855–1935) took the pseudonym G. (Gosselin) Lenotre in honor of his ancestor, André Le Nôtre, the celebrated seventeenth-century landscape architect. Contracting a passion for the period of the French Revolution and its aftermath from tales of his grandmothers, Lenotre developed the idea of chronicling with documentary fidelity the often-neglected personal tragedies that were played out against the backdrop of cataclysmic events; to his studies of private lives in turbulent times he attached the name *petite histoire*. An admirer and younger friend of dramatist Victorien Sardou, Lenotre formed his own literary circle, including historians Ernest d'Hauterive (son-in-law of Alexandre Dumas *fils*) and J. Lucas Dubreton. With his friends he met regularly to discuss historical conundrums, among them his very favorite, the fate of Louis XVII (see L.17). Lenotre was dubbed by his friend Georges Cain "the Angel of Documentation."

Lenotre's generously footnoted style is parodied in Paul Reboux and Charles Muller, *A la manière de . . .* (Paris: Bernard Grasset, 1964), 177–82.

L.15 ——— *Dossiers de police*. In series *La petite histoire* Vol. 6. Paris: Bernard Grasset, 1935.
■ These short studies include pieces on the Affair of Poisons; the Man in the Iron Mask; the Calas case; Vidocq; Clarisse Manson, the principal witness in the Fualdès murder trials; and the murder of the Duchesse de Praslin. In his review of the Calas case (see V.9), Lenotre suggests that the murder may have been committed by an intruder, either a thief or a rival of the victim for the affection of one of the fair women of Toulouse.

L.16 ——— *The Guillotine and Its Servants* [La guillotine et les exécuteurs des arrêts criminels pendant la Révolution]. Trans. Mrs. Rodolph Stawell. London: Hutchinson, n.d.
■ Lenotre presents dispassionately the manifold effects of the French Revolution on the capital punishment business, recounting the rise and decline of the Sanson family of executioners and the varying fortunes of their provincial colleagues, whose ranks were

sometimes filled out by amateur volunteers when the demands of the Terror required. It is remarkable how few eyewitness accounts of executions during the Terror survive; one rare narrative is that of the Abbé Carrichon who, having fulfilled his promise to accompany three aristocratic ladies on the way to their death, stayed on to observe the spectacle and comment on the executioners' professionalism.

L.17 ———— *Le roi Louis XVII et l'énigme du temple.* Paris: Perrin, 1921.

■ Without considering the respective claims of the principal pretenders, the Baron de Richemont and Carl-Wilhelm Naundorff, to be the real Louis XVII, Lenotre focuses his inquiry on an antecedent question: did Louis XVII die in 1795 as a prisoner of the Temple after his parents, Louis XVI and Marie Antoinette, had gone to the scaffold, or did he escape, with another child being substituted for him? The cautious author concludes that the supposition of the removal of the Dauphin from the Temple on the night of January 19, 1794, by Revolutionary leader Pierre Gaspard (Anaxagoras) Chaumette with the complicity of the prince's prison guardian, the shoemaker Antoine Simon, and his wife, "is better adapted than any other theory to the known circumstances of the captivity in the Temple." Lenotre suggests that Chaumette intended to maintain control of the Dauphin to ensure his own power (and indeed survival) upon the passing of the Revolutionary fever. Chaumette was guillotined, however, before such a plan could be implemented.

In April 2000, two scientists, Jean-Jacques Cassiman of the University of Louvain, Belgium, and Bernd Brinkmann of the University of Münster, Germany, announced that the little boy who died in the Temple prison was Louis XVII (*New York Times*, April 20, 2000). DNA samples extracted from the boy's dried heart closely matches those of other members of the French royal family, including DNA taken from a lock of Marie Antoinette's hair. See also Philippe Delorme, *Louis XVII la vérité: Sa mort au temple confirmée par la science* (Paris: Pygmalion/Gérard Watelet, 2000).

L.18 ———— *Le vrai chevalier de Maison-Rouge, A. D. J. Gonzze de Rougeville 1761–1814.* Paris: Perrin, 1912.

■ Rougeville managed to gain entrance to the Conciergerie prison during Marie Antoinette's captivity and passed the queen a white carnation boutonniere containing a message promising to rescue her. The queen's response, though, was intercepted, and nothing came of the so-called "carnation plot." As Lenotre discovered, Rougeville spent the rest of his life in shameless self-promotion and in murky royalist conspiracy, which had become second nature to him. Although Lenotre shows considerable sympathy for the quixotic intriguer, who after years of police surveillance was summarily executed in 1814 for aiding invading Russian forces, the real-life Rougeville does not match the nobility of his fictional counterpart, the eponymous hero of Alexandre Dumas's stirring *Le chevalier de Maison-Rouge* (1846). See D.44.

L.19 ———— *The Woman Without a Name* [La femme sans nom]. Trans. Doris Ashley. London: Collins, 1923.

■ In 1789 a woman claiming to be the Marquise Marie de Douhault asserted that eighteen months earlier her death had been fabricated by a greedy relative with designs on her estate and that she had been confined in the Salpétrière prison. Despite her recourse to the courts, the marquise never regained possession of her name, her title, or her estates. Lenotre does not propose his own solution of the historical puzzle, but he does cite with gusto the theory that Marie may have been imprisoned by relatives of the gloomy and violent Marquis de Douhault in retribution for her having him committed to the madhouse at Charenton. The happy end of the Douhault tragedy is that it inspired the plot of Wilkie Collins's *The Woman in White* (see c.33).

L.20 ———— *Notes et souvenirs*. Comp. Thérèse Lenotre. Paris: Calmann-Lévy, 1940.

■ Historian G. Lenotre was blessed in the literary talent of his daughter, Thérèse, who contributed a lively memoir of her father to this volume, which also includes a judicious culling from his journals for the years 1890 through 1930. Lenotre recorded many events that prefigure our own time, such as the "singular vogue" for the cutler de Cette, who sold assassin Caserio the dagger with which he assassinated President Carnot in 1894. In addition, the diarist eloquently defends his interest in petite histoire: "the history of the Revolution remains to be told. Authors have often related the succession of political events, the partisan struggles, the wars; but the annals of the people during that strange period have not been written at all; no one has said how much that immense commotion stirred the nation in its depths; nobody has shown how the different classes were so thoroughly shaken, stirred, and mixed to the same extent (if I may be permitted the comparison which seems the only accurate one) as a gigantic salad, so that society, since then, seems never to have recovered its center of gravity."

L.21 Levin, Meyer *Compulsion*. New York: Simon & Schuster, 1956.

■ Levin's popular novel, later a play and a motion picture, is, for the most part, an accurate account of the 1924 murder of Bobby Franks by Richard Loeb and Nathan Leopold and the world-famous trial in which Clarence Darrow saved the "thrill killers" from execution. Levin's murderers are named Arthur Straus (Loeb) and Judd Steiner (Leopold), and their victim is Paulie Kessler; Jonathan Wilk is an idealized portrait of Darrow. The book borrows liberally from the trial record, including extensive quotations from Darrow's celebrated closing argument against capital punishment.

In introducing as a major figure in the story an eighteen-year-old cub newspaper reporter, Sid Silver, Levin indulges in wish fulfillment. A schoolmate of Loeb and Leopold at the University of Chicago and a campus correspondent for the *Chicago Daily News*, Levin was assigned to attend the arraignment and wrote a feature article on Leopold's father; however, he did not cover the trial, preferring to carry out his previous plans for European travel. In the novel, young reporter Silver becomes an amateur sleuth, identifying the victim's body and discovering that the ransom letter was typed on Judd Steiner's portable typewriter. The reporter also attends the trial, but with distinctively mixed feelings, for

Steiner, shortly before his arrest, appears to have diverted the affections of Silver's girl friend, Ruth Goldenberg.

In his foreword, Levin states that, in using an actual case for his story, he follows in the tradition of Stendhal's *The Red and the Black* and Dostoyevski's *Crime and Punishment*, adding: "Certain crimes seem to epitomize the thinking of their era. Thus *Crime and Punishment* had to arise out of the feverish soul-searching of the Russia of Dostoevski's period, and *An American Tragedy* had to arise from the sociological thinking of Dreiser's time in America. In our time, the psychoanalytical point of view has come to the fore."

Levin's imagined psychoanalytic profile of Judd Steiner is drawn in the novel by a young Freudian, Willie Weiss. Unlike many commentators on the case, Weiss sees Steiner (Leopold) not simply as the accomplice of the habitually criminal Straus (Loeb) but as a man driven to murder by his own "compulsion." The keystone of Weiss's reconstruction of Steiner's unconscious motivation is the theory that his decision to hide Paulie Kessler's naked body in a culvert after applying acid to the victim's face and genitalia was symbolic of a desire to return to the womb, "equally understandable as a way to rectify a mistake, to say that it was as a girl that he really should have been born."

In 1958, Leopold won his parole, a measure that Levin had strongly advocated. The author's support, however, met with ingratitude, for Leopold filed suit in the circuit court of Cook County, Illinois, against Levin, the publishers, and distributors of the novel and play *Compulsion* and the producer, distributor, and Chicago-area exhibitors of the motion picture of the same name. The freed murderer asserted that the defendants had violated his "rights of privacy," more narrowly contending that they, through "knowingly fictionalized accounts," had caused the public to identify him with inventions or fictionalized episodes that were so offensive and unwarranted as to "outrage the community's notions of decency." The Illinois Supreme Court granted summary judgment for the defendants, holding that their fictionalized portrayal of a matter of public interest was a constitutionally protected exercise of free speech and that the invented aspects of the attacked works "were reasonably comparable to, or conceivable from facts of record from which they were drawn, or minor in offensiveness when viewed in the light of such facts" (*Leopold v. Levin*, 259 N.E.2d 250 (1970)). Levin believed that Leopold's outrage stemmed primarily from the scene of the novel showing the rape impulse Judd Steiner (Leopold) experienced and suppressed with difficulty during a date with Ruth Goldenberg (*The Obsession* [New York: Simon & Schuster, 1973], 225–26).

L.22 Lewis, Janet *The Trial of Sören Qvist.* Garden City: Doubleday, 1947.

■ As Lewis notes in the foreword to her novel, the story of Sören Jensen Qvist, wrongly executed in 1625 for murder on the basis of fabricated evidence, was already famous in Denmark as the theme of a short story by Steen Steensen Blicher (1782–1848). Blicher, beloved poet and short-story writer of Jutland, Denmark, altered the chronology of Sören Qvist's case in his 1829 tale "The Parson at Vejlbye" (published in English in *Twelve Stories by Steen Steensen Blicher*, trans. Hanna Astrup Larsen and intro. Sigrid Undset [Princeton:

Princeton Univ. Press/American-Scandinavian Foundation, 1945]). Himself a sixth-generation parson, Steensen portrayed Qvist as "a God-fearing and upright man, but hot-tempered and domineering, intolerant of any opposition to his will." Most of the narrative is told through the journal of incorruptible county sheriff and judge Erik Sörensen, whose harsh fate is to condemn Qvist to death after becoming engaged to his daughter, Mettë.

To compress the tragedy, Blicher has the discovery of a corpse in the parson's garden follow only a few days after the disappearance of the alleged victim (instead of some twenty years afterward, as indicated in the documents of the historical case). In the story, the inventor of the plot to frame Qvist is Morten Bruus, angered by the minister's refusal of his daughter's hand in marriage and by a failed attempt to bribe Judge Sörensen in a property dispute. Bruus encourages his brother, Niels, to enter Qvist's employ as coachman and to pick a quarrel that provokes his master to strike him with a spade. Niels scampers into the woods and is supposed by neighbors to have been murdered after a substitute body planted by the Bruus brothers is disinterred. Blicher devises an additional twist in the story by bringing Qvist to believe that he buried the coachman while in a state of somnambulism, to which he had been subject on previous occasions.

The poet Janet Lewis follows Blicher's plot quite closely but enshrines Qvist's tragedy in a lyrically evoked setting of Jutland's villages and countryside. The parson's fatal decision to retain Niels in his employ despite the servant's provocative behavior takes on religious significance. Believing fervently that even demons are the servants of God, Qvist is persuaded that Niels was sent on a divine mission to test the minister's will to confront and overcome his own disposition to violence.

Another source of the Qvist story, acknowledged by Lewis in her preface as the first version she encountered, is a chapter in S. M. Phillips, *Famous Cases on Circumstantial Evidence* (New York: James Cockcroft, 1875), 14–29. Phillips's narrative bears a strong resemblance to Blicher's.

Librarian J. Christian Dyer has argued that the trial of Sören Qvist inspired the plot of Mark Twain's *Tom Sawyer, Detective*, published in *Harper's Magazine* in 1896 (see J. Christian Bay, "Tom Sawyer, Detective: The Origin of the Plot," in *Essays Offered to Herbert Putnam* [1929], ed. William Warner Bishop and Andrew Keogh [Freeport, N.Y.: Books for Libraries Press, 1967]). In his footnote to the first publication of his story, Twain claimed that he had taken the incidents "from an old-time Swedish criminal trial," changed the actors, and transferred the scene to America. Bay, however, identifies the Qvist case as the source and speculates that Twain heard the story from Anna Lillie Greenough, who married Johan Henrik Hegermann-Lindencrone (1838–1918), Danish ambassador to the United States from 1872 to 1880.

In *Tom Sawyer, Detective*, Tom is cast as a Sherlock Holmes and Huckleberry Finn is an admiring narrator in the mold of Dr. Watson. Tom's Uncle Silas, a preacher whose Arkansas farm the two boys are visiting, is charged with the murder of farmhand Jubiter Dunlap. In a triumphant court appearance, Tom demonstrates that the corpse was in fact that of Jubiter's identical twin, Jake, who was murdered by two criminal associates from whom he had snatched a pair of valuable diamonds that the trio had stolen together. The misspellings in Huck's account of the trial are often hilarious. The case against Uncle Silas is brought by "the lawyer for the prostitution," and the dead man is referred to grandly as "the diseased."

L.23 ———— *The Wife of Martin Guerre.* 1941. Denver: Alan Swallow, 1959.

■ The long success of the Martin Guerre imposture in sixteenth-century France depended on the interaction between two mysterious personalities, those of the false Martin Guerre (Arnaud du Tilh) and Bertrande de Rols, the wife of the real Martin Guerre. In her novella *The Wife of Martin Guerre*, Janet Lewis traces the life of Bertrande from her betrothal at the age of ten and her entrance into the house of Guerre at fourteen to her growing affection for her stern husband before his departure for the wars. Lewis recounts Bertrande's eager acceptance of the impostor as her long-awaited spouse. Afterward, her growing doubts of his identity, coupled with her fear of having been "betrayed into adultery," lead her to make the accusation of fraud that brings him to his death.

Despite du Tilh's strong resemblance to her husband, psychological differences arouse Bertrande's suspicions: his affectionate treatment of the children, the indulgence and gentleness he showed her, and his "gift of tongue," which did not match her recollections of the cold and silent Martin Guerre. After these nagging doubts are confirmed by a returning soldier who recalls that Martin Guerre lost his left leg "before St. Quentin in the year fifty seven," she calls on her Uncle Pierre (who has a monetary dispute with the impostor) for help in laying her accusation before the authorities. When du Tilh's trial ends in a sentence of decapitation, the horrified Bertrande faints. But despite pressure from the Guerre family, who appeal the case in Toulouse, she does not drop the charges. Just as the appellate judges are about to reverse the conviction, the true Martin Guerre hobbles into the courtroom on his wooden leg. Brought before him, Bertrande falls to her knees and begs forgiveness, pleading, "My sin was occasioned only by my great desire for your presence." His severe response authenticates her memories of the true Martin Guerre: "Dry your tears, Madame. They cannot, and they ought not, move my pity. The example of my sisters and my uncle can be no excuse for you, Madame, who knew me better than any living soul. The error into which you plunged could only have been caused by willful blindness. You, and you only, Madame, are answerable for the dishonor which has befallen me."

An operatic setting of *The Wife of Martin Guerre*, with music by American composer William Bergsma and a libretto by Janet Lewis, was premiered by the Juilliard Opera Theater on February 15, 1956.

L.24 Lidberg, Gustaf *Geniet-Förbrytaren Martin Ekenberg: Detektivchefens Berättelser* [The Genius Criminal Martin Ekenberg: The Detective Chief's Narratives]. Stockholm: Albert Bonniers, 1919.

■ Swedish chemist and inventor Martin Ekenberg combined the vengefulness of the Count of Monte Cristo with the technological skill of the Unabomber. Between 1894 and 1909, Ekenberg sent a variety of cleverly disguised package bombs (including a Parker pen cylinder and a perfume flask) to four men; he believed that three of the addressees had frustrated his business projects, and the other was an attorney-agent with whom he had become embroiled. Two of his targets were seriously hurt, and in another case Ekenberg's bomb exploded in a post office, injuring three employees. The bomber attempted to give the last two outrages a political coloration in the wake of a large-scale Swedish strike in 1909. He wrote to newspapers under the name "Justus Felix" (the "just and lucky man," a name drawn from the hero of a children's story), attributing the attacks to a Socialist assassination bureau.

Detective chief Lidberg, who had a role in the investigation, tells how Ekenberg, after a professional colleague recognized his handwriting in a letter from the self-proclaimed Socialist "enforcer," was tracked down and arrested in London, where he had won a reputation as a promising scientist. After an often-tumultuous extradition proceeding, Ekenberg was ordered to be turned over to the Swedish authorities, but he committed suicide in Brixton jail before the ruling could be carried out. Lidberg caps his compelling account with a summary of evidence gathered by the Swedish police that Ekenberg had committed even more grievous crimes, the poisoning of two wives.

L.25 Liebermann von Sonnenberg, Erich, and Otto Trettin *Continental Crimes* [Kriminalfälle]. Trans. Winifred Ray. Foreword George Dilnot. London: Bles, 1935.

■ Although written by the heads of the Berlin Detective Service, this collection of German cases from the early nineteenth century through 1930 emphasizes unusual murders rather than feats of detection. Among the twenty-two chapters are studies of:

- The 1897 murder of Berlin widow Schultz and her daughter by Joseph Gönczy ("The Murder of the Gypsum Schultzes"), who, in a scheme reminiscent of Arthur Conan Doyle's "The Red-Headed League," obtained access to the victims' premises by establishing a fake shoe shop on the street level
- The exposure and compelled suicide of Colonel Alfred Redl, chief of staff of the 8th Prague Army Corps, who sold Austrian military secrets to Russia before World War I
- German-trained American lawyer Karl Hau's murder of his wealthy mother-in-law in Baden-Baden (see H.1)
- Robber-murderer August Sternickel, who was executed in 1913 after remaining concealed for eight years
- Marie Krüger ("Aunt Marie"), a serial matrimonial killer who turned from poisoning to throat-cutting
- Albert Ziethem, a barber who died in prison in 1901 after seventeen years' confinement for the murder of his wife, although his assistant Wilhelm had confessed the crime on several occasions ("Don't Forget the Baker")
- Saffran, convicted in 1931 with two accomplices of murdering a cyclist and burning his corpse on the premises of a failing family business in a scam designed to simulate

Saffran's death and to collect insurance. The crime was suggested by a 1929 murder scheme perpetrated by Kurt Tetzner, who set his car ablaze with a corpse at the wheel ("The Man-Hunters"). In his foreword, George Dilnot compares these cases to that of Alfred Arthur Rouse in England (see N.7).

The Redl spy case is the subject of John Osborne's play, *A Patriot for Me* (London: Faber & Faber, 1966). Although of modest family origin, Osborne's Redl wins promotions because his superiors grade him as possessing "all the qualities of first-class field officer and an unmistakable flair for intelligence"; he is "upright, discreet, frank and open, painstaking," and possesses "marked ability to anticipate, as well as initiate instructions, without being reckless." Yet he is undone by his secret homosexuality, which exposes him to the blackmail of Russian intelligence. At a drag ball, the host, Baron von Epp, describes the dangerous freedom that homosexuals like Redl dared to assert in the face of Austro-Hungarian conformism: "We are none of us safe. This . . . is the celebration of the individual against the rest, the us's and the them's, the free and the constricted, the gay and the dreary, the lonely and the mob."

Osborne's play, and novelist Joseph Roth's 1932 German-language masterpiece *The Radetsky March*, are the sources of Istvan Szabo's 1984 film *Colonel Redl*.

L.26 Locard, Edmond *Le magistrat assassiné (Affaire Fualdès)*. Paris: Éditions de la Flamme d'Or, n.d.

■ In this work on the enigmatic 1817 murder of magistrate Joseph-Bernardin Fualdès in a house of assignation in Rodez, twentieth-century scientific detective Locard delivers a crushing blow, 138 years after the fact, to the already dubious credibility of a key witness, Clarisse Manson (see L.11). Locard states that his analysis of the handwriting of one of the letters Clarisse claimed to have received from those who wanted her to remain silent shows that she had herself forged the letter.

Born at Lyon in 1877, Edmond Locard became one of France's greatest scientific detectives. A student of Dr. Alexandre Lacassagne, Locard, based in his native city, served both the Sûreté nationale and private clients. Because of his enthusiasm for Sherlock Holmes and their shared emphasis on observation of physical clues, Locard has been dubbed the "French Sherlock Holmes" by Irving Wallace, who interviewed the venerable sleuth in 1949 and again in 1963, when Locard had reached the age of eighty-six ("The French Sherlock Holmes," in *The Sunday Gentleman* [New York: Simon & Schuster, 1965]). In addition to his books on criminology, policing, forgery, poison, and forensic science, Locard has written a volume of professional reminiscences (*Confidences: Souvenirs d'un policier* [Lyon: Éditions Lugdunum. 1942]) and a monograph on the Gouffé trunk murder (*La malle sanglante de Millery* [Paris: Gallimard, 1934]) and has edited a series of causes célèbres, to which he has contributed books on poisoner Marie Lafarge; Caserio, assassin of President Carnot; anarchist Orsini; and Mata Hari. Another of his studies for the series records his first great detective triumph, the unmasking of Angèle Laval as the prolific writer of anonymous letters in Tulle, who inspired Henri-Georges Clouzot's celebrated film *Le corbeau* [The Raven] (1943).

L.27 Logan, John *Never the Sinner.* New York: Samuel French, 1999.

■ Fourteen years after its world premiere at Chicago's Stormfield Theatre, *Never the Sinner* enjoyed a successful off-Broadway run in 1999. Remaining faithful to the court record and nonfiction accounts of the Leopold-Loeb murder case, the play presents the still-ongoing clash of viewpoints regarding the application of capital punishment to unrepentant killers. Clarence Darrow, even as he rejects his clients' Nietzschean justification of their brutal murder of teenager Bobby Franks, opposes the death penalty without qualification, hating the sin but "never the sinner." Prosecutor Robert Crowe disagrees, asking acerbically, "And I wonder what Mrs. Franks would say to that?" The play's dialogue is punctuated by a heartbeat perhaps representing both the life that the killers callously ended and the humanity that they failed to consult within their own breasts.

L.28 Lo Kuan Chung *All Men Are Brothers* [Shui Hu Chuan, or "Water Margin Novel"]. Trans. Pearl S. Buck. 2 vols. New York: John Day, 1933.

■ In her introduction, Buck notes that "many Chinese scholars believe [fourteenth-century novelist] Lo Kuan Chung, the author of [*The Romance of the Three Kingdoms*], wrote "Shui Hu Chuan" also, and it seems fairly sure that at least he revised it and perhaps made substantial changes and additions, whether or not it be true that he wrote the whole."

The central figure of the sprawling novel is a historical brigand of the Sung dynasty, Sung Chiang, who established a band with a core of thirty-six loyal men at Liang Shan in Shandong Province. Folk tradition treated Sung Chiang as a patriot and friend of the poor, despite his widespread raids, and credited him with capturing the outlaw Fang La and helping the government suppress a rebellion. In fact, Sung Chiang was probably executed by imperial authorities about 1125 A.D. When the Ming dynasty began (1368), its rulers did not look kindly on literary adulation of outlaws, and the *Shui Hu Chuan* was supplemented to end with Sung Chiang's death of poisoning. The popular bandit hero had also appeared in dramas of the previous Yüan (Mongol) period.

L.29 London, Geo *Comédies et vaudevilles judiciaires.* Paris: Librairie Générale de Droit et de Jurisprudence, 1932.

■ The second chapter contains London's humorous reflections on Dr. Charles Paul, the leading forensic scientist of his time. London styles Dr. Paul, who talked confidentially to his corpses, the "eternal witness."

L.30 ——— *Les grands procès de l'année 1927–1938.* 12 vols. Paris: Les Éditions de France, 1928–39.

■ Continuing the tradition of such illustrious predecessors as Albert Bataille and Georges Claretie, reporter Geo London brought his acute powers of observation and ready wit to the coverage of French criminal trials, important or picturesque, between 1927 and 1938. As the prefaces to many of his annual trial volumes attest, he was widely admired by the lawyers and judges of his era. An anecdote of C. Campinchi, a Paris trial lawyer, illustrates London's attachment to his deadlines. After a man was condemned on the basis of a devastating piece of testimony, the defendant's outraged mother told London that she would kill the witness. The journalist is supposed to have replied with a bow: "Thanks for letting me know. Could you manage to do it before 5 o'clock? That's the hour for my provincial edition."

L.31 ———— *L'Humour au tribunal.* Paris: Librairie Générale de Droit et de Jurisprudence, 1931.

■ London's anecdotes are studded with names and personalities of the great twentieth-century French trial lawyers, including Henry Torrès and Landru's defender, Vincent de Moro-Giafferi.

L.32 ———— *Les mystères de Themis.* Paris: S.E.P.E., 1947.

■ London attended the trial of the civil suit brought by executioner Anatole Deibler asserting the right to be given a ground-floor apartment because of his weak heart.

L.33 Londres, Albert. *Au bagne* [In the Prison Camp]. Paris: Albin Michel, 1932.

■ This powerful reportage of journalist Londres's visit to French Guiana influenced the decision of the French Assembly to abolish prison camps in 1938.

L.34 Longfellow, Henry Wadsworth *Giles Corey of the Salem Farms.* In *The New-England Tragedies.* Boston: Ticknor & Fields, 1868.

■ This underappreciated verse play, published eighty-five years before the premiere of Arthur Miller's *The Crucible*, is a tragedy of two victims of the Salem witch hunt, Giles Corey (spelled Cory in the historical sources) and his wife, Martha. At the trial of Goodwife Corey, accused of afflicting Mary Walcott, Martha's husband, Giles, as in real life, is compelled to testify against her, stating that in her presence he inexplicably found it difficult to pray. Mary was executed and Giles was pressed to death for refusing to plead to the charges against him. Giles explains his adamancy in a speech that rivals the eloquence of Miller's John Proctor:

> I will not plead.
> If I deny, I am condemned already,
> In courts where ghosts appear as witnesses,
> And swear men's lives away. If I confess,
> Then I confess a lie, to buy a life
> Which is not life, but death in life.
> I will not bear false witness against any,
> Not even against myself, whom I count least.

In the Longfellow drama, John Proctor plays a treacherous role offstage; he has reportedly accused Corey of having burned his house. Other historical figures appearing in the play are the West Indian slave Tituba; Cotton Mather, shown as suffering pangs of conscience about the trials; and the archvillain of the piece, Magistrate Hathorne (who was an ancestor of Longfellow's Bowdoin College classmate, Nathaniel Hawthorne).

Longfellow anticipates the conclusions of some modern scholars (for example, Paul Boyer and Stephen Nissenbaum, in their *Salem Possessed: The Social Origins of Witchcraft* [1974]) in attributing the witchcraft allegations to social or economic grievances. Corey's farm worker John Gloyd testifies against him because he feels underpaid and overworked.

L.35 Loomis, Stanley *A Crime of Passion*. Philadelphia: Lippincott, 1967.

■ This is the principal account in English of the Duc Théobald de Choiseul-Praslin's murder of his wife in their palatial home, Hôtel Sébastiani, 55 rue du Faubourg St. Honoré, Paris, in August 1847 (see F.7). Loomis relates the crime to the period of French romanticism, a movement to which the unfortunate duchess made her own modest contribution with the letters she wrote between 1838 to the year of her murder. Many world-famous writers (including Victor Hugo and Nathaniel Hawthorne [see H.15]) took an interest in governess Henriette Deluzy, who was suspected, but ultimately cleared, of complicity in the murder, which was a strand in the public hostility to the aristocracy that ultimately precipitated the Revolution of 1848.

L.36 Lorca, Federíco García *Blood Wedding*. 1933. In *Three Plays: Blood Wedding/Yerma/ The House of Bernarda Alba*. Trans. Michael Dewell and Carmen Zapata. Intro. Christopher Maurer. New York: Farrar, Straus & Giroux, 1993.

■ Lorca was inspired to write his masterpiece *Blood Wedding* by newspaper accounts of the abduction of a bride before her wedding near the Andalusian town of Níjar in the arid province of Almería. Francisca Cañadas Morales (the model for Lorca's Bride) had been carrying on a love affair with her cousin, Curro Montes Cañadas, a dashing womanizer who refused to marry her. In spite, she agreed to wed a spiritless laborer, whose relatives saw the marriage as the best means of improving his economic lot. When Curro overheard Francisca quarreling with her fiancé before the ceremony was to begin, he concluded that she still loved him and decided to run away with her. Francisca told the judge that the decision was hers: "Since I liked my cousin more than my fiancé, and since what he offered me was better than the life I would have had with Casimiro, I thought about it alone in my room while I was putting on my wedding dress, and when my cousin, going round to the back of the house, came to my room, I said: 'It's now or never. Take me away with you before Casimiro wakes up and my brother-in-law arrives.' And we escaped on Curro Montes's horse."

The real-life murder that followed the kidnapping of the bride is much more prosaic than the duel that claims the lives of the two rivals in Lorca's play. José Perez Pino, the groom's brother, encountered the fleeing lovers on the road before the wedding guests had even noticed their absence; he shot Curro to death (see Ian Gibson, *Federico Garcia Lorca: A Life* [New York: Pantheon, 1990], 335–39).

L.37 Louis, Michel *La bête du Gévaudan: L'Innocence des loups* [The Beast of Gévaudan: The Innocence of Wolves]. Paris: Perrin, 1992.

The "Beast of Gévaudan," a real-life precursor of the Hound of the Baskervilles, is credited with having killed more than a hundred people and mauled dozens more in Gévaudan and neighboring Auvergne between 1764 and 1767. Some have blamed wolves gone homicidal, but private zookeeper Michel Louis claims that the much-maligned animals are too shy of human beings to have undertaken a murderous campaign on such a grand scale, nor do they decapitate their victims as the Beast was prone to do.

Louis finds a human agency behind the attacks in the person of Antoine Chastel, allegedly a sadist who trained as a killer a hybrid between a male wolf and a bitch. The ravening Beast remains a popular image on the French scene and graces the sign of a Left Bank tavern.

L.38 Lucas-Dubreton, J. [pseudonym of Lucas de Peslouan.] *Lacenaire, ou Le romantisme de l'assassinat.* In series *Le sphinx.* Paris: Editions de la Nouvelle Revue Critique, 1930.

■ This monograph is an effective antidote for the grandiosity, self-pity, and selective recall of the past that characterize the memoirs of sociopath killer Pierre-François Lacenaire. Lucas-Dubreton fills in many passages in Lacenaire's life that the criminal preferred to gloss over, including his undistinguished career in the Parisian gangland. In this historian's view, Lacenaire's vaunted "war against society" does not appear to have been waged relentlessly out of fixed philosophical commitment but to have consisted of sporadic acts triggered by career failures and need for ready cash.

However, Lucas-Dubreton tends to credit rumors that, if true, would enhance Lacenaire's own wish to establish links with the French romantics. Lacenaire supposedly abandoned a plan to assassinate Eugène Scribe only because the playwright made him a gift of two louis, and critic Jules Janin bought his life for 50 francs when the uninvited Lacenaire appeared at a dance with murder in his heart.

L.39 ——— *Louvel le régicide.* In series *Drames judiciaires d'autrefois.* Paris: Perrin, 1923.

■ Surely one of the longest-premeditated political assassinations in history was the stabbing of the Duc de Berry, second in line to the French throne, outside the Paris opera house on the night of February 13, 1820. The murderer, a poorly educated saddler named Pierre Louvel, plotted his crime for six years as he brooded over the Bourbon betrayal of France in alliance with invading foreign powers. Freeing his mind of monarchist prejudices such as those displayed by Chateaubriand, Lucas-Dubreton, reporting judge (*maître de requêtes*) of France's supreme administrative court (*Conseil d'Etat*), portrays Louvel as an honest patriot imbued with deistic principles of the republican era who resisted stoutly the efforts of the conspiracy theorists to wring a false admission that he had collaborated with other extremists in the murder of the duke. Among a host of fascinating revelations, Lucas-Dubreton, a close friend of historian G. Lenotre, notes that the French investigators of the early nineteenth century employed a technique anticipating the lie detector: during Louvel's questioning, a doctor felt his pulse and found that it always beat with the same regularity (146).

L.40 Lukas, J. Anthony   *Big Trouble: A Murder in a Small Western Town Sets Off a Struggle for the Soul of America.* New York: Simon & Schuster, 1997.

■ In December 1905, Idaho's former governor, Frank Steunenberg, was assassinated through the explosion of a bomb set at the gate of his home in Caldwell. Six years earlier Steunenberg, while in office, had called in federal troops to quell labor violence in the Coeur d'Alene silver and lead mining district, and his killing was suspected to be an act of revenge on the part of the Western Federation of Miners (WFM). A labor bomber, Harry Orchard (whose real name was Albert E. Horsley), was promptly arrested and confessed to famous Pinkerton detective James McParland, implicating three WFM officials as his paymasters: William Haywood, Charles H. Moyer, and George A. Pettibone.

In the Author's Note, Lukas explains that he undertook his gargantuan study of Steunenberg's assassination because he thought it would be interesting to examine that moment in American history when capital and labor came closest to plunging the nation into class warfare. Lukas describes his book as "both a narrative of a sensational murder case and a social tapestry of the land in which that case unfolded." The consideration of the social and political context of the killing is most effective when Lukas portrays the frontier community in which Steunenberg lived and flourished; the interlocks of early Idaho government with mining, railroad, timber, real estate, newspaper, and banking interests; rivalries and ideological differences that sapped the strength of the nascent labor movement; the record of black troops sent to pacify Coeur d'Alene and their uneasy relations with the community; and President Theodore Roosevelt's labor policies, which consisted mainly of railing against capitalists and unions with equal vigor. Much of the bulk of this volume is accounted for by lively but sometimes inordinately detailed portrayals of figures who played important roles in the murder case, including Governor Steunenberg; Harry Orchard; detective McParland; Bill Haywood; Clarence Darrow, one of Haywood's defense counsel who contributed signally to his acquittal; and the "gentlemen of the press" who covered the trial. Occasionally, Lukas's biographical digressions serve little purpose except to provide color and amusement, notably in an interlude entitled "Quartet," which he devotes to Ethel Barrymore, who while on tour came to court to hear Darrow's opening argument and later met Orchard in the warden's office; Hugo Münsterberg, a Harvard psychology professor who assayed Orchard's credibility for *McClure's*; Walter Johnson, pitching for a local team when the trial was going forward; and Gifford Pinchot, chief U.S. forester.

By the time Lukas's narrative ends, the prosecutions of all three labor defendants have failed, and Senator William Borah, one of the counsel for the state, has himself been tried and acquitted under a charge of fraud in the course of his client Frank Steunenberg's acquisition of federal timberland. The author comments that the opposing forces in "this nasty class war . . . had just about canceled each other out." Their tactics bore a close resemblance: "Operative for operative, hired gun for hired gun, bought juror for bought juror, perjured witness for perjured witness, conniving lawyer for conniving lawyer, partisan reporter for partisan reporter, these cockeyed armies had fought each other to an exhausted standoff."

In a short epilogue that reads like an afterthought, Lukas concludes on the basis of his review of correspondence in the files of the Socialist weekly *Appeal to Reason* that Haywood and his accused co-conspirators were guilty of ordering the murder of Steunenberg. The principal letter cited was pseudonymously written to the managing editor by George H. Shoaf, Socialist newsman and agent provocateur. Shoaf opines that "trickery and audacity liberated the miners' officials." Although this view may be correct, it is disappointing that Lukas, after such an exhaustive study, places prime reliance on the words of Shoaf, whom he consistently depicts as a liar and confidence man.

L.41 Lüsebrink, Hans-Jürgen, ed. *Histoires curieuses et véritables de Cartouche et de Mandrin.* Paris: Montalba, 1984.

■ The editor, a specialist at the University of Bayreuth on depictions of criminality in eighteenth-century French literature, here collects criminal "biographies," poems, and dialogues published in the so-called Blue Library (*Bibliothèque bleue*), a series of popular crime chapbooks published in the eighteenth and nineteenth centuries. Included are items related to the two eighteenth-century criminal heroes who have dominated the public mind in France, Parisian gangster Louis-Dominique Cartouche and smuggler–guerrilla chief Louis Mandrin. Another entry is a group of love letters of Madame Lescombat (see F.12). Lüsebrink contributes an illuminating introduction on the function of popular publications as successors to oral traditions of the "social bandit."

L.42 Lustgarten, Edgar *The Business of Murder.* London: Harrap, 1968.

■ Six serial or mass killers are the subjects of this volume: Britain's post–World War II murderers, John George Haigh, Neville George Clevely Heath, Peter Thomas Anthony Manuel, and John Reginald Halliday Christie; France's Henri Désiré Landru; and the infamous Irma Grese of the Belsen death camp.

The stories of these archcriminals are told in the author's later popular manner that reflects his work on radio and television; what they gain in fast pacing is sometimes offset by an insensitivity to human tragedies and a tendency to spout dubious generalizations about criminal behavior. As always, Lustgarten is at his best in portraying dramatic courtroom duels, such as Peter Manuel's *pro se* cross-examination of William Watt, whose wife, daughter, and sister-in-law Manuel had slaughtered (in addition to at least five other victims).

In his chapter on Christie, the 10 Rillington Place murderer, Lustgarten, unlike Ludovic Kennedy, concludes that Timothy Evans, not Christie, murdered Evans's wife, Beryl, and their daughter, Geraldine (see K.3).

Edgar Marcus Lustgarten was born in 1907, the son of a Manchester barrister. He was educated at Manchester Grammar School and at Oxford University (where, in 1930, he was president of the Oxford Union). Called to the bar, he practiced on the northern circuit. During World War II, Lustgarten broadcast propaganda on the BBC World Service. He stayed at the BBC after the war, chiefly as a producer; the "Prisoner at the Bar" series of famous trial reconstructions, which he wrote and presented, achieved a great success. He also published collections of true-crime articles and crime novels; on television, he narrated a fictional crime series and chaired political chat shows. In December 1978, he died in the reference department of the Marylebone Public Library.

Playwright and novelist Nigel Williams, in the comic novel *The Wimbledon Poisoner* (London: Faber & Faber, 1990), pays tribute to the ubiquity of Lustgarten as a crime commentator. The novel's protagonist, Henry Farr, who has decided to murder his wife, imagines that Lustgarten will one day point out his one fatal mistake: "He could see Edgar Lustgarten narrowing his eyes threateningly at the camera, as he paced out the length of Maple Drive. 'But Henry Farr,' Lustgarten was saying, 'with the folly of the criminal, the supreme arrogance of the murderer, had forgotten one vital thing. The shred of fibre that was to send Henry Farr to the gallows was—'"

L.43 ———— *The Chalk Pit Murder.* London: Hart-Davis, MacGibbon, 1974.

■ Thomas John Ley, age sixty-six, was passionately jealous of his friend and former mistress, Evelyn (Maggie) Brook, also sixty-six. Born in England, Ley had emigrated to Australia where he became Minister of Justice in New South Wales. After he and Maggie returned to England, Ley fancied that he saw rivals everywhere, and his obsession fixed on a young barman named Jack Mudie. The ex-minister formed a conspiracy for the elimination of Mudie. With the help of Lawrence Smith, a carpenter working on the renovation of his property; an unscrupulous chauffeur named John Buckingham and his son; and an unwitting woman, Lilian Bruce, Ley lured Mudie to his home at 5 Beaufort Gardens, where the young man was set upon and trussed from head to foot. Mudie's strangled body was later found in a Surrey chalk pit twenty-two miles away.

Buckingham turned Crown's evidence. Three days before the date set for his execution, Ley was reprieved and committed to Broadmoor as insane. Lustgarten explains how, in a misguided application of British principles of sportsmanship, Smith's sentence was commuted to life imprisonment once it had been determined that the instigator of the crime would not hang. In his persuasive analysis of the Home Office's leniency to Smith, Lustgarten contrasts this grant of mercy to the government's later refusal to reprieve Derek Bentley in the Craig and Bentley murder case, even though the gunman Christopher Craig, as a minor, could not be executed.

The Chalk Pit Murder is the only Lustgarten work devoted to a single case. As in the best of his crime essays, he shows less interest in the murder and its antecedents than in his analysis of the trial and the personalities of judge and counsel.

L.44 ———— *Defender's Triumph.* New York: Scribner, 1951.

■ Together with its companion volumes, *Verdict in Dispute* and *Woman in the Case*, this collection of Lustgarten's studies of criminal trials represents his finest work. Lustgarten says of the cases selected for this volume, "This is a book about four murder trials, in each of which the prisoner was acquitted. I do not suggest that any of them should have been convicted. I do suggest that *all* of them *would* have been convicted had they not been shielded by remarkable defenders."

The first essay serves up a Victorian favorite, the acquittal of Adelaide Bartlett, prosecuted for the 1886 murder of her husband, Edwin, by pouring liquid chloroform down his throat after first rendering him unconscious with chloroform fumes. The motive was allegedly provided by Adelaide's infatuation with the family's minister, the Reverend George Dyson. Lustgarten credits Adelaide's counsel, Edward Clarke (who unwaveringly believed in her innocence), as having "erected one of the greatest defences in the history of our courts." The powerful advocate was able to persuade the jury that Edwin Bartlett, suffering from depression, had committed suicide by swallowing a wineglass of chloroform while his wife was absent from the bedroom.

Patrick Hastings, in Lustgarten's view, "unquestionably takes rank among the greatest jury advocates who have ever adorned the Bar." In 1932 Hastings, who, unlike the "barnstorming" Marshall Hall, tended to underplay to the jury, achieved one of his greatest triumphs with the acquittal of socialite Elvira Barney in the shooting death of her lover Michael Stephen, who "had no genuine occupation" (he vaguely described himself as a dress designer). In her statement to police, Elvira admitted quarreling with Michael about another woman after he saw her home and claimed that her revolver discharged after he tried to wrest it from her, fearing she would harm herself. A trial highlight recreated by Lustgarten is Hastings's cross-examination of Crown expert Robert Churchill: counsel obtained the witness's admission that "if one person has the revolver in his hand and the other person seizes it and the revolver is pointing towards him, it is certain to go off if it is pressed hard enough."

Due to the "magnetic intensity and dynamic force" of the famed Edward Marshall Hall, artist-designer Robert Wood was acquitted of the 1907 slashing of prostitute Phyllis Dimmock's throat in Camden Town, London. A nettling issue facing Marshall Hall was Wood's attempt to have another girlfriend, Ruby Hall, concoct an alibi; the advocate calmly told the jury that the alibi did not cover the established time of the murder and was intended "not to prove that he did not commit the murder, but to prevent him being publicly inculpated with a harlot."

Norman Birkett's defense of Toni (sometimes spelled Tony) Mancini achieved the remarkable result of obtaining an acquittal of man who, in 1933, had stuffed a dead body of a woman in a trunk and then proceeded to share a flat with it; ordinarily, mistreatment, concealment or disposal of a corpse is regarded by juries as insuperable evidence that the defendant committed murder. A waiter, Mancini (whose real name was Cecil Lois England) lived on his mistress Violette Kaye's earnings in Brighton; he claimed to have found her dead in their flat and that panic-stricken, because of his criminal record as a thief, he had decided to hide her body. At the trial, while urging the jury not to dismiss the possibility that Kaye, drugged or intoxicated, had fallen down the stairs, Birkett laid greater stress on the alternative view that a rough "john" had done her in.

L.45 ———— *The Illustrated Story of Crime.* Chicago: Follett, 1976.

■ This illustrated omnibus is divided into chapters dealing with gangsters, financial crimes, political assassinations, kidnapping, insanity pleas, sex crimes, and unsolved cases. In his preface, Lustgarten defends the study of crime as a window that opens on human nature and maintains that "the window cannot be held responsible for the prospect." In his view crime is "fundamentally unchanging" despite social, technological, and moral developments.

L.46 ———— *The Judges and the Judged.* London: Odhams, 1961.

■ Another of the author's omnibus volumes, *The Judges and the Judged*, contains ninety brief sketches of dramatic highlights of criminal and civil trials and of the personalities who dominated them. The volume is divided into five sections dealing with:

- Eighteen judges, each of whom is discussed in the context of a significant trial over which he presided
- A group of defendants, including Alma Rattenbury, Lord Haw Haw, Mary Blandy, Herbert Armstrong, and Julius and Ethel Rosenburg
- Key expert and lay witnesses, including forensic scientists such as Sir Bernard Spilsbury and toxicologist Dr. Alfred Swaine Taylor and, among the fact witnesses, Evelyn Nesbit Thaw and Whittaker Chambers
- A group of "sensational" cases, including the treason trials of Sir Roger Casement and Alfred Dreyfus
- A concluding series of "scandalous" trials, including those of Queen Caroline and the bigamous Duchess of Kingston

L.47 ———— *The Murder and the Trial.* New York: Scribner, 1958.

■ This volume, which republishes many essays from Lustgarten's previous books, is of principal interest because of its inclusion of three pieces from his *Prisoner at the Bar* broadcasts for the BBC's "Light Programme." The subjects are: Frederick Seddon, convicted for poisoning miserly lodger Miss Eliza Mary Barrow (Lustgarten believes that Seddon, "the heartless brute, the money-mad man, the clever devil who could stand up to [cross-examination by] Rufus Isaacs," was shown to be guilty to a moral certainty); Richard Pigott, who forged a letter signed in the name of Irish patriot Charles Stewart Parnell, which expressed approval of the Dublin murder of a British government representative; and Lizzie Borden (Lustgarten's only treatment of an American case).

In an introduction, American crime novelist and critic Anthony Boucher asserts that Lustgarten possesses all the four qualities needed for outstanding true-crime writing: literacy, scholarship, insight, and "a feeling of irony, of relish."

L.48 ———— *Verdict in Dispute.* New York: Scribner, 1950.

■ Lustgarten considers six famous murder trials in which the verdicts rendered "are open to dispute"; three of the verdicts, in his belief, are "demonstrably bad."

The 1889 conviction of Florence Maybrick for the poisoning of her husband, James, with arsenic obtained by the soaking of flypapers was, in Lustgarten's view, not based on adequate proof of guilt. Had the Court of Criminal Appeal then existed, he believes that the verdict would have been quashed instead of remaining to "mock at and discredit the fair name of British justice."

The burglar and convict Steinie Morrison (an alias of Morris Stein) was tried at the Old Bailey in 1911 on a charge of murdering Leon Beron, whose body, stripped of money and valuables, had been found on Clapham Common. Two slashes on the victim's face were described as "S-shaped" by a doctor at the inquest. Lustgarten comments on the "feverish, uncontrolled excitement" inspired by the crime: "Outside the court, in London's foreign quarter, witnesses were coaxed, threatened, drilled and even beaten by partisan groups." Morrison was convicted, largely on the basis of dubious eyewitness testimony of cabmen and the introduction of the defendant's prior criminal record. Lustgarten regards the verdict as questionable "because it failed to give the prisoner the benefit of a doubt, and was rooted in a trial that gave scant cause for satisfaction."

Of the verdicts considered in the book, Lustgarten regards as least debatable the conviction of Norman Thorne for the 1924 murder of his sweetheart, London typist Elsie Cameron. Believing herself pregnant, Elsie insisted on marriage, but Thorne had set his sights on another woman. He murdered and dismembered his cast-off lover and buried her in a chicken run on his Crowborough farm. In his trial at Lewes, Thorne pleaded that he found Cameron hanging inside the farm hut, a suicide. Sir Bernard Spilsbury, the Crown's forensic expert, told the jury that he had observed eight bruises on the dead girl's body, all inflicted shortly before death, and one on the temple, caused by a crushing blow; he saw no signs of asphyxiation. Lustgarten holds open the possibility that Thorne did not wilfully murder Elsie but had become involved in a deadly struggle when he tried to leave the hut. As in many other murder trials, the concealment of the body must have told powerfully against him.

In his account of the notorious trial of Edith Thompson and Frederick Bywaters for the murder of her husband, Percy (see B.78), Lustgarten joins in the prevailing view that her conviction was unjust. He opines that her trial "was from first to last a failure in human understanding; a failure to grasp and comprehend a personality not envisaged in the standard legal textbooks and driven by forces more powerful and eternal than those that are studied at the Inns of Court."

In the epigraph of his essay on the 1931 murder of Julia Wallace (see G.23), Lustgarten quotes drama critic and crime-fancier James Agate's view: "Either the murderer was [Julia's husband, William Herbert] Wallace or it wasn't. If it wasn't, then here at last is the perfect murder. If it was, then here is a murder so nearly perfect that the Court of Criminal Appeal, after examining the evidence, decided to quash Wallace's conviction." In his summary of the trial, Lustgarten singles out for praise the trial judge, Mr. Justice (later Lord) Wright, who virtually invited the jury to acquit Wallace. The jury, however, declined to follow his lead. Lustgarten comments scathingly that "their fathers had perversely convicted Mrs. Maybrick, and now these representatives of a more enlightened epoch jealously preserved the Liverpool tradition."

The final article examines the trial of Lizzie Borden. It is Lustgarten's speculation that the small-town jury may have found defense counsel and ex-Governor George Robinson's simple language more comprehensible than District Attorney Hosea Knowlton's more elevated style.

L.49 ———— *The Woman in the Case.* New York: Scribner, 1955.
■ This collection studies four women who played important roles in famous murder cases, two as defendants, one as a victim, and another as a key witness.

In his consideration of Alma Rattenbury, acquitted of complicity in her jealous young lover George Percy Stoner's 1935 mallet slaying of her seemingly complaisant husband, Lustgarten takes issue with her common portrayal as a nymphomaniac. In his view, Rattenbury, who was a sometime song writer, had an artistic temperament that was accompanied by *nostalgie de la boue*, which he freely paraphrases as "a craving—especially a sexual craving—for the dregs." It was this impulse that led her to initiate her fatal affair with Stoner, the Rattenburys' chauffeur and handyman. After the trial, in which Stoner alone was convicted, Alma committed suicide. Lustgarten sermonizes: "Mr. Rattenbury died and Mrs. Rattenbury took her life and Stoner passed into penal servitude because a woman entered upon and idealised a sex relationship in which the seeds of catastrophe were plainly visible to any disinterested spectator from the start."

Lustgarten charges that, in the erroneous 1909 conviction of Oscar Slater for the murder and robbery of Miss Marion Gilchrist, "the Glasgow police, going all out for a conviction, employed as their main instrument [Helen Lambie] a girl of twenty-one" (see B.73). In analyzing the ability of the police to mold Lambie's testimony placing Slater at the murder scene, Lustgarten notes that she was "mulish, extremely self-opinionated, vain." Lambie, who was the victim's maid, became a nationwide celebrity. Her "name is in every newspaper and on every tongue; casual acquaintances gaze at her in awe and proudly point her out to others as she passes by." It is not surprising that she "has not emerged quite untouched from these experiences."

The starvation murder of Harriet Staunton by her husband and his brother, who coveted her modest fortune (see J.6), could, according to Lustgarten, "never have succeeded but for the victim's curious blend of childish docility and childish stubbornness." He does not regard her as insane or imbecile but "of immature mind and arrested intellect." Resenting the "white-wash on the Staunton brothers" that followed their conviction, Lustgarten argues that they and Elizabeth, wife of Harriet's brother-in-law, Patrick Staunton, were at the heart of the conspiracy against her life.

In the final essay, Lustgarten revisits the case of Madeleine Smith, whom he calls an "enigma." At the time he died of arsenic poisoning, Smith's lover, Emile L'Angelier, angered at her decision to break off their affair, had been threatening to deliver her intimate letters to her father. Although many writers roundly condemn the "Scotch verdict" of not proven that liberated Madeleine, Lustgarten shows understanding of the jury's dilemma. Smith's purchases of arsenic (supposedly for cosmetic use) were undisputed, but there was no direct evidence that she had met her lover on any of the three dates on which the prosecution claimed that poison had been administered. Lustgarten maintains that, had Smith not been disqualified from testifying by the trial procedures then in effect, her cross-examination would have resulted in conviction. In a masterstroke of imagination, he supplies the line of questioning that would have shattered her defense.

L.50 Lyttkens, Yngve *Attarpsmorden* [The Murders at Attarp]. Stockholm: Albert Bonniers, 1953.

■ Beginning in 1946, Stockholm lawyer Lyttkens wrote a fine series of monographs devoted to famous Swedish murder cases. Typically his presentation of the facts is objective and unobtrusive, and he reserves his views on guilt or innocence for a final chapter. Given his profession Lyttkens unsurprisingly emphasizes court proceedings and evidentiary issues, but the setting of many of the crimes in remote country houses lends the same nostalgic allure that can be found in the plays of Chekhov or the young Gorky.

The Murders at Attarp is Lyttkens's sixth work. On June 5, 1845, a former state controller, the fiery-tempered drunkard Per Ludvig Ekwall, his fourteen-year-old daughter Henriette, and housemaid Maja Stina Forsberg took ill. The maid died when Ekwall refused to send for a doctor, and despite the medical attentions the family procured when his own condition worsened, he expired within a few days; both deaths were shown to be due to arsenic. Fortunately, Henriette Ekwall recovered from the poisoning.

The sensational murder trial that followed was studded with confessions, retractions, charges, and countercharges by members of the Ekwall household. The first to bare her soul was a maid, Hedda Thorman, who accused herself of having murdered her newborn child, fathered (so she said) by Controller Ekwall's son Wilhelm; and of proceeding at Wilhelm's suggestion to poison spinach and a milk bowl in the family kitchen to dispose of Maja Stina Forsberg, who Hedda claimed had helped her to murder her infant. By degrees Hedda retracted her entire confession, asserting that she had made her statement for the purpose of improving her jail accommodations.

The next and champion self-denouncer was Controller Ekwall's eldest daughter, Sophie, who made a series of conflicting declarations. At first she claimed to have poisoned her father to protect her mother and herself against his violent treatment and also to remove him as a perceived barrier to her planned marriage. Later, Sophie threw the responsibility for the poisonings on her father, who, she asserted, wanted to take his own life and ordered her to procure and administer the arsenic. Finally, she retracted this statement, avowing that she had planned her father's murder in concert with her mother; the maid Maja Stina Forsberg was also liquidated because of her knowledge that the maid's brother had supplied the arsenic. The religious Mrs. Ekwall steadfastly denied any role in the poisonings.

The final judgment in the case found Sophie Ekwall guilty of participation in the murder but acquitted Mrs. Ekwall and the maid Hedda Thorman. Author Lyttkens agrees with this verdict and accepts the view of certain relatives of Mrs. Ekwall that Sophie had turned to arsenic to free herself from an incestuous relationship with her father.

The trial was reported by famed Swedish novelist and poet C. J. L. Almqvist, who compared the case to that of Marie Lafarge, of which he also published a journalistic account. Almqvist was himself later tried for attempted arsenic poisoning (see B.27); a biographer who believes him guilty has speculated that his crime was inspired by knowledge of the Lafarge and Ekwall cases (see A. Hemming-Sjöberg, *A Poet's Tragedy: The Trial of C. J. L. Almqvist*, trans. E. Classen [London: Allen & Unwin, 1932], 182–87).

L.51 ———— *Dramat på Broxvik* [Drama at Broxvik]. Stockholm: Albert Bonniers, 1948.

■ In December 1895, Chamberlain Evert Reinhold Mauritz Taube von Block died at his country house in Broxvik after a month's illness culminating in the vomiting of blood. A young family friend, Helga Fägersköld, who was visiting at the time, revealed to the chamberlain's son, Evert Jr., to whom she had subsequently become engaged, that she suspected his mother of poisoning his father with sublimate of mercury. On two occasions during Evert Taube's illness, she had come across Mrs. Taube pouring a suspect liquid into a jug of fruit soup intended for her husband; Helga also claimed that Mrs. Taube, after the chamberlain's death, had confessed to poisoning him.

An autopsy performed at the demand of Evert Taube Jr. found nonlethal traces of quicksilver and arsenic. Poisoning charges were filed against widow Taube, but the proceedings were disrupted by a bombshell of Helga Fägersjöld's own making: in an ill-conceived effort to conceal the birth of an illegitimate child, she simulated a knife attack on herself and simultaneously sent the prosecutor a written confession of Taube's poisoning (which she vainly hoped would be taken as a forgery by a third party).

As a result of Helga's twin hoaxes, she was also charged with Chamberlain Taube's death, and the inconsistent cases against her and widow Taube were consolidated. Ultimately, the court acquitted both women but grudgingly ruled that Helga was being freed despite "troubling circumstances" that weighed against her innocence.

Despite Helga Fägersköld's hoaxes impulsively concocted to cover up the birth of her child, Lyttkens essentially accepts her testimony tending to show that poison was administered to Chamberlain Taube by his wife. He theorizes that Mrs. Taube was mentally unstable, perhaps by heredity; Mrs. Taube's mother had ended her days in an asylum, and there was evidence that Mrs. Taube had tried years before to murder her husband and also attempted to poison her brother. Lyttkens observes that, to the contrary, no motive for the poisoning of Taube could be brought home to Helga Fägersköld. The prosecution suggested that she was trying to shift control of the family's estate from Mrs. Taube to her son Evert Jr., but Lyttkens points out that the chamberlain's death preceded Helga's romance with Evert Jr. The greatest remaining unsolved mystery of the case is the cause of death; the poison fed the chamberlain may not have been a lethal dose.

M

M.1 Maass, Joachim   *The Gouffé Case.* Trans. Michael Bullock. New York: Harper, 1960.

■ German journalist and novelist Joachim Maass, in his fictional rendering of the trunk murder of process server Toussaint-Augustin Gouffé (B.60), invents an epilogue to the trial, which resulted in the execution of Michel Eyraud and the sentencing of his mistress, Gabrielle Bompard, to twenty years of hard labor.

In Maass's novel, Bompard is acquitted; a young man named Edmond Jacquart pursues her across the American continent from Saratoga Springs and the forests of Vermont to California. At first Jacquart's quest is motivated by a dedication to truth and justice, but he becomes sexually obsessed with his quarry, crying at last: "You tugged me into your bed, you dragged me through the empty land. Instead of the answer I so hotly desired, I heard in my ears only the panting of your lust, the buzzing of emptiness." She shoots him, but her bullet bounces off an amulet. Only semiconscious, he seems to glimpse her retreating form: "she was carried off in [a] ghostly manner and disappeared far away among the black rock and seething mist of the cliff."

M.2 Macé, Gustave *La police Parisienne.* 5 vols. [*La service de la Sûreté: Mon premier crime; Un joli monde; Gibier de Saint-Lazare; Mes lundis en prison; Mon musée criminel.*] Paris: G. Charpentier, 1885–90.

■ Macé embarked on the publication of this series six months after his departure from service as the head of the Paris Sûreté. In *Mon premier crime* [*My First Crime*], he recounted one of his greatest triumphs, the arrest of Pierre Voirbo for the murder of Désiré Bodasse, whose head he threw into the Seine (see Armand Lanoux, *La tête tranchée* [Geneva: Famot, 1974]).

Un joli monde [A "Pretty" World] is described by its author as "the parade of the army of evil in broad daylight, from the fake beggar to the chloroformer who puts his victim to sleep scientifically, the better to rob him." In *Gibier de Saint-Lazare* [The "Jailbirds" of Saint-Lazare], Macé surveys the world of prostitution; and in *Mes lundis en prison* [My Mondays in Prison] he discusses various types of criminals under lock and key.

In the final volume of the series, *Mon musée criminel* [My Crime Museum], illustrated by thirty-one pages of photographs, Macé presents his black museum of crime. In his introduction he identifies as his proudest accomplishment the independence of the Sûreté, which in 1887 was freed of the sovereignty of the Chief of the Municipal Police and placed under the immediate direction of the Police Prefect.

M.3 McGuinness, Frank *Innocence: The Life and Death of Michelangelo Merisi, Caravaggio.* London: Faber & Faber, 1987.

■ This play, in two acts respectively titled "Life" and "Death," was first performed at Dublin's Gate Theatre in 1986. The action is set in Rome on May 29, 1606, the day on which Caravaggio killed Rannuccio Tomassoni in a brawl resulting from their earlier ball game (sometimes identified as tennis). Caravaggio is shown consorting with a golden-hearted whore named Lena and providing a pair of young male "rough trade" hookers named Antonio and Lucio to his patron and lover Cardinal Francesco del Monte. For all his violence and attraction to darkness, the painter cannot break free of memories of his childhood, which are stirred by a visit from his brother and the ghost of a sister who died in childbirth.

In the second act, Caravaggio briefly takes refuge with Lena after his murder of Tomassoni, which is variously explained by the play's characters. Lucio tells Lena that the victim "tried to do us out of some money for swag we nicked at the Cardinal's house," while to Caravaggio the tragedy seemed to have been foreordained: "I was following him. Waiting to kill him. All my life. To kill. To die. Maybe he was following me. Finally, we touched." It is the Cardinal who voices the deepest understanding of the great artist's personality: "A dangerous man, aren't you, Caravaggio? You believe with a depth that is frightening. And with a vision that is divine."

M.4 Machen, Arthur *The Canning Wonder.* New York: Knopf, 1926.

■ In the preface to his scrupulously fair account of the mysterious disappearance of Elizabeth Canning near London in 1753 (see D.15 and F.8), Machen asserts: "In our investigation . . . there is one palmary clue which we must seize firmly at the beginning, and never allow to escape us, and this is the sure and undisputed fact that Elizabeth Canning was an infernal liar."

After twenty-eight days' absence from home, Canning returned in distressing physical condition, claiming that she had been imprisoned in a brothel on little bread and a jug of water after refusing to become a prostitute. On the basis of her accusations, an elderly gypsy, Mary Squires (see Fig. 5), was sentenced to death under England's Bloody Code, not for kidnapping but for cutting off and stealing Canning's stays. When official and public sentiment turned against Canning, Squires was reprieved.

Machen's book focuses on Canning's subsequent perjury trial, which resulted in her transportation to America after two recalcitrant jurors were bullied into agreeing with the guilty verdict. Although duly noting the division in testimony concerning the whereabouts of Squires on the date of the alleged abduction (January 2), Machen seizes on the overwhelming evidence that Elizabeth's story was false. In her statements after returning home, she had failed to describe the gypsy's remarkable facial disfigurement. On being escorted by a party of warrant servers to "Mother Wells's" bordello, the house in which she had supposedly been held, she was slow to identify the room in which she claimed to have been detained, a loft that, in any event, did not correspond to her earlier descriptions; and the roof from which she dropped in her escape did not, as she had previously asserted, contain a penthouse to break her fall.

Machen speculates that Elizabeth's disappearance had a more shameful explanation that she was anxious to conceal: "I think that someone hustled her into a coach, and got in after her and proceeded to press his suit with a certain vigour and alacrity, whereupon Elizabeth squealed, but was not seriously annoyed. . . . . And then, let us conjecture, the unknown took Elizabeth to a brothel and left her there the next morning, and that Elizabeth fell into the ways of the house."

The donations of Albert and Helen Borowitz to the Kent State University Libraries include an important collection of the works and correspondence of Arthur Machen.

M.5 Mailer, Norman *The Executioner's Song.* Boston: Little, Brown, 1979.

■ Gary Gilmore, who murdered gas station attendant Max Jensen and motel manager Bennie Bushnell, died before a Utah firing squad in January 1977. His execution was the first in the United States in ten years. Gilmore had attracted national attention by refusing to contest the execution order, and his reported last words were "Let's do it."

Writer and literary promoter Lawrence W. Schiller read about the scheduled execution of Gilmore and his refusal to file an appeal; he immediately went to work interviewing the condemned man and other persons with knowledge of the case. After reading the letters of Nicole Baker, Gilmore's lover, Schiller decided that the story would be perfect for Norman Mailer (see Carl Rollyson, *The Lives of Norman Mailer: A Biography* [New York: Paragon, 1991], 281–96). Mailer agreed and, in the light of publicity surrounding Gilmore's execution, decided that Gilmore "embodied many of the themes I've been living with all my life long." For his "true life novel," Mailer conducted about fifty interviews, supplementing the sixty that Schiller had done.

Book 1 of the novel, "Western Voices," begins with Gilmore's release from prison and culminates with his two murders nine months later. In composing this narrative, Mailer chose to "move through everybody's head"; he abandoned his controlling authorial voice and spoke, instead, in what novelist Joan Didion has called a "meticulously limited vocabulary and [a] voice as flat as the horizon . . . the authentic Western voice." He makes no attempt to explain Gilmore's murders, nor, indeed, did the killer, who took refuge behind the cryptic remark "I can't keep up with life."

The second half of *The Executioner's Song*, "Eastern Voices," focuses on the process of gathering material to write the novel. Lawrence Schiller, as Mailer's stand-in, dominates this portion of the story. Schiller is prompted by Gilmore's defensiveness to wonder whether "he was qualified, at bottom, to know Gary Gilmore." In the Afterword, Mailer confesses: "The story is as accurate as one can make it. This does not mean it has come a great deal closer to the truth than the recollections of the witnesses."

Norman Mailer, unheeding of the prior experience of Richard Wright, was to learn to his chagrin that writing fact-based crime literature is a safer occupation than vouching for the rehabilitation of real-life criminals. In 1941 Wright asked the governor of New Jersey to grant parole to Clinton Brewer, a black man imprisoned since 1923 for murdering a young woman, pointing out that Brewer had taught himself music composition. Brewer murdered another young woman within months of his release. Mailer, impressed by prisoner Jack Henry Abbott's literary talent, wrote to his Utah parole board advocating his release despite his record of violence. Six weeks after Abbott was freed, he fatally stabbed Richard Aidan, a twenty-two-year-old actor, dancer, and playwright (perhaps also possessing some artistic gifts) who worked at an East Village restaurant in New York City.

M.6 Malamud, Bernard *The Fixer*. New York: Farrar, Straus & Giroux, 1966.

▓ Yakov Bok, the hero of Bernard Malamud's Pulitzer Prize and National Book Award winning novel *The Fixer*, is a carpenter, painter, and handyman who can "fix what's broken—except in the heart." After his wife, Raisl, runs off with her lover, the "fixer" leaves his Jewish village (*shtetl*) for Kiev, where he hopes to improve his lot, dim as that prospect appears for a Jew in the Russia of Nicolas II. He becomes the supervisor of a brick factory belonging to an anti-Semite but can obtain such employment only through two infractions of law: he conceals his Jewish identity papers and takes up residence at the brickyard in a district reserved for Christians. A criminal investigation of these relatively minor offenses is expanded by unscrupulous officials into a groundless charge of "ritual murder," the stabbing of twelve-year-old Zhenia Golov for the alleged purpose of collecting his blood and delivering it to the synagogue for the making of Passover matzos. (The boy was, in fact, probably killed by his mother and her lover to prevent his revealing their gangland activities.)

The heart of the novel is Bok's existential struggle for survival in a tsarist prison, where only an honest investigative magistrate and a sympathetic guard seek to shield him from injustice and humiliation. An avowed freethinker and a devotee of Spinoza's philosophy, Jakob finds, as his trial date recedes tantalizingly before him, that he can also draw comfort from the Old and New Testaments. When he is ultimately offered his freedom for a false confession that he "witnessed" the murder of Zhenia by "Jewish compatriots," Bok declines because the price of liberation on these terms would be tragedy for others. The only solution he can conceive for the plight of Russians and Jews alike is the fall of the tsarist regime: "One thing I've learned, [Bok] thought, there's no such thing as an unpolitical man, especially a Jew. You can't be one without the other, that's clear enough. You can't sit still and see yourself destroyed. Afterwards he thought, Where there's no fight for it there's no freedom. What is it Spinoza says? If the state acts in ways that are abhorrent to human nature it's the lesser evil to destroy it." As Bok is finally led to his trial, one or two people in the crowd wave at him and some shout his name.

The facts of the crime that leads to Yakov Bok's ordeal are closely patterned after the trial of Mendel Beiliss for the 1911 ritual murder of thirteen-year-old Andrei Yushchinsky, whose body, bearing forty-seven wounds and drained of most of its blood, was found in a cave on the outskirts of Kiev (see Maurice Samuel, *Blood Accusation: The Strange History of the Beiliss Case* [New York: Knopf, 1966]). More likely suspects than the hapless Beiliss were the unsavory Vera Cheberyak and a trio of hoodlum associates (dubbed the "Troika"). Cheberyak's son Zhenya (Evgeny) was a friend of the dead youth. (As can be seen from the summary of *The Fixer*, Malamud reversed the roles of the two boys, converting the son of the female criminal into the victim.)

The trial of Beiliss ended in the defendant's acquittal after two years' incarceration, but the first branch of the jury verdict offered a sop to the anti-Semites, a finding that the murder had been committed in one of the buildings of the brick factory that Beiliss oversaw. The prosecution of Beiliss was strongly condemned by Russian liberals, including short-story writer Vladimir G. Korolenko and Vladimir Dmitrievich Nabokov, father of the famed author. The memoirs of Beiliss's chief defense counsel are published in English (O. O. Gruzenberg, *Yesterday: Memoirs of a Russian-Jewish Lawyer*, ed. Don C. Rawson and trans. Don C. Rawson and Tatiana Tipton [Berkeley: Univ. of California Press, 1981]).

Another fictional working of the Beiliss case is the Yiddish novel *The Bloody Hoax* [Der Blutiger Shpas], by Sholom Aleichem (born Sholom Rabinovitch). In the 1920s the book was adapted as a popular Yiddish play produced in New York, *Hard to Be a Jew* [Shver tzu zayn a Yid]. In the novel, a Jew, Hersh Rabinovitch, and a Russian friend, Grigori Popov, trade places so that Grigori can learn a Jew's lot in tsarist Russia. Popov, taken for a Jew, is prosecuted for ritual murder but saved from being tried when the young prosecutor, Popov's cousin, recognizes him in court. The novel has appeared in an English-language edition (Sholom Aleichem, *The Bloody Hoax*, trans. Aliza Shevrin and intro. Maurice Friedberg [Bloomington: Indiana Univ. Press, 1991]). Two years later, portions of the Beiliss trial transcripts were also published in English (Ezekiel Leikin, *The Beiliss Transcripts: The Anti-Semitic Trial That Shook the World* [Northvale, N.J.: Jason Aronson, 1993]).

According to biographer Frederick Karl, Franz Kafka, near the end of his life, wrote about the Beiliss case in a story that was destroyed by Dora Dymant, with whom he was living (See Frederick R. Karl, *Franz Kafka: Representative Man* [New York: Ticknor & Fields, 1991], 75–76n). In 1899, Bohemia itself was gripped by an unjust blood-libel murder accusation against Leopold Hilsner, who was imprisoned for sixteen years before being pardoned in 1916.

M.7 Mamet, David *The Old Religion.* New York: Free Press, 1997.

■ The inspiration for this novel is the 1915 murder of Atlanta pencil factory girl Mary Phagan, for which factory manager Leo Frank was wrongly convicted and lynched. The story is told through Frank's brief interior monologues, which express the uneasiness of Jews in a Christian community and segue into speculations about divine providence and predestination. Having placed false hopes in the protections afforded by the American legal system, Frank comes to understand the Yiddish curse, "May you be involved in a lawsuit when you're right." Unfortunately, however, Mamet's work does not illuminate the course of the famous Frank murder case or the personalities who figure in it; the pathetic victim is referred to by name only once in the course of the novel and is characterized principally as having "smelled unclean," another proof of this author's pronounced misogyny.

M.8 Manzoni, Alessandro *The Betrothed* [I Promessi Sposi]. Trans. and intro. Bruce Penman. London: Penguin, 1972.

■ In this masterpiece of historical fiction that tells of the persecution of the young lovers, Renzo Tramaglino and Lucia Mondella, by a villainous nobleman with designs on Lucia, Don Rodrigo, Manzoni draws on significant events from seventeenth-century Milanese annals. The character of Gertrude, an aristocratic cloistered nun whose protection Lucia seeks, only to be betrayed, is based on Sister Virginia (born Marianna de Leyva), the so-called "Nun of Monza," who was condemned to immured confinement after carrying on a scandalous love affair with a rakish neighbor of her convent (see M.22). In chapters 9 and 10 of his novel, Manzoni portrays Gertrude's eccentricity as the joint product of her family's oppression and her own wilfulness. Her father and eldest brother had forced her to take the veil so that the inheritance of the first born would be unimpaired by a dowry. Once she was installed in the convent, however, it was Gertrude's sense of aristocratic prerogatives that led her to tyrannize her fellow nuns and to take a depraved lover.

A second historical strand in the narrative (chapters 31–33) is the bubonic plague that ravaged Milan in 1630. Manzoni emphasizes the cravenness of city officials, who, in an attempt to excuse their own inaction in the face of the advancing pestilence, purported to give credence to the public delusion that plague germs were being deliberately spread in poisonous unguents applied by "anointers." Renzo is himself set upon by a mob suspecting him of being an anointer.

Manzoni's condemnation of the city fathers' willingness to exploit the public's insane fears of plague-spreaders is devastating:

> ... when obstinate folly is finally overcome its evasions and contortions—its dying acts of revenge, so to speak—are often of such a kind that we can only wish it had held out to the end, unconquered and unshaken, against the evidence and the facts. And this was a case in point. The men who had fought so long and so resolutely against the view that a seed of disease had from the beginning been near at hand, or in their very midst, which could multiply and spread by natural means to cause a disaster—those men were no longer able to deny that the disease was in fact spreading through the city. But they could not admit that it was due to natural causes without also admitting that they had completely misled the public and done great harm thereby. This disposed them to find some other reason, and to accept any explanation of the sort that might offer itself. (578)

In a separate nonfictional work, Manzoni studied the criminal prosecution of suspected anointers in Milan (see M.9).

M.9 ———— *Storia della Colonna Infame* [The History of the Column of Infamy]. 1840. Milan: Dall'Oglio, n.d.

▪ This nonfictional pendant to the 1840 revision of Manzoni's novel *The Betrothed* is an impassioned brief for the men unjustly tortured and executed in 1630 as "anointers" thought to have deliberately spread germs in the Milanese bubonic plague epidemic. The fatal sequence of events began on the morning of June 21, 1630, when Caterina Rosa, looking through a window of a street-bridge, saw a man in a black cape and a hat pulled over his eyes who appeared to be wiping his hands on the walls of houses as he passed along the street. The thought immediately occurred to her that he might be "one of those who had been going around anointing the walls." The man she saw was later identified as Guglielmo Piazza, a subordinate official of the commission of public health. Piazza implicated a barber Giangiacomo Mora, whose only real offense appears to have been the unlicensed manufacture and sale of quack medicine that supposedly warded off the plague. Piazza and Mora were tortured and put to death after accusing others of participating in the ever-widening anointers' conspiracy.

Manzoni, the grandson of famed penological reformer Cesare Beccaria, is primarily interested in levying accountability for this bizarre miscarriage of justice. He takes issue with the conclusion of Pietro Verri, in his *Observations on Torture*, that the blame lay in the institution of torture itself and in its capacity for generating false confessions and accusations. In Manzoni's view, the ultimate responsibility must be borne by the individuals who wielded power of life and death in Milan. These dishonorable officials had carried out prosecutions for crimes that had no scientific basis, merely to appease mob passions and to shield themselves against charges of failure to protect public health. In the pursuit of these aims, they had ignored or distorted clear restrictions on the use of torture in interrogations and had shown cavalier disregard for procedural fairness. The continuing relevance of this book resides in Manzoni's insistence that, when justice fails, we cannot content ourselves with blaming the system when fair-minded prosecutors and judges could have secured a more humane outcome.

The title of this work refers to a memorial column built on the site of barber Mora's house, which had been torn down after his execution; the monument was to remind posterity of the infamous anointers' plot.

An English translation of *Storia della Colonna Infame* has been reprinted in Alessandro Manzoni, *The Betrothed*, and *History of the Column of Infamy*, ed. David Forgacs and Matthew Reynolds (London: J. M. Dent, 1997).

M.10 Marlowe, Christopher *The Massacre at Paris*. In *Plays of Christopher Marlowe*. London: Everyman's Library, 1947.

■ First acted in 1592 and 1593, this drama (which survives only in a garbled and abbreviated text) presents a series of contemporary atrocities, the St. Bartholomew's Night massacre of the Huguenots in Paris (1572); the 1588 assassination of the Duc de Guise, the leader of the Catholic extremists; and the retaliation killing of King Henry III in 1589.

The principal villains of the drama are the queen mother Catherine de Medici, who treacherously presents a gift of poisoned gloves to Jeanne d'Albret, the old queen of Navarre, and the Duc de Guise, who orders the Paris massacre with Catherine's encouragement. Human faces are given to the victims of the slaughter by a succession of murder scenes showing the killings of Protestants in a variety of social stations high and low: Admiral Coligny; a man named Seroune, stabbed before his wife's eyes; the king's professor of logic; and two schoolmasters of Henry of Navarre. At least in the version that has come down to us, the Duc de Guise, as he contemplates the butchery, has the longest soliloquy and the best lines, including these (299):

> Give me a look, that, when I bend my brows,
> Pale death may walk in furrows of my face;
> A hand, that with a grasp may gripe the world;
> An ear to hear what my detractors say;
> A royal seat, a sceptre, and a crown;
> That those which do behold them may become
> As men that stand and gaze against the sun.

M.11 Martin, Benjamin F. *The Hypocrisy of Justice in the Belle Epoque*. Baton Rouge: Louisiana State Univ. Press, 1984.

Professor Martin closely examines political corruption of the justice system under France's Third Republic, as exemplified by the murder acquittals of Marguerite Steinheil and Henriette Caillaux and the long-delayed judicial reckoning with Thérèse Humbert, who borrowed vast sums on the strength of a bogus inheritance. When Martin strays from his main theme he is susceptible to occasional error; for example, his assertion that Adolphe Steinheil, whose wife was tried for his murder, was without talent as a painter.

M.12 Martin, John Bartlow *Butcher's Dozen and Other Murders.* New York: Harper, 1950.
■ Martin is one of America's most respected twentieth-century journalists. The John Bartlow Martin Award for Public Interest Magazine Journalists cites his reportorial achievements: "During his life, John Bartlow Martin advanced the tenets of public interest journalism. His magazine stories about labor racketeering, poor working conditions, racism, crime and abuse of mental patients were marked by careful reporting, incisive writing and a palpable concern for victims. In many cases, these stories prompted public policy changes and inspired other journalists to make a difference with their own words. In his ten years at Northwestern University's Medill School of Journalism, he helped turn students into serious investigative writers." Martin also wrote a biography of Adlai Stevenson and served as U.S. ambassador to the Dominican Republic.

Butcher's Dozen contains six outstanding examples of Martin's crime articles. Ohio-born, he included two pieces on serial killers of his native state. The title article on Cleveland's Mad Butcher of Kingsbury Run, who murdered (and usually decapitated and dissected) at least twelve or thirteen victims of both genders between 1934 and 1938. Martin calls the Cleveland Butcher "America's preeminent mass murderer" and attributes his escape from detection to his own cleverness rather than to police failures. Admitting his inability to parse the motive for the mutilation of the bodies, Martin writes: "He did not dissect his victims in an insane rage. So he must have had another reason, perhaps unknown heretofore in criminal history. And unimaginable—unless we accept the theory that his rationale encompassed nothing more than murder for murder's sake. For if this is so, then dismemberment might well be the next logical step, to shock society, to complete the job."

(While paying respect to Martin's pioneering essay, a recent well-researched book on the Kingsbury Run murders provides more detailed information about the mutilation and disposal of the corpses and the course of the investigations without, however, making a choice among the suspects considered in the final chapter. James Jessen Badal, *In the Wake of the Butcher: Cleveland's Torso Murders* [Kent, Ohio: Kent State Univ. Press, 2001]. Badal utilized police and coroner's records as well as the papers of lead detective Peter Merylo and conducted extensive interviews. The author argues that the Cleveland police, unfamiliar with serial killers, were initially bewildered by the apparently motiveless butcheries of strangers, believing as they traditionally did that "murderers killed people they knew for such readily understandable reasons as anger, greed, revenge, or jealousy" [91–92].)

The other Ohio reportage ("The Chair") relates to Murl Robert Daniels's 1948 rampage with former Mansfield prison mate John Coulter West, which resulted in five holdups and six murders (including Daniels's stripping and execution of three members of the Niebel family who he feared would serve as witnesses against him). Daniels's life in crime might have been influenced by brain injuries suffered at age thirteen when he was hit by a truck while riding a bicycle. Martin attended Daniels's electrocution only after deciding to study the path that led him to the chair.

Martin brings the quality of *romans noirs* to his portrayal of modest lives disrupted by crime and of the mean streets in America's cities. "The Ring and the Conscience," which he regards as his best story, evokes the sad nightlife of wartime shore leave in Houston. Clara Belle Penn was killed by a conscience-stricken married sailor when she refused to return his wedding ring after a one-night stand; the man (whose name the author shields) was given a five-year suspended sentence.

Equally touching is "The Innocents." In 1949, nineteen-year-old Milt Babich shot to death Patricia Birmingham, suspecting (perhaps erroneously) that she was aware of his responsibility for the pregnancy of her sister, Kathleen. Babich claimed that he had intended only to frighten Patricia and that the gun had fired twice by accident. This teenage tragedy was born of ignorance about sex and contraception.

"Cops and Robbers" is an homage to the police detectives of Chicago, who broke up a gang of violent downstate criminals (the "Bookie Gang") that audaciously preyed on the bookmaking and gambling operations of the Syndicate in 1945. A famous associate of the gang was George ("Bugs") Moran, whose beer mob had been assassinated in the St. Valentine's Day massacre of 1929.

Another underworld story, which Martin describes as the only crime history in the book, chronicles the rise and fall of the Shelton Boys in southern Illinois. The Sheltons made a rare ascent from country gunmen to big-time racketeers, tangling, along the way, with the Ku Klux Klan, rival mobster Charley Birger, and the Chicago mob. The volume also includes Martin's "Notes on Crime Writing," explaining his choice of subjects and work methods, and a final chapter providing examples of the raw documentary materials on which he based his reports.

M.13 **Masefield, John** "The Campden Wonder" and "Mrs. Harrison." In *The Poems and Plays of John Masefield*. Vol. 2. New York: Macmillan, 1918.

■ These plays are based on a mysterious 1670 disappearance of William Harrison from the Cotswold town of Chipping Campden. Harrison, a seventy-year-old steward to the Viscountess Campden, vanished while supposedly collecting rents from tenants. On the highway, a poor woman reportedly picked up a hacked hat and comb and a bloody neckband all belonging to Harrison. John Perry, Harrison's servant, confessed his involvement in the killing and robbery of his master and implicated his mother, Joan Perry, a reputed witch, and his brother, Richard, in the crime; all three were executed for murder. Two years after the triple hanging, William Harrison, very much alive, returned to Chipping Campden with an unbelievable tale of having been sold as a slave to an eighty-seven-year-old Turkish physician who asserted a strong attachment to Lincolnshire (see L.8).

Long before Masefield wrote the first of the plays, *The Campden Wonder*, at the end of 1905 and in early 1906, he had heard the story of William Harrison's disappearance and its tragic aftermath. He had hoped that the one-act drama might be staged as a pageant in Chipping Campden, but it was produced instead at the Court Theatre in London in 1907 under the direction of Harley Granville Barker. The villain of the piece, John Perry, falsely confesses to the Parson that he, his mother, Joan, and brother, Dick, strangled William Harrison for his "gold." A disreputable alcoholic, John acted out of revenge against his sober brother, who had bragged about his forthcoming salary increase that would bring him to twelve shillings a week, three more than John's wages. John was also angered by Dick's "godly" lectures about his misconduct and carried out his threat to bring him "lower than the lowest." John's personal grievances appear to have had a political undertone, for he calls Dick an Oliver Cromwell man and a regicide. For melodramatic effect, Masefield concludes the play by bringing on Mrs. Harrison to announce the missing William's return just after the three Perrys have been hanged for his murder.

The sequel, "Mrs. Harrison," is a short scene between the Harrisons shortly after his return. Mrs. Harrison accuses her husband of having gone away for beer and "trollopsing" and rebukes him for having been the cause of the Perrys being hanged. He tells her that "my Lord" gave him 300 pounds to go away and that it was to the nobleman's advantage that he stay hidden awhile. Harrison threatens to kill his wife if she breathes a word of his secret. Despite the bitterness with which she greeted her long-lost mate, Mrs. Harrison sprang to his defense when the Parson arrived to obtain an explanation of the strange disappearance. All William could say was that he had been kidnapped, but Mrs. Harrison supplied all the circumstantial details, including the fact that one of his captors had the smell of onions on his breath; she also invented the tale that Harrison had been sold in slavery to a Turk and was put to work "digging in the herb beds." After her husband and their visitors depart, Mrs. Harrison laments, "I been wife to a murderer," and takes poison.

M.14 Masson, Jeffrey Moussaieff *Lost Prince: The Unsolved Mystery of Kaspar Hauser.* New York: Free Press, 1996.

■ Unlike Andrew Lang (see L.8), psychiatrist Jeffrey Masson essentially believes in the veracity of Kaspar Hauser, the German "wild child" who turned up on Nuremberg's streets in 1828 with a tale of imprisonment from babyhood and deprivation of even the minimal comfort and nurture essential for normal personality development. In an introductory essay, Masson relates his account of the German cause célèbre to his controversial advocacy of Freud's original but later abandoned position that patients' "buried memory" of child abuse usually reflects actual experience. Masson is "intrigued" by the term "soul murder" applied to Hauser's mistreatment by Anselm Ritter von Feuerbach, the kindly Bavarian jurist who investigated the Hauser case and later befriended the mysterious boy. In Masson's view, Kaspar's tale represents an extreme case of child abuse truthfully recalled in teenage years, although the youth may have "simply elected not to talk about certain things he knew."

Masson also lends credence to the suggestion of Hauser's tutor, Georg Friedrich Daumer, that the boy's death of a stab wound was due to a plot in which his guardian, Philip Henry,

Earl of Stanhope, was complicit. It may be relevant to note, however, that Daumer is also credited with inventing the theory that Mozart was murdered by the Masons.

As appendices to his essay, Masson includes English translations of Feuerbach's *Kaspar Hauser*, Kaspar's autobiography, and other documents of the case.

Another psychiatric study of the wild child is Dr. Leonard Shengold's article "A Literary/Historical Example of Anal-Narcissistic Defensiveness: The Soul Murder of Kaspar Hauser" (*Halo in the Sky: Observations on Anality and Defense* [New York: Guilford Press, 1988]). This sympathetic study, accepting the story of Kaspar Hauser's captivity as factual, likens the traumatic effects of his experience to those of brainwashing. He hypothesizes that Kaspar received satisfactory mothering prior to imprisonment at age four, so that his early intellectual growth was adequate for him to relearn powers of communication after his release. In the psychological sphere, his wounds ran deeper, for he could not free himself of a sense of isolation and depression and, when the outer world overstimulated and then disappointed him, a regressive desire to return to his jailer and the dark cellar where he had been confined.

The Borowitz True Crime Collection owns an important association copy of the first edition of Feuerbach's account of the case in an English translation, *Caspar Hauser: An Account of an Individual Kept in a Dungeon Separated from Early Childhood to about the Age of Seventeen* (London: Simpkin & Marshall, 1833). The book bears the handwritten inscription, "Presented by the Author Earl Stanhope Chevening Kent 1839" (see Fig. 10). Feuerbach had also dedicated the work to Stanhope, believing him to share his own devotion to Kaspar.

M.15 Mather, Cotton *Pillars of Salt: An History of Some Criminals Executed in This Land, for Capital Crimes. With Some of Their Dying Speeches; Collected and Published, for the Warning of Such as Live in Destructive Courses of Ungodliness.* Boston: Printed by B. Green and J. Allen for Samuel Phillips, 1699. Reprinted partially in Daniel E. Williams. *Pillars of Salt: An Anthology of Early American Criminal Narratives.* Madison: Madison House, 1993.

■ Described as "the most ambitious piece of crime literature to appear in New England up to that time," Mather's work sandwiches between the opening and close of his discourse on the execution of an infanticide, Sarah Threeneedles, texts relating to a dozen other criminals executed in New England (see Daniel A. Cohen, *Pillars of Salt, Monuments of Grace, New England Crime Literature and the Origins of American Popular Culture, 1674–1860* [New York: Oxford Univ. Press, 1993], 55). Of particular interest is the previously published dialogue of Mather with James Morgan as he accompanied the condemned man during his walk to the gallows. Morgan, whose confession and last speech are also included, had stabbed butcher Joseph Johnson to death with an iron spit after Johnson intervened in a violent quarrel between Morgan and his wife. Mather also republishes similar material relating to Hugh Stone, condemned for murdering his wife in a dispute over a sale of a piece of land. Other interpolations in *Pillars of Salt* take the form of brief case summaries. In the ensemble, these cases constitute what Mather calls "an History of Criminals, whom the Terrible Judgments of God have Thunder struck, into PILLARS OF SALT."

The principal thrust of Mather's book is cautionary; its purpose is to dissuade readers from following the examples of sinners who ended their days on the gallows. None of the cases he chose involved professional criminals or killers who acted in cold blood. Five offenses cited are the murders of illegitimate infants by their distraught mothers. Two killings arose out of domestic quarrels, and other object lessons were drawn by Mather from executions for adultery, bestiality, mutiny, the murder of an employer by resentful servants, and rape. Among the factors Mather's narratives identify as contributing to crime are intoxication, neglect of religious duties, and disrespect for parents.

M.16 Matthews, T[homas] S[tanley] *To the Gallows I Must Go.* New York: Knopf, 1931.
■ Matthews, literary editor of *Time* and previously associate editor of *The New Republic*, based this riveting novella on the case of Judd Gray and Ruth Snyder, electrocuted in 1928 for the murder of Snyder's husband, Albert (see G.38). The narrative is told by daybed salesman Todd Lorimer (Gray), whose enthrallment with Grace Hexall (Ruth Snyder) leads to his compliance with her demand to murder her husband, Foster. The ecstatic moments of Lorimer's affair cannot prevent him from realizing that Grace, who had increased Foster's insurance coverage in anticipation of the crime, had a dark side he had not suspected. When the police knock at the door of the hotel room where Lorimer is hiding after the murder, he answers almost with a sense of relief.

M.17 Matthieu, Pierre *La Guisiade.* 1589. Ed. and annotated Louis Lobbes. Geneva: Droz, 1990.
■ The first edition of this play about the assassination of French Catholic *ultra* leader, Henri, Duc de Guise, at Blois, was published about six months after the crime. Matthieu, a twenty-five-year-old jurist who ardently supported the anti-Huguenot campaigns of Guise and the "League" that he headed, was able to accomplish this feat of speed by reworking earlier plays on the biblical subject of Esther and the antisemitic minister Haman. Matthieu initially tackled this theme at age eighteen in his drama *Esther* and reset that work in 1588 as the twin plays *Aman* [Haman] and *Vashti*, to celebrate the convocation of the Estates General at Blois, an event that appeared to signal peace between the Duc de Guise and King Henri III and to promise a united Catholic front against the Huguenots. Much to the chagrin of Matthieu, the king, to whom he had dedicated *Vashti*, treacherously ordered the killing of Guise at Blois. The young playwright's new version of the drama now took the assassination as its theme with Guise protrayed as religious martyr and Henri demonized as a traitor both to the duke and the Catholic religion.

La Guisiade, which attained its final form in an updated text reflecting the revenge killing of King Henri by monk Jacques Clément in August 1589, depicts the wavering king in confrontations with his anti-Huguenot mother, Catherine de Medici; the Duc de Guise; and an unnamed evil counselor referred to only as "N.N.," a traditional designation in French of an indeterminate person. Editor Lobbes identifies this personage as the Devil, but the Argument of Act 4, Scene 1, in which he appears, likens him to other characters in drama who have approved evil decisions of kings; their names are omitted by the author "so as not to dishonor his poem." In the Argument of Act 4, Scene 3, when the king, after weighing opposing considerations, gives the assassination order, reference is made to the "evil doctrine of Machiavelli," who in his book *The Prince* excepts from the Prince's duty of good faith "the freedom to be treacherous, when he desires to take vengeance or to rule with peace of mind." Henri's final assessment of his options leaves him only Hobson's choice:

> If I have him killed, never will a king be seen
> Less feared, less revered, less obeyed than me.
> If he lives on, he will seize the rights of my empire.
> Then I must kill him; I can suffer no worse.

M.18 Maugham, William Somerset "The Letter." In *East and West: The Collected Short Stories of W. Somerset Maugham*. Garden City, N.Y.: Garden City Publishing Co., n.d.

■ This famous story is based on a case called to Maugham's attention by a Singapore lawyer, C. Dickinson, and his wife. In 1911, Ethel Mabel Proudlock, wife of a headmaster in Kuala Lumpur (now capital of Malaysia), fired six bullets into the manager of a tin mine, William Crozier Steward, on the veranda of her home while her husband was away. At trial, as in the Maugham story, it was established that Mrs. Proudlock, despite her claim of self-defense against attempted rape, was having an affair with Steward and was angered by his relationship with a Chinese woman. Unlike her fictional counterpart, Leslie Crosbie, who was freed by a verdict of justifiable homicide, Mrs. Proudlock was found guilty of murder and sentenced to be hanged. The Sultan of Selangor, who had jurisdiction over Kuala Lumpur, pardoned her. After returning to England without her husband, Mrs. Proudlock died in an asylum.

The principal plot element invented by Maugham was the letter Leslie Crosbie had written to her lover asking him to visit her; the story ends with her lawyer's purchasing the incriminating document from the dead man's Chinese mistress. The memorable 1940 film version of *The Letter* starred Bette Davis as the murderess and Gale Sondergaard as her Chinese rival. A book-length study of the Proudlock case has recently been published: Eric Lawlor, *Murder on the Verandah: Love and Betrayal in British Malaya* (London: Harper-Collins, 1999).

M.19 Mauriac, François *L'Affaire Favre-Bulle.* Paris: Grasset (Les Amis des Cahiers Verts, no. VI), 1931.

■ In 1929 Jeanne-Alphonsine Favre-Bulle, forty-five, shot and killed her young lover, Léon-Alphonse Merle, and his mistress in residence, Léonie-Julie Julliard, forty-three, in Merle's apartment in a Parisian suburb. Merle had been slow in performing his promise to send Mme. Julliard packing and appeared to prefer to live as lord and master of a ménage à trois. Mauriac attended Mme. Favre-Bulle's trial, which ended with a sentence of twenty years of hard labor. To the author it was an outrage that the judge and lawyers, preoccupied with their professional duels, failed to understand how the previously blameless defendant had been led to commit the murders. Unlike many adulteresses, she had refused to live a secret double life, had confessed the affair to her husband, and staked her future happiness on Merle's false professions of undivided love. Mauriac concludes: "The most horrible thing in the world is justice separated from charity."

M.20 Maxwell, Sir Herbert   *Inter Alia: A Scottish Calendar of Crime, and Other Historical Essays.* Glasgow: Maclehose, Jackson, 1924.

■ Maxwell's volume of historical essays collects papers published in *Blackwood's*, *Cornhill Magazine*, and *Nineteenth Century Review* and lectures given at Scottish universities. The first piece, "A Scottish Calendar of Crime," reviews highlights of crime and punishment in Scottish history as reflected in the work undertaken by Robert Pitcairn (1793–1855) at the urging of Sir Walter Scott (*Ancient Criminal Trials in Scotland*, compiled from the original records and manuscripts, with historical illus., 3 vols. in 7 [Edinburgh: The Bannatyne Club, 1833]). Showing no pity for the patriotic sensibilities of his fellow Scots, Maxwell renders a devastating portrait of a corrupt justice system that pardoned wealthy murderers in return for bribes and executed the poor for minor offenses; tolerated or incited clan feuds; and savagely pursued witches and the religious dissidents of the moment. Maxwell also deals in some detail with the Gowrie Conspiracy of 1600, concluding that "there is much reason to support the suspicion that capture [of Scotland's King James VI] and not murder was the end in view, and that Gowrie would have felt avenged had he succeeded in delivering James into the hands of the Queen of England."

In his chapter on the so-called Casket Letters incriminating Mary Queen of Scots in the murder of her husband, Henry Darnley, Maxwell argues that the purported "translations" of the letters adduced before the commissioners hearing her case at Westminster were unreliable, and, indeed, the commissioners so found. It is Maxwell's theory that conspirators desiring to exculpate themselves in the murder plot had both the motive and opportunity to tamper with the documents found in the casket.

A medieval war crime of vast proportions comes to the fore in Maxwell's essay on the Battle of Agincourt (1415). In his proclamation and general order issued on landing in the Seine River near Harfleur, King Henry V prohibited his troops from committing murder, rape, or other offenses against the civilian population, even taking care to ban destruction of vines and fruit trees. However, when word reached King Henry after the battle at Agincourt that his baggage had been plundered by country folk, his fear mounted that his outnumbered forces might face a renewed French assault that might link up with the large body of prisoners held by the English. In Maxwell's words, the king thereupon "had recourse to a desperate remedy, which even self-preservation could hardly justify": Henry sent a herald to warn the French commander that, if he initiated an offensive, the throats of all the prisoners would be cut. Contemporary French accounts maintain that the king ordered every man to kill his own prisoners, and that when his command was not carried out with enough speed to please him, "an esquire and two hundred archers were told off as butchers."

In *Henry the Fifth*, Act 4, Scene 5, Shakespeare bluntly presents this scene of carnage, giving Henry the words:

But hark! what new alarum is this same?
The French have reinforc'd their scatter'd men;
Then every soldier kill his prisoners!
Give the word through.

In his article "Take No Prisoners" (*New Yorker*, June 17, 1996), Lawrence Weschler comments: "Neither Laurence Olivier nor Kenneth Branagh, for instance, included the slightest allusion to [the atrocity] in their film versions, of 1944 and 1989, respectively; perhaps it seemed too starkly upending of the generally rising tone of celebration and pageantry." Weschler reported that the omitted scene would be restored in the production of *Henry V* in the New York Shakespeare Festival's 1996 Central Park season.

Maxwell also includes a vivacious chapter on the life of d'Artagnan (Charles de Batz-Castelmore), immortalized by Alexandre Dumas *père* in *The Three Musketeers* and its sequels. D'Artagnan rose to the captaincy of the Royal Musketeers under Louis XIV and— if Maxwell is right in trusting the gallant soldier's so-called memoirs, penned by his contemporary, Courtilz de Sandras— led a career easily as romantic as portrayed in Dumas's pages. The real d'Artagnan was a persistent womanizer (once imprisoned in the Bastille when the injured husband was a French ambassador), a secret emissary, and a royal spy given to disguise. He was not above accepting repugnant assignments, which included the arrest of disgraced Finance Minister Fouquet, whom he admired, and serving as an official eyewitness at the drowning of a Spanish agent (see Gatien Courtilz de Sandras, *Mémoires de M. d'Artagnan* [Paris: Club français du livre, 1955]).

M.21 Mayer, Edwin Justus *Children of Darkness: An Original Tragi-Comedy.* New York: Horace Liveright, 1929.

■ Mayer, perhaps best known for his screenplay for *To Be or Not to Be*, sets this romantic drama in Newgate prison in 1725. Among the inmates is the archgangster of eighteenth-century London, Jonathan Wild (see D.9), to whom Sherlock Holmes compared Professor Moriarty. Mayer's Wild believes that he is wrongly condemned to death, opining, "Why, if we are to believe what we are taught—if I am condemned justly—then it is a crime to kill one man, a virtue to kill ten thousand." This sentiment is drawn from Mayer's reading of Fielding's satirical novel *The Life of Mr. Jonathan Wild the Great*. Another semi-authentic figure appearing in the play is Lord Wainwright. This icy aristocrat who indifferently explains that he is held for poisoning his wife "and a few of her friends" is apparently an anachronistic rendering of the Victorian serial poisoner, Thomas Griffiths Wainewright (see w.20).

M.22 Mazzucchelli, Mario *The Nun of Monza.* Trans. Evelyn Gendel. New York: Simon & Schuster, 1963.

■ The tragic flaw of the Nun of Monza, Sister Virginia of the Convent of Santa Margherita, was that she could not forget that she was born Marianna de Leyva (1575–1650), the daughter of a Spanish nobleman whom she succeeded as Monza's feudal ruler. Both within and outside the convent, Sister Virginia wielded her vast power, removing a prioress who opposed her romance with a rakish neighbor, Gian Paolo Osio, and arrogantly ignoring the whispers of the community. Two children were born of her liaison, one dead and the second a daughter who was to become the all-too-visible apple of Sister Virginia's eye. To quell threats of exposure, Osio, a violent man with murders in his past and willing allies among Sister Virginia's friends in the convent, killed in succession a refractory lay nun, Caterina de Meda; a blacksmith, Ferrari, who had duplicated keys for the convent doors; and Rainerio Roncino, an apothecary. Then, having abetted the flight of two complicit nuns from the convent, he pushed Sister Ottavia into a river and battered her as she tried to reach the shore; he threw Sister Benedetta into the well already encumbered with Caterina's head. Sister Ottavia died of her injuries, but only after having given damning testimony.

The trials of Osio, Sister Virginia, and three other nuns who had assisted her love affair and the murders, resulted in severe sentences. Sister Virginia was immured for thirteen years in a cell of the "House of the Converts of Santa Valeria," euphemistically called a convent but in reality a shelter for reformed and indigent prostitutes. Condemned to death in absentia for the murder of Rainerio and other crimes, Osio was murdered and beheaded by a person unknown to history (perhaps a friend seeking to ingratiate himself with government and church authorities).

Relying heavily on records of the case, Mazzucchelli has constructed a seamless narrative that unobtrusively quotes eyewitness evidence, key documents, and the commentary of Ripamonti, secretary to Cardinal Federigo Borromeo. He assesses Sister Virginia's autocratic character without sentimentality, doubting that she genuinely repented even after the long years of solitary confinement.

Alessandro Manzoni introduces the Nun of Monza into his epic novel *The Betrothed* (see M.8).

M.23 Mellinkoff, David   *The Conscience of a Lawyer.* St. Paul: West Publishing, 1975.

■ In 1840 Lord William Russell was murdered in his home in Park Lane, London, by his Swiss valet, François Bernard Courvoisier, whom his master may have come upon in the act of taking off with the household silver. Courvoisier's trial produced a legal controversy that was still being pursued in British and American newspapers at the end of the decade. The defendant's counsel, Charles Phillips, in his closing argument to the jury, accused the police of fabricating evidence, and he was understood by some listeners to have expressed a personal belief in Courvoisier's innocence and to have cast suspicion on a housemaid, even though his client had confessed the murder to him during the course of the trial.

David Mellinkoff, a law professor at the University of California, Los Angeles, ingeniously cast the Courvoisier trial into the form of a legal treatise or "hornbook" exploring the ethical issues presented by the professional decisions made by Phillips in defending his client. The three principal questions examined are the propriety of defending a client known to be guilty; the extent to which a lawyer may "cast the guilt upon the innocent"; and the permissibility of counsel's expression of belief in a client's cause.

Mellinkoff was best known for his opposition to his profession's communication in "legalese," or what he preferred to excoriate as "contagious verbosity" (*New York Times*, Jan. 16, 2000).

M.24 Melville, Herman *Billy Budd, Sailor (An Inside Narrative)*. 1886. Ed. Harrison Hayford and Merton M. Sealts Jr. Chicago: Univ. of Chicago Press, 1962.

■ The title character of Herman Melville's semi-autobiographical novel *White-Jacket* (1850), is a young seaman on the U.S. frigate *Neversink*. The sailor nicknamed "White-Jacket" refers disapprovingly to the summary condemnation and hanging aboard the USS *Somers* in 1842. The men were sentenced to death for mutiny (despite the absence of overt acts of rebellion) by Melville's cousin, Lieutenant Guert Gansevoort, who had reported the supposed mutinous conspiracy to Captain Alexander Mackenzie. Melville's voice is probably heard in White-Jacket's comments: "The well-known case of a United States brig furnishes a memorable example, which at any moment may be repeated. Three men, in a time of peace, were then hung at the yard-arm, merely because, in the Captain's judgment, it became necessary to hang them. To this day the question of their complete guilt is socially discussed. How shall we characterize such a deed? Says Blackstone, 'If any one . . . in time of peace, hang . . . any man by color of martial law, this is murder, for it is against Magna Charta.'"

Michael Paul Rogan has shown how Melville returned to the theme of the *Somers* mutiny in *Billy Budd*, written in the last years preceding his death in 1891 (*Subversive Genealogy: The Politics and Art of Herman Melville* [New York: Knopf, 1983]). In this novella, according to Professor Rogan's analysis, Melville absolved both the condemned Billy and his executioner, Captain Vere, of bad motives. Instead, the death sentence reflected a rigid, formalistic devotion to the state that was divorced from human feeling and paradoxically left uncontaminated the love that Vere and Billy felt for each other.

M.25 "Member of the Massachusetts Bar" *Mysteries of Crime, as Shown in Remarkable Capital Trials.* By a Member of the Massachusetts Bar. Boston: Samuel Walker, 1870.

■ "The difficulty of obtaining the report of a certain celebrated capital trial" suggested to the author the preparation of this volume, one of the first significant trial collections compiled by an American author. The work is "of a popular character, designed to meet the tastes of a large class of readers." Many American cases (some later studied by Edmund Pearson) are included, as well as others from Britain and from the German original of Anselm Ritter von Feuerbach (see F.6). The principal chapters relating to American, British, and Canadian cases are:

- Trial of John W. Webster (the Harvard Murder Case of 1849)
- The Murder of Helen (Ellen) Jewett (see C.31)
- Henry G. Green, executed for the 1845 arsenic poisoning of his bride, Mary Ann Wyatt,

in Berlin, New York (see A.11, vol. 17). Green, about twenty-one, joined a traveling company of temperance performers after being smitten by the charms of one of the entertainers, Mary Ann Wyatt. While on the road, Green married Wyatt impetuously and returned home to face the disapproval of his mother and sister. Within a matter of days after his stormy family meeting, he murdered his wife with repeated administrations of arsenic. At the trial, the prosecution, according to the author, established the prisoner's motive for desiring to be freed from his new wife as "the dissatisfaction and inquietude his hasty and inconsiderate marriage had given to his family."

- Albert J. Tirrell, charged with the murder of Maria Ann Bickford (see P.5)
- The murder of Captain Joseph White (see P.7)
- William Jones, whom the author ironically dubbed "a criminal too good to be a murderer." Jones was acquitted of murdering a housemaid with a borrowed razor in connection with a burglary in Bedford Square, London on New Year's Eve. He had argued that it was his jeopardy as a forger and thief that caused him to flee the police and to make a false statement before a magistrate investigating the killing.
- Rev. Ephraim K. Avery, tried for the murder of Sarah Maria Cornell (see K.1). The author concludes: "There was no reason to suppose that the verdict [of acquittal] was not just."
- Abraham Thornton, acquitted of the murder of Mary Ashford near Erdington, England in 1817 (see N.7)
- Lucretia Chapman, acquitted of the 1831 poisoning of her husband, William, in Pennsylvania. Lucretia's "Latin lover," Leno (or Carolino) Amalio Espas y Mina, was sentenced to death in a separate trial as a principal in the second degree (see A.11, vol. 6).
- William Corder, the "Red Barn" murderer
- George C. Hersey, Massachusetts poisoner convicted in 1861
- Sawney Cunningham. With apparent gullibility, the author adapts an eighteenth-century tale about a Glasgow murderer and highwayman supposedly hanged at Leith in 1635. The story seems to be a variant of the Sawney Beane legend (see N.4).
- Moses Chapman Eliot. Moses Eliot, twelve years old, was acquitted in the 1834 shooting death of his playmate Josiah Buckland, near Springfield, Massachusetts. In a dying declaration to his mother, Josiah told his mother that Moses had persuaded him to run off with him to seek employment on a ship in Boston; that they had practiced target shooting with Moses's pistol but quarreled over his friend's demand that Josiah give him his best coat for the journey; and that Moses had intentionally fired at him when he stooped to pick up the ramrod of the gun. Although Moses did not report the shooting, the jury accepted his defense of accident, perhaps impressed by the boy's respectable upbringing.
- Assassination of Canadian politician Thomas D'Arcy McGee in Ottawa (see W.2)
- Stephen and Jesse Boorn, erroneously convicted of murdering Russell Colvin, who disappeared after their 1813 quarrel but returned in time to forestall the executioner

M.26 Mencken, H[enry] L[ouis] "Inquisition." In *Heathen Days 1890–1936*. New York: Knopf, 1955.

■ The modest punishment meted out to schoolteacher John Thomas Scopes in the famous "Monkey Trial" of 1925 for violating Tennessee's prohibition against teaching Darwinism was a fine of one hundred dollars. Mencken, who reported on the trial in terms offensive to the local citizens (whom he dubbed "yahoos"), recollects in his hilarious article "Inquisition" that "the only strangers who actually suffered any menace to lives and limbs during the progress of the trial" were chief defense counsel Clarence Darrow; a Hearst reporter who leaked an intended ruling by the judge; a YMCA secretary from Cincinnati who was mistaken (due to a hoax perpetrated by Mencken) for a mythical Bolshevik assassin; and "an itinerant atheist who came to town to exhibit a mangy chimpanzee." Mencken explodes the rumors that the townfolk, outraged by his trial reports, "formed a posse and ran [him] out of town."

M.27 Mérimée, Prosper *Carmen*. 1845. In *Mérimée, romans et nouvelles*. Intro. Maurice Parturier. Vol. 2. Paris: Garnier, 1967.

■ In his *Bandits* (see H.25) E. J. Hobsbawm asserts that José-Maria "El Tempranillo," an outlaw who operated in the Andalusian hills, was "the original Don José of *Carmen*." The link that Mérimée made between the historical bandit and his Don José may have been subtler and more personal. A biographer relates that when the young Mérimée visited Spain in 1830: "His great hope was to meet a real brigand, but though he never tired of listening to tales about bandits and smugglers, especially the famous José-Maria, the nearest he got to them was when his coach was stopped near Ecija by a ferocious-looking band of armed men, who however proved to be only the local farmers on their way to market" (A. W. Raitt, *Prosper Mérimée* [New York: Scribner, 1970], 79). When the narrator of *Carmen*, upon meeting Don José, decides that the stranger must be the bandit José-Maria in disguise, he may be indulging in wish fulfillment:

> There was in Andalusia at that time a famous bandit named José-Maria, whose exploits were on every tongue. Was I at José-Maria's side? I recounted the stories I knew of that hero, all in his praise, and I expressed highly my admiration for his courage and generosity.
> "José-Maria is ridiculous," the stranger replied coldly.
> . . . Yes, it is definitely him [the narrator thought]. Blond hair, blue eyes, a large mouth, beautiful teeth, small hands; a fine shirt, a velvet jacket with silver buttons, white skin gaiters, a bay horse . . . No more doubt of it! But I would respect his incognito.

The biography of the bandit José-Maria "El Tempranillo" is included in the first volume of a two-volume work, F. Hernandez Girbal, *Bandidos Célebres Españoles (en la Historia y en la Leyendal* (Madrid: Lira, 1993).

M.28 Merrill, Boynton, Jr. *Jefferson's Nephews: A Frontier Tragedy*. Princeton: Princeton Univ. Press, 1976.

■ In December 1811, Lilburne and Isham Lewis, nephews of Thomas Jefferson, butchered a young slave, George, in a kitchen of Lilburne's farm in Livingston County in western

Kentucky. Boynton Merrill has written a brilliant study of the depraved crime and its antecedents. A farmer and poet, Merrill more than compensates for a lack of academic theory and jargon by his knowledge of agriculture and river transportation and by his researches into genealogy and public records. He is also intimately familiar with the locality in which the murder was committed, having acquired part of the Lewises' plantation.

The Lewis brothers were the sons of Thomas Jefferson's sister, Lucy, and second cousins, once removed, of explorer Meriwether Lewis. The surviving accounts of their crime are inconsistent. It appears that George had enraged Lilburne by leaving the plantation without permission on what the Reverend William Dickey, the Lewis family pastor, referred to as a "skulking expedition." After his return, Lilburne sent George to a spring for water, and on his way back the slave dropped and broke an "elegant pitcher" that is said to have belonged to Lucy Jefferson. With Isham's help, Lilburne, in a drunken rage, dragged George into a kitchen cabin, sank an axe into his neck, and forced another slave to dismember George's body and cast the pieces onto the fire. The cremation was interrupted almost supernaturally by the first of a series of earthquakes Kentucky was to suffer over a period of many months. Most of the unburned bits of bone and flesh were raked out of the ashes and hidden in the masonry, but a subsequent tremor unearthed George's head, leading to the discovery of the crime.

After the Lewises were indicted, Lilburne accidentally shot himself to death while arranging the procedures for carrying out a suicide pact under which he and Isham were to shoot each other. Isham escaped from prison before he could be tried as an accessory to George's murder.

Merrill identifies many strands in Lilburne's murderous impulse. Violence was "a characteristic of life" in Kentucky, where the Lewises had moved in 1808 after the collapse of their father's finances in their native Virginia. In his new setting, Lilburne suffered money troubles of his own following a severe nationwide depression. He also was strongly affected by the deaths of his first wife, older brother Randolph, and mother. The existence of slavery itself was perhaps the most important secondary element in the tragedy, in that it "supplied the victim and shaped the character of the murderers." All these influences on Lilburne's conduct were exacerbated by his alcoholism.

Merrill also speculates that there may have been genetic instability in the Lewis family, citing the apparent suicide of a rather distant relative, Meriwether Lewis. Although Jefferson is not known to have commented on his nephews' crime, Merrill notes that in an 1813 letter he attributed the explorer's death to "hypochondriacal affections" that were "a constitutional disposition in all the nearer branches of the family of his name." In Merrill's view, this assertion reflects Jefferson's view that his nephews were insane at the time of their murder of George.

M.29 Michener, James *Kent State: What Happened and Why.* New York: Random House & Reader's Digest Books, 1971.

■ Novelist Michener's book is based on information he gathered in Kent, Ohio, in an effort to understand what happened on the campus of Kent State University on May 4, 1970, when rifle fire of the National Guard took the lives of four students and wounded nine others. The author's conclusions included the following:

- Experts (with whom the author agreed) concluded that there was no riot, because the students had assembled peacefully and had not acted in concert, but that there had been individual acts of "tumultuous conduct."
- The National Guard was in control at all times and present in such numbers as to protect its members from critical assault.
- There was no sniper, and General Robert Canterbury of the Guard had not given an order to fire.
- The deaths and wounds inflicted by the Guard constituted "an accident, deplorable and tragic."
- No student performed any act on May 4 for which he or she deserved to be shot.
- "The hard-core revolutionary leadership across the nation was so determined to force a confrontation—which would result in gunfire and the radicalization of the young—that some kind of major incident had become inevitable."

In 1972 Professors Carl M. Moore and D. Ray Heisey of Kent State University produced an appraisal of Michener's account, entitled "Not a Great Deal of Error . . . ?" Although Michener had written a "dramatic and powerful book" about the Kent State tragedy, the authors argued that he had made numerous errors. They had sent questionnaires to about 200 people quoted by Michener. Of the approximately one-half that were returned, the professors commented: "A casual reading through the responses made it quite apparent that misquotation and distortion of what had been said were not isolated instances."

For a balanced presentation of views a decade after the May 4 shootings, see *Kent State/ May 4: Echoes Through a Decade*, ed. Scott L. Bills (Kent, Ohio: Kent State Univ. Press, 1982).

M.30 Middleton, Thomas, and Thomas Dekker *The Roaring Girl.* Ed. Andor Gomme. London: Ernest Benn (New Mermaids series), 1976.

■ Mary Frith (1584?–1659), known to her contemporaries as Moll Cutpurse, donned men's attire to pursue her careers as thief, receiver-general of stolen goods (rivaling the prominence of her eighteenth-century successor, Jonathan Wild), fortune-teller, and bawd. During the English Civil War she served as a royalist irregular, leading a successful attack on a paywagon of the commonwealth forces. Mary was irrepressible in adversity; when she was condemned to do penance in a white sheet at Paul's Cross for the offense of wearing men's apparel, her thieving colleagues profitably fleeced the crowd in attendance on her disgrace (see Charles Andrews, "Moll Cutpurse," in *Lives of Twelve Bad Women*, ed. Arthur Vincent [London: T. Fisher Unwin, 1897], 49–60).

Moll Cutpurse is the title character in the Middleton and Dekker comedy *The Roaring Girl* (1611), in which the authors apply a generous coat of whitewash to her character. The boisterous and quarrelsome ("roaring") Moll's action in the play's plot has no biographical roots. She agrees to feign a scandalous betrothal to Sebastian Wengrave so as to overcome his father's objection to Sebastian's marriage to his true love, Mary Fitz-Allard. Moll is shown to be the victim of public prejudice. She proves to be honest and courageous; her reputation as a "cutpurse" is due to her having made a study of thieves' techniques and slanging speech (cant) so that she could serve as a conduit for the restoration of stolen property. What is more impressive to the modern reader, Moll turns out to be something of a feminist, challenging a brazen gallant, Laxton, to a duel because he has mistaken her open, friendly manners as a sign of whorishness.

M.31 Miller, Arthur *All My Sons*. 1947. In *Arthur Miller's Collected Plays*. New York: Viking, 1957.

■ In what the author calls a tragedy of "unrelatedness," Joe Keller does not recognize his kinship with the twenty-one airmen whom he has sent to their deaths by supplying cracked engine heads. Miller has explained the origin of the plot of *All My Sons* in a real-life incident: "During an idle chat in my living room, a pious lady from the Middle West told of a family in her neighborhood which had been destroyed when the daughter turned the father in to the authorities on discovering that he had been selling faulty machinery to the Army. The war was then in full blast. By the time she had finished the tale I had transformed the daughter into a son and the climax of the second act was full and clear in my mind."

M.32 ——— *The Crucible*. 1953. In *Arthur Miller's Collected Plays*. New York: Viking, 1957.

■ The central figure of *The Crucible* is a strong-willed historical victim of the Salem witch trials, John Proctor, who became enmeshed in the prosecutions while attempting to save the life of his wife, Elizabeth. He made the fatal error of arguing in his petition for transfer of the trials to Boston that the actions of the Puritan judges "are very like the Papish cruelties."

Miller turned to the Salem trials as affording a parallel to the hysteria of McCarthyism. He "wished for a way to write a play that would be sharp, that would lift out of the morass of subjectivism the squirming, single, defined process which would show that the sin of public terror is that it divests man of conscience, of himself." John Proctor, as recreated by Miller, keeps his conscience intact. After refusing adamantly to name others as consorting with the Devil, he withdraws at the last moment his own signed confession of guilt: "Because it is my name! Because I cannot have another in my life!" For a discussion of Longfellow's play on a similar theme, see L.34.

M.33 Mishima, Yukio [pseudonym of Hiraoka Kimitake] *The Temple of the Golden Pavilion*. New York: Knopf, 1959.

■ Yukio Mishima's novel, based on a shocking arson case of 1950, traces the growing resentment in the mind of an ugly young novice, Mizoguchi, of the worship of eternal beauty in the Zen Buddhist temple of Kinkakuji in Kyoto. His early obsession with looking at the temple yields to anxiety over the risk of its destruction by an American air raid. At the same time as he commits acts of sadism at the instigation of an American soldier, he tries to besmirch the honor of his Zen master by giving him the cigarettes he has received as a reward for his despicable behavior. The young stutterer's envy of the Golden Temple leads him from "small evils," such as stealing, gambling, and failing to attend classes, to the grandiose dream of committing suicide by burning down the temple. His desire for notoriety is also a strand in his design for arson. He tells a young geisha: "In a month— yes, in a month from now there'll be lots about me in the papers. Please remember me when that happens." Mizoguchi, however, decides at the last minute to flee the scene of devastation. As he gazes at the fire, he puffs on a cigarette, feeling "like a man who settles down for a smoke after finishing a job of work."

In 1976 the novel was adapted as a like-named opera by the Japanese composer Toshiro Mayuzumi.

M.34 Molière [pseudonym of Jean-Baptiste Poquelin] *The Miser.* In *Plays by Molière.* New York: Modern Library, n.d.

■ Although this play is based on Plautus's *Aulularia*, the character of Harpagon appears to have been influenced by Molière's familiarity with two renowned Parisian skinflints, police chief Jean Tardieu and his even more miserly wife Marie, who were both murdered by house-breakers in 1665 (see G.1), the year before the play's premiere. The entrance of the two victims into Hades was lampooned by Nicolas Boileau in his dialogue *Les héros de roman* (ca. 1665).

M.35 Mongrédien, Georges *L'Affaire Foucquet.* Paris: Hachette, 1956.

■ A specialist in seventeenth-century France, Mongrédien writes with equal fluency about the Grand Siècle's history, culture, and crimes. Before addressing the trial of Jean Fouquet (or Foucquet), superintendent of finances, for embezzlement and treasonous conspiracy, Mongrédien had already written volumes on the two other great causes célèbres of the era, the imprisonment of the Man in the Iron Mask (*Le masque de fer*) and the Affair of Poisons (*Madame de Montespan et l'affaire des poisons*).

Since works by earlier authors treated in detail the well-documented legal proceeding against Fouquet, Mongrédien directs much of his attention to the reflection of the trial in contemporary pamphlets and street literature, which turned predominantly favorable to the disgraced minister as the unfairness and political bias of the prosecution became apparent. Literary friends of Fouquet, including fabulist Jean de La Fontaine, Madame de Sévigné, and Paul Pellisson, also rallied to his support. The secondary charge of treason imploded before the trial ended: Fouquet, fearing that the unstable Cardinal Mazarin planned his destruction, had formulated a quixotic "project" for armed resistance should the need arise; but he took no steps to effectuate his design and had forgotten that a draft of the scheme lay hidden behind a mirror at his home in Saint-Mandé, where the authorities found it after his arrest. The principal charges against him related to financial irregularities. That some of the accusations were true there seemed little doubt. For example, he had bought up for next to nothing expired treasury bills, which he resold at their face amount after having fresh government funds earmarked for their payment. Still, the underlying motives of the trial were political: Fouquet's rival, Colbert, sought to replace him, and Louis XIV, intent on establishing an absolute monarchy, prosecuted Fouquet as the embodiment of the old regime headed by the corrupt Mazarin. When a majority of Fouquet's judges rejected the death penalty and opted for exile, the king intervened to order life imprisonment.

Mongrédien ends his account with a moving description of Fouquet's eighteen-year imprisonment in a dungeon at Pignerol, where he died. During the last five years of his life, he was served by a valet named Eustache Dauger, who Mongrédien believes may thereafter have been kept in close confinement as the Man in the Iron Mask. It is Mongrédien's thesis that Dauger's fate may have been due to the purpose of the state to suppress secrets that the valet may have learned from Fouquet, possibly including some embarrassing tidbits about the love life of Anne of Austria. This hypothesis is, however, difficult to square with indications that Louis XIV was about to release Fouquet when the prisoner died of apparent apoplexy.

See Albert Borowitz, "Fouquet's Trial in the Letters of Madame de Sévigné," in *A Gallery of Sinister Perspectives: Ten Crimes and a Scandal* (B.27).

M.36 Montarron, Marcel *Les grands procès d'assises.* Paris: Editions Planète, 1967.
■ Montarron, one of France's most highly respected court reporters, comments on fifteen famous trials in the period 1913 to 1966.

The Bonnot Gang (1913): Montarron attributes the French sentimentality about these robbers and killers (the "tragic bandits") to the fact that most of them were under age twenty and were influenced by the ideas of Parisian anarchist circles. Another factor in their popularity was the gang's innovative use of the automobile in their attacks on collecting agents and banks, as well as their resistance to massive police sieges. The criminal for whom the gang is named, Jules Bonnot, was not the most violent among them, nor was he primarily motivated by political extremism. Embittered by unemployment and his wife's desertion, Bonnot advanced from counterfeiting to thefts of motor vehicles and, an expert motor repairman and driver, invented the plan of using cars to carry out the gang's lightning attacks. Wounded in a police stakeout, he shot himself to death. Three gang members were guillotined, one took poison while awaiting execution, and others received sentences ranging from five years to life imprisonment. Montarron, who interviewed surviving members of the gang, says of Bonnot, "In sum, caring very little for anarchist theories, what he wanted was money, and by any available means, to retire, his fortune made, to the country, with the mistress, whose memory haunted him until his death." See Victor Méric, *Les bandits tragiques* (Paris: Simon Kra, 1926); Emile Becker, *La "Bande à Bonnot"* (Paris: Debresse, 1968); Bernard Thomas, *La bande à Bonnot* (N.p.: Tchou, 1968); William Caruchet, *Ils ont tué Bonnot* [They Have Killed Bonnot] (Paris: Calmann-Lévy, 1990).

Henri-Désiré Landru (1921): Montarron never tired of discussing Landru with Jean Belin, who as a young policeman had arrested the famous "Bluebeard" killer of ten "fiancées" and the son of one of them. The reporter, however, did not believe that Landru, as charged, incinerated the bodies of all his victims in a kitchen stove. To Montarron there remained two secrets of Landru: the enigma of "the man himself, the model husband, the irreproachable father of four children, prisoner of his own silence," and his other magic secret, "the paradoxical enchantment that this don Juan 'with the face of a sickly fox' exercised on all the lonely and aging women who did not want to give up on adventure and love." Accounts of the Landru trial by a trio of observers are provided in Henri Béraud, Emmanuel Bourcier, and André Salmon, *L'Affaire Landru* (Paris: Albin Michel, 1924).

Guillaume Seznec (1924): In what Montarron calls Brittany's "little Dreyfus case," Seznec, a sawmill owner, served twenty years in the penal colony of French Guiana for the murder of Pierre Quémeneur, who disappeared during a 1923 business trip with Seznec. Quémeneur's body was never found. The tragedy of the Seznec family deepened when a witness, François Le Her, who had testified on the defendant's behalf, forced Seznec's daughter, Jeannette, to marry him under threats that he had proof of her father's guilt. In a violent quarrel with her unsavory husband, Jeannette killed him; she was acquitted of homicide in 1949. The Seznec family still maintains Guillaume's innocence (Jane [Jeannette] Seznec, *Notre bagne* [Our Prison Camp], comp. Claude Sylvane [Paris: Denoel, 1950]; Denis Seznec, *Nous, les Seznec* [We, the Seznecs] [Paris: Robert Laffont, 1992]; Denis Langlois, *L'Affaire Seznec* [Paris: Plon, 1988]; Jean Rieux and Lice Nédelec, *Seznec innocent . . . ou prestidigitateur criminel?* [Lorient: Jugant, 1976]). An investigative magistrate self-published a report of an investigation he conducted at his own expense to rehabilitate Seznec (Victor Hervé, *Justice pour Seznec* [Cotes-du-Nord: Editions Hervé, 1933]).

Dr. Pierre Bougrat (1927): After receiving citations for valor in World War I and marrying well, Dr. Bougrat saw his life in Marseilles go into a steep decline. His disreputable nightlife caused his wife to leave him, and he was jailed for issuing rubber checks. His troubles deepened when the body of a friend and patient was found in his office closet. Bougrat claimed that Jacques Rumèbe, a paymaster, had poisoned himself in despair over being robbed of payroll cash. However, a forensic expert, Professor Barral, found no significant traces of poison in Rumèbe's body and speculated that the patient might have died of a "therapeutic accident" caused by an allergic reaction to Bougrat's injection. Nevertheless, Bougrat was convicted of murder and transported to Guiana; he escaped to Venezuela, where he resumed his medical practice and died rich. Montarron deplores the angry response of the presiding judge to Professor Barral's testimony, regarding the trial as one where the prosecution decides to cling to a single hypothesis, only to be confronted by evidence that an alternative explanation is plausible. For a book-length study of the Bougrat trial, see Serge Douay, *L'Affaire Bougrat* (Paris: Presses de la Cité, 1974). The defense counsel states his case in Stefani Martin, *Le Docteur Bougrat n'a pas tué* [Dr. Bougrat Did Not Kill] (Paris: Argo, n.d.).

Paul Gorguloff (1932): The author witnessed the execution of Paul Gorguloff, an anti-Bolshevik Russian who shot elderly French president Paul Doumer to death at a Paris exhibition devoted to the literary works of war veterans, including Claude Farrère, who was wounded by a bullet. Montarron does not doubt the insanity of Gorguloff, who envisioned a cult of which he was the prophet and blamed the French for not expelling the Reds from his country.

Christine and Léa Papin (1933): In his article on the butchery of Madame Lancelin and her daughter, Geneviève, by their domestic servants, the Papin sisters (see G.8), Montarron regrets that medical experts deputed to assess their mental responsibility only paid them two half-hour visits in prison. Christine, the elder sister, died in an asylum after her death sentence was commuted; Léa Papin, after eight years in prison, went to work as a domestic in a luxury hotel.

Georges Sarret (1933): With the assistance of German sisters Philomène and Catherine Schmidt, Sarret committed serial killings to acquire the victims' property and insurance proceeds. In a villa near Aix, he immersed two corpses in a bath of sulphuric acid. Sarret was executed and the Schmidts were sentenced to ten years in prison.

Eugène Weidmann (1939): See C.34.

Dr. Marcel Petiot (1946): Petiot, who admitted murdering sixty-three victims in Paris during the Nazi occupation, is to Montarron the Landru of World War II, reflecting that war's grander scale of horrors. The prosecution charged Petiot with twenty-seven murders; he denied eight of them and maintained that he killed the others for patriotic reasons. Montarron comments, "It was undeniable that he had killed Jews who wanted to escape Nazi oppression, but it is no less true than he had, in addition, eliminated informers and pimps in the service of the Gestapo. And it was troubling that German uniforms were found in the baggage of victims." It was proved that Petiot's claim to be a member of the French Resistance was false. See Thomas Maeder, *The Unspeakable Crimes of Dr. Petiot* (Boston: Atlantic–Little Brown, 1980); René Tavernier, *L'Affaire Petiot* (Paris: Presses de la Cité, 1974).

Pauline Dubuisson (1953): This article follows to its tragic end the life of Dubuisson, who inspired the character portrayed by Brigitte Bardot in Henri-Georges Clouzot's 1960 film *The Truth*. After her discharge from prison, where she had served a six-year detention for killing her former lover, Félix Bailly, Pauline fell in love again; but when the romance soured, she committed suicide. The prosecution, who viewed her as ruled by pride, had regarded earlier suicide attempts after the Bailly shooting as simulated. The Dubuisson case is studied at length in Paulette Houdyer, *Le diable dans la peau* [Devil in the Flesh] (Paris: René Julliard, n.d.).

Gaston Dominici (1954): The author calls the murder of Sir Jack Drummond, his wife, and daughter near Lurs "the mystery of the 20th century." Largely on the basis of Dominici's persuasive show of knowledge during the reconstruction of the crime, Montarron appears to believe that he was involved in the deaths of the British tourists. The motive, however, remains a mystery. Attempts at theft of the victims' property, in Montarron's view, followed the murders rather than having caused them (see G.15).

Guy Desnoyers (1958): Fearsomely determined to conceal his paternity, this randy parish priest of Lorraine, and former curé of Uruffe, murdered his sweetheart, Régine Fays, who was more than eight months pregnant, and tore the infant from her womb, mutilating its body and face.

Denise Labbé and Jacques Algarron (1956): Montarron rates this the most touching case of the post–World War II period. Believing that her cooling lover of seven months demanded the sacrifice of her two-and-a-half-year-old daughter, Catherine, to his vision of an "ideal union," Denise, after three failed murder attempts, drowned her child in a laundry boiler. She was sentenced to life imprisonment and Jacques Algarron was sentenced to serve twenty years at hard labor as instigator of her crime. Montarron regards the penal responsibility of Algarron as "juridically difficult to demonstrate." The reporter has also edited a volume of the trial documents, *L'Affaire Denise Labbé-Algarron* (Paris: Table Ronde, 1956). See also Marcel Jouhandeau, "Les amants de Vendôme," in *Trois crimes rituels* (Paris: Gallimard, 1962).

Dr. Casters and Suzanne and Jean Vandeput (1962): The acquittal of Dr. Casters, Suzanne and Jean Vandeput, and three of the Vandeputs' relatives for the mercy killing of the couple's armless thalidomide baby, with the doctor's assistance, caused Montarron to rejoice. The reporter felt that the parents had already suffered the worst that could happen. Still, he faulted the clinic in Liège, Belgium, where the baby was born, for underrating the baby's chances for survival and failing to counsel the Vandeputs on the possibility of living with a severely handicapped child.

Lucien Léger (1966): When Léger, a male nurse in a Villejuif psychiatric hospital, strangled ten-year-old Luc Taron, in the woods of Verrières, one of his principal motives may have been to gain notoriety. Nevertheless, like William Heirens, he eventually blamed the crime on a mythical third person, to whom he gave the name Georges-Henri Molinaro.

M.37 Montarron, Marcel (with Jean-Michel Charrier) *Stavisky: Les secrets du scandale.* Paris: Robert Laffont, 1974.

■ Montarron, coauthor of this absorbing account of the Stavisky scandal and its aftermath, observed and reported these events as they unfolded. Serge Stavisky was for most of his criminal career an unimaginative crook who made a living as gigolo, petty swindler, and fraudulent theatrical entrepreneur. In 1926 he was arrested for securities theft, but his growing network of political protectors won him successive trial postponements and liberation from prison. Taking on a new name of "Monsieur Alexandre," Stavisky began to spend lavishly at hotels, casinos, and racetracks and perpetrated grander frauds, capped by the issuance of close to 300 million francs in falsified bonds of the Bayonne pawnshop.

On January 8, 1934, after the police closed in at a leisurely pace, Stavisky was found dead of a gunshot wound to the head in a secluded villa near Chamounix. When the news came to Paris, two governments fell, and high functionaries were fired or transferred; M. Thomé, head of the Sûreté, became the director of the Comédie Française, prompting the tart comment that the "National Theatre is not a house of detention." Public outrage triggered by the Stavisky fraud and the subsequent firing of police chief Jean Chiappe led to bloody riots in Paris beginning February 6, 1934. A final violent echo of the Stavisky affair was heard from La Combe aux Fées near Dijon on February 20: the decapitated, mutilated corpse of Judge Albert Prince, formerly chief of the finance division of the public prosecutor's office during the period when Stavisky's criminal trial was repeatedly postponed and unfavorable police reports on his activities were pigeonholed, was found on a railroad track, his head and a severed arm nearby. A light hempen cord was bound around Prince's right leg.

Conspiracy theorists, rejecting the appearance of suicide in the deaths of Stavisky and Prince, have contended that both men were murdered to prevent revelation of the role of government officials in the Stavisky frauds. In the case of Stavisky's shooting, it is noted, for example, that the point at which the fatal bullet imbedded itself into the wall is considerably lower than the height of the hunted criminal's temple wound, assuming that he was standing upright when the shot was fired. Still, Montarron and his collaborator opt for a self-inflicted gunshot, arguing, however, that Stavisky may have died in a "suicide by persuasion" induced by the police's excruciatingly slow encirclement of his hideout.

The authors also conclude that Prince committed suicide, despite controversial forensic evidence that he may have been chloroformed prior to the approach of the train that crushed and beheaded him. The telephone call that lured Prince to Dijon with a false report of his mother's illness does not stand up to close scrutiny; Prince received this message only because he returned home to pick up a change purse he had forgotten, and he also failed to verify the false Dijon telephone number from which the call was purportedly placed.

The police and journalistic investigations into the death of Prince were farcical. Georges Simenon, engaged to write a series of articles on possible underworld involvement, was misled by fabrications that would never have fooled his Inspector Maigret.

M.38 Moravia, Alberto [pseudonym of Alberto Pincherle] *The Conformist.* Trans. Angus Davidson. New York: Farrar, Straus & Young, 1951.

■ The novel's antihero, Marcello Clerici, joins the fascist secret police, hoping that his conformity with the demands of Mussolini's regime, as well as a middle-class marriage, will help him overcome two traumas: doubt about his sexual orientation exacerbated by his childhood killing of a homosexual attacker; and fear of the Clerici genes inherited from a sadistic father committed to a mental institution. The murder of exiled antifascist Professor Quadri, in which Marcello reluctantly participates, is based on the assassination of Moravia's cousins, Carlo and Nello Rosselli.

Political activist and writer Carlo Rosselli was born in Rome in 1899. He won his university degree with a thesis on syndicalism. As a member of the Socialist Party, he organized a clandestine struggle against Mussolini, publishing protest literature after the assassination of Matteotti. He was arrested in 1926 and was sent to the fascist prison camp on the island of Lipari, from which he escaped in 1929 in the company of Francesco Fausto Nitti, who described their deliverance in *Escape* (New York: Putnam, 1930). He went to France where he organized the antifascist resistance of the group Justice and Liberty. Subsequently he fought in a contingent of Italian volunteers in the Spanish Civil War. On June 9, 1937, he and his brother Nello were murdered in Bagnoles de l'Orne, France, by French assassins in Mussolini's pay. The ideals of Carlo and Nello Rosselli are honored in present-day Florence by the activities of the Rosselli Brothers Club (Circolo Fratelli Rosselli). See Stanislao G. Pugliese, *Carlo Rosselli: Socialist Heretic and Antifascist Exile* (Cambridge, Mass.: Harvard Univ. Press, 1999).

M.39 Munro, C. K. [pseudonym of Charles W. Kirkpatrick Macmillan] *At Mrs. Beam's: A Play.* New York: Knopf, 1926.

■ The denizens of Mrs. Beam's Notting Hill Gate boardinghouse live in a world of hearsay, half-remembered conversations, news reports, and inexperience. The most feverish imagination to be found among their company belongs to Miss Shoe, an elderly busybody who is persuaded that new lodgers, Mr. Dermott and his companion, Laura Pasquale, are French serial wife-killer Henri Désiré Landru and his next victim. The suspicions of the spinster-sleuth are heightened by the trunk that graces Dermott's bedroom. It turns out that the newcomers, who are evicted by the landlady for living in sin, are criminals, just as Miss Shoe had proclaimed; they are professional thieves who have carted away their fellow lodgers' possessions in the ominous trunk. They are also thieves of hearts, each carrying on a brazen flirtation even while they are orchestrating their sudden departure.

N

N.1 Naipaul, V[idiadhar] S[urajprasad] "Michael X and the Black Power Killings in Trinidad." In *The Return of Eva Perón: with, The Killings in Trinidad.* New York: Knopf, 1980.

■ In 1967, Michael de Freitas, son of a Portuguese shopkeeper and a black woman from Barbados, was sentenced to jail for a year after his conviction under England's Race Relations Act for an anti-white speech he made in Reading under the name "Michael X." It was in London, V. S. Naipaul comments sardonically, that de Freitas "became a Negro," exploiting press interest in black militancy by his gift for public relations.

A Trinidadian of Indian origin, Naipaul narrates the murderous second chapter of Michael X's life. After fleeing to Trinidad in 1971, Michael X, who had now adopted the black Muslim name of Michael Abdul Malik, organized a small "agricultural" commune but showed a greater talent for fundraising than for effectuating his largely fictitious community projects. In January 1972 he ordered the execution and burial of Gale Ann Benson, a twenty-seven-year-old middle-class English divorcée who had been living with Malik's American Black Power henchman, Hakim Jamal. Jamal had come to believe that it did not look good for a black radical to consort with a white woman, but for Malik, according to Naipaul, the killing of Benson was a "literary murder." He had been working on a clumsy autobiographical novel with English characters, and "Benson, English and middle class, was just the victim Malik needed: his novel began to come to life."

Although plotting was beyond Malik's ability as a writer, he planned and carried out the murder with meticulous attention to detail. Shortly afterward, for no apparent reason other than that his taste for blood had been aroused, he commanded the execution of another commune member, Joe Skerritt. In 1975 Malik was hanged in the Royal Jail at Port of Spain, Trinidad.

In his portrait of Michael X, who at age thirty-seven proclaimed himself "the Best Known Black man of this entire white western world," Naipaul emphasizes the futility of importing American notions of Black Power into Trinidad, where blacks are in the majority and assertions of racial oppression can camouflage more realistic social issues.

N.2 Narayan, R[asipuram] K[rishnaswami] *Waiting for the Mahatma.* London: Methuen, 1995.

▪ The shadow of the tragic destiny to be fulfilled by Mahatma Gandhi falls on this narrative of two young lovers. The naive Smiram leaves a domineering granny in Narayan's imaginary town of Malgudi to become a follower of Gandhi and later an independence agitator (painting "Quit India" on walls) and a train wrecker, all for love of Bharati ("daughter of India"), one of the Mahatma's devoted volunteers. The title appears to have a double meaning. Indians wait for Gandhi to appear among them to preach his message of nonviolent opposition to British rule or, after liberation, to call for an end to religious massacres. In their personal lives, Smiram and Bharati endure years of imprisonment and separation before they finally receive Gandhi's permission to marry; he grants his approval only moments before he is assassinated by Hindu extremist Nathuram Godse on January 30, 1948.

Narayan suggests that Gandhi's sainthood was often a heavy burden for lesser mortals to carry, even those as well intentioned as the novel's long-parted lovers. Not all independence workers, however, are portrayed as selfless. For example, the cynical photographer, Jagadash, settles into Smiram's hideout after inventing zany missions that land the inexperienced young man in jail. After liberation, Jagadash assembles a photographic album glorifying his own role.

N.3 Nelson, Richard *Two Shakespearean Actors.* London: Faber & Faber, 1990.

▪ On the night of May 10, 1849, a riot outside New York City's Astor Place Opera House, where British tragedian William Macready was appearing as Macbeth, resulted in thirty-one deaths and 150 injuries. The disturbance arose from the seething rivalry between Macready and the more flamboyant American actor Edwin Forrest, who was playing at the Broadway Theatre at the time of the riot. What began as professional antagonism was converted into political violence by nativists led by Elmo Z. C. Judson ("Ned Buntline"), who brought rowdies (dominated by the Bowery B'hoys) into the Astor Place theater and surrounding streets with inflammatory handbills asking working men whether "Americans or English [shall] rule in this city." Judson, in the aftermath of the riot, was convicted of criminal conspiracy and given the maximum sentence of one year in jail and a fine of $250 (see Richard Moody, *The Astor Place Riot* [Bloomington: Indiana Univ. Press, 1958]).

In Richard Nelson's play, the massacre in Astor Place is moved offstage. The riot is an example, blown to disastrous proportions, of life's intrusion on the inner world of the actor. Macready tells Forrest that the world should be left behind, in the dressing room, but speculates as to how he could play Hamlet if his father had just died. Forrest responds: "But fathers don't die every time we play Hamlet. Instead, bills are sent that day which can be wrong. You step in horse shit on the street. Wives don't listen when you talk to them. You lose your favourite pen. Or hat. Or your right shoe. Or other stocking. Or you fall in love that day. Or hear a joke that you cannot forget and cannot stop smiling about. Your brother writes and says he's going to visit. The breakfast wasn't at all what you wanted. And then you play Hamlet. Then you become someone else. To do this you must learn to forget. Sometimes I think this is my favourite part of being an actor."

N.4 [Newgate Calendar]   *The Complete Newgate Calendar.* Ed. J. L. Rayner and G. T. Crook. 5 vols. London: Navarre Society, 1926.
■ This handsome set selects its narratives of murderers, robbers and highwaymen from many sources that exemplify the popular editions of criminal biographies collectively known as Newgate Calendars. These sources include:

- Captain Charles Johnson's *General History of the Lives and Adventures of the Most Famous Highwaymen, etc.* (1734)
- Captain Alexander Smith's *Compleat History of the Lives and Robberies of the Most Notorious Highwaymen, etc.* (1719)
- *The Tyburn Chronicle* (1768)
- *The Malefactors' Register* (1796)
- George Borrow's *Celebrated Trials and Remarkable Cases . . .* (1825).
- The final edition of the Newgate Calendar, by Andrew Knapp and William Baldwin (1826)
- Camden Pelham's *Chronicles of Crime* (1841)

An early criminal included in the collection is Sawney Beane, a legendary figure whose misdeeds in East Lothian, east of Edinburgh, are placed in the reign of Queen Elizabeth I of England. Inhabiting a cave with his vast brood, Beane and his family murdered and robbed passersby and then cannibalized them. The author of Beane's life in the *Newgate Calendar* asserts that these monsters were set upon by four hundred men dispatched by Scotland's King James VI and that bloodhounds led these troops into the criminals' subterranean den.

Some commentators believe that Sawney Beane inspired the story of Sweeney Todd, the Demon Barber of Fleet Street (see Peter Haining, *The Mystery and Horrible Murders of Sweeney Todd, the Demon Barber of Fleet Street* [London: Frederick Muller, 1979], 116–18). Sawney Beane also makes an appearance as a "low-browed, buck-toothed, and inhuman" villain in S. R. Crockett's novel *The Grey Man* (London: T. Fisher Unwin, 1896).

N.5 Nixon, Edna   *Voltaire and the Calas Case.* London: Gollancz, 1961.
■ In the first section of the book, Nixon places *l'affaire Calas* in the setting of the French religious wars and the Catholic extremism of Toulouse, where the tragedy unfolded. After Marc-Antoine Calas apparently hanged himself in 1761, his Huguenot father Jean was tried and executed for murder. The theory of the prosecution was that Jean had killed his son to prevent him from converting to Catholicism, as a younger brother Louis had already done without parental retribution. The second section of the book pays tribute to Voltaire's successful campaign to win the posthumous recognition of Jean Calas's innocence.

N.6 Norris, Frank *McTeague: A Story of San Francisco*. 1899. Ed. Donald Pizer. New York: Norton, 1977.

■ In this naturalistic novel reflecting its author's fondness for Emile Zola's Rougon-Macquart cycle, both the brutish dentist McTeague and his miserly wife, Trina, whom he murders, are victims of inherited traits over which they have limited control. In the course of his composition of the work, Norris came under the indirect influence of the theories of Cesare Lombroso, who believed that lawbreaking tendencies were inherited from criminal parents or parents who had suffered a degeneration of the nervous system due chiefly to alcoholism. Another more immediate source for the portrayal of McTeague was a San Francisco murder case of 1893. In that year, unemployed ironworker Patrick Collins stabbed his wife, Sarah, to death because she would not give him money for drink and would not live with him. The vicious attack, resulting in more than thirty wounds, was made in a kindergarten where Sarah worked as janitor in addition to taking in laundry to support the two Collins children. *San Francisco Examiner* articles described Collins, who had been previously jailed for slashing Sarah with a razor, as "brutish . . . not a man who has sunk, but one who was made an animal by nature to start with." Confirming his belief in criminal atavism, the reporter commented, "If a good many of Patrick Collins' ancestors did not die on the scaffold then either they escaped their desert or there is nothing in heredity."

N.7 [Notable British Trials Series] *Notable British Trials.* 83 vols. Various editors. Edinburgh and London: William Hodge, 1905–59.

■ In his article on the *Notable British Trials* and other subsequent trials series, Jonathan Goodman quotes Edmund Burke's expression of surprise that "the English language contains no book like the *causes célèbres* of the French, particularly as the openness of our proceedings renders the records more certain and accessible, while our public history and domestic conflicts have afforded so many splendid examples of the unfortunate and the guilty" ("Trials Series: Some Notable, Some Not," *Medicine, Science and the Law* 13 (Jan. 1973): 49). Goodman observes that this void was filled by the *Notable Scottish Trials* series begun by Edinburgh court reporter Harry Hodge in 1905 and then expanded into the *Notable British Trials.* Each volume is under the editorship of a professional writer, journalist, lawyer, or, occasionally, doctor who contributes an introductory essay followed by a transcript of the trial; William Roughead (see R.16) was the most prolific editor, undertaking responsibility for ten volumes. The principal trials included in the series (excluding political, financial, and civil cases), the dates of the trials, and the respective editors are listed below:

- Captain Kidd (1701). Ed. Graham Brooks
- Jack Sheppard (1724)—Hanged for burglary. Ed. Horace Bleackley
- Captain John Porteous (1736)—Convicted of illegally ordering the Edinburgh Civil Guard to fire on a crowd at a hanging. Ed. William Roughead
- Mary Blandy (1752)—Convicted of poisoning her father with arsenic. Ed. William Roughead

- James Stewart (1752)—The "Appin murder" referred to in Robert Louis Stevenson's *Kidnapped*. Ed. David N. Mackay
- Eugene Aram (1759)—Schoolmaster and murderer. Ed. Eric R. Watson
- Katherine Nairn (1765)—Convicted of participation in arsenic poisoning of her husband, Thomas Ogilvie. Ed. William Roughead
- Deacon William Brodie (1788)—Respectable house-breaker who provided one of the sources of Dr. Jekyll and Mr. Hyde. Ed. William Roughead
- "Bounty" mutineers (1792). Ed. Owen Rutter
- Abraham Thornton (1817)—Acquitted of murder of Mary Ashford in a case that belatedly led to the abolition of vestiges of trial by battle. Ed. Sir John Hall
- Henry Fauntleroy (1824)—Forger. Ed. Horace Bleackley
- John Thurtell and Joseph Hunt (1824)—See B.29. Ed. Eric R. Watson
- Burke and Hare (1828)—Body snatchers and murderers. Ed. William Roughead
- J. B. Rush (1849)—Convicted of a massacre of the inhabitants of Stanfield Hall. Ed. W. Teignmouth Shore
- William Palmer (1856)—Serial poisoner. Ed. Eric R. Watson
- Madeleine Smith (1857)—Released under Scottish verdict of "not proven," in prosecution for poisoning of her lover. Ed. F. Tennyson Jesse
- Dr. Thomas Smethurst (1859)—Pardoned after conviction of poisoning his wife whom he had married bigamously. Ed. Leonard A. Parry
- Jessie M'Lachlan (1862)—Reprieved after receiving controversial death sentence for murder of servant Jessie M'Pherson supposedly in connection with theft of household goods. Ed. William Roughead
- Franz Müller (1864)—England's first train murderer. Ed. H. B. Irving
- Dr. Edward William Pritchard (1865)—Convicted of poisoning his wife and mother-in-law. Ed. William Roughead
- Henry and Thomas Wainwright (1875)—Wealthy brush manufacturer Henry sentenced to death and his brother Thomas to prison for murder of Henry's young mistress, Harriet Lane, whose remains the brothers were transporting in parcels when arrested. Ed. H. B. Irving (published posthumously with an appreciation by barrister Sir Edward Marshall Hall)
- The Stauntons (1877)—The Penge case, in which brothers Louis and Patrick Staunton and Patrick's wife, Elizabeth, had death sentences commuted to life imprisonment in the murder of Louis's wife, Harriet, through prolonged abuse and neglect. (The Borowitz True Crime Collection holds correspondence of editor Atlay and author and columnist George Sims regarding a complaint from a friend of the Stauntons about the embarrassment caused them by Atlay's trial volume after their release from prison.) Ed. J. B. Atlay
- Eugène M. Chantrelle (1878)—Teacher of French who poisoned his wife. Ed. A. Duncan Smith
- Kate Webster (1879)—Domestic servant with long record of larceny reacted to notice

of dismissal by killing her employer, Julia Thomas, with a hatchet and boiling her remains. Ed. Elliott O'Donnell

- Charles Peace (1879)—Charlie Peace, the Banner Cross murderer, is another criminal of the Jekyll-Hyde type. A burglar who sometimes carried the tools of his criminal trade in his violin case, Peace threatened his neighbor, Katherine Dyson, after she broke off their affair, and he later shot her husband, Arthur, to death. Ed. W. Teignmouth Shore
- Dr. George Henry Lamson (1882)—The drug-addicted doctor poisoned eighteen-year-old Percy Malcolm John, his wife's physically disabled nephew, hoping for inheritance. Ed. Hargrave L. Adam
- Adelaide Bartlett (1886)—Acquitted of murdering her husband, Edwin, by pouring liquid chloroform down his throat; the charge against her young lover the Reverend George Dyson had previously been withdrawn. Ed. Sir John Hall
- Florence Maybrick (1889)—In a controversial trial, Mrs. Maybrick was convicted of arsenic poisoning of her husband, James, a Liverpool cotton broker (who in 1992 was added to the list of Jack the Ripper suspects as the author of the so-called Ripper Diaries). Mrs. Maybrick was released from prison in 1904 and died in America in 1941 at age seventy-six. Ed. H. B. Irving
- John Watson Laurie (1889)—The "Arran murder case," in which Laurie was convicted of murdering and robbing a new steamship acquaintance, young Edwin Robert Rose, on Scotland's Arran Island. Laurie, found to have been of unsound mind, was transferred to a criminal asylum at Perth Prison. Ed. William Roughead
- Thomas Neill Cream (1892)—A serial poisoner of female patients and prostitutes, Dr. Cream has joined the ranks of Jack the Ripper suspects. Ed. W. Teignmouth Shore
- Alfred John Monson (1893)—In this Ardlamont murder, Monson benefited from the Scottish verdict of "not proven" in the gunshot death of young Cecil Hambrough, whose life he had insured. Dr. Joseph Bell, Arthur Conan Doyle's medical professor on whom Sherlock Holmes is patterned, had testified that the wound had not been self-inflicted but had resulted from a shot fired more than six feet away. Ed. John W. More
- Oscar Wilde's three trials (1895). Ed. H. Montgomery Hyde
- William Gardiner (1903)—The "Peasenhall Case," in which Gardiner was released after two juries were unable to reach a verdict in the murder of twenty-three-year-old maid Rose Harsent. Her throat had been cut and an attempt made to burn her body, perhaps to conceal her pregnancy. Ed. William Henderson
- George Chapman (1903)—Still another killer whom some have identified as Jack the Ripper, Chapman, born Severin Klosowski in Poland, successively poisoned three mistresses. Ed. Hargrove L. Adam
- Samuel Herbert Dougal (1903)—In this "Moat Farm" case, Dougal shot spinster Camille Holland, whom he had wooed with an eye to profit from her assets; he buried her body in a drainage ditch on a remote Essex farm. (One of Dougal's diary leaves (from August 1900) is in the Borowitz True Crime Collection.) Ed. F. Tennyson Jesse
- The "Veronica" Trial (1903)—Murder of ship captain by three mutineers: Gustav Rau,

Otto Monsson, and Willem Smith. Ed. G. W. Keeton and John Cameron

- Adolf Beck (1896, 1904)—Twice convicted as a swindler on the basis of mistaken identity, Beck was ultimately vindicated. Ed. Eric R. Watson
- Robert Wood (1907)—Acquitted in the Camden Town murder of prostitute Emily "Phyllis" Dimmock. Ed. Basil Hogarth
- Oscar Slater (1909–28)—After nineteen years in prison, Slater, who had been convicted of murdering elderly Marion Gilchrist in Glasgow as a result of mistaken eyewitness testimony, was freed, partly due to the advocacy of Sir Arthur Conan Doyle. Ed. Wil-liam Roughead
- Hawley Harvey Crippen (1910)—The prototypical mild-mannered murderer, Crippen, born in Michigan and trained as a homeopathist in Cleveland, poisoned his wife, Belle, with hyoscine, buried her under the coal cellar floor of his London flat, and was arrested fleeing by ship for America with his mistress, Ethel Le Neve. (The Borowitz True Crime Collection holds a copy of a letter of Mrs. Crippen's sister, Louise Mills, complaining to editor Young about his unfair portrayal of her sister.) Ed. Filson Young
- John Alexander Dickman (1910)—Debt-burdened Dickman murdered John Nisbet in a railway carriage on the North-Eastern Railway. Ed. S. O. Rowan-Hamilton
- Steinie Morrison (1911)—Died in prison, ever protesting his innocence in the slaying of Leon Beron on Clapham Common. Ed. H. Fletcher Moulton
- Frederick Henry Seddon and wife Margaret Ann Seddon (1912)—Miserly Frederick was hanged for poisoning his equally miserly lodger Eliza May Barrow; Mrs. Seddon was acquitted. Ed. Filson Young
- George Joseph Smith (1915)—The so-called "brides-in-the-bath" honeymoon murderer. Ed. Eric R. Watson
- Harold Greenwood (1920)—The subject of editor Duke's novel *Bastard Verdict* (1934), solicitor Greenwood was acquitted in Wales of murdering his wife. Ed. Winifred Duke
- Jack Alfred Field and William Thomas Gray (1920)—Hanged for battering Irene Violet Munro to death on the "Crumbles" shingle beach near Eastbourne. Ed. Winifred Duke
- Frederick Bywaters and Edith Thompson (1922)—Lovers hanged for the murder of Edith's inconvenient husband, Percy. Edith's controversial conviction was based mainly on her letters to twenty-year-old Bywaters reporting her earlier attempts (perhaps imaginary) to poison her husband. Ed. Filson Young
- Ronald True (1922)—Sent to Broadmoor as criminally insane after conviction of the rolling-pin murder of prostitute Gertrude Yates ("Olive Young"), whose jewelry he stole together with eight pounds in cash. Ed. Donald Carswell
- Herbert Rowse Armstrong (1922)—Solicitor hanged for poisoning ailing wife in Hay-on-Wye. Shortly after the murder, Armstrong attempted to poison Oswald Martin, his only professional competitor in town. Ed. Filson Young
- Jean Pierre Vaquier (1924)—Poisoned Alfred Jones, proprietor of Blue Anchor Hotel, Byfleet, Surrey, with strychnine purchased for a "wireless experiment" in the hope of renewing his affair with Jones's wife, Mabel. Ed. R. H. Blundell and R. E. Seaton

- John Donald Merrett (1927)—Benefited from the Scottish verdict of "not proven" on charge of fatal shooting of his mother but found guilty of forging checks in her name. Ed. William Roughead
- Frederick Guy Browne and William Henry Kennedy (1928)—Professional thieves with long records were hanged for shooting to death Police Constable George Gutteridge, who had stopped them while driving a stolen car. Browne was convicted on the basis of Kennedy's statement blaming him for the killing. Ed. W. Teignmouth Shore
- Dr. Benjamin Knowles (1928)—Medical officer in West Africa freed on appeal, quashing death sentence for murder of wife, Madge, who accidentally sat on loaded revolver he kept at bedside as defense against prowlers. Ed. Albert Lieck
- Sidney Harry Fox (1930)—Murdered his mother at a Margate hotel and set fire to her room. Fox is one of the sources of Emlyn Williams's play *Night Must Fall*. Ed. F. Tennyson Jesse
- Alfred Arthur Rouse (1931)—Supposedly for the purpose of starting life anew, Rouse faked his death by murdering a hitchhiker and setting fire to his car and the victim. Ed. Helena Normanton
- Jeannie Donald (1934)—Aberdeen murderess who strangled eight-year-old Helen Priestly, child of neighbors with whom she was on bad terms, and created injuries that simulated a rape. Mrs. Donald's death sentence was commuted and she was released from prison in 1944. Ed. John G. Wilson
- Alma Victoria Rattenbury and George Percy Stoner (1935)—Lovers Rattenbury, aged thirty-eight, and domestic worker Stoner, aged nineteen, jointly tried for Stoner's mallet murder of Rattenbury's husband, Francis, a distinguished architect. Alma Rattenbury, acquitted, took her own life; Stoner was reprieved after receiving death sentence. (Borowitz True Crime Collection holds letters received by Jesse from Dr. William O'Donnell, who was called to the murder scene and testified at the trial.) Ed. F. Tennyson Jesse
- Buck Ruxton (1936)—Hanged for the murder of his wife, Isabella. The case is remarkable for the reconstruction of the bodies of Mrs. Ruxton and another victim, nursemaid Mary Rogerson, from remains examined by forensic scientists, including Dr. John Glaister. Ed. R. H. Blundell and G. Haswell Wilson
- Frederick Nodder (1937)—Hanged for the strangling death of ten-year-old Mona Tinsley, whose body was retrieved from the River Idle. Nodder had been a lodger of the Tinsleys evicted for nonpayment of rent. Ed. Winifred Duke
- Patrick Carraher (1938–46)—Petty criminal tried twice in Glasgow for unrelated murders and hanged for the second crime. (Borowitz True Crime Collection holds copy of correspondence complaining of editor's unsubstantiated charge [p. 10] that the criminal courts of Scotland were used as "laboratories in which the [capital punishment] abolition issue might be tested over a long period.") Ed. George Blake
- August Sangret (1943)—The "Wigwam Murder Case." Sangret, Canadian solder with Indian blood, was hanged for murdering with a knife and a birch stake nineteen-year-old Pearl Wolfe, with whom he had slept in wigwams of his construction. Ed. Macdonald Critchley

- Neville George Clevely Heath (1946)—Hanged for the sadistic murder of Margery Gardiner. At the trial evidence was also introduced identifying Heath as the brutal killer of Doreen Marshall. Ed. Macdonald Critchley
- Thomas John Ley and Lawrence John Smith (1947)—The "Chalk Pit Murder." Ley, former Minister of Justice of New South Wales, Australia, and an employee, carpenter Smith, strangled and buried in a chalk pit. John Mudie, a barman Ley delusionally believed to be carrying on an affair with Ley's sixty-six-year-old mistress. Ley was committed for insanity, and Smith's death sentence was commuted to life imprisonment. Ed. F. Tennyson Jesse
- James Camb (1948)—The "Porthole murderer," Camb, a steward aboard the ss *Durban Castle*, was convicted of strangling and pushing through her cabin porthole passenger Gay Gilson. After being sentenced to death, Camb was reprieved and ultimately released after serving a term of imprisonment. (The Borowitz True Crime Collection holds a menu of "Our Society" of September 27, 1987, signed by Henry Elam, one of the Crown counsel at Camb's trial.) Ed. Geoffrey Clark
- Peter Griffiths (1948)—The "Blackburn Baby Murder." Griffiths was hanged for the sex slaying of Anne Devaney, three years and eleven months old. The murderer was traced after England's first mass fingerprinting. (A copy of the fingerprinting form and a collection of police photographs are in the Borowitz True Crime Collection.) Ed. George Godwin
- John George Haigh (1949)—The "acid bath murderer" hanged for the murder of Henrietta Durand-Deacon, Haigh confessed to murdering Mrs. Durand-Deacon and seven other women (including two fictional victims), destroying their remains in acid and drinking their blood. Ed. Lord Dunboyne
- Timothy John Evans and John Reginald Halliday Christie (1950–53)—The murders at 10 Rillington Place. Weak-minded Evans and serial killer Christie were convicted for distinct murders in separate trials, but many writers (including Ludovic Kennedy) have since maintained that Christie was responsible for all the crimes. Ed. F. Tennyson Jesse
- John Thomas Straffen (1952)—Committed to Broadmoor after strangling two small girls, mentally deficient Straffen escaped and claimed a third victim. After being sentenced to death, Straffen was reprieved and imprisoned. Ed. Letitia Fairfield and Eric P. Fullbrook
- Christopher Craig and Derek William Bentley (1952)—Controversial case in which slow-witted Bentley was executed for murder of police constable Sidney George Miles, although underaged Craig pulled the trigger and was the ringleader in the youths' burglary attempt. Also at issue was the meaning of Bentley's ambiguous words "Let him have it, Chris," after the police asked for Craig's weapon. Ed. H. Montgomery Hyde

Other trials in the series are those of Mary Queen of Scots; Guy Fawkes; King Charles I; the Bloody Assizes; the Annesley Case; Lord Lovat; the Douglas Cause; the Duchess of Kingston; the City of Glasgow Bank; the Baccarat Case; Roger Casement; the Royal Mail Case (trial of Lord Kylsant); the IRA Coventry Explosion; and William Joyce ("Lord Haw Haw").

N.8 [Nozières, Violette] *Violette Nozières.* Brussels: Éditions Nicolas Flamel, 1933.

■ Poet E. L. T. Mesens founded this Belgian publisher for the purpose of issuing, beyond the reach of French authorities, this pamphlet in which seventeen surrealist poets and artists assemble works in defense of young Violette Nozières (sometimes spelled Nozière; see F.13), who then faced charges for poisoning her father and attempting to poison her mother. The surrealist publication included poems by André Breton, René Char, Paul Eluard, and Benjamin Peret, illustrations by Hans Arp, Salvador Dali, Max Ernst, Alberto Giacometti, René Magritte, and Yves Tanguy; and a cover attributed to Man Ray. The surrealists had made earlier interventions on behalf of: anarchist Germaine Berton, who in 1923 shot Marius Plateau to death in the offices of Charles Maurras's right-wing journal *L'Action française*, of which Plateau was secretary; and the sisters Papin, maidservants who massacred their employers in Le Mans in 1933. As in these earlier cases, the defense of Violette Nozières gave the surrealists the opportunity to defend a woman they could view as oppressed, as well as an occasion to attack the bourgeois family. They seized with particular delight on Violette's claim that since age twelve she had been subjected to repeated sexual abuse by her father. In his poem Breton noted with a sneer M. Nozières's forethought in choosing a first name for his daughter that included the word rape (*viol*) in its first four letters. On the other hand, Dali's word-play angered his comrades: he misspells Violette's surname "Naziere" to create an association with the Nazis and also distorts her features by producing a long proboscis supported on a crutch, because her name also suggested to him the French word for nose (*nez*).

O

O.1 Oates, Joyce Carol *Zombie.* New York: Dutton, 1995.

■ Oates partially based her narrator-protagonist, Quentin P., on the Wisconsin serial sex killer, Jeffrey Dahmer, who preyed on minority victims whom he picked up at shopping malls and gay bars. Like Dahmer, Quentin was set loose on society after conviction of a lesser sex offense. He becomes obsessed with the idea of reducing young men to subservient "zombies" by the performance of transorbital lobotomies, of which he has read in a psychosurgery treatise. But all his crude operations go fatally awry, as very likely he had intended. Although Quentin clearly suffers from a sexual pathology, his conduct appears to be conditioned to some degree by traits that might be found in other less violent criminals, or even in maladjusted persons who are able, more or less, to conform to society's dictates. He is an insecure loner who avoids eye contact yet feels that people look through him. His family relations are generally affectless, but he harbors a particular resentment for his father, a respected physics professor. When Dr. M.K., a Nobel laureate, is posthumously found to have conducted radiation experiments likened to Nazi crimes, Quentin "had to laugh." He wondered why people pretended to care after so much time and probably drew an analogy between the venerated scientist's misdeeds and his own undiscovered acts of sadism.

O.2 O'Hara, John *Butterfield 8.* New York: Harcourt Brace, 1935.

▪ In 1931 party girl Starr Faithfull drowned off Long Island, prompting a police investigation that could not determine whether her death was due to accident, suicide or murder (see G.25). O'Hara's novel, inspired by the case, begins: "On this Sunday morning in May, this girl who later was to be the cause of a sensation in New York, awoke much too early for her night before."

The wakening heroine is Gloria Wandrous, whose name resembles Starr Faithfull's by seeming to be pure invention; her surname is often heard as "wondrous." Gloria, like Starr Faithfull, has been traumatized by child abuse, first inflicted at age eleven in an encounter with Major Boam, a friend of her uncle, and repeated in a sexual relationship with a schoolteacher named Dr. Joab Ellery Riddington, who taught her to sniff ether, an addiction of Starr Faithfull. When love seems to come to Gloria in the persona of former Yale athlete Weston Liggett, a womanizer twice her age, her surprisingly powerful response is inhibited by the "despair" induced by meaningless couplings with many other men. Liggett, for his own part, is so overwhelmed by their few nights of boozy romance that he abandons his wife and children, but his impulse to join his life to Gloria's is blocked by the fear that she will turn out to be like the casual amours of his past. He even regards her briefly as a "common thief," because she took his wife's fur coat in resentment over his having torn her evening dress, caveman-like, on their first night together. Understanding too late that he cannot bear losing Gloria, he pursues her aboard the *City of Essex,* bound for Boston. Their conversation on deck ends with her refusal to go to his cabin, and when he hails her later sitting on the dining-saloon roof, she rushes to the rail, falls overboard and is sucked into the ship's side wheel. Liggett believed that she was "hoping to get away from him by running down the stairs" and called himself a murderer.

The narrative and dialogue of *Butterfield 8* teem with references to criminals of the era, including Nathan Leopold and Richard Loeb; Ruth Snyder and Judd Gray; Legs Diamond; and cop-killer Two-Gun Crowley.

O.3 [Old Bailey Trials Series] *Old Bailey Trials.* 7 vols. Ed. C. E. Bechhofer Roberts. London: Jarrolds, 1944–48.

▪ Jonathan Goodman, in an article reviewing British trials series, opines that the austerity of the *Old Bailey* volumes (initially published in conformity with the Book Production War Economy Standard) is matched by the inelegant writing style of C. E. Bechhofer Roberts, who edited the entire set. The trials included are those of:

- Harry Dobkin, wartime fire-spotter who strangled his estranged wife Rachel in 1941 in a dispute over maintenance payments and dismembered and burned her body in the vestry of a bombed-out chapel
- Reginald Sidney Buckfield, who was committed to Broadmoor after stabbing Ellen Ann Symes to death on a Kent road. While in jail as an army deserter, Buckfield wrote a story called "Mystery of Brompton Road Murders," which, while seeking to support his eventual alibi defense, actually persuaded the police to arrest him for the murder.

- Helen Duncan, sentenced to nine months imprisonment in 1944 for conspiring with others to engage in fake spiritualism in violation of the Witchcraft Act of 1735. She preyed on wartime grieving for lost loved ones.
- Karl Gustav Hulten, a twenty-two-year-old American private from Cambridge, Massachusetts, and his accomplice, eighteen-year-old Elizabeth (Betty) Maud Jones, who were convicted of the 1944 murder of a London taxi driver (the "Cleft Chin Case"). Hulten was hanged and Jones, reprieved less than forty-eight hours before her appointment on the scaffold, was resentenced to life imprisonment but released in 1954. In 1944, the killers' story was filmed as *Chicago Joe and the Showgirl*, with the screenplay by crime writer David Yallop.
- The Mr. A. Case, a civil lawsuit that preceded the 1925 conviction of William Cooper Hobbs, a solicitor's managing clerk, of participation in a conspiracy to blackmail Sir Hari Singh (Mr. A), heir-presumptive to the throne of Kashmir
- Thomas John Ley and Lawrence J. Smith, whose murder trial is the subject of a volume of the *Notable British Trials*
- William Joyce ("Lord Haw Haw") sentenced to death for treason during World War II. The case is also included in the *Notable British Trials*.

0.4 O'Neill, Eugene *The Iceman Cometh.* 1946. New York: Random House (Modern Library), 1957.

■ The character of the informer Don Parritt in O'Neill's play has its roots in the history of American labor violence. Two union men, the McNamara brothers, James and John, were charged with responsibility for the bombing of the *Los Angeles Times* building in 1910, in which twenty-one people died. Their defense counsel, Clarence Darrow, plea-bargained for prison sentences. After the trial private detective William J. Burns bribed Donald Vose, disaffected son of anarchist Gertie Vose, to help him trap two union agitators, Matthew Schmidt and David Caplan, whom Burns believed to be participants in the McNamara bombing. In the play, the informer's betrayal of his mother becomes more direct. Whereas Donald Vose had acted in faithlessness to Gertie's cause, Don Parritt's tip to detective Burns actually leads to his mother's arrest as one of the bombing conspirators. At first maintaining that he had been motivated solely by the need for money to finance his dissolute life, Parritt finally confesses to having acted out of hatred for his mother. After the command of his mother's former lover, the disillusioned syndicalist-anarchist Larry Slade, to "get the hell out of life," Parritt throws himself off a fire escape shortly before the play's end.

0.5 Orton, Joe [pseudonym of John Kingsley Orton] *Loot.* In *Joe Orton: The Complete Plays.* New York: Grove Weidenfeld, 1990.

■ Orton's brilliant career as a comic playwright was cut short when he was murdered by his lover, Kenneth Halliwell (see John Lahr, *Prick Up Your Ears: The Biography of Joe Orton* [New York: Knopf, 1978]).

Orton's anarchic farce *Loot* substitutes for the bedroom doors, emblematic of this time-honored stage genre, a coffin in which the embalmed body of Mrs. McLeavy is ready for funeral services. Her son, Hal, and his friend, Dennis, unceremoniously remove the body and substitute money they have stolen from a bank. The pair of crooks brings off a dizzying sequence of legerdemain to hide their loot from the prying eyes of Truscott, a Scotland Yard detective who finally stumbles onto the cache and settles for a 25-percent share. Although Truscott often adopts the mannerisms of Sherlock Holmes played by Groucho Marx, his characterization, as enriched by Orton's revisions of his original draft, owed much to the author's obsession with Detective Sergeant Harold Challenor. Orton's biographer, John Lahr, writes that Challenor's "outrageous methods of detection captured more headlines than criminals." He became "the subject of the first police inquiry into their own ranks under the 1964 Police Act." The detective's bag of tricks included fabricating evidence as well as the intimidation and abuse of prisoners. One of Challenor's widely quoted remarks on making an arrest is repeated verbatim by Truscott in corruptly arresting McLeavy (Hal's father) at the end of the play: "You're fucking nicked, my old beauty."

P

P.1 [Pao Ch'eng] *The Strange Cases of Magistrate Pao: Chinese Tales of Crime and Detection.* Trans. and retold Leon Comber. Rutland, Vt.: Tuttle, 1964.

▪ Fictionalized stories of cases of Sung dynasty district magistrate Pao Ch'eng appeared as early as the Yüan dynasty and were later collated in ten volumes by an unknown Ming scholar. Comber selects six examples and retells them effectively without doing injury to the unadorned style of the original. Although the Chinese district magistrate combined the functions of investigator, prosecutor, and judge, these tales, which are spiced with seduction, adultery, rape, and lascivious monks, emphasize detection. Traditional Chinese detective fiction caters to its readers' fondness for the supernatural. In one of these stories, the canny Judge Pao knows how to play on superstition to the advantage of justice: a monk confesses a murder after a confrontation with "ghosts" who turn out to be disguised runners sent by the magistrate.

P.2 Parker, Dorothy, and Ross Evans *The Coast of Illyria: A Play in Three Acts.* Intro. Arthur F. Kinney. Iowa City: Univ. of Iowa Press, 1990.

▪ In 1796 Mary Lamb, in a fit of insanity, stabbed her mother through the heart with a case knife after Mrs. Lamb intervened on behalf of a terrified apprentice girl whom Mary had been pursuing with the weapon. Mary's brother, Charles, "was at hand only time enough to snatch the knife out of her grasp." Charles saved Mary from commitment to Bedlam by undertaking her custody. The Parker-Evans play (first performed in 1949 by the Dallas Repertory Theater) shows the Lambs living together with terrible memories of the murder and fears of Mary's periodic relapses.

The title, drawn from the Lambs' tale of Shakespeare's *Twelfth Night* (which serves as the play's epigraph), is the kernel of Charles's outburst to his friend George Dyer in Act 3: "Oh, what a couple we are! She in her constant danger, driving me to this; I with my stinking drunkenness sending her quicker to her hells. Two shipwrecked souls. Like "Twelfth Night," isn't it? A brother and sister shipwrecked off the coast of Illyria."

The dark play, relieved by the wit of the Lambs' literary friends Samuel Taylor Coleridge, William Hazlitt, and Thomas De Quincey (who trade barbs in the manner of Parker's Algonquin circle) moves relentlessly to a shattering finale. Mary suffers a serious relapse, and Charles's beloved, the actress Fanny Kelly, gives him up, realizing that there is no room for her in the inseparable union of brother and sister.

Parker, as rehearsals of the play progressed, came to identify strongly with Mary Lamb; in much of her literary work, she addressed the fear of abandonment.

P.3 Pearson, Edmund Lester *Books in Black or Red.* New York: Macmillan, 1923.

■ Pearson's lead essay discusses literary hoaxes, which he takes pains to differentiate from literary forgeries for gain. The nicety of this distinction was not entirely without self-interest, because among the cases discussed is the author's own highly successful prank: the publication, with the collaboration of a friend John Cotton Dana, of Pearson's fabricated 1774 *Old Librarian's Almanack* (1909; reprinted, facsimile ed., Pittsburgh: Beta Phi Mu, 1979). Pearson recalls the evolution of his good-natured imposture and the gullibility of foolish critics. He dignifies his own proceedings by reference to better known forgeries, those of Denis Vrain-Lucas (see D.1), as well as the imaginary auction in Benche, Belgium, of unique book treasures dreamt up by the nonexistent Comte de Fortsas.

Another essay offers homage to the father of the English true-crime essay, Thomas De Quincey, who established mock-aesthetic criteria for evaluating great murder cases. Pearson judges that to merit study, a "pure murder" must have an element of mystery and, applying that standard with humorous rigor, purports to exclude most homicidal genres: political assassination, crimes of passion, murders committed by madmen, killings accompanying robbery, and serial murders. From most of these disfavored categories Pearson is careful to except some of his favorite cases.

Edmund Lester Pearson (1880–1937) was the leading American crime historian during the first half of the twentieth century. A humorous New Englander educated at Harvard College, Pearson later received a degree in library science from the New York State Library School and became editor of publications at the New York Public Library in 1914. After two decades of varied literary activity as columnist, reviewer, and author on subjects relating to books, libraries, and book collecting, Pearson devoted the last twelve years of his life to his interest in murder cases. His passion for this subject had been stirred by his Harvard literature professor George Lyman Kittredge, who opined that "murder is the material of great literature." Although some of Pearson's articles, read today, are more notable for wit and charm than for depth of research, he deserves credit for defining the canon of notable American, English, and French murder cases for a broad readership. His sole extended study, which related to Lizzie Borden's trial, has been criticized by Edward D. Radin (see R.3) as distorting the trial record to establish her guilt. But some commentators do not support Radin's charges. My own view is that Radin's charges are justified in some respects but do not, in the aggregate, overcome Pearson's demonstration of Lizzie's probable guilt.

See Biographical Note in Edmund Pearson, *The Librarian: Selections from the Column of That Name*, ed. Jane B. Durnell and Norman D. Stevens (Metuchen, N.J.: Scarecrow Press, 1976), xvi–xxiv. Pearson's boyhood is recounted in his *The Believing Years* (New York: Macmillan, 1912).

P.4 ———— *Five Murders, with a Final Note on the Borden Case.* Garden City, N.Y.: Doubleday Doran (Crime Club), 1928.

■ Dedicated to his "leader in writing" on crime, William Roughead, this volume consisting principally of extended essays is one of Pearson's finest. In these pieces, Pearson mutes his characteristic facetiousness as he undertakes scholarly studies that, for the most part, are based on original court records and contemporary newspaper accounts.

Throughout his life, fires seemed to follow Frederick Small ("The Man Who Was Too Clever"). When he planned the near-perfect murder of his recently insured third wife, Florence, arson played a major part. He set a fire-raising device to operate in his remote New Hampshire home at an hour when he was in Boston with a business associate. Florence was to be completely incinerated by the blaze; but the heat was so intense that her body crashed through to the cellar, where it was preserved by invading lake waters. The head and trunk were almost intact, and the examining doctors found that Mrs. Small had been strangled, shot in the skull, and struck by a heavy instrument. Frederick Small went bravely to the gallows. Pearson ends with a regretful observation: "It is one of the tormenting ironies of life that many good men do not make as good an end as those whose death is obscure and shameful."

Pearson turns to the neighboring state of Maine to retell the Hart-Meservey murder case of 1877 ("The Mystery of Tenants Harbour"). Sarah Meservey's strangled body was found in her Tenants Harbor house five weeks after the thirty-seven-year-old seaman's wife had been last seen on December 22. A neighbor, Nathan F. Hart, was convicted after telling local residents before the discovery of the corpse that he had dreamed Sarah was strangled. Hart claimed, however, that the dream *followed* the finding of the body. Pearson records the case's greatest mystery: "Five weeks had elapsed before this strangely incurious village, at last noticing the letters left unclaimed at the post office, as well as other unusual facts, thought that perhaps some inquiry should be made."

A companion piece to "Mate Bram!" (Pearson's better known study of maritime murder; see P.10), "Aboard the 'Glendower'" reports the murder of Captain Charles P. Wyman on the three-master *Glendower*. Clearly the murderer had acted in a frenzy, for "there were more than twenty wounds, either cuts or bruises, upon the head, as if he had been struck alternately with the blade and then the head of a hatchet." Ship's cook William De Graaf, tried for the crime in a Boston court, was found not guilty. In preparing his article on the case, Pearson uncovered a legend that, when he returned to the jail after the acquittal to reclaim his clothes, De Graaf confessed his guilt to a bailiff. According to the bailiff, the cook told him that his deformity had been caused by harsh treatment by Wyman many years before and that he had bided his time to take revenge. Pearson is properly skeptical of the truth of the bailiff's story.

In "The Doctor's Whisky," Pearson provides a summary account of Dr. Thomas Thatcher Graves's 1890 murder of wealthy Josephine Barnaby by mailing her a poisoned bottle of whisky as a "New Year's gift." Mrs. Barnaby had foolishly allowed the doctor to assume charge of her financial affairs.

"The Firm of Patrick and Jones" tackles the famous chloroform murder of William Marsh Rice, benefactor of Rice Institute, by crooked lawyer Albert T. Patrick and Rice's secretary-valet Charles F. Jones. Patrick had forged a will, assignments, and checks in his victim's name. When Patrick's murder conviction was sustained on appeal by a 4 to 3 vote, his death sentence was commuted to life imprisonment. In 1912 New York governor John A. Dix granted Patrick a pardon, making the astounding statement that "there had always been an air of mystery about the case."

The occasion for Pearson's postscript, "The End of the Borden Case," was the death of Lizzie Borden at age sixty-six in Fall River and the passing of her estranged elder sister, Emma, nine days later. The two women were buried in the family lot near the graves of their father, mother, infant sister, and stepmother. Pearson believes that Lizzie's acquittal was practically ensured by the presiding judge's exclusion of her contradictory inquest evidence about her whereabouts (yard or barn?) at the moment of her father's murder and by the judge's refusal to admit the testimony of three witnesses to Lizzie's attempt to buy prussic acid on the day before the killings. In his conclusion, Pearson reconstructs the chronology that would have permitted Lizzie, with nerves of steel and plenty of luck, to hatchet both victims without being discovered.

P.5 ——— *Instigation of the Devil*. New York: Scribner, 1930.
■ The brief chapters of this book are culled from forty to fifty articles that appeared in *Vanity Fair*. The titles of the pieces and their subjects (where not self-evident) are:

- Chapter 1. "Mrs. Wharton's House-Party": At her trial in 1871–72, Mrs. Elizabeth Wharton of Baltimore was acquitted of poisoning her creditor, General William Scott Ketchum, with tartar emetic. Pearson is grateful that she didn't use the time-worn excuses of having purchased the poison to kill rats or improve her complexion; she cited some ailment for which she needed tartar emetic as an external application.
- Chapter 2. "The Colt-Adams Affair": Brother of the gun inventor, Samuel, John Colt chose in 1841 a more primitive weapon, a hatchet, to dispatch Adams, whom he boxed for shipment to New Orleans; Colt stabbed himself one hour before he was to be hanged.
- Chapter 3. "What Does a Murderer Look Like?": Pearson playfully attacks a number of his bêtes noires: Lombroso's principles of criminal physiognomy and sentimentalists who are persuaded of innocence by a murderer's respectable looks or fine words.
- Chapter 4. "The Wicked Duke": Pearson relies on Armand Fouquier's nineteenth-century *Causes Célèbres* in briefly retelling this French criminal case. This is an account of the Duc de Choiseul-Praslin's murder of his wife (see L.35).
- Chapter 5. "Five Times Convicted of Murder": Black Alabama farmer Ervin Pope had

his death sentence commuted after five trials for the murder of miller James McClurkin in 1909 resulted in conviction.

- Chapter 6. "For the Borgia Medal, Connecticut Presents": Pearson discusses Lydia Sherman (called Connecticut's Lucrezia Borgia), who admitted to poisoning two husbands and six children with arsenic. She was at last convicted of second-degree murder in the poisoning of her spouse, Horatio Nelson Sherman.

- Chapter 7. "What Makes a Good Murder?": Pearson, in considering the criteria for the "good murder," rejects political assassinations and crimes of passion. He opines, "The good murder, the really desirable performance, beloved by the collector, is committed not by a habitual criminal, but by some one of blameless life. . . . The victim of the good murder is not a complete stranger, nor a passing acquaintance, but preferably some one near and it may be even dear to the murderer."

- Chapter 8. "The Tichborne Case"

- Chapter 9. "A Young Lady Named Perkins": Josephine Amelia Perkins of Devonshire developed an uncontrollable passion for riding and stealing horses.

- Chapter 10. "The First Butterfly of Broadway": Richard P. Robinson was acquitted of murdering a prostitute, Helen Jewett, in nineteenth-century New York City.

- Chapter 11. "'You Murdering Ministers'": Pearson illustrates the pun of his title by recounting the violent career of a Baptist preacher George Washington Carawan, which culminated in his murder of a neighbor, schoolmaster Clement H. Lassiter, whom he suspected of attempting to rape his wife. While his jury was out, Reverend Carawan shot the prosecutor, causing no injury, and then killed himself.

- Chapter 12. "That Damned Fellow Upstairs": This is a brief account of the Northumberland Street affray in London (see A.8).

- Chapter 13. "Precedents in the Hall-Mills Case": Pearson finds ample precedents in crime history for many of the elements of New Jersey's famous Hall-Mills murder case brought to trial in 1926: love-letters; hordes of volunteering witnesses, honest, dishonest or deluded; unreliable eyewitnesses; and the "marvellous female witness," a role played to the hilt in the Hall-Mills trial by the so-called "Pig-Woman," Jane Gibson, whom the jury believed to be a liar.

- Chapter 14. "Was Poe a Detective?": Pearson was skeptical about Edgar Allan Poe's claim to have anticipated, in his story "The Mystery of Marie Roget," discoveries that were subsequently made regarding the murder of Mary Cecilia Rogers.

- Chapter 15. "The Occasionally Veiled Murderess": Henrietta Robinson wore a veil when tried for the 1853 arsenic poisoning of Timothy Lanagan and Catherine Lubee in 1853. Dubbed the "Veiled Murderess," she died in an asylum. Her veil led to fevered speculations about a romantic identity.

- Chapter 16. "The Man Pays—Sometimes": In 1869 George S. Twitchell Jr. was convicted of beating his mother-in-law to death with a poker, and his possibly complicit wife went free. Pearson regards such a result as not uncommon.

- Chapter 17. "The Hanging of Hicks the Pirate": In 1860 Albert W. Hicks was executed on Bedloe's Island, New York Bay, for killing Captain Burr and brothers Smith and

Oliver Watts aboard the oyster sloop *E. A. Johnson*. Hicks had been tried for piracy rather than murder.

- Chapter 18. "The Mysterious Murder of Cécile Combettes": Drawing again on Armand Fouquier's *Causes célèbres*, Pearson revisits the unjust conviction and execution of Frère Léotard for the murder of a girl he may never have met (see B.54).

- Chapter 19. "Eight Professors from Yale": In the Reverend Herbert H. Hayden's trial for the murder of his pregnant servant girl, Mary Stannard, a Connecticut jury disagreed, with eleven favoring acquittal. Stannard's throat had been cut and her stomach contained crystals of arsenic that Yale professor Edward S. Dana found to be identical with the poison sold in a shop in the town.

- Chapter 20. "The Tirrells of Weymouth": Pearson recalls two trials involving Tirrells of Weymouth (who were unrelated). In 1846, advocate Rufus Choate secured the acquittal of Albert John Tirrell, charged with cutting the throat of prostitute Maria Bickford, arguing that if his client attacked Bickford, he was then subject to "somnambulism." In 1860 George Canning Hersey poisoned his pregnant sweetheart, Mary Tirrell, with strychnine, which he had represented was an abortifacient.

- Chapter 21. "The 'Learned' Murderer": Edward Rulloff (or Ruloff) murdered his wife and child at Ithaca, New York, and was jailed only for "abduction," since his victims' bodies were not discovered. During his incarceration he studied languages and developed a philological theory. Crime, however, remained his first love. He was hanged for the murder of Frederick Mirick (Merrick). A postmortem examination of the killer revealed that the scholar-murderer's brain weighed nine or ten ounces more than the average and that "he had the forehead which indicates intellect."

- Chapter 22. "Accomplished Female Liars": Among leading female practitioners of the art of lying, Pearson cites Elizabeth Canning, who falsely claimed to have been abducted (see M.4); and Marie de Morell, who fraudulently accused Lieutenant de la Roncière of sending her obscene letters and of attempting to rape her (see D.19).

- Chapter 23. "A Rather Mysterious Chancellor": Pearson relates the unsolved disappearance of well-known judge Chancellor John Lansing in New York City in 1829.

- Chapter 24. "The Death of Gulielma Sands": Levi Weeks, defended by future foes Alexander Hamilton and Aaron Burr, was acquitted in 1800 of murdering Gulielma Sands, whose body was found in a well. John Lansing presided at the trial.

- Chapter 25. "The Crime in the Sunday School": Thomas W. Piper confessed to beating five-year-old Sunday school student Mabel Young to death with a cricket bat in a church belfry in 1875, as well as an earlier murder and assault.

- Chapter 26. "Mr. Spooner's in the Well": This is one of the first famous murder cases in the United States, the slaying of Joshua Spooner by three men at the behest of the victim's wife, Bathsheba.

- Chapter 27. "Rules for Murderesses": Based on his study of classic cases, Pearson proposes four rules to be observed rigorously by women who want to get away with murder: (1) "If you decide to murder your husband never act in concert with a lover"; (2) "It is inadvisable for a maidservant to murder her mistress under circumstances of extreme barbarity" (Kate Webster violated this injunction); (3) Even in the murder of a father or mother the astute murderess will take care that no lover appears upon the scene (according to Pearson, Lizzie Borden, unlike poisoner Mary Blandy, passes this test with flying colors); and (4) "If you commit murder for insurance money or for mere pleasure make it wholesale. Never stop at one."

P.6 ———— *More Studies in Murder.* New York: Harrison Smith & Robert Haas, 1936.
■ This collection of short pieces (which originally appeared in *Vanity Fair*, the *New Yorker*, *Mystery*, and *Liberty*) is divided into two sections, "Part One: More Studies in Murder" and "Part Two: Other Studies." A list of the titles and subjects of the murder articles follows:

- "The Corpse on the Speak-Easy Floor": A Harlem murder case, described in a bantering manner that now would be regarded as racist
- "Sarah Jane Robinson": A famous nineteenth-century Massachusetts serial poisoner
- "The Death of Bella Wright": The "Green Bicycle Case," a 1919 gunshot murder of a factory girl near Leicester, with no apparent motive. Ronald Light was acquitted. See H. R. Wakefield, *The Green Bicycle Case* (London: Philip Alan, 1930).
- "The Sleepy Hollow Massacre": Isaac Buckhout, on New Years Day, shot two neighbors visiting his Tarrytown home and then beat his wife to death, suspecting her of infidelity.
- "The Days of Floradora," consisting of:
  - "The Wicked Hansom": *Floradora* showgirl, Nan Patterson, benefited from a hung jury when tried for shooting Frank T. Young in a New York City hansom cab in 1904. See Newman Levy, *The Nan Patterson Case* (New York: Simon & Schuster, 1959).
  - "Murder in Greenwich Village": Dr. Robert Buchanan, though boasting he was cleverer than famed poisoner Carlyle Harris, was executed for the 1892 poisoning of his wife, Annie, in New York City.
  - "Mr. Elwell": The unsolved murder of bridge expert Joseph B. Elwell (see G.26)
  - "Willie's Legs": A masseur, Willie Guldensuppe, was murdered and dismembered in 1897 by Martin Thorn, who had quarreled with him over Augusta Nack's favors.
- "Nineteen Dandelions": Major Herbert Armstrong of Hay-on-Wye poisoned his wife with weed killer.
- "Mrs. Costello Cleans the Boiler": In 1933 Jessie Costello, of Peabody, Massachusetts, was acquitted of poisoning her husband, Bill, a fireman, with potassium cyanide.
- "Miss Holland's Elopement": The Moat Farm murder (see W.15)
- "Legends of Lizzie": Lizzie Borden, Pearson's favorite figure in crime history
- "Malloy the Mighty": Indestructible Michael Malloy, victim of a Bronx underworld murder, proved as difficult to kill as Rasputin. He was poisoned, run down by a taxi, and gassed.
- "Four Infamous Names": Jack the Ripper; Charlie Peace; J. P. (California "Bluebeard") Watson, who confessed that he married many women and murdered four of them;

Peter Kürten, the "Monster of Düsseldorf" who after World War I perpetrated and attempted numerous murders

- "The Great Chowder Murder": "Mrs. Fleming" (Mary Alice Almont Livingston) was acquitted of 1895 poisoning of Mrs. Bliss's chowder in New York City.
- "The Third Passenger": The Wainwright brothers, Henry and Thomas, murdered Harriet Lane in London in 1874.
- "Birth of the Brainstorm": Daniel McFarland, having murdered his ex-wife's lover, Albert Richardson, in the offices of the *New York Tribune*, successfully pleaded temporary insanity. Pearson comments: "His was the first 'brainstorm,' the first case of 'dementia Americana.'"
- "Bertram the Burglar": In Springfield, Massachusetts, Bertram Spencer supplemented his daily income with burglaries, in the course of which he shot Martha Blackstone, a schoolteacher, through the heart in 1919.
- "Sob Sisters Emerge": Maria Barberi, a darling of sob-sister journalism, slit a faithless lover's throat in New York City and was acquitted in 1896.
- "Mr. Bravo's Burgundy": This is one of Victorian England's greatest mysteries, the poisoning of Charles Bravo (see J.5).

The miscellaneous cases included in Part 2 of the book include the disappearance of Elizabeth Canning; and the immoral Rector of Stiffkey, who had a weakness for models and dancing girls.

P.7 ——— *Murder at Smutty Nose, and Other Murders*. New York: Doubleday Page, 1926. *Murder at Smutty Nose* is one of Pearson's best volumes, containing:

■ "Murder at Smutty Nose; or, The Crime of Louis Wagner": The title essay returns to the two axe murders committed by seaman Louis Wagner on Smutty Nose Island in the Isles of Shoals off the New Hampshire coast in 1873. Pearson's study is a worthy successor to the 1875 account of Isles of Shoals resident Celia Thaxter, "A Memorable Murder (see T.8)," on which Pearson draws, particularly for descriptions of the remote setting of the crime. While pronouncing himself (as he regularly does) an enemy of armchair psychologists who venture to explore the minds of people they have never met, Pearson makes a blunt assessment of Wagner's character: "He was a simple savage; with a child's cruelty, a child's selfishness, a child's readiness to burst into tears. He could have trampled another human being under foot, and then wept for an hour over the death of his canary bird." Wagner must also not have blushed easily, for until his execution at Thomaston, Maine, he attributed the murders to the heads of the Smutty Nose family, Maren and John Hontvet.

The picturesque surroundings of the Smutty Nose murders were one of the sources of its strong appeal to Pearson. He cited the double atrocity as an exception to his master William Roughead's dictum that a murder "has seldom a setting worthy of the horror of the deed."

"A Demnition Body; or, The Embarrassments of Mr. Udderzook": Pearson's essay on the Goss-Udderzook insurance murder case is derived from the discussion of the affair in John B. Lewis and Charles C. Bombaugh, *Stratagems and Conspiracies to Defraud Life Insurance Companies*, 2d ed. (Baltimore: James H. McClellan, 1896). In 1872 William E. Udderzook and his heavily insured brother-in-law, inventor Winfield Scott Goss, conveyed a dead body to a Maryland cottage rented by Goss and set it ablaze. Goss disappeared; Udderzook and the Goss family, claiming that a charred corpse in the cottage ruins was Goss's, sued life insurance companies to recover under his policies. The trouble with the scheme was that the bibulous Goss kept popping up, and Udderzook, to keep the insurance litigation heading in the right direction, murdered and buried his inconvenient partner. Udderzook was hanged, none the richer for his pains. Pearson's narrative of the bizarre case is one of his sprightliest.

"America's Classic Murder; or, The Disappearance of Doctor Parkman": The subject of this essay is the "Harvard murder case" of 1849, in which Harvard chemistry professor John W. Webster murdered, bathed in acid, and incinerated his pressing creditor, Dr. George Parkman, a benefactor of the Harvard Medical College (see B.27). Pearson notes that many persons have believed Webster's assertion that his fatal blow was struck in anger, but the grisly and unsuccessful means he employed to do away with the body (which Pearson believes to cast doubt on premeditation) probably doomed him.

The Borowitz True Crime Collection holds a scrapbook of contemporary articles on the case that was compiled by A. Oakey Hall, a future mayor of New York, who was a harsh critic of the trial.

"The People *versus* Molineux; or, Two Tragedies and a Farce": Roland Molineux is the central figure in the 1898 poisonings of two members of the New York City's Knickerbocker Athletic Club, which were forerunners of the twentieth century's Tylenol murders. The unusual poison employed was cyanide of mercury, contained in bottles of medicine mailed to club member and house committee member H. C. Barnet and athletic director Harry Cornish. Barnet and Katherine Adams, an elderly relative of Cornish with whom he boarded, died after taking the medicine; Cornish became gravely ill but recovered. Former Knickerbocker member Molineux, suspected because of the similarity of his handwriting to that on the mailing label of the poisoned Bromo-Seltzer sent to Cornish, had quarreled with him and resigned from the club when he failed to get him removed. Molineux's feud with Barnet seems to have resulted from their rivalry for the love of Blanche Chesebrough, whom Molineux married after Barnet's death. Molineux's conviction in his first trial for the murder of Mrs. Adams was overturned in a controversial decision of the New York Court of Appeals, which ruled erroneous the admission of evidence regarding the Barnet murder. On retrial, Molineux was acquitted by the jury in four minutes. In 1917 he died in an insane asylum.

"Three Footnotes to De Quincey": Three Victorian murderers are bracketed in this chapter: Doctor Thomas Neill Cream; Doctor Hawley Harvey Crippen; and bathtub murderer George Joseph Smith.

"The Salem Conspiracy; or, The Lamentable Death of Captain White": In 1830, a wealthy octogenarian, Captain Joseph White, was murdered in his Salem, Massachusetts, house, receiving a heavy blow on the temple and thirteen stab wounds. In a retrial, Daniel Webster, delivering one of the most famous prosecution speeches in American history, secured the conviction and hanging of Joseph J. Knapp Jr., who had hired assassin Richard Crowninshield Jr. Knapp, husband of White's grandniece, had labored under the false belief that, on the old man's death, his mother-in-law would inherit half of the estate. In a separate trial, Webster obtained the conviction and execution of Joseph Knapp's brother, John Francis Knapp, a participant in the plot. Richard Crowninshield, the professional criminal who murdered White, hanged himself in jail before he could be brought to trial.

Pearson relates the amazing report that "Webster's speeches were taboo in the [Salem] schools if they included his argument in the White case." He adds: "In no other town, in all probability, would any one try to treat a scandal nearly a century old as if it happened yesterday."

"The Sixth Capsule; or, Proof by Circumstantial Evidence": In 1891, New York City medical student Carlyle W. Harris poisoned his secret wife Helen Potts by placing a capsule of pure morphine in a box of three other capsules containing a harmless mixture of morphine and quinine. He had forgotten that the strong dose of morphine would cause the pupils of his victim's eyes to contract, signaling narcotic poisoning to the examining physicians. Harris went to the electric chair proclaiming his innocence. Pearson attributes such protestations to the hope for a last-minute reprieve; avoidance of family disgrace; and "the wish to deny satisfaction to jury, judge, and lawyers, who are responsible, in his estimation, for his plight."

"The Tiverton Tragedy; or, The Strange Case of Miss Cornell and Rev. Mr. Avery": Methodist minister Ephraim K. Avery was acquitted of murdering pregnant Fall River, Massachusetts, factory worker Sarah Maria Cornell, thirty, whose body was found hanging from a stake in Tiverton, Rhode Island, on a December morning in 1832. She had left a note in her bandbox advising that if she should be missing, Avery would know where she was.

Pearson hesitates between murder or suicide as the cause of Cornell's death, but notes: "If murder it was, there were evidently other men, aside from Mr. Avery, who may have had a motive to wish her out of the way."

Avery moved to Pittsfield, Ohio, and lived a quiet life as a farmer; he died in 1869. See K.1.

"Two Victorian Ladies": Madeleine Smith and Constance Kent

"Hell Benders; or, The Story of a Wayside Tavern": In Pearson's narration, the chronicle of the tavernkeeping Benders' serial killings in Kansas is pure American gothic, the New World's equivalent of France's Red Inn murders and England's legends of Sawney Beane and Sweeney Todd. The Benders' homicidal operations may have been concentrated in a six-month period of 1872 and 1873. The search for Dr. William H. York, who disappeared after visiting the Benders' tavern in March 1873, led to the discovery of his body and of about ten others, buried in the adjoining garden.

The fate of the Benders, who fled in advance of the search party, is disputed. By far the most colorful of the clan was Miss Kate Bender, who, when not engaged in felonious employment, lectured on spiritualism.

"The Bordens: A Postscript": On the occasion of the death of the Bordens' neighbor, Mrs. Churchill, who discovered Abby Borden's body, Pearson returns to a discussion of his favorite murder case. He now exculpates by name three trial witnesses who had been suspected of involvement in the crime or its aftermath: the maid, Bridget Sullivan; Lizzie's uncle, John Vinnicum Morse; and the family physician, Dr. Bowen. Pearson also notes that the emotional wave of support for Lizzie ended soon after her acquittal. While denying the reports that she lived as a recluse, he observes that as late as 1926, "she was not often seen in public."

"Number 31 Bond Street; or, The Accomplishments of Mrs. Cunningham": Pearson's charming finale is an account of the Cunningham-Burdell murder case. A self-proclaimed widow, "Mrs." Emma Cunningham was acquitted of the 1857 knife murder of dentist Harvey Burdell in his house on Bond Street, New York City, where Cunningham lived as a tenant and boardinghouse keeper for the numerous residents. Long boasting the position of the dentist's fiancée, Cunningham claimed to have married him shortly before his death, despite their violent quarrels that once resulted in police intervention. The ceremony, however, may have been fraudulently celebrated by Cunningham with a man posing as Burdell. Certainly she was capable of such an imposture, because, after her acquittal, she was caught in a sting operation while trying to pass off a borrowed infant as the fruit of her union with Burdell.

P.8 ——— *Murders That Baffled the Experts*. New York: Signet, 1967.

■ This is a posthumous paperback collection of short articles previously appearing in Liberty. For the most part, the articles reprise material treated at greater length by Pearson in his other books. The titles of the *Liberty* pieces and, in parenthesis, the criminal or suspect discussed, are:

- "The Mystery of the Cottage by the Lake" (Frederick Small)
- "The Mystery of the Green Bicycle" (Ronald Light)
- "Scotland Yard's Strangest Case" (Constance Kent)
- "The Blue-Blood Mystery of Boston" (Harvard professor John W. Webster)
- "The Mystery of the Dancing Shoes" (Abraham Thornton): Pearson discusses the 1817 drowning of Mary Ashford of which Thornton was acquitted. When her family sought a retrial under an obscure legal procedure ("appeal of murder"), Thornton, invoking another relic of judicial history, successfully demanded trial by battle. The offer was declined by his puny opponent. In 1813 Parliament abolished both appeals of murder and trial by battle (see N.7). Pearson inclines to the belief that Ashford drowned by accident.
- "The Case of Tommy Tucker" (Charles L. Tucker, who raped and murdered Mabel Page)
- "The Locked Room" (Patrick Mahon): Pearson briefly retells Patrick Mahon's murder

and dismemberment of Emily Kaye (see F.1). Pearson regarded Mahon as "a complete egotist" who "could act without compassion or pity, as some folk lack the musical sense or the mathematical faculty."
- "The Petal of the Red Geranium" (Frère Léotade)
- "The Case of Mr. Wainwright" (Henry Wainwright)
- "Miss Holland's Elopement" (Samuel Dougal, the Moat Farm murderer). See w.15.

P.9 ———— *Queer Books*. Garden City: Doubleday, Doran, 1928.

■ In his two-part article "From Sudden Death," Pearson sketches the development of true-crime writing in England and America from gallows sermons and pamphlets devoted to murders, capital trials, condemnations, dying confessions, and executions through the works of his favorites among crime historians and essayists: Thomas De Quincey, J. B. Atlay, H. B. Irving, William Roughead, Sir John Hall, F. Tennyson Jesse, and William Bolitho. He proffers no explanation for the popularity of books about murder, commenting that "people like to read such books because they like to do so." Pearson also comments favorably on the *Notable British Trials* series and hopes for the appearance of a similar edition of American trials.

Other articles in this volume include an essay on Henry Tufts, a late-eighteenth-century thief, counterfeiter, jail breaker, and seducer whose ghostwritten memoirs Pearson was later to edit (see P.10). Other pieces in the collection deal with temperance fiction and two nineteenth-century American crime novels falsely claimed to be factual by their publisher, Arthur R. Orton.

P.10 ———— *Studies in Murder*. New York: Macmillan, 1924.

■ The first of Pearson's collections of crime essays begins with his masterpiece, a study of Lizzie Borden, acquitted by a New Bedford jury in 1892 of the hatchet murders of her stepmother, Abby, and her father, Andrew, in their Fall River, Massachusetts, home. Although Pearson's belief in Lizzie's guilt is palpable, he presents lucidly the strengths and weaknesses of the cases for both the prosecution and the victorious defense. His summary is evenhanded:

> The points which had told against her were the seemingly impossible nature of the story about the visit to the barn or yard; the alleged attempt to buy poison; the lapse of time between the two murders, which appeared to shake the theory of an outside murderer; the failure to find the sender of the note to Mrs. Borden; and the fact that from the stairs which she descended when her father entered the house, the body of her step-mother could have been visible. But, on the other hand, the glaring improbability of such murders being committed by a woman; combined with the failure to find any definitely determined weapon; and above everything, the absence of blood from the clothing or person of the accused,—all these not only strengthened the faith of those who were sure of her innocence, but convinced the authorities that they were far from having a strong case.

The introductory essay in *Trial of Lizzie Borden* (ed. and case history Edmund Pearson [Garden City: Doubleday Doran, 1937]) follows similar lines of narrative and analysis. Here Pearson suggests that "the death of Mr. Borden was possibly not part of the original plan." Addressing the often-asked question of how Lizzie (assuming her guilt) could have "expected to avoid interruption, and not be caught red-handed," he comments that "she acted, as others have done, with great boldness—foolhardiness, if you like. Although such daring is inconceivable to most of us cautious folk, that does not alter the fact that, every day in the year, crimes occur which are characterized by audacity."

Other essays included in the 1924 edition of *Studies in Murder* are:

- "The Twenty-Third Street Murder": The unsolved 1870 killing of Benjamin Nathan in his New York City house. Suspects ranged from the victim's son to a safecracker. The case is fictionalized in Arthur Train, *The Confessions of Artemas Quibble* (New York: Scribner, 1911).
- "'Mate Bram!'": Pearson's account of first mate Thomas Bram, who axed Captain Charles Nash, his wife, Laura, and second mate August Blomberg to death aboard the *Herbert Fuller* in 1896. Bram, in different versions of the bloody events, advanced "the curious but convenient notion that the dead alone were guilty." One of his proffered explanations was that Blomberg intended to "insult Mrs. Nash"; seeing this, the captain had rushed to her defense and was overpowered by the second mate, who then committed suicide. Twice convicted, Bram served fifteen years; he was pardoned by President Wilson. To Pearson the crime was "a nocturne, a sea-piece, with a vague suggestion of piracy, and more than a slight odor of strong drink." Mary Roberts Rinehart's novel *The After House* (Boston: Houghton Mifflin, 1914) exculpates Bram and attributes the murder to the helmsman.
- "The Hunting Knife": The discovery of a fragmented bloody hunting knife and a pin belonging to the victim Mabel Page in the pocket of Charles L. Tucker's coat, and the delivery to police of an empty knife sheath bearing his teeth marks led to Tucker's murder conviction and execution in 1906. Pearson excoriates the mawkish agitation in behalf of Tucker as a mere "boy" of twenty-four.
- "Uncle Amos Dreams a Dream": This article relates the Enoch Arden–like adventures of Vermonter Russell Colvin, who disappeared in 1812 and returned seven years later after Stephen and Jesse Boorn had been condemned for his murder. Both Boorns were released.

The Modern Library edition of *Studies in Murder*, first published in 1938, the year after Pearson's death also included: "Malloy the Mighty" (see P.6); "Hauptmann and Circumstantial Evidence," in which Pearson argues that "the conviction of [Bruno Richard] Hauptmann was *not* based entirely on circumstantial evidence. And it is wholly unnecessary to be perturbed about an innocent person in a position similar to Hauptmann's, because an innocent person never gets in such a position. Not in a million years would the powers of Heaven and earth unite to entangle an innocent person in a net of so many strands"; and "Do

We Execute Innocent People?" where Pearson contends (optimistically) that the execution of the innocent is a phenomenon encountered only in the distant past.

P.11 [Edmund Lester Pearson, ed.] *The Autobiography of a Criminal: Henry Tufts.* New York: Duffield, 1930.

■ Having two years earlier written an essay on Henry Tufts (see P.9), Pearson edited his 1807 ghostwritten autobiography, which he rated as "probably the first extensive American criminal biography." After studying the appealing crook's career, Pearson was "impressed with the difficulty of discovering him at all, outside the brown covers of his old book." He therefore relished the opportunity of confronting with an extant Massachusetts court record of 1794 Tufts' account of having been wrongly convicted and sentenced to be hanged for the theft of six silver spoons sold to him by a man named John Stewart. The actual indictment charged Tufts with a burglary in which he carried off eight spoons, a "washed beer glass," a beaver hat, a walking staff, two pairs of leather slippers, and a pair of shoes. In Tufts's successful application for reprieve, there is no mention of the mysterious Mr. Stewart, from whom Tufts supposedly purchased six spoons.

P.12 Perelman, S[idney] J[oseph], and Ogden Nash *One Touch of Venus.* Score Kurt Weill. Boston: Little, Brown, 1944.

■ Suggested by F. Anstey's story "The Tinted Venus," this 1943 Broadway musical plays a variation on the Pygmalion/Galatea myth by bringing a statue of Venus to life (in the person of Mary Martin). Act 1, Scene 6, laid in the roof garden of the Whitelaw Savory Foundation of Modern Art, shows a party of Foundation students in full progress; the participants are dressed in the period of 1910 and dancing a variation of the can-can. The curtain of a small stage parts to reveal a series of tableaux portraying the murder of Belle Elmore by her mild-mannered husband, Dr. Hawley Harvey Crippen, and his love affair with a pretty typist, Ethel Le Neve (see W.23). The dumb show accompanies the ballad "Doctor Crippen," sung by the Foundation's benefactor, Savory. The burden of the song is that all the doctor did and suffered was for love of the fair stenographer:

> Here's to Doctor Crippen,
> Hawley Harvey Crippen,
> Lying in a felon's grave.
> But he didn't mope
> When they cut the rope,
> It was all for Ethel Le Neve.

In 1961, Dr. Crippen and his two women returned to the musical stage in a full-length work. *Belle: or, The Ballad of Doctor Crippen*, with music and lyrics by Monty Norman and a book by Wolf Mankowitz, ran for only forty-four performances at London's Strand Theatre. The piece was vilified by critics, who did not approve of the choice of a brutal murder case as the fare for music-hall parody. A recent admiring review of the original-cast album suggests that the rejection of the Strand production was also inspired by the fact that Ethel Le Neve was still living in 1961 ("Murder, Mystery and Mayhem," in *Record Cabinet*, http://www.musical-theatre.net/html/recordcabinet/murder.html).

P.13 Plato *The Trial and Death of Socrates.* Trans. G. M. A. Grube. Indianapolis: Hackett, 1975.

▪ Plato's account of the trial and death of Socrates in 399 B.C. is told from different vantage points in four dialogues. In the early work, *Euthyphro*, the Athenian of that name is surprised to encounter Socrates near the king-archon's court and inquires as to the nature of his business there. The philosopher informs him that Meletus has indicted him for corrupting the youth, commenting ironically that "it is no small thing for a young man [like Meletus] to have knowledge of such an important subject." (For Xenophon's version of Socrates's ordeal, see x.1.)

The famous *Apology* purports to record the actual speech that Socrates delivered at his trial. In *Crito*, Socrates explains to an old friend after his condemnation to death why he declines to attempt an escape into exile: such flight would have violated his obligation to observe the laws of Athens.

Plato's final reflection of Socrates's ordeal is the renowned death scene in *Phaedo*, where, Socrates, feeling his body grow cold with the advance of the hemlock he has drunk, requests his friend Crito to make the traditional offering of the sick to the god of healing, Asclepius.

P.14 Plomer, William *The Case Is Altered.* New York: Farrar & Rinehart, 1932.

▪ South African William Plomer (1903–1973) based this novel on facts too close for comfort: insane jealousy and murder in a Victorian house in Bayswater where the author was a lodger. On Sunday morning, November 24,1929, James Achew, partly of Native American origin, cut the throat of the landlady, Sybil de Costa, while a six-year-old daughter, born of their liaison, looked on in horror. The obsessively jealous Achew went looking for Plomer but found his room to be empty, because, luckily, the writer was away for a weekend in the country. Before the police arrived, Achew cut his own throat and put his head in the kitchen's gas oven, but his injuries were not severe.

To spare the feelings of the victim's woman friend who shared the building management, Plomer, after his return to London on the afternoon following the crime, helped remove the bloody traces of the razor slaying. According to his friend and publisher Virginia Woolf, he had to clean scraps of flesh from the carpet.

At the murder trial of Achew, the jury, in returning a guilty verdict, followed Mr. Justice Avory's instruction that legal insanity was not established by proof that the defendant harbored a delusional belief in Sybil de Costa's infidelity. The Home Secretary, however, reprieved the prisoner, who was removed to Broadmoor Criminal Lunatic Asylum (see *The Crime Annual 1931*, ed. Robert Curzon [London: F. V. White, 1931]; Peter F. Alexander, *William Plomer: A Biography* [Oxford: Oxford Univ. Press, 1989]).

In the novel, the crime is set in a lodging house, which serves as a symbol of the disintegrating class structure of England. Among its inhabitants are the attractive Jewish landlady Beryl Fernandez (a stand-in for Sybil de Costa, whom Plomer found "quite sympathetic") and her murderous companion; Beryl's close friend and co-manageress Mrs. Gambitt, "whose chief aim in life is to be taken for [a] decayed gentlewom[a]n"; Miss Brixworth, a "lonely woman, with few resources either inside or outside herself," who is keen on being addressed as "madam"; and Eric Alston, a young fruiterer's assistant, whose impulses toward power, speed, and male companionship apparently encourage Plomer to glimpse signs of a more vital Britain of the future.

The title of the novel has multiple meanings. In the neighborhood of the lodging house is a pub called "The Case Is Altered." In the eighteenth century a famous highwayman was caught there unawares by a young lord whom he had robbed; as soon as he made sure of his capture, the peer exclaimed, "Now, sir, the case is altered." The words reverberate throughout the novel, as Plomer invokes them to reflect the reduced social circumstances of the lodgers and, more broadly, the decline of English middle-class values.

P.15 Plutarch "Caesar" and "Tiberius Gracchus." In *The Lives of the Noble Grecians and Romans*. Trans. John Dryden. Rev. Arthur Hugh Clough. New York: Random House (Modern Library), n.d.

■ Plutarch's *Lives* contains two of the earliest descriptions of famous Roman political assassinations, those of dictator Gaius Julius Caesar on March 15, 44 B.C., and of tribune of the people Tiberius Sempronius Gracchus in 133 B.C.

Plutarch's account of the murder of Caesar by conspirators as he entered the senate on the Ides of March reaches its peak when the dictator catches sight of Brutus among his attackers:

> . . . Brutus also gave him one stab in the groin. Some say that he fought and resisted all the rest, shifting his body to avoid the blows, and calling out for help, but that when he saw Brutus's sword drawn, he covered his face with his robe and submitted, letting himself fall, whether it were by chance or that he was pushed in that direction by his murderers, at the foot of the pedestal on which Pompey's statue stood, and which was thus wetted with his blood. So that Pompey himself seemed to have presided, as it were, over the revenge done upon his adversary, who lay here at his feet, and breathed out his soul through his multitude of wounds, for they say he received three-and-twenty. And the conspirators themselves were many of them wounded by each other, whilst they all levelled their blows at the same person.

The enemies of Tiberius Gracchus, incited by a violent speech in the senate by Publius Cornelius Scipio Nasica Serapio, followed him into the street with togas wrapped around their heads for concealment. The senators' attendants followed them, armed with makeshift weapons:

> The attendants [whom the senators] brought with them had furnished themselves with

clubs and staves from their houses, and they themselves picked up the feet and other fragments of stools and chairs, which were broken by the hasty flight of the common people. Thus armed, they made towards Tiberius, knocking down those whom they found in front of him, and those were soon wholly dispersed and many of them slain. Tiberius tried to save himself by flight. As he was running, he was stopped by one who caught hold of him by the gown; but he threw it off, and fled in his under-garment only. And stumbling over those who before had been knocked down, as he was endeavouring to get up again, Publius Satureius, a tribune, one of his colleagues, was observed to give him the first fatal stroke, by hitting him upon the head with the foot of a stool. The second blow was claimed, as though it had been a deed to be proud of, by Lucius Rufus. And of the rest there fell above three hundred killed by clubs and staves only, none by an iron weapon.

A drawing executed by Théodore Géricault (Fig. 1) at the time of his first voyage to Rome in 1816–17 is the study of a man in a toga beset by a group of five male figures, of whom one brandishes a cudgel. To the right of the attackers stands a Fury handling snakes. A Géricault expert has suggested that the scene depicted may be the assassination of Caesar (Germain Bazin, *Théodore Géricault: Étude critique, documents et catalogue raisonné, tome II, l'oeuvre: Période de formation*, no. 517 [Paris: La Bibliothèque des Arts, 1987]). A comparison of the above Plutarch texts indicates, however, that the murder of Tiberius Gracchus is a more likely subject. Caesar died of multiple stab wounds, but no swords or daggers appear in the drawing, where the victim, like Gracchus, is attacked by a club. Moreover, the assailants depicted by Géricault, like those who pursued the tribune, include commoners as well as their senatorial leaders, who may be represented in the drawing by a dominant turbaned figure in their midst, pointing toward the victim.

P.16 Poe, Edgar Allan "The Mystery of Marie Roget." 1842–43. In *The Complete Poems and Stories of Edgar Allan Poe*. Ed. Arthur Hobson Quinn and Edward H. O'Neill. Vol. 1. New York: Knopf, 1951.

■ Worried over his wife's ill health and his precarious financial situation, Poe in 1842 designed a new literary genre in his second detective story featuring French sleuth Auguste Dupin. In "The Mystery of Marie Roget," Poe based the narrative on a thinly veiled and superficially Gallicized version of a contemporary unsolved American murder case in which the body of twenty-one-year-old Mary Cecilia Rogers was found floating in the Hudson River near Hoboken, New Jersey. John Walsh, in his *Poe the Detective: The Curious Circumstances Behind "The Mystery of Marie Roget"* (New Brunswick: Rutgers, 1968), attracted renewed attention to scholar William Kurtz Wamsatt's earlier discovery that Poe, in revising the story for his *Collected Tales* of 1845, made fifteen changes harmonizing his narrative with police discoveries in late 1842 that attributed Mary's death to a bungled abortion by Mrs. Frederica Loss (Poe's Madame Deluc) at her New Jersey inn. Walsh argued further that, before the first periodical appearance of the story was complete, Poe journeyed to New York (in November 1841) to defer the publication of the third installment so that he could make revisions that would suggest abortion as the cause of death. According to Walsh, Poe's original solution was that Mary had been killed by her abductor, a naval officer, in a sexual frenzy.

In 1971, Raymond Paul, author of excellent novels based on historical murders, published a nonfictional analysis of Mary Rogers's murder, *Who Murdered Mary Rogers?* (Englewood Cliffs, N.J.: Prentice-Hall, 1971), in which he proposed a new solution: that her abortion under the knife of Mrs. Loss had been a success but that on the Tuesday following her disappearance she was murdered near Mrs. Loss's inn by her rejected fiancé, Daniel Payne.

A more recent addition to the study of the case is Amy Gilman Srebnick's *The Mysterious Death of Mary Rogers: Sex and Culture in Nineteenth Century New York* (New York: Oxford Univ. Press, 1995). Srebnick questions John Walsh's hypothesis that Poe deferred and altered the third installment of "Marie Roget" to accommodate the botched-abortion theory that had just appeared in the press. In any event, Srebnick's interest lies elsewhere: "The historical significance of 'Marie Roget' lies not in Poe's ability or inability to solve a real crime, or in his faithfulness, or lack of it, to the circumstances of the 'real' event, but rather in his understanding of the crime as a quintessential event of modern urban culture."

The Borowitz Collection holds a color lithograph portrait of Mary Roget issued by her canny former tobacconist-employer as point-of-sale material. The legend reads: "MARY C. ROGERS: Known as the beautiful Cigar Girl Murder'd at Hoboken on Sunday July 25 1841. Aged 21 Years. Drawn by the direction of Mr. J. Anderson her late Employer No. 2 Wall Street 321 Broadway N.Y." See Fig. 11.

P.17 ——— "Scenes from 'Politian,' an Unpublished Drama." 1835–36. In *The Complete Poems and Stories of Edgar Allan Poe*. Ed. Arthur Hobson Quinn and Edward H. O'Neill. Vol. 1. New York: Knopf, 1951.

■ As he was later to do in the story "The Mystery of Marie Roget," Poe, in this unfinished verse play, shifted the scene of an American crime to Europe, in this case Italy. The drama is based on the so-called "Kentucky tragedy," in which Jereboam Beauchamp stabbed to death Colonel Solomon P. Sharp, who had refused his challenge to a duel. Beauchamp had proposed marriage to Ann Cooke, and she accepted on the condition that he avenge her dishonor by Sharp, who had impregnated and abandoned her. In "Politian," Lalage (Ann Cooke) stokes her melancholy over the forthcoming marriage of her faithless lover Castiglione (Sharp) to Alessandra with readings from *The Duchess of Malfi* and *Antony and Cleopatra*. But her prospects brighten when she meets the equally gloomy Politian, Earl of Leicester. Immediately enflamed with love, Politian, as Lalage's champion, challenges Castiglione to a duel, but Lalage's seducer, acknowledging his guilt, refuses to fight. As the fragmentary play breaks off, Politian threatens Castiglione with public humiliation.

Despite its Italian setting, "Politian" is bound to its American origins in a speech of Lalage invoking "a land new found— / Miraculously found by one of Genoa– / A thousand leagues within the golden west."

P.18 Porter, Katherine Anne *The Never-Ending Wrong*. Boston: Little, Brown, 1977.

■ Porter, best known for her fiction, here recalls her activities as picketer and as typist for a Communist-controlled organization in the last days of the campaign to save the lives of anarchists Nicola Sacco and Bartolomeo Vanzetti, who had been convicted of murder in the 1920 holdup of a payroll truck in South Braintree, Massachusetts. Never able to decide whether Sacco and Vanzetti were guilty, Porter opposed their conviction as a "terrible miscarriage of justice," a "most reprehensible abuse of legal power, in [government's] attempt to prove that the law is something to be inflicted—not enforced—and that it is above the judgment of the people." She retained a "lifelong sympathy for the cause to which [Sacco and Vanzetti] devoted their lives—to ameliorate the anguish that human beings inflict on each other—the never-ending wrong, forever incurable."

In stark contrast with Porter's humanitarian instincts stands the callousness of her Communist supervisor, Rosa Baron, who did not share her wish to save the lives of the two condemned men: "Alive—what for?" Baron asked her mockingly. "They are no earthly good to us alive."

P.19 Praviel, Armand *L'Incroyable odysée de Martin Guerre* [The Incredible Odyssey of Martin Guerre]. In series *Les histoires extraordinaires*. Paris: Gallimard, 1933.

■ From a psychological point of view, this book furnishes one of the best analyses of the imposture of sixteenth-century French swashbuckler Arnaud du Tilh, who usurped the personality, wife, and property of his comrade-in-arms, Martin Guerre of Artigat, and expiated his crime on the gallows. Many other authors have concluded that Guerre's wife, Bertrande, abandoned by her husband for eight years, was readily complicit in the fraud (see D.2), but Praviel also addresses an even thornier issue: how did du Tilh arrive at the hazardous wager that his hoax would succeed? Praviel believes that the imposture was not premeditated from afar.

Bearing an uncanny resemblance to Guerre, du Tilh, while passing through the environs of Artigat, was greeted as the long-missing Martin by Dominique Pujol and Pierre de Guithet. Remembering the stories his fellow soldier had told him about his life, du Tilh decided on the spur of the moment that he could substitute for Guerre and that his abandoned wife would likely greet him with open arms: "As for [du Tilh], he knew now that everything Martin Guerre had told him was true, and that Bertrande would hope for nothing better than to welcome him. He started Pujol and Pierre de Guithet talking as he was always able to do. He had the lively feeling that with a little daring, he would be the master of his destiny, a tranquil and prosperous destiny, which would bear no resemblance to the wandering, half-starved life he had led."

P.20 Pringle, Patrick *Stand and Deliver: The Story of the Highwaymen*. New York: Norton, n.d.

■ On his rollicking tour through the contemporary chapbook biographies of England's highwaymen, Pringle debunks the reputations of some famous robbers but for the most part is delighted to serve up fiction along with the few ascertainable facts. The love affair of the English with their highwaymen (many originating in the upper classes) is possibly due to the national passion for horses as well as the pathos that is attached to a set of criminals who, though rarely murderous, often died on the gallows while still in their twenties or thirties. Among the highwaymen Pringle discusses are:

- John Popham (born in 1531), who decided that "he could, with application, make as much money by the Law as by highway robbery" and became Lord Chief Justice
- Captain James Hind, Pringle's favorite among gallant cavaliers who took to the road during the Commonwealth period
- Jonathan Simpson, a late-seventeenth-century innovator who put on ice skates to rob Londoners flocking to the frozen Thames
- The eighteenth-century's fabled Dick Turpin, whose ride to York astride Black Bess, popularized by Harrison Ainsworth in his novel *Rookwood*, never happened, argues Pringle
- The "Gentleman Highwayman," James Maclaine, who in 1749 robbed writer Horace Walpole and then offered to sell back any goods Walpole might want at a midnight rendezvous at Tyburn; Walpole wisely declined the meeting.
- George and Joseph Weston, rare examples of a brother act in highway robbery

Pringle attributes the decline of the highwaymen by the early nineteenth century to the organization of an efficient police force and banking legislation that relieved travelers of the necessity of carrying large sums.

P.21 Proust, Marcel *Jean Santeuil*. 1896–99. Trans. Gerard Hopkins. Preface André Maurois. New York: Simon & Schuster, 1956.

■ In this precursor of *Remembrance of Things Past*, Proust reflected on two causes célèbres of the 1890s, the scandals relating to the financing of the Panama Canal project and the prosecution of Captain Alfred Dreyfus for treason.

The protagonist, Jean Santeuil, who serves as the author's alter ego, recalls the downfall of Monsieur Marie, a deputy and former minister who is tainted by financial irregularities reminiscent of the Panama affair. Because of his close friendship with Marie, Jean's father rallies to the disgraced politician's defense even though he believes him guilty. Jean believes that Marie was tempted to his ruin by the comfort he took in the religious doctrine that no one is without sin. Marie found it easier to call himself a "miserable sinner" than to acknowledge "I have been taking money to which I was not entitled."

The chapters on the Dreyfus case mirror Proust's own impressions as an ardent Dreyfusard observer of the criminal defamation trial of Emile Zola. Jean Santeuil, attending sessions of the trial, focuses on two army witnesses from opposing sides, General de Boisdeffre, the chief of staff commanding respect as the embodiment of France's military grandeur despite his lankiness, stiff gait, and preoccupied expression; and Colonel Picquart, imprisoned for his challenge to the errors of the prosecution and viewed by Jean Santeuil as a philosopher motivated not by ideology but by fidelity to his own mental processes.

In *Remembrance of Things Past*, it is not the narrator (Marcel) who most passionately espouses the Dreyfusard cause, but a stereotypically Jewish character, Bloch. In a rare melodramatic development, however, it is ultimately revealed that the Prince and Princess de Guermantes, unbeknownst to each other, offered prayers for Dreyfus (see Jean Recanati, *Profils juifs de Marcel Proust* [Marcel Proust's Jewish Characters] [Paris: Buchet/Chastel, 1979]).

P.22 ———— "Sentiments filiaux d'un parricide" [Filial Feelings of a Parricide]. In *Contre Sainte-Beuve* [Against Saint-Beuve], preceded by *Pastiches et mélanges* and followed by *Essais et articles*. Paris: Gallimard, 1971.

■ In 1906 Marcel Proust learned of the death of a Monsieur van Blarenberghe, with whom his parents had been friendly. On their behalf, he sent a letter of condolence to Henri, the deceased man's young son. Early in the following year, Proust was shocked to read that Henri had stabbed his mother to death and committed suicide. In an article written for *Le Figaro*, "Filial Feelings of a Parricide," Proust generalized the significance of the family tragedy, concluding, as Oscar Wilde had done in *The Ballad of Reading Gaol*, that each man kills the one to whom he is bound by love. He felt that, like Henri, he had killed his own mother through the sorrows and disappointments he had inflicted on her: "The reality is that we age, we kill everyone who loves us by the worries we give them, by the very uneasy tenderness that we inspire and ceaselessly alarm" (158–59). George Painter, Proust's biographer, concludes that the composition of the article enabled Proust to forgive his own deceased mother and to begin the journey toward the creation of his great novel *Remembrance of Things Past* (*Proust: The Later Years* [Boston: Little, Brown, 1965], 67–71).

P.23 Pushkin, Aleksandr *Mozart and Salieri*. In *The Poems, Prose and Plays of Alexander Pushkin*. Ed. Avrahm Yarmolinsky. New York: Modern Library, n.d.

■ The tradition of Mozart's poisoning has produced one authentic masterpiece, Pushkin's short dramatic dialogue *Mozart and Salieri*, conceived in 1826—only one year after Salieri's death, when rumors of his confession of Mozart's murder were still in the air—and completed in 1830. In the Pushkin play (later set by Rimsky-Korsakov as a like-named opera), Salieri poisons Mozart both because Mozart's superior gifts have made Salieri's lifelong devotion to music meaningless and because Mozart has introduced Salieri's soul to the bitterness of envy. Unlike many of Mozart's later admirers, Pushkin does not depict Salieri as a mediocre hack but rather as a dedicated musician who was intent on the perfection of his craft and was able to appreciate innovative genius (as in the case of his master, Gluck) and to assimilate it into his own development. However, Salieri refers to himself as a "priest" of music to whom his art is holy and serious. He is enraged by Mozart's free, creative spirit and by what he sees as Mozart's lighthearted, almost negligent, relation to the products of his genius. Salieri's assessment of his rival is confirmed for him by the joy Mozart takes in a dreadful performance of an air from *Figaro* by a blind fiddler. As was true in their real lives, both Salieri and Mozart, in Pushkin's pages, inhabit a world where poisoning is assumed to be a possible event even in the lives of famous and civilized men.

Mozart refers to the rumor that "Beaumarchais once poisoned someone," and Salieri alludes to a tradition that Michelangelo murdered to provide a dead model for a Crucifixion. In Pushkin's version, the murder of Mozart provides no relief for Salieri's torment but only furnishes final proof of his inferiority. At the close of the play, Salieri is haunted by Mozart's observation immediately before being poisoned that "genius and crime are two incompatible things."

The theme and language of Pushkin's *Mozart and Salieri* are echoed in Peter Shaffer's immensely successful play *Amadeus* (New York: Harper & Row, 1981). See Albert Borowitz, "Salieri and the 'Murder' of Mozart," in *Innocence and Arsenic: Studies in Crime and Literature* (B.28).

Q

Q.1 Queiroz, Rachel de *Lampião.* 2d ed. Rio de Janeiro: José Olympio, 1954.

■ The most famous bandit chief (*cangaceiro*) in the scrubland (*sertão*) of northeastern Brazil was Virgulino Ferreira da Silva, known as Lampião, the "Lantern." Lampião, despite many acts of cruelty, has acquired many of the traits of Robin Hood in the ballads, fiction, and drama of his country since he was shot and decapitated.

The five-act play by Rachel de Queiroz (also a novelist and a translator of classic European authors, including Tolstoy and Dostoyevski) follows the outlaw's career from his abduction of a shoemaker's wife who became his mistress, Maria Bonita, to his death at the hands of pursuing troops. While emphasizing her hero's courage, Queiroz is not blind to the defects in his character: inhumanity, egoism, megalomania, and tyrannous control over his followers. His grandiosity leads him to offer the governor of Recife a division of the northeastern region, and he is offended when the secessionist proposal is contemptuously declined. Lampião is capable of actions of unbelievable savagery and can rationalize the worst of them as appropriate measures of self-defense or revenge against enemies and would-be traitors. A woman he set afire was a "witch" who informed against him, and a younger brother he killed in a duel was making eyes at Maria Bonita.

Soon after the curtain rises, Queiroz shows the legend of Lampião in the process of formation. The shoemaker's wife, who is about to run off with Lampião, tells her husband that the bandit's reputation is undeserved: "Lampião lived in peace until the age of 16 and only became an outlaw because the police bandits killed his father. What can a man do but take vengeance?" The shoemaker has a less flattering explanation for Lampião's choosing a life of crime: he began by killing a neighbor because of a straying goat.

R

R.1 R—— and P.V—— *Annales du crime et de l'innocence: ou Choix de causes célèbres anciennes et modernes, réduites aux faits historiques.* 20 vols. Paris: Lerouge, 1813.

■ The Bibliothèque Nationale online catalog identifies the author of this early compilation of criminal cases as Pierre-Joseph-Alexis Roussel. In a rather condescending introduction, he states his purpose: "There is a mass of *causes célèbres*, curious and interesting, which ladies, and even men not destined for the bar, cannot undertake to read, because they become tiresome. In stripping these cases of their legal element, in putting aside doctrinal discussions, arguments, and legal citations, and limiting ourselves to a simple factual narrative, we believe we are able to furnish to the great majority of readers the simultaneous means of education and enjoyment." The series is remarkable for including not only famous French cases (e.g., Joan of Arc; the false Martin Guerre; the Calas affair; Cartouche; Desrues; Madame Lescombat; Mandrin; and Ravaillac) but crimes in many other countries, including England, Germany, Portugal, Poland, and Russia.

R.2 Racine, Jean *Britannicus*. 1669. Paris: Larousse, 1991.

■ Based primarily on the *Annals* of Tacitus, this tragedy portrays Roman emperor Nero on the day he embarks on his infamous career as a serial killer. In his preface, Racine acknowledges that he always regarded the emperor as a monster but chose to put him on the stage as a "monster aborning," before he set fire to Rome and murdered his mother, Agrippina, and his wife, Poppea. The action of the drama focuses on the emperor's young cousin and stepbrother, Britannicus, the legitimate successor to Claudius's throne whom Agrippina had shunted aside in favor of Nero as her only son. Before giving his consent to the assassination, Nero was regarded as a "good" ruler. In fact, Racine, relying on an anecdote reported by Suetonius and Seneca, has the ethical counselor Burrhus remind the emperor that early in his reign he had resisted signing the death warrant of a criminal with the remark: "I wish I didn't know how to write." Still, if the cunning Agrippina is to be believed about matters of family history, Nero, if not genetically predestined for criminality, was affectless from the days of his youth. Upbraiding him for distancing her from the corridors of power after she had him crowned, she cries: "You are an ingrate, you always were. From your earliest years, you returned my care and tenderness with no more than feigned caresses. Nothing could win you over; and your hardheartedness should have stalled my acts of kindness in mid-course."

R.3 Radin, Edward D. *Lizzie Borden: The Untold Story*. New York: Simon & Schuster, 1961.

■ In this contrarian study, respected crime reporter Radin pins the Borden murders on housemaid Bridget Sullivan, who, he theorizes, might have become enraged when Mrs. Borden refused her requested postponement of window washing on a hot day. En route to this dubious conclusion, Radin sharply criticizes Edmund Pearson for compressing, misrepresenting, or deleting evidence favorable to the defense in his edited transcript of Lizzie Borden's trial and in his essays on the case. Radin stumbles a bit over Lizzie's testimony that Mrs. Borden had mentioned having received a "note" summoning her to pay a sick call on the day of the murder; facing the unyielding fact that the author of the note never stepped forward to support Lizzie's testimony, Radin hypothesizes that the writer was a foreigner who did not want to get involved with the law.

R.4 Rand, Ayn [pseudonym of Alice or Alissa Rosenbaum] *Night of January 16th*. 1934. New York: Plume, 1987.

■ Originally entitled *Playhouse Legend* and subsequently *Woman on Trial*, this audience-participation courtroom drama took as its springboard, according to Rand, the collapse of the Swedish financier and "Match King" Ivar Kreuger, who committed suicide in 1932 amid the ruins of his fraudulent corporate empire (see G.39). In her introduction, Rand explains: "Bjorn Faulkner, the hero who never appears in the play, is not Ivar Kreuger; he is what Ivar Kreuger might have been or, perhaps, ought to have been. The two sides in the play are represented, on the one hand, by Bjorn Faulkner and Karen Andre, his secretary-mistress who is on trial for his murder—and, on the other, by John Graham Whitfield and his daughter [Faulkner's wife]. The factual evidence for and against the accused is (approximately) balanced. The issue rests on the credibility of the witnesses. The jury [drawn nightly from the audience] has to choose which side to believe, and this depends on every juror's own sense of life."

Rand's own verdict, unexpressed in the play, was that Karen Andre was not guilty of the charge that she had thrown Faulkner over a penthouse parapet. Taking that view, Rand appears to endorse a "sense of life" (shared by Faulkner and Andre) that values power and self-assertiveness over morality. Andre became the magnate's devoted mistress after he raped her on the first day of her employment and was not troubled by her lover's failure to distinguish between right and wrong: "Bjorn never thought of things as right or wrong. To him, it was only: you can or you can't. He always could."

R.5 Rattigan, Terence *Cause célèbre*. London: Hamish Hamilton, 1978.

■ In 1935, fortyish Alma Victoria Rattenbury and her eighteen-year-old lover, George Percy Stoner, the family chauffeur and handyman, were jointly tried for the mallet slaying of her husband, Francis, a distinguished architect. Alma was acquitted, and Stoner, because of his youth, was reprieved after being sentenced to death. Alma committed suicide after the trial. The young Stoner took part in the Normandy landings, survived the war, and married. The most recent accounts of the case conclude that Alma Rattenbury neither wielded the mallet nor conspired in the murder, but the trial judge and public opinion castigated her "immorality." See Michael Havers QC, Peter Shankland, and Anthony Barrett, *Tragedy in Three Voices: The Rattenbury Murder* (London: William Kimber, 1980); Sir David Napley, *Murder at the Villa Madeira: The Rattenbury Case* (London: Weidenfeld and Nicolson, 1988). In *Tragedy in Three Voices*, the authors give credence to a recent interview with a fellow prisoner of Alma Rattenbury claiming that Alma had told her the cause of Stoner's murderous rage: the chauffeur had overheard Francis Rattenbury pressing his wife to seduce a man who could provide financing for a projected block of flats.

Rattigan's play, *Cause Célèbre*, based on the Rattenbury murder case, premiered at London's Her Majesty's Theatre on July 4, 1977, with Glynis John in the role of Alma Rattenbury. Since Stoner was still living, the playwright renames him George Wood. The drama, which shifts between Court Number One at the Old Bailey and the outside world, draws parallels between the Rattenburys' dysfunctional marriage (from which sex had disappeared since the birth of a child six years earlier) and inharmonious male-female relationships among the other characters. One of the reluctant jurors, Edith Davenport, has commenced divorce proceedings against her errant husband, John, who offers to return if she will overlook casual transgressions. Their son Tony contracts a venereal disease from a prostitute he visits to assuage the excitement caused by reading too many newspaper articles about Alma Rattenbury's love life; in his distress, the young man attempts suicide. The two worlds of the play converge when Edith Davenport, prejudiced against Alma from the start, is strongly moved by her testimony that "when an older person loves a younger, it's the younger who dominates because the younger has so much more to give." The juror thinks immediately of her own relationship with her son Tony, who keeps her in thrawl because of her excessive maternal love; discovering her empathy with Alma, she changes her vote to not guilty and all the other holdouts give way.

R.6 ———— *The Winslow Boy.* New York: Dramatists Play Service, n.d.

■ First produced at London's Lyric Theatre in 1946, *The Winslow Boy* is based on the case of thirteen-year-old cadet George Archer-Shee, who was dismissed from the Royal Naval College, Osborne, in 1908, charged with the theft and forged signing of a five-shilling postal order. George's father, Martin Archer-Shee, in spite of advanced age and ill health, sought to clear his son's name. A preliminary hearing denied the father's right to bring suit against the Crown regarding a dismissal from naval service. On appeal, without deciding this legal issue, the Court persuaded Solicitor-General Sir Rufus Isaacs (later Lord Reading), to proceed directly to a trial on the merits. The subsequent trial, which pitted Sir Rufus against another great barrister, Sir Edward Carson, did not result in a jury verdict. The trial was ended by the solicitor-general's announcement, on behalf of the admiralty, that he accepted "the statement of George Archer-Shee that he did not write the name on the postal order, and did not cash it, and consequently that he is innocent of the charge."

Ewen Montagu, in the introduction to his admirable 1974 edition of the Archer-Shee case in the *Celebrated Trials* series (see c.19), does not reach a conclusion on the merits of the controversy, remarking, "A careful and open-minded study of the sworn testimony of the relevant witnesses may lead some to one conclusion and some to the other."

Rattigan's drama stays away from the courtroom; all four acts are set in the drawing room of the dismissed cadet's family (the Winslows) in their South Kensington house. The focus of the play is on the high price paid by young Arthur Winslow's parents and siblings for the father's decision to pursue the cadet's cause to the end. Arthur, by contrast, seems to take the issue rather lightly, passing the final day of the trial at the "flicks" near the courthouse.

David Mamet's 1999 film adaptation of the play is faithful to Rattigan, except for its hint in the last frames of a possible future romance between Catherine Winslow and defense counsel Sir Robert Morton (a suggestion that must have caused chagrin to the ghost of Sir Edward Carson).

R.7 Raymond, Ernest *We, the Accused.* London: Cassell, 1935.

■ Ernest Raymond's novel *We, the Accused* explores a triangular relationship that is reminiscent of the Crippen case. Small, mild-mannered schoolteacher Paul Arthur Presset (Hawley Harvey Crippen), married to an older, unattractive, and hectoring wife, Elinor (Belle Elmore), falls in love with a young teacher, Myra Bawne (Ethel Le Neve), who becomes his mistress. Presset drifts into poisoning his wife when she is ill so that the cause of death appears natural, and she is buried in the churchyard. Later, the local gossips, headed by her doctor, whom Presset has called "a second class brain," bring the adulterous affair and their suspicions to the attention of the police.

Raymond's sympathetic account of his doomed lovers shunts aside the grisly details of Crippen's disposal of his wife's corpse, which he decapitated and deboned before burying most of the remains beneath the cellar floor. Myra has no advance knowledge of the crime, but she stands by Paul, who defends her against charges of complicity. The final section of the novel is an unrelenting description of the cruel execution process that torments Presset before taking his life. The title of the novel serves the same double function that Truman Capote later assigned to the words *In Cold Blood*; Raymond refers simultaneously to the man and woman who face criminal prosecution, as well as to the general public, which he "accuses" of heartlessly tolerating capital punishment.

In James Thurber's famous Crippenesque sketch "Mr. Preble Gets Rid of His Wife," Mrs. Preble continues her henpecking to the last fatal moment, criticizing her husband for his slow-moving adultery and his inadequate preparations for her burial (*Thurber on Crime* [T.11]). The best nonfictional account of the Crippen case is Tom Cullen, *Crippen: The Mild Murderer* (London: Bodley Head, 1977).

R.8 Reade, Charles *The Courier of Lyons.* 1854. In *Plays by Charles Reade*. Ed. Michael Hammet. Cambridge: Cambridge Univ. Press, 1986.

■ The blindness of nineteenth-century French justice in mistaking Joseph Lesurques for Dubosc, one of the Lyon mail-coach murderers, was the subject of popular melodrama on both sides of the Channel. The principal appeal of the plot was the opportunity it provided for a single actor to play two characters who looked alike. English actor Charles Kean had scored a resounding success as identical twins in *The Corsican Brothers*. It was therefore with great delight that in 1854 he accepted Charles Reade's adaptation of *The Courier of Lyons [Le Courrier de Lyon]*, by Moreau, Siraudin, and Delacour. In the stage work, unlike real life, tragedy is averted at the last moment: before Lesurques mounts the scaffold, Dubosc's coconspirators identify him as the murderer, and Lesurques is restored to his loving daughter, Julie, and her fiancé, Didier. Along the way to this happy ending, the identities of Lesurques and Dubosq are confounded time and again. The most poignant error is made by Lesurques's father, Jerome, who believes until the final act that the criminal who shot him at his inn near the site of the mail-coach attack was his own beloved son.

In 1877 Henry Irving produced a revised version of the play, renamed *The Lyons Mail*, and took the two main roles, which were re-created in a later generation by his son, the actor-manager and crime essayist H. B. Irving.

R.9 [Regional Murder Series] *Regional Murder.* Ed. Marie F. Rodell. 9 vols. New York: Duell Sloan & Pearce, 1944–48.

■ Each volume in this series, under the general editorship of Marie Rodell, literary agent and expert in the art of mystery fiction writing, contains articles on murders in a single American city. The cities included are Boston, Charleston, Chicago, Cleveland, Denver, Detroit, Los Angeles, New York, and San Francisco. Among the authors are famous true-crime and mystery authors as well as journalists and local historians.

R.10 Réouven, René *Dictionnaire des assassins.* Paris: Denoël, 1974.

■ Despite the facetious manner of the author, this is a useful dictionary of murderers containing 230 biographical entries in which French malefactors are given pride of place. Réouven often prefaces an entry by brief allusions to other similar cases.

R.11 Reynolds, John *The Triumphs of God's Revenge against . . . Murder.* 5th ed. London: William Lane, 1670.

■ This was an early example of a purported true-crime work. Reynolds (fl. 1621–50) claimed to have drawn his stories from authentic crime records that he collected while voyaging in Europe as a commercial traveler. There is, however, no evidence that the collection is anything but the fruit of its author's imagination. Belonging to a field of popular realistic fiction that has been dubbed "warning literature," each story shows how crime is inexorably uncovered and punished by divine retribution. One of the stories included in the first edition of this work published in 1621 was the primary source for *The Changeling*, a 1652 drama by Thomas Middleton and William Rowley. Reynolds's work was so favored by the public that it appeared in various editions over the span of a century and a half. (See Fig. 3 a & b for the illustrated title pages of the 1670 edition, owned by the Borowitz True Crime Collection.)

R.12 Richer, François *Causes célèbres et intéressantes, avec les jugements qui les ont décidées* [Famous and Interesting Cases, with the Judgments]. 22 vols. Amsterdam: Michel Rhey, 1772–88.

■ Richer (1718–1790), a lawyer before the Parlement, revised Gayot de Pitaval's work, attempting to retrieve the facts from "the chaos in which [critics of Pitaval] claim they have been swallowed up."

R.13 Rilke, Rainer Maria "Der Knabe" [The Boy]. 1906. In *Rainer Maria Rilke, Sämtliche Werke*. Vol. 1: *Gedichte* [Poems]. Frankfurt am Main: Insel, 1955.

■ Poet Rilke utilizes two of the motifs commonly employed in twentieth-century lyrics mythifying Kaspar Hauser, who appeared in Nuremberg in 1828 with a tale that he had been imprisoned since childhood (see M.14): the horse and the rider. In Rilke's poem these two images contribute to the representation of the mysterious youth's isolation as well as his magical power. The narrator describes a wishful dream in which he would lead a troop of torch-bearing horsemen riding through the night astride wild horses. It would be dark but he would wear a helmet of gold and at his back, emerging from the same darkness, ten men in similar helmets would be arrayed. One of them, standing by, would clear their way with the blast of a trumpet, which would blow them "a dark solitude." As their steeds' hoofbeats rattle like rain,

> Houses fall to their knees behind us,
> Streets bow down to meet us;
> Town squares recede.

R.14 ["Robert the Devil"] *Robert the Devil.* In *Four French Plays.* Trans. W. S. Merwin. New York: Atheneum, 1985.

▪ Robert I, a duke of Normandy who died in 1035, was father of William the Conqueror. Accused of poisoning his brother, Duke Richard III, whom he succeeded in 1028, Robert passed into legend with the unflattering nickname "Robert the Devil." The anonymous fourteenth-century French play translated in this volume attributes his love of evil to a desperate vow his mother made to the Devil in pleading for a cure of her infertility. She informs her husband of the hellish pact:

> 'The devil's own may he be;
> Since God will not quicken me
> If I should have a child of you
> To the devil I owe him.'

True to his infernal ancestry, Robert gave himself over to robbery, pillaging abbeys, sacking monasteries, the violation of nuns, and the murder of seven hermits. After repenting, he obtains God's forgiveness by living in poverty and feigned madness, from which he emerges as a mysterious knight in white armor who saves Christian lands from a pagan invasion.

"Robert the Devil" is the title character of an 1831 opera by Giacomo Meyerbeer, set to a libretto by Eugène Scribe and Germain Delavigne.

R.15 Rosenberg, Charles E. *The Trial of the Assassin Guiteau: Psychiatry and Law in the Gilded Age.* Chicago: Univ. of Chicago Press, 1968.

▪ Even prior to his assassination of President James Garfield in 1881, Charles J. Guiteau's life had been marked by eccentricity and violence. A shabby lawyer and bill collector, an incoherent evangelist and political pamphleteer, and a dreamer of grandiose business schemes, he had, without apparent provocation, threatened his devoted sister with an axe. After his arrest immediately following his shooting of the president in Washington's railroad station, he justified his act both as a divinely commanded mission and as a patriotic deed to end internecine strife between the "Stalwart" and "Half-breed" wings of the Republican Party.

The unique value of Rosenberg's study is his analysis of the professional politics and divergent scientific theories that divided late-nineteenth-century American psychiatrists and alienists into warring camps. Disagreements were particularly intense when the definition of insanity was at issue, as in Guiteau's trial. The Old Guard, led by the asylum superintendents' association, tended to view insanity as a concomitant of physical disease and to emphasize society's right to defend itself against aberrant behavior by distinguishing between insanity and vice. A younger and more "liberal" generation of "neurologists," influenced by European and particularly German theory, was more willing to associate insanity with emotional impairment. Rosenberg identifies "one sensitive point upon which disagreement was absolute," namely, "the role of heredity in the causation of mental illness and criminality; could it in some cases autonomously produce insanity and antisocial behavior—without the intervention, that is, of environmental factors?" This was the position of Dr. Edward C. Spitzka, who testified on behalf of Guiteau's insanity plea.

On the scaffold, Guiteau read his poem "I Am Going to the Lordy," intended as the dying words of an innocent child. The condemned man spoke favorably of his verses: "If set to music they may be rendered very effective." Stephen Sondheim evidently agreed, for he composed music for the bizarre poem in the ill-fated musical *Assassins*.

R.16 Roughead, William *Bad Companions*. Edinburgh: W. Green, 1930.

■ As noted in the foreword of Hugh Walpole, Roughead, in this volume, generally turns away from major criminals to cases that are often slight but "human and moving." The highlights include:

- The conviction of late-eighteenth-century eccentric Welshman Rhynwick Williams (extravagantly dubbed the "Monster"), who was given to pricking the thighs of young women with his sword and tearing their undergarments. A recent study minimizes the likely responsibility of Rhynwick Williams for the attacks attributed to London's Monster (Jan Bondeson, *The London Monster: A Sanguinary Tale* [Philadelphia: Univ. of Pennsylvania Press, 2001]). Bondeson argues that the long series of attacks included copycat crimes and hoaxes. Assuming "the gown and wig of the judge" in the case against Williams, the author concedes that he certainly "abused and insulted several women" and probably "cut the clothes and sometimes the flesh of some early Monster victims." Moreover, it was "by no means unlikely that his actions set off the Monster hysteria, which then mushroomed out of proportion." Still, Bondeson concludes, there would not be sufficient evidence to convict Williams in a modern court, because the eighteenth-century proceedings were infected by anti-Monster mania, the unholy influence of rewards, and conflicting eyewitness testimony.
- The frauds of Rachel Leverson (Madame Rachel), the seller of cosmetics advertised as rendering clients "beautiful for ever." In 1868 Leverson was convicted of bilking Mary Borradaille on the strength of the beautician's promises to arrange a marriage to a peer.
- The essay "Closed Doors; or, The Great Drumsheugh Case," concerning an 1810 defamation action based on a schoolgirl's false accusations of lesbianism against two schoolmistresses. Roughead briefly considered filing a plagiarism case against Lillian

Hellman, who, without attribution, based her successful play *The Children's Hour* on Roughead's article (see H.19).

- "Mrs. Jeffray's Rats," in which Roughead deplores Elizabeth Jeffray's lack of originality in citing a plague of rats as the reason for her purchases of arsenic with which she dispatched lodgers Mrs. Ann Carl and Hugh Munro in 1838

- "The Great Burdon Mystery," a study of the slow arsenic poisoning of Mrs. Joseph Wooler near Darlington in the English county of Durham in 1855. Roughead believes that the victim's husband, who was acquitted after the trial judge's charge swayed the jury, poisoned her with repeated injections. The essay is uncharacteristically harsh; Roughead compares the blustering defense counsel, Serjeant Wilkins, to Dickens's Serjeant Buzfuz.

- The 1929 conviction of twenty-year-old Bertie Willox of the hammer slaying of his father, Robert ("The Edge of Circumstance"), which Roughead compares to Lizzie Borden's famous parricides. Despite the bloodiness of the attack, only minute stains could be detected on Bertie's clothing, but circumstances told against the young man, whom his father had employed as housekeeper: it was proved that the defendant had forged book entries to cover up embezzlement of household funds. The jury verdict against Bertie was rendered by a slim majority (9 to 6), and the death sentence was commuted to life imprisonment. Roughead notes that Scottish parricides, once rare, had become more common in the twentieth century.

The son of a prosperous Edinburgh shirtmaker, Roughead (1870–1952) was comfortably fixed for life and able to give up a brief legal career as a solicitor for the pursuit of his true passion, the study of criminal cases of Scotland and of the even more murderous nation south of the border. Roughead's essays and his introductions to several volumes he edited in the *Notable British Trials* series set a high standard for meticulous treatment of trial records. He personally attended almost all the significant Edinburgh trials of his time and made it a point, whenever possible, to visit scenes associated with the crimes of which he wrote. Although sometimes criticized for excessive irony in describing "criminous" conduct, Roughead leaves no doubt of his belief in evil and the value of capital punishment.

This deeply rooted son of Edinburgh rarely visited England and never traveled abroad. A touching illustration of his literary generosity and personal warmth was his strong friendship and admiration for his American disciple, Edmund Lester Pearson, who paid a visit to his home in 1930. Roughead is the subject of a biography by the eminent crime historian and literary critic Richard Whittington-Egan, *William Roughead's Chronicles of Murder* (Moffat, Scotland: Lochar, 1991).

R.17 ———— *The Fatal Countess and Other Studies*. Edinburgh: W. Green, 1924.

■ The title essay is devoted to Lady Frances Howard, who in 1613 devised the poisoning in the Tower of London of Sir Thomas Overbury, a severe critic of her adulterous affair with Robert Carr, destined to become her second husband under the title of Earl of Somerset. The countess and the earl, her co-conspirator, were spared the scaffold but, by what

Roughead calls "an ingenious refinement of cruelty," were compelled by Order of Council to live together at one of two designated county seats.

Other essays in the collection consider:

- The 1780 poisoning of Sir Theodosius Boughton by his brother-in-law, Captain John Donellan, who had administered essence of laurel water in the hope of succeeding to his victim's estate. In his published defense, Donellan admitted to having used laurel leaves as an "aromatic bath for his feet."
- Mary Elizabeth Smith's 1846 suit against Earl Ferrers for breach of promise of marriage, a proceeding involving a series of letters beside which, according to Roughead, the Bardell-Pickwick correspondence "pales into insignificance." The love letters were persuasively demonstrated to have been fabricated by the plaintiff.
- The controversial conviction and transportation of William Burke Kirwan for the 1852 murder of his wife, Maria Louisa, on the island of Ireland's Eye near Dublin. Roughead subtitles his account "a Detective Story" and withholds any definitive judgment on Kirwan's guilt or innocence.
- The conviction of Dr. Dionysius Wielobycki in 1857 for forging the will of an elderly female patient. As a young boy, Roughead had had his fancy caught by the doctor's "outlandish" name on a tombstone in a suburban cemetery and later elucidated his shameful, though bloodless, secret.

R.18 ———— *Glengarry's Way and Other Studies.* Edinburgh: W. Green, 1922.

■ The spirits of Sir Walter Scott and Robert Louis Stevenson hover over this delightful collection. The title essay recalls how the hot-tempered Alistair Ranaldson Macdonell, fifteenth laird of Glengarry, who inspired certain traits of Fergus MacIvor in Scott's *Waverly*, came to kill Lieutenant Norman Macleod in 1798 following a trivial dispute over the belle of a subscription ball. After his acquittal, Glengarry plunged into other quarrels. In another article ("Plagium"), Roughead, displaying his antiquarian flair, uncovers an eighteenth-century precedent relevant to the ruling on the kidnapping of Harry Bertram in Scott's *Guy Mannering*. In the historical case, Sir Alexander Anstruther won an amazing acquittal on charges of kidnapping and imprisoning two sailors to prevent them from giving incriminating testimony in a smuggling prosecution.

Two pieces concern Lord Braxfield, an eighteenth-century Scots judge whom Roughead admired and gracefully defended against the posthumous libels of his Whig critic, Lord Cockburn (see "The Bi-Centenary of Lord Braxfield"). Braxfield was the original of Lord Hermiston in Robert Louis Stevenson's novel *Weir of Hermiston*. The young Walter Scott attended the last criminal trial over which Braxfield presided, that of James M'Kean ("The Hanging of James M'Kean"), who pleaded guilty to the murder and robbery of James Buchanan, parcel carrier between Lanark and Glasgow. Scott regarded M'Kean's original defense of accidental killing in sudden passion as "apocryphal," observing that "the contrary was manifest from the accurate preparation of the deadly instrument, a razor strongly lashed to an iron bolt, and also from the evidence on the trial, from which it seems he had invited his victim to drink tea with him on the day he perpetrated the murder, and that this was a reiterated invitation."

A pair of essays deal with Scottish poisoning trials. In "Locusta in Scotland," Roughead surveys the poisoning cases of his nation from the burning of Lady Glammis (for disposing of her first husband, John, in 1527 by means of drugs, charms, and enchanted potions) through the nineteenth-century conviction of William Bennison, an Irishman, for bigamy and the arsenic poisoning of his second wife, Jane, after apparently dispatching his first spouse by similar means. A separate essay ("Poison and Plagiary") illustrates the copy-cat crime phenomenon: in 1857 James Thomson, an apprentice tailor, poisoned a fellow lodger, Agnes Montgomery, with prussic acid after reading a newspaper report of Madeleine Smith's trial (see s.32) relating to Smith's attempt to purchase the same poison prior to the death of her lover, Emile L'Angelier.

Three pieces in the collection exemplify the baleful effects of community oppression of the innocent. In "The Last Tulzie," Roughead relates with satisfaction the acquittal of Edinburgh college students in a nineteenth-century riot instigated by a street mob with the support of police. "The Twenty-Seven Gods of Linlithgow" is the story of the belatedly successful legal struggle of an Episcopalian schoolmaster against his unjust dismissal by a town council come under Presbyterian control. Roughead's third assault on local prejudice is made in "The Hard Case of Mr. Oliphant." In a case bearing a strong resemblance to France's Calas affair, the Oliphant family was groundlessly prosecuted in 1764 for the murder of their servant, Dinah Armstrong, who was probably a drowning suicide after implication in domestic thefts. Unlike Jean Calas, Mr. Oliphant and his co-defendants were acquitted.

R.19 ———— *In Queer Street.* Edinburgh: W. Green, 1932.

■ "Queen's Evidence," which begins this collection, reports a curious Glasgow trial of 1932 in which counsel for thirty-one-year-old murder defendant Peter Queen failed to persuade the jury that his alcoholic mistress, Christina Gall, had quietly committed suicide by strangling herself in the bed in their apartment kitchen while Queen was in an adjoining room looking for pillow slips she had told him she wanted to embroider. Remarkably, the eminent forensic expert Sir Bernard Spilsbury made one of his rare appearances for the defense, arguing unsuccessfully in support of the suicide theory.

The second essay ("Andrew Merrilies' Tale") recalls a Scottish case of "mysterious disappearance" (paralleling the affairs of Elizabeth Canning in eighteenth-century England and Tawana Brawley in twentieth-century America) in which the person gone missing falsely blamed third parties for assault and kidnapping. Roughead (proclaiming himself in an aside a stout believer in Elizabeth Canning's innocence) has no doubt that Merrilies fabricated his tale of the assault and abduction he had supposedly suffered in a bog near Edinburgh but blames him chiefly for slaughtering his dog in an effort to substantiate his wild tale.

In another entry ("My First Murder: Featuring Jessie King"), Roughead recollects the first murder trial he attended, the 1889 proceeding in which Jessie King was convicted of murdering two infants whom she had agreed to adopt for a paltry sum; a third victim was never found. One of the postmortem examinations was performed by Dr. Joseph Bell, on whom Sir Arthur Conan Doyle based the character of Sherlock Holmes. Between sessions of Jessie King's trial, Roughead visited sites associated with the testimony, anticipating the advice that crime historian Andrew Lang was to give him a quarter of a century later: "Never write about a case until you have seen the *locus*."

A long essay, "The Wandering Jurist," has a strong literary flavor, for it relates the courtroom battles of one of James Boswell's most litigious clients, an Edinburgh solicitor and compulsive pamphleteer named James Gilkie, who failed in his persistent efforts to obtain justice for an old man who had apparently been murdered in an affray with three creditors. Roughead also includes another account of a crazed litigant who unsuccessfully pursued the Royal Bank of Scotland on a claim that it had disbursed £1,000 of her deposited funds without authorization ("Betsy Mustard: or, Hot Stuff"). The remaining cases considered in the volume are:

- Margaret Tindal Shuttleworth's 1821 murder of her vintner husband, Henry, at Montrose with a poker while apparently in a drunken rage, her habitual state ("The Vintner's Wife")
- The 1828 laudanum poisoning and robbery of elderly Robert Lamont by John and Catherine Stuart aboard the steam-packet *Toward Castle*, making its return run to Glasgow from Inverary. After conviction Mr. Stuart confessed six similar crimes; the case gave to English slang the phrase "tipping the Doctor," which means the administration of laudanum with a view to robbery. Scots must have been greatly edified by Mr. Stuart's avowal that he had learned his sinister trick in London (see "The Crime on the *Toward Castle*").

R.20 ———— *Knave's Looking Glass.* London: Cassell, 1935.

■ This volume includes four essays that retell in "popular fashion" Roughead's introductions to cases that he had edited for the *Notable British Trials* series: Oscar Slater, J. D. Merrett, Deacon William Brodie, and Jessie M'Lachlan (the "Sandyford Mystery"; see N.7). The Slater case had a strong personal appeal to the author, who had attended the trial that ended with the unjust conviction of the defendant for the 1908 murder of Marion Gilchrist. After years of advocacy in collaboration with Sir Arthur Conan Doyle and others, Roughead rejoiced when the newly created Scottish Court of Criminal Appeal quashed conviction of Slater in 1928 on the basis of erroneous jury instructions (see C.35). Roughead had testified in the appeal regarding the opinion of Dr. John Adams, the first physician to view the body, that the murder blows had been delivered with a rear leg of a chair.

Roughead also had a soft spot in his crime historian's heart for Jessie M'Lachlan, whom he regarded as erroneously condemned for the murder of housemaid Jess M'Pherson. His essay on the case leaves little doubt of his belief that the real culprit was the Crown's principal witness, James Fleming, the "old gentleman" whom Jessie had served as accessory after the fact (see B.73). Roughead found persuasive Jessie's detailed statement, read in court after the guilty verdict, in which she described Fleming's murder, motivated by his desire to prevent the maid from disclosing his unwanted sexual advances.

The essay entitled "Mrs. Donald's Crime: or, The Force of Circumstance" (published the year before in the *Juridical Review*) is a brilliant and courageous analysis and reconstruction of the case of Mrs. Jeannie Donald of Aberdeen, convicted in 1934 of murdering Helen Priestly, the eight-year-old daughter of upstairs neighbors with whom Mrs. Donald was not on good terms. The asphyxiated girl's body was found in a sack stowed in a recess of the apartment building's hallway; brutal sexual injuries had been inflicted to simulate a male rape. The most persuasive forensic evidence at trial showed that an uncommon coliform bacillus was identified in both the dead girl's underwear and in a washcloth in the Donalds's apartment.

Much to the distress of the Aberdeen citizenry, the death sentence imposed on Mrs. Donald was commuted to life imprisonment. However, Roughead, who had attended the trial, did not disagree with the moderation of the penalty. He surmised that, in an altercation, Mrs. Donald may have shaken the child, unintentionally causing her to collapse because of an enlargement of the thymus gland revealed by the autopsy. Panic-stricken in the belief that Helen was dead, Mrs. Donald might then have proceeded to simulate a rape and, through the shock induced by the fearful injuries to the girl's sex organs, caused her to choke on her vomit. If Roughead is right, the Donald case takes its place among those causes célèbres where a murder conviction may well have been based on the mistreatment of a victim's body after an accidental death or injury.

The gracefulness of the newly written essays included in this volume is enhanced by the simplified literary style that Roughead developed in his later years.

R.21 ——— *Mainly Murder*. London: Cassell, 1937.

■ This varied collection is dedicated to playwright James Bridie in friendship and because of his drama, *The Anatomist*, based on the Burke and Hare body snatching case. The first essay, "Death in Cuddies Strip: A Tale of Three Handkerchiefs," relates the 1935 trial of a Peeping Tom, John M'Guigan, for the fatal shooting of Danny Kerrigan in Cuddies Strip, a popular lovers' lane of Perth, Scotland, and the rape of Kerrigan's girlfriend Marjory Fenwick. Three handkerchiefs figure in the evidence, of which the most important was an Indian handkerchief with which Marjory's wrist was bound. It was established at trial that this handkerchief was stolen in a burglary of a neighboring mansion at Aberdalgie and that M'Guigan, whose fingerprints were found at the house, had also left there his own blue handkerchief. The jury returned what Roughead, who attended the trial, regarded as an illogical verdict, finding the defendant guilty of the burglary and the rape but, by a majority vote, deciding that the murder charge was not proven.

Like the trial of Captain Porteous (see N.7), to which it has been compared, the conviction of midshipman Thomas Whyte in 1814 for manslaughter in the killing of seaman William Jones demonstrates the severity with which Scottish justice views the use of military force against an unarmed adversary. In Roughead's account "The Intemperate

Midshipman: or, Trouble on Leith Pier," it appears that the victim had at worst angered the defendant by failure to follow promptly an order to return to his ship. More likely, both men had had too much to drink.

In "The Weaver's Hand: A Tale of Two Graves," Roughead addresses an 1830 trial in Perth, Scotland, in which a dishonest weaver's employee, John Henderson, murdered and robbed his master, James Millie. The essay focuses on a similarity of the case to the Thurtell-Hunt murder (see B.29): quickly perceiving that corpse he had buried under the workshop floor produced a noisome smell, the murderer "dug a fresh grave in the garden—as an airier situation—a little distance from the well, and having disinterred the body from the workshop floor, he dragged it to the garden path and there re-buried it."

In "The Shadow on Shandy Hall: or, 'What Love Costs an Old Man,'" Roughead makes one of his rare excursions into the world of Irish crime to retell the 1887 trial in which Dr. Philip Cross was convicted of slowly poisoning his wife, Mary, with arsenic and strychnine. The motive could not have been plainer, because within two weeks of his wife's death, Dr. Cross, who had entered a prayer for her in his diary and paid all of five guineas for a funeral, married a young former governess, known in the trial reports as "Miss Skinner." Dr. Cross was hanged by English executioner James Berry, whose expert services were called upon by the Irish authorities. The notebook of press clippings on which Roughead based his account also included news of an 1888 inquest in which the jury found that a first cousin of Dr. Cross, Jane Cross Crooke, had caused the death of her husband by willful neglect and starvation. Roughead concluded: "Members of the Cross family were plainly ill-cast as ministers to the sick."

The final entry in the volume is "To Meet Miss Madeleine Smith: A Gossip on the Wonder Heroine of the 'Fifties." Madeleine's jury in 1857 found not proven the charge that she had laced her lover Pierre Emile L'Angelier's chocolate with arsenic to prevent him from disclosing her ardent love letters to her father (see N.7). Rating Miss Smith one of his five favorite murderesses, Roughead reviews the comments of contemporary journalists on her trial. He regards as the best of the lot an article in the *Saturday Review*, which, assuming her guilt, attributed the crime to her discovery that L'Angelier was capable of blackmail:

> The deep fountains of her passion were, on discovering her paramour's character, frozen up. She found that she had ventured everything on an unworthy object; and the very depth of her love was changed, on the complete and perfect sense of utter loss, into the corresponding depth of hatred.

R.22 ——— *Malice Domestic.* Edinburgh: W. Green, 1928.

■ As promised by its title, this splendid collection is mainly devoted to murders within the family. The first essay, "Malice Domestic: or, The Balham Mystery," is Roughead's retelling of the mysterious antimony poisoning of Charles Bravo. The author theorizes that the fatal dose came from a lotion of tartar emetic that had been kept in the stable cupboard for administration to horses. The essay appears to exculpate Florence Bravo of any role in her husband's death, implying instead that the guilty person may have been the housekeeper, Mrs. Jane Cox, whom Bravo had threatened to discharge in a fit of economy. Roughead even suggests that Mrs. Cox might have earlier poisoned her late husband in Jamaica.

"Poison in the Pantry" does full literary justice to one of Roughead's favorite Scottish murderers, the disreputable physician Edward Pritchard, who poisoned his wife and mother-in-law; his wife died from the administration of tartar emetic in small doses over a long period, and both antimony and aconite appear to have been administered to Pritchard's mother-in-law. Roughead is very critical, as was the court, of the professional conduct of attending physician James Paterson, who, in the interest of protecting his own reputation, declined to take any action on signs that a slow poisoning was in progress.

In "Miss Fenning's Misfortune? or, The Proof of the Pudding," Roughead lines up with the majority of commentators over the years in opining that the young cook Elizabeth Fenning was convicted and hanged in error on the charge that in 1815 she had attempted to poison members of the Turner family by salting dumplings with arsenic.

Detective-Lieutenant John Trench appears as a defender of truth in "Warner's Warning: or, The Perils of Identification." He triumphantly established an alibi for Charles Warner, who had been accused of the murder of reclusive householder Jean Milne on the basis of faulty eyewitness evidence; the detective confirmed that the suspect had pawned his waistcoat in Antwerp at the time of the murder. Trench's similar effort to refute dubious eyewitness testimony in the case of Oscar Slater (see c.35) resulted in his dismissal from the police force.

John Adam, the protagonist of "The Mulbuie Murder: or, When Adam Delved," led a double life. While enjoying connubial bliss under the name of Anderson, he enhanced his household resources by wedding and murdering Jane Brechin. Her battered body, still clad in her wedding dress, was found buried in a ruined hut on the moorland of Mulbuie in the Scottish Highlands. Roughead cites this case as a prime example of the force of circumstantial evidence. He laments that "there is a certain type of mind that would only be satisfied by a murderer sending, the day before the deed, a post-card to intimate his purpose, or committing the crime in presence of two witnesses above fourteen years of age, acquainted with the nature of an oath."

The essay titled "The Stolen Heiress: or, The Biter Bit" recounts the trial of Edward Gibbon Wakefield and his brother William for conspiracy to abduct heiress Ellen Turner, a fifteen-year-old schoolgirl. Both men were sentenced to three years in prison, and Edward's marriage with Ellen at Gretna Green, Scotland, under the false pretense that the marriage would save her father from pressing creditors, was declared null and void. After his release from Newgate prison, Edward Wakefield became a distinguished colonial statesman, thereby inspiring one of Roughead's greatest lines: "The evil that men do lives after them, the good is oft interred in the Dictionary of National Biography." Wakefield's colonial papers are collected in Edward Gibbon Wakefield, *A Letter from Sydney and Other Writings on Colonization* (London: Dent, 1929).

Another essay in the collection, "Conrad on Crime," discusses crime in the fiction of Joseph Conrad, with whom Roughead conducted a literary correspondence.

R.23 ———— *Neck or Nothing*. London: Cassell, 1939.

■ The first essay, "Enjoyment of Murder," is reprinted from an American collection of Roughead's crime studies. In this charming piece, Roughead identifies his favorite true-crime writers as J. B. Atlay, H. B. Irving, Edmund Pearson, Tennyson Jesse, and William Bolitho. He shares with his readers a generalization he has made from the study of many sorts of murderers: "However disparate their methods may be, all have this common characteristic: self-conceit, so abnormally developed as to become a sort of moral cancer—an overweening sense of their individual importance in the scheme of creation, and a corresponding indifference to, and disregard for, the claims and feelings of others."

"The Boys on the Ice: or, The *Arran* Stowaways" tells the horrifying tale of six young stowaways on the *Arran*, whom the ship's captain, Robert Watt, abandoned on an ice field off the coast of Newfoundland; only four of the youths arrived safely on shore. The jury found Captain Watt guilty of culpable homicide and of compelling the boys to leave a British ship, but he received the remarkably lenient penalty of eighteen months' imprisonment.

In "Killing No Murder: or, Diminished Responsibility," Roughead takes a dim view of findings of diminished responsibility in the trials of two Edinburgh sex slayers of the 1930s, Alexander Toomey and the epileptic James Boyd Kirkwood.

"Wicked Madam Branch: or, Cruelty in the Kitchen" relates one of the most frightful examples of cruelty to servants. In 1740 Elizabeth Branch and her daughter were hanged for beating to death their servant Jane Buttersworth. Roughead highlights the most macabre detail of the crime, Madam Branch's indignation that her dairymaid Ann James showed an initial reluctance to share a bed overnight with the corpse.

The collection also includes Roughead's account of the last trial for piracy in Scotland, which resulted in the 1822 execution of Peter Heaman and François Gautier for piracy and murder aboard the schooner *Jane* of Gibraltar, bound for Bahia in Brazil.

In 1913 gamekeeper John Saunders was acquitted of the attempted murder of his wife, Elizabeth, by poison ("Strychnine on Toast: or, The Gamekeeper at Home"). She complained of bad-tasting toast, and strychnine was found to be present in cream, marmalade, and a wheat biscuit. Saunders was unanimously found not guilty, and Roughead agrees, suspecting that Elizabeth, who suffered from "nerves" and dyspepsia, "doctored" the food herself.

The final essay, "The Frightfulness of Mr. Williams: A Nocturne in Green," was designed to inspire fresh admiration for Thomas De Quincey's famous essay on John Williams, the "Ratcliffe Highway Murderer." Reviewing contemporary pamphlets, Roughead shows how they laid out only the bare facts of Williams's massacres of the Marr and Williamson families, leaving it to De Quincey to recreate the full horror of these crimes by the force of his empathetic imagination.

R.24 ———— *The Rebel Earl, and Other Studies*. Edinburgh: W. Green, 1926.

■ The gems of this miscellany are Roughead's classic essays on the Victorian murder cases of Constance Kent and Adelaide Bartlett.

Roughead accepts the veracity of Constance Kent's belated confession of the murder of her four-year-old stepbrother, Francis Saville Kent, whose body, almost decapitated and bearing a stab wound in the chest, was found in a privy of the family's Wiltshire house ("Constance Kent's Conscience: A Mid-Victorian Mystery"). Inspector Whicher had suspected Constance of the crime and theorized that the girl had destroyed her blood-stained nightdress. The inspector's personality and his speculation about destruction of evidence were utilized by Wilkie Collins in his pioneering detective novel *The Moonstone* (see C.32).

Even though Roughead believes in Constance Kent's guilt, he finds it difficult to accredit the view of Dr. John Charles Bucknill, who examined her, that Constance had been actuated by a desire to avenge disparaging remarks that her stepmother (formerly the housekeeper) had made about the first Mrs. Kent, who had died insane. To Roughead, it seemed that "the monstrous character of the crime, the pitiful inadequacy of the alleged motive, and the hideous heritage of the mad mother, jointly and severally predicate a mind diseased."

Bernard Taylor, in his *Cruelly Murdered: Constance Kent and the Killing at Road Hill House* (London: Souvenir, 1979), believes that Constance murdered her stepbrother by suffocation and the stab wound to the little boy's chest. He attributes the decapitation, however, to Constance's father, Samuel Saville Kent. Taylor would have us believe that Samuel discovered the body after rising from a bed he was sharing with the nurse, Elizabeth Gough, and slashed his son's throat to divert suspicions from the family by simulating an intruder's savage attack.

In "The Luck of Adelaide Bartlett: A Fireside Tale," Roughead retells with obvious pleasure the trial of Adelaide for the poisoning of her husband, Edwin, by the unprecedented administration of liquid chloroform. Adelaide had been carrying on an affair with the family's Wesleyan pastor, the Reverend George Dyson, with the apparent consent of Edwin, who, according to Adelaide, had, except on one ill-considered occasion, ceded his marital rights to the young minister. Roughead has doubts that the marriage was as platonic as Adelaide claimed, for the police discovered condoms in the pockets of the dead husband's clothes.

Adelaide Bartlett was acquitted by the jury after two hours of deliberation, the foreman explaining to the court that they did not think there was "sufficient evidence to show how or by whom the chloroform was administered." Roughead identifies as a key prosecution error its initial theory that Adelaide first administered chloroform vapor in the traditional manner and then forced the liquid poison down her husband's throat after he had become unconscious. The judge did not permit the submission of an alternative possibility that liquid chloroform had been mixed with the victim's brandy.

Other interesting essays in the collection are:

- In "The Scotch Triumvirate: A Caledonian Caricature," Roughead elucidates a rare 1752 print showing three Scots on the gallows. These include Captain James Lowry, hanged for the murder of one of his crew on the ship *Molly*; William Henry Cranstoun, confederate of Mary Blandy in her poisoning of her father; and Major James Macdonald, whom Roughead, despite his best efforts, was unable to identify.

- In "A Case for De Quincey: A Footnote to the Famous Essay," Roughead identifies a melodramatic murder case that he deemed worthy of De Quincey's pen, the Haddington affair, in which Robert Emond brutally slew a widow named Mrs. Franks and her fifteen-year-old daughter, Madelina. Emond threw Mrs. Franks's body into her pigsty, but the animals, more humane than he, refused to devour the corpse as he had intended.
- In "An Academic Discussion: A Macabre Conceit," Roughead produces a fantasy mimicking the humor of De Quincey. He imagines a special meeting of the Society of Scottish Criminals in which Madeleine Smith, Dr. Edward Pritchard, and others dispute the claims of America's Lizzie Borden to supremacy over her Scottish rivals.

R.25 ———— *Reprobates Reviewed*. London: Cassell, 1941.

■ Dedicated to crime novelist Joseph Shearing, this volume, mostly consisting of articles that appeared in earlier Roughead collections, offers a new treasure, a captivating biography of Mary Moders, bigamist, imposter, flim-flammer, and thief. Samuel Pepys rejoiced when Mary, then posing as Lady Henrietta Marie de Wolway, sole daughter of a German earl, was for the second time acquitted of bigamy, but he was less impressed by her stage debut in *The German Princess* (1664), in which she played herself. After a career of truly creative deceptions, Mary died at age thirty-eight on the gallows for her participation in the robbery of a Southwark brewer.

Prompted by the grandson of nineteenth-century Philadelphia prosecutor George Ross, Roughead wrote one of his infrequent essays on American crime, "Lucretia Carries On: A Transatlantic Idyll." In separate 1832 trials prosecuted by Ross, Bucks County schoolmistress Lucretia Chapman was acquitted of poisoning her husband with arsenic, but her young Latin boarder and lover, Carolino (Lino Amalia) Espos y Mina, was convicted. The poison was purchased by Mina under a false pretext and mixed with chicken soup, disproving the adage that this fabled panacea can do no harm.

R.26 ———— *The Riddle of the Ruthvens, and Other Studies*. Edinburgh: W. Green, 1919.

■ This collection contains a rich trove of Scottish crime and historical mystery. The title essay examines the puzzling 1600 murder of two members of the Ruthven family, the Earl of Gowrie and his younger brother Alexander, while they were entertaining King James VI of Scotland (later James I of England). Roughead rejects James's official version that the Ruthvens (who were posthumously convicted of treason and witchcraft) planned to assassinate him and that his followers succeeded miraculously in turning the tables on the "Gowrie Conspiracy." It also strikes Roughead as unlikely that the murders were premeditated by the king, who, coward that he was, would have preferred his enemies to be dispatched while he was not on the scene. Most probable in Roughead's view is the theory of Sir William Bowes expounded within a month of the tragedy: "This matter seeming to have an accidental beginning, to give it an honorable cloak is pursued with odious treasons, conjurations, etc. imputed to the dead Earl."

Roughead devotes two articles to his favorite Scots judge, Robert M'Queen, Lord Braxfield, the original of Lord Hermiston in Robert Louis Stevenson's unfinished novel *Weir of Hermiston*. In "The Real Braxfield," Roughead provides a biography and character sketch of Braxfield and defends him against charges of injustice in the Scottish Sedition Trials of 1793 and 1794. Reports of two other significant criminal cases tried before Braxfield survive. One is the 1788 trial of Deacon William Brodie who, town councillor by day and burglar by night, is one of the sources of Robert Louis Stevenson's Dr. Jekyll and Mr. Hyde. The other trial (described in Roughead's essay "With Braxfield on the Bench"), in which Major Sir Archibald Gordon Kinloch was prosecuted for the murder of his brother, Sir Francis Kinloch of Gilmerton, was the first case in Scotland in which the criminal responsibility of the insane was seriously considered. After compassionate instructions by Braxfield, the jury found, in a special verdict, that the defendant was insane at the time he shot his brother, who was attempting to put him under restraint. Major Gordon was under the delusion that Sir Francis had poisoned him.

With the aid of his friend Simon Fraser, Lord Lovat (later executed for treason in the Tower of London), Scottish judge James Erskine, Lord Grange, had his quarrelsome wife kidnapped and transported in 1732 to an island in the Outer Hebrides, where she remained in captivity until her death thirteen years later. In his essay "The Husband of Lady Grange," Roughead reports speculation that Lady Grange was sequestered to prevent her disclosing her husband's complicity in Jacobite plots, but, since she was the grand-daughter of a man who had assassinated a judge, her threats against her husband's life may sufficiently explain her disappearance.

The 1830 murder and robbery of peddler Murdoch Grant in Scottish moorlands ("The Pack of the Travelling Merchant") appealed to Roughead partly because of its location. "Murder," he maintains, "to be fully effective, should be done out of doors, and if possible amid surroundings agreeably savage." Another asset of the case was an apparently supernatural element: Kenneth Fraser, known as "The Dreamer," had a dream vision of a cairn (a pile of stones serving as memorial or landmark), under which the murdered peddler's pack lay buried. Accompanied by a police officer, Fraser located the site revealed by his dream, but a search there was unsuccessful. Pursuing their investigations nearby, however, the searchers discovered in a hole among stones certain articles that were later identified as the peddler's property. A dissolute young schoolteacher named Hugh Macleod was hanged for the murder. Roughead speculates that Macleod may have first concealed the peddler's pack in a cairn and unwittingly revealed this incriminating fact to Kenneth the Dreamer.

The essay "Auld Auchindrayne" is a narrative of murders arising out of feuds between the Cassillis and Bargany families during the reign of Scotland's King James VI. In 1611 John Mure and his son, James, of Auchindrayne, having gone over to the Bargany side of the inveterate quarrel, were hanged for instigating the murder of Sir Thomas Kennedy of Colzean and for their subsequent assassination of young William Dalrymple to eliminate his evidence regarding the murder plot. The saga of the Mures forms the basis of S. R. Crockett's novel *The Grey Man* (London: T. Fisher Unwin, 1896).

Literary forgery is the theme of the essay "'Antique' Smith." A copying clerk, Alexander Howland Smith, was convicted of massive fabrications of documents purportedly in the hand of such luminaries as Scotland's national poet, Robert Burns.

Three sons of Scotland's notorious outlaw Rob Roy MacGregor were pursued for their kidnapping of propertied widow Jean Kay ("The Abduction of Jean Kay") and her forced marriage to one of the abductors, fugitive murderer Robert MacGregor. In 1754 Robert was hanged for his part in the crime. Roughead believes that Robert's brother James was permitted to escape from prison because of his cooperation with the Crown in connection with the prosecution of James Stewart in the so-called Appin murder case.

Roughead recalls that a crucial scene of Sir Walter Scott's *The Heart of Midlothian* is set at the memorial cairn of infamous murderer Nicol Muschet. After repeated failed attempts to catch his wife in orchestrated adulteries, to poison her, and to lead her into ambush where a hired assassin waited, Muschet took a more direct approach by murdering her brutally in Edinburgh's King's Park. He was deservedly hanged in 1721, and his co-conspirator, James Campbell Burnbank, was banished to America ("Nicol Muschet: His Crime and Cairn").

David Haggart, hero of the essay "The Adventures of David Haggart," was, in Roughead's words, a "thief, murderer, and man of letters." Since he was executed in 1821 at the age of twenty, his criminal career did not amount to much, but his autobiography, spiced with thieves' slang, gave him a unique place in the literature of Scottish crime. Jail-breaking was Haggart's principal nonliterary talent, and a killing that mars his generally nonviolent career occurred in the course of an escape. According to Roughead, "David wanted to die a great man, at the head of the profession of crime—Scotland's Jack Sheppard." Even if he fell short of that goal, he figured prominently in the romance of escapes, once fleeing in women's clothes and on another occasion exchanging garments with a scarecrow.

Another essay relates one of Edinburgh's great unsolved murder cases, the stabbing and robbing of William Begbie, porter to the British Linen Company, in Tweeddale's Close ("Mackcoull and the Begbie Mystery"). Sir Walter Scott and his friends speculated fruitlessly about the killer's identity. Suspicions came to center on a notorious criminal named James Mackcoull, alias Captain Moffat, who died in Edinburgh's county jail in 1820 while under sentence of death for robbing the Glasgow branch of the Paisley Union Bank of £20,000. Despite the fact that Mackcoull's criminal career eminently suited him for the commission of the Begbie murder, the crime could not be brought home to him.

R.27 ——— *Rogues Walk Here.* London: Cassell, 1934.

■ In a preface Roughead assesses modestly the attractions of his true-crime writing: "Plain, simple food is all I have to set before you, though I warrant it prepared and served to the utmost of my skill. Here is no psychological sauce to whet the appetite, no Freudian ornament to bedeck the board; while for accompaniment to promote digestion there is only a muted murmur of ironic comment, instead of the syncopated blare of brazen instruments."

The youthful Roughead, shortly after qualification as solicitor, attended every session of the Edinburgh trial of Alfred John Monson for the murder of his tutee Cecil Hambrough; in Roughead's opinion, this was the "outstanding murder trial of [the] generation." (See "The Ardlamont Mystery; or, The Misadventures of Mr. Monson.") After angling unsuccessfully to acquire control of Hambrough family property, the financially pressed Monson turned to simpler measures. He had the life of Cecil, who had not yet reached his majority, insured for £20,000 and persuaded the boy to assign the policies to Mrs. Monson. Roughead argues that when Monson's attempt to drown the young boy in a faked boating mishap failed, he staged a hunting "accident" resulting in a fatal gunshot wound to Cecil's head. The Edinburgh jury found the charges against Monson not proven, but the compulsive swindler was convicted in 1898 of an unrelated conspiracy to defraud a life insurance company. Roughead's persuasion of Monson's guilt in Percy Hambrough's hunting death was not universally shared. He notes the conclusion of a 1909 book review in the *Academy* (edited by Lord Alfred Douglas, whom he suspects also authored the review): "The verdict of the jury was a cowardly and wicked verdict . . . . An English jury would unhesitatingly have acquitted Monson."

With regret, Roughead concludes in "The Monster of Ballantrae: or, The Last of the Ogres" that the cave-dwelling cannibal Sawney Beane, supposedly executed with his brood of ogres by order of King James VI, is pure invention. He consoles his readers with the opinion that an actual case of Scottish cannibalism mentioned in 1460 was "the fount and origin" of the Sawney Beane legend.

Roughead was apparently predestined from early childhood to immersion in Scottish murder cases; he recalls how he met the poisoner-to-be Eugène Marie Chantrelle when he accompanied his mother on her visit to Madame Chantrelle to obtain a reference for a housemaid ("The Mélanges of Monsieur Chantrelle: French Master, Physician and Murderer"). A French instructor of English children in foreign languages, Chantrelle was also an amateur physician, wife abuser, and bordello habitué. He was hanged for poisoning his English wife, born Elizabeth Cullen Dyer, with opium after insuring her life. Having administered a lethal dose of the drug, Chantrelle, who Roughead believes was then acting in an alcoholic haze, clumsily simulated a break in a gas pipe to explain Elizabeth's sudden demise.

The principal point of interest in the grisly murder case of Elizabeth Jeffries is that, while awaiting execution in 1752, he engaged in correspondence with a far more famous Scottish murderess, Mary Blandy, to whom she ultimately acknowledged her guilt ("The Indiscretions of Miss Jeffries: or, The Naughty Niece"). Elizabeth became the mistress of her uncle, butcher Joseph Jeffries, and a miscarriage and abortion resulted from their liaison. When Uncle Joseph threatened to disinherit her after discovering that Elizabeth had taken a younger lover, John Swan, she and Swan shot the old man in the head and stabbed him while he lay in bed early in the morning. The small shot from the gun lodged in the old man's tongue and mouth, rendering him speechless and unable to identify the guilty persons before he died in the evening following the attack.

"Poison in the Parlour: or, Round the Tea-Table" recreates a well-staged arsenic poisoning that Roughead discovered in a rare pamphlet. In November 1816, after a failed attempt a month before, Dr. Robert Sawle Donnall successfully poisoned his mother-in-law, Elizabeth Downing, so that his wife would share in the inheritance. Donnall apparently added the poison to the first cup of cocoa that he served Mrs. Downing at a family party. Instead of bringing the death-bearing cup directly to his victim, who sat apart, he circled the table where the other guests were placed, and distracted attention by spilling brother-in-law Edward Downing's cup on Mrs. Downing's dress. Perhaps the purpose of this charade was to facilitate an argument that the poison was stealthily administered by another guest. If this was Donnall's original plan, he changed strategy after the fact, for he threw out the contents of Mrs. Downing's stomach at the postmortem examination and claimed that her death was due to cholera morbus; the jury needed only twenty minutes to acquit him.

In introducing the essay, "'Holy Willie' Bennison: or, Sinner Into Saint," Roughead confides, "In studying the habits of our Scots workers of iniquity I am often struck by the strange affinity observable in their conduct between religious enthusiasm and crime.... I rather incline to think these evil-doers as sincere in their piety as in their wickedness."

William Bennison, active in the spiritual exercises of the local Primitive Methodist chapel, was convicted of bigamy and arsenic poisoning of his second wife, Jane Hamilton. Bennison had probably poisoned his first wife as well, and the murder of Hamilton was to clear the way for the zealous Methodist's new romance.

The last piece is a Roughead rarity, a comic playlet in one scene where the subjects of his favorite essays foregather at the home of Mrs. Mary Mackinnon, a brothel keeper. Among her guests, many in a quarrelsome mood, are Jessie M'Lachlan and the lecherous grandpa, James Fleming; the murderers Dr. Edward Pritchard, Eugène Chantrelle, and Nicol Muschet; Dr. Robert Knox, purchaser of dead bodies from Burke and Hare; and the man Roughead would rate the darkest-hued of Scotland's villains, King James VI.

R.28 ———— *The Seamy Side.* London: Cassell, 1938.

■ In the first essay, "Death Comes to Supper: or, Domestic Tragedy," Roughead brackets two cases in which arsenic appears to have been administered to family members at table. In 1911, wastrel and speculator John James Hutchison committed suicide with prussic acid as he was about to be arrested for poisoning his parents, Mr. and Mrs. Charles Hutchison, and guests at a party in celebration of their silver wedding. Charles Hutchison and Mr. Clapperton, the grocer who had supplied the coffee in which the poison was mixed, had died, but fortunately all the other guests who had taken ill (including John Hutchison's fiancée) recovered.

A similar tragedy occurred in 1924 when James Ray King and his wife, Agnes, ingested arsenic while eating bread and cheese with their sons; Mrs. King died of the poison. The trial of son William Laurie King, Roughead states, "is the only important criminal trial occurring in my day in the High Court of Justiciary at Edinburgh that I have failed to attend." The defendant was acquitted of the poisonings, although he appeared to be a young man of doubtful veracity. Under pressure from his father to join the parental accountancy practice, William had only belatedly admitted his failure to sit for his intermediate chartered accountant's examination. He had purchased arsenic supposedly for use in making an aniline dye, but he claimed to have forgotten about his possession of the poison until after his mother's death. In view of the verdict, Roughead regarded any discussion of the merits of the case as "plainly impertinent." However, William King's forgetfulness about the poison struck him as "to say the least, remarkable."

The collection contains another essay on an unusual poisoning case, "Death Comes by Post: or, Friendship's Offering." In 1906 a cake of shortbread covered with icing containing strychnine was mailed to William Lennox; the lethal gift claimed the lives of Lennox and his housekeeper, Grace M'Kerrow. When Lennox's epileptic nephew, Thomas Mathieson Brown, was put on trial, the usual positions of prosecution and defense on legal insanity were oddly reversed. The Crown asked the jury to find that the prisoner was insane and unable to stand trial, while the defense urged that he should be acquitted on the merits in view of the insufficiency of evidence to establish that he was in fact the poisoner. The Crown's case that Brown had committed the apparently motiveless crime rested mainly on the similarity of his handwriting to that on the mailing label; Brown's possession of strychnine; and the fact that Brown had traveled to Glasgow on the day the package of cake was posted. The jury, at the trial judge's strong urging, found Brown insane by majority vote, and he was sent to the Criminal Lunatic Department at Perth, Scotland. The decision was strongly criticized as supporting commitment for criminal insanity even where proof of a criminal act is slight.

R.29 ———— *Twelve Scots Trials.* Edinburgh: William Green, 1913.

■ In this first collection of his crime essays, dedicated to H. B. Irving, Roughead credits his having undertaken "adventures in criminal biography" to the suggestion of Andrew Lang. Explaining his own enthusiasm for the true-crime genre, Roughead concedes that truth "is alone enough to alienate the sympathy of a fiction-loving public," but adds, "yet here we have characters and incidents as curious, and problems in psychology as perplexing, as any wherewith the modern novelist delights his votaries; and although the fitness of my rascals to adorn a tale may be questioned, their ability to point a moral is beyond dispute."

The cases included in this maiden volume, spanning over three centuries, 1570–1889, are:

• John Kello, parson of Spott (near Dunbar), who murdered his wife in order to prepare the way for a more profitable marriage. Having first taken care to spread the report that his wife, Margaret, had suicidal thoughts, he strangled her with a towel, tied a rope around her neck, and hung the body from a hook in the ceiling of her own room in order to simulate the advertised suicide. When he had set this scene, he locked the front door of his house, leaving the key on the inside, and rushed out by the back way to the church, where he delivered an eloquent sermon. Kello was hanged for his crime after the Reverend Andrew Simpson, of Dunbar, secured his confession. In the novel *Mr. Kello* (London: Harrap, 1924), by the pseudonymous John Ferguson (who has been

identified as Frederick Watson), the murder is related to witchcraft and witch burn-
ings in the Spott area, which were actually a much later phenomenon.

- Lady Warriston, who, with the help of her nurse Janet Murdo, hired a groom named
  Robert Weir to murder her unwanted husband, John Kincaid, in 1600

- Major Thomas Weir and his sister Jean, Edinburgh's famed sorcerors who were executed in 1670—Jean for witchcraft and the major apparently for sins of the flesh on
  which Roughead does not elaborate. The ghosts of the unholy pair reportedly were
  still disturbing the peace of Edinburgh as recently as 1909.

- Philip Stanfield, a profligate first-born executed in 1688 for murdering his father, who
  had threatened to change his will in favor of a younger son. Sir Walter Scott doubted
  the justice of the verdict, which was the last recorded in Scottish criminal annals in
  which the conviction was based on the ancient ordeal called the Law of the Bier: the
  corpse of Philip Stanfield's father had bled afresh at the murderer's touch.

- The murder of English sergeant Arthur Davies while hunting in "occupied" Scotland
  in 1749. Duncan Clerk and Alexander Macdonald, reputed thieves, were tried for the
  crime in 1754 partly on the basis of an identification made by the ghost of the dead
  sergeant. This apparition had (in Gaelic, a tongue foreign to Davies) allegedly disclosed
  the names of the guilty pair to Alexander M'pherson after accurately indicating where
  the sergeant's remains could be found. Roughead, astounded by the verdict of acquittal, surmises that the defendants were actually identified by informers and that the
  appearance of Davies's specter may have been staged.

- Katharine Nairn, whose trial Roughead edited for the *Notable British Trials* series
  (see N.7)

- The 1766 trial of Mrs. Helen Keith of Northfield and her son, William, who, on the
  complaint of her stepson George, the new laird (lord), had been arrested for the murder of his father, Alexander Keith, at the Northfield house. Roughead strongly approves
  of the royal pardon that followed the conviction of the pair of defendants. The long
  delay in prosecution had made important defense testimony unavailable. Neither Mrs.
  Keith, as the dead man's second wife, nor their son William seemed to have an adequate motive, since their small legacies left them less prosperous than they had been
  while Alexander Keith lived. And no physician had an opportunity to inspect the signs
  of strangulation that lay witnesses thought they observed on the dead man's body.

- Mrs. Mary Smith, who benefited from the Scotch verdict of "not proven" when charged
  in 1827 with the arsenic poisoning of her servant Margaret Warden, whom she believed pregnant with the child of her youngest son, George Smith. Sir Walter Scott
  attended the trial of Mrs. Smith, who was known in local ballads as "The Wife o' Den-
  side." Dissatisfied with the verdict, he declared: "Well, sirs, all I can say is, that if that
  woman was my wife, I should take good care to be my own cook!"

- Christina Gilmour, who in 1844 faced charges of having poisoned with arsenic her bridegroom of six months, John. The marriage was apparently never consummated, since
  Christina strongly preferred a previous wooer. As in the case of Mary Smith, which
  her counsel cited as a precedent, the jury found the charges not proven.

- The "St. Fergus Affair," in which Roughead relates the 1853 trial of Dr. William Smith on charges of having shot and killed a young farmer named William M'Donald after insuring his life. The origin of the murder weapon found near the body was in dispute, and the jury returned a not proven verdict, by a majority, after an absence of only ten minutes.
- "The Dunecht Mystery" recalls a bizarre trial of 1882, in which poacher Charles Soutar was convicted of stealing the body of the Earl of Crawford and Balcarres with the motive of obtaining a ransom for recovery of the corpse.
- An account of the 1889 trial of the "Arran Murderer," J. W. Laurie, which Roughead also edited for the *Notable British Trials* series (see N.7).

R.30 Rowland, John *Murder Mistaken: An Analysis of Two Unsolved Murders.* London: John Long, 1963.

■ A prolific crime historian as well as author of crime novels, biography, and popular science, John Rowland pairs studies of the "Rising Sun Case" (1907) in which Robert Wood was acquitted of slitting the throat of Camden Town (London) prostitute Emily (or Phyllis) Dimmock; and the "Green Bicycle Case" (1919), in which war veteran Ronald Light was found not guilty of the shooting of fellow cyclist Bella Wright in a Leicestershire lane. Both defendants had the good fortune of retaining the services of one of England's greatest barristers, Sir Edward Marshall Hall, who extricated them from the results of their own follies: providing false information to the police in a misguided effort to divert the investigation. Rowland theorizes that Dimmock was murdered by one of the sailors she brought home for sex and that Wright may have been accidentally shot at long range by a man unaware that he had hit the girl as she cycled down the lane. The accident theory espoused by Rowland in the latter case resembles the "magic bullet" theory in the assassination of President Kennedy. A dead crow or raven was found near Wright's body, and a bullet was retrieved from the road. Rowland suggests that the bullet "could have killed the mysterious bird, then penetrating the head of Bella Wright as she cycled along that lane." Then, "having done its worst, it might have lost its momentum, and have fallen into the road."

R.31 Runyon, [Alfred] Damon *Trials and Other Tribulations.* Philadelphia: Lippincott, 1947.

■ Runyon, best known as a humorist and sports reporter, demonstrates in this volume that he was also a perceptive and lively crime journalist. The book includes his reports on famous criminal trials and other headline-grabbing legal proceedings of the 1920s and 1930s: the Hall-Mills and Snyder-Gray murder cases; the failed prosecution of George McManus for the killing of New York City gambler Arnold Rothstein; the conviction of Al Capone for tax evasion; the domestic imbroglio of "Daddy" Browning and his teenage wife, "Peaches"; and a Senate investigation of J. P. Morgan. Many of the pieces are in the light vein of the author's famous Broadway stories, but the Halls-Mills and Snyder-Gray coverage provides valuable eyewitness commentary on the trials. Description of the participants is delightfully quirky and unforgettable. Here, for example, are his introductory renderings of Ruth Snyder and

Judd Gray: "A chilly looking blonde with frosty eyes and one of those marble, you-bet-you-will chins, and an inert, scare-drunk fellow that you couldn't miss among any hundred men as a dead set-up for a blonde, or the shell game, or maybe a gold brick."

In his assessment of the Hall-Mills trial, Runyon takes what might now be regarded as a contrarian position, attributing the acquittal not so much to the weakness or mere-triciousness of the prosecution as to an inattentive and possibly corrupted jury bent on favoring its local plutocracy, in which the defendants prominently figured. In one respect the case prefigured the O. J. Simpson trial: the defense team was referred to as the "million-dollar defense."

S

s.1 Sade, Donatien Alphonse François, Marquis de *La Marquise de Ganges.* 1813. Foreword Gilbert Lely. Paris: Pierre Amiot, n.d.

■ In this fictionalized account of the murder of the marquise de Ganges by her brothers-in-law, with the tacit support of her husband, Sade ranges himself firmly on the side of persecuted virtue. His unwonted moralizing even leads him to invent appropriate punishment for the principal malefactor, the abbé de Ganges, who at the end of the novel has his brains blown out by a mysterious stranger who proclaims, "Die, monstrous criminal; I avenge your victim." Sade characterizes the respective roles of the three Ganges brothers in the murder as follows: "the marquis [the husband] lent himself to the evil that the abbé advised and the chevalier [the younger brother] carried out" (91).

s.2 Saint-Edme, B. *Répertoire général des causes célèbres anciennes et modernes.* 3 series in 13 vols. Paris: Rosier, 1834–35.

■ The director of this compilation by a "society of men of letters" was also author of a dictionary of criminal punishments. Among the reasons he cited for these series of trial accounts was to produce a "complete collection" of causes célèbres previously published; to create a history of the French penal system; and to provide, when possible, information regarding events subsequent to the judgments rendered in the cases. The second of the three series is principally devoted to the criminal cases of the French Revolution and Napoleon's reign.

s.3 Sanson, H[enri] *Mémoires de Sanson: Sept générations d'exécuteurs 1688–1847* [Memoirs of the Sansons: Seven Generations of Executioners]. 6 vols. Paris: Dupray de la Mahérie, 1862–63.

■ After providing a historical overview of modes of criminal punishments, Henri Sanson traces his family's service as France's executioners through seven generations. The fount of this tradition was a Norman, Charles Sanson de Longval, who made an inauspicious debut in the execution of Angélique Nicole Carlier (Madame Tiquet), condemned for plotting unsuccessfully to murder her husband. Sanson struck the back of Madame Tiquet's neck with a heavy double-edged épée, which was the instrument of death in the late seventeenth century. But her head did not fall:

A cry of horror arose in the crowd.

Sanson de Longval struck again. This time as before, a whistle was heard in the air, and the sound of the sword which resounded on the block; but the head was not severed. It seemed to the spectators who were closest that the body had quivered.

The roar of the crowd became menacing.

Blinded by the blood that spurted at each blow, Charles wielded his lethal weapon for the third time and brought it down with a sort of frenzy.

Finally Angélique's head rolled at his feet.

In spite of this unpromising beginning, the Sansons performed their bloody functions until 1847, when Henri Sanson was discharged. He remarks with satisfaction, "A cloud of competitors fought over the ancient heritage of my family; but none of those who had coveted it obtained it."

In an epilogue, Sanson foresaw the end of capital punishment: "The death penalty has served its time. In abolishing it, one will liberate from painful duties a class of functionaries for whom I may more easily raise my voice now that I have ceased my activity. One will return to the esteem of their fellow citizens men who have failed to merit it only under the sway of the most illogical of prejudices."

s.4 Sardou, Victorien *La Tosca: The Drama Behind the Opera.* Ed. and trans. W. Laird Kleine-Ahlbrandt. Lewiston: Edwin Mellen Press, 1990.

■ Although Sardou, a master of the French "well-made" play, larded his melodrama *La Tosca* (1887), starring Sarah Bernhardt, with references to real events and figures of Napoleon's Italian campaign of 1800, the historicity of the play's plot and principal characters is disputed. Sardou maintained rather vaguely that Tosca's tragic fate was based on an actual incident in French history. George Jellinek, in his article "Napoleon and the Prima Donna" (*Opera News*, Feb. 8, 1975), asserts that Sardou's republican patriot Angelotti and brutal Roman police chief Scarpia actually existed: "As they retreated from Italian cities, the pro-Napoleonic Roman Republic collapsed, Consul Angelotti was imprisoned, and Baron Vitellio Scarpia's reign of terror began."

Baron Vitellio Scarpia, described as exceptionally cruel and passionate, also appears in Susan Sontag's romance *The Volcano Lover* (New York: Farrar, Straus & Giroux, 1992). But Sardou translator Kleine-Ahlbrandt states that Scarpia was fictional and that the character of Angelotti "was quite possibly suggested by the real-life political pamphleteer, Luigi Angeloni (1759–1842), whose doctrinaire ideas were inspired by Rousseau and the encyclopedists." The only Sardou character for whom Kleine-Ahlbrandt vouches is deceased at the time of the play's action: Count Palmieri, whom Scarpia had deceptively executed in the same manner as he plans to shoot Mario Cavaradossi, Tosca's lover. In real life, Marquess Palmieri, a Neapolitan army colonel, was hanged for conspiracy in 1807 on orders of Joseph Bonaparte's ruthless police chief, A. Saliceti. Amid all this confusion of fact and invention, we can be thankful for Puccini's glorious operatic setting of the play.

s.5 Sartre, Jean-Paul "Erostratus." In *The Wall and Other Stories*. 1939. Trans. Lloyd Alexander. New York: New Directions, 1948.

■ Sartre's antihero, Paul Hilbert, cannot bring himself to love his fellow men and resents his inability to detach himself from their words and thoughts. To his coworkers he announces his preference for "black" heroes. A man named Masse, who had "some education," proposes as Hilbert's ideal Erostratus, who "wanted to become famous and . . . couldn't find anything better to do than to burn down the temple of Ephesus, one of the seven wonders of the world." When Masse confesses that he cannot recall the name of the temple's builder, Hilbert comments, "Really? But you remember the name of Erostratus? You see, he didn't figure things out too badly."

Emulating the ancient temple destroyer, Hilbert goes into a Montparnasse street determined to claim a life with each of the six bullets in his revolver. His scheme, however, miscarries. He shoots a big red-necked man three times in the belly but fears he may have only wounded him. After firing two more shots at random in a café, he locks himself in a lavatory but finds that he is unable to carry out his planned suicide. See Eric Gans, "Herostratus Forever," in *Chronicles of Love and Resentment* no.1997 (Apr. 5, 1997), www.humnet.ucla.edu/humnet/anthropoetics/views/views87.htm.

When tried for the murder of his high-school friend Alain Guyader in 1948, Claude Panconi claimed that the crime had been inspired by his reading of Sartre's "Erostratus" (see B.24). The theme of the ancient Greek temple arsonist has been reprised by Soviet playwright Grigory Gorin in his *Forget Herostratus!* (see G.28).

s.6 Schama, Simon *Dead Certainties (Unwarranted Speculations)*. New York: Knopf, 1951.

■ Schama's title jokes about the inability of historians to establish the truth about two famous deaths: British general James Wolfe's death in battle at Quebec in 1759 and the murder of George Parkman at Harvard Medical College in 1849. The book establishes an attenuated link between the two events by drawing attention to their common connection with the Parkman family of Boston. Famed historian Francis Parkman re-created Wolfe's battlefield death in tones less glorious than the apotheosis depicted in Benjamin West's heroic painting. Parkman's interpretation reflected his own neurasthenic constitution, which influenced his description of the sickly Wolfe summoning energy from "his feeble body to bear him on till the work is done."

The killing of Parkman's uncle George, a benefactor of the Harvard Medical College, is the subject of the second and major part of the book. In 1849 Harvard chemistry professor John White Webster murdered his demanding creditor, Dr. George Parkman, and then dismembered and incinerated his body. As events proved, it was not Parkman's enormous height that made his remains a poor choice for concealment but his identifiable dental work. Schama reads the Webster case as "a squalid and shocking reproach to the governing class of Harvard and Boston." He withholds judgment on many questions raised during the trial, stating in his Afterword that, "though a verdict is rendered and a confession delivered in the case of John Webster, the ultimate truth about how George Parkman met his end remains obscure."

Schama's technique is to substitute for certainties several disparate views of reality. In "The Many Deaths of General Wolfe," he introduces a purely imaginary narrator, a foot soldier who saw the dying general "lying on a mound beside a sorry little bush attended by just two men." When he retells the Webster crime, Schama explores the divergences among versions given by Webster, the trial lawyers, and the chief prosecution witness, janitor Ephraim Littlefield (see B.27). The richness of historical archives still leaves historians, as Schama laments, "painfully aware of their inability ever to reconstruct a dead world in its completeness, however thorough or revealing their documentation."

s.7 Schevill, James *The Death of Anton Webern.* In *Collected Short Plays.* Athens: Ohio Univ. Press (Swallow Press), 1986.

■ Composer Anton Webern was tragically shot to death by a panicky American army cook serving with U.S. occupation forces in Austria at the end of World War II. The cook, who had never handled a gun before, participated in an amateurish "sting" operation against Webern's son-in-law, who was suspected of black market activity. See Hans Moldenhauer, *The Death of Anton Webern: A Drama in Documents* (New York: Philosophical Library, 1961).

Schevill's "counterpoint for voices" was intended to be performed as a radio play, a concert reading, or a television piece with film or projections. Schevill attempted to imitate in Webern's role the jagged rhythms and enigmatic silences of the composer's style. Webern's wife reports that his last words were "It's over." The musician, however, prefers to recall the subtler markings in his scores:

> Like a whisper
> > Scarcely audible
> > Dying away
> > > The directions of my music,
> Desires of intense, natural change,
> the constant changes of inconstancy,

A later collection, *5 Plays* (1993), includes *Ape-God, or Who Killed Dian Fossey?* The famed student of mountain gorillas bravely defends her beloved animals against pygmy poachers, but others are skeptical of Fossey's motives. Her friend Rosamond warns her that "we whites who like to live here can't defend Africa against Africans," and a fellow researcher opines: "She made so many enemies that one was bound to kill her."

s.8 ——— "The Images of Execution" and "A Woman Staring through a Telescope at Alcatraz." In *The Complete American Fantasies.* Athens: Ohio Univ. Press (Swallow Press), 1996.

■ Two poems in Schevill's collection evoke the soullessness of punishments. The gassing of

Caryl Chessman at San Quentin on May 2, 1960, is the theme of "The Images of Execution." The death penalty, in the poet's eye, meaninglessly ends a cycle of "sin and no redemption." He broods that

> the ancient game of punishment
> Tortures player as well as victim,
> Racks us with endgame, ironic images of justice . . .

In "A Woman Staring through a Telescope at Alcatraz," the prison-gazer's stare at the Rock calls to mind one of its most famous inmates, two-time murderer Robert Stroud, nicknamed "the Birdman of Alcatraz" because of his ornithological studies. For Schevill, it was Stroud's unwillingness to compromise that led to his isolation from society:

> This dangerous mind, reformer in the quicksands of change,
> Prisoner in the comforting climate of compromise
> Where each servile hand must be shaken for advancement.

S.9 Schiller, Johann Christoph Friedrich *The Robbers*. 1781. In *Sturm und Drang: The Soldiers, the Child Murderess, Storm and Stress and the Robbers*. Ed. Alan C. Leidner. New York: German Library, 1992.

■ In this play, on which Verdi based his opera *I Masnadieri*, Karl von Moor, outraged by his brother's plot to have him disinherited, becomes the leader of a robber band. But all ends well with Karl's making amends to society. Schiller's ultimate sources in crime history have been identified. The first is a "malevolent rabble" of as many as 1,500 members who infested the wooded mountains of Thuringia, Bohemia, and Franconia in the early and mid–eighteenth century. A document of 1753 records details that would readily appeal to romantic writers: the band was observed to camp in the open near a ruined castle and to engage in free love.

The activity of Schiller's Karl von Moor as a bandit chief also accords in part with the contents of the "Butlar Record" of 1734, which refers to the links of a feudal family with a band of robbers.

Schiller (1759–1805) played an important role in persuading Germans that valuable psychological insights were to be gained from the study of crime. In addition to basing imaginative works on crime (including the assassination of Wallenstein), Schiller contributed a foreword to a 1792 German-language edition of selections from Gayot de Pitaval's groundbreaking *Causes Célèbres* series.

S.10 —— *Der Verbrecher aus verlorener Ehre* [The Criminal Because of Lost Honor]. 1786. Stuttgart: Reclam, 1981.

■ The antihero of this story, Christian Wolf, is physically ill favored and poor. To win the favor of a young girl, he turns to poaching so as that he can afford to buy her gifts. Nothing goes according to plan. Wolf's beloved rejects him; he is caught red-handed by a gamekeeper; and he then begins a downward path to prison, recidivism, murder, and leadership of a robber band. At last, conscience stings, and Wolf, after detention as a suspicious character, reveals his true identity to his captors.

The narrative is based on the history of a criminal named Christian Schwan. Schiller lent authenticity to his account by adding a subtitle, "A True History," and by telling the heart of the tale in Christian Wolf's voice. Schiller's only authorial intervention comes in an introductory passage in which he expounds his views on methodology in making literary use of historical materials. He concludes that the hero must be presented at the same low emotional temperature as the reader is likely to maintain. Moreover, the principal focus should be on motivation rather than action: "We must wish to see [the hero] not only *accomplishing* his action but also willing his action. We are infinitely more interested in his thoughts than in his deeds, and even more interested in the sources of his thoughts than in the consequences of his actions."

Schiller's concept of the criminal motivated by his sense of lost honor, and the objectivity of the narrative style, look forward to Heinrich von Kleist's "Michael Kohlhaas" (see K.8).

s.11 Schulberg, Budd *On the Waterfront: The Final Shooting Script with an Afterword by the Author.* Hollywood: Samuel French, n.d.

■ In his Afterword, Schulberg tells how this film evolved as an artistically brave collaboration with director Elia Kazan. Following leads provided by Malcolm Johnson's Pulitzer Prize–winning *Crime on the Waterfront*, Schulberg made his own investigations of the docks. At the time Manhattan's westside waterfront was run by the Bowers mob, and Brooklyn was controlled by the Anastasia family. Schulberg met the insurgent longshoremen and the "waterfront priest," Father John Corridan of St. Xavier's Church in the Dunn-McGrath neighborhood. Father John, "a tall, fast-talking, chain-smoking, hard-headed, sometimes profane, Kerryman," became Karl Malden's character in the film, and the fighting speech comparing a labor insurgent's death to the Crucifixion was "taken almost verbatim from Father Corridan's daring sermon on the Docks."

s.12 Sciascia, Leonardo *"The Moro Affair" and "The Mystery of Majorana."* Manchester, England: Carcanet, 1987.

■ The major work in this volume is a polemical commentary on the Red Brigades' 1978 kidnapping and execution of Aldo Moro, president of the Christian Democrats. Sciascia's ire is aroused by the random police search for Moro, which was aimed at dazzling the public instead of pursuing significant leads, and by the politicians and journalists who reconciled the public mind to Moro's eventual killing by the erroneous contention that his appeals for a negotiated prisoner exchange were dictated by his captors. Sciascia subjects the successive communications from Moro and the Red Brigades to the kind of close critical elucidation that would be merited by worthier texts. Even the Italian press of the era played word games with Moro's life; when a Red Brigades' communiqué referred to "carrying out" the sentence passed upon Moro, the editor of a Christian Democratic paper took heart in the terrorists' use of the gerund, suggesting that the period for the execution could be extended.

In his second essay, "The Mystery of Majorana," Sciascia tackles one of twentieth-century Italy's most puzzling historical enigmas, the unexplained disappearance of Sicilian physicist Ettore Majorana from Naples in 1938. The highly speculative hypothesis at which the article arrives is that Majorana, although hinting at suicide, went into hiding (perhaps in a Carthusian monastery) to divorce himself from the world of science, which he saw to be headed toward the discovery of atomic power. Physicist Erasmo Recami, however, in his book *Il Caso Majorana* [The Majorana Case] (Milan: Mondadori, 1987), rejects this theory, believing that Majorana fled from his total personal environment in which his "hypersensitive spirit suffered from the difficulty of human contact."

During a visit to Germany in 1933, Majorana made the acquaintance of atomic physicist Werner Heisenberg. Addressing briefly the issue of Heisenberg's motivation in visiting Niels Bohr in 1940 (the subject of Michael Frayn's play *Copenhagen*), Sciascia suggests that the aging Danish scientist misread as a threat Heisenberg's message intending to assure the West that Nazi Germany was in no position to develop an atomic weapon.

S.13 Scott, Sir Walter   *The Heart of Midlothian.* 1818. In *The Works of Sir Walter Scott.* Vols. 11 and 12. Boston: Houghton Mifflin, 1912–13.

■ Scott interweaves two historical eighteenth-century tales of royal pardon. The first concerns the fate of John Porteous, captain-lieutenant of the City Guard of Edinburgh, convicted of murder and wounding in 1736 after he ordered his troops to fire on a crowd gathered at the hanging of Andrew Wilson, robber of an excise collector. A stay of the captain's execution was granted by Queen Caroline, but a mob took Porteous from the Tolbooth prison and hanged him in the Grassmarket.

In the novel the fate of Captain Porteous is linked with the story of two sisters, Effie and Jeanie Deans. Effie is a prison mate of the captain in the Tolbooth, having been charged with statutory infanticide because of her inability to account for the whereabouts of a newborn child. Her lover, George Robertson, a real-life accomplice of excise robber Andrew Wilson, pleads in vain with Effie to flee the Tolbooth in the confusion caused by the irruption of Captain Porteous's lynch mob.

It remains for Jeanie Deans to save her sister through religious faith and simple eloquence. Jeanie refuses to give false trial testimony to save her sister's life. Instead, setting off to London on foot, she persuades the queen and the Duke of Argyll of Effie's innocence. Jeanie and Effie Deans are based on Helen and Isobel Walker. At the request of a woman who was touched by Helen Walker's devotion to her sister, Scott arranged for an Edinburgh architect to erect a tombstone in her memory with an inscription in the author's words (see W. S. Crockett, *The Scott Originals* [New York: Scribner, 1912], 233–40).

S.14 ——— *Kenilworth.* 1821. In *The Works of Sir Walter Scott.* Vols. 21 and 22. Boston: Houghton Mifflin, 1912–13.

■ The denouement of this novel is the mysterious death in 1560 of Amy Robsart, wife of

Queen Elizabeth I's favorite, Lord Robert Dudley (the future Earl of Leicester). Amy's body was found at the foot of a staircase in Cumnor Hall, the property of Dudley's retainer Anthony Forster, and the politically correct view was that she had accidentally fallen to her death. However, darker rumors implicated Dudley and Queen Elizabeth, who were suspected of carrying on a love affair and of planning to marry after the death of inconvenient Amy.

Scott's novel is replete with distortions of historical fact. Amy Robsart did not marry Dudley in secret, as Scott relates; nor did Dudley become Earl of Leicester or live at Kenilworth until after her death. Scott absolves Queen Elizabeth and Dudley of complicity in Amy's death, which he attributes to the disloyal plot of Lord Robert's henchman, Sir Richard Varney, who rigged a trapdoor through which Amy fell.

Nonfictional studies have offered varying explanations of Amy's death. George Adlard, in *Amye Robsart and the Earl of Leycester* (London: John Russell Smith, 1870), surmises that Amy fell either accidentally or as a suicide despairing of her husband's neglect. More recently, Hugh Ross Williamson, revealing his strong anti-Tudor bias, asserts that "no one who has seriously studied the matter is likely to doubt that the queen had guilty foreknowledge of the murder of her lover's wife, though the Tudor-Protestant propaganda line, obscuring this, is still potent in 'popular' history" (*Historical Whodunits* [New York: Macmillan, 1956], 63).

**s.15 ——— ** *Rob Roy*. 1817. In *The Works of Sir Walter Scott*. Vols. 7 and 8. Boston: Houghton Mifflin, 1912–13.

■ It is difficult to disentangle the historical Robert MacGregor Campbell (Rob Roy), who was born around 1671 and died in 1735, from his legend. Once a cattle-drover on a large scale, he was ruined financially and turned to raiding the herds of others. Still, Highland traditions portrayed him as a champion of his dispossessed MacGregor clan and "the friend of the poor and oppressed, as Robin Hood was, not given to wanton cruelty, not a monster thirsting for blood, but drawing the sword only when generous motives inspired him" (W. S. Crockett, *The Scott Originals* [New York: Scribner, 1912], 197–98).

Sir Walter Scott was an admirer of the Highland hero, acquiring a long-barreled Scottish gun bearing his initials for his collections at Abbotsford. In the novel *Rob Roy*, the outlaw plays a beneficent role as the defender of Frank Osbaldistone against the villainies of his cousin Rashleigh, who caps his transgressions by supporting the English cause in the Jacobite rising of 1715.

s.16 Sen, Mala *India's Bandit Queen: The True Story of Phoolan Devi*. London: Harvill (HarperCollins), 1991.

■ For centuries the deeply ravined Chambal Valley south of Agra, India, has been infested by bands of criminals worshiping Kali, the Hindu goddess of revenge. The Thugs, ritual stranglers who preyed on Indian travelers (see s.33), were suppressed by the British in the nineteenth century, but the armed robbers called *dacoits* persist to the present day. The dacoits prefer the designation *baghis* (rebels) and often fancy themselves as "social bandits," robbing the rich to benefit the oppressed. Oddly, India's religious antagonisms are forgotten among the dacoits, but caste differences fuel gang warfare.

Against this historical backdrop, Sen has written one of the best accounts of India's modern "bandit queen," Phoolan Devi. Born into the Mallah (fishermen) subcaste of the lowly Sudras, Phoolan was kidnapped by dacoits and took one of the robbers, Vikram Mallah, as her lover and protector. When he was killed, she was chloroformed and gang-raped by a group of upper-caste Thakurs in the village of Behmai. In 1981, she had her revenge when twenty-two Thakur men were shot in cold blood (twenty fatally) in the so-called Behmai Massacre. She denied any involvement in the slaughter, but her companion and joint gang leader, Man Singh, admitted the responsibility of their gunmen. In 1983, Phoolan Devi and Man Singh surrendered to the police of Madhya Pradesh in a well-publicized ceremony after obtaining Indira Gandhi's promise that they would be spared from capital punishment.

Mala Sen based her fine work on interviews with Phoolan and her relatives and utilized "prison diaries" dictated by the illiterate bandit queen. Despite the bloodiness of Phoolan's revenge, the book is a powerful indictment of abuse of Indian women, police brutality and incompetence, and sinister ties between upper-caste string-pullers and government officials.

After her release from prison in 1994, Phoolan Devi's life remained eventful. She was elected a member of India's parliament in 1996 as a candidate of the low-caste Samajwadi Party for the constituency of Mirzapur, Uttar Pradesh. Survivors of the Behmai massacre, unimpressed by her new political credentials, sought to put her on trial for murder. In 1998, her name was floated as a candidate for the Nobel Peace Prize. The name "Phoolan Devi" was also proposed as a baby name that "gives you an intense desire to be of service to others." On July 25, 2001, Phoolan was killed by masked gunmen outside her home.

See also Richard Shears and Isobelle Giddy, *Devi: The Bandit Queen* (Hemel, Hempstead: George Allen & Unwin, 1984); Phoolan Devi, with Marie-Thérèse Cuny and Paul Rambali, *I, Phoolan Devi: The Autobiography of India's Bandit Queen* (London: Little, Brown, 1996).

s.17 Sereny, Gitta *The Case of Mary Bell.* London: Eyre Methuen, 1972.

■ Gitta Sereny, a Hungarian writer who has worked with disturbed French and German children, explores in *The Case of Mary Bell* the background of the two horrifying murders committed within six weeks in Newcastle-upon-Tyne in the spring of 1968. The victims, Martin Brown, aged four, and Brian Howe, three, were found strangled in the working-class Scotswood district, the neighborhood of the eleven-year-old Mary Bell and her thirteen-year-old girlfriend, who were accused of the murders. Sereny attended the trial, held in assize court, where little interest was exhibited during the proceedings in the causes of the crime. The older girl was acquitted, probably partly due to her slow-wittedness and her obvious submission to the younger, brighter, and more dominant Mary Bell. Mary was found guilty of manslaughter rather than murder due to "diminished responsibility" resulting from her diagnosed psychopathic personality. The judge sentenced her to be detained for life and recommended that she receive psychiatric treatment, but no mental hospital would admit her.

Though the court considered Mary's mental condition in sentencing, no effort was made by the authorities to investigate the causes (such as childhood traumas) of her compulsion to kill. Instead the authorities and the public viewed her as a "bad seed," a child-monster, clever and cunning. Sereny expresses her dissatisfaction with this attitude toward a minor she regards as sick, a child whose actions should be understood as "a cry for help." By interviewing members of the staff who cared for her during and after the trial, as well as family and neighbors, Sereny begins to see a pattern of rejection and deprivation suffered by Mary at the hands of her emotionally disturbed mother, Betty Bell, who frequently disappeared from the family home and occasionally offered Mary to others to care for or even to adopt. The large and close extended family kept Betty's illness hidden during the trial to protect her from public scrutiny, as they had all through her troubled life. Sereny decries the English public's lack of curiosity about Mary's life story, an indifference that she thinks arose out of their acceptance of the "bad seed" theory: "Unprecedented in a country famous for its murder trials and literature, the press and public not only resisted but rejected the case of Mary Bell. 'I don't want to read about it,' people said, 'it's too horrible.'"

S.18 ———— *Cries Unheard: The Story of Mary Bell.* London: Macmillan, 1998.

■ In *Cries Unheard: The Story of Mary Bell* Gitta Sereny returns to the case that is the subject of her 1972 book (see S.17). She presents the material gathered in five months of intensive interviews with Mary Bell, who agreed to talk to the author twenty-seven years after her conviction. The publication of this book caused a furor in the press due to the fact that Bell was paid for the interviews, although the money was put in a trust fund for her daughter. Speaking at the age of forty, Bell describes her troubled relationship with her mother, whose death preceded her agreement to grant interviews. She also speaks of her life in prison, the difficulties she encountered after release, and the structure given to her life by the birth of her child. Her attachment to her child brings her to a confrontation with the horror of her crime, which during her years in prison she had suppressed.

The first part of the book overlaps the story told in *The Case of Mary Bell*. Only at the end of the interviews, after long years of denial, does Mary Bell retrieve her memory of the murders and of her sexual abuse from the age of four at the hands of her prostitute mother who used her as a pawn in her "business." Sereny believes these "childhood experiences . . . to be the key to the tragedy that happened in Scotswood in 1968." She also states that "if properly investigated, comparable childhood traumas will be found in the background to most similar cases wherever they have occurred." In part she blames the British "fetish of privacy" that led Mary's family, neighbors, social workers, and police (all of whom had seen several examples of her extreme aggressive behavior toward little children prior to the murders) to ignore her "cries for help." Social workers, for example, are faulted for protecting "their relationship with parents at the expense of children." But regardless of these failures of the system, Mary herself is painfully aware of the guilt of which she will never be free: "There are many unhappy, very disturbed kids out there who don't end up robbing families of their children."

s.19 Shakespeare, William *King Richard III.* First performed ca. 1594. Ed. Janis Lull. The New Cambridge Shakespeare. Cambridge: Cambridge Univ. Press, 1999.

■ In his famous opening soliloquy, Richard confides that he is "determinèd to be a villain." It is sometimes argued that Shakespeare's portrayal of Richard as a villainous serial murderer, whose horrors culminate in the ordered slaying of the young princes in the Tower, reflected the "Tudor Myth" propagated by Sir Thomas More's *History of Richard III* (ca.1513). However, editor Janis Lull notes that "the earliest known portrait of Richard as a usurper . . . was recorded by an Italian priest Dominic Mancini [in 1483], when the victory of Henry Tudor over Richard III was still two years in the future."

Shakespeare's dark image of the homicidal Richard is relieved by the king's sense of humor, cleverness, bravery, and heroic refusal to repent in the face of his final defeat. Aware of his own high birth, Richard aspires to rise in power rather than to grow morally. In the words of romantic critic William Hazlitt, he "is not a man striving to be great, but to be greater than he is" (*Characters of Shakespeare's Plays* [1817; London: Oxford Univ. Press (World's Classics), 1939], 188).

s.20 ———— *The Merchant of Venice.* In *The Comedies of Shakespeare.* New York: Random House (Modern Library), n.d.

■ English public opinion was strongly moved in 1594 by the trial and hanging of Roderigo Lopez, Portuguese-Jewish physician to Queen Elizabeth. Lopez had been convicted of attempting to poison the Queen in exchange for a reward from the Spanish government. Catering to public furor over the case, the "Admiral's men" revived Christopher Marlowe's *The Jew of Malta,* which registered fifteen performances between the end of the Lopez trial and the end of 1594. A. L. Rowse believes that *The Merchant of Venice* was conceived by Shakespeare and his "Chamberlain's men" in a desire to outdo the rival theatrical company. Shylock is a greatly humanized version of Marlowe's Jew, Barnabas. Many scholars, however, see an allusion to Dr. Lopez in Gratiano's speech in Act 4, scene 1, comparing Shylock to the offspring of a wolf (*lupus* in Latin and therefore a near-homonym of the name Lopez). The passage cited occurs in the courtroom scene, when Gratiano rails against Shylock:

> Thou almost mak'st me waver in my faith
> To hold opinion with Pythagoras,
> That souls of animals infuse themselves
> Into the trunks of men: thy currish spirit
> Govern'd a wolf, who hang'd for human slaughter,
> Even from the gallows did his fell soul fleet,
> And whilst thou lay'st in thy unhallow'd dam,
> Infus'd itself in thee; for thy desires
> Are wolfish, bloody, starv'd, and ravenous.

s.21 Shearing, Joseph [pseudonym of Gabrielle Margaret Vere Campbell Long] *Airing in a Closed Carriage.* New York: Harper, 1943.

■ In the novel *Airing in a Closed Carriage*, Joseph Shearing retells the controversial Maybrick case and searches for the truth by studying character and motivation. When the Liverpool cotton merchant James Maybrick died in 1889, his young and pretty American wife, Florence, was accused by his brothers and servants of having administered arsenic to him. Underlying the accusation in Shearing's account was the hostility of the family, friends, and staff of James Maybrick (whom the novelist calls John Tyler) toward the Southern belle he married (renamed May), whose elegant upper-class style had never been accepted in Liverpool. Shearing downplays Florence Maybrick's real-life love affair with Alfred Brierley (Jerome Thorne in the novel) and conflates the several Maybrick brothers into a single character, Richard Tyler, who seeks revenge against May after she repels his advances. The author emphasizes May's girlhood use of arsenic under the supervision of her mother as a cosmetic face wash and traces John Tyler's long-standing arsenic-eating habit. The novel shows that with such a quantity of arsenic in the house, it would be difficult to point a finger at a poisoner; but the police found no problem in accepting Richard's accusations after being presented with "evidence" of arsenic he planted among May's belongings as well as the flypapers from which she extracted arsenic for cosmetic use, as Florence Maybrick claimed to have done.

In actuality, the motive that the Maybrick entourage presented to the police for murder was Florence's adultery and her expressed desire for a divorce. What the police and public did not know was that James Maybrick had struck his wife before witnesses, an act that, coupled with his adulterous relationship with a woman who had borne him several illegitimate children, would have given her the right to divorce without having to resort to murdering her husband.

Nonfictional studies of the Maybrick case have concluded that the evidence was insufficient to support the murder conviction, which led to Florence's imprisonment for fifteen years after commutation of the death sentence. Queen Victoria was adamantly opposed to Mrs. Maybrick's release, which was not ordered until after the queen's death. Whether guilty or innocent, Florence deserves credit for an important legal reform spawned by dissatisfaction with the verdict in her trial, the 1907 creation of the Court of Criminal Appeal. See Bernard Ryan with Michael Haver, QC, MP, *The Poisoned Life of Mrs. Maybrick* (London: William Kimber, 1977); Trevor L. Christie, *Etched in Arsenic* (Philadelphia: Lippincott, 1968).

Gabrielle Margaret Vere Campbell Long (1886–1952) wrote more than a hundred books under the pseudonyms Marjorie Bowen, Joseph Shearing, George Preedy, John Winch, Robert Page, and Margaret Campbell. In 1932 she began writing under the Joseph Shearing name novels based on famous crimes, most readily identifiable. Under that same pseudonym she also published nonfictional studies of Charlotte Corday (*The Angel of the Assassination*) and the poisoner Marie Lafarge (*The Lady and the Arsenic*). Under the name Marjorie Bowen, she wrote a biography of Sophie Dawes, a suspect in the mysterious death of her elderly lover, the Prince de Bourbon Condé (*The Ordeal of Sophie Dawes*). Also as Marjorie Bowen, she produced a novel about the Glencoe Massacre (*Glen O'Weeping*), and as George Preedy, fictional accounts of France's "Affair of the Poisons" (*The Poisoners*) and the mysterious Comte de Saint-Germain (*The Courtly Charlatan: The Enigmatic Comte de St. Germain*).

S.22 ———— *Blanche Fury*. London: Heinemann, 1939.

■ English obsessions with genealogy and estates in land converge in the James Blomfield Rush murder case, which is the basis for the novel *Blanche Fury* by Joseph Shearing. The 1849 massacre of the inhabitants of Stanfield Hall was motivated by Rush's harboring the groundless belief that he was the rightful owner of the Jermy family properties. Already in debt to the Jermys, Rush purchased the lease on Potash Farm, bringing himself to the verge of bankruptcy. To avoid foreclosure he forged documents canceling his debt to the Jermys and had his mistress/housekeeper Emily Sandford sign as a witness. To avoid exposure he disguised himself as a gypsy woman, broke into the house, and shot the Jermy father and son.

The novel, written in the style of a gothic romance, retells the case through the eyes of Blanche Fury, a governess and distant impoverished relative of the Furys of Clerc Hall (Stanfield Hall). She becomes the lover of Phillip Strangeways (Rush) and shares with him a hatred of the father and son who live in the great house. Strangeways feels a kinship with her but notes (perhaps with uncanny foresight) that the name Blanche Fury echoes the title of John Webster's drama *The White Devil*, quotations from which are scattered throughout the novel.

Although Blanche mirrors Emily Sandford in her love affair with the murderer and in her witnessing the forged document, there are several important differences between the two women. Blanche, as a relative of the Fury family, inherits the estate after the murders, while Emily Sandford was a complete outsider. In the novel Blanche's passionate love for Strangeways and hatred of the landowners suggest that she has a greater culpability in the crime. Her decision in the end to inform on Strangeways may also be partly designed as protection against the suspicions of the community. Emily Sandford, by contrast, tried to support Rush's alibi; but under pressure from the magistrate, she retracted her false statements and then remained immovable even under a vigorous cross-examination by Rush himself.

The Borowitz True Crime Collection holds four pieces of Staffordshire pottery memorializing the "popular" Rush murders: figurines of Rush and Sandford and miniatures of Stanfield Hall and Potash Farm.

S.23 ———— *The Crime of Laura Sarelle*. New York: Smith & Durrell, 1941.

■ This novel is a ghost story that links two Laura Sarelles who figure in murders separated by sixty years. The first Laura's husband murders her brother and is hanged. His crime weighs on the mind of his wife's later namesake. As in the case of John Donellan (hanged in 1781), on which the ancestral crime in the novel is based, the poison used is a distillation of the cherry laurel leaves that yield laurel water (prussic acid). The name of the poisonous plant is echoed in the first syllable of Laura's Christian name and the second syllable of her last name. Haunted by her predecessor, the second Laura poisons a hated brother and attempts to cast the guilt on her husband so that she will be free to marry the man she loves. Her brother, Sir Theodosius Sarelle (named after Donellan's victim Sir Theodosius Boughton, a brother-in-law whose wealth he coveted), had forbidden the love match. Another echo of the Donellan case is the name of the family house, Leppard Hall, recalling the Boughton residence, Lawford Hall. Shearing emphasizes that both Leppard Hall and its inhabitants are possessed by the past, when Laura's lover warns her brother: "You cannot get away from it, Theo, especially in an old place like Leppard Hall. You're living in those dead people's house, using their furniture, sleeping in their beds, with their portraits hanging on your walls. Everything you spend or have was theirs, or earned by them, or left by them. Their graves are only a few yards away, and there is some story about them that you very carefully conceal."

S.24 ——— *For Her to See.* [American title: *So Evil My Love.*] London: Hutchinson, 1947.
■ Joseph Shearing, in the novel *For Her to See*, interweaves two famous murder cases: the poisoning of Charles Bravo (see J.5) and the Brighton trunk murder for which Toni Mancini—waiter, companion of prostitutes, and man of many aliases—was tried and acquitted (see Jonathan Goodman, "A Coincidence of Corpses," in *The Railway Murders* [London: Alison & Busby, 1984], 131–66). Olivia Sacret (Mrs. Cox), the friend and companion of Susan Rue (Florence Bravo), is led by infatuation with her artist-lodger Mark Bellis (Mancini) to blackmail and murder. Bellis's charm and good looks work their spell on Mrs. Sacret, a naive widow of a missionary who fails to recognize clues to Bellis's criminal past even when he recounts several murders, including an unsolved case involving a body in a trunk. After he has run off with her valuables instead of eloping with her as promised, she examines one of his possessions he has left behind: "the old wide trunk that had served as a model's throne when he had painted her portrait. . . . It was empty, smelt unpleasantly and was smeared with dark brown stains. . . . There were coarse grey hairs stuck to the torn linen lining." But rather than link the trunk to Bellis's tales of murder, Mrs. Sacret assumes it had been used to hold paints or a dog. Only later does she discover from her lawyer that the name Bellis was one of many aliases of the artist-criminal who lived with various "unfortunates" and defrauded "foolish, inexperienced women who, romantic or sentimental, are easily gulled." The title, *For Her to See*, refers to Bellis's use of artistic means to show Mrs. Sacret how to get rid of George Rue (Charles Bravo): "He took his palette, thinned his colours with turpentine and quickly drew in little scenes. . . . First there was a man in bed, a group of figures standing by, then the women, one giving the other a small bottle, then a woman, painted large, pouring the contents of the bottle into a glass, then the man in bed again, receiving a glass from his nurse, then a shrouded corpse, and a funeral." The title can also be read figuratively to indicate Mrs. Sacret's blindness to the criminal character of Bellis. It is her failure "to see" his motives that makes the novel tantalizing, for the unreliable perceptions of Mrs. Sacret force the reader to question her understanding of events as they unfold.

S.25 ———— *The Lady and the Arsenic.* New York: A. S. Barnes, 1944.

■ Shearing describes this book as "a biography in the form of a novelette, such a tale as our grandparents might have read in the pages of *The Family Herald*." Yet her account, to which she applies modest fictional touches, scrupulously follows French nonfiction sources and ends with a nuanced weighing of the evidence. Although Shearing regards the prosecution as excessively zealous and the medical proof as weak, she looks for the solution of the mystery in the personality of Marie Lafarge, agreeing with the assessment of M. de Léautaud that she had a "romantic and extravagant character." Acknowledging the possibility that some of the arsenic might have been administered by Denis Barbier (who had committed forgeries in support of Charles Lafarge's business dealings and might have wished him dead), Shearing still concludes that Marie could well have fed her husband lethal doses of the poison. To complete her portrait of Madame Lafarge as a self-deluding fantasist, the author ends the book with Marie's exalted 1846 love letter to M. Cavel, inspector of the Central prison, whom she believed to share her passion.

In the course of her narrative, Shearing relates the tasty rumor that Marie Lafarge was an illegitimate grandniece of Louis-Philippe; she states that the king's refusal to intercede on her behalf was motivated by a desire to avoid the "scandal [that] would be caused by showing favour to one now well known to be closely, if illegitimately, connected with the House of Orleans."

S.26 ———— *Moss Rose.* London: Heinemann, 1934.

■ Shearing based her novel on the "Great Coram Street Murder" (London, 1873), in which Harriet Buswell was stabbed to death on Christmas Eve; a ship's chaplain, Dr. Gottfried Hessel, was acquitted of the crime and received the court's apology in addition to substantial compensation. The principal character in the novel, a dancer-prostitute named Belle Adair, who dances to the Moss Rose Waltz, suppresses evidence that incriminates murder suspect Pastor Morl, first extorting payments for her silence and later hoping to link her life with his. Ignoring a warning from police that he is likely to kill again, she becomes his next victim. Belle's fatal miscalculation was a belief in her power to dominate a violent man. She deluded herself with the thought that "however dangerous, strange or unstable he was, she could control him."

S.27 ———— *The Strange Case of Lucile Cléry.* New York: Harper, 1932.

■ This is the first of the fact-based crime novels to be written by Gabrielle Campbell Long under the pseudonym "Joseph Shearing." It is the tale of a French governess patterned after Henriette Deluzy, a central figure in the Duke de Praslin's butchery of his wife in their palace on the Faubourg St. Germain in 1847.

Shearing's vision of the governess, an illegitimate offspring of Bonapartists (named Lucile Cléry after her mother but working in Paris as Lucile Debelleyme), is markedly contrarian. Whereas most authors exculpate the real-life governess of having instigated the Duke of Praslin's crime, Shearing paints a merciless portrait of Lucile's character. Ambitious, proud, envious of her "betters," almost automatically manipulative, crippled by sexual repugnance, she seeks to acquire dominion over the household of the Duke du Boccage once she finds that he lives in estrangement from his neurasthenic, laudanum-addicted wife. Much to her surprise, Lucile falls in love with the duke even as she urges him to take extreme measures to remove his wife as an obstacle to their happiness. A weak man, he follows her hint that he should tamper with the heavy baldaquin above the duchess's bed; but that does not succeed. When the allies of the duchess succeed in driving Lucile out of the household, she arranges a secret interview with the duke and declares her love. Purporting to request only that he obtain a written recommendation from his wife, Lucile also demands that the duke take some unspecified "action" to remedy her plight. The murder follows, and the duke takes arsenic. Upon her release from prison after evidence of her involvement in the duke's crime is found insufficient, Lucile secretly rejoices that the scandal she caused has led to the downfall of Louis Philippe and the aristocrats who supported him: "she had always hoped to see a return of the Bonapartes, to whose patronage her family had owed whatever they possessed. Now this moment had really come. Prince Louis Napoleon was supposed to be hastening to Paris, there might be another Empire ruled over by a Bonaparte—and she had had some hand in it ... not through any direct interest or interference in politics, but merely as a governess in the household of M. du Boccage."

s.28 Shelley, Percy Bysshe   *The Cenci.* 1819. In *Complete Poems of Keats and Shelley*. New York: Modern Library, n.d.

■ The youth of Count Francesco Cenci was stormy and was marked not only by amorous adventure with the women of Rome but also by signs of perversion and a strain of violence that found frequent release in street brawling and attacks on servants and tenants. He was often imprisoned, but fines and money damages won him freedom. Most of his sons grew up in his own image of violence, but he liked them no better for the resemblance. Ironically bearing a surname meaning "rags," Cenci kept his sons in a state of destitution until three of them obtained a papal decree ordering him to provide them with maintenance. Francesco was also caught in a maze of lawsuits with his creditors, who challenged the restrictions he had placed on family properties, and with the Church, to which he twice made reparation for his father's thievery. He was always in litigation with members of his own family, his most sensational controversy being his unsuccessful (but prescient) claim that his son Giacomo was attempting to poison him.

Two of his sons died violently, Rocco being killed in the aftermath of a street fight and Cristoforo being murdered in Trastevere, in a love triangle. Tradition has Francesco rejoicing in his sons' deaths, but his joys were numbered. Creditors were closing in on the stingy count and a dowry was required for the marriage of his daughter Antonina. Worst of all, he was convicted in 1594 of sodomy and saved himself from the stake only by a payment of one-third of his estate to the Roman government.

In 1597, Francesco, with his daughter Beatrice and his second wife, Lucrezia, moved from Rome to the Castle of Petrella, perched high on a crag in the Abbruzzi. The castle was situated in the Kingdom of Naples just beyond the borders of the Papal States. Rumor was divided as to whether his purpose in moving was to devise new crimes beyond the reach of vigilant Roman authorities or, more prosaically, to escape his creditors. In any event, he seemed intent on keeping Beatrice under his control in the castle indefinitely so as to prevent her marriage and the burden of another dowry. What began as residence passed into imprisonment, with Beatrice and her stepmother being confined in a room whose windows were walled up and replaced by air vents. He beat Lucrezia with a riding spur when she upbraided him for an attempted sexual assault on her young son and struck Beatrice with a bullwhip after he discovered a letter she had written to her brother Giacomo seeking his help in obtaining her release.

From the violence and degradation to which he subjected his daughter and wife in the castle and from the largely financial grievances of his son Giacomo, a murder conspiracy gradually took form. Beatrice's lawyer, the eminent Prospero Farinaccio, was later to argue unsuccessfully, on the basis of inconclusive and conflicting testimony of two maids, that the principal murder motive was an incestuous attack by Francesco on Beatrice. The tradition and literature of the case seized on the incest claim as central to the tragedy. But nobody can read of the wretched treatment of the two women at La Petrella without finding Francesco's cruelty to be unnatural even in the absence of incest.

The murder conspiracy may be described as a tragedy of errors. Beatrice appears to have been the main force behind the crime, but the murderer was Olimpio Calvetti, castellan of La Petrella, with whom Beatrice had been having a love affair. Giacomo gave his consent to the murder from Rome but lent little assistance, except a supply of poison that could not be administered to Francesco because of his suspicious nature. Lucrezia wavered, but when the murder hour arrived, it was she who unlocked the door to her husband's bedroom. Assisted by Marzio Catalano, a tinker and sometime guitar teacher, Olimpio killed Francesco with a hammer. The count's body was thrown from the castle after the murderers clumsily enlarged a hole in a balcony in order to make it appear that the floor had given way. Suspicions of murder were immediately aroused, and they were increased by the overhasty burial of the count and the inept attempts of the conspirators to cover up evidence of the murder. On the orders of the Cenci family and their ally, Monsignore Mario Guerra (whom tradition later incorrectly identified as a suitor of Beatrice), Olimpio was assassinated to eliminate his testimony. However, Olimpio's accomplice, Marzio, who had been wandering through neighboring villages giving guitar lessons with Count Cenci's cloak on his back as payment and proof of his crime, was captured and confessed his part in the murder. After initial arrogant denials leading to continued questioning and to torture, Giacomo, Lucrezia, and Beatrice ultimately confessed. Giacomo and Lucrezia put the principal blame on Beatrice, and Beatrice blamed her dead lover, Olimpio.

Beatrice, Lucrezia, Giacomo, and a teen-aged brother, Bernardo (who at most may have concurred passively in Giacomo's consent to the murder), were sentenced to death in 1599. The brief of their principal defense counsel, Farinaccio, survives. He argued that Beatrice's part in the murder was justified by her father's incestuous assault and by her fear of its repetition. (In a note that he appended to a final edition of his brief prepared years later, Farinaccio conceded that the claim of the act of incest had not been proved.) The lawyer contended that Lucrezia had withdrawn from the conspiracy, and Giacomo, he urged, should not be punished more severely than his sister for coming to her defense. Finally, he argued that Bernardo was entitled to clemency because of his minority and dimwittedness. Bernardo was only seventeen at the time of the murder, but his mental incapacity was demonstrated by no better evidence than that he had difficulty with his Latin lessons.

All the defendants were condemned to death. It is conjectured that Pope Clement VIII might have been inclined to mercy had not another murder of a noble parent, Costanza Santacroce, entirely without extenuating circumstances, occurred in Rome while he was considering the Cenci case. In any event, the Pope granted a reprieve only to young Bernardo, who was, however, condemned to witness the executions and thereafter to serve in prison galleys.

The executions were cruel. Giacomo was clubbed to death and the two women were beheaded. Beatrice was only twenty-two when she died, but she looked younger and is remembered as a beauty. Even at the execution, her unusual hold on the public sympathy and imagination was apparent. Young girls placed garlands on her head while it lay at the foot of the scaffold, and large mourning crowds followed as her body was taken to its resting place in the Church of San Pietro in Montorio.

In the seventeenth century fanciful accounts of the case were published that purported to have been written immediately after the executions but may have been written decades later. One such version inspired Shelley to write his drama *The Cenci* in 1819. A manuscript purporting to have been copied from the archives of the Cenci Palace was given to the poet during his travels in Italy. In a preface to his play, he recalled that when he arrived in Rome, he "found that the story of the Cenci was a subject not to be mentioned in Italian society without awakening a deep and breathless interest." Shelley was strongly drawn to the figure of Beatrice, "a most gentle and amiable being, a creature formed to adorn and be admired, and thus violently thwarted from her nature by the necessity of circumstance and opinion." At the same time, his anticlerical emotions were aroused by what he saw as evidence of corruption at work in the Pope's judgment. "The old man [the count] had during his life repeatedly bought his pardon from the Pope for capital crimes of the most enormous and unspeakable kind," and the Pope, as a consequence, "probably felt that whoever killed the Count Cenci deprived his treasury of a certain and copious source of revenue." Shelley even asserted that the papal government had attempted to suppress the facts relating to its handling of the Cenci case and that the circulation of the manuscript he had received had been "until very lately, a matter of some difficulty."

Shelley intended his play for public performance and even dreamt of Edmund Kean in the role of Count Francesco. But he recognized that "the story of the Cenci is indeed eminently fearful and monstrous: anything like a dry exhibition of it on the stage would be insupportable." It was necessary, therefore, to "increase the ideal, and diminish the actual horror of the events." As one concession to public taste, Shelley muted the incest theme;

Mary Shelley thought that his strongest allusion was a curse of Cenci that if Beatrice should have a child, it may be

> A hideous likeness of herself, that as
> From a distorting mirror, she may see
> Her image mixed with what she most abhors,
> Smiling upon her from her nursing breast. (4.1.146–49)

According to Shelley, the highest moral purpose of drama was "the teaching of the human heart, through its sympathies and antipathies, the knowledge of itself." The drama was not, in his view, the place for the enforcement of dogmas. Therefore, though Beatrice might have done better in life to win Count Francesco from his evil ways by peace and love, a theater audience would yawn at his conversion; the real themes of the case—revenge, retaliation, and atonement—were also the fabric of effective drama.

Holding these opinions on the function of drama, Shelley set out to focus his play on the clash of passionate human beings. Although his treatment of the case is consequently less ideological than some of the modern settings, images repeatedly used by the poet highlight themes of the inadequacy of human justice and the struggle of youth with old age and authority. These two themes are combined in Cardinal Camillo's quotation of the Pope's explanation of unwillingness to punish Francesco for an impious celebration of the death of two sons:

> In the great war between the old and young
> I, who have white hairs and a tottering body,
> Will keep at least blameless neutrality. (2.2.38–40)

In Shelley's version, Beatrice and her co-conspirators are selfishly urged on by the young priest Orsino (the poet's name for the historical Monsignore Guerra) in the hope that the murder will put Beatrice and the family fortune in his power. Beatrice, however, dominates the play. After her father's crime against her (which gains in horror by never being expressly named), Shelley's heroine moves successively from a sense of degradation to a desire for self-purification, revenge, declaration of moral innocence, and resigned preparation for death (see Albert Borowitz, "Portraits of Beatrice: The Cenci Case in Literature and Opera," in *A Gallery of Sinister Perspectives: Ten Crimes and a Scandal* [Kent, Ohio: Kent State Univ. Press, 1982], 11–20).

s.29 Shew, E. Spencer   *A Companion to Murder* and *A Second Companion to Murder*. New York: Knopf 1961, 1962.

■ These "dictionaries of death" were written by a former criminal-court reporter who became Honorable Secretary of the Parliamentary Lobby Journalists, the elite press corps of political journalists attached to the House of Commons. Since the entries are models of concise crime narration, the books can be read from cover to cover for pure enjoyment as well as providing a reliable research source. The two volumes, each arranged alphabetically by criminal, are divided according to the weapons used; the first volume deals with poison, shooting, suffocation, drowning, and strangling; and the second with blunt and sharp instruments of great variety and inventiveness.

S.30 Sinclair, Upton   *Boston*. 2 vols. New York: Albert & Charles Boni, 1928.

■ Sinclair's massive novel of the trial of anarchists Nicola Sacco and Bartolomeo Vanzetti for a holdup murder has been judged by scholar Louis Joughin to contain "a thorough review of almost all the [case's] important features" and to be "accurate in detail to the degree that one would expect of a scientific study" (G. Louis Joughin and Edmund M. Morgan, *The Legacy of Sacco and Vanzetti* [New York: Harcourt Brace, 1948], 448).

Cornelia Thornwell, widow of a former governor of Massachusetts, asserts her new independence by leaving home to take a job in Plymouth's cordage works. There she meets Vanzetti. After learning of the charges brought against her new friend, she and another liberal maverick of the Thornwell clan, her granddaughter, Betty Alvin, join the struggle to defend the two anarchists.

Cornelia, wedded to the hopeless cause, becomes increasingly aware that her allegiance to Sacco and Vanzetti has severed her from the more comfortable allegiances of the past: "A world of lies, a world run on the basis of lies, so that when you talked about truth-telling you were a Utopian and a dreamer; worse yet, a traitor to your friends, to your business associates, your family, your class! A fastidious person, an ivory-tower esthete, preferring your own peace of mind to the rights of those who had taken you into their confidence, assuming that you would play the game as everybody else played it, for your profit and comfort as well as their own!"

Another true-crime-based work by Sinclair is his self-published 1925 play *Bill Porter: A Drama of O. Henry in Prison*.

S.31 Sitwell, Osbert, and Margaret Barton   *Sober Truth: A Collection of Nineteenth-Century Episodes Fantastic, Grotesque and Mysterious*. 1930. Preface Osbert Sitwell. London: Macdonald, 1944.

■ In his preface, Sitwell credits his childhood nurse with imparting enthusiasms (including her love of murder reports) that were at odds with the "certainty and security" of the Victorian age. *Sober Truth* is a collection of firsthand accounts of Victorian crimes and sensations which "show that under the stream of high-minded platitudes the most extraordinary events, that should have been enough to induce in any mind that followed them both a certain scepticism and a terror and respect for the unknown and unknowable, were in progress."

In Sitwell's view, the "icy-hearted, calculating slaughters" that opened and closed the era could only have occurred in the science-worshiping nineteenth century: "for with Burke and Hare the murders were committed in order to gain money by supplying the medical market with enough fresh corpses for dissection while Jack the Ripper displayed an anatomical skill."

The collection also documents other persons and subjects (mainly English and French) that were popular with nineteenth-century readers fond of true crime, scandal, and historical mystery: the impostor who called herself Caraboo, Princess of Jevasu (inspiring the 1994 film *Princess Caraboo*, with Kevin Kline and Phoebe Cates); Prince Louis Napoleon's escape from Ham prison; the ardently pursued dancer Lola Montez; the Duc de Praslin, who murdered his duchess in Paris; the "false dauphins" who claimed to be Louis XVII; Madeleine Smith, accused of poisoning her lover; Constance Kent, confessed killer of her little stepbrother; the Tichborne impostor; and the arrest and trial of Captain Alfred Dreyfus.

s.32 Sitwell, Sacheverell *Ames Damnees* [Damned Souls]. In *Splendours and Miseries*. London: Faber & Faber, 1943.

■ This four-part narrative of the case of Madeleine Smith, released by the Scottish verdict of "not proven" from charges of poisoning her blackmailing lover, Emile L'Angelier, is one of the most beautifully written crime essays in English (see Fig. 13). The first section is a revery, in prose-poetry, that evokes the first night of love spent by the doomed couple in the Woods of Rowaleyn. Emile's journey from Glasgow to meet Madeleine is recalled from the young Frenchman's viewpoint, and his emotions are recreated with more sympathy than is generally shown by crime writers for this pomaded lady-killer: "And now the storm blows into his heart and blood. Beginning with a gentle torment that is mostly pleasure. With pauses of dread, and moments when he wonders why he was ever born. When he wishes he were a small babe, but born to this opportunity. For he was destined to this."

In the following chapters of his story, Sitwell adopts a cooler style as he recounts the familiar tale of Madeleine's engagement to her wealthy neighbor, Mr. Minnoch, and Emile's threats to deliver Madeleine's love letters to her father. In a reconstruction of the former lovers' final meeting, Sitwell speculates that Madeleine gave herself to Emile one last time to put him in the mood to accept a cup of poisoned cocoa. At the end, the mood of the essay's prelude returns: "But, if the soul be immortal, they will have met again. For ever, in deception and concealment. This young girl, who lived to be so old, lies restless, and gets up, continually, to see if her little sister is asleep beside her. She does not haunt us with the cup and spoon, as she stirs the poison. But she dissimulates, and is awake while all are sleeping. Listening for the tap of his stick upon the railing outside her window; and coming to the door to open it. A ghost in the big city; and in the woods of Rowaleyn. Upon a May evening, when blood fell on the anemone and the compact of tragedy was sealed and signed."

s.33 Sleeman, James L. *Thug, or, A Million Murders*. London: Sampson, Low, Marston, ca. 1930.

■ Colonel Sleeman pays tribute to the accomplishments of his illustrious grandfather, Major General Sir William Henry Sleeman, who, between 1829 and 1840, largely suppressed the three-hundred-year-old hereditary cult of the Thugs ("deceivers"). These mysterious slayers ritually strangled Indian travelers with a yellow-and-white strip of cloth (*ruhmal*) in obedience to Kali (or Bhowani), the goddess of destruction or retribution. The Thugs often occupied respectable positions in the community and spent their vacations as members of murder gangs that worked India's roads and rivers. The Thugs' technique was to win the confidence of their intended victims by posing as merchants, soldiers, or paupers willing to join forces with other wayfarers against the dangers that lay ahead. After traveling and camping with their prey, frequently for many days, the Thugs led them to prearranged places of murder and burial (*beles*), where they then strangled and robbed them.

Author Sleeman describes the mythical origin of the cult of Thuggee:

The legendary origin of this strange and horrible religion, according to the Thugs, dated back to a time when the world was pestered with a monstrous demon, so gigan-tic in stature that the deepest ocean reached no higher than its waist, who devoured mankind as fast as it was created. Bhowani, or Kali, as she is variously called, tried to kill this horrid prodigy with a sword, but from every drop of blood spilt there sprang a new demon, until the hellish brood multiplied to such a degree that she realised the impossibility of completing her task unaided. In this dilemma Bhowani brushed the sweat from her arm and from it created two men, to each of whom she gave a strip of cloth, torn from the hem of her garment, and commanded them to strangle the de-mons, thus overcoming the blood difficulty. These legendary progenitors of Thuggee worked with such skill and vigour that soon all the demons were slain, and the goddess gave them the *ruhmal*, or strip of cloth, as a reward for their assistance, bidding them transmit it to their posterity with the injunction to destroy all men who were not of their kindred.

In homicidal worship of their dark goddess, the Thugs claimed only Indian victims and generally spared women unless their killing was necessary to eliminate witnesses.

William Sleeman's triumphant campaign against the Thugs in his roles as investigator and magistrate was based on a three-part strategy. Among the first Englishmen to understand the hereditary and religious bases of Thug murder, he painstakingly prepared genealogy charts of the ritual killers so that he could eliminate them root and branch. He also drew on his linguistic skills to elucidate the secret language that had permitted the Thugs to communicate without fear of discovery. Finally, as his successes mounted, he was able to pressure many cult members to inform on their comrades.

Heroic efforts of individual administrators, however, were not in themselves sufficient to eradicate Thuggee. Just as America's battle against twentieth-century organized crime was aided by the RICO statute criminalizing racketeering activity, Sleeman's crusade required the backing of special legislation. An 1836 act made membership in a Thug gang punishable with life imprisonment at hard labor and authorized the trial of Thugs in centralized courts rather than mandating proceedings at widely scattered crime scenes.

To dramatize the remorselessness of the Thugs, James Sleeman quotes liberally from their courtroom confessions to his grandfather. Among the most prolific of the killers was the gang chief Feringeea, who, as the author observes, was immortalized in Eugène Sue's novel *The Wandering Jew* (1844–45).

Another biography of Sir William Henry Sleeman is Sir Francis Tuker's *The Yellow Scarf* (London: J. M. Dent, 1961). An early account of Thuggee was published in an 1839 three-volume novel by Captain P. Meadows Taylor, *Confessions of a Thug*. Meadows Taylor was a pioneering investigator of Thuggee while briefly serving as superintendent of police in Bolarum. The Borowitz True Crime Collection holds the first edition of *Confessions of a Thug*, together with an abridged one-volume edition, with an introduction by Brian Rawson (New York: Stein & Day, 1968), as well as a copy of James Sleeman's *Thug*, inscribed by the author in 1938 for Air Chief Marshal Sir Philip E. Brooke-Popham, governor and commander-in-chief, Kenya.

s.34 Smith, Edward H. *Famous Poison Mysteries.* New York: Dial Press, 1927.

■ Smith's purpose in assembling this collection of twenty-two poisoning cases, famous and obscure, is to demonstrate his thesis that the poisoner's craft "is by long odds the least secure, the most telltale of all the methods of murder." The cases he studies all have ties with America, either because the crime was committed in the United States or because the accused, like Dr. Crippen and Florence Maybrick, was American-born.

Of special interest are Smith's chapters on two linked poisoning trials, those of Carlyle W. Harris and Dr. Robert W. Buchanan. Harris, a medical student at Columbia University's College of Physicians and Surgeons, was apparently inspired by lectures on the pharmaceutical and toxicological properties of morphine to turn the drug to practical application. He was executed in 1893 for the poisoning of his secret wife, Helen Potts, after the administration of morphine was detected by observation of the victim's symmetrically contracted pupils. Two years later an unlicensed Canadian physician practicing in Greenwich Village, Robert Buchanan, followed Harris to the electric chair, although he had told friends the bungling Harris could have covered up his crime by adding belladonna to the toxic capsule so as to counteract morphine's impact on the pupils. When Buchanan followed his own advice in disposing of a wealthy but otherwise inconvenient second wife, restaurateur Richard Macomber remembered and testified to his damning words. The Buchanan case is the basis of John Dickson Carr's mystery novel *The Sleeping Sphinx* (New York: Harper, 1947).

Smith believes that Harris was guilty but insane; nevertheless, he concludes that "a verdict of guilty has rarely been returned against a man upon more incomplete evidence." Buchanan—who "died the death of a rogue who is also a fool"— was convicted partly on the strength of a vulgar letter that he wrote to a friend shortly after the death of his second wife.

Other poisoners considered in Smith's volume are candy poisoner Cordelia Botkin; Roland Molineux; and Dr. J. Milton Bowers.

s.35 Smith-Hughes, Jack *Eight Studies in Justice.* London: Cassell, 1953.

■ "Puzzled Justice, or Temptation and the Elder" relates with anti-Puritanical delight the two inconclusive trials of William Gardiner, Primitive Methodist elder, for the 1902 stabbing murder of pregnant chorister Rose Harsent in the Suffolk village of Peasenhall. Gardiner, father of eight children, had been suspected of carrying on an affair with Rose, partly on the basis of rumors spread by a pair of Peeping Toms. Although the two juries that heard the case failed to reach a verdict, Smith-Hughes agrees with the eleven jurors on the first panel who voted in favor of conviction. Regarding Gardiner's possible motive, Smith-Hughes comments: "The murderer might not have been the father of the girl's unborn child, but he probably had good reason to suppose that he would be given the credit for her condition." See w.16.

In "Retarded Justice, or The Wicked Squire," Smith-Hughes discusses the 1759 trial of licentious William Andrew Horne for murder of his illegitimate child 35 years before. According to Smith-Hughes, Horne "established a British record for retarded vengeance on a capital charge that is unlikely to be beaten." Horne, who by primogeniture had become a Buckinghamshire squire, was condemned on the testimony of his brother Charles, who had participated in the crime. William had made the fatal error of turning Charles out of the family home and thereafter "would not give the least assistance to him, nor a morsel of bread to his hungry children begging at their uncle's door."

"Outraged Justice, or The Perils of a Lapsed Craft" recounts the trial of English body snatchers John Bishop and Thomas Williams. The two men were in-laws, but it is not easy to define their relationship: Smith-Hughes comments that since Bishop had married Williams's stepmother, and Williams subsequently wed Bishop's half-sister Rhoda, Bishop was either his father-in-law or brother-in-law. More to the point was their collaboration in the 1831 murder of a young boy (identified by some witnesses as Carlo Ferrari, an Italian street performer who slung a cage with two white mice around his neck). Bishop and Williams were arrested while making a clumsy attempt to sell the body of the youth to hospital anatomists with the participation of a middleman named James May. After conviction of murder, Bishop and Williams were hanged, and May, benefiting from a reprieve, was transported to Australia. As a result of the public outcry over the crime, England, ten days after the executions of the two murderers, passed a law regulating dissection. Smith-Hughes regards the statute as "a piece of more or less panic legislation [that] has, for once, stood the test of time." (The Borowitz True Crime Collection owns a nineteenth-century English child's plate depicting Carlo Ferrari, who was known as "the Poor Italian Boy" [Fig. 9].)

The article "Republican Justice, or Who Killed the Judge?" examines the mysterious 1934 death of Judge Albert Prince in the wake of the Stavisky fraud and corruption scandals in France (see M.37). Prince, who, as second in command of the financial section of the French prosecutor's office (the Parquet), had postponed legal action against Stavisky in a period ending in 1931, was found decapitated by a train near Dijon, his wrist bound to a rail. He had been summoned to Dijon by a false telephone call reporting that his mother had been taken to a clinic for emergency treatment of a strangulated hernia. Smith-Hughes theorizes that Prince, who was under investigation for his role in the government's failure to move against Stavisky, committed suicide, possibly in a manner calculated to simulate murder. The author also suggests, rather fancifully, that in placing the fictitious telephone call Prince may have been inspired by the Wallace murder case in Liverpool (see G.23).

In another essay, "Royal Justice, or The Conscience of a Citizen-King," Smith-Hughes concludes that King Louis-Philippe stifled a murder prosecution in the mysterious death of the Duke de Bourbon, elderly protector of Baroness de Feuchères (Sophie Dawes) (see A.13).

Barrister Smith-Hughes subjects the evidence in each case to close examination. However, his narratives are sometimes impeded by ironic use of euphemism and circumlocution, a stylistic quirk found in many admirers of William Roughead. For example, if a cat has killed pet mice, Smith-Hughes writes that "the cat had terminated their existence after a two-month sojourn."

s.36 ——— *Nine Verdicts on Violence*. London: Cassell, 1956.

■ Two Victorian murder cases launch this varied collection. In "Slaughter in Slough, or Who Swung the Chopper?" Smith-Hughes presents a tantalizing riddle. Augustus Payne, an employee in the Revilles' butcher shop, was found not guilty of having wielded the chopper that severed the head and neck of Mrs. Ann Reville as she sat unsuspecting at her desk. Smith-Hughes suspects that the killer was butcher Hezekiah Reville, who "had decided to kill his wife and to put the blame on Payne who, perhaps only because he was growing up, had been something of a nuisance of late."

The second Victorian case is a milestone in the history of England's treatment of the insanity defense ("The Broken Engagement: A Controversial Reprieve"). In 1863 George Victor Townley stabbed Elizabeth Caroline (Bessie) Goodwin to death in a country lane after she broke off their engagement. After the jury rendered a guilty verdict, Baron Martin, the trial judge, imposed the death sentence while sobbing, because he suspected Townley might no longer be sane. Before Home Secretary Sir George Gray could consider the insanity issue, the condemned man's solicitor hastily secured a certification of Townley's lunacy under a forgotten statute and thereby obtained a respite from the scheduled execution. A firestorm of controversy arose regarding Townley's legal responsibility, but Gray, following tradition, converted the respite from capital punishment into a permanent reprieve. In 1865 Townley committed suicide in prison by vaulting over a staircase railing.

Two essays on nineteenth-century French trials follow. Captain Auguste Doineau was twice convicted of crimes: complicity in the 1856 murder of an Algerian chieftain and participation in the liberation of Marshal Bazaine, who had been imprisoned on the island of Sainte Marguerite for surrendering too readily to the Prussians at Metz ("Death in the Desert: A Study in Political Morality"). Smith-Hughes also writes of Abbé Albert Bruneau, whom he regards as justly convicted of murdering Abbé Constant Fricot in 1894 ("Unpleasantness at the Rectory, or A Wolf in Priest's Clothing"; see B.64). And a trio of Kenyan cases includes the acquittal of five Samburu tribesmen charged with murdering Theodore Cowper Powys, son of novelist T. F. Powys. The younger Powys most likely cracked his skull in falling from a horse that reared before a lion ("Song of the Vultures, or Samburu Witchcraft").

Two cases from Georgian England complete the volume. One of these, "Who Killed Lord Charles? or A Conspiracy of Silence," reports the bewildered investigation into the death of Lord Charles Townshend, who was shot by pistol (placed in his mouth) while riding with his brother in a carriage after being returned to his seat in Parliament. He and his brother, Lord Frederick Townshend, rector of Stiffkey (less famous than his modern successor, who sought to win the souls of prostitutes), were both lunatics, so murder, suicide, or an accident occurring in extravagant horseplay were all equally plausible explanations.

S.37 ———— *Six Ventures in Villainy*. London: Cassell, 1955.

■ The first essay, "Lord Cochrane's Uncle Andrew," relates the audacious 1814 London stock-trading fraud that led to Lord Cochrane's sentence to the pillory and twelve months' imprisonment after trial before Lord Ellenborough. One of the principal conspirators was a former vintner named Peter Holloway, whose speculations left him with stock, currently valued at £20,000, that he desired to unload at a higher price. Lord Cochrane's rascally uncle, Andrew Cochrane Johnstone, had also been plunging on the stock exchange, and neither he nor his nephew were averse to turning a quick profit. Holloway conceived a brilliant plan: he would drive up the stock-exchange prices by spreading a rumor that Napoleon was dead and that Paris had declared for Louis XVIII. The false report would be spread by a party of bogus French military officers who would parade through London with the white cockade of the Bourbons in their hats. This scheme was somehow communicated to a bankrupt adventurer, Charles Random de Berenger, who was a dining companion of Cochrane Johnstone and his brother. De Berenger supported the rumors of Napoleon's fall in the guise of uniformed Lieutenant-Colonel du Bourg, who claimed to be newly arrived from France with dispatches confirming the change of regime.

When the rumors were abroad and stocks skyrocketed, the conspirators sold out at handsome prices; the Stock Exchange found that Cochrane Johnstone and Lord Cochrane registered gains of £4,931 and £2,470, respectively. At his ensuing trial, Lord Cochrane was incriminated by evidence that de Berenger had taken refuge at a new address of Cochrane in London that was not widely known. Smith-Hughes has no doubt of Lord Cochrane's guilt but attributes a more central role in the conspiracy to his uncle.

Richard Patch is the villain of the piece in "Dissolution of Partnership: A Shot in the Dark." Previously foreman of Isaac Blight's ship-dismantling business at Rotherhithe, South London, Patch was taken into partnership but fraudulently avoided paying his capital share while at the same time helping Blight evade the firm's creditors. Having decided to eliminate his majority partner, Patch first stage-managed a murder attempt by persons unknown, firing a shot through Blight's shutters at night when he was away on business. When Blight returned, Patch made a second nocturnal attack with deadlier effect, killing Blight with a bullet fired through the back parlor window where his partner, contrary to custom, was sitting. Patch was convicted and hanged on the strength of circumstantial evidence, including proof of his schemes to avoid financial obligations to his victim. Though he accepts the verdict, Smith-Hughes suggests that the evidence of fraud and propinquity to the fatal shot was no stronger than in the case of Donald Merrett, acquitted in the death of his mother whose name he was convicted of forging (see N.7).

Other cases studied in this collection are the rebellion against William Bligh's rule as governor of New South Wales, Australia ("Macarthur's Sheep: The Reluctant Mutineer"); and the acquittal of the lascivious Lord Baltimore of the rape of Sarah (Sally) Woodcock, a milliner whom he had abducted and brought to his house. In the latter case, the jury returned its verdict for the defendant one hundred minutes after the Lord Chief Justice had instructed that "however unwarrantable Lord Baltimore's conduct in gaining possession of Miss Woodcock, he would not be guilty of rape if she had consented before he lay with her."

s.38 ———— *Unfair Comment upon Some Victorian Murder Trials.* London: Cassell, 1951.
■ Barrister Smith-Hughes closely analyzes the records of courtroom proceedings in seven murder trials, including three in which he believes male murderers were wrongly acquitted. Of these, the most famous is twenty-nine-year-old Edmund Pook, epileptic son of a Greenwich printer, prosecuted for battering to death with a lathing hammer seventeen-year-old Jane Clouson, his family's former domestic servant. Clouson, two months pregnant, was found in the early morning of April 26, 1871, clinging to life in a country lane near Eltham. It was the police theory that she had been Pook's mistress and that he had smashed her face to prevent identification. Smith-Hughes attributes amorous Edmund's acquittal to police bungling, the hostility of the trial judge, and the hearsay rule's exclusion of Clouson's expectation, confided to a friend shortly before her death, that Pook planned on elopement. In the author's view, Pook's guilt was established conclusively by the fact that Edmund took pains to establish a false alibi even before the police had identified the victim.

The collection also includes the celebrated prosecution of Captain Thomas Dudley and Edwin Stephens for the 1884 murder and cannibalization of cabin-boy Richard Parker in a lifeboat on the high seas (killed in order to provide nourishment for the other shipwreck survivors). The defendants' death sentence was commuted to six months' hard labor. Smith-Hughes quotes an anonymous letter to the *Times* noting the strong similarity of the case to Edgar Allan Poe's tale "The Narrative of Arthur Gordon Pym"; the correspondence called the Dudley-Stephens murder "nature's most outrageous plagiarism in fiction."

s.39 Snow, C[harles] P[ercy] *The Sleep of Reason.* New York: Scribner, 1968.
■ This novel in Lord Snow's *Strangers and Brothers* series is derived from the so-called Moors murder trial. In 1966, Ian Brady, aged twenty-seven, and his mistress, Myra Hindley, twenty-three, were sentenced to life imprisonment for the murder of seventeen-year-old Edward Evans and two preadolescent children, Lesley Ann Downey and John Kilbride. (More specifically, Brady was convicted of the murder of all three victims; Hindley was found guilty of the murder of Evans and Downey and of harboring Brady in connection with his murder of Kilbride.) The trial derived its sobriquet from the fact that the victims' bodies were discovered buried on the moors near Manchester. All the murders were brutal and preceded by either sexual assault or torture. The interest of the murderers

in de Sade, torture, and Nazism was documented by Brady's collection of books, which he bundled into suitcases and checked at a parcel room at Manchester Central Station prior to the last murder. The sufferings of little Lesley Downey and her pleas for mercy were recorded by the murderers on a tape stored with their pornography collection, and they had also recorded their questioning of a friend of Lesley's with respect to the missing girl.

In determining to insert a crime resembling the Moors case into his roman fleuve, C. P. Snow was able to select from a number of alternative methods of relating the trial to the lives of the principal characters: the use of the trial as a public event in which the characters would express and develop views purely in the roles of citizens; the introduction of a character into the processes of the trial in a professional capacity; or the establishment of a personal relationship among the principal characters and the participants in the crime. Snow elected to make one of the accused murderesses Cora Ross, a niece of George Passant (childhood friend of Lewis Eliot, protagonist of the *Strangers and Brothers* series). She and Kitty Pateman, with whom she is having a love affair, are accused of torturing and murdering an eight-year-old child. Snow's decision to establish Passant's personal tie with one of the murderesses does not appear to have been made for technical considerations alone. The close relation between the observers and the trial is very much in keeping with the point of view from which events are generally seen in Snow's fiction. He is primarily concerned in his novels with personal and social relations within relatively small groups, and the impact of the outside world and of contemporary history is recorded in the reactions and interreactions of the group members.

Lewis Eliot seems to speak for Snow in rejecting the possibility of identifying specific ideological influences as the sources of the criminal act committed by Pateman and Ross: "Was there ever any single cause of any action, particularly of action such as this? Yes, they must have been affected by the atmosphere around them; yes, they were more likely to go to the extreme in their sexual tastes. Perhaps it made it easier for them to share their fantasies. But between those fantasies and what they had done, there was still the unimaginable gap. Of course, there were influences. But only people like them—predisposed to commit sadistic horrors, anyway, would have played on to the lethal end. If they had not had these influences, there would have been others."

In expressing this view, Snow appears to part company with his wife, the novelist Pamela Hansford Johnson, who, in her book *On Iniquity* (New York: Scribner, 1967), blamed the Moors murders on pornography and the affectless society.

The views of Snow, Johnson, and other writers on the Moors murders are discussed in Albert Borowitz, "The Snows on the Moors: C. P. Snow and Pamela Hansford Johnson on the Moors Murder Case," in *Innocence and Arsenic: Studies in Crime and Literature* (see B.28).

s.40 Soulié, Maurice *La mort et la résurrection de M. de la Pivardière*. In series *Énigmes et drames judiciaires d'autrefois*. Paris: Perrin, 1926.

■ On the evening of August 15, 1698, Charles-Louis de la Pivardière was received coldly by his wife Marie at their home in Berry—for good reason, since Marie had discovered that her husband was living a bigamous life in Auxerre as Monsieur Duboucher, a bailiff married to an innkeeper's daughter. By the morning after the quarrel, Charles-Louis had disappeared. A housemaid declared that she had seen Marie and her reputed lover, the family chaplain Sylvain Charotz, murder their master, and another deposed to having seen him weltering in blood on his bed. Murder proceedings ensued, but under the protection of a safe conduct obtained from Louis XIV by "Madame Duboucher" to ward off bigamy proceedings, Charles-Louis de la Pivardière appeared in court to proclaim his survival and Madame de la Pivardière's innocence. Accused of imposture, Monsieur de la Pivardière ultimately proved his identity to the satisfaction of Attorney General (later Chancellor) Henri-François d'Aguesseau, whose powerful arguments resulted in dismissal of the murder charges. Purporting to rely on "oral history," author Soulié casts his narrative in the form of a nonfiction novel, inventing dialogue and thoughts but remaining true for the most part to the eighteenth-century accounts of this intriguing identity controversy.

s.41 Soyinka, Wole   *Death and the King's Horseman.* New York: Hill & Wang, 1987.

■ In 1986 Nigerian playwright Soyinka became the first African to win the Nobel Prize for Literature. Based on events that took place in 1946 in Oyo, a Yoruba city dating from ancient times, *Death and the King's Horsemen*, regarded as Soyinka's masterpiece, portrays the disastrous confrontation between British criminal laws and ritual suicide mandated by Nigerian religion. When the village king died, it was the duty of his ritual attendant, or Horseman, to "commit death" and accompany him to their ancestral heaven. British District Officer Simon Pilkings is informed by his Nigerian subordinate, Sergeant Amusa, of the Horseman Elesin's intention to kill himself that night "as a result of native custom." Amusa's report concludes with a bow to Western law proscribing suicide attempts: "Because this is criminal offense I await further instruction at charge office." In order to prevent Elesin's suicide, Pilkings orders him imprisoned in the barred cellar of the British residency, where slaves used to be stored. Pilkings's plan goes tragically awry, for Elesin's son, Western-educated Olunde, assumes the role of the Horseman by killing himself in his disgraced father's place. When his son's body is brought to him, Elesin strangles himself with the loop of his chain.

Soyinka decries the interpretation of his play as a "clash of cultures," explaining that "the confrontation in the play is largely metaphysical, contained in the human vehicle which is Elesin and the universe of the Yoruba mind—the world of the living, the dead and the unborn."

s.42 Spark, Muriel   *Aiding and Abetting.* New York: Doubleday, 2001.

■ John Bingham, the seventh Earl of Lucan and descendant of the major-general who ordered the ill-fated "Charge of the Light Brigade," was apparently as clumsy as he was brutal. If the verdict of a coroner's jury is to be credited, in November 1974 Lord Lucan bludgeoned to death his children's nanny, Sandra Rivett, in the darkened cellar of his family home in Lower Belgrave Street, London, and stuffed her corpse into a mailbag, having mistaken her for the intended victim, his estranged wife, Veronica. When Veronica came upon the scene looking for Sandra, Lucan attacked her with the same weapon, a length of lead piping bound in surgical tape; but Lady Lucan, bleeding from head wounds, escaped to a neighborhood pub to raise an alarm.

Patrick Marnham, a journalist for *Private Eye* at the time of the murder, believes that Lord Lucan was guilty of conspiracy to kill his wife but that the attacks were carried out by a hit man who had not performed up to professional standards. See Patrick Marnham, *Trail of Havoc: In the Steps of Lord Lucan* (London: Viking, 1987).

The motive for the murder plot is hard to unriddle. Lord Lucan, whose misfortunes in gambling belied his nickname "Lucky," was heavily in debt and may have hoped to regain control of the family home. Marnham, however, places primary emphasis on the fact that Lucan had lost custody of his children to Veronica after a bitter court battle in which evidence was offered that he had tried to strangle her. The adverse court ruling, according to Marnham, set Lucan on his fatal course: "Lucan wanted to recover custody of his children and continue to live in England. Having exhausted his legal remedies, he was driven to extra-legal action: crime. Having concluded that his wife was mad, unfit to look after his children, implacable and a more plausible witness than he, he decided that she would have to die."

Lucan disappeared shortly after the Belgravia attacks and has never resurfaced to the present day. Marnham presents a compelling case that Lucan's friends, blinded as he was by outdated notions of class honor and privilege, aided him to elude the police and maintained him in his long years of hiding.

Perhaps Marnham's theory that Lucan employed a killer (to which Muriel Spark refers in *Aiding and Abetting*) influenced the novelist to introduce two characters, "Lucky" and Walker, who pretend with equal adamancy to be the fugitive Lucan. One may in fact be the earl and the other a confederate who assists him in raising funds to defray the expenses of life on the run. In Paris the two men consult Dr. Hildegard Wolf, a self-styled psychiatrist who once, like Lucan, had blood on her hands: as Beate Pappenheim, she had worked "miracles" as a fake stigmatic who had smeared her simulated wounds with menstrual blood. Threatened by Walker with exposure of her fraudulent past, Dr. Wolf flees from the Lucan doubles, while Lacey Twickenham, daughter of one of the earl's friends, follows the trail of the real murderer, hoping for an interview. The ensuing complications are resolved when Hildegard's lover has "Lucky" and Walker hired for tutorial service in Africa, where one meets a fate that will remind Sparks's readers of Evelyn Waugh.

Hildegard Wolf attributed to the real Lord Lucan the belief that "people like us don't go to prison." Lucan might also have been persuaded that "people like us" knew how to deal with other people, and he was possibly moved by this conviction "when he 'dealt' with the woman he thought was his wife, when he 'dealt' with the knowledge of his blunder that he killed only the children's nurse." When the Lucan murder case is summarized early in the book, Spark, apparently speaking in her own voice, recalls a "strongly felt complaint" by the police: "the missing Earl had been aided and abetted in his movements subsequent to the murder. His upper-class friends, said the police, had helped the suspect to get away and cover his tracks. They mocked the police, they stonewalled the enquiries."

It is left, however, to a fictional acquaintance of Lord Lucan to explain, in response to

Lacey Twickenham's questions, the mind-set of the aiders and abettors: "There was a kind of psychological, almost an unconscious conspiracy to let him get away. It was not only that he was a member of the aristocracy, a prominent upper-class fellow, it was that he had pitched his life and all his living arrangements to that proposition. . . . He was seen by friends with blood on his trousers but they couldn't, or in other words didn't, want to believe he had perpetrated all that violence. In those first days, and even first weeks, he managed to get away. He did so on the strength of his own hypnotic act. A similar case, before your time, was the escape of the traitors Maclean and Burgess."

s.43 Spicer, Henry *Judicial Dramas: or, The Romance of French Criminal Law.* London: Tinsley, 1872.

■ This work, dedicated to Serjeant William Ballantine of the English Bar, was intended to introduce English readers to French "drames judiciaires." Spicer's chapters include the impersonation of Martin Guerre; the murder of the Marquise de Ganges by her brothers-in-law; the erroneous conviction of Monsieur and Madame d'Anglade for burglary of the Paris apartments of François Comte de Montgomery; Cartouche; Martin Dumollard, the farmer who serially murdered housemaids (1862); and the Duc de Praslin's murder of his wife. Spicer drew from a number of sources rather than pilfering the French collections of causes célèbres and, during a trip to France in 1862, was a direct observer of the furor aroused by the Dumollard murder case.

s.44 Springsteen, Bruce "American Skin." First performed by the singer-composer on June 4, 2000, Baltimore.

■ Protesting the killing of Amadou Diallo, a black street vendor, by four New York police officers in 1999, the song begins with the words "41 shots" and repeats the phrase nine times. The lyric sermonizes—"You can get killed just for living in your American skin"—and questions the reality of the danger perceived by the policemen: "Is it a gun? Is it a knife? Is it a wallet? This is your life."

s.45 [State Trials Series] *A Complete Collection of State Trials and Proceedings for High Treason and Other Crimes and Misdemeanors from the Earliest Period to the Present Time, with Notes and Other Illustrations.* Comp. J. B. Howell, William Cobbett, and David Jardine. London: Longman, Hurst, Rees, Orme, & Brown, 1809–28.

■ This last edition of Howell's *State Trials*, which concludes with an index volume, includes many famous British murder trials, including those of Mary Blandy, Earl Lawrence Ferrers, Captain Samuel Goodere, Captain William Kidd, Captain John Porteous, and Robert Carr, Earl of Somerset. The set begins with proceedings against Thomas Becket in 1163 for high treason.

s.46 Stead, Philip John *The Police of Paris.* London: Staples, 1957.

■ This is one of the best brief surveys in English of the history of the French police, outlining its development from the Age of Louis XIV to the 1950s. The author served as director of studies at the Police College, Bramshill, and is a biographer of Eugène-François Vidocq, the founder of the Sûreté, and the translator of many French works, including the memoirs of nineteenth-century murderer-sociopath Lacenaire (see L.3).

S.47 ——— *Vidocq: A Biography*. London: Staples, 1953.

■ This lively biography of Vidocq is made especially valuable by Stead's knowledge of Vidocq's London tour and his influence on English detective literature and stage thrillers, including Tom Taylor's *Ticket-of-Leave Man*, which introduces the Vidocq-like Hawkshaw the detective.

S.48 Stendhal [pseudonym of Marie-Henri Beyle] *The Red and the Black*. 1830. New York: Modern Library, 1995.

■ A small-town carpenter's son named Julien Sorel, the ambitious protagonist of *The Red and the Black*, had a strong will to power and, despite his contempt for middle-class society, a desire to rise above his station. Had the Napoleonic empire survived, he would have pursued military glory (the "Red" of the title), but under the Restoration he is compelled to settle for the "Black," symbolizing the priesthood that Stendhal sees as allied with the bourgeoisie in maintaining dominion over France. Admitted as tutor to the household of M. de Rênal, the town mayor, Julien, with almost mathematical calculation, seduces his wife. When the affair is discovered, the mayor sends him to a religious seminary in Besançon. After leaving the seminary, Julien stops en route to Paris to persuade the remorseful Madame de Rênal to yield to his embraces again. Once he enters his new service in the home of the Marquis de la Môle, Julien resumes his pattern of cold conquests by impregnating the Marquis's daughter Mathilde. The sophisticated nobleman offers Julien Mathilde's hand in marriage, but the match is frustrated when Madame de Rênal, writing a letter dictated by her confessor, reveals Julien's villainy. Julien takes his revenge by shooting his former mistress during services in her town church. His victim is taken to the hospital (where she recovers); he is led off to prison and convicted of the murder attempt. While in prison, Julien is visited by Madame de Rênal and Mathilde, who both responded to his coldness with ardor. At last, he feels regret in having failed to accept the happiness that Madame de Rênal had offered him: "In the past, . . . when I could have been so happy during our walks in the woods of Vergy, a fiery ambition dragged my soul off to imaginary lands. Instead of pressing to my heart this charming arm that was so close to my lips, my plans for the future carried me away from you; I was involved in innumerable battles that I had to win in order to build a colossal fortune. . . . I would have died without knowing the meaning of happiness if you hadn't come to see me in this prison."

The narrative of Julien Sorel's two romances and of his murder attempt is based with considerable accuracy on the record in the trial of Antoine Berthet, guillotined in Stendhal's native city of Grenoble for wounding Mme. Michoud de la Tour (Mme. de Rênal) in the church of Brangues in 1827. The principal factual issues in the Berthet case were reconsidered by René Fonvieille in his study *Le véritable Julien Sorel* (Paris: Arthaud, 1971). Among his principal conclusions are the following:

- Despite lack of strong evidence in the historical record, it appears that Mme. Michoud and Antoine Berthet were in fact lovers.
- The dismissal of Berthet from the Michoud household may have been due in part to Berthet's Bonapartist leanings.
- Berthet believed himself betrayed by Mme. Michoud in the frustration of his plan to marry Henriette de Cordon, daughter of the Count de Cordon ("Mathilde," in the novel). He became subject to a persecution mania that caused him to attribute to Mme. Michoud a conspiracy to destroy him. Therefore, he planned to murder her in a spectacular manner that would make the entire community aware of his grievance and his revenge.

Another criminal case in which Stendhal took great interest, the slaying of an unfaithful mistress by Adrien Laffargue, a young cabinetmaker, may also have influenced the characterization of Julien Sorel. Stendhal remarked in his *Roman Journal* (see s.49) that all great men would probably come from the class to which M. Laffargue belonged.

s.49 ———— *A Roman Journal*. 1827–29. Ed. and trans. Haakon Chevalier. New York: Collier, 1961.

■ Ever fascinated by crimes of his day and of distant times and locales, Stendhal included in his *Roman Journal* a detailed report of the trial of twenty-five-year-old cabinetmaker Adrien Laffargue (sometimes spelled Lafargue), who, overcome by jealousy, shot and decapitated his faithless mistress Thérèse in her room in the town of Bagnères. Later to furnish one of the sources for *The Red and the Black*, the trial of Laffargue (who was sentenced to five years' imprisonment) drew the following comment from Stendhal: "While the upper classes of Parisian society seem to lose the faculty of feeling with force and constancy, the passions display a frightening energy in the petty bourgeoisie, among the young people who, like M. Laffargue, have received a good education, but whom the absence of fortune forces to work and brings into conflict with real needs."

Other crime-related entries in Stendhal's journal concern Italian poisoning techniques (including a seventeenth-century procedure for cutting a peach into halves with a gold knife poisoned only on one side); a recent serial poisoner who plied a beggar's trade in the streets of Rome; the origin of Italian banditry in resistance to Spanish domination; and a report of his friend M. R. Colomb, who "had the good fortune of seeing those robbers whom we have heard mentioned perhaps a hundred times during these eighteen months."

s.50 ———— *The Shorter Novels of Stendhal*. Trans. C. K. Scott-Moncrieff. New York: Liveright, 1946.

■ Volume 2 includes five short novels of Italian murder and violence, including "Vittoria Accoramboni," which purports to be a translation of a narrative written at Padua in 1585 of the woman whom John Webster made the protagonist of his drama, *The White Devil* (see w.9); and "The Cenci," briefly relating the 1599 parricide committed by Beatrice Cenci and her brothers (see s.28).

s.51 Stephenson, Shelagh *An Experiment with an Air Pump.* London: Methuen Drama, 1998.

■ Borrowing the time-shifting device of Tom Stoppard's play *Arcadia*, Stephenson gives us a present-day perspective on the interplay of science and art during the late eighteenth and early nineteenth centuries. The issues remain constant: whether scientists' devotion to research is tainted by impure passion and whether the humanism instilled by the study of art and literature is freighted by excessive preoccupation with the past.

The play takes its title and dominant image from the masterpiece (1767–68) of painter Joseph Wright of Derby, which demonstrates a cruel experiment in which a bird suffocates as air is pumped out of a glass globe, only to have its life spared at the last moment. Stephenson suggests analogies among the use of air pump; the supply of "fresh" corpses to anatomists by William Burke and William Hare, Edinburgh body snatchers and murderers (see T.9), and their English counterpart, John Bishop; and twenty-first-century controversy regarding prefetal genetic research.

In the course of the drama, Tom, a present-day English professor, discovers beneath his venerable house in Newcastle-upon-Tyne, a skeleton with its upper spine missing. The audience knows what Tom does not: that the remains belong to an eighteenth-century hunchbacked Scottish servant named Isobel Bridie. Scientist Thomas Armstrong cynically wooed her so that he might examine her anatomical anomaly. Learning of his treachery, she unsuccessfully attempted to hang herself. When Armstrong found her still breathing, he suffocated her, like the bird in the air pump. It is implied that he later removed her hump for closer study.

s.52 Stevenson, Robert Louis *Kidnapped* and *David Balfour.* [In England *Catriona.*] In *The Works of Robert Louis Stevenson.* Vailima Edition. Vols. 9 and 10. New York: Scribner, 1921–23.
■ In 1752 red-haired Colin Roy Campbell of Glenure (the "Red Fox") was shot to death in a wooded ambush while walking home in the Appin area of the Scottish Highlands. Campbell, as King George II's agent, was in the process of evicting tenants from lands belonging to an exiled Jacobite landlord to whom they remained loyal. James Stewart was tried and hanged for complicity in this Appin murder; his kinsman Allan Breck, who was suspected of being one of the assassins, fled abroad. Scottish historian Andrew Lang claimed to have learned the identity of the true murderer (whom he believed to have acted alone) but refused to divulge the secret in his article on the case (see L.8).

In the novel *Kidnapped* (1886), young David Balfour witnesses the Appin slaying and comes upon his friend Allan Breck Stewart nearby. Although David suspects Allan Breck of the crime because of menacing statements he had previously made about the hated royal agent, Breck is firm in his denial, declaring that "if I were going to kill a gentleman, it would not be in my own country, to bring trouble on my clan."

David Balfour (1893; known as *Catriona* in Britain) follows the course of James Stewart's murder trial. Balfour, doubtless speaking for Stevenson, is scandalized by the address of the Duke of Argyll, presiding as Lord Justice-General, to the condemned man; seething with political partisanship Argyll told Stewart that had the rising of 1745 succeeded, the prisoner "might have been satiated with the blood of any name or clan to which you had an aversion." David Balfour comments: "James was as fairly murdered as though the Duke had got a fowling-piece and stalked him." He also noted that a juryman had scandalously interrupted the speech for the defense with the words: "Pray, sir, cut it short, we are quite weary."

S.53 ——— *The Strange Case of Dr. Jekyll and Mr. Hyde.* In *The Works of Robert Louis Stevenson*. Vailima Edition. Vol. 7. New York: Scribner, 1921–23.

■ The image of Jekyll and Hyde (conceived in a feverish nightmare experienced by Stevenson) appears to have had its origin in a real personage of the author's native city of Edinburgh, Deacon Brodie (1741–1788). William Brodie was a successful carpenter and cabinetmaker and so highly regarded in his craft that he became "deacon" or president of the Edinburgh carpenters' trade. Far from having the solid churchgoing habits that his title might suggest to those unacquainted with its professional significance, Deacon Brodie spent many happy hours on Sunday mornings making wax impressions of the door locks of friends and neighbors who were at services. Brodie led a double life: by day he practiced his carpentry; at night he was a daring housebreaker.

The houses and office he raided (at first alone and later as leader of a gang of four) included many he had previously visited to make repairs or perform other work of his trade. Between blows of hammer and strokes of saw, he had taken the opportunity to make copies of keys and locks and to observe room arrangements and the arrival and departure schedules of inhabitants and workers. Some victims who witnessed his nighttime incursions thought they recognized him under his black gauze mask, but they kept their own counsel, out of either friendship or disbelief. The next morning Brodie would condole with them on their losses or would be in attendance at the town council, of which he was an ex officio member, helping formulate plans to catch the audacious criminal.

Brodie's career ended when a member of his gang gave him away to the authorities after a disappointing raid on the Scottish Excise Office. Brodie fled and was caught in Holland, where he was making profitable use of his fugitive hours learning the art of forgery from an itinerant expert. The Deacon was hanged in 1788 at the Edinburgh Tolbooth prison. Legend has it that he was hanged on a gallows that he had built in the course of his carpentry for the city. Unfortunately, this supreme irony is not borne out by chronology.

In the night nursery where Robert Louis Stevenson slept as a child were a bookcase and a chest of drawers made by Deacon Brodie. There is little doubt that his devoted nurse, Alison Cunningham ("Cummie"), who had the odd notion that the way to put an impressionable child to sleep is to tell him terrifying stories, regaled him with the exploits of Edinburgh's famous Deacon. When Stevenson was thirteen or fourteen years old, he made his first attempt at a play based on Deacon Brodie, and at nineteen, in 1869, he wrote a later draft. In 1879 his friend W. E. Henley (the hot-tempered, red-bearded, one-legged poet and critic who was to serve as the model for Stevenson's immortal character Long John Silver) "fished" the 1869 draft out of a trunk and persuaded Stevenson to collaborate with him on a new version. In their play, Deacon Brodie pursues his burglar's trade partly for the economic purpose of restoring his sister's dowry, which he had dissipated by gambling. At the same time, Stevenson and Henley introduce a philosophical interpretation that is underscored by the play's subtitle, "The Double Life." Deacon Brodie feels that his "naked self" is stifled by the social restrictions and hypocrisy of daytime Edinburgh and leaps into his nights of crime as into a "new life." He invokes the night as "the grimy, cynical night that makes all cats grey, and all honesties of one complexion." When at the end of the play the Deacon, in a departure from his historical fate, dies in a duel with the police, he cries that he has found the "new life" at last. Unfortunately, *Deacon Brodie*, like Stevenson's other dramatic collaborations with Henley, was unsuccessful, and its American performances were not helped by the fact that Henley's brother, an untalented actor, was cast in the title role.

The disappointing fate of the play by no means ended Stevenson's fascination with the figure of Deacon Brodie or his speculations about the existence of the unknown dark sides of men whose public characters were beyond reproach. Eve Blantyre Simpson, the sister of Stevenson's close friend Walter Simpson, reports that Stevenson would pace up and down before the Simpsons' library fire and "expatiate on the double life, speaking again of the Deacon. He would wonder what burglary some esteemed citizen of his own day was guilty of in the . . . [night]." The respected Dr. Henry Jekyll and his alter ego, the unspeakable Mr. Hyde, are the permanent embodiment of Stevenson's obsession with the double soul of man.

To a modern generation, which has learned, through such studies as Steven Marcus's *The Other Victorians* (New York: Basic Books, 1966), of the unpleasant aspects of the private conduct of the Victorians, Stevenson's tale seems to be as well suited to nineteenth-century England as to Deacon Brodie's Edinburgh of a century earlier. In fact, in a striking exception to the rule that history never repeats itself, a notorious criminal case was tried at Sheffield in 1879 that presented a close parallel to the exploits of Brodie. Charlie Peace—known to his suburban community in London as "Mr. Thompson," a proper, violin-playing citizen busy with his great assortment of pets, a regular attendant at parish church services, and an outspoken critic of the pro-Turkish policies of the government—was a professional housebreaker by night. When he was arrested in the course of a burglary and his identity was discovered, it was found that he had committed two murders, one of them years before. Peace was hanged for his crimes. His violin is now one of the prime exhibits in Scotland Yard's Black Museum.

S.54 Stoker, Bram *Dracula.* London: Constable, 1897.

■ Vlad Tepes, a fifteenth-century prince of Walachia (now part of Romania), impaled masses of captives on spikes. According to legend, he took dinner amid rows of his suffering victims. From researches in the British Library, Bram Stoker, author of *Dracula*, appears to have obtained information about fifteenth-century Hungarian military campaigns against the Turks; as a result of Stoker's reading, there emerged "a composite picture—admittedly sketchy—of an authentic character who bore at least some of the characteristics of the historical Dracula" (see Barbara Belford, *Bram Stoker* [New York: Knopf, 1996], 259–60;

Raymond T. McNally and Radu Florescu, *In Search of Dracula* [Greenwich: New York Graphic Society, 1972], 35–81). It was Stoker, however, who was responsible for combining vampirism with the Vlad Tepes traditions to create his undead count.

s.55 Sullivan, Robert *Goodbye Lizzie Borden.* Brattleboro, Vt.: Stephen Greene, 1974.
■ This volume, written by a judge of the Massachusetts Superior Court, is the first book-length study of the Borden case by a jurist. Judge Sullivan regards as erroneous two evidentiary exclusions made by the trial judge: the ruling that Lizzie's sworn statements at the inquest could not be admitted since she was then constructively under arrest; and the exclusion of evidence that shortly before the axe murders Lizzie attempted to purchase prussic acid in order, so she said, to mothproof a fur cape. Nevertheless, Sullivan believes that the evidence before the jury established Lizzie's guilt beyond a reasonable doubt.

Sullivan speculates that the jury may have been influenced by news reports of the unrelated axe murder of Bertha Manchester in Fall River shortly before the Borden trial began.

s.56 Swift, Jonathan "Clever Tom Clinch Going to Be Hanged" (1726) and "Blue-Skin's Ballad" (1724). In *The Poems of Jonathan Swift.* Ed. Harold Williams. 3 vols. 2d ed. Oxford: Oxford Univ. Press (Clarendon Press), 1958.
■ Undoubtedly the greatest contribution Swift made to crime literature was persuading John Gay to write a "Newgate pastorale," which became *The Beggar's Opera.* Among his own poems, a ballad describes the hanging of "Clever Tom Clinch." Clever Tom has been identified as a highwayman named Tom Cox, who had been executed more than thirty years before the appearance of Swift's verses. The criminal's last actions were unrepentant:

> And when his last Speech the loud Hawkers did cry,
> He swore from his Cart, it was all a damn'd lie.
> The Hangman for Pardon fell down on his knee;
> Tom gave him a Kick in the Guts for his Fee. (2:399–400)

"Blue-Skin's Ballad," a 1724 poem attributed to Swift, celebrates a violent incident in the life of Joseph Blake, nicknamed Blueskin, a companion of the thief and jail-breaker Jack Sheppard. During the Old Bailey trial of Blueskin and Sheppard, Blueskin used his penknife to cut the throat of the gangster and informer Jonathan Wild (see F.10), who had betrayed them. The ballad's author rejoices:

> Attend and draw near,
> Good News you shall hear
> How honest Wild's Throat was cut Ear to Ear
> Now Blueskin's sharp Penknife has set you at Ease,
> And ev'ry Man round me may rob if he please. (3:1113–15)

S.57 Swinburne, Algernon Charles *Bothwell: A Tragedy*. London: Chatto & Windus, 1874.

■ The action in Swinburne's five-act verse drama is dated with precision, beginning on March 9, 1566, as Lord Darnley, second husband of Mary Queen of Scots, broods over the wrongs that will lead him to order the murder of his wife's secretary and favorite, David Rizzio. Darnley voices to James Douglas, Earl of Morton, his suspicion that Rizzio is the queen's lover; but perhaps of more substance is his grievance that the secretary has opposed his request to be vested with the "crown matrimonial," which would grant him an independent royal station for life. The final act ends on March 16, 1568, when Mary flees into exile in England after the rout of her troops at Langside.

The dramatic apex of the tragedy is Act 2, which culminates with the assassination of Darnley at Kirk o'Field near Edinburgh by accomplices of James Hepburn, Earl of Bothwell, Mary's third husband-elect. As Bothwell contemplates the execution of his plot, the act of murder shrinks in significance before its design:

> . . . what is here to do
> Is less now than the least I yet have done,
> Being but the putting once of the mere hand
> To the thing done already in device,
> Wrought many times out in the working soul.

T

T.1 Taylor, Katherine Fischer *In the Theater of Criminal Justice: The Palais de Justice in Second Empire Paris*. Princeton: Princeton Univ. Press, 1993.

■ In this extended essay, Professor Taylor, an architectural historian, demonstrates that Louis Duc, who designed the 1868 wing of Paris's Palais de Justice to house the criminal courts, created a facade and interior that reflected changes in the justice system. Taylor illustrates the arrangement and functioning of the principal courtroom by describing the course of mass murderer Jean-Baptiste Troppmann's 1869 trial (see B.68), the first cause célèbre to be heard in the new facility. In Taylor's view, the courtroom layout presented in visual terms the shift in French criminal procedure from an emphasis on codified law and the judge's inquisitorial role toward presentation of oral testimony, greater jury discretion, and an "accusatorial" system enhancing the participation of opposing counsel in the truth-determining process. In keeping with these legal developments, Duc's courtroom facilitated theatricality and psychological observation. The "handsome distances" within the bar of the court (*barreau*) permitted counsel to make telling gestures, and "the jury sat below large clerestory windows which illuminated the dock and highlit the defendant's every movement."

The richness of the courtroom décor aroused controversy among art critics. Charles Blanc wrote: "I conjure up a poor man, in the grip of poverty, having been stupefied by ignorance, who is brought there in worker's clothing to account for a theft or a murder, under those gilded ceilings, vermilioned and illustrated with splendid paintings." To Félix Narjoux, however, the courtroom's majesty was necessary to inspire awe in defendants and jurors alike. In designing the facade of the criminal wing in a style that mingled masculine and feminine aspects of the classical orders, Taylor argues that Duc sought to reflect the increased leniency of French criminal justice but faced a difficult problem: "how public architecture might represent or interpret publicity and authority where post-Revolutionary ideology requires that authority be diffused or internalized in individualized conscience."

T.2 Tennyson, Alfred Lord   *Becket.* 1884. In *The Complete Poetical Works of Tennyson.* Ed. W. J. Rolfe. Boston: Houghton Mifflin, 1898.

■ An aficionado of criminal cases, Tennyson devoted this late play to the tumultuous events that began with the installation of Thomas Becket as archbishop of Canterbury and culminated in his assassination in Canterbury Cathedral in 1170. After Tennyson's death in 1892, Sir Henry Irving achieved outstanding success in the lead role both in England and America.

Although Tennyson's Becket is ennobled by his resolution in the face of death and by the very meanness of his enemies' motives, he is not free of character flaws. Even after becoming the leader of England's Church, he shelters King Henry II's mistress, Rosamund de Clifford, in a secret "bower," and the zeal with which he pursues the claims of religion may be tainted by personal animus. John of Salisbury could well have been justified in warning him:

> We are self-uncertain creatures, and we may,
> Yea, even when we know not, mix our spites
> And private hates with our defence of Heaven.

Tennyson has Henry throw out the crucial hint that legend attributes to the king: "Will no man free me from this pestilent priest?" The poet, however, yields to his penchant for melodrama in placing the "fair Rosamund" on the scene when the assassination plot begins to form. Queen Eleanor and her henchman, Sir Reginald Fitzurse, one of Becket's sworn foes and a disappointed suitor of Rosamund de Clifford, discover the young woman's hiding place, and the queen's threats to poison or stab her are stymied by the sudden arrival of Becket. In their frustration, Eleanor and Fitzurse arrange for the archbishop's murder.

T.3 Tey, Josephine [pseudonym of Elizabeth MacKintosh]   *The Daughter of Time.* New York: Macmillan, 1952.

■ In this masterpiece of historically based crime fiction, Detective Inspector Alan Grant is laid up in a hospital due to injuries suffered from a fall through a trap door. To while away the days of his recovery, he devotes himself to Clio, the muse of history (the "daughter of Time"), by solving the mystery of the murder of the princes in the Tower of London. To the delight of Ricardians worldwide, Grant exculpates Richard III (whose painted portrait suggests to him "someone used to great responsibility, and responsible in his authority") and puts the blame on Henry VII.

T.4 Thackeray, William Makepeace "The Case of Peytel." 1839. In *The Paris Sketch Book*: *The Works of Thackeray*. Kensington Edition. Vol. 17. New York: Scribner, 1904.

■ In this article, Thackeray attacks the conviction and hanging of *notaire* Sébastien Peytel for the premeditated killing of his wife, Félicie, and his valet, Louis Rey, during a carriage journey on a French country road (see B.69). It was Peytel's story that Rey had fired at his wife from a distance with the motive of robbery and that he had then pursued the servant, striking murderous blows with a blunt instrument in retribution. Thackeray thought that the prosecution smacked too much of theater and made a point-by-point rebuttal to show that the inferences on which the conviction was based could all be reversed in Peytel's favor. The principal goal of the article was to protest against the execution of Peytel, based as it was on dubious evidence (see B.28).

T.5 ———— *Catherine: A Story*. 1839–40. London: Smith Elder, 1869.

■ William Makepeace Thackeray was a harsh critic of the so-called Newgate novels published in England between 1830 and 1847, which seemed to present crime and criminals in an appealing or sentimentalized manner. Thackeray's major attack on this fiction was made through his comic novel *Catherine*. Instead of parodying the work of Newgate novelists (such as William Harrison Ainsworth and Edward Bulwer Lytton), as he had done in the past, Thackeray dipped into the pages of the *Newgate Calendar* to find a criminal who would be particularly revolting. He hit upon Catherine Hayes, wife of a London tradesman, who conspired with two lodgers, including one who may have been her illegitimate son, to murder her husband. Her biography featured the beheading and dismemberment of the victim and Catherine's burning at the stake and was described by its editor as "altogether too shocking for a single comment." Thackeray's budding skill as a novelist overcame his original satiric intent, and he elaborated the plot of *Catherine* far beyond the facts of the case.

T.6 ———— *Denis Duval*. In *The Works of Thackeray*. Kensington Edition. Vol. 28. New York: Scribner, 1904.

■ In this novel left unfinished at Thackeray's death, the famous highwaymen, George and Joseph Weston, play inglorious roles. Joseph, the younger of the Weston brothers, is introduced unflatteringly as "a red-eyed, pimple-faced, cock-fighting gentleman for ever on the trot, and known, I dare say not very favourably, all the country round." Joseph becomes a bitter enemy of the novel's hero Denis Duval, after the youthful Denis repels an attack by the highwayman on a coach with a volley of shot from a little pistol. Thackeray's notes indicate that he planned for Denis to attend the trial of the two Westons, who were hanged for their crimes. The portrayal of the brothers as unredeemed villains is in keeping with Thackeray's disapproval of romanticizing criminals in fiction. For a description of the Weston brothers's career, see Patrick Pringle, *Stand and Deliver* (P.20).

T.7 ——— "Going to See a Man Hanged." In *Sketches and Travels in London: The Works of Thackeray*. Kensington Edition. Vol. 21. New York: Scribner, 1904.

■ This piece, originally published in *Fraser's Magazine*, records Thackeray's emotions in attending the hanging of the valet Courvoisier, who murdered his master, Lord William Russell. The greatness of the article lies in its eloquent peroration against capital punishment and public hanging. Although he had no doubt of Courvoisier's guilt, the experience left Thackeray with "an extraordinary feeling of terror and shame," springing from his partaking with 40,000 others in "this hideous debauchery, which is more exciting than sleep, or than wine, or the last new ballet." See Albert Borowitz, "Why Thackeray Went to See a Man Hanged," in *Innocence and Arsenic: Studies in Crime and Literature* (B.28).

T.8 Thaxter, Celia "A Memorable Murder." 1875. In *The Portable Murder Book*. Ed. Joseph Henry Jackson. New York: Viking, 1945.

■ Poet Celia Thaxter was the daughter of the lighthouse keeper on White Island in the Isles of Shoals, ten miles out to sea from Portsmouth, New Hampshire. In this classic among early American crime essays, she produced a gripping account of a contemporary murder case on the neighboring island of Smutty Nose. On March 5, 1873, Louis Wagner, an unemployed sailor and fisherman of Prussian origin, axed and strangled two sisters-in-law, Anethe and Karen Christensen, in the single household on Smutty Nose. Wagner rowed to the island in a stolen dory in the hope of robbing the isolated house while the men of the family, as he knew, were in Portsmouth waiting to bait their nets. He knew the Hontvet-Christensen home well, for he had lived there in the previous year while working as a fisherman in the islanders' trawling activities.

Thaxter captures the landscape of the Isles of Shoals with the eye of a native and the soul of a poet. She spins the bloody tale in the empathetic and suspenseful style of Thomas De Quincey while taking pains not to overheat her imaginative rendering of the killer's mind. She writes: "The whole affair shows the calmness of a practiced hand; *there was no malice in the deed*, no heat; it was one of the coolest instances of deliberation in the annals of crime." Wagner, whose booty amounted to less than twenty dollars, was hanged in Maine, to which Smutty Nose belonged.

T.9 Thomas, Dylan *The Doctor and the Devils, and Other Scripts*. New York: New Directions, 1966.

■ Fallon and Broom are Thomas's recreations of William Burke and William Hare, notorious Edinburgh body snatchers and murderers who sold corpses in the 1820s to Dr. Robert Knox, anatomy professor (renamed Dr. Thomas Rock). The greatest strength of this film script is the evocation of the city streets in the prose-poetry of Thomas's stage directions: "The straw-strewn cobbles of the Market are crowded with stalls. Stalls that sell rags and bones, kept by rags and bones. Stalls that sell odds and ends of every odd kind, odd boots, bits of old meat, fish heads, trinkets, hats with feathers, broadsheets, hammers. Stalls like ash bins. Anything that is marketable, to the poor."

For a long time the stiff-necked Rock denies responsibility for his suppliers' crimes; he maintains that the end of advancing science justifies any means and that "the Resurrectionists who dig up the dead and sell them to the Anatomical Schools are a direct result of the wrongness of the Law." In the final scene, however, Rock's voice is heard revealing his awareness that Fallon and Broom had produced "fresh" corpses by resorting to murder: "My name is a ghost to frighten children. . . . Will my children cry '*Murder*' and '*Blood*' when I touch them . . . as if my hands were Fallon's hands? . . . Did I set myself above pity? . . . *Oh, my God, I knew what I was doing!*"

In 1985, Thomas's script, as adapted by dramatist Ronald Harwood, was filmed with Jonathan Pryce and Stephen Rea playing Fallon and Broom, respectively. The contemporary documents of the Burke and Hare case are collected in Jacques Barzun, ed., *Burke and Hare: The Resurrection Men* (Metuchen, N.J.: Scarecrow Press, 1974).

T.10 Thompson, C. J. S. *Mysteries of History, with Accounts of Some Remarkable Characters and Charlatans.* Philadelphia: Lippincott, 1928.

■ Dr. Thompson, who held the title of Honorary Curator of the Historical Collection of the Museum of the Royal College of Surgeons of England, studied the history of medicine, pharmacy and quackery; historical mysteries; and poisonings through the ages. *Mysteries of History* tackles such conundra as

- The death of Amy Robsart. Thompson concludes: "She [Amy] stood in the way of the realization of his [Robert Dudley's] great ambition to marry Elizabeth, and the Queen's words, 'none of his were at the attempt at his wife's house,' but adds to the strong suspicion that Dudley was the instigator of a plot against his wife's life."
- The transvestite adventurer, the Chevalier d'Eon, on whom an autopsy was performed by Thomas Copeland. The surgeon certified that "d'Eon de Beaumont was of the masculine sex and of that sex only."
- The mysterious Count de Saint Germain, alchemist and political agent of Louis XV.
- The "king of charlatans," Cagliostro (Giuseppe Balsamo).

Among other books by Thompson are *Poison Mysteries in History Romance and Crime* (London: Scientific Press, 1923); and *Poison Mysteries Unsolved: "By Person or Persons Unknown"* (London: Hutchinson, 1937).

T.11 Thurber, James *Thurber on Crime.* Ed. Robert Lopresti. New York: Time Warner (Mysterious Press), 1991.

■ Among this largely humorous collection are two crime reportages. In "A Sort of Genius" Thurber recalls the triumph of reputedly dim-witted defendant Willie Stevens in his cross-examination at the Hall-Mills murder trial of 1922. Stevens broke the back of the prosecutor's case by his wit, courtesy, and clear account of his whereabouts on the night of the crime. Reviewing Willie's life in the fourteen years after the trial, Thurber finds him to be eccentric but far from deserving his reputation for mental deficiency. In reality, Willie was given to reading on engineering, entomology and botany and dipped into what he called the "worthwhile poets."

Another true-crime article relates the murder of New York City gambler Herman Rosenthal at the behest of corrupt police officer Charles Becker, an affair that disputed headlines with the sinkings of the *Titanic* and the *Lusitania*. The collection also includes an affectionate memoir of *New Yorker* editor Harold Ross's loss of $71,000 to the unobtrusive forger Harold Winney, who served as his private secretary. Finally, Thurber, assuming the style of Horatio Alger, parodies the success story of Walter McGee, who kidnapped Mary McElroy in 1915, winning not only a ransom but also the intercession of his tender-hearted victim for the commutation of his death sentence.

T.12 Toobin, Jeffrey *The Run of His Life: The People v. O. J. Simpson.* New York: Random House, 1996.

■ In many respects the criminal trial of O. J. Simpson for the stabbing murders of his wife Nicole and Ron Goldman resembles the celebrated case of Lizzie Borden. Both trials illustrate the difficulty American prosecutors traditionally have in convicting celebrity defendants (O.J., of course, was a national sports hero; Lizzie and her family were prominent citizens of Fall River, Massachusetts, where the crimes were committed). Both trials featured "million-dollar" defense teams (Lizzie's counsel, former Massachusetts governor George D. Robinson, had appointed one of the trial judges). And both trials presented similar enigmas: a missing weapon, an accused killer whose person and clothes were free of bloodstains shortly after a gory attack, and serious problems in reconstructing the chronology of the defendant's movements before and after the crime.

New Yorker staff writer Jeffrey Toobin has written the most lucid and objective contemporary account of Simpson's criminal trial. Amply persuaded at the trial's end that Simpson was guilty, Toobin perhaps regretted his acceptance of defense attorney Robert Shapiro's invitation, while the case was still pending, to examine Detective Mark Fuhrman's psychological disability file at the Los Angeles Police Department. When Toobin's article on his investigation appeared in the *New Yorker*, it included Shapiro's allegation that Fuhrman was a racist, and the detective's credibility as a prosecution witness was accordingly impaired in advance. Shapiro immediately called his co-counsel F. Lee Bailey in London and crowed, "It's over. I won the case." (Dominick Dunne included his reportages of the Simpson murder trial in *Justice: Crimes, Trials, and Punishments;* see D.51.)

O. J.'s subsequent civil trial resulting in the imposition of $33.5 million for the two wrongful deaths, is recounted by the victorious trial counsel Daniel Petrocelli (writing with Peter Knobler), in *Triumph of Justice: The Final Judgment on the Simpson Saga* (New York: Crown, 1998). See also D.51.

T.13 Trilling, Diana *Mrs. Harris: The Death of the Scarsdale Diet Doctor.* New York: Harcourt Brace Jovanovich, 1981.

■ Critic and social commentator Diana Trilling changed her mind about Jean Harris after attending the trial in which the headmistress of the Madeira School in Virginia was convicted of second-degree murder in the 1980 shooting of her long-time lover, Dr. Herman Tarnower, inventor of the "Scarsdale Diet." Trilling's "initial response was one of unqualified sympathy for the headmistress," whose action "forced upon us a fresh realization that behind the contained and orderly lives we lead as members of the respectable middle class there's a terrible human capacity that may one day overwhelm any of us."

Many factors caused Trilling to lose "this earlier tenderness." Harris's accounts of her purposes on the night of the killing were inconsistent. Her first story was that she had driven to her unfaithful lover's house with the intention of having him kill her, but later she claimed that she had set out to commit suicide. At the trial, Trilling learned that in addition to the five bullets with which she had loaded her gun, she "had brought at least five more rounds into the house with her—for suicide this surely constitutes a considerable overkill." (The presence of thirty-four more rounds of live ammunition and two spent shells in her car was excluded from evidence because of an illegal police search.) Still, Trilling believes that the jury would have voted acquittal had not the judge admitted the vitriolic and mean-spirited "Scarsdale Letter," which Harris mailed to Tarnower before she set out on her fatal drive to his home.

In her final pages, Trilling asserts rather grandly that Harris "belongs to the novel in the way that Emma Bovary does, or Anna Karenina." Jean did, however, have a better job.

T.14 Trollope, Anthony *The Way We Live Now.* 1875. London: Oxford Univ. Press (The World's Classics), 1951.

■ In an interesting article in August 4, 1995, issue of the *Times Literary Supplement*, entitled "Is Melmotte Jewish?" John Sutherland concludes that the swindler and member of Parliament Augustus Melmotte was intended to be a cosmopolitan crook of uncertain ethnic origin, perhaps a Jew but just as credibly Irish, American, German, or English. In fact, the character of Melmotte appears to be patterned on an Irish forger and swindler, John Sadleir.

A member of an old firm of solicitors in Tipperary, Sadleir moved to England where he entered the House of Commons and became a Junior Lord of the Treasury. He was also active in the city, associating himself with ventures in railways, banks, and industrial companies and winning an appointment as chairman of the London and County Bank.

It is unclear why Sadleir turned to financial crimes, but he was said to have suffered immense losses in stock exchange speculations. Whatever the reason, he engaged in forgery and fraud on a wide scale. When the Tipperary Joint Stock Bank, into which Sadleir's Bank (operated by his family for two generations) had been converted, defaulted, it was found that Sadleir had embezzled funds amounting to £400,000. He had also issued false stock in a Swedish railway and forged mortgages and commercial paper. As his fraudulent empire crumbled, Sadleir could not face the consequences and took prussic acid on Hampstead Heath. On his hall table he left a note for his solicitor: "I cannot live. I have ruined too many. I could not live and see their agony. I have committed diabolical crimes unknown to any human being."

In *The Way We Love Now*, Anthony Trollope paints a dark canvas of the destruction of English social and cultural values by dishonesty in many forms: business fraud, lavish expenditure for the purpose of self-aggrandizement, political corruption, marriage for money and position, and literary buccaneering. Like Sadleir, the swindler Melmotte ends his days by taking prussic acid. Trollope's diatribe against the dead criminal is pitiless; he calls him "a man who has become horrid to the world because of his late iniquities, a man who has so well pretended to be rich that he has been able to buy and to sell properties without paying for them, a wretch who has made himself odious by his ruin to his friends who had taken him up as a pillar of strength in regard to wealth, [and] a brute who had got into the House of Commons by false pretences."

Anthony Trollope was accused of having copied Melmotte from Mr. Merdle in Charles Dickens's *Little Dorrit* (1855–57), a character also based on John Sadleir; however, in his defense, Trollope asserted that he had not read *Little Dorrit* until 1878, three years after the appearance of *The Way We Live Now*. Mr. Merdle, like Sadleir and Trollope's Melmotte, was ubiquitous in the spheres of profit-making: "He was in everything good, from banking to building. He was in Parliament, of course. He was in the City, necessarily. He was Chairman of this, Trustee of that, President of the other. The weightiest of men had said to projectors, 'Now what name have you got? Have you got Merdle?'"

Fact-based crime fiction is the subject of Mr. Chaffanbrass's browbeating cross-examination of novelist Mr. Bouncer in Trollope's novel *Phineas Redux* (1876). Defending Finn against a charge of murder in an alleyway shortly after quarreling with the victim at a club, Chaffenbrass obtains the witness's concession that no novelist well versed in plots based on the crimes committed by Eugene Aram or the assassins of Amy Robsart "would contrive a secret hidden murder,—contrive it and execute it, all within a quarter of an hour."

T.15 Turgenev, Ivan "Kazn' Tropmana" [The Execution of Troppmann]. *Sochineniya* [Writings]. Vol. 11. Moscow: Naúka, 1983.

■ In 1870 Turgenev was invited by French writer Maxime du Camp to attend the Paris guillotining of the mass murderer Jean-Baptiste Troppmann (see B.68). Despite his squeamishness the Russian author impulsively accepted and was too embarrassed to change his mind. Like Thackeray at the London hanging of Courvoisier (see B.28), Turgenev could not bring himself to look when the moment of execution arrived. However, he was one of an elite group of onlookers during the repulsive private ceremonies that preceded death on the scaffold: a visit to the condemned man's cell, Troppmann's last haircut, the prisoner's transfer from straitjacket to execution attire, the pinioning of his arms, the dimly lighted and jostling march to the gallows. Turgenev's ultimate indignity was being mistaken for the chief executioner by someone in the huge crowd.

Turgenev concluded by arguing, as had Dickens in the aftermath of the Mannings' execution (see B.30), for an end to capital punishment (previously abolished in Russia for all nonpolitical crimes) or at least the cessation of public executions. He wrote that "decidedly none of us looked like a man who recognized that he had been present at the accomplishment of an act of public justice; everyone tried to turn his back as if to cast off responsibility for this murder (p. 150)."

A partial English translation of Turgenev's article by David Magarshack appears in Simon Rae, ed., *The Faber Book of Murder* (London: Faber & Faber, 1994), 168–79.

In the famous article "I Cannot Be Silent" (1908), Leo Tolstoy raised his influential voice to denounce the widespread use of the death penalty against revolutionists, rejecting the argument that "an evil deed committed for the benefit of many ceases to be immoral." Two other articles written by Tolstoy during 1908 also address violence and executions: "The Law of Violence and the Law of Love" and "Christianity and the Death Penalty." See Ernest J. Simmons, *Leo Tolstoy* (Boston: Little, Brown, 1946), 692–94.

Vladimir Nabokov's opposition to capital punishment, reflected in his Russian-language novels *The Gift* (first published serially in 1937 and 1938) and *Invitation to a Beheading* (1935), followed a family tradition. In 1906, his father, Vladimir Dmitrievich Nabokov, had introduced a bill abolishing the death penalty in the Russian Duma, but the legislation was blocked by the State Council. Literary biographer Brian Boyd suggests that in opening *Invitation to a Beheading* with a judge's whispered communication of the hero Cincinnatus's death sentence imposed for having private thoughts, Nabokov was echoing the mock executions of Dostoyevsky and critic and radical journalist Nikolay Chernyshevsky (*Vladimir Nabokov: The Russian Years* [Princeton: Princeton Univ. Press, 1990], 35). The simulated execution of Chernyshevsky is described in chapter 4 of *The Gift*.

T.16 Twain, Mark [pseudonym of Samuel Langhorne Clemens] *Adventures of Huckleberry Finn.* 1876. Ed. Scully Bradley, Richmond Croom Beatty, E. Hudson Long, and Thomas Cooley. 2d ed. New York: Norton, 1977.

■ Chapter 18 of *Huckleberry Finn* reflects the Darnell-Watson Feud described by Twain in his *Life on the Mississippi*. In the novel the feuding clans are the Grangerfords and the Stephensons, who have been battling so long that nobody can recall the origin of their quarrel. The feud reaches its bloody pitch after young Sophia Grangerford, with Huck Finn's unwitting aid, elopes with Harney Stephenson.

In chapters 21 and 22 of his novel, Twain adapts the first premeditated murder to be committed in the area of Hannibal, Missouri. On January 24, 1845, when Sam Clemens was ten, a prosperous merchant, William Owsley, shot "Uncle Sam" Smarr twice in the back at four paces as the two men were walking on a street in Bricksville. When drinking Smarr had publicly described Owsley as a "damned pickpocket, a damned son of a bitch" and swore that "if he ever does cross my path I will kill him." Twain's father, John M. Clemens, justice of the peace, recorded twenty-eight depositions in the case for which he received the modest sum of $13.50. Owsley was acquitted, but, according to Twain, "there was a cloud upon him—a social chill—and he presently moved away."

In Twain's fictional rendering, it is Colonel Sherburn who shoots down the verbally abusive Boggs, who is "in from the country for his little old monthly drunk." After his acquittal, Sherburn disperses a mob that has come to lynch him by daylight, telling them that they are cowards led by "half a man" and can only assume the appearance of bravery when they don masks at night. There is no record that the historical Owsley faced down a lynch mob, but in writing of the cowardice of lynchers Twain recalled: "When I was a boy I saw a brave gentleman deride and insult a mob and drive it away."

T.17 ———— *Following the Equator: A Journey Around the World*. Hartford: American Publishing Co., 1897.

■ Twain's travels described in *Following the Equator* took him to the Australian town of Wagga Wagga, where a quarter-century before, Arthur Orton, destined to win fame as the Tichborne Claimant (see A.26), had kept his butcher shop. In Twain's estimation, the Tichborne imposture was the "most intricate and fascinating and marvelous real-life romance that has ever been played upon the world's stage to unfold itself serenely, act by act, in a British court, by the long and laborious processes of judicial development."

Twain was in London when the Tichborne claimant stood trial for perjury, and in June 1873 he attended the proceedings. In chapter 15 of *Following the Equator*, Twain records his impressions as a guest at one of the Claimant's receptions: "I attended one of his showy evenings in the sumptuous quarters provided for him from the purses of his adherents and well-wishers. He was in evening dress, and I thought him a rather fine and stately creature. There were about twenty-five gentlemen present; educated men, men moving in good society, none of them commonplace; some of them were men of distinction, none of them were obscurities. They were his cordial friends and admirers. It was 'S'r Roger,' always 'S'r Roger,' on all hands; no one withheld the title, all turned it from the tongue with unction, and as if it tasted good."

In chapter 17 of his *More Tramps Abroad* (1897), Twain treated the Tichborne case at greater length. It has been noted that "Orton's attempt to claim the baronetcy helped inspire Mark Twain to write *The American Claimant* (1892), in which Colonel [Mulberry] Sellers claims to be an English earl" (R. Kent Rasmussen, *Mark Twain A to Z: The Essential Reference to His Life and Writings* [New York: Oxford Univ. Press, 1995], 458).

T.18———— *Life on the Mississippi*. 1883. Intro. James M. Cox. New York: Penguin Classics, 1986.

■ John A. Murel (or Murrell), bandit chief and slave stealer, terrorized travelers along the Natchez Trace until his imprisonment in 1834. He had also been reportedly planning a slave revolt and the seizure of New Orleans. In chapter 29 of *Life on the Mississippi*, Mark Twain quotes at length contemporary accounts of Murrell's gang and rates the blood-thirsty outlaw's criminal enterprise as vastly surpassing the misdeeds of Jesse James, who had been assassinated in 1882:

Murel was [Jesse James's] equal in boldness; in pluck; in rapacity; in cruelty, brutality, heartlessness, treachery, and in general and comprehensive vileness and shamelessness;

and very much his superior in some larger aspects. James was a retail rascal; Murel, wholesale. James's modest genius dreamed of no loftier flight than the planning of raids upon cars, coaches, and country banks; Murel projected negro insurrections and the capture of New Orleans; and furthermore, on occasion, this Murrel could go into a pulpit and edify the congregation. What are James and his half-dozen vulgar rascals compared with this stately old-time criminal, with his sermons, his meditated insurrections and city-captures, and his majestic following of ten hundred men, sworn to do his evil will!

R. Kent Rasmussen comments, "The tradition of Murrell's gang pillaging Mississippi River settlements and hiding their loot in secret caches forms part of the atmospheric background of Mark Twain's boys' stories, in which Tom Sawyer and Huck Finn often fantasize about finding PIRATE treasures" (in *Mark Twain A to Z: The Essential Reference to His Life and Writings* [New York: Oxford Univ. Press, 1995], 327).

In chapter 26 of *The Adventures of Tom Sawyer* (1876), Tom and Huck overhear Injun Joe's comrade tell him, after they unearth a box of treasure, "'Twas always said that Murrel's gang used to be around here one summer."

T.19 ——— "The Memorable Assassination." In *What Is Man? And Other Essays*. Ed. Albert Bigelow Paine. New York: Harper, 1917.

■ In 1898, while in Kaltenleutgeben, near Vienna, Twain was shaken by the news that Empress Elizabeth of Austria had been fatally stabbed by Italian anarchist Luigi Luccheni. In an essay published after his death, Twain judged the tragedy memorable because assassinations of European empresses were extremely rare and the news of the tragedy was carried throughout the world with "lightning swiftness." He attributed the crime to Luccheni's "hunger for notoriety," a motive that, Twain observed, linked the murderer with Herostratus, the destroyer of the temple of ancient Ephesus (see G.28). At the end of his article Twain gives a firsthand account of the empress's funeral.

T.20 ——— *Roughing It*. Hartford: American Publishing Co., 1872.

■ In 1857, in a Utah valley called Mountain Meadows, Indians and a group of Mormons under the leadership of John D. Lee massacred immigrant farmers who were on their way west from Missouri, Illinois, and Arkansas. Brigham Young excommunicated Lee, who was shot by a firing squad.

In chapter 17 of *Roughing It*, Mark Twain, in the course of an unflattering discussion of the "Mormon question," refers to varying accounts of the Mountain Meadows massacre that he heard during his two-day stay in Salt Lake City. Years later he was persuaded by his reading of Catherine Waite's book *The Mormon Prophet*, which included Judge Cradlebaugh's trial of the accused parties, that the Mormons "were almost if not wholly and completely responsible for that most treacherous and pitiless butchery." An appendix to *Roughing It* paraphrases Waite's interpretation of the tragic event and includes her summary of the trial testimony.

T.21 Twain, Mark, and Charles Dudley Warren   *The Gilded Age.* 1873. 2 vols. *The Writings of Mark Twain.* Author's National Edition. Vols. 10 and 11. New York: Harper, n.d.

▪ Walter F. Taylor, in *The Economic Novel in America* (1942), comments on the historical origin of Mark Twain's first novel: "Laura Hawkins was certainly suggested by Mrs. Laura Fair of California who had recently been acquitted of murder on the ground of emotional insanity. Senator Dilworthy was drawn from Senator Pomeroy of Kansas, and the activities of William M. Weed and his associates so closely resemble those of the Tweed Ring of New York that the picture is practically undisguised" (124–25).

In 1870, Laura Fair had given up hope that her lover, Alexander P. Crittenden, a California lawyer and politician, would keep his promise to divorce his wife and marry her. While Crittenden (in the company of his wife and two of seven children) was crossing San Francisco Bay on a ferryboat, Laura shot him to death. Her lawyers pleaded "emotional insanity" causing her to black out before the shooting, and a jury in her second trial acquitted her. See Kenneth Lamott, *Who Killed Mr. Crittenden?* (New York: McKay, 1963). In Twain's novel, Laura Hawkins murders her faithless lover, Colonel Selby, in a Washington hotel. A newspaper comments that the shocking crime is "the direct result of the socialistic doctrines and woman's rights agitations, which have made every woman the avenger of her own wrongs, and all society the hunting-ground for her victims." Hawkins, like her real-life model, Laura Fair, is acquitted.

U

U.1 Uhry, Alfred   *Driving Miss Daisy.* New York: Theatre Communications Group, 1988.

▪ Daisy Werthan, the elderly heroine of this Pulitzer Prize–winning play, is a socially prominent member of Atlanta's German-Jewish community. When her black chauffeur, Hoke Coleburn, tells her that the temple she attends has been bombed, Miss Daisy is unwilling to concede that the little world in which she has lived serenely is under attack. "Well, it's a mistake," she snaps. "I'm sure they meant to bomb one of the conservative synagogues or the orthodox one. The temple is reform. Everybody knows that." Despite these brave words, the perceptive Hoke Coleburn compares the outrage to the lynching of his friend Porter's father in Macon when Hoke was about ten or eleven. Hoke notices that the usually stoic Miss Daisy has begun to cry.

The 1958 bombing of Atlanta's Temple, on which this incident is based, is the subject of Melissa Fay Greene's historical work, *The Temple Bombing* (Reading, Mass.: Addison-Wesley, 1996).

V

V.1 Valdez, Luis   *Zoot Suit and Other Plays.* Houston: Arte Publico Press, 1992.

▪ Luis Miguel Valdez, a leading figure in Chicano theater and a successful filmmaker, founded El Teatro Campesino (Farmworkers' Theater) in 1965. His play *Zoot Suit* (1978) presents two inflammatory incidents in the uneasy history of Chicano-Anglo relations in Los Angeles, the Sleepy Lagoon Murder Trial of 1942 and the Zoot Suit Riots of the following year. When a young man was murdered in a brawl at a popular lovers' rendezvous known as the Sleepy Lagoon, Los Angeles police made mass arrests of zoot-suited gang members; several were convicted and sent to San Quentin, later to be set at liberty when their appeals succeeded. The Zoot Suit Riots were sparked by armed incursions by United States servicemen into Chicano neighborhoods in June 1943.

Throughout the Valdez play, the leader of a zoot-suit or Pachuco gang, Henry Reyna, converses with his alter ego, called El Pachuco, who embodies the alienation and braggadocio of the marginalized Chicano youth. When El Pachuco is stripped of his zooter's garb by hostile servicemen, he is revealed to be wearing the loincloth of his Aztec forebears. According to a character representing the press, community hostility to the zoot suit's mountainous shoulder pads, wide lapels, and "drape shape" is due to cheated ethnic preconceptions: "You are trying to outdo the white man in exaggerated white man's clothes."

Although Henry Reyna is unjustly imprisoned in the Sleepy Hollow case, he is more willing than El Pachuco to envision the possibility of assimilation into America's mainstream. Valdez proposes three alternative destinies for his hero: recidivism; posthumous receipt of the Congressional Medal of Honor after death in the Korean War; or marriage to his Chicano sweetheart, who gives him five children (three of whom become university students).

A second play in the collection, *Bandido! The American Melodrama of Tiburcio Vásquez Notorious California Bandit* (1982), is based on the life and legend of a Chicano horse thief and stagecoach robber who was the last man to be publicly hanged in California. On a split stage, Valdez creates an interplay between realistic scenes in the bandit's death cell and episodes from his life acted in the style of a melodrama. The Impresario responsible for producing the cliché-ridden melodrama acknowledges that even his claptrap cannot hide the ambiguity of Vásquez, in whom Anglos see a stereotypical Mexican and the Chicanos recognize an avenging ethnic hero: "The moral vagaries of your life confound the melodrama, sir. Are you comic or tragic, a good man or a bad man?"

v.2 Vargas Llosa, Mario "The Story of a Massacre" and "The Penis or Life: The Bobbit Affair." In *Making Waves*. Ed. and trans. John King. London: Faber & Faber, 1996.

■ Peruvian novelist Vargas Llosa served on a Commission of Investigation established by the government to conduct an inquiry into the 1983 killing of eight journalists by Indians in the Andean village of Uchuraccay. Vividly reconstructing the crime in "The Story of a Massacre," Vargas Llosa speculates that the peasants of Uchuraccay probably mistook the reporters for *Sendero Luminoso* (Shining Path) guerrillas, whom they opposed after the *Senderistas* attempted to impose economic isolation on the mountain community. It is even possible, Vargas Llosa suggests, that the men and women who unapologetically admitted participation in the ritualistic slayings (recorded in photographs taken by one of the victims) had no notion of what journalists were. He concludes: "The double threat—

the Pinochet model or the Fidel Castro model—will continue to haunt democratic regimes for as long as there are people in our countries who kill for the reasons that the peasants of Uchuraccay killed."

A lighter tone is sounded in the author's article on Lorena Gallo Bobbit's notorious sexual mutilation of her abusive husband, John Wayne Bobbit, in 1992. Although he does not take issue with Lorena Bobbit's acquittal, Vargas Llosa satirizes the feminists who turned her into "a Joan of Arc of the struggle for women's emancipation" and mocks the woman doctor who testified for the defense: "For Lorena Bobbit the choice was simple: the penis or life. And what is more important? The penis of a man or the life of a woman?"

Lorena Bobbit was a young Ecuadorian woman educated in Venezuela. Vargas Llosa notes that the fervor of Lorena-advocacy did not spare Latin America: "In Ecuador a female crowd caught up in the debate threatened to 'castrate one hundred gringos' if Lorena was sentenced to just one day in prison."

v.3 Verlaine, Paul "Peaceful Eyes My Only Wealth." In *Paul Verlaine, Selected Poems.* Trans. Martin Sorrell. Oxford: Oxford Univ. Press (Oxford World's Classics), 1999.

■ Verlaine emphasizes the alienation of Kaspar Hauser (see L.8 and w.7) from everyone he meets and everything he experiences after his release from a mysterious childhood imprisonment. Big-city men saw nothing in him but innocence; lovely women found him unattractive; and when he wanted to go to war, even death turned him down. He laments: "Was I born too early? / Or too late? Or why at all?"

v.4 Vidocq, Eugène-François *Les chauffeurs du nord* [The Northern "Feet-Warmers"]. 1845–46. Paris: Editions du Seuil, n.d.

■ The word "chauffeurs" in this novel's title does not refer to drivers but to violent brigands during the period of the Revolutionary Terror who held the feet of householders to the fire so as to induce them to reveal the places where they hid their valuables. During his years on the run from the law, Vidocq briefly associated with a chauffeur gang.

A French critic attributes the editing of this novel to Auguste Vitu, a man of letters appointed subprefect in 1851, but many of the characters are drawn from Vidocq's life. The villainous leader of the "chauffeurs," François Salembrier, was well known to Vidocq, as was Jacquard, commissioner of police at Lille who failed to catch Vidocq after his escape from a prison in that city.

Eugène-François Vidocq (1775–1857), a titanic brawler and womanizer, spent his earlier years fleeing the police after daring prison escapes; he had been jailed for minor acts of violence and ultimately condemned to the galleys for his role in forging a document releasing a prison mate who was serving a sentence for stealing cereal to feed a populous family. In 1809 Vidocq made his peace with the forces of law and order, becoming successively police spy and founder of the Paris Sûreté. On his retirement from public service, Vidocq organized a private detective agency, which became the object of police harassment. Vidocq's career and personality are reflected in the characters of Vautrin in Balzac's *La comédie humaine* and Hugo's Jean Valjean in *Les misérables.* He also influenced the portrayal of classic fictional detectives, such as Poe's Auguste Dupin, as well as Sherlock Holmes. With heavy-handed editorial assistance, Vidocq wrote his internationally best-selling memoirs and two novels based on his knowledge of the underworld. See s.47.

v.5 ——— *Les voleurs* [The Thieves]. 1836. Ed. Jean Savant. Paris: Éditions de Paris, 1957. ■ In the present edition of Vidocq's nonfictional work on French thieves, Jean Savant claims to have restored material that the original editors deleted from the manuscript. The work is divided into three sections. The first is a series of narratives regarding the exploits of well-known thieves and other criminals, including an account of one of Vidocq's greatest triumphs at the Sûreté, the foiling of a plot to rob a coach in the Forest of Sénart. The second section contains eleven short "portraits" of thieves, including François Salembrier, chief of the violent brigands known as the *Chauffeurs du Nord*, who also appears in Vidocq's novel about the gang (see v.4). The third subdivision of the book is devoted to descriptions of larcenous "specialties." An entry on the subject of business swindlers (*faiseurs*), against whom Vidocq's private detective bureau directed its principal energies, is evidence that this book was intended to advertise the success of the agency. In the chapter on swindlers, Vidocq railed against his detractors and proposed that his agency be turned over to the business community so that its operations could be widened under more respectable ownership; he agreed, however, to stay on to handle the initial organization and dreamed of the day when subscribers to his service would affix a plaque in the most conspicuous location on their premises, reading in large letters: "VIDOCQ! Insurance against business swindlers." An appendix to the text furnishes a glossary of thieves' slang.

v.6 ——— *Les vrais mémoires de Vidocq* [The Real Memoirs of Vidocq]. 1828–29. Ed. Jean Savant. Paris: Editions Corréa, 1950. ■ Vidocq's original manuscript of his memoirs was adulterated by two successive editors, Emile Morice and L. F. l'Héritier, who unscrupulously portrayed his life in the lurid tones of popular melodrama. The *Real Memoirs,* issued in 1950, reflect the successful effort of Vidocq's modern historian, Jean Savant, to disentangle Vidocq's authentic narrative from these catchpenny excrescences. The result is a spellbinding account of an adventurous life (see Albert Borowitz, "Which the Justice Which the Thief? The Life and Influence of Eugène-François Vidocq," Kent State University Libraries [Special Collections] *Occasional Papers* 3d ser., no. 4 [1997]).

A reprint of the first edition of the English translation of the memoirs was issued by Arno Press in 1976. The Borowitz Collection also holds volumes 1, 3, and 4 of the four-volume French first edition. See also Fig. 8.

v.7 ——— *Les vrais mystères de Paris* [The Real Mysteries of Paris]. 1844. Ed. Jean Savant. Paris: Club Français du Livre, 1950. ■ When Eugène Sue's novel *The Mysteries of Paris* appeared, Vidocq, who had furnished its author with information about the Paris underworld, was very pleased, particularly with the character of slum-dwelling German prince Rodolphe, which he regarded as highly instructive and true to life. Balzac, however, persuaded Vidocq to write *The Real Mysteries* in order to reflect more accurately the detective's intimate knowledge of the dark side of Paris. The production of the manuscript is almost as mysterious as its theme. Dissatisfied with the editorial work of Horace-Napoléon Raisson on the first volume, Vidocq chose another collaborator whose identity is in dispute. In view of frequent grammatical lapses in the final text, Savant suggests that Vidocq may have decided to proceed with his wife's assistance rather than entrust the fate of the novel to another literary professional.

Vidocq claimed that *The Real Mysteries* was true in its overall substance as well as in its details However, he places the beginning of the action in 1839 whereas the events he describes are attributable to the underworld as he came to know it during the period of the Bourbon Restoration and the July Monarchy.

The Borowitz True Crime Collection owns the first edition of *The Real Mysteries,* signed by Vidocq to secure copyright.

v.8 Vishakadatta   *The Signet Ring of Rakshasa* [Mudra-Rakshasa]. In *Great Sanskrit Plays in Modern Translation.* Trans. P. Lal. New York: New Directions, 1964.

■ Translator Lal believes that Vishakadatta wrote this play in the ninth century and that he was born in Pataliputra (the modern Patna), northeast India, where many of the drama's events are set; other scholars place the work centuries earlier. *The Signet Ring* is unusual among classic Sanskrit stage works in being based (at least partially) on history and focusing on murder and espionage as instruments of statecraft. The plot concerns the successful scheme of minister Chanakya (or Kautilya) to win over to the service of his royal master, Chandragupta Maurya (who usurped the throne in 321 B.C.), the able first minister of the rival Nandas, Rakshasa. Among the means employed in the secret war between the two sides are "poison girls" (seductresses ordered to poison political enemies), forgery, employment of spies and double agents, and a faked execution. The elaborate trickery is crowned by Chanakya's simulation of a falling-out with his king that provides a strong incentive for Rakshasa to join the Maurya cause.

The rumored pervasiveness of political crimes in the Maurya capital is reflected by an inquiry Rakshasa puts to Viradhagupta, who, unbeknownst to him, is a spy in the pay of Chanakya:

> Rakshasa: Tell me, how are things in Pataliputra?
> Viradhagupta: A bagful of news. I don't know where to begin.
> Rakshasa: Begin with the assassins and poisoners.

v.9 Voltaire, Francois-Marie Arouet de   *L'Affaire Calas et autres affaires.* Preface Jacques Van den Heuvel. Paris: Gallimard, 1975.

■ This edition includes the texts of Voltaire's interventions on behalf of victims of religious persecution: Huguenot Jean Calas, wrongly executed in 1762 for the murder of a son (see N.5); Pierre-Paul Sirven and his wife, who escaped trial and execution for the murder of a daughter only by flight to Switzerland; and the young chevalier de La Barre, executed for mutilating a wooden crucifix and other alleged acts and words of a sacrilegious character. Also in this collection is Voltaire's *Treatise on Tolerance on the Occasion of the Death of Jean Calas*. Particularly apparent in his treatment of the Calas case is that Voltaire preferred to dissect the flawed motives of the prosecution rather than to engage in detailed analysis of evidence. Preface author Van den Heuvel catches the master in occasional error if not chicanery. For example, Voltaire cites as proof of Jean Calas's religious tolerance his long-time employment of a Catholic maid; according to Van den Heuvel, engagement of Catholic maids in Protestant households was required by law.

W

w.1 Walbrook, H. M.   *Murders and Murder Trials 1812–1912*. London: Constable, 1932.

■ Walbrook, a former member of the literary staff of the *Pall Mall Gazette*, briefly studies twenty-nine famous murderers, many of whom are among those included in the *Notable British Trials* series: John Bellingham, assassin of Prime Minister Spencer Perceval; John Thurtell; Burke and Hare; William Corder, the "Red Barn" murderer; Thomas Griffiths Wainewright; John William Holloway, who murdered his wife Celia in Brighton's "Lovers' Walk"; François Courvoisier, Swiss valet who murdered his master, Lord William Russell (J. B. Atlay told Walbrook that a man from an opposite window saw the murder committed, but did not reveal the secret for fear of compromising a lady "in whose house he was a temporary guest"); Maria Manning; William Palmer; Madeleine Smith; Constance Kent; Franz Müller, England's first railway murderer; Dr. Edward Pritchard; Christiana Edmunds, insane killer in Brighton's "poisoned chocolates case"; Henry Wainwright, murderer of Harriet Lane; the murder of Harriet Staunton (the "Penge Mystery"); Charles Peace; Kate Webster; Percy Lefroy Mapleton, youthful murderer of Frederick Isaac Gold on a train; Dr. George Harvey Lamson; murderer John Lee, who was reprieved after three attempts to hang him failed; Adelaide Bartlett; Jack the Ripper; serial poisoner Dr. Thomas Neill Cream; trooper Charles Thomas Wooldridge, who murdered his estranged wife and was immortalized in Oscar Wilde's "The Ballad of Reading Gaol"; failed actor Richard Arthur Prince, who murdered Lyceum Theatre star William Terris at the stage door in 1897 because "he kept me out of employment for ten years and I had either to die in the street or kill him"; Dr. Hawley Harvey Crippen; Steinie Morrison; Frederick Henry Seddon.

Walbrook observes that "in nearly every case we find a monstrous, half-lunatic egotism speeding the criminal to his fate."

w.2 Wallace, W. Stewart   *Murders and Mysteries: A Canadian Series*. Toronto: Macmillan, 1931.

■ Canadian criminal cases share elements with those of the United States, including the vastness of the two countries that complicates police efforts to trace malefactors and their victims, as well as the ease with which their inhabitants obtain and use firearms. A lively introduction to Canada's classic cases is provided by this collection of sixteen of Wallace's articles, half of which originally appeared in *Maclean's Magazine*. The chapters are:

- Chapter 1. "The Delorme Case": This is a rare example of a Canadian priest prosecuted for murder. After an initial trial in which Abbé J. Adelard Delorme of Montreal was found to be insane, and two retrials resulting in hung juries, the abbé was ultimately acquitted in a fourth proceeding of the 1922 murder of a younger half-brother who was to inherit the family estate and had just had his life insured for $25,000 under a policy paid for by the abbé.
- Chapter 2. "The Mystery of Ambrose Small": One of Canada's most famous mysteries is the unsolved 1919 disappearance of unscrupulous theater owner Ambrose Small from Toronto after receiving a million-dollar certified check as the down payment in the sale of his theater interests. Wallace has "little doubt" that Small, whom many loved to hate, was murdered. At the end of his essay, the author makes a common blunder, identifying the legal term *corpus delicti* (the requisite proof that a crime has been committed) with the word "corpse."
- Chapter 3. "The Kinrade Mystery": In his study of the shooting death of Ethel Kinrade at her family's house in Hamilton in 1909, while only she and her sister Florence were at home, Wallace theorizes that the killer was most likely a mad intruder, despite Florence's inconsistent stories. The case bears some resemblance to the case of Lizzie Borden.
- Chapter 4. "The Case of Clara Ford": Even more clearly than the Kinrade case, the 1895 shooting of eighteen-year-old Frank Westwood in his Toronto home was the work of an intruder. Wallace approves the acquittal of Clara Ford, a mulatto who, the prosecution charged, had disguised herself as a man and shot the youth to avenge an unwanted advance. After making an apparently forced confession, Ford recanted in a brilliant appearance as a witness on her own behalf.
- Chapter 5. "The Case of H. H. Holmes": Wallace properly claims a Canadian interest in the crimes of H. H. Holmes, famous U.S. insurance swindler and serial killer. Holmes began his career in crime as a life-insurance swindler who obtained policy proceeds by falsely identifying a corpse as that of the assured. In a murderous variant of the scam, he insured the life of a confederate, Benjamin Pitezel, and then converted him into a genuine cadaver, probably by administering chloroform. To cover up his crime, he murdered Pitezel's two daughters in Canada.
- Chapter 6. "The Death of David Scollie": Thomas Gray and his wife were acquitted of murder and arson when the decapitated body of elderly farmer David Scollie was found in the smoldering ruins of his farm house near Peterborough, Ontario, in 1895. Scollie had deeded the property to the Grays in exchange for their promise to maintain him for life, which, Mrs. Gray complained to a neighbor, had been continuing longer than she had hoped. The Grays were tracked to Florida by Canadian detective and memoirist John Wilson Murray.
- Chapter 7. "The Case of the Hyams Twins": After their first jury failed to agree, identical

twins, Harry Place Hyams and Dallas Theodore Hyams, were acquitted of murdering their warehouse employee, sixteen-year-old William Chinook Wells, in Toronto in 1893. Defense experts supported the twins' claim that Wells's head was accidentally crushed by the falling weight of a defective elevator.

- Chapter 8. "The Crimes of Dr. Cream": Dr. Thomas Neill Cream, first abortionist and then serial strychnine poisoner of London prostitutes and blackmailer, was raised and educated in Canada and therefore included in Wallace's patriotic collection.

- Chapter 9. "The Birchall Case": The trial of Oxford-educated Reginald Birchall, who shot Fred C. Benwell to death in a Canadian swamp in 1890, caused a worldwide sensation. Hoping to raise money to bet on a horse he correctly predicted would win the year's derby, Birchall lured Benwell and Douglas Pelly to Canada as prospective farm investors. Once again, Detective John Wilson Murray cracked the case and sent his man to the gallows.

- Chapter 10. "The Lucan Murders": Perhaps the most famous crime in Canadian history is the murder of five members of the Donnelly family at their farm in Lucan, western Ontario, in the early morning hours of February 4, 1880. The massacre was the culmination of a feud among Irish immigrants. James Donnelly, the head of the family who was among the victims, had served seven years in prison for killing his neighbor Patrick Farrell in 1857. Further violence was sparked by rivalry in the coaching business and Lucan became gripped by arson and other acts of terror often attributed to the Donnellys. The 1880 murders followed the organization of a vigilante group aimed at the Donnelly family. James Carroll, the local constable, was tried for the crime on the basis of eyewitness testimony of eleven-year-old Johnny O'Connor, and acquitted; none of the other marauders was brought to justice. Full-length accounts of the feud include Ray Fazakas, *The Donnelly Album* (Toronto: Macmillan, 1977); and Orlo Miller, *The Donnellys Must Die* (Toronto: Macmillan, 1962). Poet James Reany has written a stage trilogy, *The Donnellys*, published with scholarly apparatus by James Noonan (Victoria, B.C.: Press Porcépic, 1983).

- Chapter 11. "The McCarthy Mystery": Two juries failed to agree on a verdict when John and Martha Osborne, proprietors of a hotel in Shediac, New Brunswick, were charged with murdering and robbing their guest, Timothy McCarthy, in 1877, although their employee, Annie Parker, swore that she had witnessed the crime and identified with close approximation the place where the corpse was found in the Sadouac River.

- Chapter 12. "The Death of D'Arcy McGee": A rebel in his native Ireland, Thomas D'Arcy McGee changed his views after emigrating to Canada where he became one of the "Fathers of the Canadian Confederation" in 1867 and served in Parliament. Because of his opposition to Fenian penetration of Canada, his life was in danger from attack by Irish extremists. In April 1868 he was shot dead from behind as he was about to enter his Ottawa lodging house after delivering an effective speech in the House of Commons. Patrick James Whelan was hanged for the crime, and although the only eyewitness testimony was effectively demolished by the defense, Wallace believes that sufficient evidence remained of Whelan's threats against McGee to support the verdict.

- Chapter 13. "The Hogan Murder": James Brown, a member of the Brooks' Bush gang, which waylaid and murdered legislator John Sheridan Hogan on Don Bridge to the east of Toronto in 1859, was the only one of the assailants to hang.
- Chapter 14. "The Strange Case of Dr. King": Wallace cites Dr. William Henry King as an example of a criminal "found guilty for the wrong reason." It was the prosecution's case that Dr. King, smitten by the charms and romantic advances of young Melinda Vandervoort, poisoned his wife with arsenic at Brighton, Canada, in 1858. Actually, as King confessed before mounting the gallows, he had used chloroform. Wallace wonders: "Who then put eleven grains of arsenic into the stomach of the dead woman, either after death or so soon before death that the lining of the stomach showed little or no inflammation?"
- Chapter 15. "The Townsend Case": This is a brain-teasing identity mystery. The Crown tried two murder cases against a man they claimed to be William Townsend. In the first trial the defendant was charged with having murdered shopkeeper John Hamilton Nelles in a village a few miles north of Lake Erie in 1854; in the second prosecution, he was accused of the subsequent killing of a constable. The jury failed to reach a verdict in the trial for the Nelles murder in which the defendant asserted mistaken identity, and in the trial for the constable's murder he was acquitted, persuading the jury that he was Robert McHenry, who had spent 1854 in California. On the basis of information he received from a Scottish neighbor of the so-called McHenry, Wallace believes the man who stood trial in the two cases was neither McHenry nor the bandit Townsend.
- Chapter 16. "The Mystery of Walker's Ear": Capping a battle for power between military and civil authorities in newly born British Canada, six disguised soldiers cut off the ear of Montreal justice of the peace Thomas Walker in 1764 and got off scot-free. Wallace does not regret the outcome, since "Thomas Walker was apparently a most poisonous person."

w.3 Walling, George W. *Recollections of a New York Chief of Police.* New York: Caxton, 1887.
■ One of the principal nineteenth-century American police memoirs, this book records Walling's thirty-eight years as patrolman, detective, captain, inspector, and chief of the New York City police. Among the cases of which he gives firsthand accounts are the murder of prostitute Helen Jewett; the abduction and killing of cigar girl Mary Rogers (Poe's "Marie Roget"); the Astor Place Riot; the foiled 1861 attempt to assassinate President Lincoln; the Draft Riots; the murder of Civil War journalist Albert D. Richardson; the kidnapping of Charley Ross; and the abortion "palace" of Madam Restell, who committed suicide after Anthony Comstock procured her arrest.

Walling took a dim view of New York City's party politics and the screen it provided for criminals. He summarized bluntly the "intimate" relations between politics and crime: "All the sneaks, hypocrites and higher grade of criminals, when questioned upon the subject, almost invariably lay claim to be adherents of the Republican party; while, on the other hand, criminals of the lower order—those who rob by violence and brute force—lay claim in no uncertain tones to being practical and energetic exponents of true Democratic principles" (597).

W.4 Warren, Robert Penn   *All the King's Men*. New York: Harcourt Brace, 1946.

■ Warren asserted that Willie Stark, the protagonist of *All the King's Men*, "was not Huey Long" but "only himself, whatever that self turned out to be, a shadowy wraith or a blundering human being." Still, Stark's career has many points of resemblance to the notorious governor and boss of Louisiana, including his birth in a rural district of a Southern state that enjoys only brief prosperity while its sawmills last; his self-education and door-to-door peddling of a dubious product; his rise to the governor's mansion and ultimate assassination.

In 1935 Long was murdered in the Capitol at Baton Rouge by Dr. Carl Austin Weiss Jr. Despite fanciful conspiracy theories of some historians, the killer seems to have been actuated by revenge; Long had destroyed the judicial career of Weiss's father by gerrymandering his district and spreading the rumor that he had Negro blood. In Warren's novel, Willie Stark's murder is spurred by political retaliation and "Southern honor." The governor outrages politician Tiny Duffy by ending dealings with a corrupt contractor. Duffy gets even by informing Adam Stanton that Stark is having an affair with his sister Anne, and Adam turns assassin.

W.5 ———   *Brother to Dragons: A Tale in Verse and Voices*. New York: Random House, 1953.

■ This verse novel is Warren's set of variations on a horrifying Kentucky murder of the early nineteenth century, the axe slaying of a slave named George by Thomas Jefferson's nephew, Lilburn (correctly spelled Lilburne) Lewis. George had angered Lilburn by breaking a favorite pitcher of his deceased mother Lucy Lewis (see M.28). In Warren's poem the principal figures in the case meet in eternity to reflect on the tragedy, and a commentary is provided by a poet identified by the author's initials, R.P.W. The personality and voice of Thomas Jefferson dominate the work. Jefferson's idealistic view of human nature has been shattered by his nephew's crime, which has caused him to recognize the beast in man, symbolized by the Minotaur:

> The beast waits. He's the infamy of Crete.
> He is the midnight's enormity. He is
> Our brother, our darling brother.

W.6 ———   *World Enough and Time: A Romantic Novel*. New York: Random House, 1950.

■ This novel is based on the so-called Kentucky Tragedy, which has spawned many works of imaginative literature, including a fragmentary play by Edgar Allan Poe (see P.17). In 1825 Jereboam O. Beauchamp, a young Kentucky lawyer, stabbed Colonel Solomon P. Sharp to death after Sharp, state solicitor-general, declined a dueling challenge. Beauchamp had won Ann Cooke's consent to marry him on the condition that he act as her champion against Sharp, who had impregnated and jilted her. After following the narrative of the historical case with great fidelity, Warren invented a wildly romantic ending. In real life, Beauchamp mounted the gallows after stabbing Ann Cooke to death in his cell and wounding himself. In the novel, Beauchamp's counterpart, Jeremiah Beaumont, escapes with Rachel Jordan (Ann Cooke renamed) into the wilderness; she commits suicide and he is murdered before he can return to Frankfort to give himself up. For Jeremiah, his flight westward had been a failed attempt to "embrace the world as all." See Charles H. Bohner, *Robert Penn Warren* (New York: Twayne, 1964).

w.7 Wassermann, Jakob *Caspar Hauser: The Inertia of the Heart*. 1908. Trans. and intro. Michael Hulse. London: Penguin, 1992.

■ Wassermann's influential novel revealed him as an ardent partisan of Caspar (or Kaspar) Hauser, the mysterious youth who appeared out of nowhere in 1828 to tell burghers of Nuremberg in his halting words that he had been imprisoned since early childhood and denied even a rudimentary opportunity for personality development. Many of the principal figures in Hauser's short, unhappy life are introduced by Wassermann under their actual names, with the exception of the boy's last, venomous foster parent, teacher Johan Georg Meyer, who is thinly disguised as Quandt.

Wassermann embraces a theory advanced by many writers to this day, that Hauser was the rightful heir to the princely throne of Baden (as the son of Prince Karl and his wife, Stéphanie Beauharnais), stolen in infancy to clear the path for a rival line and murdered in 1833 to hide his secret. The heroes of the narrative are Hauser's first guardian, Georg Friedrich Daumer (1800–1875); and reformist Bavarian judge Anselm von Feuerbach (1775–1833), who studied the boy's case with sympathetic belief in his veracity and suffering. Wassermann suggests, as do modern conspiracy theorists, that Feuerbach may have been poisoned for coming too close to the truth of Hauser's origin, and he identifies as archvillain Philip Henry, Earl Stanhope (1781–1855), who moves like a spider at the heart of an international plot against Hauser's life. In Wassermann's subtle portrayal, even Stanhope, Kaspar's guardian, cannot resist the charm of his ward's innocence, and he commits suicide before the murderous attack is made on the young man in a public garden of Ansbach.

In his 1921 memoir (published in the United States as *My Life as German and Jew* [New York: Coward-McCann, 1933]), Wassermann noted that his grandfather had seen Kaspar Hauser and "spoke of him as of a very mysterious person." In the same year, Wassermann commented that the idea behind his novel was "to show how people of every quality of spirit and intellect, from the coarsest to the most sophisticated, the ambitious utilitarian and the philosopher, the servile toady and the apostle of humanity, the hired scoundrel and the pedagogue, the sensual woman and the noble crusader for earthly justice, are all without exception utterly dull and utterly helpless when confronted with the phenomenon of innocence." See M.14.

The results of DNA analysis reported in the *International Journal of Medicine* in 1998 tended to prove that Kaspar Hauser was not the Prince of Baden. See http://link.springer.de/link/service/journals/00414/bibs/8111006/81110287.htm. A bloodstain from a garment believed to be Hauser's underpants was divided and analyzed independently by the Institute of Legal

Medicine, University of Munich, and the Forensic Science Service Laboratory, Birmingham, England. Mitochondrial DNA from the clothing was compared with DNA obtained from two living maternal relatives of Stéphanie de Beauharnais. Differences in sequences were found in the two reference blood samples at seven confirmed positions, proving that the Hauser bloodstain did not originate from a son of Stéphanie de Beauharnais, as believers in the foundling's Baden royal birth had maintained.

w.8 Webster, John *The Duchess of Malfi*. 1614. Ed. John Russell Brown. Manchester: Manchester Univ. Press (Revels Plays), 1974.

■ Webster's tragic heroine was, in real life, Giovanna d'Aragona, married in 1490 at age twelve to Alfonso Piccolomini, who became Duke of Amalfi in 1493; in 1498 she was widowed. Giovanna governed the duchy in behalf of her son Alfonso for more than ten years. In 1510 she left Amalfi on the pretext of making a pilgrimage to Loreto but detoured to Ancona, where she joined Antonio Bologna, formerly master of her household, whom she secretly married. The ill-matched menage was of short duration; in October 1513 Antonio was killed in Milan, and Giovanna was probably assassinated at Amalfi several months earlier. It is thought that Bandello, who based a novella on the murders, knew Antonio personally (see Gunnar Boklund, *The Duchess of Malfi: Sources, Themes, Characters* [Cambridge, Mass.: Harvard Univ. Press 1962]). Webster's masterpiece enriches the historical narrative, presenting one of the most erotic courtship scenes in seventeenth-century theater and excruciatingly prolonging the suffering of the duchess before her death at her brother Ferdinand's hands.

w.9 ———— *The White Devil*. 1612. Ed. John Russell Brown. Manchester: Manchester Univ. Press (Revels Plays), 1960.

■ Webster based his play on the criminal career of Vittoria Accoramboni. Married unhappily to Francesco Peretti, nephew of Cardinal Montalto, the childless Vittoria came under the spell of Paolo Giordano Orsini, first Duke of Bracciano. In 1576, four years before meeting Vittoria, the Duke strangled his Medici wife and subsequently also procured the murder of her lover. In 1581 Vittoria's husband was lured from his house and murdered at the orders of Paolo Giordano and Vittoria, now lovers. Shortly thereafter they married secretly in an irregular ceremony witnessed by Vittoria's maid, and over the years they defied papal disapproval by remarrying twice with greater formality. The criminal pair's situation became more precarious in 1585 with an election of a new pope, Cardinal Montalto, the uncle of Vittoria's murdered husband. Later that year, Paolo Giordano died, apparently of natural causes; Vittoria and one of her brothers were murdered a month later by three disguised assassins who broke into her home. The killers had been sent by Lodovico Orsini, a distant kinsman of Paolo Giordano, who had chosen murder as the most expeditious means of terminating Vittoria's claims on the Orsini family property (see Gunnar Boklund, *The Sources of the White Devil* [New York: Haskell House, 1966]).

By the time Act 5 arrives, Webster commits many more homicides than did the historical Vittoria and her husband. In the stage finale, one of Vittoria's two brothers,

Flamineo, stabs the other, Marcello; their mother Cornelia rushes at her murderous child with a knife; Paolo Giordano is strangled by two adversaries before Vittoria's eyes after his helmet has been sprinkled with poison to induce drowsiness; and at last Vittoria is herself stabbed to death.

w.10 Wedekind, Frank *Pandora's Box.* 1904. In *Five Tragedies of Sex.* Trans. Frances Fawcett and Stephen Spender. Intro. Lion Feuchtwanger. New York: Theatre Arts Books, n.d.
■ In this second of the Lulu plays, Wedekind brings into confrontation a male and female who both embody the sexual impulse distorted by repressive society: Lulu, fallen into a life of prostitution, receives a dangerous customer, Jack the Ripper. The renowned "lady killer" does not seem to have the gift of gab, nor does Lulu's professional repartee sparkle:

> Jack: You seem to have a pretty mouth.
> Lulu: I get it from my mother.
> Jack: It looks it.—How much do you want?—I haven't much money left.
> Lulu: Don't you want to stay all night, then?
> Jack: No, I haven't time. I must go home.
> Lulu: You can tell them at home tomorrow morning that you missed the last omnibus and spent the night with a friend.

Lulu's bargaining is unsuccessful. Jack turns the tables by insisting that she give him all the money she has in her pockets; she complies and pleads: "I won't do you any harm! I like you so much. Don't let me beg any longer!" Jack stabs Lulu's lesbian companion, Countess Geschwitz, in the belly and carries Lulu into a closet where he murders her. After a while he reemerges, congratulating himself on "a good piece of work"; he regrets, however, that "they haven't even got a towel."

In 1929, G. W. Pabst directed a silent-film version of the two Wedekind plays under the title *Pandora's Box*, with Louise Brooks in the starring role. The third act of Alban Berg's operatic setting, which ends with Jack's murder of the heroine, was posthumously scored for the Paris premiere of 1979.

w.11 Weiss, Peter *The Persecution and Assassination of Jean-Paul Marat as Performed by the Inmates of the Asylum of Charenton under the Direction of the Marquis de Sade [Marat/Sade].* English version Geoffrey Skelton. Verse adaptation Adrian Mitchell. Intro. Peter Brook. Music by Richard Peaslee. New York: Atheneum, 1965.
■ In this multilayered play-within-a-play, inmates of the insane asylum of Chartenton near Paris enact, under the direction of the Marquis de Sade, the assassination of French revolutionary firebrand and gifted scientist Jean-Paul Marat. The characters all have their say but win nobody to their point of view on the individual's place in the world's scheme, freedom, revolution, or class antagonisms. In an extended conversation with Marat, Sade laments the "total indifference of Nature" in which the cruelest death achieved by revolutionary excess loses itself. Marat responds: "Against Nature's silence I use action."

Charlotte Corday, in preparing to stab Marat, cites Judith, slayer of Holofernes, as her inspiration, but her assumption of a martyr's role will accomplish nothing. By 1808, the date of the imaginary performance at Charenton, the legacy of the Revolution has been erased by Napoleon's bloody march across Europe. As Sade's production reaches its finale, the mad actors lead an uprising against their keepers, perhaps to reflect German dramatist Weiss's glum prediction that the cycle of repression and revolt is eternal. See Fig. 6.

w.12 Welty, Eudora *The Robber Bridegroom.* 1970. New York: Harcourt Brace Jovanovich, 1978.

■ Feared highwaymen, the Harpe brothers, William "Big" Harpe and Wiley "Little" Harpe, murdered and robbed travelers on the Natchez Trace in late-eighteenth-century America. Trapped in 1799 by a posse in the Ohio wilderness, Little Harpe escaped. But Big Harpe was less fortunate: his head was cut off by a man whose wife and child he had butchered. Four years later, Little Harpe and a member of the Samuel Mason gang he had joined decapitated their leader with an axe and carried their trophy, packed in clay, to Natchez to claim a reward. While awaiting their payment, they were recognized. Both were hanged at Greenville, Mississippi, in 1804; their heads were then severed and displayed as warnings to the miscreants of the Natchez Trace. See Otto A. Rothert, *The Outlaws of Cave-in-Rock* (Cleveland: Arthur H. Clark, 1924).

The brothers Harpe (respelled Harp) appear in Eudora Welty's spellbinding novella *The Robber Bridegroom*, in which frontier legend blends with ancient myth. The king of the bandits, Jamie Lockhart, his face stained with berry juice to hide his identity, steals the beautiful Rosamond's clothing and then purloins her heart. Like Psyche, desperate to behold the features of her divine lover, Cupid, the beautiful Rosamond applies a brew to dissolve the berry stains and sends her gallant outlaw fleeing from her bed until all ends happily for the couple, who join the respectable merchant class of New Orleans.

In the course of his adventures, Jamie becomes the antagonist of Little Harp, who travels with a trunk containing the severed head of his brother, who vainly cries, "Let me out!" After they are captured by Indians seeking revenge for Little Harp's murder of a young girl of their tribe, Lockhart and Little Harp fight "the whole night through, till the sun came up," and Jamie kills his opponent.

In Welty's poetic version of the Trace, banditry and murder come to serve as symbols of the fleeting nature of human experience and joy as the seasons turn. Rosamond's father, the planter Clement Musgrove, ruminates: "Wrath and love burn only like the campfires. And even the appearance of a hero is no longer a single and majestic event like that of a star in the heavens, but a wandering fire soon lost. A journey is forever lonely and parallel to death, but the two watch each other, the traveler and the bandit through the trees. Like will-o'-the-wisps the little blazes burn on the rafts all night, unsteady beside the shore. Where are they even so soon as tomorrow? Massacre is hard to tell from the performance of other rites, in the great silence where the wanderer is coming."

In 1976 *The Robber Bridegroom* was first presented as a Broadway musical, with book and lyrics by Alfred Uhry and music by Robert Waldman. The decapitation theme is sounded when Little Harp and the portable head of his brother sing: "Two heads are better than one, brother / When everything's said and done."

One of the most sensational events in the mythical narratives of Mississippi settlement that introduce the three acts of William Faulkner's novel-drama, *Requiem for a Nun* (New York: Random House, 1951) is an escape of Natchez Trace bandits from the Jefferson jail. In time it was maintained that the imprisoned gang had included the Harpes: "twenty-five years later legend would begin to affirm, and a hundred years later would still be at it, that two of the bandits were the Harpes themselves, Big Harpe anyway, since the circumstances, the method of the breakout left behind like a smell, an odor, a kind of gargantuan and bizarre playfulness at once humorous and terrifying, as if the settlement had fallen, blundered, into the notice or range of an idle and whimsical grant. Which—that they were the Harpes—was impossible, since the Harpes and even the last of Mason's ruffians were dead or scattered by this time."

On the night of the sniper slaying of Medgar Evers in 1963, Eudora Welty wrote the short monologue of a bigoted assassin, "Where Is the Voice Coming From?" (*The Collected Stories of Eudora Welty* [New York: Harcourt Brace Jovanovich, 1980]). The killer triumphs over his victim's aspirations: "We ain't never now, never going to be equals and you know why? One of us is dead."

w.13 West, Rebecca [pseudonym of Cicily Isabel Fairfield] *The New Meaning of Treason.* New York: Viking, 1964.

▪ The most detailed study in West's revised book on treason is her consideration of William Joyce, known throughout England as "Lord Haw Haw" when he broadcasted for the Nazis during World War II. The conviction and execution of Joyce turned on the British court's determination of a gnarled issue regarding the legal basis for allegiance. Born in Brooklyn in 1906, William was a U.S. citizen at birth, the son of a naturalized American from Galway and a Lancashire woman. At first glance, therefore, it seemed that Joyce committed no offense against England when he became a naturalized German in 1940 and undertook propaganda activity on behalf of his adopted fatherland. The court, however, found a duty of British allegiance arising from the fact that, after thirty years of residence in England, Joyce traveled to Germany and began his hostile activity while holding a renewed British passport that had not expired. Dame Rebecca approved, noting that a contrary ruling would have authorized resident alien spies to flit back and forth across the English Channel without fear of prosecution.

Facing the mystery of Joyce's disloyalty, West perceives his sense of triumph over his own mediocrity: "His faint smile said simply, 'I am what I am.' He did not defend the faith which he had held, for he had doubted it; he did not attack it, for he had believed in it. It is possible that in these last days fascism had passed out of the field of his close attention, that what absorbed him was the satisfaction which he felt at being, for the first time in his life, taken seriously."

Other traitors examined by West include Alan Nunn May, the Rosenbergs, Klaus Fuchs, Burgess and Maclean, George Blake, Gordon Lonsdale, and William John Christopher

Vassall. Although she regards all traitors as thieves and liars, Dame Rebecca expresses nostalgic regret that the earlier generation of revolutionaries have been replaced by mercenary scavengers of ever-proliferating secrets, many of them obsolete when delivered to foreign enemies.

West has written a separate account of Vassall's espionage in *The Vassall Affair* (London: Sunday Telegraph, 1963).

w.14 ———— *A Train of Powder.* London: Macmillan, 1955.

■ Inserted between chapters on the Nuremberg war crimes trials are essays on murder cases, "Opera in Greenville" and "Mr. Setty and Mr. Hume." The first of these two pieces reports a 1947 lynching trial in Greenville, South Carolina. West observed with fascination the courtroom theatrics that attended the defense and acquittal of thirty-one white men (mostly taxi-drivers) charged with abducting and murdering a twenty-four-year-old black man, Willie Earle, who had been jailed for robbing and killing white cabbie Willie Brown. West regarded the lynching participants as moved by a misguided friendship rather than blood lust and believed that the trial brought home to them and their families the horror of what they had done. She is, by contrast, pitiless in the contempt she lavishes on the race-baiting defense counsel, including a lawyer with labor union ties and a "liberal" reputation. West was perhaps unduly optimistic in her conclusions regarding the impact of the trial on the mind of the South: "There was a historic change in tempo to be felt at the Greenville Trial; wickedness itself had been aware of the slowing of its pulse. The will of the South had made its decision, and by 1954 three years had gone by without a lynching in the United States."

The second murder essay is West's eyewitness account of the trial of compulsive impostor Brian Donald Hume, who dumped the decapitated and legless corpse of Stanley Setty from a rented airplane into the Essex marshes, mistaking them for the high seas. Acquitted of killing Setty, Hume pleaded guilty as an accessory after the fact and, upon his release from prison, sold his "confession" of the murder to a newspaper. In 1959 Hume was sentenced to life imprisonment for killing a taxi-driver in connection with a bank raid. In West's sensitively crafted rendering of the Setty case, violence is overcome by the cycle of birth and natural death. The essay begins with West's reflections on her visit to the dignified fisherman-fowler whose discovery of Setty's torso reanimated his trauma over his wife's sudden death by heart attack. The conclusion of the piece shifts away from the crime to the tranquil image of Mrs. Hume caring for her baby daughter in suburban London. The prospect pleases: "The snarl in Hume's genetic line would be disentangled. The mystery that involved him with Mr. Setty will be written about as long as there is a literature of crime; but it will exist only on the printed page. Day by day, through the years, somewhere in the outer suburbs of London, its practical effects will have been quietly smoothed away, and it will be as if it had never happened."

w.15 White, R[eginald] J[ames] *The Smartest Grave.* New York: Harper, 1961.

■ A mysteriously frequent widower and a lustful pursuer of housemaids, "Moat Farm murderer" Samuel Herbert Dougal was finally overtaken by justice in 1903, four years after he shot his wealthy wife, Camille Holland, in the head and buried her in the drainage ditch of a moated English farm property bought with her funds. *The Smartest Grave*, based on the Moat Farm case, is the prize-winning first detective novel of an English university don. White's fictional sleuth, Detective Inspector David Brock, discovers the body of Cecile Lucille Germaine (Camille Cecile Holland) in a filled and planted drainage ditch after his perceptive wife, Agnes, points out that the victim's diminutive body would not have sunk below the muddy water of the farm moat. In his death cell the remorseless murderer (renamed Sid Dugdale) explains his crime: "Why should an old woman with six thousand pounds and no sense stand in the way of a man with brains and energy and no capital?"

White's novel is stronger in its persuasive recreation of period and setting than in its plotting, detection, or portrayals of Victorian policemen. White's title is a quotation from Sir Thomas Browne's description of the Flood: "Though earth hath engrossed the name, yet water hath proved the smartest grave."

w.16 ——— *The Women of Peasenhall.* New York: Harper, 1969.

■ This mystery novel derives its factual basis from William Henderson's 1934 edition of *The Trial of William Gardiner* in the *Notable British Trials* series and John Rowland's 1962 monograph on the case, *The Peasenhall Mystery.* Gardiner, a "Bible-banging" Primitive Methodist choirmaster in Peasenhall, Suffolk, twice benefitted from hung juries when tried for the stabbing murder of a pregnant housemaid, Rose Harsent, with whom some villagers suspected he was having an affair. White solves the crime by attributing the crime to the "women of Peasenhall," whom he likens to a witches' coven. Rose, fictional Detective Inspector David Brock suggests, was what anthropologists term a "proxymater," who served as Georgina Gardiner's proxy in providing sexual services to her husband, William, during her numerous pregnancies. When the housemaid herself became pregnant, however, the female community of Peasenhall took umbrage; Georgina Gardiner murdered her with the aid of Rose's employer Mrs. Crisp and perhaps of the Gardiners' neighbor Amelia Pepper. White regards the 1902 Peasenhall case as a harbinger of the new century: "It was the first case in [Brock's] experience in which all the characters involved were poor persons. If, as people were saying, the new century was to be the century of the common people, the Peasenhall case was an appropriate overture."

w.17 Whittington-Egan, Richard *The Ordeal of Philip Yale Drew.* London: Harrap, 1972.

■ On a fine summer evening in 1929, Alfred Oliver, proprietor of a superior tobacconist's ship in Reading, was bludgeoned unconscious when he was behind his counter. He died twenty-four hours later. The coroner's inquest aroused enormous interest, the prime suspect being Philip Yale Drew, a popular actor, American and well known for his flamboyant personality and eccentric dress. The evidence against him seemed conclusive but was, in fact, based on rumors, conjecture, and coincidence. The conduct of the inquest led to a change in the law. Whittington-Egan exposes the bias of the coroner and the police, discusses the personalities and backgrounds of those involved in a fascinating case set against the colorful backdrop and nostalgic glitter of the theater, and concludes by rating Drew's innocence of the murder as a very high probability.

The outstanding crime historian and literary critic Richard Whittington-Egan, a descendant of Dick Whittington, Lord Mayor of London, was born in Liverpool in 1924. After studying medicine, he served in British Army Intelligence during World War II. From 1957 to 1986, he worked as a Fleet Street journalist. His works in crime history are noted for stylistic elegance as well as probing research, and he is a towering authority on Jack the Ripper. He is married to crime historian Molly Whittington-Egan.

w.18 ———— *The Riddle of Birdhurst Rise.* London: Harrap, 1975.

■ Within a year, three members of a family in South Croydon near London (Edmund Duff; his sister-in-law, Vera Sidney; and his mother-in-law, Mrs. Violet Sidney) died from massive doses of arsenic. Exhumations were ordered and three lengthy inquests held, but the authorities could find no hint of a motive and no clue as to the killer. In August 1929 the case was officially closed; the secret poisoner remained free, and the papers in the case lay gathering dust for almost half a century. Then Whittington-Egan began his own investigation: he talked to the surviving principals, reexamined the documentary evidence, and steadily drew back the lace curtains that had closed around the drawing-room drama. He found, interviewed, and accused face-to-face the person he believed to be the killer: Edmund Duff's widow, Grace. This is one of the most spellbinding modern murder narratives, and Whittington-Egan's investigation of the long unsolved poisonings was both scholarly and courageous.

w.19 Wilde, Oscar   "The Ballad of Reading Gaol." In *The Works of Oscar Wilde*. Ed. and intro. G. F. Maine. London: Collins, 1949.

■ In July 1896, a thirty-year-old trooper in the Royal Horse Guards, Charles Thomas Wooldridge, was hanged in Reading prison. In March Wooldridge waited on the road near the house of his wife, twenty-three-year-old Laura Ellen, who had aroused his jealousy; he slit her throat three times with a razor he had borrowed from a friend. Wooldridge's execution inspired his fellow prisoner Oscar Wilde to write "The Ballad of Reading Gaol." The crime of passion had suggested a parallel to what Wilde perceived as his betrayal by Lord Alfred Douglas, and his famous lines pointed the moral:

> And all men kill the thing they love,
> > By all let this be heard
> Some do it with a bitter look,
> > Some with a flattering word,
> The coward does it with a kiss,
> > The brave man with a sword!

Wilde, of course, was straining poetic license, for Wooldridge's razor was not a sword, nor had he murdered his beloved "in her bed," as the ballad proclaims, but had, less romantically, ambushed her on the road (see Richard Ellmann, *Oscar Wilde* [New York: Knopf, 1988], 503–4).

W.20 ———— "Pen, Pencil and Poison." In *The Works of Oscar Wilde*. Ed. and intro. G. F. Maine. London: Collins, 1949.

■ Wilde borrows his title from a phrase coined by poet Algernon Swinburne to describe the triple career of Thomas Griffiths Wainewright as painter, art critic, and poisoner. In assessing Wainewright's professional attainments, Wilde emphasizes his innovations in aesthetic criticism, ranking him as "one of the first to recognize . . . the true harmony of all really beautiful things irrespective of age or place, of school or manner." In the world of crime, Wainewright, in Wilde's words, was "one of the most subtle and secret poisoners of this or any age." His first victim was his uncle, Thomas Griffiths, whom he poisoned in 1829 to gain possession of Linden House, a property to which he was greatly attached. For no clear reason he then poisoned his mother-in-law, Mrs. Abercrombie, and then her daughter Helen, whose life he and his wife had insured for £18,000. With delight Wilde quoted Wainewright's answer to a friend's reproach for Helen's murder: "Yes; it was a dreadful thing to do, but she had very thick ankles."

In punishment for his crimes, Wainewright was eventually transported to Van Diemen's Land, where Wilde asserts that he never gave up his habit of poisoning. Still, he asserts as a riposte to those who would deny Wainewright's literary power, "The fact of a man being a poisoner is nothing against his prose."

Wainewright's writings are published in *Essays and Criticisms by Thomas Griffiths Wainewright*, collected with some account of the author by W. Carew Hazlitt (London: Reeves & Turner, 1880). Books on Wainewright include: a biography, Jonathan Curling, *Janus Weathercock: The Life of Thomas Griffiths Wainewright 1794–1847* (London: Thomas Nelson, 1938); a partially fictionalized biography, Charles Norman, *The Genteel Murderer* (New York: Macmillan, 1956); and a mystery novel, Ladbroke Black, *The Prince of Poisoners* (New York: Dial Press, 1932).

Wilde's theory that an artist's criminality should not infect the appraisal of his creative career is applied with a vengeance by Andrew Motion, Poet Laureate of Great Britain, in his novel *Wainewright the Poisoner: The Confession of Thomas Wainewright* (New York: Knopf, 2000). As the subtitle indicates, the work is in the form of a fictional "confession" of Wainewright; at the end of each chapter Motion appends notes comparing the text with biographical and historical sources. One of the book's purposes is to demonstrate the elusiveness of documentation and the unreliability of firsthand accounts. At the novel's midpoint, Wainewright warns the reader that "no confession may be believed, however heartfelt."

Regarding the extent of Wainewright's guilt, the confession of the artist-criminal and Motion's personal view (stated most explicitly in the note to chapter 14) are at odds. The fictional Wainewright admits only to having forged trustees' signatures for the purpose of obtaining outright control of stock certificates from which he had been receiving trust income. Motion, on the other hand, believes that, in addition, the self-styled "follower of the Ideal" poisoned his sister-in-law, Helen Abercrombie, with strychnine, possibly with the help of his wife.

Two other works by Wilde are linked to crime history: his 1880 play *Vera, or The Nihilists,* inspired by Vera Zassoulich's attempted assassination of St. Petersburg police chief Fyodor Trepov; and "The Harlot's House," a poem reflecting his disgust after a night with Parisian prostitute Marie Aguétant, later murdered by Louis Prado (see B.39).

w.21 Wilder, Thornton   *The Ides of March.* New York: Harper & Row, 1948.

▪ Wilder calls this work "a fantasia on certain events and persons of the last days of the Roman republic." The story, which transfers to 45 and 44 B.C. many earlier occurrences, is told through letters and documents imagined by the author (with the exception of poems of Gaius Valerius Catullus and a passage from Suetonius's *Lives of the Caesars* that describes the assassination of Julius Caesar on March 15, 44 B.C.).

The portrait of Caesar that emerges from the words of his friends and enemies and from his own letters is predominantly favorable. He seems to be tolerant of human limitations and forgiving of his adversaries; espousing a proto-existentialist worldview, the dictator writes to his friend Lucius Mamilius Turrinus that "life has no meaning save that which we may confer upon it" and that Rome became a city for him only in so far as he shaped it to his idea. Marcus Junius Brutus, most celebrated of his assassins, does not emerge as a hero. Reputed by Roman gossip to be Caesar's illegitimate son, Brutus mouths a concept of freedom that is mainly literary and opposes the expansion of citizenship. A week before the murder, Caesar writes to Brutus commending his new wife, Calpurnia, to his care as he contemplates leaving for war against the Parthians. Brutus drafts, but cannot bring himself to deliver, an insincere reply.

Wilder's apparent sympathy for Caesar is at odds with his dedication of the book to Lauro de Bosis, who lost his life opposing Mussolini's absolutism and had circulated chain letters against his regime, supposedly at the suggestion of George Bernard Shaw.

w.22 Williams, Emlyn   *Beyond Belief.* London: Hamish Hamilton, 1967.

▪ Emlyn Williams's *Beyond Belief* (1967), which fleshes out a factual account of the Moors case (see S.39) with the author's fictional "surmises," emphasizes the murderers' readings in sadism and the prevalence of portrayed violence. The place of cinematic violence in the atmosphere in which Brady and Hindley grew up is marked by continual quotations of lurid titles from movie marquees. But Williams is also concerned about the impact of the pornography of historic violence. In fact, he theorizes that the murder of John Kilbride may have been suggested by the assassination of President Kennedy the day before. Beyond this reference to the aura of violence, Williams portrays the crime, in rather traditional terms, as growing from the roots of childhood experiences and from the poor quality of urban life. Ultimately, however, he pauses before the "mysteries of identity . . . the spells which are woven after birth, the subtle processes working from day to day in the darkness of the young head, as it grows from childhood to adolescence and maturity."

w.23 ———— *Dr. Crippen's Diary: An Invention.* London: Robson, 1987.

■ In this fictional diary, Williams puts himself inside the mind and voice of Dr. Hawley Harvey Crippen. Born in Coldwater, Michigan, and trained as an homeopath in Cleveland, Crippen became England's most famous murderer after Jack the Ripper. In 1910 he poisoned his wife, a minor-league singer who called herself "Belle Elmore"; he dismembered her body and buried it in the cellar of their North London home. Fleeing to America aboard the SS *Montrose* with his mistress, typist Ethel Le Neve, Crippen became the first murderer to be apprehended by use of the wireless.

The Crippen diary, as imagined by Williams, combines black humor with macabre details of Belle Elmore's dissection. When he drops his wife's head in the sea en route to Dieppe, Crippen notes in his diary: "The fishes are welcome. As the French put it, *bon appétit.*" To provide stylistic verisimilitude, Williams imitates the stilted expressions, repetitive phrasings, and punctuation errors of an unschooled writer. The dramatic high spot of the diary is the tense cat-and-mouse game between Crippen and his pursuer, Chief Inspector Walter Dew of Scotland Yard. It is a prank of literary history that this pastiche of a Crippen journal (first published by Reader's Digest in 1978) preceded by a decade and a half the 1992 announcement of the discovery of the so-called diary of Jack the Ripper.

In the course of the narrative, and his factual Afterword, Williams addresses some of the abiding puzzles of the Crippen murder:

- Did Crippen intentionally poison his wife? In the diary the doctor records a plan to throw his wife overboard during a Channel crossing; but shortly before they were to embark, she died by accident. Crippen had been administering moderate doses of hyoscine to Belle to quiet her sex drive and bad temper; one evening, suffering from an overpowering headache, she had mistaken the hyoscine bottle for a painkiller and downed a lethal quantity.
- Why did Crippen wrap his wife's remains in his incriminating pajama top? The Afterword suggests that this was a foolish act of bravado; according to the diary, Belle had made humiliating remarks about Crippen's habit of wearing the pajama top when they had sex.
- Did Ethel Le Neve know about the murder? Williams believes that Crippen kept her persuaded of his innocence.

W.24 ———— *The Druid's Rest: A Comedy in Three Acts.* London: Heinemann, 1944.

■ This play, which introduced the young Richard Burton as Glan, is a comic echo of *Night Must Fall*. The action takes place at a Welsh pub, the Druid's Rest, operated by Job and Kate Edwards. Their two sons are Glan, who dreams of the sky, beer, and girls, and his younger brother, Tommos, who lives in an imaginative world of blood-and-thunder fiction and newspaper reports of crime. Tommos has spread a story that Miss Perry, spinster sister of Constable Zachariah, was walking in the woods with a hymnal under her arm and carrying a gardening spade and a cardboard box containing her illegitimate baby. Another suspicion rises when a guest calling himself Mr. Smith arrives at the pub seeking a room. Although the hatbox he carries (unlike that belonging to Dan in *Night Must Fall*) contains nothing more incriminating than books, the pub dwellers believe that its owner must be G. J. Smith, England's notorious Brides-in-the-Bath Murderer, who has been falsely reported to be on the run in Wales. It turns out that the pub's mysterious client is actually Lord Ffynnon, a nobleman mad about poetry who has decided to enjoy Welsh country life incognito before assuming his Druid's robes at the National Eisteddfod, which he has arranged to bring to Ffynnon. When the lord's true identity is revealed, Glan Edwards muses, "I know he took the name o' Smith, which happened to be the same as the other . . . But aside from that, what made us so *dead* sure he was the murderer?"

In 1997 G. J. Smith returned to the West End as the title character in Karoline Leach's two-person play *The Mysterious Mr. Love*. Although Mr. Love reflects coldly on the serial victims he drowns in honeymoon hotel bathtubs in order to collect life insurance, he experiences at moments a surprising attachment to his current target, a millinery shop assistant named Adelaide. Critic Benedict Nightingale of the London *Times* found difficulty in accepting the playwright's premise that "somewhere deep inside [Mr. Love] is a rejected, embittered slum-kid."

w.25 ———— *Night Must Fall.* 1935. In *The Collected Plays of Emlyn Williams*. London: Heinemann, 1961.

■ *Night Must Fall* builds suspensefully to the murder of an elderly hypochondriac, Mrs. Bramson, by Dan, a hotel page boy whom she has taken into her isolated Essex bungalow as an attendant and flatterer. In order to provide a realistic quality to his drama, Williams drew on his memories of many English murder cases of the preceding fifteen years. For details about the disposal of a corpse, Williams had cast his mind back to Patrick Mahon's murder of his mistress, Emily Kaye, in a Sussex bungalow (1924) and to Toni Mancini's clumsy concealment of the body of Violette Kaye (alias Joan Watson) in his Brighton lodging (1934). In fact, it was Patrick Mahon's crime that gave Williams the idea for what was to become one of the most celebrated (and certainly one of the most horrific) props in modern stage history—the hat box in which a previous victim's head is hidden.

In the personality and motivation of Williams's murderer appear reflections of at least three cases in which a young man killed an elderly woman for gain. The earliest of the cases was that of Henry Jacoby, an eighteen-year-old pantry boy in a London hotel who was executed in 1922 for battering to death a hotel guest, Lady Alice White, as she lay in her bed. The prosecution argued that Jacoby had gone to Lady White's room to steal but, when she awakened, murdered her. Jacoby excited considerable public sympathy because of his youth and possible insanity. He claimed that he had heard "whisperings" in the hotel basement earlier in the night and that he entered Lady White's room because of murmurs he thought indicated the presence of "some other person who had no right to be there."

Other homicidal models for Williams's Dan are John Donald Merrett and Sidney Fox, whose cases are included in the *Notable British Trials* series (see N.7).

A striking feature of the play is the hostility expressed by acquaintances of Mrs. Bramson, the victim-to-be. Olivia Grayne, the elderly woman's companion, cannot restrain herself from saying to Dan, "I could kill her"; and Olivia's phlegmatic suitor, Herbert

Laurie, correctly predicts, "She'll be found murdered one of these days." In giving his characters these angry lines, Williams not only builds suspense but also appears to apply a theory commonly held by crime writers of his era: that many victims have personal characteristics that attract murderers. See Albert I. Borowitz, "'The Sinister Behind the Ordinary': Emlyn Williams's *Night Must Fall*," in *A Gallery of Sinister Perspectives: Ten Crimes and a Scandal* (see B.27).

w.26 ———— *Someone Waiting*. London: Heinemann, 1954.

■ First performed in 1954, this tense thriller introduces the mild-mannered Mr. Fenn, who seeks revenge against John Nedlow, who has procured the execution of Fenn's son for a murder committed in the Nedlow flat. According to a biographer of Emlyn Williams, the loveless marriage of John and Vera Nedlow is inspired by the Wallace murder case (Liverpool, 1931), one of Williams's favorites (James Harding, *Emlyn Williams: A Life* [London: Weidenfeld & Nicolson, 1993], 161–62). One of the characters in *Someone Waiting*, Mrs. Danecourt, has attended many Old Bailey trials, including those of murderers Neville Heath and Brian Donald Hume (whom she calls Herbert Bart).

w.27 Williams, Roger L. *Manners and Murders in the World of Louis-Napoleon*. Seattle: Univ. of Washington Press, 1975.

■ This study of causes célèbres from the period of Louis-Napoleon (later Napoleon III) includes: Louis-Napoleon's failed coup attempt at Boulogne in 1840; the 1857 assassination of Paris archbishop Sibour by disaffected priest Jean-Louis Verger; bomber Felice Orsini's 1858 attempted assassination of Napoleon III; Jean-Baptiste Troppmann's murders of the Kinck family (see B.68); and Prince Pierre Bonaparte's murder of Victor Noir, who had visited the prince to make dueling arrangements in behalf of a journalist who had quite accurately suggested that Pierre was a "ferocious beast." The author explains that he chose legal cases "to exemplify the French courtroom as a political arena in the nineteenth century."

w.28 Williams, Tennessee *Not About Nightingales*. New York: New Directions, 1998.

■ This fourth long play of Williams (which he dedicated to the memory of defense lawyer Clarence Darrow) was based on a 1938 atrocity in a high-security prison in Holmesburg, Pennsylvania: twenty-five convicts who staged a hunger strike there were locked into the "Klondike," a steam-heated cell with little ventilation, and four died from the ordeal. Originally titling the work *Hell: An Expressionistic Drama Based on the Prison Atrocity in Philadelphia County*, Williams drew on material in his earlier sketch on a hunger strike, *Quit Eating*, which he had set at the Stateville, Illinois, prison where Darrow's famous clients, thrill killers Leopold and Loeb, were confined. Allean Hale has called *Not about Nightingales* (which is divided into twenty-two short "episodes") Williams's "most cinematic" play and has pointed out similarities to the 1935 prison film *The Big House*.

Although the social realism embodied in the play would not turn out to be the playwright's characteristic voice, the trustie "Canary Jim," who has a poetic vision of life's potential and its limitations, seems often to speak for Williams. The play's title is explained in what is Episode One of Act 2 in the acting version. Tormented by his fore-knowledge of the grim retribution that the hunger strike will bring, Jim tears the "Ode to a Nightingale" from a volume of Keats's poetry, denouncing the subject as "sissy stuff" that would be forsworn by "literary punks" forced to "spend a few years in stir before they select their subjects." Jim tells stenographer Eva Crane, with whom he is falling in love, that on his own release he might start writing "but not about nightingales."

w.29 Williamson, Hugh Ross *The Arrow and the Sword: An Essay in Detection*. London: Faber & Faber, 1947.

■ In this book, in which T. S. Eliot, as author of *Murder in the Cathedral*, took great interest, Williamson argues that the slayings of King William Rufus in the New Forest and of Thomas Becket in Canterbury Cathedral both constituted "the ritual killing of the Divine King in the witch-cult" having pre-Christian origins. Rufus's death was "consummated in the depths of a forest at sunset on the site of an ancient church—and thus, presumably, a pre-Christian holy place." As evidence of Becket's ritual death, Williamson cites "the recurrence of the number four" in the four knights who assassinated him and the four steps he was said to have ascended before the blows were struck.

w.30 ———— *The Butt of Malmsey*. London: Michael Joseph, 1967.

■ This historical novel champions the cause of George, Duke of Clarence, in his political struggle against his older brother, King Edward IV. Rejecting Shakespeare's portrait in *Richard III* of "false, fleeting, perjured Clarence," Williamson writes that George was "demonstrably the more popular" because of "the golden charm of his looks, deepened by sadness" and "the winning affability of his manner." Williamson accepts the tradition that the Duke was drowned in a butt of malmsey after a bill of attainder was passed against him and maintains that the bizarre mode of execution was his own choice.

w.31 ———— *The Gunpowder Plot*. London: Faber & Faber, 1951.

■ Williamson seizes on apparent weaknesses in the tradition that Parliament was miraculously saved from destruction at the hands of Catholic fanatics responsible for the Gunpowder Plot. He argues that William Parker, fourth Baron Monteagle, who received and delivered to the King's secretary an anonymous letter warning Monteagle to absent himself from Parliament on the day of the planned explosion, was a government agent provocateur who nursed and monitored the conspiracy. Also noted with suspicion are the doubtful authenticity of conspirator Thomas Winter's crucial confession and the absence of Ordnance accounts of stores of gunpowder during the period of the plot.

w.32 ———— *Historical Whodunits*. New York: Macmillan, 1956.

■ These articles are rewritten versions of the author's two radio series, "Historical Who-dunits." Despite his animus against Tudor and Protestant "propaganda," the contrarian Williamson often proposes fascinating solutions to historical enigmas. His subjects include: the death of King William Rufus, which Williamson construes as a pre-Christian ritual sacrifice; the princes in the Tower, who, according to the author, were victims of Henry VII; the identity of the impostor Perkin Warbeck, who claimed to be Richard, Duke of York; the death of Amy Robsart (see s.14); the murder of Darnley at Kirk o' Field; the Gowrie Conspiracy; the Gunpowder Plot, which Williamson believes was nursed by a Protestant agent provocateur William Parker, Baron Monteagle; the murder of Sir Thomas Overbury in the Tower; the Campden Wonder (see m.13); the murder of Sir Edmund Berry Godfrey, which ushered in the "Popish Plot" hysteria; the Appin Murder (see s.52).

w.33 Woollcott, Alexander *The Portable Woollcott.* New York: Viking, 1946.

■ Two collections included in this volume, *While Rome Burns* (1934) and *Long, Long Ago* (1943), include some of America's most sophisticated articles on classic criminal cases, most of them home-grown:

- Nan Patterson ("The Mystery of the Hansom Cab")
- The murder of Helen Jewett
- Ameer Ben Ali ("Frenchy"), tried for a New York City murder first thought to have been the handiwork of Jack the Ripper
- The Hall-Mills murder
- The Lindbergh kidnapping
- The Snyder-Gray murder
- The murder of bridge expert Joseph Elwell (see G.26)
- Carl Wanderer, hanged for the 1920 murders of his wife and a "ragged stranger" named Al Watson. Wanderer hired Watson to participate in a "robbery" of Wanderer's wife, staging the crime to make it appear that Watson had acted alone and that he had killed the attacker in revenge. Journalist Ben Hecht's skepticism about Wanderer's story led to the cracking of the case.
- The Archer-Shee case (see R.6)
- The murder of Harriet Staunton (see J.6).

Particularly delightful is Woollcott's account of the acquittal of Myrtle Adkins Bennett for the fatal shooting of her husband after he rebuked her for overbidding a bridge hand. With quicksilvered irony, Woollcott evokes the defendant's fanciful defense of accident that was accepted by the jury: "It seems the dutiful Mrs. Bennett had merely gone for the revolver because her husband wanted to take it with him to St. Joe; that in stumbling over a misplaced chair in the den she fired the first two shots unintentionally and that her husband (pardonably misreading her kind intentions) had sought to disarm her. In the ensuing Apache dance of their struggle for the gun, it had gone off and wounded him fatally."

Harpo Marx had suggested the Bennett case as a subject for an article and proposed that Woolcott entitle it "Vulnerable."

w.34 Wright, Richard *Native Son.* New York: Harper, 1940.

■ Fusing literary technique of the American naturalists (such as his beloved Theodore

Dreiser) with his own insight into the urban slum experience of African Americans, Wright creates the disturbing portrait of Bigger Thomas, who experiences his first sense of freedom when he kills (albeit perhaps unintentionally) Mary Dalton, the daughter of white liberal philanthropists and slum landlords. A twenty-year-old prone to violence born of fear, Bigger despises the acceptance of poverty and racism by his religious mother and his younger siblings, whom he regards as afflicted by "blindness"; yet, he feels keenly his exclusion from the mainstream of American life while he is simultaneously attracted by its materialistic lures embodied in films and magazines.

When Wright had half-completed his first draft of *Native Son*, a Chicago murder was committed that resembled the case the novelist had been imagining. Robert Nixon, an eighteen-year-old black man, was charged with entering the apartment of Mrs. Florence Johnson for the purpose of a burglary and murdering her by blows to the head with a brick when she was wakened by his intrusion (see *People v. Nixon*, 371 Ill. 318, 20 N.E.2d 789 [1939]). At Wright's request, aspiring poet (and his future biographer) Margaret Walker mailed him every article published on the Nixon trial over a period of a year, as shocked as her friend Wright by the crudely racist epithets applied to the defendant (*Richard Wright: Daemonic Genius* [New York: Amistad, 1988], 121–50). Nixon's defense that his accomplice in the burglary, Earl Hicks, had wielded the brick failed; the Illinois Supreme Court ruled that, under principles of felony murder, both burglars were equally responsible for the ensuing murder. Nixon was executed in 1939. The racist atmospherics of the Nixon trial are reflected in *Native Son*, and, like Nixon, Bigger Thomas uses a brick as his murder weapon in silencing his girlfriend, Bessie Mears.

w.35 Wyatt-Brown, Bertram   *Southern Honor: Ethics and Behavior in the Old South*. New York: Oxford Univ. Press, 1982.

■ In this greatly praised study of ethics and behavior in the antebellum American South, Professor Wyatt-Brown stresses the key role played by honor, which he defines as "the cluster of ethical rules, most readily found in societies of small communities, by which judgments of behavior are ratified by community consensus." The ethic of honor is composed of elements that are ages old: "inner feelings of self-worth, gentility, and high-mindedness or public repute, valor for family and country, and conformity to community wishes."

Part 3 of *Southern Honor* examines structures of social control based on honor, including the Old South's unlovely practices that replaced or, in Wyatt-Brown's analysis, complemented the civil and criminal justice system. These measures of community retribution included kangaroo-court procedures for the alleviation of periodic fears about slave insurrections, usually figments of imagination or the pretexts for reasserting white dominion and unity; lynch law and its less-violent alternate, the *charivari* (pronounced *shivaree*), in which the victim, freed by court processes or punished too lightly by judicial authorities to satisfy the mob, was subjected to dehumanizing rituals, such as tar-and-feathering.

Wyatt-Brown strongly advocates the close examination of literary narratives and court records as sources of social history. He brackets his monumental work with Nathaniel Hawthorne's classic story "My Kinsman, Major Molineux," describing a fictional eighteenth-century tar-and-feathering in New England, and a factual narrative of the similar ordeal of James Foster Jr. after he beat his teenaged wife, Susan, to death near Natchez in 1834. In the mob action that followed the quashing of the jury drawn up for Foster's trial, the defendant was saved from lynching only when the opposing lawyers for the defendant and for the interests of his victim joined forces to lead the crowd in the brutal charivari. Only by appearing to support this manifestation of community vengeance were the lawyers, whose professional positions commanded respect, able to save Foster from death.

w.36 Wyndham, Horace *Feminine Frailty.* London: Ernest Benn, 1929.

■ Essayist Wyndham created a large body of work divided between crime and high-society scandal. The characteristic volume, *Feminine Frailty*, features among its transgressors Maria Manning, Victorian murderess; Edith Carew, convicted by a British court in Yokohama of poisoning her husband, Walter; Lola Montez, dancer and beloved of "princes, illustrous personages, writers and painters;" *demi-mondaine* Cora Pearl; and Mary Anne Clarke, who profited from her love affair with the Duke of York by the sale of army commissions. The Clarke scandal was well remembered by the Victorians; in Thackeray's *Vanity Fair* (1847–48), frequenters of the "famous petits apartements of Lord Steyne" include "Marianne Clarke" and "the Duke of ——" (chap. 45).

X

x.1 Xenophon *Memorabilia.* Trans. E. C. Marchant. And *Apology.* Trans. O. J. Todd. Cambridge, Mass.: Harvard Univ. Press (Loeb Classical Library), 1923.

■ Xenophon, who was in Asia at the time of the trial and execution of Socrates, devoted the first two chapters of Book 1 of his *Memorabilia* to his own defense of Socrates against the principal charges brought against him: impiety and corrupting the youth. He argued further that Socrates could not be held responsible for the political misdeeds of Critias and Alcibiades after they abandoned the philosopher's company and teachings of virtue. Xenophon concluded that Socrates deserved honor rather than death at the hands of the state: "Under the laws, death is the penalty inflicted on persons proved to be thieves, highwaymen, cutpurses, kidnappers, robbers of temples; and from such criminals no man was so widely separated as he."

Rather than setting out, as does the comparable work by Plato, to mirror Socrates's actual defense speech to his jury, Xenophon's *Apology* is primarily an informal essay on the philosopher's deliberations regarding his prosecution and death. Socrates declines to prepare a persuasive defense because he regards a painless death as a blessed release from the ills of old age. To a friend who deplores his being put to death unjustly, the Master responds with a smile: "My beloved Apollodorus, was it your preference to see me put to death justly?"

Y

Y.1 Yamazaki Masakazu *Sanetomo.* In *Mask and Sword: Two Plays for the Contemporary Japanese Theater by Yamazaki Masakazu.* Trans. J. Thomas Rimer. New York: Columbia Univ. Press, 1980.

■ The author, born in 1934, has taught Japanese culture and literature at Yale University and modern Japanese intellectual history at Columbia University and has been a professor at Osaka University, where he received his doctorate in aesthetics.

The protagonist of his play, *Sanetomo,* is the third Kamakura Shogun, Minamoto Sanetomo, who was assassinated by his nephew, Kugyo, on the steps of the Hachiman Shrine in Kamakura in 1219 A.D. Sanetomo was a gifted poet who wrote in a thirty-one-syllable verse form called *tanka.* An annual Sanetomo Festival is celebrated in his honor by lovers of *tanka,* painting, and dancing.

In Yamazaki's drama, ghosts of Sanetomo and his circle, attired in modern clothes that might be worn at a rehearsal, reenact the events that led to his death. It is a task that the phantom courtiers are condemned to repeat throughout eternity in a fruitless effort to understand Sanetomo's enigmatic nature. The relived events bear overtones of *Hamlet.* Sanetomo's elder brother, Yoriie, his predecessor in the shogunate, has been murdered at the direction of their mother, Masako, and her brother, Yoshitoki, members of the powerful Hojo family. In the eyes of Kugyo, Yoriie's young son, Sanetomo, was tainted by the crime, and his decision to assassinate Sanetomo is motivated by revenge and ambition to become his father's successor. Yoshitoki, as portrayed by the dramatist, assented to the killing of Sanetomo, fearful of the young ruler's impenetrable mind and his growing independence, demonstrated by a sudden access of religiosity, his insistence on advancement in ministerial rank, and an unsuccessful scheme to build a gigantic ship that would carry him on a state visit to China. Sanetomo's mother appears to support her brother when her hopes to keep the Shogun in a permanent state of childishness prove to be in vain. Even Sanetomo's wife, Azusa, cannot give her husband unqualified loyalty and laments after his death that she had not "taken him into [her] possession." Above all these lesser souls, Sanetomo rises serenely, able to find happiness in the midst of his enemies' plots: "Deeply involved in some momentous task, the act of straightening things up in some little bookcase may be a source of deep joy. I'm not talking about the kind of consciousness you need to be a poet. If you want to be Shogun, you've got to forge your temperament, in just that way, so that you can become a happy human being."

Z

Z.1 Zuckmayer, Carl *Der Hauptmann von Köpenick* [The Captain from Köpenick]. 1931. In *Karl Zuckmayer Meisterdramen* [Karl Zuckmayer's Master Dramas]. Frankfurt am Main: S. Fischer, 1966.

■ This is one of the most brilliant stage comedies to be based on a real-life hoax. In 1906, cobbler and ex-convict Wilhelm Voigt donned the uniform of a Prussian captain, commandeered a detachment of grenadiers, and seized the town treasury of Köpenick near Berlin. Kaiser Wilhelm II, perhaps amused by the exploit and pleased by Voigt's demonstration of German submissiveness to the military uniform, freed the impostor after twenty months' imprisonment. Voigt joined an American vaudeville company with whom he barnstormed prior to his death in 1914.

Zuckmayer's play about a victimized Everyman, written mostly in Berlin dialect, is heavily indebted to Georg Büchner's *Woyzeck*. In the dramatist's imaginative reconception of the imposture, Voigt seizes the town hall for the primary purpose of obtaining a residence permit, or passport, which German authorities have denied him as a former convict, thereby barring him from seeking an honest livelihood in Germany or abroad. Fate's last laugh frustrates the fake captain's scheme, because Köpenick is too small to be authorized to issue identity documents. In a devastating final scene in Berlin police headquarters, Voigt for the first time gazes at his mirror image in military garb. So strong was his belief that the uniform makes the man that he had never reviewed his captain's attire before embarking on the Köpenick raid. As his shoulders quake with convulsive laughter, he finally is able to form a single word that describes both his oppression by society and his feat of revenge: "Impossible!"

Zuckmayer's amusing plot follows the peregrinations of the captain's uniform. The outfit is created by a Jewish tailor to the order of a demanding military officer. When the captain leaves the service in disgrace, his uniform passes into the ownership of a reservist who becomes mayor of Köpenick. Returned to the tailor in exchange for a newer model that better fits the mayor's expanded girth, it is spoiled at a fancy dress party and sold to a Jewish-owned old-clothes shop, where it is purchased by Voigt. These linked chapters in the uniform's "biography" anticipate Julien Duvivier's 1942 film *Tales of Manhattan*. The adventure of the Captain from Köpenick has also inspired two German movies, which appeared in 1933 and 1956.

z.2 —— *Schinderhannes.* 1927. In *Carl Zuckmayer Meisterdramen* [Carl Zuckmayer's Master Dramas]. Frankfurt am Main: S. Fischer, 1966.

■ Johann Bückler, nicknamed Schinderhannes, headed a robber gang in the central Rhineland during the Napoleonic period. He was executed at Mainz. In Zuckmayer's dialect play, Schinderhannes grows from a trickster and feared robber into a rebel martyr. In the opening scene at the Green Tree Inn, he assumes the disguise of a merchant and sells a tanner some leather that he has previously stolen from him. At the same time he begins his amorous pursuit of a ballad singer's daughter, Julchen Blasius, who becomes his devoted mistress and bears him a child.

Schinderhannes's choice of a criminal career was influenced by childhood deprivations and rebuffs: "For half of my childhood I stood at your courtyard gate and begged for a crust of bread. Always the same litany: the poor give you a piece of their scanty bread and the rich set their dogs on you."

When Schinderhannes enlists as a German soldier, his promised immunity is rescinded, and he is arrested as a "political criminal." As the bandit awaits death on the scaffold in the Mainz prison, his condemned followers sing his ballad and softly stamp their feet. Schinderhannes's blind father, Kasper, imagines that he hears 15,000 men marching to rally around his son.

Resources

ENCYCLOPEDIAS OF CRIME

Frasier, David K. *Murder Cases of the Twentieth Century: Biographies and Bibliographies of 280 Convicted or Accused Killers.* Foreword Michael Newton. Jefferson, N.C.: McFarland, 1996.

Gaute, J. H. H., and Robin Odell. *Murder "Whatdunit": An Illustrated Account of the Methods of Murder.* London: Harrap, 1982.

———. *Murder Whereabouts.* London: Harrap, 1986.

———. *The New Murderers' Who's Who.* Forewords Colin Wilson and Richard Whittington-Egan. London: Harrap, 1989.

Kohn, George C. *Dictionary of Culprits and Criminals.* Metuchen, N.J.: Scarecrow Press, 1986.

Kurland, Michael. *A Gallery of Rogues: Portraits in True Crime.* New York: Prentice Hall General Reference, 1994.

Lane, Brian, and Wilfred Gregg. *The Encyclopedia of Mass Murder.* London: Headline, 1994.

———. *The Encyclopedia of Serial Killers.* London: Headline, 1992.

Mortimer, John, ed. *The Oxford Book of Villains.* Oxford: Oxford Univ. Press, 1992.

Nash, Jay Robert. *Encyclopedia of World Crime.* 6 vols. Wilmette, Ill.: CrimeBooks, 1989.

Sifakis, Carl. *The Encyclopedia of American Crime.* New York: Facts on File, 1982.

Wilson, Colin. *A Casebook of Murder.* New York: Cowles, 1969.

———. *A Criminal History of Mankind.* London: Granada, 1984.

———. *The Mammoth Book of True Crime.* New York: Carroll & Graf, 1998.

———. *Order of Assassins: The Psychology of Murder.* London: Rupert Hart-Davis, 1972.

Wilson, Colin, and Pat Pitman. *Encyclopedia of Murder.* New York: Putnam, 1962.

Wilson, Colin, and Donald Seaman. *Encyclopedia of Modern Murder 1962–1982.* London: Arthur Barker, 1983.

BIBLIOGRAPHIES, CATALOGS, AND SURVEYS OF FICTION AND NONFICTION RELATING TO CRIME HISTORY

Barzun, Jacques, and Wendell Hertig Taylor. *A Catalogue of Crime: Revised and Enlarged Edition.* New York: Harper & Row, 1989.

Chandler, Frank Wadleigh. *The Literature of Roguery.* 1907. New York: Burt Franklin, 1958.

Harrison, Ben. *True Crime Narratives: An Annotated Bibliography.* Lanham, Md.: Scarecrow Press, 1997.

Haste, Steve. *Criminal Sentences: True Crime in Fiction and Drama.* London: Cygnus Arts (Golden Cockerel Press), 1997.

Kelly, Alexander, with David Sharp. *Jack the Ripper and Review of the Literature.* N.p.: Association of Assistant Librarians, 1995.

McDade, Thomas M. *The Annals of Murder: A Bibliography of Books and Pamphlets on American Murders from Colonial Times to 1900.* Norman: Univ. of Oklahoma Press, 1961.

Ross, John M[urray]. *Trials in Collections: An Index to Famous Trials Throughout the World.* Metuchen, N.J.: Scarecrow Press, 1983.

Sandoe, James. "Criminal Clef: Tales and Plays Based on Real Crimes." In *Murder Plain and Fanciful.* New York: Sheridan House, 1948.

Index

Bold entries identify fictional characters; asterisked page numbers denote biographical information.

Ging, Kitty, H.27

Ginzburg, Carlo, *Judge and the Historian, The: Marginal Notes on a Late-Twentieth-Century Miscarriage of Justice*, 32, G.14

"Gioconda Smile, The," H.38

Giono, Jean: *Notes sur l'affaire Dominici suivies d'un essai sur le caractères des personnages*, G.15

Girbal, F. Hernandez, 33, M.27

Girl in Lover's Lane, The, G.19

Girl in Poison Cottage, The, G.19

Girl in the Belfry, The, G.19

Girl in the Death Cell, The, G.19

Girl in the House of Hate, The, G.19

Girl in the Murder Flat, The, G.19

Girl in the Red Velvet Swing, The, G.19

Girl in the Stateroom, The, G.19

"Girl of the Golden West," H.4

Girl on the Gallows, The, G.19

Girl on the Lonely Beach, The, G.19

Girl with the Scarlet Brand, The, G.19

Girls in Nightmare House, The, G.19

Gisquet, M., *Mémoires de M. Gisquet, ancien préfet de police*, G.16

Glaister, John, N.7

Glammis, Lady and Lord, R.18

Glaser, Justice, F.6

Glaspell, Susan, *Trifles*, G.17

Glass, Alan, *Love in a Thirsty Land*, G.18

Glass, William, J.11

Glen O'Weeping, S.21

Glengarry's Way and Other Studies, R.18

Gloyd, John, L.34

Godefroy, Robert, 24

Godfrey, Sir Edmund Berry, C.14, H.7, L.9, W.32

Gods of the Lightning, A.12

God's Revenge Against Murder, 15

Godse, Nathuram, N.2

Godwin, George, N.7.65

Godwin, William, 5, B.83

Goehr, Alexander, *Arden Muss Sterben*, A.15

"Going to See a Man Hanged," 11, B.28, T.7

Gold Medal Series of Classic Murder Trials, G.19

Gold, Frederick Isaac, W.1

Golden Flood, The, A. 23

Golden, James P., A.11.7

Goldman, Ron, D.51, T.12

Goldsmith, Oliver, *Mystery Revealed, The: Containing a Series of Transactions and Authentic Testimonials Respecting the Supposed Cock-Lane Ghost; Which Have Been Concealed from the Public*, G.35

Goll, Iwan, D.30

Golov, Zhenia (Andrei Yushchinsky), M.6

Gönczy, Joseph, L.25

Gondreville, Malin de, B.7

Gonsse, Alexandre-Mominique-Joseph, marquis de Rougeville, D.44

Goodbye Lizzie Borden (Sullivan), S.55

Goodbye, Miss Lizzie Borden (De la Torre), D.16

Goodchild, George, and Bechhofer Roberts, *The Dear Old Gentleman*, B.73

Goodere, Samuel and John, I.5, S.45

Goodman, Alice, and John Adams, *The Death of Klinghoffer*, G.20;

Goodman, Jonathan, xiii, 8, C.19, G.21,* J.1, N.7, O.3; *Acts of Murder*, G.21; *The Burning of Evelyn Foster*, G.22; *The Killing of Julia Wallace*, G.23; *Murder in High Places*, G.24; *Murder in Low Places*, G.24; *The Passing of Starr Faithfull*, G.25; *The Slaying of Joseph Bowne Elwell*, F.14, G.26; *The Stabbing of George Harry Storrs*, 4, G.27

Goodwin, Bessie, C.39

Goodwin, Elizabeth Caroline, S.36

Gordon, Basil H., A.11.10

Gordon, Dame Helen Cumming, H.19

Gordon, James, C.42

Gordon, Lord George, D.23

Gorguloff, Paul, M.36.5

Gorin, Gregory, *Forget Herostratus!*, 39, G.28, S.5

Goron, Marie-François, 23, B.39, B.60; *L'Amour à Paris: Nouveaux mémoires*, G.29; *Behind the French C.I.D.: Leaves from the Memoirs of Goron, Former Detective Chief*, G.30; *Les mémoires de M. Goron ancien chef de la Sûreté*, G.31; *The Truth About the Case: The Experiences of M. F. Goron*, G.32

Gorse, Ernest Ralph (Neville George Clevely Heath), H.9

Gorse Trilogy, The, H.9

Gorsse, Pierre de, *La justice égarée par les femmes*, G.33

Goss, Winfield Scott, P.7.2

Gosselin, Louis-Léon-Théodore. *See* Lenotre, G.

Gouffé, Toussaint-Augustin, B.60, G.29, G.34, M.1, H.21

Gough, Elizabeth, R.24

Gough, Orlando, C.25

Gourevitch, Philip, G.11

Gould, Maud E., "Entreating," Fig.17

Gow, Captain, D.9

Gowrie Conspiracy, L.8, M.20, R.26, W.32

"Gowrie Conspiracy, The," L.8

Gowrie, Alexander, earl of. *See* Gowrie Conspiracy

Gracchus, Tiberius Sempronius,15, P.15, Fig.1

Graeme, Bruce, *Passion, Murder and Mystery*, G.34

Graham, Barbara, D.12

Graham, Thomas, A.11.13

Blood & Ink

was designed by Will Underwood

and composed by Christine Brooks

in 10/13 Stone Print

on a Macintosh G4 using PageMaker 6.5;

printed by sheet-fed offset lithography

on 55-pound Supple Opaque stock

(an acid-free recycled paper),

Smyth sewn and bound over binder's boards

in Arrestox B cloth, and wrapped with

dust jackets printed in four color process

by Thomson-Shore, Inc.;

and published by

THE KENT STATE UNIVERSITY PRESS

Kent, Ohio 44242